The **Rough Guide** to

Los Angeles
& Southern California

written and researched by

JD Dickey

NEW YORK · LONDON · DELHI

www.roughguides.com

Contents

Sun, sand, and surf
color section following
p.144

The Sounds of LA color
section following p.304

Color maps following
p.464

◄◄ Los Angeles beach at sunset ◄ Los Angeles skyline

Introduction to

Los Angeles

& Southern California

**It's almost impossible not to hold an opinion about Los
Angeles, a city that's loved and scorned in equal measure.
Some see it as a health, environmental, and cultural
quagmire, its freeways, smog, and Hollywood drivel
polluting countless bodies and minds. Others consider
it the lodestar of urban America, its great diversity of
peoples, culture, and geography woven into a rich tapestry
that's far too complex to describe or dismiss in a few
words. Indeed, despite the city's problems, for many
residents there's no place in the country or world like it, a
veritable crazy quilt of light, color, and energy.**

More relaxed altogether than LA itself, the surrounding
region of Southern California is well known for its
laissez-faire lifestyle of suntanning and surfing along
serpentine beaches, posing in the latest fashions along
palm-lined boulevards, and skiing and hiking in the
mountains above it all. The region's urban nodes of San
Diego, Santa Barbara, and Palm Springs are among the
wealthiest communities in the nation, and often flaunt
it quite openly. But there's more to the region than the
stereotype – the craggy Indian canyons, sun-blasted deserts, and ocean coves
are a haven from human bustle, and the cities stimulate the eye, mind, and
palate with plenty of good museums, restaurants, and cultural treasures.

The region's centerpiece, Los Angeles is a model for modern city development, having traded urban centralization for suburban sprawl and high-rise
corporate towers for strip malls. Although the city had a significant Spanish
and Mexican presence through the mid-nineteenth century, it was only after
California became an American state in 1850 that LA began to grow into
a metropolis, marketing itself as a sunny arcadia full of orange groves, clean,

fresh air, and wide-open space. When the film and aerospace industries were added to the mix in the early twentieth century, the place truly boomed, eventually displacing Chicago as America's second-largest city. Nowadays, LA's explosive population growth has brought a tumult of peoples and languages from nearly every corner of the earth to a freeway-draped landscape of glaring neon signs and towering palm trees.

The largest port in the country (and biggest in the world outside of China and Singapore), LA is a burly center for transpacific trade and a dominant financial hub. It's a magnet for immigrants with newcomers from Armenia, Zimbabwe, and everywhere in-between teeming in pockets large and small. LA's social gaps remain quite broad, and there appears to be no end in sight for the nasty racial divisions broadcast to the world during the 1992 riots. Still, the metropolis has slowly accommodated its multicultural character; Mexican-Americans in particular, whether newly arrived or of ancient lineage, are doing much to remind the city of its Hispanic origins.

Though there's plenty to see here, Los Angeles and Southern California do not reward an attraction-oriented itinerary of dutiful trotting from one museum or exhibit to the next. While there are world-class sights on offer – the Getty Center and San Diego Zoo foremost among them – the big-ticket sights in most of the region's cities (with the exception of Santa Barbara) tend to be separated by vast distances, and you'll doubtless spend much of your time on the freeway if you try to see them all. Rather, the best approach to the area is to experience those things that really make the area a great place to spend a week – especially the free-spirited bars, upscale restaurants, dynamic clubs, hedonistic beaches, and quirky shopping strips and boardwalks.

Surprisingly, many of these attractions cluster in fairly compact districts, from Venice to Old Pasadena in Los Angeles, or Coronado to La Jolla in San Diego, so you can leave your car in a parking lot or just use public transit to get there. To really get into the urban spirit, make sure to try a bit of unstructured wandering around the region's less glitzy zones, where you may stumble upon that perfect diner or funky shoe store, discovering hidden charms away from the theme parks and klieg lights.

◄ Newport Harbor in Orange County

Suggested LA itineraries

The following are suggested **itineraries** for trips up to a week. They're mainly designed around the key sights and include suggestions for where and when to have lunch. Of course, if any of the days seem too jam-packed for you, skip any of these stops and just wander – or drive – around.

Two days
• Griffith Park; Hollywood Boulevard/Sunset Strip (lunch); Melrose Avenue; Rodeo Drive.
• Getty Center (lunch); Third Street Promenade; Santa Monica Pier; Venice Boardwalk.

Four days
• Disney Hall; Museum of Contemporary Art; Little Tokyo (lunch); Exposition Park; West Adams.
• Griffith Park; Hollywood Boulevard/Sunset Strip (lunch); Miracle Mile; Los Angeles County Museum of Art.
• Melrose Avenue; Greystone Mansion; Rodeo Drive (lunch); Westwood; Getty Center.
• Venice Boardwalk; Santa Monica Pier; Third Street Promenade (lunch); Malibu; Santa Monica Mountains.

One week
Four-day plan above plus . . .
• Old Pasadena (lunch); Norton Simon Museum and Gamble House, or Universal Studios.
• Palos Verdes Peninsula; Wayfarer's Chapel; Downtown Long Beach (lunch); *Queen Mary*; Aquarium of the Pacific.
• Disneyland or Magic Mountain.

What to see

Most of Los Angeles lies in a flat basin, contained within and around the Santa Monica, San Gabriel, Santa Ana, and Verdugo mountains, and hemmed in by the Pacific Ocean to the west. From the crest of the Hollywood Hills on any given night you can see the city lights spread out before you in a seemingly endless illuminated grid. Though etched with a vast network of freeways, the landscape also features undulating hills, coastal bluffs, mountain ranges, and rocky canyons – variously home to movie stars, shopping malls, and theme attractions, not to mention impressive museums, rugged parks, and expansive gardens.

Starting in the center of the region, at the junction of the Hollywood, Santa Monica, Harbor, and Santa Ana freeways, **Downtown** has always been the hub of LA's political and financial life, a district that has long tried to match the cultural cachet of the Westside and Hollywood – to no avail. Still, there's nowhere else in the city with as much variety of class, culture, and design, all within a fairly compact area. Just west, the loosely defined district of **Mid-Wilshire**, built around part of the commercial strip of Wilshire Boulevard, is home to some of LA's best Art Deco architecture and finest

▲ Downtown's Disney Hall

residential designs. It's also a good place to take in some culture along "Museum Row" – overlapping the old Miracle Mile commercial zone – where you can find the city's widest selection of art at the LA County Museum of Art.

Due north is LA's most famous zone, **Hollywood**. Despite its well-worn patina of grime, the birthplace of the American movie business is still an essential stop, the site of grand old cinema palaces like the Chinese Theatre and the ever-popular "Walk of Fame." Hollywood, Sunset, Santa Monica, and Melrose boulevards are the district's main drags, all of which lead to the chic boutiques and trendy clubs of **West Hollywood**, a center for gays, seniors, and Russian immigrants. In the hills above Hollywood, you can take a break in **Griffith Park**, location of LA's famed observatory.

West of here, in the heart of the city's Westside, **Beverly Hills** and **West LA** are where visitors often base themselves, keeping close to the all-out glitz of Rodeo Drive or Westwood's movie theaters and affordable shops. In the latter district, there's also the picturesque UCLA campus, and further

▶ Angelenos celebrating Cinco de Mayo

Stargazing in LA

If you really want to catch a glimpse of the glitterati in LA, you can do much better than riding around on a tour bus staring at the mansion gates and shrubs of the rich and famous – and paying plenty for the privilege. You can often catch a glimpse of your favorite movie heroes and TV stars as well as has-beens and pseudo-celebrities in the city's latest bars and clubs (see listings in the *LA Times'* weekly Calendar Live entertainment section) and in the celeb-oriented restaurants listed in the box on p.279. You can sometimes get movie stars to sign autographs if you approach the rich and/or famous when they're "performing" for the public – attending a movie premiere, showing off their new duds at a flashy club, or doing anything in the company of a publicist or reporter. They're much less likely to blow you off in full public view than they are if you invade their privacy in a secluded beach cabana, back-corner dining booth, or on the Stairmaster at an upscale gym, where you can expect the quick embrace of a bodyguard and a curt, "Sir, you're making a scene," before being ushered to the exit.

west, in the Sepulveda corridor, sits LA's showpiece, the colossal Getty Center.

Santa Monica and **Venice** lie at the ocean's edge, sixteen miles from Downtown. These towns give LA its popular beach image (though the waters are cleaner further north), and are highlighted by such favorite attractions as the relaxed Santa Monica Pier, the shopping strips of the Third Street Promenade and Main Street, and the freewheeling Venice Boardwalk and body shrine of Muscle Beach.

Well off the path of most tourists and dogged by crime, **South Central** holds a few scattered but notable sights like the Watts Towers, plus the fine array of historic architecture along West Adams and several good cultural institutions in Exposition Park. East of Downtown, **East LA** is the heart of the city's Mexican-American community, with a fairly vibrant street life. To the south, the largely residential and industrial **South Bay** and **LA Harbor** respectively feature some compelling oceanside scenery and charming architecture, and the grittier port cities of San Pedro and Long Beach – best known as the anchorage of the *Queen Mary* ocean liner. Back up the coast, the **Palos Verdes Peninsula** is home to some of the city's most dramatic ocean vistas.

The sprawling suburbs of the **San Gabriel** and **San Fernando valleys**, east and north of the Hollywood Hills, bustle with

Traffic and smog

Among LA's downsides, it's likely you'll only face the typical pitfalls of traffic and smog. The latter, while still virulent, has slowly improved in recent decades. Smog reports, broken down by geographic area, are published daily in the *LA Times*. As for traffic hassles, gridlock can sometimes be avoided if you stick to one place, as many neighborhoods are surprisingly compact and can be seen on foot. Still, you'll likely need a car to jump around from place to place, or to get a real sense of the city sprawl. Driving on LA's myriad freeways can be a challenge, but as long as you don't try to emulate some of the crazier local  motorists, you should have few problems. Whatever your transportation plan, make sure to budget plenty of time for your travels. While you can theoretically go from Santa Monica to Downtown LA in twenty minutes by freeway, most likely it will take twice that amount of time, or more than seventy-five minutes on side streets.

dining, shopping, and cultural activities, from Burbank's working movie studios and Glendale's famed Forest Lawn cemetery to the historic town of Pasadena, home to the Old Pasadena shopping strip and the magnificent Gamble House. The best natural turf in LA is around **Malibu** and the **Santa Monica Mountains**, where the many state and regional parks are ideal for exploring on foot, or by car along the scenic Mulholland Highway. Nearby, the exclusive enclave of Pacific Palisades is home to a handful of architectural highlights, while the city of Malibu to the north is a surfside celebrity enclave whose beaches are famously difficult, though not impossible, to access. More beach options abound in the shoreline communities of **Orange County**, though the area is best known for inland sights like Knott's Berry Farm and Disneyland, and the Richard Nixon Library.

Once you've had your fill of LA proper, venture out into greater Southern California. **San Diego** is one of the most populous cities in the US, and best for its many fine beaches. It's also terrific for its collection of museums set amid the leafy confines of Balboa Park, for the magisterial ships docked on its harborfront, and for the grand Victorian architecture enlivening the nightlife precinct of the Gaslamp District. Two hours east of LA in the desert, **Palm Springs** is best known for the golf and sporting activities that attract the nouveau riche and tourists alike. Also worth a look are its splendid mid-twentieth-century modern architecture and surrounding

Indian canyons, and especially the eerie expanse of Joshua trees on the edge of the Mojave desert. Finally, **Santa Barbara** is the old-money redoubt of the Central Coast, gleaming with a grand old mission and handsome Spanish Colonial Revival architecture. Along with

▼ Santa Monica Pier

an array of fine hotels and dining options, a number of fascinating art and history museums heighten a genteel old-money air that's otherwise absent from Southern California's whiz-bang pop-cultural landscape.

When to go

Los Angeles holds several types of warm **climate zones**, including desert, semi-arid, and Mediterranean areas. Differences between temperatures across the area can be great: for example, Pasadena is ten to fifteen degrees hotter on average than Santa Monica, whose climate is decidedly maritime at times. Due to the enclosed topography of the LA basin, high levels of smog can accumulate, worst during the summer months in the eastern parts of the region; torrential rainstorms occur during the winter months. Monthly city temperatures range less than twenty degrees throughout the year, and in general, toasty air and sunny skies reign: summer and fall months are fairly warm and dry; winter and spring periods are cooler and wetter, but still quite warm. The right time to travel to Los Angeles depends less on the weather than on cultural events – parades, festivals, movie previews, surfing tournaments.

Average daytime temperatures in LA

	Jan	Feb	Mar	Apr	May	Jun	Jul	Aug	Sep	Oct	Nov	Dec
Max °F	65	66	68	71	73	77	83	82	81	77	73	68
Max °C	18	19	20	22	23	25	28	28	27	25	23	20
Min °F	47	48	49	53	55	60	63	63	60	57	53	49
Min °C	8	9	9	12	13	16	17	17	16	14	12	9

things not to miss

It's not possible to see everything Los Angeles and Southern California have to offer in one trip – and we don't suggest you try. What follows is a subjective selection of the area's highlights, from verdant mountain parks to unique art museums, arranged in color-coded categories. All entries have a page reference to take you straight into the guide, where you can find out more.

01 Malibu Creek State Park Page **222** • Expansive park in the Santa Monica Mountains offering terrific camping and hiking, as well as striking natural vistas memorable from many movies and TV shows, including M*A*S*H*.

02 **Sunset Strip** Page **111** • The essential axis of the California music scene, jammed with groovy bars and clubs as well as swanky hotels, oddball boutiques, and towering billboards advertising fashion, liquor, and starlets.

04 **Getty Center** Page **129** • This colossal arts center, looming above West LA and stuffed with the glory of the Old World, has done much to help Los Angeles shake off its reputation as a culture-free zone.

03 **Watts Towers** Page **165** • These spiny towers built from cast-off glass and pottery are a welcome sight in South Central LA, where their graceful silhouettes lend an otherworldly touch to the scruffy neighborhood.

05 **Hotel del Coronado** See **372** • Huge, eye-catching centerpiece of the San Diego coastline, which has graced the sands since 1888 and has appeared in several notable Hollywood movies.

06 Amoeba Music

Page **103** • The reigning king of California record stores, with acres of space housing thousands of CDs, tapes, DVDs, and vinyl records, including some classic favorites.

07 Disney-land

Page **226** • Much more than a theme park, the "Magic Kingdom" is a carefully planned resort where you can eat, sleep, and take a spin on the family-oriented rides without ever leaving its gates.

08 Venice Boardwalk

Page **145** • Mix with itinerant artists, rollerbladers, street preachers, T-shirt and trinket vendors, and hordes of tourists at this free-spirited beachside strip.

09 **Pacific Coast Highway** Page **233** • A favorite setting for biker flicks and road movies, the sinewy stretch of asphalt winds around coastal cliffs and legendary beaches from Malibu to Orange County.

11 **Egyptian Theatre** Page **100** • The stylishly preserved zenith of movie palaces in the 1920s, with ancient-looking columns, scarabs, and friezes, and a solid diet of art-house and independent fare.

10 **Angelino Heights** Page **68** • Located just beyond Downtown, a lovely stretch of Victorian homes and mansions that harkens back to a long-forgotten era of LA design and culture.

12 **Griffith Park** Page **92** • A verdant swath of urban greenery on the hills overlooking the city, containing several museums, bucolic glades, great trails, and the signature Observatory.

13 **LA County Museum of Art** Page **81** •
Now undergoing massive renovation, this huge storehouse of old and new art presents the broadest collection of art in the western US.

14 **Whisky-a-Go-Go** Page **304** •
Perhaps the most famous rock club on the West Coast, a proving ground for punk and metal groups and a classic venue that's hosted the likes of Buffalo Springfield, Janis Joplin, and The Doors.

15 **Hayden Tract** Page **136** •
Experimental architect Eric Owen Moss's enclave of bizarre, risk-taking buildings in Culver City, including everything from a business beehive to a stairway to nowhere. A must-see for fans of modern architecture and art.

16 **Canter's Deli** Page **352** • One of LA's better delis and an inspired 24-hour spectacle, with brassy waitresses, an eclectic clientele, and an adjoining cabaret.

17 Rodeo Drive Page

118 • A compact axis of downtown Beverly Hills featuring countless jewelry, fashion, and beauty merchants, that cater to both elite customers and window-shopping tourists.

19 Gamble House Page 196 •

This 1908 Craftsman-style treasure is one of Pasadena's gems, blending elements of rustic native design with touches of Swiss-chalet and Japanese decoration.

18 San Diego Zoo Page 372 •

Simply put, the greatest zoo in the country, and one of the best in the world, featuring thousands of animals, including some famous Chinese pandas.

21 Queen Mary Page 181 •

Docked in Long Beach, this striking Art Deco-styled ocean liner is open for tours – and you can also step inside a Russian sub moored nearby.

20 Natural History Museum of LA County Page 160 •

A terrific institution that holds a number of treasures, from ancient dinosaur bones to precious gemstones to three hundred pounds of gold.

Basics

Basics

Getting there

Unless you are within a half-day's drive of Southern California, the quickest way to get to the Los Angeles area is by flying into Los Angeles International Airport (LAX) or Orange County's John Wayne International. Amtrak trains provide an alternate approach to LA within the US, though this is typically a rather leisurely and expensive choice, while Greyhound buses are a cheaper, if much less enjoyable, option. If you're driving to LA, as many do, it pays to familiarize yourself with the freeway layout beforehand.

Flights from the US and Canada

Located just south of the major beach cities of Santa Monica and Venice, LAX is the destination for most flights into LA, though alternatives include John Wayne (in Orange County), Long Beach, Burbank, Van Nuys, or Ontario (thirty miles east of Downtown).

For airfares, week-to-week **prices** can vary dramatically. Published round-trip prices during the midweek in summer — the high season — on the major airlines start at around $350 from New York and other eastern seaboard cities, $270 from Midwest cities, and $500 from Toronto and Montréal, although regular airline **promotions and savers** can substantially reduce that price at slack times. What makes more difference than your choice of carrier are the conditions governing the ticket – whether it's fully refundable, the time and day, and, most importantly, the **time of year** you travel. You'll get the best prices during the low season, mid-January to the end of February, and October to the end of November; shoulder seasons cover the rest of the year. Least expensive is a non-summer-season midweek flight, booked and paid for at least three weeks in advance. Keep in mind too that one-way tickets are sometimes more expensive than round-trip tickets.

You can also cut costs by going through a specialist flight agent – either a consolidator, who buys up blocks of tickets from airlines and sells them at a discount, or a discount agent who, in addition to dealing with discounted flights, may also offer special student or youth fares.

Flights from the UK and Ireland

The only nonstop flights from Britain to California are from London, most of which land in LA. The nonstop flight time is around eleven hours. Flights are often advertised as "direct" because they keep the same flight number but actually land elsewhere first. The first place the plane lands is your point of entry into the US, which means you'll have to collect your bags and go through customs and immigration formalities there, even if you're continuing on to California on the same plane. Many other routings involve a change of aircraft.

Britain remains one of the best places in Europe to obtain flight **bargains**, though fares vary widely according to season, availability, and the current level of inter-airline competition. Be sure to shop around carefully for the best offers by cross-checking the prices quoted by travel agents and websites with those quoted in travel ads in the weekend papers and other publications. Prices definitely rocket up if you do not stay over a Saturday night.

Aer Lingus operates the only **nonstop flight** to Los Angeles from Dublin five times a week. The cheapest flights from Ireland – if you're under 26 or a student – are available from USIT (see p.24). Student-only return **fares** directly to LA range from €450 to €850, depending on the time of year; non-students can expect to pay €550 to €1000. Flights via London may cost less, but you pay slightly more tax.

Another convenient option is a fly-drive deal, which gives cut-rate (and sometimes free) car rental when you buy an air ticket.

Many airlines also offer **air passes**, which allow foreign travelers to fly between a given number of US cities for one discounted price.

Packages – fly-drive, flight-accommodation deals, and guided tours – can work out cheaper than arranging the same trip yourself, especially for a short-term stay. The obvious drawbacks are the loss of flexibility and the fact that most schemes use hotels in the mid-range bracket, but there is a wide variety of options available.

One word of **warning**: it's not a good idea to buy a **one-way** ticket to the States. Not only are they rarely good value compared to a round-trip ticket, but US immigration officials usually take them as a sign that you aren't planning to go home and may refuse you entry. With increased airport checks, you are unlikely to be allowed even to board your flight to begin with.

Flights from Australia, New Zealand, and South Africa

If you are coming from Australia or New Zealand, there's very little price difference between airlines and no shortage of flights, via either the South Pacific or Asia. Most flights crossing the Pacific are nonstop, with twelve to fourteen hours' travel time between Auckland/Sydney and LA, though some include stopovers in Honolulu and a number of the South Pacific islands. If you go via Asia (a slightly more roundabout route that can work out a little cheaper), you'll usually have to spend a night, or the best part of a day, in the airline's home city.

Traveling from **Australia**, fares to LA from eastern cities cost the same, while from Perth they're about Aus$400 more. Flights from Sydney or Melbourne to LA range between Aus$1800 and Aus$2200, depending on the season, with airline specials and student fares sometimes reducing that to around Aus$1500. Seat availability on most international flights is limited, so it's best to book at least several weeks ahead.

From **New Zealand**, most flights are out of Auckland; add about NZ$200 for Christchurch and Wellington departures. Seasonal prices vary between around NZ$1950 and NZ$2400, again with occasional special deals and student fares reducing those figures significantly.

Travel to California is not particularly cheap from **South Africa**; prices are about the same out of Cape Town or Johannesburg but several hundred rand more from Durban and other smaller cities. Fares start at around R10,000, including all taxes, and rise as high as R14,000 at peak times, which are roughly the same as those from Australia. Direct flights with US or South African carriers invariably involve a refueling stop, though a more roundabout route with one of the national airlines from further north in Africa can be cheaper.

If you intend to take in California as part of a world trip, a **round-the-world** (RTW) ticket offers the greatest flexibility and can work out far more economically than booking separate flights. The most US-oriented are the seventeen airlines making up the "Star Alliance" network; for more details, visit ⓦwww.staralliance.com.

By train

If you don't want to fly, **Amtrak** (☎1-800 /USA-RAIL, ⓦwww.amtrak.com) is a leisurely but expensive option. Although financially precarious for years, the company has

---

Sample airfares from Britain

The prices given below (in £ sterling) are a general indication of the minimum transatlantic round-trip **airfares**, including **taxes**, you are likely to find at the given periods; youth discount fares and special deals may be cheaper. Each airline decides the exact dates of its seasons. Prices are for departures from London to LA or San Francisco.

low	Nov–March (except Christmas)	340
shoulder	April, May, Sept, Oct	450
high	June–Aug, Christmas	700

B

BASICS | Getting there

Fly less – stay longer! Travel and climate change

Climate change is a serious threat to the ecosystems that humans rely upon, and air travel is among the fastest-growing contributors to the problem. Rough Guides regard travel, overall, as a global benefit, and feel strongly that the advantages to developing economies are important, as is the opportunity of greater contact and awareness among peoples. But we all have a responsibility to limit our personal impact on global warming, and that means giving thought to how often we fly, and what we can do to redress the harm that our trips create.

Flying and climate change

Pretty much every form of motorized travel generates CO_2 – the main cause of human-induced climate change – but planes also generate climate-warming contrails and cirrus clouds and emit oxides of nitrogen, which create ozone (another greenhouse gas) at flight levels. Furthermore, flying simply allows us to travel much further than we otherwise would do. The figures are frightening: one person taking a return flight between Europe and California produces the equivalent impact of 2.5 tons of CO_2 – similar to the yearly output of the average UK car.

Fuel-cell and other less harmful types of plane may emerge eventually. But until then, there are really just two options for concerned travelers: to reduce the amount we travel by air (take fewer trips – stay for longer!), and to make the trips we do take "climate neutral" via a carbon offset scheme.

Carbon offset schemes

Offset schemes run by ⓦclimatecare.org, ⓦcarbonneutral.com and others allow you to make up for some or all of the greenhouse gases that you are responsible for releasing. To do this, they provide "carbon calculators" for working out the global-warming contribution of a specific flight (or even your entire existence), and then let you contribute an appropriate amount of money to fund offsetting measures. These include rainforest reforestation and initiatives to reduce future energy demand – often run in conjunction with sustainable development schemes.

Rough Guides, together with Lonely Planet and other concerned partners in the travel industry, are supporting a carbon offset scheme run by climatecare.org. Please take the time to view our website and see how you can help to make your trip climate neutral.

ⓦ**www.roughguides.com/climatechange**

managed to keep running – though rarely ever on time. Expect delays when traveling by rail. The trains themselves vary in style, amenities, and speed, so it can be worth checking ahead on the type of train that services your route.

To arrive by way of the Midwest and Southwest, ride on the **Southwest Chief**, which begins in Chicago and travels through Kansas City, Albuquerque, and Flagstaff before reaching LA (Las Vegas is connected by bus line to this route through Needles, California). The **Sunset Limited** covers more of the South and the Southwest, taking you from Orlando through New Orleans, Houston, and Tucson, and arriving in LA via Palm Springs and Pomona. Another memorable route is the **Coast Starlight**, which runs between Seattle and San Diego and passes some of the most appealing scenery anywhere, from coastal whale-watching between San Luis Obispo and Santa Barbara, to an evening trip around Mount Shasta and a journey through the wooded terrain of the Pacific Northwest. The shortest route of all, the **Pacific Surfliner**, connects San Diego to San Luis Obispo, with LA roughly on the mid-point of the journey.

One-way cross-country fares can be as low as $200 during the off-season, or as high as $330 during peak periods; always check for **online discounts** of up to 70 percent first, though such fares are offered irregularly. While Amtrak's basic fares are good value, the cost rises quickly if you want to travel more comfortably. **Sleeping**

21

Rail passes

Travelers have a choice of several **rail passes** that cover California, which can be useful if you're on an extended tour of the state and have plenty of time to explore your destinations.

	15-day (June–Aug)	15-day (Sept–May)	30-day (mid-May–Oct)	30-day (Nov–mid-May)
North America	–	–	$999	$709
USA Rail–West	$369	$329	$459	$359

The **North America** pass is available to all travelers, issued in conjunction with Canada's VIA Rail and valid for 30 consecutive days of travel up to one year from the date of purchase; you may travel up to four times, one way, over any given route segment. The pass is valid for coach (second-class) travel, but can be upgraded for an additional charge. The **USA Rail** pass covers different segments of the US (in this case, the West) and is available only to foreign travelers. A **Rail 2 Rail** pass offers free travel on Amtrak trains for riders of LA's Metrorail and San Diego's Coaster systems (see p.28 and p.368), for linking between stations. The **California** pass ($159) is available to all, covering any seven days of travel in a 21-day window for in-state routes such as Capitols, Coast Starlight, Pacific Surfliner, and San Joaquin. Many trains fill quickly, so it's worth making reservations.

For all information on Amtrak **fares and schedules** in the US, use the toll-free number ☎1-800/872-7245, or use the reservation facility on their website ⊛www .amtrak.com; do not phone individual stations.

compartments, which include small toilets and showers, start at around $150 for one or two people, but can climb as high as $400, depending on the class of compart-ment, number of nights, season, and so on, but all include three meals per day.

By bus

Bus travel is a slow, often agonizing way to get to LA, and in the end you won't really save that much money. **Greyhound** (☎1-800/231-2222, ⊛www.greyhound.com) is the sole long-distance operator servicing LA, and charges begin at $200 round-trip, paid at least seven days in advance, from major cities like New York, Chicago, and Miami. The main reason to take Greyhound is if you're planning to visit other places en route.

Foreign visitors and US and Canadian nationals can buy a **Greyhound Discovery Pass**, offering unlimited travel within a set time limit: you can order online at ⊛www .discoverypass.com. A seven-day pass costs $283, fifteen days for $415, thirty days for $522, and the longest, a sixty-day pass, is $645. The company website has a list of international vendors if you don't want to purchase online. The first time you use your pass, the ticket clerk will date it (which becomes the commencement date of the pass), and you will receive a ticket that allows you to board the bus. Repeat this procedure for every subsequent journey. Greyhound's nationwide toll-free **informa-tion service** can give you routes and times, plus phone numbers and addresses of local terminals. You can also make reservations at ☎1-800/231-2222.

By car

Obviously, as a city built on concrete and asphalt, LA is the perfect place to reach by **car**. There are numerous freeways within the region to hasten your trip (see p.27), and there are three main routes outside Southern California leading to the metropolis: **Inter-state 5**, the north–south corridor that connects LA to Mexico and Canada along the West Coast; **I-10**, a transcontinental east–west route that begins in Jacksonville, Florida, and ends in Santa Monica (or branches off to I-8 south of Phoenix to terminate in San Diego); and **I-15**, running along a mostly deserted stretch of desert before it reaches Las Vegas and drops down into LA's eastern San Gabriel Valley. Another option is **US Highway 101**, the famed coastal route that takes you along cliffs overhanging the Pacific Ocean and terminates in Downtown LA, after traveling through the San Fernando Valley and Hollywood, where it is known as the "Hollywood Freeway." If traveling on Hwy-101 beyond LA to the north, you can expect almost double the travel time as on Interstate 5, which goes in the same general direction.

Airlines, agents, and operators

Online booking

@ www.expedia.co.uk (in UK),
@ www.expedia.com (in US),
@ www.expedia.ca (in Canada)
@ www.lastminute.com (in UK)
@ www.opodo.co.uk (in UK)
@ www.orbitz.com (in US)
@ www.travelocity.co.uk (in UK)
@ www.travelocity.com (in US),
@ www.travelocity.ca (in Canada),
@ www.zuji.com.au (in Australia),
@ www.zuji.co.nz (in New Zealand)

Airlines in North America

Air Canada ☎ 1-888/247-2262, @ www.aircanada.com
Air France US ☎ 1-800/237-2747, @ www.airfrance.com, Canada ☎ 1-800/667-2747, @ www.airfrance.ca
Alaska Airlines ☎ 1-800/252-7522, @ www.alaska-air.com
American Airlines ☎ 1-800/433-7300, @ www.aa.com
Continental ☎ 1-800/523-3273, @ www.continental.com
Delta Airlines ☎ 1-800/221-1212, @ www.delta.com
Frontier Airlines ☎ 1-800/432-1359, @ www.flyfrontier.com
Hawaiian Airlines ☎ 1-800/367-5320, @ www.hawaiianair.com
JetBlue ☎ 1-800/538-2583, @ www.jetblue.com
Northwest/KLM ☎ 1-800/225-2525, @ www.nwa.com, @ www.klm.com
Southwest ☎ 1-800/435-9792, @ www.southwest.com
United Airlines ☎ 1-800/864-8331, @ www.united.com

US Airways ☎ 1-800/428-4322, @ www.usair.com
Virgin Atlantic Airways ☎ 1-800/821-5438, @ www.virgin-atlantic.com

Airlines in the UK and Ireland

Aer Lingus UK ☎ 0800/587 2324, Ireland ☎ 0818/365 000; @ www.aerlingus.com
Air Canada UK ☎ 0871/220 1111, Ireland ☎ 01/679 3958; @ www.aircanada.com
American Airlines UK ☎ 0845/778 9789, Ireland ☎ 01/602 0550; @ www.aa.com
British Airways UK ☎ 0870/850 9850, Ireland ☎ 1890/626 747; @ www.ba.com
Continental UK ☎ 0845/607 6760, Ireland ☎ 1890/925 252; @ www.continental.com
Delta Airlines UK ☎ 0845/600 0950, Ireland ☎ 1850/882 031; @ www.delta.com
Northwest/KLM UK ☎ 0870/507 4074, @ www.nwa.com, @ www.klm.com
United Airlines UK ☎ 0845/844 4777, @ www.united.co.uk
US Airways UK ☎ 0845/600 3300, Ireland ☎ 1890/925 065; @ www.usair.com
Virgin Atlantic Airways UK ☎ 0870/380 2007, @ www.virgin-atlantic.com

Airlines in Australia, New Zealand, and South Africa

Air New Zealand Australia ☎ 132 476, @ www.airnz.com.au; New Zealand ☎ 800/737 000, @ www.airnz.co.nz
Air Pacific Australia ☎ 1800/230 150, New Zealand ☎ 800/800 178; @ www.airpacific.com
Cathay Pacific Australia ☎ 131 747, New Zealand ☎ 09/379 0861, South Africa ☎ 11/700 8900; @ www.cathaypacific.com
China Airlines Australia ☎ 02/9244 2121, New Zealand ☎ 09/308 3364; @ www.chinaairlines.com
Continental Airlines Australia ☎ 02/9244 2242, New Zealand ☎ 09/308 3350; @ www.continental.com
Delta Air Lines Australia ☎ 1300/302 849, New Zealand ☎ 09/977 2232, South Africa ☎ 011/482 4582; @ www.delta.com
EgyptAir South Africa ☎ 011/880 4126, @ www.egyptair.com
JAL (Japan Airlines) Australia ☎ 2/9272 1111, New Zealand ☎ 09/379 9906, South Africa ☎ 011/214 2560; @ www.jal.com
Kenya Airways South Africa ☎ 011/881 9795, @ www.kenya-airways.com
Korean Air Australia ☎ 02/9262 6000, New Zealand ☎ 09/914 2000; @ www.koreanair.com

Qantas Australia ☏ 131 313, New Zealand ☏ 9/357 8900, South Africa ☏ 011/441 8550; ⒲ www.qantas.com

Singapore Airlines Australia ☏ 131 011, New Zealand ☏ 800/808 909, South Africa ☏ 011/880 8560; ⒲ www.singaporeair.com

South African Airways South Africa ☏ 011/978 1133, ⒲ www.flysaa.com

United Airlines Australia ☏ 131 777, New Zealand ☏ 9/379 3800; ⒲ www.unitedairlines.com.au

Virgin Atlantic Airways Australia ☏ 1300/727 340, South Africa ☏ 011/340 3400; ⒲ www.virgin-atlantic.com

Travel specialists and tour operators

In the US

Abercrombie & Kent ☏ 1-800/323-7308 or 630/954-2944, ⒲ www.abercrombiekent.com. Well-tailored but rather upmarket tours.

Adventure Center ☏ 1-800/228-8747 or 510/654-1879, ⒲ www.adventurecenter.com. Hiking and "soft adventure" specialists.

Backroads ☏ 1-800/462-2848 or 510/527-1555, ⒲ www.backroads.com. Cycling, hiking, and multisport tours.

Mountain Travel Sobek ☏ 1-888/687-6235 or 510/527-8100, ⒲ www.mtsobek.com. Conducts hiking, kayaking, and rafting tours.

REI Adventures ☏ 1-800/622-2236, ⒲ www.rei.com/travel. Climbing, cycling, hiking, cruising, paddling, and multisport tours.

STA Travel ☏ 1-800/781-4040, ⒲ www.statravel.com. Nationwide student agency that also does good deals for older travelers.

In the UK and Ireland

American Holidays Northern Ireland ☏ 028/9023 8762, Republic of Ireland ☏ 1/673 3840, ⒲ www.american-holidays.com. All sorts of package tours to the US, including California, from Ireland.

Bon Voyage UK ☏ 0800/316 3012, ⒲ www.bon-voyage.co.uk. Flight-plus-accommodation deals in Los Angeles, Palm Springs, and Las Vegas.

Bridge the World UK ☏ 0870/443 2399, ⒲ www.bridgetheworld.com. Good all-around agency that specializes in USA travel.

Contiki Travel UK ☏ 020/8290 6777, ⒲ www.contiki.co.uk. West Coast coach tours aimed at 18–35-year-olds willing to party.

Flight Centre UK ☏ 0870/890 8099, ⒲ www.flightcentre.co.uk. Near-ubiquitous high-street agency frequently offering some of the lowest fares around.

Holiday America UK ☏ 01424/224 400. Flight-plus-accommodation and fly-drive combinations.

Kuoni UK ☏ 1306/747 002, ⒲ www.kuoni.co.uk. Flight-plus-accommodation-plus-car deals featuring Los Angeles and San Diego. Special deals for families.

North South Travel UK ☏ 01245/608 291, ⒲ www.northsouthtravel.co.uk. Nonprofit agency offering friendly and efficient service.

STA Travel UK ☏ 0870/160 0599, ⒲ www.statravel.co.uk. A major player in student, youth, and budget travel with branches in or near many universities.

Trailfinders UK ☏ 020/7938 3939, ⒲ www.trailfinders.com, Ireland ☏ 1/677 7888, ⒲ www.trailfinders.ie. Well-established travel specialists, particularly adept at organizing RTW tickets.

TrekAmerica UK ☏ 01295/256 777, ⒲ www.trekamerica.com. Touring adventure holidays, usually small groups in well-equipped 4WD vans.

USIT Northern Ireland ☏ 028/9032 7111, ⒲ www.usitnow.com, Republic of Ireland ☏ 0818/200 020, ⒲ www.usit.ie. Ireland's premier student travel centre, which can also find good nonstudent deals.

Virgin Holidays UK ☏ 0870/220 2788, ⒲ www.virginholidays.co.uk. Packages to a wide range of California destinations.

In Australia, New Zealand, and South Africa

Canada & America Travel Specialists Australia ☏ 02/9922 4600, ⒲ www.canada-americatravel.com.au. North American specialists offering everything from flights and hotels to travel passes and adventure sports.

Flight Centre Australia ☏ 133 133, ⒲ www.flightcentre.com.au; New Zealand ☏ 800/243 544, ⒲ www.flightcentre.co.nz; South Africa ☏ 0860/400 727, ⒲ www.flightcentre.co.za. Near-ubiquitous high-street agency frequently offering some of the lowest fares around.

Journeys Worldwide Australia ☏ 07/3221 4788, ⒲ www.journeysworldwide.com.au. All US travel arrangements available.

Peregrine Adventures Australia ☏ 03/9663 8611, ⒲ www.peregrine.net.au. With offices in Brisbane, Sydney, Adelaide, and Perth, Peregrine offers active small-group holidays, from short walking and camping tours to longer overland trips through California.

STA Travel Australia ☏ 1300/733 035, ⒲ www.statravel.com.au; New Zealand ☏ 508/782 872, ⒲ www.statravel.co.nz. A major player in student, youth, and budget travel with branches in many universities.

Sydney International Travel Centre Australia ☏ 02/9250 9320, ⒲ www.sydneytravel.com.au.

Individually tailored holidays, Disneyland passes, flights, and bus and rail tours.

Trailfinders Australia ☎02/9247 7666, ⊛www .trailfinders.com.au. Knowledgeable staff skilled at turning up odd itineraries and good prices.

Travel.com.au Australia ☎02/9249 5444, ⊛www.travel.com.au; New Zealand ☎800/788 336, ⊛www.travel.co.nz. Youth-oriented center with an efficient travel agency offering good fares, a travel bookshop, and Internet café.

USA Travel Australia ☎02/9250 9320, ⊛www .usatravel.au. Good deals on flights, accommodation, city stays, car rental, and trip packages.

Arrival

Depending on how you travel, arriving in LA can place you at any number of locations scattered across the city – from the train and bus stations Downtown to the main air terminal by the ocean to the freeways coming in from all directions. However you arrive, you're faced with an unending sprawl that can be a source of bewilderment even for those who've lived in it for years. Provided you don't panic, however, this ungainly beast of a city can be managed and even easily navigated, if not necessarily tamed.

By air

All international and most domestic flights use Los Angeles International Airport (**LAX**) sixteen miles southwest of Downtown LA (☎310/646-5252, ⊛www.los-angeles-lax.com). **Shuttle bus A** is for intra-airport connections (carrier-to-carrier), while buses B and C serve their respective parking lots around the clock, with parking lot C being the place to board city buses (the citywide MTA and individual lines to Santa Monica, Culver City, and Torrance) – see p.29 for more details.

To travel between LAX and Downtown's Union Station, the UCLA campus in Westwood (at parking structure 32 on Kinross Avenue), or the private Van Nuys Airport, the direct-routed **LAX Flyaway** service uses buses in freeway carpool lanes to provide the most direct airport access on public transit; buses leave every 30 minutes around the clock, except at Westwood, where the service runs from 5–1am ($4 one-way; information at ☎1-866/435-9529).

Another way into town is to ride a town car such as **LAX Chequer Shuttle** (☎310/670-1731, ⊛www.laxchequer.com) or minibuses like **SuperShuttle** (☎1-800/BLUE-VAN, ⊛www.supershuttle.com) and **Prime Time Shuttle** (☎1-800/RED-VANS, ⊛www.prime timeshuttle.com), which run to Downtown, Hollywood, West LA, and Santa Monica, as well as Long Beach and Disneyland. They'll have signs on their windshields advertising their general destination. Fares depend on the destination, but are generally around $15–20 for minibuses and $30 for town cars, plus tip for both. The shuttles run around the clock from outside the baggage reclaim areas, and you should never have to wait more than fifteen or twenty minutes; pay the fare when you board.

Taxis charge at least $35 to West LA or Hollywood, around $100 to Disneyland, and a flat $42 to Downtown from LAX; a $2.50 surcharge applies for all trips starting from LAX (all airport trips are a minimum of $17.50). For more information check out ⊛www.taxicabsla.org.

Using the **Metro** system to get to your destination from LAX is difficult. The nearest light-rail train, the **Green Line**, stops miles from the airport, and the overall journey involves three time-consuming transfers (very difficult with luggage) before you even arrive in Downtown Los Angeles. If you'd like to try anyway for $1.25, shuttle service leaves from the lower level of the terminal to access the Metro stop at Aviation Station.

If you're arriving from elsewhere in the US or from Mexico, you can land at one of the **smaller airports** in the LA area – Burbank, Long Beach, Ontario, or Orange County's John Wayne Airport in Costa Mesa. These are similarly well served by car rental firms; if you want to use public transportation, phone the MTA Regional Information Network on arrival (Mon–Fri 6am–7pm, Sat 8am–6pm; ☎1-800/ COMMUTE, ⊛www.mta.net), and tell them where you are and where you want to go.

By train

Arriving in LA by **train**, you'll disembark at Union Station (☎213/624-0171), on the north side of Downtown at 800 N Alameda St. (You can also connect to regional bus lines next door at the Gateway Transit Center.) Union Station is the hub for three main rail lines: **Metrorail**, the subway and light-rail system (see p.28), **Metrolink**, a commuter rail line servicing distant suburbs (see p.29), and Amtrak (☎1-800/USA-RAIL, ⊛www.amtrak .com), whose long-distance trains also stop at outlying stations in the LA area.

Amtrak: departures for Downtown

Anaheim	12 daily	40min
Fullerton (for Disneyland)	8 daily	35min
Las Vegas	3 daily	6hr, with bus connection
Oceanside	6 daily	1hr 35min
Oxnard	6 daily	1hr 35min
Palm Springs	2 daily	2hr 35min
Sacramento	1 daily	14hr
San Bernardino	1 daily	1hr 45min
San Diego	9 daily	2hr 50min
San Francisco	3 daily	9–12hr, with bus connection
San Juan Capistrano	9 daily	1hr 20min
Santa Barbara	6 daily	2hr 35min
Tucson	2 daily	10hr
Ventura	5 daily	1hr 50min

By bus

The main **Greyhound** bus terminal, at 1716 E Seventh St (☎213/629-8401, ⊛www .greyhound.com), is in a seedy section of Downtown – though access is restricted to

ticket holders and it's safe enough inside. There are other Greyhound terminals elsewhere in LA handling fewer services: in Hollywood at 1715 N Cahuenga Blvd (☎323/466-6384); Pasadena at 645 E Walnut St (☎626/792-5116); Glendale at 400 W Cerritos Ave (☎818/244-7295); Long Beach at 464 W 3rd St (☎562/218-6113); and Anaheim at 101 W Winston Rd (☎714/999-1256). Only the Downtown terminal is open around the clock.

Greyhound: departures for Downtown

Las Vegas	15 daily	6–8hr
Bakersfield	13 daily	2hr 45min
Palm Springs	4 daily	2hr 40min
Phoenix	8 daily	7–9hr
Sacramento	8 daily	7–10hr
San Diego	16 daily	3hr
San Francisco	14 daily	8–12hr
Santa Barbara	6 daily	2–4hr
Santa Cruz	6 daily	9hr
Tijuana, Mexico	16 daily	3hr 30min–4hr
Tucson	7 daily	10–12hr

By car

The **main routes** by car into LA are the inter-state highways, all of which pass through or by Downtown. From the east, I-10, the **San Bernardino Freeway**, runs south of Downtown then heads to the Westside and the coast, where it's called the **Santa Monica Freeway**. US-60, the **Pomona Freeway**, parallels the faster I-10 through the eastern suburbs, providing a less hair-raising inter-change than I-10 when it reaches Downtown. The **Foothill Freeway**, I-210 (formerly Route 66), mainly serves the San Gabriel Valley; while the **Golden State Freeway**, or I-5, is the chief north–south access corridor, with the **San Diego Freeway**, I-405, used commonly as a Westside alternative.

Alternative routes into the city include US-101, the scenic route from San Francisco, which as the **Ventura Freeway** cuts across the San Fernando Valley and Hollywood into Downtown. Hwy-1 follows the entire coast of California and links up with US-101 in Ventura County.Through much of southern California it's known as **Pacific Coast Highway** (PCH), and in LA it uses surface streets through Santa Monica, the South Bay, and Orange County.

Getting around

Wherever and however you're going in LA, you should allow plenty of time to get there. This is partly due to the sheer size of the city, but the tangle of freeways and the gridlock common throughout the day can make car trips lengthy undertakings – and with most local buses stopping on every corner, bus travel is hardly a speedy alternative. The Metrorail subway and light-rail system are increasingly attractive options, though at present they serve too few parts of the city to be your only transit option.

Driving and car rental

The best way to get around LA is to **drive**. All the major car rental firms have branches throughout the city, and most have their main office close to LAX, linked to each terminal by a free shuttle bus. A number of smaller rental companies specialize in everything from Gremlins to Bentleys; the best known, and one of the cheapest, is Rent-a-Wreck; a close second for more modern vehicles is Fox Rent-a-Car.

Parking is a particular problem Downtown, along Melrose Avenue's trendy Westside shopping streets, and in Beverly Hills and Westwood – the latter with one of the nation's most aggressive meter-enforcement policies. Also watch out for restrictions – some lampposts boast as many as four placards listing dos and don'ts. If you're staying at a major chain hotel in a high-ticket area (especially Downtown and Beverly Hills), be prepared to plunk down an average of $25–30 per day for hotel parking; otherwise, at cheap motels and hotels in lower-rent areas, it'll cost you nothing to keep your vehicle overnight.

Car rental companies

Advantage ☎1-800/777-5500, ⊛www.arac.com
Alamo ☎1-800/462-5266, ⊛www.alamo.com
Avis ☎1-800/230-4898, ⊛www.avis.com
Budget ☎1-800/527-0700, ⊛www.budget.com
Dollar ☎1-800/800-3665, ⊛www.dollar.com
Enterprise ☎1-800/261-7331, ⊛www.enterprise.com
Fox Rent-a-Car ☎1-800/225-4369, ⊛foxrentacar.com
Hertz ☎1-800/654-3131, ⊛www.hertz.com
National ☎1-800/CAR-RENT, ⊛www.nationalcar.com

Payless ☎1-800/PAYLESS, ⊛www.paylesscarrental.com
Rent-a-Wreck ☎1-800/944-7501, ⊛www.rentawreck.com
Thrifty ☎1-800/847-4389, ⊛www.thrifty.com

LA's freeways

Despite traffic being bumper-to-bumper much of the time, the **freeways** are the only way to cover long distances quickly; with more than 250 miles of asphalt and twenty major routes, the LA freeway system is the largest in the world.

The system, however, can be confusing, especially since each stretch might have two or three names (often derived from its eventual destination, however far away) as well as a number. Out of an eye-popping, four-level interchange known as "**The Stack**," four major freeways fan out from Downtown: the Hollywood Freeway (a section of US-101) heads northwest through Hollywood into the San Fernando Valley; the Santa Monica Freeway (I-10) runs south of Mid-Wilshire and West LA to Santa Monica; the Harbor Freeway (I-110) goes south to San Pedro – heading northeast it's called the Pasadena Freeway; and the Santa Ana Freeway (I-5) passes Disneyland and continues south through Orange County – north of Downtown it's called the Golden State Freeway. **Other freeways** include the San Diego Freeway (I-405), which roughly follows the coast through West LA and the South Bay; the Ventura Freeway (Hwy-134), which links Burbank, Glendale, and Pasadena to US-101 in the San Fernando Valley; the Long Beach Freeway (I-710), a truck-heavy route connecting East LA and

Road conditions

The California Department of Transportation (CalTrans) operates a toll-free **24-hour information line** (☎1-800/427-7623) giving up-to-the-minute details of road conditions throughout the state. On a touch-tone phone, simply input the number of the road ("5" for I-5, "299" for Hwy-299, etc) and a recorded voice will tell you about any relevant weather conditions, delays, detours, snow closures, and so on. From out of state, or without a touch-tone phone, road information is also available on ☎916/445-1534. You can also check online at ⊛www.dot.ca.gov/.

Long Beach; and short routes like Hwy-2, which serves the San Gabriel Valley, and Hwy-90, which runs through Marina del Rey. For **shorter journeys**, especially between Hollywood and West LA, the wide avenues and boulevards are a better option (sometimes the only one), not least because you get to see more of the city.

Freeway driving strategies

Although LA freeway travel presents its own unique challenges, keeping a few things in mind will go some way toward reducing the time spent in gridlock. For one, alternate route planning is critical, especially when traveling to Orange County, because **gridlock** can occur at any time of the day. To assist your planning, AM news radio stations (see p.34) provide frequent **traffic updates** identifying where the nasty tie-ups are.

The **busiest roads** are Highway 101 and the 405 freeway, with particularly hellish confluences at the Downtown "Stack" and the section of the 405 at the 10 freeway. Individual roads present their own difficulties, including the creaky 101 south through Universal City, and the antiquated 110 freeway in Highland Park, where exit-ramp speeds suddenly drop to 5 mph. At the LA River, transferring from the south 5 to the south 110 is a hair-raising merge around the base of a cliff, while following the 10 freeway through East LA plunges you briefly,

and chaotically, into the confusion of Interstate 5. Finally, tractor-trailer trucks are almost ubiquitous on the Terminal Island Expressway, a short road near the harbor, and on the Long Beach Freeway, or 710, where most of your neighbors on the road will have at least sixteen wheels.

Public transportation

The bulk of LA's **public transportation** is run by the LA County Metropolitan Transit Authority (MTA or "Metro"), whose massive **Gateway Transit Center**, Downtown to the east of Union Station on Vignes Street, serves commuters traveling by Metrorail, light rail, commuter rail, Amtrak, and regional buses. The Center comprises **Patsaouras Transit Plaza**, from where buses depart, the glass-domed **East Portal**, which leads to train connections, and the 26-story Gateway Tower, which has an MTA **customer service office** on the ground floor (Mon–Fri 6am–6.30pm; ☎1-800/COMMUTE, ⊛www.mta.net).

Metrorail

LA's **Metrorail** subway and light-rail system has tried for nearly two decades to expand and access areas of the city that its critics claimed it would never reach. The system has generally been successful in reaching its geographic goals, and more commuters are riding it each year. For tourists, much depends on location – if you're staying in Hollywood, Pasadena, or Long Beach and want to go Downtown without a car (or vice versa), it's pretty useful. Otherwise, the city's other popular areas – notably the Westside – are well out of its reach.

LA's **Metrorail** system encompasses six lines, though extensions are planned in coming years. The **Orange Line** crosses the San Fernando Valley and links Canoga Park with North Hollywood, where it connects to the northern terminus for the underground **Red Line**, heading south under the Hollywood Hills to connect Central Hollywood and Downtown (stopping at the Gateway Transit Center, as do all Downtown routes); the **Purple Line** covers the last part of the same ground, from Vermont Avenue to Union Station, but also extends a short distance west to Western Avenue. Of more use to residents than tourists, the **Green Line** runs between industrial El Segundo (where you can pick up an LAX shuttle at Aviation Station; see p.25) and colorless Norwalk in South LA. The **Blue Line** leaves Downtown and heads overland through South Central to Long Beach, while the more appealing **Gold Line**, another light-rail route, connects Downtown with northeast LA, Highland Park, and Old Pasadena, before ending at drab Sierra Madre; another section of the Gold Line, to East LA, is due to open in late 2009. **Fares** are $1.25 one way, with day passes available for $3. Trains run daily from 5am to 12.30am, at five- to six-minute intervals during peak hours and every ten to fifteen minutes at other times. No smoking, eating, or drinking is allowed while on board.

Other forms of rail transit mainly serve more distant parts of the city. Amtrak, for example, connects to points in Ventura, Riverside, and Orange counties and beyond (see p.20).

Metrolink

As one rail alternative, **Metrolink** commuter trains ply primarily suburban-to-Downtown routes on weekdays, which can be useful if you find yourself in any such far-flung districts, among them places in Orange, Ventura, Riverside, and San Bernardino counties. Although casual visitors may find the service useful mainly for reaching the outlying corners of the San Fernando Valley, the system does reach as far as Oceanside in San Diego County, where you can connect to that region's Coaster commuter rail (see p.368) and avoid the freeways altogether. One-way Metrolink fares range from $4.75 to $12.50, depending on when you're traveling (most routes run during daily business hours, often to LA in the morning and back to the suburbs in the evening) and how far you're going. For information on specific routes and schedules, call ⓣ1-800/371-LINK or visit ⓦwww.metrolinktrains.com.

Buses

Car-less Angelenos not lucky enough to live near a train route have to settle for **buses**. Although initially bewildering, the MTA network is really quite simple: the main routes

MTA offices and information

For **MTA route and transfer information**, phone ⓣ213/626-4455 or 1-800/COMMUTE; be ready to give precise details of where you are and where you want to go. Otherwise, you can check out the MTA website (ⓦwww.mta.net) or go in person to Downtown's Gateway Transit Center, Chavez Avenue at Vignes Street (Mon–Fri 6am–6.30pm), or to Mid-Wilshire at 5301 Wilshire Blvd (Mon–Fri 9am–5pm).

run east–west (eg, between Downtown and the coast) and north–south (eg, between Downtown and the South Bay). Establishing the best transfer point if you need to change buses can be difficult, but with a bit of planning you should have few problems – though always allow plenty of time.

Free brochures are available from MTA offices, as are diagrams and timetables for individual bus routes and regional bus maps showing larger sections of the metropolis. Buses on the major arteries between Downtown and the coast run roughly every fifteen minutes between 5am and 2am; other routes, and the **all-night services** along the major thoroughfares, are less frequent, usually every thirty minutes or hourly. At night, be careful not to get stranded Downtown waiting for connecting buses.

The standard **one-way fare** is $1.25, except for night routes (9pm–5am), when the cost is only 75¢; **express buses** (a limited commuter service) and any others using a freeway are usually $1.75–2.25. Put the correct money (coins or bills) into the slot when getting on. If you're staying in LA for a while, you can save some money with a **weekly** or **monthly pass**, which cost $14 and $52, respectively, and also give reductions at selected shops and travel agents. If you're staying about two weeks, consider a semi-monthly pass, sold for $27. Finally, "EZ Transit" passes give you the option of traveling on MTA and DASH buses, as well as Metrorail trains, for a flat $58 per month.

Metro Rapid routes run throughout the region, offering a modified bus service (along special #700 lines) with particular red-colored identification, waiting kiosks with enhanced displays, and technology to reduce waiting times at red lights. There are also the mini **DASH** buses, which operate through the LA Department of Transportation, or LADOT (☏808-2273 for area codes 213, 310, 323, and 818; ⊛www.ladottransit.com), with a flat fare of 25¢ for broad coverage throughout Downtown and limited routes elsewhere in the city. The LADOT also operates quick, limited-stop routes called **commuter express**, though these cost a bit more (90¢–$3.10) depending on distance.

Other **local bus services** include those for Orange County (OCTD; ☏714/636-7433, ⊛www.octa.net), Long Beach (LBTD; ☏562/591-2301, ⊛www.lbtransit.org), Culver City (☏310/253-6500, ⊛www.culvercity .org/depts_bus.html), and Santa Monica (☏310/451-5444, ⊛www.bigbluebus.com), which is the best option for reaching the Getty Center (see p.129).

Bus routes

MTA's bus routes fall into six categories, as outlined below. Whatever bus you're on, if traveling alone, especially at night, it's best to sit up front near the driver.

#1–99 Local routes to and from Downtown
#100–299 Local routes between other areas
#300–399 Limited-stop routes (usually rush hour only)
#400–499 Express routes to and from Downtown
#500–599 Express routes for other areas
#600–699 Special service routes (for sports events and the like)
#700–799 Metro Rapid service

Major LA bus lines

Metro routes unless otherwise stated.

From LAX bus center to:
Beverly Hills Santa Monica line #3 or Culver City line #6 to Metro #720
Culver City: Culver City line #6
Downtown #42, #439
Hollywood: Santa Monica line #3 to Metro #4 or #304
Long Beach #232
Santa Monica Santa Monica line #3
Watts Towers #117
West Hollywood Santa Monica line #3 to Metro #4 or #304

To and from Downtown along:
Beverly Blvd #14, #714

Hollywood Blvd #2, #4, #10, #11, #14, or #714, then connect at La Brea Ave onto #212 or #312 north
Melrose Ave #10, #11
Olympic Blvd #28, #328
Santa Monica Blvd #4, #304
Sunset Blvd #2, #302
Venice Blvd #33, #333
Wilshire Blvd #20, #21, #720

From Downtown to:

Beverly Hills #14, #20, #21, #714, #720
Burbank Studios #96
Exposition Park #81, #381
Forest Lawn Cemetery, Glendale #90, #91
Getty Center #2 or #302 then transfer at UCLA to #761
Hermosa Beach/Redondo Beach #130, then transfer to #444
Hollywood #2, #302
Huntington Library #79
Long Beach #60, #360
Orange County, Knott's Berry Farm, Disneyland #460
Rancho Palos Verdes #444
San Pedro #445, #446, #447
Santa Monica #4, #20, #304, #720
Venice #33, #333

Taxis

You can find **taxis** at most transit terminals and major hotels. Among the more reliable companies are Independent Cab Co (☏1-800/521-8294), Checker Cab (☏1-800/300-5007), Yellow Cab (☏1-800/200-1085), and United Independent Taxi (☏1-800/411-0303). Fares, which are set by the city, start at $2.65 plus $2.45 for each mile (or 44¢ per minute of waiting time), with a $2.50 surcharge if you're picked up at LAX. The driver won't know every street in LA but will know the major ones; ask for the nearest junction and give directions from there. If you encounter problems, call ☏1-800/501-0999, or visit ⊛www.taxicabsla.org.

Bikes

Cycling in LA may sound perverse, but in some areas it can be one of the better ways of getting around. There is an excellent **beach bike path** between Santa Monica and Redondo Beach, and another from Long Beach to Newport Beach, as well as many equally enjoyable inland routes, notably

Guided tours of LA

One quick and easy way to see LA is on a guided tour. The mainstream tours carry large busloads of visitors to the major tourist sights; specialist tours usually carry smaller groups and are often a better, quirkier value; and media studio tours are available on day-trips by most of the mainstream operators, though again you'll save money by turning up on your own.

Mainstream tours

By far the most popular of the mainstream tours is the half-day "stars' homes" jaunt. Usually including the Farmers' Market, Sunset Strip, Rodeo Drive, the Hollywood Bowl, and, of course, the "stars' homes," these tours are typically the most visible, and the area around the Chinese Theatre is thick with tourists lining up for tickets. Other programs include tours around the Westside at night, to the beach areas, the Queen Mary, day-long excursions to Disneyland, and shopping trips to Tijuana.

Costs are $30–95 per person, with some simple hour-long trips around Hollywood for around $20. You can make reservations at – and be picked up from – most hotels. Otherwise contact one of the following booking offices:

Hollywood Fantasy Tours ☏323/469-8184, ⍟www.hollywoodfantasytours.com.

LA Tours ☏323/460-6490, ⍟www.latours.net.

Red Line Tours ☏323/402-1074, ⍟www.redlinetours.com.

Starline Tours ☏1-800/959-3131, ⍟www.starlinetours.com.

VIP Tours ☏310/641-8114, ⍟www.viptoursandcharters.com.

Specialist tours

The specialist tours listed are also generally $30 or more per person.

Architecture Tours LA ☏323/464-7868, ⍟www.architecturetoursla.com. Driving tours of the master buildings of the LA region, with packages focusing on Hollywood, West LA, Pasadena, and Downtown. Cost varies depending on itinerary.

Architours ☏323/294-5821, ⍟www.architours.com. Walking, driving, and custom tours of the art and architecture highlights of the city. Multiday trips also available. Prices vary according to itinerary.

Neon Cruises ☏213/489-9918, ⍟www.neonmona.org. Popular, three-hour evening tours of LA's best remaining neon art, once a month on Saturdays (June–Oct), organized by the Museum of Neon Art. You may need to book months in advance. $45.

SPARC tours: the Murals of LA 685 Venice Blvd, Venice ☏310/822-9560, ⍟www.sparcmurals.org. Enlightening tour of the "mural capital of the world." Along with being an excellent art center, SPARC conducts two-hour mural tours ($400), personalized to your interests and sometimes including discussions with the artists.

To Fly LA 16303 Waterman Drive, Van Nuys ☏877/TO-FLY-LA, ⍟www.toflyla.com. Tours by helicopter of some of the more prominent visual sights in the region, such as movie studios, skyscrapers, and the Hollywood sign, for $225–395, with dinner packages available.

Studio tours

For some insight into how a film or TV show is made, or just to admire the special effects, there are guided studio tours at Warner Brothers ($35; ⍟www.burbank.com /warner_bros_tour.shtml), NBC ($7.50; ☏818/840-3537), Sony ($25; ☏323/520-TOUR), Paramount ($35; ⍟www.paramount.com/studio), and Universal ($53, plus $7 parking; ⍟www.universalstudioshollywood.com), all near Burbank except for Sony, in Culver City, and Paramount, in Hollywood. If you want to be part of the **audience** in a TV show, Hollywood Boulevard, just outside the Chinese Theatre, is the spot to be: TV company reps regularly appear handing out free tickets, and they'll bus you to the studio and back. All you have to do once there is be willing to laugh and clap on cue.

around Griffith Park and the grand mansions of Pasadena. For maps and information, contact AAA, 2601 S Figueroa Street (Mon–Fri 9am–5pm; ☎213/741-3686, ⓦwww.aaa-calif.com), or the LA office of the state's Department of Transportation, known as CalTrans, 100 S Main Street (Mon–Fri 8am–5pm; ☎213/897-3656, ⓦwww.dot.ca.gov). Bike rental prices range from $10 a day for a clunker to $15–20 a day or more for a mountain bike (see "Sports and Outdoor Activities," p.326, for a list of vendors). Many beachside stores also rent **roller skates** and **rollerblades**.

Walking

Although some people are surprised to find sidewalks in LA, let alone pedestrians, walking is in fact the best way to see much of Downtown and districts like central Hollywood, Pasadena, Beverly Hills, Santa Monica, and Venice. You can structure your stroll by taking a guided walking tour (see box), the best of which are organized by the Los Angeles Conservancy (☎213/623-CITY, ⓦwww.laconservancy.org), whose treks around Downtown are full of Art Deco movie palaces, once-opulent financial monuments, and architectural gems. You can enjoy guided hikes through the wilds of the Santa Monica Mountains and Hollywood Hills free of charge every weekend with a variety of organizations and bureaus, including the Sierra Club (☎213/387-4287, ⓦwww.angeles.sierraclub.org), the State Parks Department (☎818/880-0350, ⓦwww.parks.ca.gov), and the Santa Monica Mountains National Recreation Area (☎805/370-2301, ⓦwww.nps.gov/samo).

The media

Known for its helicopter pursuits of police chases and for constant celebrity gossip, LA's local press has a deserved reputation for sensationalism, but you can still find good regional and national media outlets, typically of the print variety. With the growth of cable TV, there are more television viewing choices than ever, though since most channels are owned by the same handful of multinational corporations, the quality has not improved one bit. The same is true for area radio stations; hunt down LA's public-radio affiliates for relief from the inane talk-show chatter and rigid pop-music playlists.

Newspapers and magazines

For such a large city, LA supports surprisingly few daily **newspapers**. At the top of the list is the *Los Angeles Times* (ⓦwww.latimes.com), the most widely read newspaper in Southern California, available at news boxes and dealers throughout town. Friday's "Calendar" section is an essential source for entertainment and cultural listings (with much of the information also available online for a fee at ⓦwww.calendarlive.com). Upscale hotels often distribute the newspaper to your door for free, sometimes along with a copy of the *New York Times* or *Wall Street Journal*. However, most other major newspapers, whether domestic or foreign, tend to be found mainly at city and university libraries, and a few large magazine stands.

As far as **other dailies** go, the *Los Angeles Daily News* (ⓦwww.dailynews.com) is more conservative than the *LA Times*, with a near-militant suburban slant; while *La Opinion* (ⓦwww.laopinion.com) is one of the country's major Spanish-language newspapers, and has a large readership in LA. The *Orange County Register* (ⓦwww.ocregister.com), a right-of-center paper, is mainly found in its namesake macro-suburb and offers little for LA readers.

There are a few good **alternative weeklies**, most notably the free *LA Weekly* (Ⓦwww.laweekly.com), found at libraries and retailers everywhere, providing engaging investigative journalism and copious entertainment listings. The *OC Weekly* (Ⓦwww .ocweekly.com), the liberal Orange County counterpart of the *LA Weekly*, is a fine alternative source. Valuable substitute for the *Weekly* is the relatively recent *Los Angeles CityBeat* (Ⓦwww.lacitybeat.com), which like its competitor is free and found in boxes throughout town.

Every community of any size has at least a few free newspapers that cater to the local scene. Many of these are also good sources for listings for bars, restaurants, and nightlife within their areas. Both the USC and UCLA campuses have libraries carrying recent overseas newspapers, while day-old **foreign papers** are on sale in Hollywood at Universal News Agency, 1645 N Las Palmas Ave (daily 7am–midnight), and the 24-hour World Book and News, 1652 N Cahuenga Blvd.

LA has a few style-conscious **magazines**, foremost among them the monthly *Los Angeles* magazine (Ⓦwww.lamag.com), packed with gossipy news and profiles of local movers and shakers, as well as reviews of the city's trendiest restaurants and clubs. There are also dozens of less glossy, more erratically published **zines** focusing on LA's diverse gay and lesbian culture and nightclubs. As for **free** magazines, the touristy *Where LA* (Ⓦwww.wherela.com) is a monthly public-relations magazine found in many hotel rooms, and has both glossy reviews and more straightforward listings.

Television

LA **network television** generally offers a steady diet of talk shows, sitcoms, soap operas, and the ubiquitous "reality shows," with some Spanish-language and Asian stations on the UHF portion of the dial. An ad-free alternative to the standard fare is KCET, on UHF channel 28 (Ⓦwww.kcet.org), LA's public television station and one of the nation's top producers of educational programs.

Most motel and hotel rooms are hooked up to some form of **cable TV**, though the number of channels available to guests depends on where you stay. (See the daily papers for channels, schedules, and times.) Most cable stations are actually no better than the big broadcast networks, though some of the specialized channels are occasionally interesting. Cable News Network (CNN) and Headline News both have round-the-clock news, with Fox News providing a right-wing slant on the day's events. ESPN is your best bet for all kinds of sports, MTV for youth-oriented music videos and programming, and VH-1 for Baby Boomer shows. Home Box Office (HBO) and Showtime present big-budget Hollywood flicks and excellent TV shows, while Turner Classic Movies takes its programming from the Golden Age of Hollywood cinema (1930s to 1950s).

Many major **sporting events** are transmitted on a pay-per-view basis, and watching an event like a heavyweight boxing match will set you back at least $50, billed directly to your motel room. Most hotels and motels also offer a choice of **recent movies** that have just finished their theatrical runs, at around $10 per film.

Major LA broadcast TV stations

KCBS CBS channel 2
KNBC NBC channel 4
KTLA CW channel 5
KABC ABC channel 7
KCAL CBS channel 9
KTTV Fox channel 11
KCOP MyNetwork channel 13
KCVR PBS channel 24 UHF
KCET PBS channel 28 UHF
KMEX Univision channel 34 UHF (Spanish language)
KVEA Telemundo channel 52 UHF (Spanish language)

Radio

Radio stations are even more abundant than broadcast TV stations, and the majority stick to mainstream commercial formats. **AM stations** are best for news, traffic reports, and talk radio, while **FM stations**, particularly the federally and subscriber-funded **public** and **college stations** found between 88 and 92 FM, broadcast diverse programming, from bizarre underground rock to obscure local theater. Of these stations, KCRW (89.9) has some of the most diverse programming in LA, from public affairs to dance music, which at night can be anything from trance, dub, and trip-hop to ambient. LA also has a range of decent **specialist music** stations – classical, jazz, and so on – as well as a sizable number of Spanish-language stations. Finally, check out LA Radiowatch (@www.radiowatch.com) for information on up-and-coming **Internet** stations playing tunes over the Web – often more unusual and daring than their broadcasted counterparts.

LA radio stations

AM

KFI 640 right-wing talk radio
KFWB 980 news, traffic, talk, sports
KNX 1070 CBS radio: traffic, news, sports
KDIS 1110 Radio Disney
KTLK 1150 left-wing talk
KMZT 1260 "K-Mozart" – classical

FM

KKJZ 88.1 blues and jazz @www.kkjz.org
KXLU 88.9 alternative, progressive, and eclectic @www.kxlu.com
KPCC 89.3 news, talk, arts, and (National Public Radio) NPR @www.scpr.org
KCRW 89.9 one of the country's best NPR affiliates, with new music, transatlantic imports, and world news @www.kcrw.com
KPFK 90.7 leftist opinions, news, and music, Pacifica affiliate @www.kpfk.org
KUSC 91.5 classical and opera @www.kusc.org
KCBS 93.1 oldies
KMVN 93.9 pop
KLOS 95.5 album rock
KLSX 97.1 talk
KRBV 100.3 soul, R&B, and rap
KRTH 101.1 golden oldies
KIIS 102.7 Top 40 pop
KBIG 104.3 pop and dance
KPWR 106 rap and R&B
KROQ 106.7 indie and grunge rock

Culture and etiquette

If you regularly watch the sort of mainstream movies and TV shows that feature life in California, you'll find you're already familiar with many aspects of the area's culture and etiquette before you arrive. A few points do warrant a mention, though.

Some form of picture ID should be carried at all times. A driver's license will probably do the trick, though having a passport as well should diffuse any suspicion. If you're stopped when driving you'll be required to produce a driver's license, the car's registration papers, and verification of insurance (though the latter two will be waived if you are driving a rental).

One point of eternal discussion is tipping. Many workers in service industries get paid very little and rely on tips to bolster their income. Unless you've had abominable service (in which case you should tell the management), you really shouldn't leave a bar or restaurant without leaving a tip of at least fifteen percent, and about the same should be added to taxi fares. A hotel porter deserves roughly $1 for each bag carried to your room; a coat-check clerk should receive the same per coat. When paying by credit card you're expected to add the tip to the bill before filling in the total amount and signing. Smoking is a much frowned-upon activity in California, which has banned it in all indoor public places, including bars and restaurants. In fact, you can spend weeks in the state barely ever smelling cigarette smoke. Nevertheless, cigarettes are sold in virtually any food shop, drugstore, or bar, and also from the occasional vending machine.

Possession of under an ounce of **marijuana** is a misdemeanor in California, and the worst you'll get for holding a little of the widely consumed herb is a $100 fine. Being caught with more than an ounce, however, means facing a criminal charge for dealing, and a possible prison sentence – stiffer if you're caught anywhere near a school. Other **drugs** are, of course, completely illegal and it's a much more serious offense if you're caught with any.

Shopping

Not surprisingly, the richest state in the US is something of a shopper's paradise where you'll be able to find just about anything your heart may desire. Details of specific shopping locations are given throughout the guide, but here is a general indication of what you are likely to come across.

Malls

Visitors to LA, especially on their first visit to the US, cannot fail to be impressed by the ubiquitousness of the ultimate American shopping venue, the mall. Whether these are of the "strip mall" variety, strung out along major arteries, or showpiece complexes in desirable neighborhoods, they unabashedly glorify commercialism and consist mostly of well-known multinational chains. The summit of commercial excess is Rodeo Drive (see p.118) in Beverly Hills, where the older

Clothing and shoe sizes

Women's dresses and skirts

American	4	6	8	10	12	14	16	18
British	8	10	12	14	16	18	20	22
Continental	38	40	42	44	46	48	50	52

Women's blouses and sweaters

American	6	8	10	12	14	16	18
British	30	32	34	36	38	40	42
Continental	40	42	44	46	48	50	52

Women's shoes

American	5	6	7	8	9	10	11
British	3	4	5	6	7	8	9
Continental	36	37	38	39	40	41	42

Men's suits

American	34	36	38	40	42	44	46	48
British	34	36	38	40	42	44	46	48
Continental	44	46	48	50	52	54	56	58

Men's shirts

American	14	15	15.5	16	16.5	17	17.5	18
British	14	15	15.5	16	16.5	17	17.5	18
Continental	36	38	39	41	42	43	44	45

Men's shoes

American	7	7.5	8	8.5	9.5	10	10.5	11	11.5
British	6	7	7.5	8	9	9.5	10	11	12
Continental	39	40	41	42	43	44	44	45	46

Hollywood stars go to shop. Many chic designers have flagship boutiques on the strip, and menswear merchant Bijan, at no. 420, claims to be the most expensive shop in the world, with the average customer dropping $100,000 at one visit.

Arts and crafts

LA is home to many artists, whose paintings, sculptures, and other creations can easily be found both in big galleries on the Westside and in smaller shops with a reputation for creativity, such as those around northeast LA Original artworks will set you back a fair penny, maybe even thousands of bucks, depending on how established the artist is. Quaint gift shops selling attractive items from all over the world also abound and are a good source of souvenirs and presents, even if they are not specifically local.

Farmers' markets, food, and drink

One fine tradition that has survived since California's earlier times are "farmers' markets," which pop up regularly around the city. It can come as a pleasant surprise to stumble on a street full of stalls selling fresh country fare in the middle of Hollywood, for example. Most concentrate solely on edible goods, but the larger ones may have a few gift stalls as well.

LA's countless ethnic eateries, bakeries, cake shops, cheese dealers, and other delicacy suppliers can be well worth seeking out, even though it can be time-consuming to reach the many purveyors spread widely across the metropolitan basin. Check out p.352 for a list of selected shops.

Travel essentials

Costs

Given the historically low value of the American dollar, there's rarely been a better time for foreign travelers to visit LA. The city is less expensive than San Francisco or New York, and with a minimum of effort you can find plenty of bargains and reasonably priced goods and services, though of course you won't lack for choice should you want to splurge at one of the city's swankier restaurants or trendy bars.

Accommodation is likely to be your biggest single **expense** in LA: adequate lodging is rarely available for less than $70 per night, although hostels will of course be cheaper (usually $18–25 per night in a dorm bed). An acceptable hotel room will run from $80 to100, with fancier hotels costing much more – upwards of $400 in some cases. **Camping** is an alternative only if you're staying in more isolated areas like

San Clemente, or in other spots on the fringes of the metropolis (see "Accommodation," p.255).

Unlike accommodation, prices for **good food** range widely, as do the types of places that serve it, from hot-dog stands to chic restaurants. You could get by on as little as $20 a day per person, but realistically you should aim for around $50 – and remember, too, that LA has plenty of great spots for a splurge. Beyond restaurants, the city has many bars, clubs, and live-music venues to suit all tastes and wallets.

In terms of **transportation**, your best bet is probably to rent a car from any of the rental outlets around the airport, for anywhere between $40 and 80 per day. Regional distances are huge, and if you're headed anywhere beyond central LA or, more specifically, beyond the Westside, you'll undoubtedly find public transit to be a time-consuming hassle. US gas prices, despite passing $3 per gallon in recent years, are still relatively cheap compared to those in Europe.

Added to the cost of most items you purchase is an 8.25 percent sales **tax**. Additionally, many LA-area municipalities tack on a hotel tax of around 14–15 percent, which can drive up accommodation costs dramatically.

For attractions in the main part of the Guide, **prices** are quoted for adults, with children's rates listed only if they are more than a few dollars less; at some spots, kids get in for half price, or for free if they're under eight. Seniors may sometimes get a break, too, with admissions that usually run a few dollars less than the standard adult rate. Los Angeles also has a few **free** attractions for everyone, but these are mostly historical and cultural monuments like adobes and old railroad stations – with the major exceptions of the Getty Center and Getty Villa (though parking for each is $8).

Crime and personal safety

Though California isn't trouble-free, you're unlikely to have any run-ins if you stick to the tourist-friendly confines of the major areas. The lawless reputation of Los Angeles is far in excess of the truth; at night, though, a few areas – notably Compton, Inglewood, and East LA – are off-limits. By being careful, planning ahead, and taking care of your possessions, you should be able to avoid any problems.

If you're unlucky enough to get **mugged**, just hand over your money; resistance is generally not a good idea. After the crime occurs, immediately report it to the police so you can later attempt to recover your loss from an insurance provider – unlikely, but worth a try. One prime spot to be mugged is at an **ATM** outside the tourist areas, where you may be told to make the maximum withdrawal and hand it over. Needless to say, you should treat ATM use with the strictest caution and not worry about looking paranoid.

If your passport is stolen (or if you lose it), call your country's consulate (see list on p.39) and pick up or have sent to you an application form, which you must submit with a notarized photocopy of your ID and a reissuing fee, often at least $30.

Car crime and safety

When driving, under no circumstances should you stop if you are "accidentally" rammed by the driver behind you; instead, drive on to the nearest well-lit and busy spot and phone the police at ☏911. Keep doors locked and hide valuables out of sight, either in the trunk or the glove compartment, and leave any valuables you don't need for your journey back in your hotel safe. Should a relatively uncommon "carjacking" occur, in which you're told at gunpoint to hand over your car, you should flee the vehicle as quickly as possible, get away from the scene, and then call the police. If your car breaks down at night while on a major street, activate the emergency flashers to signal a police officer for assistance. During the day, find the nearest phone book and call for a tow truck. Should you be forced to stop your car on a freeway, pull over to the right shoulder – never the left – and activate your flashers. Wait for assistance either in your vehicle, while strapped in by a seatbelt, or on a safe embankment nearby.

Breaking the law

Whether intentionally or not, foreign visitors may find themselves breaking the law on occasion. Aside from speeding or parking violations, one of the most common ways visitors bring trouble on themselves is through jaywalking, or crossing the road against red lights or away from intersections. Fines can be stiff, and the police will most assuredly not take sympathy on you if you mumble that you "didn't think it was illegal."

Alcohol laws provide another source of irritation to visitors, particularly as the law prohibits drinking liquor, wine, or beer in most public spaces like parks and beaches, and, most frustrating of all to European tourists, alcohol is officially off-limits to anyone under 21. Some try to get around this with a phony driver's license, even though getting caught with a fake ID will put you in jeopardy particularly if you're from out of the country. Driving under the influence, or drunk driving, is aggressively punished throughout the state, with loss of license, fines, and potential jail time for those caught breaking the law with a police-enforced "Breathalyzer" test. The current limit is a blood-alcohol level of .08, or three drinks within a single hour for a 150-pound person. Other infringements include insulting a police officer (ie arguing with one) and riding a bicycle at night without proper lights and reflectors.

Entry requirements and visas

Basic requirements for entry to the US are detailed (and should be frequently checked for updates) on the US State Department website (ⓦtravel.state.gov).

Under the Visa Waiver Program (VWP), if you're a citizen of the UK, Ireland, Australia, New Zealand, most western European states, or other selected countries (27 in all), and visiting the US for less than ninety days, at a minimum you'll need an onward or return ticket, a visa waiver form, and a Machine Readable Passport (MRP). The **I-94W Nonimmigrant Visa Waiver Arrival/ Departure Form** will be provided either by your travel agency or embassy or when you board the plane. The same form covers entry across the US borders with Canada and Mexico (for non-Canadian and non-Mexican citizens). Under no circumstances are visitors who have been admitted under the Visa Waiver Program allowed to extend their stays beyond ninety days. If you're in the Visa Waiver Program and intend to work, study, or stay in the country for more than ninety days, you must apply for a **regular visa** through your local US embassy or consulate.

Canadian citizens, who have not always needed a passport to get into the US, should have their passports on them when entering the country. If you're planning to stay for more than ninety days you'll need a **visa.** Without the proper paperwork, Canadians are barred from working in the US.

Citizens of all other countries should contact their local US embassy or consulate for details of current entry requirements, as they are often required to have both a valid passport and a nonimmigrant visitor's visa.

For further information or to get a **visa extension** before your time is up, contact the nearest US Citizenship and Immigration Service office, whose address will be at the front of the phone book under the Federal Government Offices listings, or call ☎1-800/877-3676. You can also contact the National Customer Service Center at ☎1-800/375-5283.

US Customs

Upon your entry to the US, Customs officers will relieve you of your customs declaration form, which you receive on incoming planes, on ferries, and at border crossing points. It asks if you're carrying any fresh foods and if you've visited a farm in the last month.

As well as food and anything agricultural, it's prohibited to carry into the country any articles from such places as North Korea, Iran, Syria, or Cuba, as well as obvious no-nos like protected wildlife species and ancient artifacts. Anyone caught sneaking **drugs** into the country will not only face prosecution but be entered in the records as an undesirable and probably denied entry for all time. For duty-free allowances and other information regarding customs, call ☎202/354-1000 or visit ⓦwww.customs.gov.

US embassies and consulates abroad

Australia

Canberra (embassy) 21 Moonah Place, Yarralumla ACT 2600 ☎02/6214 5600, ⓦcanberra .usembassy.gov
Melbourne (consulate) 553 St Kilda Rd, VIC 3004 ☎03/9526 5900
Perth (consulate) 16 St George's Terrace, 13th Floor, WA 6000 ☎08/9202 1224
Sydney (consulate) MLC Centre, Level 10, 19–29 Martin Place, NSW 2000 ☎02/9373 9200

Canada

Ottawa (embassy) 490 Sussex Drive, ON K1N 1G8 ☎613/238-5335, ⓦcanada.usembassy.gov
Calgary (consulate) 615 Macleod Trail SE, Room 1000, AB T2G 4T8 ☎403/266-8962
Halifax (consulate) Wharf Tower II, 1969 Upper Water St, Suite 904, NS B3J 3R7 ☎902/429-2480
Montréal (consulate) 1155 St Alexandré St, QC H3B 1Z1 ☎514/398-9695, ⓦmontreal.usconsulate .gov
Québec City (consulate) 2 Place Terrasse Dufferin, QC G1R 4T9 ☎418/692-2095, ⓦquebec.usconsulate.gov
Toronto (consulate) 360 University Ave, ON M5G 1S4 ☎416/595-1700, ⓦtoronto.usconsulate.gov

Vancouver (consulate) 1095 W Pender St, 21st Floor, BC V6E 2M6 ☎604/685-4311, ⓦvancouver .usconsulate.gov

Winnipeg (consulate) 201 Portage Ave, Suite 860, MB R3B 3K6 ☎204/940-1800, ⓦwww .usconsulatewinnipeg.ca

Ireland

Dublin (embassy) 42 Elgin Rd, Ballsbridge 4 ☎01/668 8777, ⓦdublin.usembassy.gov

New Zealand

Wellington (embassy) 29 Fitzherbert Terrace, Thorndon ☎04/462 6000, ⓦnewzealand .usembassy.gov

Auckland (consulate) 3rd Floor, Citibank Building, 23 Customs St ☎09/303 2724

South Africa

Pretoria (embassy) 877 Pretorius St, 0083 ☎12/431 4000, ⒻA12/342 2299, ⓦusembassy .state.gov/pretoria

UK

London (embassy) 24 Grosvenor Square, W1A 1AE ☎020/7499 9000, visa hotline ☎09042/450 100, ⓦlondon.usembassy.gov

Belfast (consulate) Danesfort House, 223 Stranmillis Road, Belfast BT9 5GR ☎028/9038 6100

Edinburgh (consulate) 3 Regent Terrace, EH7 5BW ☎0131/556 8315

Consulates in California

Australia

Los Angeles 2049 Century Park E, 19th Floor, CA 90067 ☎310/229-4800, ⓦwww.dfat.gov.au /missions

Canada

Los Angeles 550 S Hope St, 9th Floor, CA 90071-2627 ☎213/346-2700, Ⓕ213/620-8827, ⓦwww .dfait-maeci.gc.ca

San Diego 402 W Broadway, 4th Floor, CA 92101 ☎619/615-4287, Ⓕ619/615-4286

Ireland

San Francisco 100 Pine St, Suite 3350, San Francisco, CA 94111 ☎415/392-4214, Ⓕ415/392-0885

New Zealand

Los Angeles 2425 Olympic Blvd, Santa Monica, CA 90404 ☎310/566-6555, ⓦwww.nzcgla.com

South Africa

Los Angeles 6300 Wilshire Blvd, Suite 600, CA 90048 ☎323/651-0902, Ⓕ323/651-5969, ⓦwww.link2southafrica.com

UK

Los Angeles 11766 Wilshire Blvd, Suite 1200, CA 90025 ☎310/481-0031, Ⓕ481-2960, ⓦwww .britainusa.com/la

Electricity

The US operates on 110V 60Hz and uses two-pronged plugs with the flat prongs parallel. Foreign devices will need both a plug adapter and a transformer, though laptops and phone chargers usually automatically detect and cope with the different voltage and frequency.

Health

Foreign travelers should be comforted that if you have a serious accident while you're in California, emergency services will get to you sooner and charge you later. For **emergencies**, dial toll-free ☎911 from any phone. For medical or dental problems that don't require an ambulance, most hospitals have a walk-in emergency room: for your nearest hospital or dental office, check with your hotel or dial information at ☎411.

Should you need to see a **doctor**, lists can be found in the *Yellow Pages* under "Clinics" or "Physicians and Surgeons." Be aware that even consultations are costly, usually around $75–125 each visit, which is payable in advance. Keep receipts for any part of your medical treatment, including prescriptions, so that you can claim against your insurance once you're home.

For minor ailments, stop by a local **pharmacy**, a few of which are open 24 hours. Foreign visitors should note that many medicines available over the counter at home – codeine-based painkillers, for one – are **prescription-only** in the US. Bring additional supplies if you're particularly brand-loyal.

By far the most common tourist illness in California is **sunburn**: the sun can be fierce, so plenty of protective sunscreen (SPF 30 and above) is a must. Surfers and swimmers should also watch for strong currents and **undertows** at some beaches: we've noted in the text where the water can be especially treacherous.

Travelers from Europe, Canada, and Australia do not require inoculations to enter the US.

Medical resources for travelers

US and Canada

CDC ⓦwww.cdc.gov/travel. Official US government travel health site.
International Society for Travel Medicine ⓦwww.istm.org. Has a full list of travel health clinics.

Australia, New Zealand, and South Africa

Travellers' medical and Vaccination Centre ⓦwww.tmvc.com.au, ☎1300/658 844. Lists travel clinics in Australia, New Zealand, and South Africa.

UK and Ireland

British Airways Travel Clinics ☎012776/685-040 or ⓦwww.britishairways.com/travel/healthclinintro/public/en_gb for nearest clinic.
MASTA (Medical Advisory Service for Travellers Abroad) ⓦwww.masta.org or ☎0113/238-7575 for the nearest clinic.
Travel Medicine Services ☎028/9031 5220.

Insurance

As most people know by now, the US has no national health-care system. You're well advised to protect yourself from exorbitant medical costs should any injury occur while in the country. Even though EU health-care privileges apply in America, UK residents would do well to take out an **insurance** policy before traveling to cover against theft, loss, and illness or injury. Before paying for a new policy, however, it's worth checking whether you are already covered – some all-risks home insurance policies may cover your possessions when overseas, and many private medical schemes include coverage when abroad. Holders of official student/teacher/youth cards in Canada and the US are entitled to meager accident coverage and hospital in-patient benefits. Students will often find that their student health coverage extends during vacation periods and for one term beyond the date of last enrollment.

After exhausting the possibilities above, you might want to contact a **specialist travel insurance** company. A typical travel insurance policy usually provides cover for the loss of baggage, tickets, and – up to a certain limit – cash or checks, as well as cancellation or curtailment of your journey. Most of them exclude so-called dangerous sports unless an extra premium is paid: in America, this can mean scuba diving, white-water rafting, and windsurfing, though probably not kayaking. Many policies can be changed to exclude coverage you don't need – for example, sickness and accident benefits can often be excluded or included at will. If you do take medical coverage, ascertain whether benefits will be paid as treatment proceeds or only after return home, and if there is a 24-hour medical emergency number. When securing **baggage coverage**, make sure that the per-article limit – typically under £500 – will cover your most valuable possession. If you need to make a claim, you should keep receipts for medicines and medical treatment, and in the event you have anything stolen, you must obtain an official theft report from the police.

Rough Guides has teamed up with Columbus Direct to offer you travel insurance that can be tailored to suit your needs. Products include a low-cost **backpacker** option for long stays; a **short break** option for city getaways; a typical **holiday package** option; and others. There are also annual **multitrip** policies for those who travel regularly. Different sports and activities can usually be covered if required. See our website (ⓦwww.roughguides.com/website/shop) for eligibility and purchasing options. Alternatively, UK residents should call ☎0870/033 9988, Australians ☎1300/669 999, and New Zealanders ☎0800/55 99 11. All other nationalities should call ☎+44 870/890 2843.

Internet

The proliferation of wireless hot spots all over the region means anyone traveling with a WiFi–enabled laptop or PDA should have no trouble getting connected to the **Internet**, often at fast speeds at no cost. At some cafés you'll need to use your credit card to sign up for a service, though many other cafés have unsecured access or will give you the password when you buy a coffee or muffin.

If you need to borrow a computer to log on, the best bets are **public libraries**, which almost invariably have **free Internet access**, usually available for an hour a day – just ask at the front desk. You may have to wait for an opening, or sign up for a later slot. Espresso **cafés** are another good bet. You'll sometimes find a couple of computers in the corner for which there'll be a small charge, though these are becoming increasingly rare as places have taken out their machines when they've installed a WiFi network. You'll also come across dedicated **cybercafés** with a dozen or more machines usually charged at around $5–10 an hour. Many motels, hotels, and hostels also offer Internet access with a machine or two in the lobby, but again, WiFi is taking over.

If you are traveling with a **laptop** and want to get connected, visit ⓦ www.kropla.com, which gives details of how to plug your laptop in when abroad, phone country codes around the world, and information about electrical systems in different countries.

Laundry

The larger hotels provide laundry service at a price. Cheaper motels and hostels may have self-service laundry facilities, but in general you'll be doing your laundry at a laundromat. Found all over the place, they're usually open fairly long hours and have a powder-dispensing machine and another to provide change. A typical wash and dry might cost $4–6.

Mail

Post offices are usually open Monday through Friday, from 9am to 5pm, although some are also open on Saturday from 9am to noon or 1pm.

Ordinary **mail** within the US costs 41¢ for letters weighing up to an ounce; addresses must include the zip code, which can be found at ⓦ www.usps.com. The return address should be written in the upper left corner of the envelope. **Airmail** from California to Europe generally takes about a week. Letters weighing up to an ounce (a couple of sheets) cost 84¢, and postcards

cost 75¢ (63¢ to Canada and 55¢ to Mexico).

Drop mail off at any post office or in the blue mailboxes found on street corners throughout LA. Domestic letters that don't carry a **zip code** are liable to get lost or at least seriously delayed; phone books list zip codes for their service area, and post offices – even abroad – should have zip-code directories for major US cities.

You can have mail sent to you c/o General Delivery (known elsewhere as poste restante), at the main post office in Downtown LA, north of Union Station, at 900 N Alameda St, Los Angeles, CA 90012 (Mon–Fri 8am–5.30pm, Sat 8am–4pm; ☎213/617-4404), which will hold mail for thirty days before returning it to the sender – so make sure the envelope has a return address. Alternatively, any decent hotel will hold mail for you, even in advance of your arrival.

Rules on sending **parcels** are very rigid: packages must be sealed according to the instructions given at the start of the *Yellow Pages*. To send anything out of the country, you'll need a green **customs declaration form**, available from the post office. Postal rates for airmailing a parcel weighing up to 1lb to Europe, Australia, and New Zealand are $14–18.

Maps

The **maps** in this book should be sufficient in helping you find your way around the main parts of town and their key attractions, with the exception of the Hollywood Hills, whose serpentine passages and switchbacks require highly detailed maps to navigate (and even then, with difficulty). For a folding map, try Rand McNally's excellent Los Angeles/Hollywood map ($4.95) focusing on central LA, or our own rip-proof *Los Angeles Rough Guide Map* ($8.95).

For a more detailed view of the city, Thomas Brothers Publishing has the hefty, spiral-bound, 2008 editions *LA County Thomas Guide* ($19.95), and *Thomas Guide to Los Angeles and Orange Counties* ($34.95), sold at most bookstores. Published yearly for counties across Southern California, the Thomas guides are the best maps available for regional travel, especially for venturing beyond the easily accessed parts of the city into more unfamiliar territory – like the northern deserts, eastern suburbs, or Hollywood Hills. If you're staying for several weeks, consider purchasing one if you're traveling anywhere outside central LA. If you're interested in highly detailed views of rural terrain, as well as the urban layout, consider DeLorme's large-format *Atlas and Gazetteer of Southern and Central California* ($19.95, last updated in 2005), which best shows national forests, parkland, hiking trails, and minor dirt and gravel roads. The colorful *Benchmark California Road and Recreation Atlas* ($24.95, published 2002) is also excellent for showing the same features.

If you happen to be a member, stop by the Automobile Club of Southern California, 2601 S Figueroa St, south of Downtown (Mon–Fri 9am–5pm; ☏213/741-3686, ⊛www .aaa-calif.com), for free maps, guides, and other information. The national office of the AAA also provides maps and assistance to its members, as well as to British members of the AA and RAC, and Canadian members of the CAA (☏1-800/222-4357, ⊛www.aaa.com).

LA-area travel bookshops can be found under "Shopping," p.356.

Money

With an **ATM card**, you'll be able to withdraw money just about anywhere in LA, though you'll be charged $2–4 for using a different bank's network. Foreign cash-dispensing cards linked to international networks, such as Plus or Cirrus, are also widely accepted. Make sure you have a **personal identification number** (PIN) that's designed to work overseas.

Bank hours are generally from 9am to 5pm Monday to Thursday, and from 10am to 6pm on Friday; the big local names are Wells Fargo and Bank of America. For banking services – especially currency exchange – outside normal business hours and on weekends, try major hotels or Travelex outlets.

Credit cards are the most widely accepted form of payment for most hotels, restaurants, and retailers. Using a credit card can save on exchange-rate commissions. Most major credit cards issued by foreign banks are honored in the US. Visa, MasterCard, American Express, and Diners Club are the most widely used.

If your credit cards are **stolen**, you'll need to provide information on where and when you made your last transactions, and to access the specific credit card company emergency numbers (on the back of your card).

Opening hours and public holidays

The opening hours of specific attractions – including museums, theme parks, public offices, and homes open for tours – are given throughout the Guide, with phone numbers for those sights that are open irregularly, closed until further notice, or accessible only via advance reservation. It's always worth checking ahead, especially if you're planning to visit attractions far from central LA.

As a general rule, most museums are open Tuesday through Saturday (occasionally Sunday, too) from 10am until 5 or 6pm, with somewhat shorter hours on the weekends. Many museums will also stay open late one evening a week – usually Thursday, when

---

Money: a note for foreign travelers

Given its recent decline in value, one **US dollar** is now the rough equivalent of .50 pound sterling, .68 euro, one Canadian dollar, 1.14 Australian dollars, 1.28 New Zealand dollars and 6.7 South African rand – all of which makes visiting LA an attractive budget vacation.

US currency comes in bills of $1, $5, $10, $20, $50, and $100 **denominations**. All are the same size, though denominations of $10 and higher have in the last few years been changing shades from their familiar drab green. The dollar comprises one hundred cents, made up of combinations of one-cent pennies, five-cent nickels, ten-cent dimes, and 25-cent quarters. Quarters are most useful for buses, vending machines, parking meters, and telephones, so always carry plenty.

ticket prices are sometimes reduced. Government offices, including post offices, are open during regular business hours, typically 8 or 9am until 5pm, Monday through Friday (though some post offices are open Sat morning until noon or 1pm). Most stores are open daily from 10am until 5 or 6pm, while specialty stores can be more erratic, usually opening and closing later in the day, from noon to 2pm until 8 or 9pm, and remaining shuttered for two days of the week. Malls tend to be open from 10am until 7 or 8pm daily, though individual stores may close before the mall does.

While some diners stay open 24 hours, the more typical restaurants open daily around 11am or noon for lunch and close at 9 to 10pm. Places that serve breakfast usually open early, between 6 to 8am, serve lunch later, and close in the early or mid-afternoon. Dance and live music clubs often won't open until 9 or 10pm, and many will serve liquor until 2am and then either close for the night or stay open until dawn without serving booze. Bars that close at 2am may reopen as early as 6am to grab bleary-eyed regulars in need of a liquid breakfast.

On the national public holidays listed below, banks, government offices, and many museums are likely to be closed all day. Small stores, as well as some restaurants and clubs, are usually closed as well, but shopping malls, supermarkets, and department and chain stores increasingly remain open, regardless of the holiday. Most parks, beaches, and cemeteries stay open during holidays, too. Some tourist attractions, information centers, motels, and campsites are only open during the traditional tourist season, from Memorial Day to Labor Day, though California's benign weather extends that considerably.

National holidays

New Year's Day Jan 1
Martin Luther King's Birthday observed third Mon in Jan
Presidents' Day third Mon in Feb
Memorial Day last Mon in May
Independence Day July 4
Labor Day first Mon in Sept
Columbus Day second Mon in Oct
Veterans' Day Nov 11

Thanksgiving fourth Thurs in Nov
Christmas Dec 25

Phones

Like most major US cities, LA has an excellent communications infrastructure, with countless high-tech links to the rest of the country and the world. Although some areas are better hooked up than others – the Westside, for example – most communication services are more than adequate throughout the region, especially telephone service and email.

If you're making a **telephone** call, Los Angeles has almost a dozen area codes (listed below) that, with the rise of ten-digit dialing, you may need to use even if calling from within the same area code. A local call on a public phone usually costs 50¢. Outside the immediate calling zone, you'll have to dial a 1, plus the area code, then the telephone number. Unless you're using a cell phone (and not paying a roaming fee), you'll be

Telephone charge cards

Most long-distance companies enable customers to make **calling-card** calls billed to their home number. Call your company's customer-service line to find out if it provides this service, and if so, what the toll-free access code is.

An alternative to telephone charge cards is cheap, **pre-paid phone cards** allowing calls to virtually anywhere in the world. Most convenience stores sell them; look for signs posted in shop windows advertising rates, which can vary dramatically, and check the fine print to make sure you're getting a good deal. Some cards allow you to add time to them as their minutes elapse through the use of a unique PIN number, while others only have a set number of minutes available. Finally, pre-paid calling-card companies may change their rates, policies, or deals on a month-to-month basis, or go out of business altogether, so if you're buying a card, make sure to use it within a reasonable amount of time, lest you end up with a worthless piece of plastic.

charged quite a bit more for out-of-area-code calls than for calls within them. For detailed information about calls, area codes, and rates in the LA area, consult the front *White Pages* of the telephone directory.

Of course, **mobile phones** are ubiquitous, and with excellent reception in all but the remotest areas, taking your phone to California makes a lot of sense. Ask your provider to confirm that your phone will work on US frequencies (most do these days) and get it set up for international use. **Roaming** calling rates can be pretty high and if you're planning to make a lot of calls it may work out cheaper to **buy a phone** in California, though the lower cost is counterbalanced by the need to tell all your friends your new phone number. Basic, new phones can be picked up for as little as $30.

Calling from your **hotel room** will cost considerably more than if you use a public phone. Fancy hotels often charge a connection fee of at least $1 for most calls (waived if they're toll-free), and international calls will cost a small fortune. While an increasing number of public phones accept credit cards, these can incur astronomical charges for long-distance service, including a high "connection fee" that can bump charges up to as much as $7 a minute.

Any number with ℡800, ℡866, ℡877, or ℡888 in place of the area code is **toll-free**. Most major hotels, government agencies, and car rental firms have toll-free numbers, though some can be used only within the state of California – dialing is the only way to find out. Numbers with a ℡1-900 prefix are toll calls, typically sports information lines, psychic hotlines, and phone-sex centers, and will cost you a variable, though consistently high, fee for just a few minutes of use.

Calling home from LA

Australia 00 + 61 + city code
Canada 1 + area code
New Zealand 00 + 64 + city code
UK and Northern Ireland 00 + 44 + city code
Republic of Ireland 00 + 353 + city code
South Africa 00 + 27 + city code

Useful numbers

Emergencies ℡911; ask for the appropriate emergency service: fire, police, or ambulance.

Directory information ℡411
Directory inquiries for toll-free numbers ℡1-800/555-1212
Long-distance directory information ℡1- (area code)/555-1212
International operator ℡00

LA area codes

213 Downtown
310 West Hollywood, Beverly Hills, West LA, Westwood, Santa Monica, Venice, Malibu, South Bay, San Pedro
323 Mid-Wilshire, Hollywood, South Central LA, East LA
562 Long Beach, Whittier, Southeast LA
626 Pasadena, Arcadia, San Gabriel Valley
661 Santa Clarita, far northern LA
714 Northern Orange County – Anaheim, Garden Grove, Huntington Beach
805 Lancaster, northern deserts
818 Burbank, Glendale, San Fernando Valley
909 Pomona, Inland Empire
949 Southern Orange County – Costa Mesa, Newport, and Laguna beaches

Photography

With fabulous scenery and great light much of the time, many parts of the LA area can be a **photographer's** paradise. Bring plenty of digital memory or be prepared to period- ically visit photo shops and burn your images onto CD. As ever, try to shoot in the early morning and late afternoon when the lower-angled light casts deeper shadows and gives greater depth to your shots.

It is never a good idea to take photos of military installations and the like, and with the current heightened security, airports and some government buildings may be consid- ered sensitive.

Senior travelers

Seniors are defined broadly in the US as anyone older than 55–65 years of age. Those traveling can regularly find discounts of anywhere from 10 to 50 percent at movie theaters, museums, hotels, restaurants, performing arts venues, and the occasional shop. On Amtrak, they can get a 15% discount on most regular fares, and 10% off the purchase of a North America Rail Pass. On Greyhound the discount is smaller, in the range of 5 to 10 percent. If heading to a national park, don't miss the **America the Beautiful Senior Pass**, which, when bought at a park for a mere $10, provides a lifetime of free entry to federally operated recreation sites, as well as half-priced discounts on concessions such as boat launches and camping. In California, low-income seniors can apply for a **Golden Bear Pass** ($5; ⓦwww.parks.ca.gov), which allows complimentary parking at all state-operated facilities, though it doesn't cover boating fees, camping, and the like.

Time

California runs on **Pacific Standard Time** (PST), which is eight hours behind GMT, and jumps forward an hour for Daylight Savings Time (the second Sunday in March to the first Sunday in November). During most of this eight-month period, when it is noon Monday in California it is 3pm in New York, 8pm in London, 5am Tuesday in Sydney, and 7am Tuesday in Auckland.

Tourist information

California's official tourism website (ⓦwww .visitcalifornia.com) is a reasonable starting point for advance information. Much of the same material is available in its free tourism information packet, which can be ordered online, by calling ⓣ1-800/GOCALIF, or by contacting California Tourism, PO Box 1499,

Sacramento, CA 95812-1499 (ⓣ916/444-4429 or 1-800/862-2543).

Visitor centers go under a variety of names, but they all provide detailed information about the local area. Typically they're open Monday through Friday 9am–5pm and Saturday 9am–1pm, except in summer, when they may be open seven days a week from 8am or 9am until 6pm or later. These promotional offices will send you copious material on their respective areas, including glossy promos advertising the swanky hotels and restaurants, plugs for the top sights, and, occasionally, a simple map or two.

You can also pick up free promotional material such as maps, hotel and restaurant pamphlets, and magazine-sized city guides at small kiosks across the city, or at stands in most hotels.

Travelers with disabilities

The US is keen to accommodate travelers with mobility problems or other physical disabilities. All public buildings have to be **wheelchair accessible** and provide suitable toilet facilities, almost all street corners have dropped curbs, public telephones are specially equipped for hearing-aid users, and most public transport has accessibility aids such as subways with elevators and buses that "kneel" to let riders board. Even movie theaters have been forced by courts to allow

Visitor centers in and around LA

Downtown: 685 S Figueroa Street (Mon–Fri 9am–5pm; ⓣ213/689-8822, ⓦwww .lacvb.com) and at the Hollywood & Highland mall, 6801 Hollywood Boulevard (Mon–Sat 10am–10pm, Sun 10am–7pm; ⓣ323/467-6412)

Beverly Hills: 239 S Beverly Drive (Mon–Fri 8.30am–5pm; ⓣ1-800/345-2210, ⓦwww.beverlyhillscvb.com)

Long Beach: 1 World Trade Center, 3rd Floor (Mon–Fri 9am–5pm; ⓣ1-800/452-7829, ⓦwww.visitlongbeach.com)

Orange County: near Disneyland at 640 W Katella Avenue (daily 8am–8pm; ⓣ714/991-INFO, ⓦwww.anaheim411.com or ⓦwww.anaheimoc.org)

Pasadena: 171 S Los Robles Avenue (Mon–Fri 8am–5pm, Sat 10am–4pm; ⓣ626/795-9311, ⓦwww.pasadenacal.com)

Santa Monica: 1400 Ocean Avenue (daily 10am–4pm, summer 9am–5pm; ⓣ310/393-7593, ⓦwww.santamonica.com) and in the Santa Monica Place mall, Colorado Boulevard at Third Street (daily 9am–6pm; ⓣ1-800/544-5319)

West Hollywood: in the Pacific Design Center, 8687 Melrose Avenue #M38 (Mon–Fri 9am–5pm; ⓣ310/289-2525, ⓦwww.visitwesthollywood.com)

people in wheelchairs to have a reasonable, unimpeded view of the screen.

The major hotel and motel chains, such as Embassy Suites, Hilton, Hyatt, Radisson, and Best Western, are your best bet for accessible **accommodation**.

Transport

Major **car rental** firms can provide vehicles with hand controls for drivers with leg or spinal disabilities, though these are typically available only on the pricier models. Parking regulations for disabled motorists are now uniform: license plates for the disabled must carry a three-inch-square international access symbol, and a placard bearing this symbol must be hung from the car's rearview mirror.

American **air carriers** must by law accommodate customers with disabilities, and some even allow attendants of those with serious conditions to accompany them for a reduced fare. Almost every Amtrak train includes one or more cars with accommodation for disabled passengers, along with wheelchair assistance at train platforms, adapted on-board seating, free travel for guide dogs, and discounts on fares, all with 24 hours' advance notice. Passengers with hearing impairment can get information by calling ☎1-800/523-6590 (TTY) or checking out ⊛www.amtrak.com.

By contrast, traveling by **Greyhound** and **Amtrak Thruway** bus connections is often problematic. Buses are not equipped with platforms for wheelchairs, though intercity carriers are required by law to provide assistance with boarding, and disabled passengers may be able to get priority seating. Call Greyhound's ADA customer assistance line for more information (☎1-800/752-4841, ⊛www.greyhound.com).

Information

The California Office of Tourism (⊛www.gocalif.ca.gov) has lists of handicapped facilities at places of accommodation and attractions. National **organizations** facilitating travel for people with disabilities include SATH, the Society for the Advancement of Travelers with Handicaps (☎212/447-7284, ⊛www.sath.org), a nonprofit travel-industry grouping made up of travel agents, tour operators, and hotel and airline management; contact them in advance so they can notify the appropriate members. Mobility International USA (☎541/343-1284, ⊛www.miusa.org) answers transportation queries and operates an exchange program for people with disabilities. Access-Able (☎303/232-2979, ⊛www.access-able.com) is an information service that assists travelers with disabilities by putting them in contact with other people with similar conditions.

The City

The City

Downtown LA

V isible from a distance as a small patch of skyscrapers caged by freeways, **DOWNTOWN LA** makes a fair attempt to act as an urban center, and in recent years has added a clutch of interesting new sights to broaden its appeal. Still, for many visitors it's an easily missed neighborhood that gets overlooked in favor of Burbank movie studios, Westside shopping districts, or Orange County theme parks.

Downtown was once the social and cultural hub of the region, where the masses worked, dined, shopped, and came to be entertained. With the advent of the automobile, however, Angelenos moved away from the city center, paving over orange groves and beanfields in their march outward. Downtown was given over to commercial activity, if little else: most of the middle and working classes escaped, or were forced out when their homes were destroyed by dubious urban-renewal schemes.

Still, for all its failings, boosters kept trying to make Downtown into an actual attraction for visitors. In this they have finally succeeded, for in the last decade Downtown has re-emerged as an enjoyable place to visit during the day (though this corporate-dominated zone still shuts down at night), with a smattering of grand old movie palaces, modern museums, and a few interesting pieces of architecture – along with some of the city's best hotels and restaurants.

It's only fairly recently that Downtown has become vertical at all. Until 1960, **City Hall** was, at 28 stories, the town's tallest structure, but from the 1960s to the end of the 1980s, LA saw a building boom spurred on largely by Canadian and Japanese venture capital. Development replaced the creaky Victorians atop Bunker Hill with glass curtain-walls and Brutalist concrete monsters. The boom faded during LA's near-depression during the early 1990s, but since then, the area has made a slow recovery. To many, the monumental construction of Disney Hall is the singular symbol of Downtown's long-awaited rebirth, while less high-minded souls point to the sports complex of the Staples Center as providing the real lifeblood of the area.

Although the gleaming modernity of Bunker Hill is immediately tempting, a trip Downtown is best experienced beginning at **the Plaza**, the original nineteenth-century town site and now the remodeled focus of "**El Pueblo de Los Angeles**," a state park that also holds the historic, if over-commercialized, **Olvera Street**. To the south, LA's **Civic Center** is a bland seat of local government, enlivened by the classic form of City Hall and the startling modern assertiveness of the new Caltrans building.

Further south stand the antique facades along Spring Street and Broadway. Since their heyday in the 1920s as the respective financial and cultural axes of the city, the two streets have changed considerably. **Broadway** is still a thriving commercial area (but now has a Hispanic flavor), with T-shirt stands and fast-food vendors lining its corridor. Many of its once-grand movie palaces now host fiery evangelist churches, hectic' swap meets, or the occasional Hollywood action flick. **Spring Street**, on the other hand, became largely deserted through the 1980s and 90s, but since then some of its grand Neoclassical buildings have been renovated into artist's lofts and a few smart shops and restaurants.

Replacing Spring Street as LA's financial axis, **Bunker Hill** has rather limited charms – mainly museums and modernist architecture. North and east of Downtown, **Chinatown** and **Little Tokyo** are interesting for their predictable wealth of ethnic restaurants, though neither is a vital cultural center – the city's Asian immigrants tend to migrate toward livelier places like Monterey Park and Alhambra. Central American newcomers, by contrast, often end up in **Westlake** or **MacArthur Park**, west of Downtown, while hipsters gravitate to funky, working-class **Echo Park**. To the northeast of Downtown, the **Lummis House** and **Heritage Square** offer more sedate trips through local culture and history, with a smattering of worthwhile artist's studios and galleries open to the public.

Finally, sealing off Downtown from the spiderweb of freeways to the east, the **LA River** is a bleak concrete channel designed for flood control and, not surprisingly, the forbidding setting for dramatic scenes in assorted TV shows and Hollywood action flicks.

Downtown can easily be seen in a day, and if your feet get tired you can hop aboard the **DASH buses** that run frequently to major tourist destinations. The area is also the hub of the MTA networks and easily accessible by public trans- portation, based around the colossus of Union Station. **Parking** in lots is expensive on weekdays ($8–10 per hour), but on weekends is more affordable (a flat $7–10 for up to eight hours); street parking is a good alternative, except on Bunker Hill, where the meters cost at least $2 per hour.

Some history

For more than two hundred years, the center of Downtown LA has been slowly shifting. **Spanish colonizers** constructed the first town site, the Plaza, in 1781, but the tract was soon destroyed by fire and rebuilt further southeast in 1818, at the present site of El Pueblo de Los Angeles. Encompassing the historic Pico House and Plaza Church, the district was the focus of commer- cial activity during the Mexican years of rule and the early American period, though even then other parts of the LA basin were developing as alternative nodes for housing and commerce, independent of the growth of Downtown LA itself.

By the end of the nineteenth century, Downtown's **commercial hub** had relocated to Broadway, thick with department stores and vaudeville theaters, while Spring Street had become the financial axis. The Plaza was left to decay until the 1920s, when renovation projects slowly brought the area back, this time as a tourist center. Meanwhile, Broadway and Spring were, along with City Hall (completed in 1928), the most visible emblems of LA as an emerging American **metropolis** – by then numbering over a million people within its city limits and over two million in surrounding LA County. This trend (assisted in part by the devastating earthquake and fires of 1906) sent San Francisco into permanent eclipse as the largest and most powerful California city.

Although the Civic Center is still LA's seat of government, its financial and cultural counterparts have since relocated. Cold War-era urban renewal projects shoved the city center six blocks to the west and doomed the great boulevards in the process. Bunker Hill replaced Spring Street in the 1960s as Downtown's

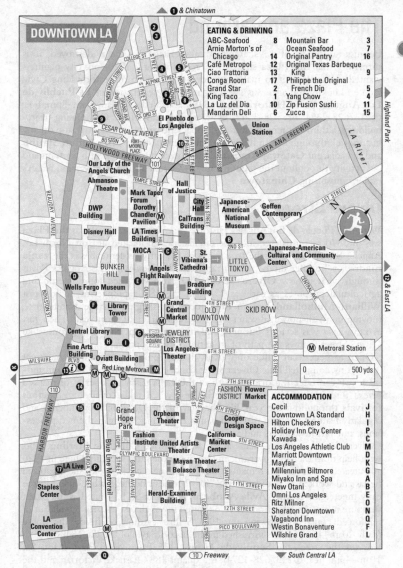

DOWNTOWN LA

▲ ❶ & Chinatown

EATING & DRINKING

ABC-Seafood	8	Mountain Bar	3
Arnie Morton's of		Ocean Seafood	7
Chicago	14	Original Pantry	16
Café Metropol	12	Original Texas Barbeque	
Ciao Trattoria	13	King	9
Conga Room	17	Philippe the Original	
Grand Star	2	French Dip	5
King Taco	1	Yang Chow	4
La Luz del Dia	10	Zip Fusion Sushi	11
Mandarin Deli	6	Zucca	15

ACCOMMODATION

Cecil	J
Downtown LA Standard	H
Hilton Checkers	I
Holiday Inn City Center	P
Kawada	C
Los Angeles Athletic Club	M
Marriott Downtown	D
Mayfair	K
Millennium Biltmore	G
Miyako Inn and Spa	A
New Otani	B
Omni Los Angeles	E
Ritz Milner	O
Sheraton Downtown	N
Vagabond Inn	Q
Westin Bonaventure	F
Wilshire Grand	L

Ⓜ Metrorail Station

0 — 500 yds

▶ Highland Park

▶ ⑫ & East LA

▼ ❶ ▼ ⑩ Freeway ▼ South Central LA

financial nucleus, thanks to a drastic facelift engineered by LA's fumbling **Community Redevelopment Agency (CRA)**. While Spring Street's financial center re-emerged on the western side of Downtown, nothing so far has re-created Broadway's buzzing entertainment zone. Ultimately, it took a handful of huge new showpieces, most prominently Disney Hall, Our Lady of the Angels Catholic Church, and the Staples Center, to begin drawing the city's attention back from the Westside, with the hopes of civic boosters and investment gurus riding on the public's appreciation for eye-catching architecture and sports enthusiasm – so far, a moderately successful gamble.

The Plaza and around

Because so much of LA's architectural heritage has been destroyed, it is surprising that **the Plaza** still exists. From the early 1920s on, city planners wanted to demolish it to make way for a larger, even more forbidding Civic Center. Luckily, the area was saved by its 1953 designation as **El Pueblo de Los Angeles State Historic Park**, 845 N Alameda St (daily 9am–5pm; free; ☎213/628-2381 or 628-3562, ⓦwww.ci.la.ca.us/ELP). Comprising thirty buildings, a third of them open to the public, the park is an essential stop on any history trek through LA. In the immediate vicinity of the Plaza, **Union Station** and the adjacent **Gateway Transit Center** make up a sizable hub for train and bus activity throughout the region, while just north sits the latest version of LA's rather uninspiring **Chinatown**.

Olvera Street

Within El Pueblo de Los Angeles Historic Park, the square known as **the Plaza** was in 1870 reconstructed into the circular design located just off North Los Angeles Street. However, the true focus of the early settlement was the **zanja madre**, or "mother ditch," which ran from the then-wild Los Angeles River through what is now **Olvera Street**. The canal was used for domestic and agricultural purposes as early as 1781; in the 1870s, pioneering hydrologist **William Mulholland** had an early job ditch-digging on the watercourse, moving up to all-powerful water superintendent in eight short years. Then, just as now, *agua* was serious business, and it's no accident that a key route like Olvera Street follows the path of an antique irrigation ditch.

Open to pedestrian traffic only (daily 10am–7pm; free; ⓦwww.olvera-street.com), tiny, congested little Olvera Street has been closed since 1930 to automobiles; you can trace the original path of the *zanja madre* by a series of marked bricks throughout. The street is at its best when taken over for numerous **festivals** throughout the year, like the Day of the Dead on November 2, and regularly features strolling mariachi bands, Aztec and Mexican-themed processions, and various dancers and artisans.

Olvera Street's re-emergence was the work of one **Christine Sterling**, who, with help from the city government, tore down the slum she found here in 1926 and created much of what remains today. For the next twenty years, she organized fiestas and worked to popularize the city's Mexican heritage while living in the early nineteenth-century **Avila Adobe** at 10 Olvera St. It's touted as the oldest structure in Los Angeles, from 1847, although it was almost entirely rebuilt out of reinforced concrete following the 1971 Sylmar earthquake. Inside, the house (daily 10am–4pm; free), is furnished in the historic style of the the 1840s.

Across the street, the **Sepulveda House**, 125 Paseo de la Plaza (Mon–Sat 10am–4pm; free; ☎213/628-1274), is a quaint 1887 Eastlake Victorian and the park's visitor center, with rooms highlighting different eras in Hispanic cultural history and an informative free film on the history of LA. Las Angelitas, a docent group, offers regular free tours of this and Olvera Street (Wed–Sat 10am, 11am & noon; ☎213/628-1274, ⓦwww.lasangelitas.org); there are also tour brochures available at the plaza's central information desk at 130 Paseo de la Plaza.

South and west of Olvera Street

Just west of the Plaza, the Catholic Plaza Church, or **La Placita**, 535 N Main St (daily 6.30am–8pm; ☎213/629-3101, ⓦwww.laplacita.org), is a small adobe structure with a gabled roof that has long been a sanctuary for Central American refugees. From 1861 to 1923 the building was remodeled or reconstructed four times, but it still evokes a sense of the local heritage. Church **masses** (occasionally with mariachi bands) occur three or four times daily, with twelve Eucharist services on Sunday.

Just south of Olvera Street, across the Plaza, is a small collection of historic buildings that are in various states of renovation and public use. From the east, the red-brick **Old Plaza Firehouse** (Tues–Sun 10am–3pm; free) was only operational for thirteen years, beginning in 1884, subsequently becoming a saloon, lodging house, and pool hall before reaching museum status in 1960. If you like old firefighting equipment, this is the place for you. Around the corner, LA's original Chinese settlement was centered on the **Garnier Building**, an 1850 brick-and-stone structure that now houses the **Chinese American Museum**, 425 N Los Angeles St (Tues–Sun 10am–3pm; $5; ℡213/485-8567, ⓦwww.camla.org). Inside, local Chinese history, society, and culture is detailed, with items from the nineteenth and twentieth centuries including revealing letters, photos, and documents, as well as a smattering of contemporary art and the re-creation of a Chinese herb shop *c*.1900.

West across tiny, pedestrianized Sanchez Street, handsome Italianate arches grace the **Pico House**, opened in 1870 as LA's most luxurious hotel; the last Mexican governor of California, Pio Pico, lived here. Pico House is closed to the public, as is the adjacent **Merced Theater**, which dates from the same year and was the city's first indoor theatre. The **Old Masonic Hall** next door (Tues–Fri 10am–3pm; free) was the first of its kind in the city when built in 1858. It still holds the occasional Freemason meeting and displays artifacts such as swords, compasses, and jewels.

Lastly, three blocks west, at the top of the hill marking the junction of Sunset Boulevard and Hill Street, the **Fort Moore Pioneer Memorial** is a series of bas reliefs depicting early political and social figures who provided "for [LA's] citizens water and power for life and energy." This heroic inscription is written on the adjacent wall of what has been described as "the most spectacular man-made waterfall in the United States": an 80-foot-wide, 50-foot-high torrent serving as a colossal monument to the city's aqueous needs. Not surprisingly, it was shut off thirty years ago.

Union Station and around

The Mission-style **Union Station**, across from the Plaza at 800 N Alameda St, is an impressive architectural landmark that stands on an early site of LA's Chinatown; the local Chinese community was forcibly evicted when the station was constructed in the 1930s. Despite rail travel's precipitous decline in the US, the terminus remains one of the city's best-preserved monuments to the golden age of railways, replete with grand arches, a high clock tower, Spanish-tiled roof, and Art Deco verticality, grand arches, and Streamline Moderne lettering. The heart of the region's public transit system, the station serves as the confluence for Amtrak, Metrolink, and Metroline commuter trains (see Basics, p.26), as well as the occasional shooting location for all kinds of Hollywood movies. It was used most memorably in *Blade Runner*, as the gloomy, atmospheric police station where Harrison Ford's Deckard is given his mission to kill off four alien "replicants"; you may recognize the location (minus the film's smoky darkness) by peering into the now-closed north wing to the left, just after you enter.

Less interesting is **Gateway Transit Center**, connected to Union Station by tunnel below the train tracks and comprising three distinct parts: the 26-story

Gateway Tower, with a customer service center on its ground floor; **Patsaouras Transit Plaza**, the bus mall itself, decorated with insipid public art and worth avoiding at night; and, under a glass ceiling, the **East Portal**, a light and airy space marred by an Orwellian-looking mural supposedly celebrating LA's ethnic diversity. There's nothing much to see beyond here, just the largest municipal **jail** in the US – where Paris Hilton cooled her heels for three weeks in 2007.

Chinatown

If you visit LA's **CHINATOWN** expecting to see a bustling affair, you will be sadly disappointed. Located between North Broadway and North Hill streets, the center of the enclave is rather touristy: small and hemmed in by wide boulevards, with its maze of ersatz-Chinese architecture, and narrow pedestrian alleys featuring inauthentic names like Bamboo Lane. The area was established in 1938 along North Broadway and North Spring Street following its residents' abrupt transplant from the current site of Union Station. Unless it's **Chinese New Year**, when there's a parade of dragons and firework celebrations, there's little point in turning up here except to eat in one of the good, affordable **restaurants**. Apart from this, Chinese culture here consists of a handful of small shopping malls, where you can pick up an assortment of lanterns, teapots, and jade jewelry. On the outlying streets away from the hub, there's an assortment of pan-Asian diners and stores that perhaps give a better sense of the gritty neighborhood's vitality.

For a more well-rounded sense of contemporary Chinese culture, visit **Alhambra** and **Monterey Park**, both lively ethnic suburbs located several miles east of Downtown.

▲ Chinatown

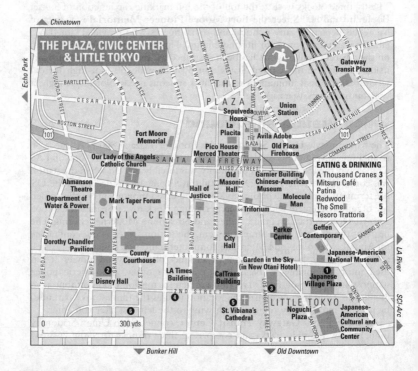

THE PLAZA, CIVIC CENTER & LITTLE TOKYO

EATING & DRINKING
A Thousand Cranes 3
Mitsuru Café 1
Patina 2
Redwood 4
The Smell 5
Tesoro Trattoria 6

▼ Bunker Hill   ▼ Old Downtown

Civic Center

Marked by City Hall's great white pillar, the **Civic Center** is the seat of government for the city and county of LA. Bounded on the east and west by San Pedro and Figueroa streets and on the north and south by the Hollywood Freeway and First Street, this hive of bureaucracy offers only a few interesting cultural and architectural sights. There is, to be sure, much activity during weekday office hours, but apart from that it's a rather strange scene of desperate homeless people wandering in an often-deserted landscape of spartan modern architecture and ugly public artworks.

City Hall and around

City Hall, 200 N Spring St, is still visible in TV reruns as Dragnet's imposing symbol of civic virtue and as the *Daily Planet* office in the original Superman show. Once LA's tallest structure, its silhouette is now dwarfed by the office blocks of Bunker Hill. The building's crown is as close as most visitors will ever get to seeing the Mausoleum at Halicarnassus, one of the seven ancient wonders of the world, which provided a curious, only-in-LA architectural inspiration. You can still get a good look at the inside of the building on free **tours**, which include its 28th-story 360-degree observation deck (Mon–Fri 10am–4pm; free), but for a more in-depth view of the building and its architecture, the LA Conservancy offers monthly tours (first Sat of month 11am; 1hr 45min; $5; ☎213/623-CITY, @www.laconservancy.org).

Less inspiringly, there's plenty of bad, unavoidable public art hereabouts, especially at the corner of Main and Temple, where the monstrous, six-story **Triforium**, from 1975, is decorated with shafts of colored glass, flashing lights, and loudspeakers strategically placed between its massive concrete legs. After being silent for decades and surviving numerous demolition threats, the sound system in the "polyphonoptic" carillon was finally reactivated at the end of 2006. The behemoth occasionally offers up arbitrary (CD-based) music selections, though its accompanying light show still isn't synchronized with them, as was the original plan. More compelling is **Molecule Man**, 255 E Temple St, in which sculptor Jonathan Borofsky (better known for his *Ballerina Clown* in Venice; see p.145) used perforated figures to supposedly illustrate the watery composition of the human body. Some see the figures as bullet-riddled bodies – a jab at the adjacent **Parker Center**, headquarters of the LAPD. The building is named for arch-crimefighter **William Parker**, whose iron reign in the 1950s resulted in the paramilitary mentality that still plagues the force.

Just to the south, near Spring and First streets, the concrete and glass **Times–Mirror Complex** houses the production facilities for the *Los Angeles Times*, the West Coast's biggest newspaper. Built in the colossal PWA Moderne style in the mid-1930s, and given a drab expansion in 1973, the building supplanted an earlier version, closer to Broadway, that was bombed, rebuilt, then torn down. Take one of its free **public tours** (hours vary; by reservation only at ☎213/237-5757, @www.latimes.com) if you're interested in seeing how the paper operates.

Much more eye-opening and engaging is the colossal modernist pile of the new **CalTrans Building**, at Main and First streets (Mon–Fri 8am–5pm; free), which features some of the most groundbreaking architecture in the country. The spectacle starts at the ground-level Broad Plaza, where the uneven glass-and-aluminum facade towers over the visitor, its exterior panels opening and closing depending on weather and sunlight. Closer to the entrance, in the

The LA Times dynasty

The *Los Angeles Times* began life in 1881 as the mouthpiece for **Harrison Gray Otis**, the arch-conservative publisher whose virulently anti-labor opinions and actions led union chiefs to call him the most "unfair enemy of trades unionism on the North American continent." Having already kept the Southern Pacific Railroad from monopolizing development of the LA Harbor, Otis also engineered public support for the giant construction projects that stole water from Northern California's Owens Valley and carried it to LA, or, more precisely, to the San Fernando Valley, where he and other investors made a fortune in shady real-estate dealings.

The *LA Times* directly reflected Otis's sharp opinions and, when he died in 1917, his legacy was passed to his son-in-law, **Harry Chandler**, who maintained the paper's fight against unions and political reform until his death in 1941. His personal fortune was worth up to a billion dollars, much of it made in San Fernando Valley real estate, thanks in large part to the newfound water source irrigating freshly built suburbs. Chandler was a plutocrat and mayoral kingmaker who usually got his way with city politicians, controlling them much like his father-in-law had.

In 1960, the *LA Times* changed course dramatically with the ascension of Harry's son **Otis** to the publishing throne. Through his progressive efforts, the paper finally rejected its provincial conservatism and became nationally recognized for its journalistic quality. In later decades, with the demise of rivals like William Randolph Hearst's once-powerful *Los Angeles Herald-Tribune*, the *Times* would nearly monopolize local journalism and emerge as an **international news organization**, with bureaus around the world. More recently, however, the paper was gobbled up in a media **megamerger** by the *Chicago Tribune*. Most agree that the merger was a disaster for the *Times*, resulting in mass layoffs and a broad decline in the paper's coverage and quality. In 2007, plans were announced for the Tribune Company itself to be swallowed up by financier Sam Zell, who in turn may sell the *LA Times*. In the meantime, this once-towering journalistic icon continues to languish.

"outdoor lobby," a number of banded neon tubes spray colored light in various patterns across four stories, making it the largest public-art sculpture in the city. Inside, assorted minimalist art pieces decorate the lobby and elevator banks, and on the east side of the building, the large, glassy curtain wall is actually made up of hundreds of photovoltaic cells, contributing five percent of the building's power needs. For this building and others, pioneering designer Thom Mayne won architecture's highest honor, the Pritzker Prize, in 2005.

Civic Center West

The municipal buildings in the **Civic Center West** are fairly bland, though not entirely without interest. The **Department of Water and Power Building**, at the corner of Hope and First streets, is a pleasing modern pile that casts an appealing glow at night with its narrow horizontal bands of light – though its array of once-gleaming fountains have been turned off to save water. Nearby is the 1925 **Hall of Justice**, Broadway and Temple streets, a compelling counterpart to City Hall, with high granite columns typifying the late Beaux Arts style of the time, and famous for hosting the turbulent trial of the Manson Family. The building closed in 1994, after being damaged by the Northridge earthquake, but it is set to be renovated and re-opened as headquarters for the LA County sheriff's office.

A block west is LA's ecclesiastical colossus, **Our Lady of the Angels** Catholic church, 555 W Temple St (Mon–Fri 6.30am–6pm, Sat 9am–6pm, Sun 7am–6pm;

tours Mon–Fri 1pm; free; T 213/680-5200, W www.olacathedral.org). The $200-
million concrete centerpiece of the local archdiocese is a truly massive structure,
standing eleven stories tall and capable of holding three thousand people. Dressed
in an unattractive shade of ochre, the church's fortress-like exterior suggests a
parking garage or prison. The interior is the undeniable highlight, with its grand
marble altar and giant bronze doors, tapestries of saints, and ultra-thin alabaster
screens for diffusing light – not to mention the $30 million worth of art and
furnishings laid out in a space longer than a football field.

Little Tokyo and around

Southeast of the Civic Center, **LITTLE TOKYO** is a more vital ethnic core than
Chinatown – if not quite a flourishing residential neighborhood – full of smart
shops and restaurants, well-heeled visitors, and a handful of business and cultural
institutions. Originally named in 1908, the area, bound by First and Third streets
north and south, and Central Avenue and San Pedro Street east and west, was
home to 30,000 Japanese immigrants before they were forced into internment
camps in 1942. While the district has returned to prominence, thanks in no small
measure to the 1980s real estate bubble that created numerous offices and hotels,
most of LA's Japanese-Americans now live well outside the area.

Little Tokyo

Little Tokyo is best explored on foot, starting at the **Japanese American
Cultural and Community Center**, 244 S San Pedro St (T 213/628-2725,
W www.jaccc.org), reached via the gentle contours and heavy basalt rocks of
Noguchi Plaza, designed by modern sculptor Isamu Noguchi, who grew up
in nearby Boyle Heights. Inside the center, the **Doizaki Gallery** (Tues–Fri
noon–5pm, Sat & Sun 11am–4pm; free) shows traditional and contemporary
Japanese drawing and calligraphy, along with costumes, sculptures, and other
media. Also on site is the **Japan America Theater** (box office Mon–Sat
noon–5pm; T 213/680-3700), which hosts cultural events such as kabuki
theater, as well as more contemporary plays. Shoehorned between the two and
easy to miss is the stunning **James Irvine Garden** (daily 9am–5pm; free), with
a 170-foot stream running along its sloping hillside. Although it was named after
its biggest donor it really owes its existence to the efforts of two hundred volun-
teers who gave up their Sundays to carve the space out of a flat lot, turning it
into the "garden of the clear stream" and making the area seem a world away
from LA's expanse of asphalt and concrete. Nearby, the more authentically
Japanese **Garden in the Sky**, 120 S Los Angeles St, located on the *New Otani
Hotel*'s third-floor terrace, uses local materials native to Japan. This half-acre
strolling garden, or *shuyu*, works the skyline into the setting – a technique
known as "borrowed scenery," or *shakkei* – allowing you to contemplate the
grandeur of City Hall during your walk around the premises.

The most active part of Little Tokyo is **Japanese Village Plaza** (most stores
daily 9am–6pm), an outdoor mall near First Street and Central Avenue lined
with sushi bars, upscale retailers, and Zen rock gardens; built in 1971, it's due to
be renovated in the coming years. Adjacent to the plaza is the area's signature
icon: the **Yagura Tower**, a small canopy sitting atop slender wooden beams,
built in the style of a traditional Japanese fire tower used to spot forest fires.

Across the road at 369 First Street, the **Japanese American National Museum** (Tues–Sun 11am–5pm, Thurs closes at 8pm; $8; ℡213/625-0414, Ⓦwww.janm.org), housed in a former Buddhist temple constructed in 1925, has exhibits on everything from origami to traditional furniture and folk craftwork to the internment of Japanese-Americans during World War II.

Just north from the museum is the **Geffen Contemporary**, Central Avenue at First Street (same hours and website as MOCA, to which a ticket entitles same-day admission). The Frank Gehry-designed museum, which occupies an old city warehouse and police garage, was initially opened in 1983 as overflow space for the main facility on Bunker Hill. Though there are no permanent installations on view, you're likely to find anything from temporary exhibits on the latest LA architecture to small abstract paintings lining the walls to huge pieces occupying similarly huge galleries.

West of Little Tokyo, **St Vibiana's Cathedral**, 114 E Second St, is a modest replica of Barcelona's church of San Miguel del Mar, with a simple white Italianate design. For years the regional seat of the Catholic Church, as well as a sanctuary for recently arrived Latin American immigrants, the 1871 cathedral fell on tough times after it was damaged in the 1994 Northridge earthquake and the archdiocese abandoned it to build Our Lady of the Angels further west, absconding with some of its stained glass and its sarcophagus in the process. Saved from demolition, the cathedral has been redeveloped as a rental complex, making for a wonderfully elegant spot for weddings, art shows, and the like (information at ℡213/622-4949, Ⓦwww.vibianala.com). There's also a new, Little Tokyo branch of the LA Public Library system on site (Mon & Wed 10am–8pm, Tues & Thurs noon-8pm, Fri-Sat 10am-6pm; ℡213/612-0525, Ⓦwww.lapl.org).

SCI-Arc and the Arts District

East of Little Tokyo, not far from the LA River, intriguing art is on display in the **Freight Depot** of the Southern California Institute of Architecture, or **SCI-Arc**, 960 E Third St, parking at 345 Merrick St (daily 10am–6pm; free; ℡213/613-2200, Ⓦwww.sciarc.edu), housed in a renovated train depot from 1907. Founded in 1972 by Thom Mayne (best known for his CalTrans Building; see p.55), "SCI-Arc" devotes its flowing horizontal spaces to experimental architectural instruction, and has as its director the great modernist maverick Eric Owen Moss, whose own work in Culver City alone merits a visit to that town (see p.136). Not surprisingly, the depot's public gallery hosts all manner of quirky and avant-garde exhibits by its students and faculty, from high-tech computer models to minimalist installations that play off light and shadows. In the neighborhood just west of the depot, an independent cultural scene is developing around classic old industrial buildings that have been renovated into lofts and branded as the **Arts District**. Despite the promising name, there are no official sights here yet, but some visitors drop in for the handful of funky bars or cafés; if arriving by night, take a cab, as the area's a bit too close to Skid Row for comfort.

Old Downtown

Spring Street, Main Street, and Broadway form the axes of **Old Downtown**, a once-thriving district that has in recent years tried to recapture its old spark with scattered new investment. To the east, the **Garment District** and

Flower Market are hives of mercantile energy, representing an urban vitality that the antique banking corridor of Spring and Main streets can only hope to achieve with a smattering of new condos and cafés. Paralleling Spring to the west, Broadway buzzes with colorful street life, though its character has changed, too: whereas movie palaces and fine restaurants once drew white middle-class crowds, its current swap meets and bargain discounters now draw working-class Hispanics.

Spring and Main Streets

As the one-time "Wall Street of the West," the imperious banking and commercial buildings of **Spring** and **Main streets** no longer serve their original functions, almost all of them victims of Downtown's financial relocation to Bunker Hill. Still, for those with an interest in LA history, or with a nose for sniffing out the area's emerging arts scene, the streets may offer a few worthwhile attractions (many of which are viewable on LA Conservancy tours of the old strip; see p.55). South from the Civic Center, begin your wanderings at peaceful **Biddy Mason Park**, 333 S Spring St (daily 8am–8pm, weekends open 9am; free), which commemorates a former midwife and slave who won her freedom in an 1855 legal challenge. The small memorial, adorned with camphor and jacaranda trees, provides a timeline of her life, from when she was purchased for $250 (on the property that is now the park), to when she became one of the founders of the local First African Methodist Episcopal Church.

Less than a block away begins the strip that redevelopers have christened as the **"Old Bank District,"** a collection of stately Beaux Arts buildings from one hundred years ago that are now, in various stages, being converted into upmarket housing, smart shops, chic eateries, and the like. Fourth Street is the main crossing axis of the area, and most of the worthwhile buildings lie along Spring. At no. 408, the 1904 Braly Block is home to the **Continental Building**, which was LA's first "skyscraper," though it only boasts twelve stories. The imposing structure has been transformed into artists' lofts and condos, as has the nearby **Farmers and Merchants Bank**, at no. 401. The eye-catching Neoclassical pile from 1908, rich with grand columns and possessing a stately presence, is popular for film shoots and special events. The also-remodeled **Security Trust and Savings Bank**, at no. 514, is home to four small theaters presenting intermittent productions and special events. Further south, the one-time **Pacific Coast Stock Exchange**, no. 618, bears an inscription stating that it was "created for the economic welfare of the community, state and nation." Ironically, the Moderne structure was completed in 1930 – the first full year of the Great Depression. Nearby, at Spring Street's intersection with Seventh Street, the 1910 **I.N. Van Nuys Building** celebrates one of the city's early titans, a San Fernando Valley land baron and wheat farmer, in grand Beaux Arts style, with ornamental Ionic columns and white terracotta walls adorning the old office space.

Skid Row and the Fashion District

East of Spring Street, a portion of LA County's homeless population (estimated at around forty to sixty thousand people) can be found on **Skid Row**, which begins just south of Little Tokyo and continues down past Seventh Street. Further south, the **Fashion District** (formerly the Garment District; most businesses Mon–Sat 10am–5pm; ☏213/488-1153, ⓦ www.fashiondistrict.org), is one of the area's most appealing attractions, with twenty square blocks of

OLD DOWNTOWN & BUNKER HILL

EATING & DRINKING

Angelique Café	18	Cole's Pacific Electric Buffet	12	Mayan	21
Café Pinot	6	Ciudad	5	New Moon	20
Casey's Bar	13	Emerson's	11	Pete's Café and Bar	3
Checkers	7	Engine Co. No. 28	10	Standard Bar	9
Cicada	14	Grand Central Market	2	Water Grill	8
Clifton's Cafeteria	16	L.A. Prime	4	Wood Spoon	19
Club 740	17	La Cita	1	Yorkshire Grill	15

clothing manufacturers and discounters selling everything from fabric for as little as $2 per yard, to designer suits and exquisite silk and velvet draperies. On Saturdays, the wholesalers open their doors to the general public, prompting a free-for-all among the fabric-obsessed. The biggest retailer here, the **California Market Center**, at Ninth and Los Angeles streets (typically Mon–Fri 9am–5pm; ☏213/630-3600, ⓦwww.californiamarketcenter.com), fills three million square feet and seemingly has just as many visitors, especially during the hectic mid-October "Fashion Week" (ⓦwww.fashionweekla.com). Just across Los Angeles Street at Santee, the **Cooper Design Space** (☏213/627-3754, ⓦwww.cooperdesignspace.com) offers designer merchandise in a bevy of showrooms, as well as designer studios and offices. Most shrewd Angelenos avoid the high-priced Westside boutiques and head to this district to buy clothing.

To plunge into the fabric-shopping experience at its most colorful and robust, head for the area along Maple Avenue between Sixth and Ninth streets, where businesses (often run by first-generation immigrant families) sell bolts of serviceable fabrics for ultra-cheap prices. Keep in mind, however, that street parking is meager and traffic maddening. Nearby, at the atmospheric **Flower Market**, 766 Wall St (public hours Mon, Wed & Fri 8am–noon, Tues, Thurs & Sat 6am–noon; entry $2, Sat $1; ☏213/627-5527, ⓦwww.laflowerdistrict.com), trade buyers make the rounds as early as 2am, though the public has to wait a few more hours to get its hands on a voluminous selection of blooms; you can buy them for a fraction of the prices charged elsewhere.

Much more tumultuous is **Santee Alley** (between Maple Ave and Santee St, running from Olympic Blvd to 12th St), a visual-information-overloaded agora thick with hundreds of vendor shops and little stalls selling everything from the cheapest junky sunglasses to the chicest designer suits; the quality of the goods (and honesty of the dealers) varies, so you should haggle without hesitation.

Broadway and the Theater District

Broadway was once the proud center of LA's most fashionable shopping and entertainment district, brimming with movie palaces and department stores. Although identified by tourist agencies as the Theater District, Broadway today is largely taken over by the clothing and knick-knack stores of a bustling Hispanic community, which operate out of the ground floors of otherwise empty hundred-year-old buildings. Combined with blaring salsa music and a hectic street scene, this is one of the city's most electric environments, which can only really be experienced on foot.

An instructive place to begin exploring the strip's former color is at its southern end, with the **Herald-Examiner Building**, 1111 S Broadway, a grand Mission-style edifice occupying a city block and featuring blue-and-yellow domes and (now boarded-up) ground-level arcades. The building was first home to William Randolph Hearst's *Los Angeles Examiner*, the progressive counterpart of the *Los Angeles Times*, which grew to have the widest afternoon circulation of any daily in the country. After it merged with Hearst's *Herald-Express*, though, trouble soon began, and the paper went out of business in 1989. Although the building is closed to the public, redevelopment plans are taking shape and, thanks to its opulent setting, it frequently hosts movie crews.

The Theater District begins one block to the west, at 1040 S Hill St, with the wild **Mayan Theater**. A stunning remnant of the pre-Columbian revival, its ornamental design, including sculpted reliefs of Aztec gods and bright paintings of dragons and birds, is every bit as outlandish as its Chinese Theatre counterpart in Hollywood. The building is still in use as the *Mayan* dance club (see "Drinking," p.298). The neighboring **Belasco Theater**, 1050 S Hill St, has similar brash appeal, with a Spanish Baroque design and a bright green color, though its partially restored interior is only open to film crews as a shooting location.

Nearby, the **United Artists Theater**, 929 S Broadway, is a 1927 Spanish Gothic movie palace with a lobby designed after a cathedral nave – appropriate, since the theater is now the site of a church (you can get a look inside on an LA Conservancy tour; see p.55). A block away, stuck amidst the theaters, is the Art Deco **Eastern Columbia Building**, 849 S Broadway, with terracotta walls of gold and aquamarine, a giant clock face, and sleek dark piers on its roof, all essential viewing for anyone remotely interested in 1920s architecture. Further along, at no. 760, the **Globe Theater** is a 1913 Beaux Arts design that has been reimagined as the splashy, atmospheric, multistory nightclub known as *Club 740* (T213/627-6277, W www.740la.com); it's well worth a visit to dance to Latin electronica and view some eye-opening Art Deco architecture inside.

The street continues with a rash of old moviehouses, notably the **Los Angeles**, 615 S Broadway, built in ninety days for the world premiere of Charlie Chaplin's *City Lights* in 1931, crowning what had become the largest concentration of film theaters in the world – then around twenty, now thirteen. Considered by some to be the best movie palace in the city, the theater's plush lobby behind the triumphal arch facade is lined by marble columns supporting an intricate mosaic ceiling, while the 1800-seat auditorium is enveloped by trompe l'oeil murals and lighting effects. Although the theatre is no longer open to the public for regular screenings, a June program called *Last Remaining Seats* draws huge crowds here and to the nearby **Orpheum Theatre**, 842 S Broadway – a monumental French Renaissance palace of grand staircases and chandeliers, now a special-event venue – to watch revivals of classic Hollywood films. If you're in town at the time, don't miss it (tickets $20 per film, often with live entertainment; call T213/623-CITY or visit W laconservancy.org for details). Near the Los Angeles Theatre, you can take in the Renaissance Revival charm of the **Palace Theatre**, 630 S Broadway, a remodeled nickelodeon from 1911, during one of its occasional public events; check entertainment listings for details.

A few blocks north, the **Million Dollar Theater**, no. 307, has appeared in numerous Hollywood movies and is renowned for its whimsical terracotta facade, mixing buffalo heads with bald eagles. The former moviehouse was built in 1906 by theatre magnate Sid Grauman, who went on to build the Egyptian and Chinese theaters in Hollywood. The building is now closed to the public, but there are plans to develop condos on the upper stories and show movies and stage performances in the auditorium. Across the street, the 1893 **Bradbury Building**, no. 304 (lobby open Mon–Sat 9am–5pm; free), has perhaps the finest atrium of any structure in the city, each level of its glazed-brick court adorned in wrought-iron railings and open-cage elevators, all atmospherically lit by a skylight. The lobby, which is as far as the public can go, should be recognizable from films such as *Blade Runner*, and LA Conservancy tours often begin here. As you exit on Third Street, the colorful **Grand Central Market**, between Third and Fourth (daily 9am–6pm; T213/624-2378, W www.grandcentral square.com), provides a good taste of modern Broadway – everything from apples and oranges to pickled pig's feet and sheep's brains.

Pershing Square and around

The city's oldest park, the uninspiring but unavoidable **Pershing Square**, acts as a buffer between Bunker Hill and Old Downtown. Constructed in 1866 and known variously as Public Square, City Park, La Plaza Abaja, and St Vincent's Park, it was renamed for the last time in 1918, in honor of World War I general **John Pershing**. However, decades of efforts to revitalize the park have resulted only in a bright purple campanile towering over charmless concrete benches and a dearth of grass and foliage.

The buildings around the square hold more appeal, including the **Millennium Biltmore Hotel**, on the west side of the park, its three brick towers rising from a Renaissance Revival arcade along Olive Street. Inside, the grand old lobby has an intricately painted Spanish-beamed ceiling, plus all manner of Baroque flourishes and an elegant bar, exquisite ballrooms, and a dark, luminous pool facility. The hotel's accommodation is also outstanding (see p.243).

To the east lies the heart of the **Jewelry District** (most businesses at least Mon–Fri 10am–5pm; ☎213/622-3335, ⓦwww.lajd.net), a wholesale and retail zone to which diamond shoppers come to hunt down the cheapest prices for the rock of their choice. One of the more prominent spots, the **International Jewelry Center**, 550 S Hill St, holds more than six hundred jewelers and dealers in precious stones and metals. If this doesn't satisfy your passion for gem shopping, try the **California Jewelry Mart**, 607 S Hill St, a green Art Deco structure; the **St Vincent Jewelry Center**, 640 S Hill St, a sizable complex with some of the best deals; or the grand **Jewelry Theater**, 411 W Seventh St, which occupies the former Warner Brothers Theater.

Finally, at 617 S Olive St, the Art Deco **Oviatt Building** once housed on its ground floor LA's most elegant haberdashery, catering to dapper types such as Clark Gable and John Barrymore, which has since been converted into the *Cicada* restaurant (see p.268). The building's elevators, which open onto the street-level exterior lobby, feature hand-carved oak paneling designed and fashioned by elegant Parisian craftsman René Lalique. Equally striking is the intricate 1928 design of the building's exterior, especially its grand sign and **clock** high above, as well as the exquisite **penthouse**, a regular host of weddings and public events (event-related showings Tues noon–5pm, Thurs 2–8pm; by reservation only at ☎310/286-2989, ⓦwww.oviatt.com).

Bunker Hill

Developed as a middle-class neighborhood in the 1870s, **Bunker Hill** was an upscale district for just a few decades; by the 1940s it was little more than a collection of fleabag dives and crumbling Victorian mansions, providing the seedy *film noir* backdrop for detective films such as the apocalyptic 1955 Mike Hammer movie *Kiss Me Deadly*. With its middle class having long since moved to the suburbs, in the 1960s the whole thing was plowed under, and Bunker Hill became the nucleus for Downtown's massive redevelopment as a high-rise corporate enclave, a hive of activity from nine-to-five, and deserted after hours.

The best way to approach Bunker Hill's **Financial District** used to be the **Angels Flight Railway**, a short section of track that leads up from the corner of Hill and Fourth streets to the top of Bunker Hill. The funicular was a throwback to the long-departed Victorian era, but the inclined train cars were removed in 1969 during the urban-renewal period, later to be restored and repainted orange and black in 1996. The railway was again closed in 2001 after the death of a passenger in an accident, and it may begin operation once more by 2008.

Breaching the fortress of Bunker Hill

Bunker Hill, filled with freeway access ramps, giant boulevards without sidewalks, walled-off corporate landscapes, and even signs prohibiting pedestrians, has been, sadly described as true to its name – a sealed-off high-rise enclave, with automatically controlled security doors and private guards to ward off interlopers. When Bunker Hill was being developed in the 1960s and 70s, the financial forces behind the project never considered creating a pedestrian-friendly space downtown and instead followed the logic of much late-modern design: bigger is better, impersonal is ideal, and cars are always king – a formula that, unfortunately, still persists in much of LA's municipal planning.

Still, there are a few remedies for dealing with Bunker Hill's layout if you're on foot. The first is to explore the area from the north or south – via Flower and Hope streets and Grand Avenue. Because of poor planning and a greater incline, the east and west sides of the hill are its most "fortified" and difficult to navigate. If you're coming from the east, however, the Angels Flight Railway (when running) is your best bet; if you're coming from the west, try Fifth Street, as the east–west streets to the north are among the most inaccessible to pedestrians. Motorists should also realize that while Bunker Hill was made expressly for their driving pleasure, it was not made for convenient, or cheap, parking. Find a lot below the hill and hike up the incline from there, or be prepared to cough up $2 in quarters per hour for street parking. Finally, resist the temptation to walk under the hill by way of the Third Street Tunnel; despite its gleaming appearance in films like *Blade Runner*, it remains quite deadly to careless pedestrians.

The Music Center and Disney Hall

On the north end, LA has lumped together three leading music and theater venues – the Dorothy Chandler Pavilion, the Ahmanson Theatre, and the Mark Taper Forum – as the blandly modern **Music Center**, north of First Street at 135 Grand Ave (see "Performing arts and film," Chapter 15). However, **Disney Hall**, First Street at Grand Avenue, is a true jewel of modern architecture, a headline-grabbing spectacle based on a 1987 design by architect Frank Gehry and similar to his Guggenheim Museum in Bilbao, Spain. Finished in 2003, the Hall is a 2300-seat acoustic showpiece whose stainless-steel exterior resembles something akin to colossal origami or broken eggshells and is so shiny that the county had the metallic facade sanded down in order to reduce its glare. The interior is just as impressive, with a mammoth, intricate pipe organ and rich, warm acoustics; indeed, the Hall is already considered one of the best places in the country to hear music, which you can do courtesy of the LA Philharmonic (W www.laphil.com; see p.309). Hours and days vary for tours, which run between 10am and 2pm and cost $12–15 for an hour-long visit (information at T 213/972-7211 or 323/850-2000).

The Museum of Contemporary Art

Just south and across the street from Disney Hall, the **Museum of Contemporary Art** (MOCA; Mon & Fri 11am–5pm, Thurs 11am–8pm, Sat & Sun 11am–6pm; $8, students $5, free Thurs; T 213/626-6222, W www.moca .org) is the leading institution for contemporary art in Southern California, designed in 1986 by showman architect **Arata Isozaki** as a "small village in the valley of the skyscrapers." MOCA justifies a look for its exterior alone, its playful red pyramids a welcome splash of color in a high-rise sea of black, white, and brown.

The **main entrance** to the galleries is below the barrel-vaulted pavilion on Grand Avenue (which opens onto an outdoor sculpture plaza and a gift shop), in a smaller plaza down the stairs from the upper plaza. Much of the museum is used for **temporary exhibitions**, which may include the likes of Donald Judd's prefabricated metal boxes and Ed Kienholz's perverse assemblage art. The bulk of the **permanent collection** draws heavily from the Abstract Expressionist period and features pieces by Franz Kline and Mark Rothko, an important Jackson Pollock work – his imposing, hypnotic *Number Three* – plus ten of Sam Francis's vivid splashes of color. You'll also find plenty of pop art, in Claes Oldenburg's papier mâché representations of hamburgers and gaudy fast-foods, Andy Warhol's print-ad black telephone, and Robert Rauschenberg's *Coca-Cola Plan*, a battered old cabinet containing three soda bottles and angelic wings tacked onto the sides. Jasper Johns's well-known *Map* – a blotchy diagram of the US states – is also here.

Many newer art-world stars are represented as well; highlights include Alexis Smith's quirky collages, Lari Pittman's painted postmodern hallucinations, and Martin Puryear's anthropomorphic wooden sculptures. The museum's strong **photography** collection celebrates the work of Diane Arbus, Larry Clark, and Robert Frank, while the impressive selection of **Southern California artists**, which ranges from Chris Burden's polemical sculptures to Robert Williams' feverishly violent and satiric comic-book-styled paintings, is not to be missed.

The best time to visit MOCA is during an **evening concert** in summer, when jazz and classical music is played outdoors under the silhouette of the red pyramids. At other times, a ticket to MOCA also entitles you to same-day entrance to the Geffen Contemporary, the museum's renovated warehouse for temporary exhibitions on the east side of Downtown (see p.58), and to the branch at the Pacific Design Center in West Hollywood (p.113).

▲ Museum of Contemporary Art

The Financial District

South of MOCA is the bulk of office towers that make Downtown visible from a distance. Known as the **Financial District**, the area became LA's money center in the 1960s and 1970s, making the antique buildings of Spring Street and the Old Bank District obsolete. There are a handful of interesting sights here if you feel like giving your legs a stretch. A good place to start is the **Wells Fargo History Museum**, just south from MOCA at 333 S Grand Ave (Mon–Fri 9am–5pm; free; ☎213/253-7166, ⓦwww.wellsfargohistory.com). Located at the base of the Wells Fargo Center, and one of nine Wells Fargo museums in the US, the museum displays photographs, a two-pound chunk of gold, a re-created assay office from the nineteenth century, and an original Concord stagecoach.

A block away, the shining glass tubes (or, to some, giant cocktail shakers) of the **Westin Bonaventure Hotel**, 404 S Figueroa St (see p.244), have become one of LA's most unusual landmarks since the late 1970s, giving Downtown as close to a showpiece postcard pile as it's likely to get. The only LA building by architect John Portman, the structure doubles as a shopping mall and office complex, and is built with a flurry of ramps, concrete columns, and catwalks in a soaring atrium that is one of the city's most eye-popping interiors. Step inside for a ride in the glass elevators that climb up the outside walls of the building, giving views over much of Downtown and beyond. From the hotel's rotating bar, *Bona Vista* (see p.291), you'll get a bird's-eye view of Bunker Hill's skyline, including the **Gas Company Tower**, 555 W Fifth St, a stunning modern high-rise whose crown symbolizes a blue natural-gas flame on its side.

The biggest of the skyscrapers, though, is the cylindrical **Library Tower**, at Grand Avenue and Fifth Street, designed by I.M. Pei's firm and, at 73 stories, the tallest building west of Chicago. Now owned by US Bank (which has named the tower after itself, with little public effect), the off-white, cylindrical tower is open to tours run through operators such as Red Line Tours (see box, p.31). In exchange for planning permission and air rights, the developers of the tower agreed to pay some $50 million toward the restoration of the neighboring **Richard J. Riordan Central Library**, 630 W Fifth St (Mon–Thurs 10am–8pm, Fri & Sat 10am–6pm, Sun 1–5pm; ☎213/228-7000, ⓦwww.lapl.org/central), named for LA's billionaire mayor of the 1990s. The concrete walls and piers of the lower floors form a pedestal for the squat central tower, which is topped by a brilliantly colored pyramid roof. The library, built in 1926, was the last work of architect Bertram Goodhue, and its striking, angular lines set the tone for many LA buildings, most obviously City Hall. Across Fifth Street, Lawrence Halprin's huge **Bunker Hill Steps**, supposedly modeled after the Spanish Steps in Rome, curve up Bunker Hill between a series of terraces with uneventful outdoor cafés, and ultimately end at the **Source Figure**, one of sculptor Robert Graham's small, creepy nudes, at the top.

On the downslope, a reminder of old LA sits at Sixth and Flower streets. **The California Club**, an exclusive men's social club, was a favorite spot for the **Committee of 25**, an informal group of conservative politicians and bigwigs who secretly decided important issues behind the club's (still) closed doors. Just over a block away is the more welcoming **Fine Arts Building**, 811 W Seventh St (Mon–Fri 8.30am–5pm; free; ☎310/286-2989), notable for its grand entry arch featuring gargoyles and griffins, and eye-catching lobby where you'll find medieval-flavored carvings and the odd modern art exhibit.

Finally, the peripheral attractions in the area include two of artist Kent Twitchell's massive murals. The first, **Harbor Freeway Overture**, decorates the side of a parking lot and is visible from the northbound 110 freeway at Seventh Street. In it, members of the LA Chamber Orchestra stare out at the traffic, with the mural sponsor, and CEO of Mitsubishi, hiding somewhere among the musicians. Several blocks to the southeast, at 1031 S Hill St, Twitchell's **Ed Ruscha Monument** was the piece that first brought the muralist to fame, showing Ruscha, the quintessential California artist, looming high above a parking lot, with the blank expression and rigid pose of Frankenstein's monster.

South Park

In the vicinity of the Ruscha mural, the mostly colorless blocks south of Bunker Hill have been named "**South Park**" by developers apparently lacking irony or access to cable TV. Serene **Grand Hope Park**, a grassy public space between Grand Avenue and Hope Street, just south of Ninth Street, was designed by Lawrence Halprin, and features a whimsical clock tower, wooden canopies, and concave fountains with gilt mosaics. The park's former most prominent resident, the **Museum of Neon Art**, 501 W Olympic Blvd, is relocating to a site yet to be determined (information at ☎213/489-9918, ⓦwww.neonmona.org); however, it still offers monthly bus tours of LA's best neon sights (see box, p.31). Across the park, the **Fashion Institute of Design and Merchandising**, 919 S Grand Ave (Tues–Sat 10am–4pm; free; ☎1-800/624-1200, ⓦwww.fashionmuseum.org), trains would-be couturiers and costume designers, throwing the odd fashion exhibition, with items drawn from its collection of ten thousand pieces of costume and apparel. While the French gowns, Russian jewels, and quirky shoes sometimes on display are appealing, the highlight is the annual "**Art of Motion Picture Costume Design**" show that runs from February to April and displays colorful outfits from the golden age of cinema to the present, from Liz Taylor's Cleopatra garb to Austin Powers's retro 1960s outfits.

Finally, three blocks to the southwest, the LA **Convention Center**, 1201 S Figueroa St (☎213/741-1151 or 800/448-7775, ⓦwww.lacclink.com) and the **Staples Center**, 865 S Figueroa St (☎213/742-7340, ⓦwww.staplescenter.com), are sleek modern structures that have led the way for the redevelopment of the area, but otherwise offer little of interest beyond conventions and Lakers games. Opening just north of the Staples Center in the coming years, and to be finished in full by 2010, is a behemoth called **LA Live** (information at ⓦwww.nokiatheatrela.com/lalive.php), which will feature a multi-venue theatre complex, sports facilities and broadcast studios, a pair of upper-end hotels, a sizable central plaza, a museum devoted to the Grammy Awards, a bowling alley, and numerous arcades, restaurants, clubs, and shops. The main thrust of the complex is to attract convention visitors and keep them – along with denizens of planned surrounding condos – in the same general area and where they'll feverishly consume.

Around Downtown

Just west of the Harbor Freeway, the **Temple–Beaudry** and **Pico–Union** barrios are home to thousands of newly arrived immigrants from Central America, areas more depressed in many ways than the noted ghettos of South Central LA – so avoid getting lost on one of the minor side streets. Also potential trouble, **MacArthur Park** and the **Westlake** neighborhood along

Wilshire Boulevard, despite the appeal of their faded Victorian architecture, should only be viewed by car when arriving at night – when petty theft and drug dealing are rampant. In the daytime it's safer, though it's best not to linger. (The one essential reason to come here is the renowned *Langer's Deli*, p.261, which offers curbside pickup.) North of Westlake, **Echo Park** has a pleasantly faded charm and a hipster vibe, and, like **Angelino Heights** to its east, is safer and quite picturesque. Further east is car-friendly **Elysian Park**, a green space that surrounds **Dodger Stadium**. Finally, **Highland Park**, northeast of Downtown, has two decent museums, none very far from the grim concrete channel of the **LA River**.

Westlake and MacArthur Park

Westlake is the tumultuous center for countless newcomers to the city, thronged with Panamanians, Hondurans, Salvadorans, and others. The activity centers on the intersection of **Wilshire and Alvarado**, where street vendors hawk their wares in front of busy swap meets, overlooked by the classy sign for the departed **Westlake Theater**, 638 Alvarado St, now promoting a flea market. A few Angelenos drop by the area for cheap and tasty Mexican food, since the place has something of the atmosphere of Broadway; you're advised to be wary, though, and stick to the well-trafficked areas during the day (avoiding the whole thing after dark).

Across Alvarado, **MacArthur Park** was developed in the 1890s when its surrounding area was a prime LA suburb, and strolling was a favorite pastime (these days it's drug dealing). Although the Red Line subway passes under the park, there's not much here to detain you, though the area still has a faded charm. To the south, **Bonnie Brae Street** and **Alvarado Terrace** continue to have a number of quaint Victorian houses. The one functional museum of note in the area is the **Grier–Musser Museum**, 403 S Bonnie Brae St (Wed–Sat noon–4pm; $6; ☎213/413-1814), offering a glimpse of the luxurious furnishings and stylish architecture of the nineteenth century, overflowing in six rooms with all manner of Victorian bric-a-brac and precious decor.

Echo Park and Angelino Heights

About a mile north of Westlake along Glendale Boulevard, **Echo Park**, a tranquil arrangement of lotuses and palm trees set around an idyllic lake, was the setting for several scenes in Roman Polanski's film *Chinatown*. In one memorable sequence, detective Jake Gittes follows the town water boss to a clandestine meeting, spying on him in a rowboat – the kind which you can still rent (along with paddleboats; typically $10 per hour) from vendors flanking Echo Park Avenue, running along the eastern edge of the lake. In 2008 Echo Park began to be drained and its wetlands restored to something resembling their original state. Water or not, the park also appeals for its funky, **bohemian atmosphere**, with countless affordable (for LA) bungalows and apartments around the park housing the city's next generation of painters, musicians, and filmmakers. To get a flavor of the scene, wander over to the gritty stretch of Sunset Boulevard just north, especially around the Alvarado junction, where the cheap clubs and diners provide just the sort of creative ferment that stirs the souls of the city's next generation of homegrown artists.

As a different sort of inspiration, in the large, white **Angelus Temple** on the northern side of the lake, evangelist **Aimee Semple McPherson** used to preach to some five thousand people, with thousands more listening in on the

▲ Haskins House on Carroll Avenuel

radio. The first in a long line of media evangelists, "Sister Aimee" was tainted by a later romantic scandal and died in 1944, but the building is still used for services by her Four Square Gospel ministry, which dunks converts in its huge water tank during mass baptisms.

Just east of Echo Park on a hill overlooking the city, **Angelino Heights** was LA's first suburb, laid out in the flush of a property boom at the end of the 1880s and connected by streetcar to Downtown. Although the boom soon went bust, a dozen elaborate houses that were built here, especially along **Carroll Avenue**, have survived and been restored – their wraparound verandas, turrets, and pediments set oddly against the Downtown skyline and occasionally used in ads for paint, among other things. One, with a weird pyramid roof, was used as the set for the haunted house in Michael Jackson's *Thriller* video. The best of the lot is the **Sessions House**, no. 1330, a Queen Anne masterpiece with Moorish detail, decorative glass, and a circular "moon window." On the first Saturday of the month, you can take a two-and-a-half-hour tour of the neighborhood through the LA Conservancy (Sat 10am; $10; reserve at ☎213/623-CITY, Ⓦlaconservancy.org), and visit the interiors of two of these classic homes as well.

Elysian Park

Two miles north of the Civic Center, quiet **Elysian Park** was laid out in 1886 and has been shrinking ever since. The LA Police Academy first commandeered a chunk of the park for its training facility; later, the Pasadena Freeway sliced off another section. Finally, after city bureaucrats booted a good number of poor tenants from the land, **Dodger Stadium** was constructed in the early 1960s to host the transplanted Brooklyn baseball team, and the park became a fraction of its former self. However, even crisscrossed by winding roads, it's still worth a look, especially for its awe-inspiring views of the metropolis – when the smog doesn't intercede. Parking can be nightmarish, but it's often easy and cheap to get tickets to a game, unless the hated Yankees or Giants are in town – the antipathy for the former being the last holdover from the Dodgers' Gotham days.

Beyond the stadium, **Angels Point**, on the upper western rim of the park, is your best vantage point of the city, marked by an abstract sculpture with a palm tree growing out of its center.

Highland Park

Beside the freeway, a mile from Elysian Park, Highland Park is one of several neighborhoods north of Downtown that has established a surprising beachhead for the arts in a once-depressed part of the city (see box below). It was the very first district annexed to LA, in 1895, and is linked up with the Gold Line Metrorail, with a stop at the **Southwest Museum of the American Indian** (☎323/221-2164, ⓦwww.southwestmuseum.org), which rises castle-like below Mount Washington. The museum is the oldest in Los Angeles, founded in 1907 to house tribal artifacts from all over North America. However, while this facility continues to operate as a cultural center, the museum collection is in the process of being relocated (ongoing through 2009 or beyond), so check the website for the latest details.

Just down the road, at 200 E Ave 43, the **Lummis House** (Fri–Sun noon–4pm; free; ☎323/222-0546, ⓦwww.socalhistory.org) is the well-preserved home of

---

Art in post-industrial LA

Although the Westside grabs most of the attention for attracting artists, in recent years the leading edge of LA's **underground art movement** has been located much further east, in the neighborhoods of northeast Los Angeles, which have increasingly drawn some of the city's most interesting and enterprising painters, sculptors, and architects to the districts of Highland Park, Eagle Rock, Mount Washington, and Lincoln Heights.

A good place to start is **The Brewery**, north of Downtown at 676 S Ave 21 (information at ☎323/222-0222, ⓦwww.oversight.com), a renovated 1920s complex of twenty buildings that's gone from brewing suds to exhibiting designers and architects, with some three hundred artists occupying space in a variety of galleries and art annexes that are open to the public (typically Fri–Sun noon–5pm; free). Most prominent in the complex is Michael Rotundi's striking **Carlson-Reges Residence**, a converted electrical utility building, noteworthy for its jagged architecture and post-industrial decor. (It's not open to the public, but is viewable from outside.) Another worthwhile site is the **Judson Gallery for Contemporary and Traditional Art**, in Highland Park at 200 S Ave 66 (1hr tours Wed 10am & 2pm; $5; ☎800/445-8376, ⓦwww.judsonstudios.com), which displays contemporary stained glass along with periodic exhibitions in a variety of media.

To learn more about northeast LA's art scene, check out the websites of the community-oriented **Northeast LA Network** (ⓦwww.nelanet.org) and the more comprehensive **Arroyo Arts Collective** (☎323/850-8566, ⓦwww.ArroyoArts Collective.org), which also organizes an annual November Discovery Tour ($10 in advance, $15 on the day), a self-guided tour of around eighty of the best and quirkiest of the area's galleries and private studios.

Charles F. Lummis, the city librarian who helped develop the Southwest Museum and was at the heart of LA's nineteenth-century boom. An early champion of civil rights for Native Americans, and one who worked to save and preserve many of the missions, Lummis built his late-nineteenth-century home as a cultural center, where the literati of the day would meet to discuss poetry and the art and architecture of the Southwest. The house, named "El Alisal" after the many large sycamore trees that shade the gardens, is an ad hoc mixture of Mission and Medieval styles; its thick walls were made out of rounded granite boulders taken from the nearby riverbed and the beams over the living room are old telephone poles. The solid wooden front doors are similarly built to last, reinforced with iron and weighing tons, while the plaster-and-tile interior features rustic, hand-cut timber ceilings and home-made furniture. It's all a fitting reflection of its rugged owner, one of the few individuals to reach LA by walking – from Cincinnati.

Across the Pasadena Freeway, and two miles north of Downtown, the fenced-off, ten-acre park of **Heritage Square**, 3800 Homer St (Fri–Sun noon–5pm, tours on the hour Sat & Sun noon–3pm; $10; ☏323/225-2700, Ⓦwww .heritagesquare.org), is an outdoor museum featuring a jumble of Victorian structures collected from different places in the city, most transported from Bunker Hill. The strip uncomfortably sites a railway station next to an octagonal house next to a Methodist church, and although the buildings are interesting enough, the adjacent freeway makes this a less than ideal spot to imagine a Victorian world of buggies and gingerbread.

The LA River

"A beautiful, limpid little stream with willows on its banks" is how water czar William Mulholland once described the **LA River**, the long concrete gutter that serves as Downtown's eastern border. While the river may have often been tranquil, it was also quite volatile, periodically flooding neighboring communities until, in 1938, a typically drastic solution was imposed: its muddy bottom was transformed into cement and its earthy contours into a hard, flat basin. The river mutated into a flood channel, which it remains, snaking through the city for 58 miles. Although some of the northern sections of the river (mainly through the San Fernando Valley) have been reseeded with trees and foliage, efforts to return the Downtown stretch to its natural state have met with predictable bureaucratic resistance.

Still, the fight continues, with groups like **Friends of the LA River** (☏1-323/223-0585, Ⓦwww.folar.org) arguing for the restoration of the watercourse's old natural contours, and hosting curious monthly "**river tours**" (April–Nov once a month 10am–4.30pm) exploring the high- and lowlights of different sections of its length, either by bus ($55) or car caravan ($25). To learn more about the character of the waterway and the potential for resurrecting its much-abused ecosystem, you can stop by the idyllic **Los Angeles River Center and Gardens**, 570 W Ave 26 (Mon–Fri 9am–5pm; free; ☏323/221-9939, Ⓦwww .lamountains.com/planning_river.html), for its informative "living river" presentation and exhibit showing the rebirth of the river along eleven upstream miles. A **bike-staging area** here has a repair station, restroom, and basic facilities for cyclists making the rugged trek along the various trails that link this terrain with the more verdant expanses of Pasadena's Arroyo Seco (see p.196).

You can also get a good Downtown river view by driving across several eastside bridges, designed in various revival styles – from mild Gothic to quasi-Baroque – or by renting movies. The empty riverbed has been used in numerous films, notably *Grease*, in which the channel hosts a wild drag race, and the *Terminator* series, in which cyborgs run amok in its bleak setting.

Mid-Wilshire and the Miracle Mile

The ethnically diverse territory of **MID-WILSHIRE** takes in the general area around **Wilshire Boulevard** between Downtown and Beverly Hills, running parallel to Hollywood to the north. Beyond motoring down the prime traffic corridor of Wilshire itself, many visitors overlook the area, despite its being one of LA's best bets for revisiting the architecture of the early twentieth century, having escaped much of the redevelopment that has drastically transformed the more famous parts of town – at least until recently. The recent demise of the fabled *Ambassador Hotel*, where Robert Kennedy Jr was killed, seems to have heralded a new burst of development, with shuttered properties suddenly given new life, a handful of important historic structures renovated, and everything else in the way unceremoniously demolished. Because Wilshire was the principal route of LA's first major suburban expansion in the 1920s, when the middle class began migrating west along the expanding strip, you can literally take a chronological tour of LA history simply by driving west from Downtown along it, from the Art Deco piles of its eastern end, to the auto-centric precinct of the mid-century Miracle Mile, to today's upscale shops and office blocks of the Westside.

Communities of middle-income Asians, old-money whites, working-class African Americans, diverse groups of Hispanics, and a small but growing bohemian contingent live within a few miles of each other along the Wilshire corridor. LA's most industrious ethnic enclave, **Koreatown**, has experienced renewed growth in recent decades with a slew of modernist office towers and three-story strip malls. To the west, just north of Wilshire Boulevard, many of the old Anglo-Saxon estates in places like **Hancock Park** visually recall their 1920s heyday, and are now populated by members of various ethnic groups, though still only one class – rich.

Further along Wilshire, the **Miracle Mile** is a classic shopping strip that boasts enough remaining Art Deco architecture to make a visit worthwhile, while the area's western side has been reincarnated as **Museum Row**, a collection of institutions celebrating everything from tar-soaked fossils to automobile culture, but especially noted for the presence of the huge, recently renovated **LA County Museum of Art** – one of the city's essential stops. **Fairfax Avenue**, west of Museum Row, takes you up to the human hive of the **Farmers Market** and through the geographical heart of the city's Jewish population. Further

The millionaire socialist

Aline Barnsdall, the 1920s heiress who commissioned Frank Lloyd Wright to build her Hollyhock House in Hollywood (see p.91), was not the only socialist who became rich thanks to oil. Decades earlier, **Henry Gaylord Wilshire** gained his notoriety from the petroleum industry (also making a fortune selling an electrical device that claimed to restore gray hair to its original color), and, like Barnsdall, was a scion of a family dynasty, as well as an entrepreneur. By the time he was 30, in the 1880s, he had already come to California and founded the Orange County town of Fullerton. Shortly thereafter, he became heavily involved in progressive causes and took up the **Socialist** banner in two unsuccessful runs for Congress, losing both in New York and California. These defeats did not deter his frenetic activity, however, and before long he was in London hanging out with members of the **Fabian Society**, as well as a then-unknown George Bernard Shaw. The turn of the century found Wilshire back in LA, this time buying up chunks of land from Pasadena to Santa Monica, including some of the Westlake neighborhood west of Downtown, site of now-faded MacArthur Park (see p.68).

Although Wilshire is often credited with creating his eponymous boulevard, the strip had actually been a wagon trail well before the Spanish had begun to settle in the area; by Wilshire's time it had become known as the **"Old Road,"** though it was actually little more than an uneven dirt path. The oil baron soon developed the street and the property around it, eventually helping the boulevard to connect Downtown with the ocean and creating one of the city's biggest thoroughfares in the process. Wilshire, though, had worse luck than the street he named. After another failed congressional attempt, he lost much of his money in foolhardy investments, managing to drop a cool $3 million. Still, he survived long enough to see his beloved route become one of the city's most important streets, a role that it holds to this day.

west, the **Third Street** shopping district, along with **La Brea Avenue** to the east, is where the trendy buy the latest designer clothes, eat in the smartest cafés, and hobnob with other would-be hipsters. Fittingly perhaps, the west side of Mid-Wilshire is marked by an imposing symbol of mass consumerism, the concrete monstrosity of the **Beverly Center mall**.

Wilshire Boulevard

Named for oil magnate and socialist H. Gaylord Wilshire – a unique individual even by LA standards (see box above) – **Wilshire Boulevard** runs from Downtown to Beverly Hills and Santa Monica, and is at its most historic from Vermont to Fairfax avenues. This latter stretch of road was for many decades LA's prime shopping strip, until the same middle class that supported this **"linear city"** in the 1920s and 1930s disappeared for good in the 1970s and 1980s. After a couple of lean decades, many of the strip's once-vacant buildings have begun to re-emerge as the homes of cheap ethnic diners, offices for entertainment companies, and various independent businesses. While the Art Deco piles have experienced only scattered renovation (and, occasionally, demolition), they continue to serve as beacons of a lost era, when Zigzag and Streamline Moderne architecture were the rage, and designers built apartment blocks to resemble Egyptian temples and French castles.

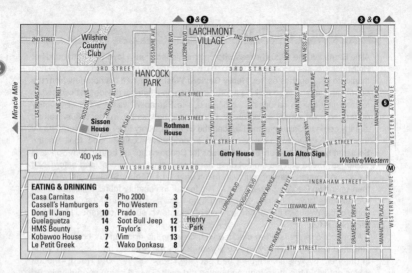

EATING & DRINKING

Casa Carnitas	4	Pho 2000	3
Cassell's Hamburgers	6	Pho Western	5
Dong Il Jang	10	Prado	1
Guelaguetza	14	Soot Bull Jeep	12
HMS Bounty	9	Taylor's	11
Kobawoo House	7	Vim	13
Le Petit Greek	2	Wako Donkasu	8

East of Vermont Avenue

The section of Mid-Wilshire closest to grim MacArthur Park and Westlake is predictably dicey (see "Downtown," p.68), but around **Lafayette Park**, between Wilshire and Sixth Avenue, are a few excellent examples of various historic-revival architectural styles. The **Park Plaza Hotel**, 607 S Park View St, a mixture of Romanesque Revival and Art Deco designs, was once the celebrity-frequented Elks Lodge; built in 1925, it is adorned by intricately crafted sculptures of stern angels on the facade, with an exquisite marble lobby (closed to public view) regularly used in film shoots. Nearby, the **First Congregational Church**, 540 S Commonwealth Ave, is a 1930 English Gothic–styled cathedral known for its huge and glorious set of pipe organs (half-hour concerts Thurs 12.10pm; free) and, appropriately, the annual Bach Festival (information at ⊤213/385-1341, ⓦwww.fccla.org). The best example of the period-revival styles may be the historic **Granada Buildings**, 672 S Lafayette Park Place, a shopping and residential complex posing as a charming Spanish Colonial village. It was here that the great Hollywood photographer George Hurrell shot many of the greats of the golden age, including Greta Garbo, and where today (at Starlight Studios, in Suite 48) you can watch many of the better films of the era in special weekly screenings (Sat 7pm; screenings free, pre-show lecture $10; ⊤213/383-2448, ⓦwww.thestarlightstudio.com).

Overall, though, the best and most famous icon in the neighborhood is the former **Bullocks Wilshire** department store, 3050 Wilshire Blvd, the most complete and unaltered example of Zigzag Moderne Art Deco architecture in the city, with a proud terracotta base and dazzling green oxidized-copper tower. Built in 1928, in what was then a suburban beanfield, it was the first department store in LA outside Downtown, and the first to construct its main entrance, a porte-cochere entry for cars, at the back of the structure adjacent to the parking lot – pandering to the automobile in a way that was to become the norm. The era's obsession with modernity and transport extended to the inside, where murals and mosaics featured planes and ocean liners abuzz with activity. Badly vandalized during the 1992 riots, the store subsequently closed, but the building

has since reopened as the law library of adjacent **Southwestern University**, which gave it a monumental, $29 million restoration to bring the old beauty back to its original glamour; to inquire about visiting during special events, visit Ⓦwww.swlaw.edu/campus/building.

West of Vermont Avenue

Now that the LA Unified School District has gotten its way and destroyed the landmark **Ambassador Hotel**, formerly located just west of Vermont Avenue at 3400 Wilshire Blvd (see box, p.76), the last remaining LA icon on this stretch is the bizarrely re-sited **Brown Derby** restaurant, across the street from the hotel lot (now being redeveloped for a high school). Once the city's prime example of programmatic architecture (or buildings shaped like objects – in this case, a hat), the Derby now sits on the roof of a minimall, where a coat of orange paint and a stripped brim have made it all but unrecognizable.

A few blocks west, the strikingly modern **St Basil's Roman Catholic Church**, 3611 Wilshire Blvd, was once the seat of the Church in Los Angeles (now Downtown at Our Lady of the Angels; see p.56), and is still LA's foremost example of contemporary ecclesiastical architecture, dating from 1969; the church features twelve severe, looming concrete columns interspersed with stained-glass windows, resplendent teak altars and pews, and a ceiling decorated with over two thousand twisted aluminum tubes. For a particularly vivid experience, come during one of the church's periodic **choral concerts** (for information, check listings or call Ⓣ213/381-6191). Built forty years earlier and somewhat more traditional, the lustrous mosaics, marble, and gold of the Byzantine **Wilshire Boulevard Temple**, nearby at no. 3633 (Ⓣ213/388-2401, Ⓦwww.wilshireboulevardtemple.org), are appropriately stunning.

At the corner of Wilshire and Western Avenue, you can find one of LA's great Art Deco monuments: the **Wiltern Theater**, a former movie palace featuring a bluish Zigzag Moderne facade and narrow windows that make the building seem larger than it actually is. Not to be missed is the theater's dazzling interior, notable for its opulent sunburst motifs and grand Art Deco columns and friezes.

75

The sad fate of the Ambassador Hotel

From the early 1920s to the late 1940s, the **Ambassador Hotel** was one of the essential centers of LA's social, political, and entertainment worlds. Occupying a sizable tract of land in what were then the automobile suburbs of the city, the hotel, when built in 1921, stood out prominently in the landscape of low-slung development and a few remaining agricultural tracts. But LA developed quickly, and the complex soon became the winter home of transient Hollywood celebrities, and its **Cocoanut Grove** club was a favorite nightspot, attracting singers and musicians like Bing Crosby and Duke Ellington on stage (its glossy character was recently re-created in Martin Scorsese's *The Aviator*). The large ballroom also hosted some of the early Academy Award ceremonies and appeared in the first two versions of *A Star is Born*. Politically, too, it hosted events with significant consequences: **Richard Nixon** wrote his immortal "Checkers" speech here in 1952, and on June 5, 1968, **Bobby Kennedy** was fatally shot in the hotel kitchen as he tried to avoid the press after winning the California presidential primary.

Despite its considerable history and impressive architecture, though, the building's future was in doubt since the hotel closed almost twenty years ago. At first, Donald Trump battled the **LA Unified School District** to win control of the site, and the latter won the legal fight many years after, only to dither over the hotel's fate for some time. Then in late 2004 it was announced that most of the complex would be unceremoniously destroyed and replaced with a sorely needed high school. Due to lawsuits, it took nearly three years to knock the hotel down, but knock it down the LAUSD did. The district promises to preserve and has put into storage a handful of remnants from the site — a facade here, a chunk of the old Cocoanut Grove there— but for the most part this was a battle LA's preservationists lost badly, thanks to the city's shockingly weak historic preservation laws, and the hotel's presence in a city ruled by indifferent developers and bureaucrats.

Known as the Warner Bros Western Theater upon its completion in 1930, the building was nearly demolished in the 1980s until, unlike other threatened structures in the vicinity, conservationists were able to save it. It's now a concert hall (see p.302), and you'll need a ticket for a look inside.

Decades ago, countless **neon signs** used to illuminate the bustling blocks of the Wilshire corridor. Some of them still survive. City redevelopment money has helped to relight a few, though the repair list is quite long and most landlords can't afford the upkeep and electric cost that the signs require. Because there's no guarantee that these signs will be lit when you arrive, neon lovers may want to hedge their bets by viewing them in the daylight. Neon of note includes the elegant **Gaylord sign**, 3355 Wilshire Blvd, the stylishly Art Deco **Asbury sign**, 2505 W Sixth St, the faux-French **Du Barry sign**, 500 S Catalina Ave, and the gentle script of the **Los Altos Hotel sign**, 4121 Wilshire Blvd. The Museum of Neon Art offers monthly tours of these and many other historic signs (see box, 31), or check out Ⓦ www.publicartinla.com/neon_signs if you'd like to do your own tour.

Koreatown

To get a good look at LA's cultural diversity, head south to Olympic Boulevard, between Vermont and Western avenues, to find the center of **KOREATOWN**, the largest concentration of Koreans outside Korea (around

200,000 people) and five times bigger than touristy Chinatown and Little Tokyo combined. Unlike the latter two, Koreatown is an active residential and commercial district, noticeably lacking the low-rise buildings and mom-and-pop stores that fit the stereotype of ethnic enclaves elsewhere: the district is loaded with glossy modern buildings and huge, multistory minimalls that contain several of the city's better restaurants, especially for Korean barbecue (see p.271). Except for dining, though, you really won't linger here, as there aren't enough key sites to warrant a lengthy trip. A good place to start any visit, however, is the **Korean Cultural Center**, further west at 5505 Wilshire Blvd (Mon–Fri 9am–5pm; free; ☎323/936-7141, ⓦwww.kccla.org). Along with a museum displaying photographs, antiques, and craftwork from Korea and local immigrants, the center features an art gallery with rotating exhibits of fine art, folk work, and applied crafts, and puts on periodic theatrical and performing arts productions.

Hancock Park and around

Further west, Wilshire passes through the sloping, tree-lined neighborhood of **Hancock Park**, named after yet another oil magnate, G. Allan Hancock, who developed this expansive parcel of real estate in the 1920s as an elite suburb. The area has managed to retain both its charm and its well-heeled residents, thanks to its carefully preserved historic revival architecture, especially the restored 1920 **Getty House**, 605 S Irving at Sixth Street, the mayor's official residence. In 2005 the house was reoccupied by the LA mayor after a twelve-year absence (the two previous leaders lived elsewhere). However, just two years after re-establishing the mayoral presence there, Antonio Villaraigosa moved out in the wake of an affair with a TV reporter, leaving his wife and kids as the mansion's current occupants. Getty House is open periodically for free tours and public events (check ⓦwww.gettyhouse.org for details), but can be readily appreciated from the street. As for the suggestive name, J. Paul Getty himself didn't reside here – his oil company owned it, along with the surrounding blocks, before donating it to the city in 1975.

There are plenty of other lovely houses, mock-Tudor and otherwise, in the neighborhood, though none are regularly open to the public. Still, you can check out some grand exteriors, such as Paul R. Williams's magnificent **Rothman House**, 541 Rossmore Ave, a half-timbered Tudor jewel, and, further west, a bizarre example of Medieval Norman, the **Sisson House**, Hudson Avenue at Sixth Street, featuring a gloomy facade and three-story tower. In early October, in the small subdistrict of Windsor Square, a few blocks east of Rossmore Avenue, a number of elegant homes are open for public tours; contact the Windsor Square-Hancock Park Historical Society for more information (tickets $35; ☎213/243-8182, ⓦwww.wshphs.org).

Bordering Hancock Park to the west and Wilshire Boulevard to the north, the Mid-Wilshire blocks of **La Brea Avenue** have emerged as one of the city's trendier shopping districts, with weekend visitors coming to sample the edgy galleries, hip boutiques and restaurants, and antique furniture dealers. As a more relaxed, though similarly well-heeled, alternative, **Larchmont Village** also has its share of high-end shops and restaurants, located just around Larchmont and Beverly boulevards, on the northern edge of Hancock Park.

The Miracle Mile

Like so many of LA's iconic districts, the **Miracle Mile**, along Wilshire Boulevard between La Brea and Fairfax avenues, was created by a property developer, in this case A.W. Ross, who realized the growing importance of the city's car culture and quickly began developing this stretch of road in 1921. Designed to be best viewed at 25–30mph, the strip's buildings used a horizontal layout, clear and large signage, simplified ornament, and novelties like timed traffic lights to cater to drivers. It worked. And though it never became LA's version of Fifth Avenue as Ross thought it would be, the Miracle Mile was quite a successful enterprise in its time, luring once-big-name department stores like Coulter's, Desmond's, Orbach's, and May Company to the then fringes of the city. Inevitably, the westward suburban shift that helped create the Miracle Mile also doomed it, and by the 1970s the area had fallen into decline, its vivid Art Deco designs left to fade and crumble after its department stores had moved away. In recent years, however, the strip has experienced a minor commercial upturn, with the arrival of nightclubs, galleries, ethnic diners, and offices for movie producers and agents (though a few shuttered storefronts and unrestored facades are still evident here and there). There are few stretches where you can reach 30mph these days, and the Miracle Mile has some of LA's worst **congestion**, leading many residents to heretically call for an extension of the city's Purple Line subway to serve the area.

LA's greatest unknown architects

Frank Lloyd Wright's forays into pre-Columbian styles in 1920s Los Angeles are well known, as are Rudolf Schindler's and Richard Neutra's early modernist efforts. However, the firm of **Morgan, Walls and Clements** had equal, if not greater, success in the age of Art Deco, even though its name is now largely forgotten.

The most conspicuous works of Octavius Morgan, J.A. Walls and Stiles O. Clements were the beloved Art Deco movie palaces that have survived the years and re-emerged as shrines to the golden age of Hollywood. The old **Warner Bros Western Theater**, now called the Wiltern (see p.75) and transformed into a performing-arts complex, was a triumph of the Zigzag Moderne style saved from the wrecking ball by community activism in the 1980s. Other of the firm's theaters, such as the **El Capitan** (see p.101), have survived through massive renovation, or by being converted into nightclubs, as in the pre-Columbian fantasy of the **Mayan Theater** (see p.61). Moviehouses aside, the firm's best work included a variety of commercial buildings in a range of styles, most notably the monumental Assyrian design of the **Samson Tyre and Rubber Company**, now The Citadel shopping complex (see p.167) – an ersatz temple stranded alongside a busy freeway.

Besides being skilled in period-revival architecture, Morgan, Walls and Clements also produced superb Beaux Arts designs, as in Downtown's **I.N. Van Nuys Building** (see p.59) and the stately classicism of the **Farmers and Merchants Bank**, 401 S Main St, and the Streamline Moderne, shown best in the sleek and towering **Owl Drug Company**, 6380 Hollywood Blvd. Perhaps their most impressive remaining structure is the Spanish Colonial **Chapman Building and Market** (now known as the Granada Buildings; see p.74), a fanciful creation occupying a full city block and hiding an interior courtyard with assorted clubs and restaurants.

Although many of the firm's structures were built for commerce, their Andalusian **Adamson House** in Malibu (see p.219), was not, offering the best chance to see what made their romantic escapist designs of the period so appealing to the private, as well as the public, world.

The route begins with the **Security Pacific Bank Building**, just east of La Brea Avenue at 5209 Wilshire Blvd, now the home of *LA CityBeat* weekly news, which gives you a small hint of what LA's greatest Art Deco structure, the **Richfield Building** Downtown, must have looked like before it was summarily destroyed in 1968. Both the original, and the current black-and-gold version, were designed by the firm of Morgan, Walls and Clements, perhaps LA's greatest purveyor of Art Deco and historic revival styles (see box opposite). Just past this is the **Wilson Building**, 5217 Wilshire Blvd, a grand Zigzag tower known for the colossal neon ad on its roof; the former **Dark Room**, no. 5370, a Streamline Moderne retail shop with a facade shaped like a huge camera; and, another Art Deco classic, the former home of **Desmond's Department Store**, no. 5514, with its bold Moderne tower and wraparound corners. The most vibrant classic Deco building may be the **El Rey Theater**, no. 5519, a thriving concert venue (see p.303) with its sleek king's head and flashy neon marquee, while just to the north, a series of **period-revival apartment blocks**, between Burnside and La Brea avenues around Sixth Street, manages to impress with wild 1920s and 1930s styling, everything from French chateaux to Hansel-and-Gretel cottages to pop-Baroque confections, many of them preserved with their original designs.

ACCOMMODATION		EATING & DRINKING							
Beverly Laurel	A	Amalfi	17	El Coyote	14	Insomnia	15	Rosalind's	33
Bevonshire		Angelini Osteria	8	Erewhon	6	Ita-Cho	9	Singapore's	
Lodge	B	Ca' Brea	25	Flora Kitchen	28	Largo	3	Banana Leaf	18
Farmer's		Campanile	29	Genghis Cohen	2	Luna Park	30	Sofi	24
Daughter	C	Canter's Deli	1	Grace	12	Mimosa	5	Surya	16
Orlando	D	Cobras and		Gumbo Pot	20	Molly Malone's		Swingers	11
Wilshire Crest	E	Matadors	7	Hatfield's	13	Irish Pub	27	Tasca	26
		Du-Par's	22	Inaka Natural		Nova Express	4	Tom Bergin's	31
		El Carmen	23	Foods	19	Nyala	32		
				India's Oven	10	Pampas Grill	21		

Museum Row

As you continue west, the Art Deco monuments of the Miracle Mile give way to the cultural behemoths of **Museum Row**. The museums begin at **La Brea Tar Pits**, Wilshire at Curson Avenue, where a large pool of smelly tar (*la brea* in Spanish, making the name redundant) surrounds full-sized models of mastodons struggling to free themselves from the grimy muck, a re-creation of prehistoric times when such creatures tried to drink from the thin layer of water covering the tar in the pits, only to become entrapped. Millions of bones belonging to some 230 kinds of animals (and one set of human bones) have been found here and reconstructed in the adjacent **George C. Page Discovery Center**, 5801 Wilshire Blvd (daily 9.30am–5pm, Sat & Sun opens 10am; $7, students $4.50; ☎ 323/934-PAGE, ⓦ www.tarpits.org), a Westside branch of the Natural History Museum in Exposition Park. During the summer, the outside "Pit 91" presents researchers on view, cleaning and categorizing the bones of recent finds (summer 10am–4pm daily; free). Inside, you can examine the mounted remains of many early or extinct creatures, including bison, saber-toothed tigers, and giant ground sloths, who met their fate here during the last Ice Age, from 40,000 to 100,000 years ago. More recently, oil drillers pumped the liquid black gold from the ground and created an industry as endemic to Southern California as the movie business. In fact, it was a petroleum geologist, **William Orcutt**, who found the modern world's first saber-toothed tiger skull here in 1916, and an oil magnate, G. Allan Hancock, who in the same year donated this property to the county (not far from his later Hancock Park development). Outside, tar still seeps through the grass, but most of it oozes behind chain-link fences.

Across the street, the **Craft and Folk Art Museum**, 5814 Wilshire Blvd (Tues, Wed & Fri 11am–5pm, Thurs 11am–7pm, Sat & Sun noon–6pm; $5; ☎ 323/937-4230, ⓦ www.cafam.org), has a small selection of handmade objects – rugs, pottery, clothing, and more. The limited gallery space also hosts a few rotating exhibitions, including vintage circus posters, ceramic folk art, and highly

▲ La Brea Tar Pits

detailed Japanese paper arts-and-crafts. Further west, the **Architecture + Design Museum**, 5900 Wilshire Boulevard (Mon–Sat 10am–6pm, Sun 11am–5pm; $5; ⓦ www.aplusd.org), puts on rotating exhibits of the latest trends in art, photography, and architecture, with a number of famous international names represented; however, the place is more of a showroom for interesting design than a conventional museum, so only true aficionados should bother to take a look. At the intersection of Fairfax Avenue, the **Petersen Automotive Museum**, 6060 Wilshire Blvd (Tues–Sun 10am–6pm; $10, parking $6; ⓣ 323/930-CARS, ⓦ www.petersen.org), is spread over three floors, showcasing cars of all makes and models, from the splashiest muscle cars to "million-dollar" vehicles like the 1919 Bentley and 1961 Ferrari. The second floor is mainly given over to temporary exhibits, where you might find anything from a Ferrari retrospective to a series of pint-sized mini-cars, and much more. On the ground floor, after you enter, an asphalt path leads you on a winding trek through the city's vehicular past, heading past dioramas of LA car worship past and present – from the reconstruction of a Streamline Moderne gas station to a mock-1950s car-hop diner to a 1960s hot-rod body shop in a suburban garage. The museum's most memorable image may be its re-creation of the *Dog Café*, a departed LA landmark of roadside pop architecture shaped like a giant bulldog smoking a pipe.

The Los Angeles County Museum of Art

On the west side of the La Brea Tar Pits, the **Los Angeles County Museum of Art**, or LACMA, 5905 Wilshire Blvd (Mon, Tues & Thurs noon–8pm, Fri noon–9pm, Sat & Sun 11am–8pm; $9, students $5; ⓣ 323/857-6000, ⓦ www .lacma.org), is one of the least-known of the important museums in the US, dwarfed in national prestige by the Getty Center even though its collection is considerably broader and, in fact, one the largest west of the Mississippi. Since its creation in 1965, the museum's homely beige-and-green blocks have attracted the scorn of architecture critics and have served as plodding, uninspired places to show world art. Following a Renzo Piano blueprint, LACMA is currently undergoing an extensive renovation and expansion, which will make it the kind of celebrated art venue it should have been all along.

Unless you come during a period of reconstruction (the schedule is still up in the air), make sure to check out as much of LACMA's collection as you can – the place is enormous, so there's no way you could see everything in one visit. The first phase of the reconstruction ends in 2008 with the opening of the new **Broad Contemporary Art Museum**, located between LACMA West and the rest of the facility, and highlighting a range of current art from LACMA's permanent collection and temporary shows. Also being refurbished are older structures, such as the **Ahmanson Building**, which houses a fine selection of world art, and the **Art of the Americas Building**, which contains US and Latin America art. Most big-budget traveling exhibitions will continue to take place in the Hammer Building, on the north side of the site. Get a map of the complex from the **information desk** in the central courtyard, and note that with the expansion, many of the pieces described below may be shifting around – final details are still in flux. Along with everything else, a new **sculpture court** will be installed, which promises to include a Jeff Koons installation of a full-sized locomotive engine hanging from a crane.

The Art of the Americas Building
The rearranged and rechristened **Art of the Americas Building** (formerly the Anderson Building) is home to the museum's surprisingly spotty collection

of **American art**; although the collection is rotated, typical highlights include the work of John Singleton Copley (the regal *Portrait of a Lady*), Winslow Homer (the dusty realism of the *Cotton Pickers*), Albert Pinkham Ryder (the murky, alluring landscape of *The River*), and Thomas Eakins, whose writhing, nude *Wrestlers* is the sort of expertly crafted, almost erotic work that has made him a favorite among contemporary critics.

Better than most of the paintings on display, though, is the impressive assortment of American and Western **furniture**, including bureaus from the Federal period, rough-hewn Craftsman designs, and machine-molded 1950s modern seats, the best of which are the familiar but fetching laminated-wood chairs of Charles and Ray Eames. Also in the building is a striking selection of Central and South American art, the highlight of which is the **Fearing Collection**, consisting of funeral masks and sculpted guardian figures from the early civilizations of pre-Columbian Mexico.

The Ahmanson Building

Although the structure is in the process of being renovated, the **Ahmanson Building**'s collection is in many ways the centerpiece of a trip to LACMA. Below the first floor, on a small lower level, is the museum's growing collection of **Chinese and Korean art**, of primary interest for its ancient lacquerware trays, hanging scrolls, bronze drinking vessels, glazed stone bowls, and jade figurines all covering nearly seven thousand years of East Asian history. Outside, in the sculpture court, the **B. Gerald Cantor Sculpture Garden** is mostly noteworthy for its cast of characters from Rodin's *Gates of Hell*, as well as his towering Balzac, along with a few other of the great French sculptor's works.

The central attractions of the second floor are undoubtedly the **European art rooms**, which begin with a good overview of Greek and Roman art and continue into the medieval era with religious sculptures, notably a series of stone carvings of the Passion cycle and various shards of ecclesiastical architecture such as Romanesque capitals, Gothic reliefs, and so on. The Renaissance and Mannerist eras are represented by compelling works such as Veronese's *Two Allegories of Navigation*, great Mannerist figures filling the frame from an imposing low angle; El Greco's *The Apostle Saint Andrew*, an uncommonly reserved portrait; and Titian's *Portrait of Giacomo Dolfin*, a carefully tinted study by the great Venetian colorist. Northern European painters are well represented by Hans Holbein's small, resplendent *Portrait of a Young Woman with White Coif*, a number of Frans Hals's pictures of cheerful burghers, and Rembrandt's probing *Portrait of Marten Looten*.

In adjacent galleries are Georges de la Tour's *Magdalen with Smoking Flame*, a Caravaggio-influenced chiaroscuro work of a girl ruminating by candlelight while holding an ominous skull; Jean-Jacques Feuchère's wickedly grotesque bronze sculpture, *Satan*; and an excellent cache of Rodin's smaller works. Elsewhere are some lesser works by Degas, Gauguin, Renoir, and the like, and rounding out the second floor are a few rooms containing ancient **Egyptian and Persian** sculptures and icons, including bronze figures and stone reliefs of Egyptian deities dating back to 3000 BC.

The third floor is most interesting for its **South and Southeast Asian** and Islamic art, notably the selection of richly detailed sculptures of Buddha in copper and polychromed wood, watercolor images of Tibetan monks inlaid with gold, and a pantheon of Hindu gods carved in stone, copper, and marble. The adjacent **costume and textile gallery** presents a wide assortment of fabrics and clothing from many different eras and cultures – including ancient

The people vs Ed Kienholz

Twenty years before Robert Mapplethorpe and Andres Serrano stirred up controversy in the art world of the 1980s, **Ed Kienholz** was making waves with his *Back Seat Dodge '38*, a broken-down old Dodge with faded blue paint and dim headlights sitting on an artificial grass mat surrounded by empty beer bottles. An open door reveals two wire-mesh bodies, their grubby clothes ripped and torn, intertwined in an act of sexual frenzy and looking thoroughly decomposed. Ominous, crackly music adds to the sordid effect. Now recognized as a triumph of early social-protest art, Kienholz's piece was called many other things upon its debut in the mid 1960s – indecent, morally depraved, pornographic.

LA County Supervisor **Kenneth Hahn** was one of the loudest voices to vilify both Kienholz and the museum for exhibiting the work, calling for the museum to be shut down unless it was removed. The battle that ensued was resolved with an appropriately ridiculous solution: the piece would be left in the gallery, but its car door would have to be closed most of the time; only when an adult over 18 asked to see the work could the door be opened by a museum guard, and only then if no minors were present in the room.

Both Kienholz and Hahn moved on from the fight relatively unscathed: Hahn became a local legend for securing support for rapid transit, building Martin Luther King Jr General Hospital, creating the freeway emergency "call box" system, and funding sports complexes (he had earlier successfully lured the Dodgers away from Brooklyn); Kienholz went on to establish an international reputation for daring assemblage art, becoming especially influential in Europe, though largely unheralded in his native country.

Appropriately, Kienholz carried his fixation with cars to the grave. When he was buried in 1994, in a strangely modern version of an Egyptian funeral rite, his wife drove him and his possessions down into the grave, burying him along with his favorite car – a Packard.

Persian rugs, embroidered Jacobean gauntlets made of gold and silk, kimonos from feudal Japan, and nineteenth-century New England quilts – but really draws the crowds with occasional shows on **Hollywood costume design**, featuring elegant gowns and outlandish headpieces from the likes of studio legends Edith Head and Adrian.

The Broad Building

Contemporary art is showcased in the brand-new **Broad Contemporary Art Museum** (opening in 2008), where American and international **modernist** art is the focus; among the more prominent pieces of twentieth-century art are works by Picasso and Magritte and abstract expressionists like Mark Rothko and Franz Kline, as well as the splashy, colorful paintings of Sam Francis, which hypnotically occupy a gallery to themselves. Less celebrated, but just as appealing, are Mariko Mori's hypnotic video presentation *Miko No Inori*, in which the platinum-blonde artist stares at the viewer with ice-blue eyes, manipulating a glowing orb to a hushed and haunting soundtrack; Bill Viola's *Slowly Turning Narrative*, a huge, rotating projection screen displaying discordant images; and Ed Kienholz's *Back Seat Dodge '38*, looking just as perverse as it did in the 1960s when it caused political outrage (see box above). On a similar note, Michael McMillen's multimedia assemblage *Central Meridian* is a creepy walk-in garage, decorated with occult symbols and other mysterious ornaments, that showcases an old beater propped up on blocks and eerily lit by red neon under its chassis.

The Pavilion for Japanese Art and Bing Center

On the northeast side of LACMA, adjacent to the tar pits, is the **Pavilion for Japanese Art**, easily the most effective building in the museum complex with its striking design, and the only one that will be completely spared when the LACMA remodeling job ends. This traditional–modern hybrid was designed by maverick architect Bruce Goff, and modeled after traditional *shoji* screens to filter varying levels and qualities of light through to the interior. Rivaling the holdings of the late Emperor Hirohito as the most extensive in the world, the pavilion's collection includes delicately painted screens and scrolls, while elegant ceramics and lacquerware are arranged beside a gradually sloping ramp that starts at the entrance and meanders down through the building, until it reaches a small, ground-floor waterfall that trickles pleasantly in the near-silence of the gallery.

Just across from the Pavilion, the **Leo S. Bing Theatre** in the **Bing Center**, presents a regular series of film programs that focus on classic Hollywood, art-house, and foreign favorites, for about the cost of a regular movie ($9; ☎323/857-6010). Additionally, the center houses a research library and the dramatic prints and drawings of the **Robert Gore Rifkind Center for German Expressionist Studies**, which includes a compelling library of magazines and tracts from Weimar Germany (by appointment only; call LACMA for details).

LACMA West

LACMA continues on to the western end of Museum Row (and the Miracle Mile), inside the former May Company department store at Fairfax Avenue. Built in 1934 as a great westward leap over other local retail stores, the building – whose eye-catching facade brings to mind an oversized perfume bottle – is home to **LACMA West**, which has finally been connected to the museum proper with LACMA's expansion. When this building isn't showing big-ticket blockbusters, it presents children's art in a special gallery – with pieces made to be jumped on, played with, and laughed at.

Around Museum Row

Just **west of Museum Row** is the harrowing **Museum of the Holocaust**, 6435 Wilshire Blvd #303 (Mon–Thurs 10am–5pm, Fri 10am–2pm, Sun noon–4pm; free; ☎323/651-3704, ⊛www.lamuseumoftheholocaust.org), which recounts the history of anti-Semitism and serves as a memorial to those who died in the Holocaust, as well as an affecting presentation of survivors' thoughts and memories; look for the intricate model of the Sobibor death camp, created by one of its survivors. Different sections of the museum reflect on Nazi atrocities, and illustrate the various means of resistance – violent or non-violent – employed by victims, and offer the overall timeline by which German hatred of Jewish people and culture led to the Nuremberg laws, Kristallnacht, and eventually the "Final Solution" of state mass murder. All manner of vividly evocative and disturbing photos, film, artifacts, and icons make this trip through the blackest page of modern European history a grim, but essential, stop.

On a very different note, a few blocks **south of Wilshire**, around San Vicente Boulevard, the period-revival architecture of **Carthay Circle**, a 1920s property development, is one of LA's best spots to see classic Spanish Colonial homes. A few more blocks to the south, **South Carthay** preserves plenty of 1920s and 1930s Historic Revival styles, and also has the added benefit of being one of the region's few protected architectural areas (and toured periodically by the LA Conservancy; see p.55). On the western edge of the neighborhood, the attractive **Center for Motion Picture Study**, 333 S La Cienega Blvd (Mon, Thurs & Fri 10am–6pm, Tues 10am–8pm; ☎310/247-3000, ⓦwww.oscars.org/mhl), houses the esteemed **Margaret Herrick Library**, whose voluminous and non-circulating collection includes books on actors, filmmaking, and festivals, as well as screenplays, film production photographs, and etchings. Formerly the home of the Beverly Hills Water Department, it was given a 1988 renovation by the Academy of Motion Picture Arts and Sciences, though its original spirit was kept intact – a municipal shrine to water, designed to look like a Spanish Mission church.

A mile from Wilshire down La Brea Avenue, **St Elmo's Village**, 4836 St Elmo Drive (☎323/931-3409, ⓦwww.stelmovillage.org), is a community arts project now forty years old, worth a look for its colorful murals and sculptures, with many of the local artists present for Sunday-afternoon presentations. It's now also the site of the **Festival of the Art of Survival**, an annual celebration of folk and popular art and music held each Memorial Day, and periodic jazz and poetry events.

Fairfax Avenue and around

Just beyond Museum Row, **Fairfax Avenue**, between Santa Monica and Wilshire boulevards, was long the backbone of the city's Jewish culture, full of temples, yeshivas, kosher butcher-shops, and delicatessens. The ethnic presence is still around, even as encroaching development from all sides threatens to turn the area into another homogenized LA retail zone.

At Fairfax's junction with Third Street are the creaky buildings and white-clapboard tower of the **Farmers Market** (Mon–Fri 9am–9pm, Sat 9am–8pm, Sun 10am–7pm; free; ☎323/933-9211, ⓦwww.farmersmarketla.com). Created in 1934 in an act of civic boosterism, it was intended to highlight the region's agrarian heritage, much of which was being paved over to make way for new suburbs. Inside the market is a bustling warren of food stalls and produce stands, popular with locals and out-of-towners to the point where it now sees tens of thousands of visitors daily. This growth has helped fund a monstrous mall next door: **The Grove** (☎323/900-8080, ⓦwww.thegrovela.com), a three-level, $100 million complex that has taken over much of the market's parking lot; there's nothing here you haven't seen anywhere else, but it's a pleasant enough place to get your shopping fix, and there's a diverting fountain in the center with kinetic jets to keep the young ones occupied. Also on the Farmers Market property is the 1852 **Gilmore Adobe**, named for the company that financed the Grove's creation and has also helped renovate some of the classic structures of Downtown's Old Bank District. As one of the oldest dwellings in LA, the adobe was once surrounded by a dairy farm, but has since been converted into private corporate offices.

Just north at the corner of Beverly Blvd, **CBS Television City** is a thoroughly contemporary, sprawling black cube – and something of an architectural eyesore – but also a worthwhile destination if you're in town to sit in

▲ Eating lunch at Farmers Market

an audience for a sitcom, game show, or the network's *Late Late Show* (call ☎ 323/852-2624, or ☎ 818/295-2700 for other programs); note, however, that many sitcoms – including those on other networks such as Fox – are taped in the San Fernando Valley at CBS Studio Center (ⓦ www.cbssc.com; to attend a taping, call Audiences Unlimited at ☎ 818/753-3470). To the east, pleasant **Pan Pacific Park**, 7600 Beverly Blvd, once featured the wondrous Pan Pacific Auditorium, a masterpiece of late Art Deco architecture and filming location for the Olivia Newton John kitsch classic *Xanadu*. Although the structure burned down in a 1989 fire, a hint of its breezy architectural style is still visible in the lettering and curving pylon of an adjacent sports facility. Also at the site is a moving **Holocaust Memorial** (☎ 310/204-2050, ⓦ www.laholocaust-monument.com), featuring six black-granite columns (each representing a million Jews killed by the Nazis) inscribed with the events of that dark period from 1933 to 1945.

West of the Farmers Market, the **Third Street** shopping district, running from La Jolla Avenue to La Cienega Boulevard, is another of LA's trendy retail zones. Although there are numerous good antique stores, restaurants, and coffee shops, most visitors are actually drawn by the huge shopping mall nearby – the imposing **Beverly Center**, Third Street at La Cienega Boulevard, a hideous brown-plaster fortress that serves as the hub of weekend activity for LA teenagers.

Hollywood and West Hollywood

Ever since movies and their stars became international symbols of the good life, **HOLLYWOOD** has epitomized the American dream of glamour, money, and overnight success, acting as a magnet to both tourists and hopefuls drawn by the prospect of riches and glory. Even if their real chances of success were infinitesimal, enough people were taken in by the dream to make Hollywood what it is today – a charged combination of optimism and despair. Nathanael West memorably captured its dark side in his 1938 novel, *The Day of the Locust*, Raymond Chandler made a career out of telling bleak stories of its violence and corruption, and James Ellroy has mined its depravity in lurid detail. Nonetheless, this dark side has only served to enhance Hollywood's romantic appeal, giving it an allure that no amount of myth-busting or bad press can taint.

Hollywood's uniqueness was enshrined by the California state legislature in 2006, when it established the **exact borders** of the area – one of the rare times in US history when a state has gotten involved with marking the perimeter of a city district. More or less, the state's version of Hollywood follows the contours of Griffith Park, the lower stretch of the eastern Hollywood Hills, Melrose Avenue, and part of Sunset Boulevard, excluding West Hollywood. Just beyond the eastern edge, at Griffith Park Boulevard, is a district whose early development was similar to Hollywood's. **Silver Lake**, the initial site of the movie studios, is now a center for Latin American immigrants and a well-established gay community. To the northwest, **Los Feliz** was home in the 1920s to many of the residences of Hollywood bigwigs, and nowadays is a charming mixed-income community with a few examples of notable architecture on its northern slope. Further north lies **Griffith Park**, the site of LA's famed **observatory**, among other less well-known institutions, and offering some excellent recreational opportunities.

The district's main drag, **Hollywood Boulevard**, is still essential viewing – the basis for much LA myth and lore, epitomized by the ever-popular **Walk of Fame**. This strip and its southern neighbor, **Sunset Boulevard**, were the central axes of the golden age of Hollywood, from the 1920s through the early 1950s; even now the stars live above it in exclusive homes in the **Hollywood Hills**, perched on snaking driveways behind locked gates – the most tangible reminders of the wealth generated in the city. The **lower Hollywood** stretches of **Santa Monica Boulevard** and **Melrose Avenue** are known for a famous film studio, cemetery, and shopping strip, while the economic core of the area lies further west in **WEST HOLLYWOOD**, actually a separate city, attracting a diverse mix of gays and lesbians, pensioners, bohemians, and a fast-growing community of Russian immigrants. Youthful poseurs and music lovers congregate on the legendary **Sunset Strip**, a traffic corridor loaded with legendary, divey, and posy nightclubs and bars, and huge, towering billboards.

Some history

Although you'd never believe it these days, Hollywood started life as a **temperance colony**, created to be a sober, God-fearing alternative to raunchy Downtown LA, eight miles away by rough country road. Laid out and named by real estate wizard H.J. Whitley — justly known as the Father of Hollywood — in 1887, Hollywood was a typically LA property development. The place grew and became an independent city in 1903, still dry enough to keep the teetotalers happy, but linked by streetcar with the rest of the region, giving sinners easy access to the vices of Downtown LA. The district's pious nature was forever changed in 1911, though, when residents were forced, in return for a regular water supply, to be annexed to the now-booming city of Los Angeles. The film industry, meanwhile, gathering momentum on the East Coast, needed a place with guaranteed sunshine, cheap labor, low taxes, diverse scenery, and most importantly, enough distance to dodge Thomas Edison's patent trust, which tried to restrict filmmaking nationwide. Southern California was the perfect spot.

A few offices affiliated to Eastern film companies started appearing Downtown in 1906 and the first true studios opened in nearby Silver Lake, but independent hopefuls soon discovered the cheaper rents in Hollywood (for the full story, see "The Rise of Hollywood," p.407). Of considerable influence was **Thomas Ince**, a producer who set up shop here and established a production studio that would become a template for later filmmaking companies. While Hollywood soon vaulted to domestic economic success, its international rise was only assured after the first world war; World War II crippled Europe's vibrant film industry, ensuring American pop-culture hegemony until the 1950s. At that time, government antitrust actions, television, and revitalized European competition damaged the US movie industry, and by the 1960s large-scale financial flight further weakened LA's film business.

In recent years, even the industrial companies involved in motion pictures – support facilities for editing, lighting, and props – have been underbid by outside competitors based in Canada, and shooting locations have migrated there – as well as to more far-flung spots such as Eastern Europe. While offices for big-name producers, directors, actors, and agents are still based in LA, all of the major studios, except for **Paramount**, have long since moved from Hollywood to digs in Burbank, Culver City, and elsewhere.

Not surprisingly, the district was hobbled by the departure of the studios, and for many decades after, novels and films depicted it as rife with two-bit thugs, skanky hookers, and drug-dealing scamps. The image kept tourists well away (except from icons like the Chinese Theatre), even as it attracted slumming hipsters. Since the late 1990s, a new influx of urban-renewal money and increased tourism have helped to brighten up the place, and city redevelopment schemes are always in the works – including the massive **Hollywood and Highland mall**, site of the Academy Awards. Shocking to many, the tourists have now returned in full force, at least on the stretch of Central Hollywood from Vine Street to La Brea Avenue. Beyond this, Hollywood may never be totally sanitized, and most of its true denizens – rock musicians, struggling writers, club-hoppers, and petty criminals – prefer it to stay that way.

Silver Lake and Los Feliz

As the original home of the region's film studios, **Silver Lake** and **Los Feliz** are fitting places to begin any in-depth tour of Hollywood (though the former is located just beyond its official eastern border). Unfortunately, Silver Lake's movieland heritage survives in only a few dusty pockets; it's more noteworthy now for its striking views of the city and fine modern architecture. Los Feliz has preserved slightly more of its history and maintains a number of landmark buildings, thanks to the financial wherewithal of its richer residents, and remains a pleasantly low-key area with less of the pretension found in the Hollywood Hills.

Silver Lake

As a city district, **SILVER LAKE** is something of a transitional zone between the creative grunge of Echo Park and the upscale comfort of Los Feliz, its lower section having a decidedly funky, grimy feel and its upper-slope denizens looking down with well-heeled wariness. As a body of water, Silver Lake is not a pretty sight – little more than a utilitarian reservoir, built in 1907, just before the area around it briefly became LA's movie capital. With its mainly Hispanic parts near Sunset Boulevard, Silver Lake also has sizable white and Latino gay populations, and the combination gives the place a real vitality, especially evident in the area's varied bars and clubs, where you're apt to come across anything from old-fashioned cocktail lounges to free-wheeling drag shows. The intersection of **Sunset** and **Silver Lake boulevards** is the funky heart of the neighborhood, crowded with grubby-chic dance clubs, dingy bars, art studios, offbeat shops, and cheap restaurants. The best time to come is during the **Sunset Junction Street Fair** in August (see p.336), a bohemian carnival known for its loud music, ethnic food, and vintage-clothing stalls, which draws everyone from aging hippies with their families to pierced and tattooed youth looking for a little raucous amusement.

Above Sunset, Silver Lake's hills rise around the reservoir, and from the aptly-named **Apex Street** to the east, wealthy residents are afforded great views of the city, which you can get too, if you don't mind driving up the precipitously steep incline to reach the top. The hills to the west are peppered with prime examples of modernist homes by the likes of Gregory Ain, Richard Neutra, R.M. Schindler, and Harwell Harris. Two bravura examples of mid-twentieth-century design are Schindler's cliff-hugging masterpiece of projecting roofs and glass corners, the **Van Patten House**, 2320 Moreno Drive, and John Lautner's **Silvertop House**, 2138 Micheltorena St (best viewed from 2100 Redcliff Drive), with its cantilevered roofs and balconies, wraparound glass windows, and sweeping concrete curves. Occasionally, houses such as these are open to the public for classical-music concerts presented by the Da Camera Society (see "Performing arts and film," p.307).

The east side of Silver Lake is an area once known as **Edendale**. Although most of the district's movie history has been paved over or altered beyond recognition (such as the long-gone Walt Disney studio formerly at 2719 Hyperion Ave), an indication of its fleeting glory is at 1712 Glendale Blvd, currently a storage facility but once the place where movie pioneer Mack Sennett's **Keystone Film Company** employed such legends as Fatty Arbuckle, Charlie Chaplin, Gloria Swanson, and the Keystone Kops, using much of the surrounding terrain for shooting locations. If you're a devotee of Laurel and

Hardy, wander south to one such location on Vendome Street where, near no. 930, a **long stairway** saw the duo trying to move a grand piano up its incline, in the 1932 film *The Music Box*.

③ Los Feliz

Named after nineteenth-century soldier and landowner José Feliz, **LOS FELIZ** is a mixed-class neighborhood with large numbers of Hispanic and gay residents, though it used to hold the glittering mansions of movie stars and studio bosses, a legacy that has left it with no small amount of eye-opening architecture. Just northwest of Silver Lake and occupying a prime perch below Griffith Park, the district numbered among its 1920s denizens Cecil B. DeMille, W.C. Fields, and Walt Disney. The legendary animator had his first "studio" here, at 4649 Kingswell Ave, which was actually little more than rental space in a realty office, where the bathroom had to double as a darkroom.

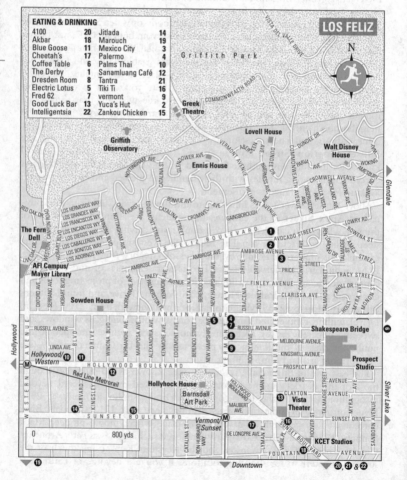

EATING & DRINKING

4100	20	Jitlada	14
Akbar	18	Marouch	19
Blue Goose	11	Mexico City	3
Cheetah's	17	Palermo	4
Coffee Table	6	Palms Thai	10
The Derby	1	Sanamluang Café	12
Dresden Room	8	Tantra	21
Electric Lotus	5	Tiki Ti	16
Fred 62	7	vermont	9
Good Luck Bar	13	Yuca's Hut	2
Intelligentsia	22	Zankou Chicken	15

KCET Studios, 4401 Sunset Blvd, constructed in 1912 and now housing the local public-TV station, is Hollywood's oldest film studio in continuous use. Its hundred-year-old lot was first home to forgotten studios like Lubin, Essanay, Monogram, and Allied Artists, but was later to become the birthplace of great films like the original *Invasion of the Body Snatchers*, and execrable ones like Zsa Zsa Gabor's *Queens of Outer Space*. When tours are running, you can poke around this studio for free, unlike on any other movie-studio tour in town (though the trek is more TV-oriented; 90min tour; Fri only; by reservation at ☎ 323/953-5289, ⓦ www.kcet.org).

Also remodeled for TV, the old **Vitagraph Studios**, 4151 Prospect Ave, was one of the first movie studios to go under, and is now the home of Prospect Studios, which mainly uses the facility for taping soap operas like *General Hospital* and dramas like *The Shield* and *Grey's Anatomy*. Melodrama and mystery junkies may also want to pass by **4616 Greenwood Place**, the apartment complex that was used as the exterior of TV's *Melrose Place*, and where Raymond Chandler lived in the 1930s.

More atmospheric is the **Vista Theater**, at the convergence of Sunset and Hollywood boulevards, a lovely, quasi-Egyptian moviehouse (see p.317). Across the street is the vacant site where **D.W. Griffith** constructed his Babylonian set for the 1916 film **Intolerance**, which cost $2 million and employed fifteen thousand extras. The movie was a parable about social bigotry and a response to critics of his earlier hit, *The Birth of a Nation*, which glorified the Ku Klux Klan; however, audiences were largely intolerant of *Intolerance*, and as a reminder of the movie's failure, the colossal film set (featuring elephant statues, hanging gardens, and massive pillars) sat for three years, becoming a perverse sort of tourist attraction as it became more decrepit. As an odd epilogue, a stripped-down "re-creation" of the gargantuan film set – complete with elephant pillars and a massive pseudo-Babylonian arch – is now the centerpiece of the giant Hollywood and Highland mall in Central Hollywood (see p.101), and of a Disneyland fake studio lot (see p.229).

Just after the original movie set's destruction, Frank Lloyd Wright began building his first LA house up the road, on a picturesque hillside overlooking the city. Construction of the 1921 **Hollyhock House**, close to the junction of Vermont Avenue at 4800 Hollywood Blvd (Wed–Sun tours at the bottom of the hour 12.30–3.30pm; $7; ☎ 323/662-8139, ⓦ www.hollyhockhouse.net), was largely supervised by Wright's student, **Rudolf Schindler**. Covered with Mayan motifs and stylized, geometric renderings of the hollyhock flower, the house is an intriguingly obsessive dwelling — complete with a fireplace moat — whose original furniture (now replaced by detailed reconstructions) continued the conceptual flow. The bizarre building was obviously too much for its oil-heiress owner, Aline Barnsdall, who lived here only for a short time, complaining of its leaks, cramped space, and inhuman geometry, before donating both the house and the surrounding land to the city authorities. Without question, the heiress was right to some degree, as the house works much better as a piece of sculpture than it does as an actual, functional home. It now sits in the **Barnsdall Art Park**, where a number of galleries devoted to the work of regional artists make a pleasant stop while you're waiting for the Hollyhock tour to begin.

Further into the residential heart of Los Feliz are a number of notable sights, including the **Shakespeare Bridge** on Franklin Avenue near St George Street, a 1925 quasi-Gothic charmer with turrets, which leads toward several notable private homes, and the **Walt Disney House**, 4053 Woking Way, an oversized Tudor cottage perched on a high slope, where the cartoon magnate lived for a period in his early career. Further into the hills, Richard Neutra's **Lovell House**, 4616 Dundee Drive, is a stack of blindingly white concrete slabs balanced on delicate stilts that looks quite contemporary for a 1929 building, and in fact was the first steel-frame house in the US. One of LA's landmarks of early modernism, the so-called "Health House" (the name reflects the original owner's dedication to wholesome living) was used to striking effect in the film *L.A. Confidential*, as the home of a wily pornographer. More garish is the **Sowden House**, 5121 Franklin Ave, a pink box with concrete Aztec-looking jaws designed by Frank Lloyd Wright's son Lloyd; you can get a pretty good look at this curiosity from the street.

Much higher on the slopes above Los Feliz, the **Ennis House**, 2655 Glendower Ave, is the elder Wright's own design, a fascinating experiment built from hundreds of bulky concrete blocks to look like a monumental Mayan temple – one of four similar Wright oddities in LA. The house's imposing, pre-Columbian appearance has added atmosphere to over thirty TV shows and movies, from Vincent Price's *The House on Haunted Hill* to David Lynch's *Twin Peaks* to Ridley Scott's *Blade Runner*. Unfortunately, due to earthquake and flooding damage, the place is in sorry shape, its south-facing wall partially collapsed in 2004. If you'd like to contribute to this essential, pricey renovation, call ☎323/660-0607 or visit ⓦwww.ennishouse.org.

Finally, Los Feliz is home to the **American Film Institute** campus, Los Feliz Boulevard at Western Avenue, whose **Louis B. Mayer Library** (Mon, Tues & Thurs 9am–5pm, Wed 9am–7pm, Sat 10am–4pm; free; ☎323/856-7654, ⓦwww.afi.com) doesn't mount exhibits – it's a non-circulating research facility stuffed with 14,000 books, 5000 scripts, and all manner of archives on classic and contemporary movies, with special collections devoted to Martin Scorsese, Sergei Eisenstein, and many others. AFI's annual **film festival** is the most important such event in Southern California (ⓦwww.afi.org), its screens attracting silver-screen aspirants from around the country and world.

Griffith Park

Griffith Park (daily 5am–10.30pm, mountain roads close at dusk; ☎323/913-4688), north of Los Feliz, is the nation's largest municipal park, a sprawling combination of gentle greenery and rugged mountain slopes that makes for a good day out – an escape from LA's traffic and chaos, if not its smog. The park was acquired by mining millionaire **Griffith J. Griffith** in 1884, but almost immediately, Griffith wanted to be rid of it; he could find no buyers and, in 1896, deeded the space to the city for public recreation. With its picture-postcard vistas and striking silhouette, it has since become a standard field trip for grade-school kids and a requisite stop for anyone taking a trip through Hollywood. Above the landscaped flat sections, where the crowds gather to picnic, play sports, or visit the fixed attractions, the hillsides are rough and wild, marked only by foot and bridle paths, leading into appealing terrain that gives great views over the basin and out towards the ocean. Unfortunately, in May 2007 a good chunk of the park **burned** in one of the LA area's regular conflagrations, charring more than 800 acres (about a fifth of the park) and wiping out such favorite spots as the bird sanctuary and Dante's View. The major attractions were (barely) saved, though, and the park is still an essential, if partially carbonized, stop for city visitors.

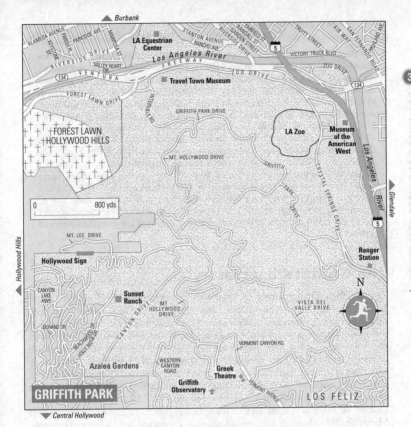

Near the entrance to the park off of Los Feliz Boulevard, Fern Dell Drive leads into the **Fern Dell**, a bucolic glade of ferns that acts as a border between the park to the east and an exclusive neighborhood to the west. Along Canyon Drive to the northwest, a hiking trail leads past a rock quarry to the lush **azalea gardens**. Elsewhere, the **Greek Theatre** (T 323/665-1927, W www.greektheatrela.com), is an open-air amphitheater that seats nearly five thousand beneath its quasi-Greek columns – though if you're not coming for a show (mostly summertime rock, jazz, and country concerts), you'll see just the bland exterior.

More entertaining for some are the caged animals in the **LA Zoo**, 5333 Zoo Drive (daily 10am–5pm, summer closes 6pm; $10, kids $5; W www.lazoo.org), one of the biggest zoos in the country and home to more than 1600 creatures, divided by continent, with pens representing various parts of the world. Despite the zoological inventory, it's crammed and uninspired, especially compared to its San Diego counterpart (see p.375). In the **recreation center**, Los Feliz Boulevard at Riverside Drive, are various sports facilities, as well as an old-fashioned **carousel** (11am-5pm: summer daily, rest of year Sat & Sun; free) with 68 sprightly horses first carved in 1926 and a rather sizable organ. In the summer the park hosts periodic, free classical-music **concerts** (information at W www.symphonyintheglen.org).

Park activities

The steeper parts of Griffith Park, which blend into the foothills of the Santa Monica Mountains, offer a variety of **hiking trails,** with some 55 miles in the park overall. You can get maps at the park centers at 4400 and 4730 Crystal Springs Rd (daily during daylight hours; ☏323/664-6611). The highest point in the area – the summit of Mount Hollywood — is a good trek for those in shape, but there are plenty of lesser jaunts if you're not quite up for it. From no. 4730, you can also rent a bike (summer Fri–Sun 2–8pm, rest of year Sat & Sun noon–dusk; $8–10 per hour; ☏323/653-4099). If you'd rather go horseback riding, the **Sunset Ranch**, 3400 N Beachwood Drive, provides one- or two-hour horse rides through the area for $25 and $40 (daily 9am-3.30pm; ☏323/469-5450, ⓦwww.sunsetranchhollywood.com), and the **LA Equestrian Center**, just across the LA River at 480 Riverside Drive, offers horse rentals for $20 per hour or evening rides for $40 (daily 5am-9pm; ☏818/840-8401, ⓦwww.la-equestriancenter.com). The park also offers basketball and tennis courts, a swimming pool, a golf course, and a baseball field, among other things; contact the park's main number for information on these sites (most are open during general park hours).

The Griffith Observatory

The **Griffith Observatory**, at 2800 East Observatory Rd (Tues–Fri noon–10pm, Sat & Sun 10am–10pm; free; ☏213/473-0800, ⓦwww.griffith observatory.org), is unquestionably one of LA's monuments, a domed Art Deco shrine to science, and a favorite shooting location for Hollywood filmmakers, but it got off to a less than auspicious start. Just after the turn of the twentieth century, Griffith J. Griffith offered $700,000 to the city to build the observatory and theater on the parkland he had previously donated. The city declined, principally because "the Colonel" had just been released from California's San Quentin Prison for trying to murder his wife – a 1903 incident in which Griffith, drunk and convinced that his wife was plotting a papal conspiracy, shot Mary Griffith through the eye. Although convicted of attempted murder, Griffith only spent a year in prison, and it wasn't until 1919, after his death, that LA finally took his money and later built the observatory and theater.

The observatory, finished in 1935, is perhaps most familiar from its use as a backdrop in *Rebel Without a Cause* and numerous sci-fi flicks, ranging from *The Amazing Colossal Man* to *The Terminator*. One of the city's most enjoyable spots, it was closed for several years for a massive **renovation** (and nearly burned up in the wildfire soon after), but has now been re-opened to glorious effect. It presents an array of high-tech exhibits for young and old alike – highlighted by the twelve-inch Zeiss refracting telescope, a trio of solar telescopes for viewing sunspots and solar storms, and other assorted, smaller telescopes set up on selected evenings for inspecting the firmament at your own pace. A full range of modern exhibits covers the history of astronomy and human observation, including a camera obscura, and a 150-foot timeline of the universe provides the lowdown on cosmological history and explains wormholes, black holes, and other out-of-this-world notions. For planetarium shows you'll need to reserve seats at the observatory and pay $7 for tickets. There's so much at the facility – which has quickly become a contender among the nation's top observatories and museums – that general reservations for visiting are required and parking disallowed; to visit, call ☏1-888/695-0888 and prepare to pick up the shuttle ($8 per person) at the Hollywood & Highland mall, LA Zoo parking lot, or Greek Theatre.

▲ Griffith Park

Northern Griffith Park

The **northern end** of the park, over the hills in the San Fernando Valley, is best reached directly by car from the Golden State Freeway (I-5), although you can take the park roads (or explore the labyrinth of hiking trails) that climb the park's hilly core, past some of its wildlife lurking in the brush. The most worthwhile museum in these parts is undoubtedly the **Museum of the American West**, near the junction of the Ventura and Golden State freeways at 4700 Western Heritage Way (Tues–Sun 10am–5pm; $9, students $5; ⊤323/667-2000; Ⓦwww.museumoftheamericanwest.org). The museum was founded by **Gene Autry**, the "singing cowboy" who from 1929 cut over six hundred discs and was the star of Hollywood Westerns during the 1930s and 1940s as well as his own TV show in the 1950s. Autry fans hoping for a shrine to the man who penned the immortal *That Silver-Haired Daddy of Mine* are in for a surprise, however: the **collection** – from buckskin jackets and branding irons, to Frederic Remington sculptures of turn-of-the-century Western life, to the truth about the shoot-out at the OK Corral – is a serious and thoughtful examination of Western history and legends. The comprehensive collection of artifacts is organized into engaging sections on native peoples, European exploration, nineteenth-century pioneers, the Wild West, Asian immigrants, and, of course, Hollywood's versions of all of the above. Catholic missionaries, gunslinging criminals, tribal medicine men, Romantic painters, and Tinsel-town directors are but a few of the colorful figures the museum honors, and sometimes criticizes.

Less intriguing is the nostalgic **Travel Town Museum**, 5200 Zoo Drive (Mon–Fri 10am–4pm, Sat & Sun 10am–5pm; free; ⊤323/661-8958, Ⓦtravel town.org), touted as a transportation museum but more a dumping ground for old trains and fire engines. Still, there are more than enough creaky locomotives and antique trucks, plus a miniature train to ride ($2.50), to keep the little ones occupied, perhaps far longer than their parents can stand. Bounding Griffith Park's northwest rim, **Forest Lawn Hollywood Hills**, 6300 Forest Lawn Drive (daily 8am–5pm; ⊤800/204-3131, Ⓦwww.forest lawn.com), is a cemetery of the stars that, while not quite as awe-inspiringly vulgar as its Glendale counterpart (see p.204), is no less pretentious, with showy gravestones and fancy memorials to such luminaries as Buster Keaton, Stan Laurel, Marvin Gaye, and Charles Laughton, as well as the likes of Andy Gibb, Liberace, and Jack Webb.

Hollywood Boulevard

From the 101 freeway to the edge of West Hollywood, the central section of Hollywood runs along **Hollywood Boulevard**, whose hub from Vine Street to La Brea Avenue contains the densest concentration of faded glamour and film mythology in the world, with a pervasive sense of nostalgia that draws tourists the world over. The decline that blighted the area from the early 1960s is receding in the face of prolonged efforts by local authorities – including repaving Hollywood Boulevard with a special glass-laden tarmac that sparkles in the streetlights and inviting all manner of new malls to take root here. Nevertheless the place still has its grungy side after dark away from the main tourist zones, when the assorted scenesters, drunks, drug addicts, and prostitutes create a lively, if not entirely savory, mix. Still, the contrasting qualities of faded glamour, modern hype, and deep-set seediness also make Hollywood one of LA's best spots for funky bar-hopping and nightclubbing, with a range of cheap, affordable options.

Once you cross the freeway and reach Gower Street, you enter the most celebrated stretch of the boulevard. An unofficial dividing line between the east and west sides of this historic district is **Highland Avenue**.

HOLLYWOOD

EATING & DRINKING

25 Degrees	21
Arena	43
Avalon	5
Bar Sinister	27
Beauty Bar	2
Boardners	23
Bourgeois Pig	2
Burgundy Room	26
Café des Artistes	32
Cat 'n Fiddle	37
Catalina Bar and Grill	25
Chan Darae	34
Cyber Java	20
Dar Maghreb	40
El Floridita	42
Frolic Room	11
Goldfinger's	4
Highlands	8
Hollywood Canteen	41
Hotel Café	29
King King	23
The Knitting Factory	2
Little Hong Kong Deli	38
Miceli's	26
Moun of Tunis	7
Music Box @ Fonda	22
Musso and Frank Grill	31
Off Vine	10
Pig n Whistle	18
Powerhouse	42
The Room	30
Roscoe's Chicken and Waffles	4
The Ruby	35
Shintaro Sushi	19
Taipan	1
Tiny's K.O.	36
Tommy's	13
Uzbekistan	6
Vanguard	24
The Well	22
The Woods	31
Yamashiro	33
Yonni's	9

ACCOMMODATION

Banana Bungalow	A
Best Western Hollywood Hills	C
Comfort Inn & Suites	B
Dunes Sunset	O
Holiday Inn Hollywood	G
Hollywood Celebrity	J
Hollywood Hills Magic Hotel	D
Hollywood International Hostel	K
Hollywood Liberty	I
Hollywood Metropolitan	P
Hollywood Roosevelt	L
Orange Drive Manor	H
Orchid Suites	F
Renaissance Hollywood	E
Saharan	Q
Sunset-La Brea Travelodge	N
USA Hostels – Hollywood	M

East of Highland Avenue

Perhaps the most famous intersection in Los Angeles, the junction of **Hollywood and Vine** still tingles the spines of dedicated Hollywoodphiles. During the early years of film, the rumor spread that any budding star had only to parade around this junction to be "spotted" by big-name film directors, who nursed coffees behind the windows of neighboring restaurants, as the major studios were in those days all concentrated nearby. In typical Hollywood style, the whole tale was blown wildly out of proportion, and while many real stars like Tom Mix and Rudolph Valentino did pass by, it was only briefly on their way to and from work. The most visible reminder of the legend today is located underground, where the **Red Line** subway stops on its way from Downtown up to North Hollywood in the San Fernando Valley. This subterranean station is decorated with film reels and familiar cinematic imagery. For a look at this and other subway-art highlights, the MTA transit system sponsors free two-hour tours of the most noteworthy and eye-catching installations (first Sat & Sun of month; 10am; information at ⓣ213/922-2738 or ⓦwww.mta.net/metroart).

Nowadays, few aspiring stars loiter at Hollywood and Vine, but many visitors do come to trace the **Walk of Fame**, which officially begins here (see box below), and just north of Hollywood and Vine is a small array of historic pop-culture buildings. The most familiar, the **Capitol Records Tower**, 1750 Vine St, resembles a stack of 45rpm records with its circular floors and top spire; Capitol was the first major record company based on the West Coast, and used this as its headquarters until the building was sold to a developer in 2006. Nearby, at 6233 Hollywood Blvd, the 1929 **Pantages Theater** (ⓣ323/468-1770) has a bland facade but one of the city's greatest interiors, a melange of Baroque styling and ornate Art Deco friezes that mainly sees touring stage productions these days, but also served as the glossy site of the Academy Awards throughout the 1950s. Next door, the **Frolic Room** is an old-time watering hole (see p.292) that has

Sidewalk stargazing

As practically any visitor to Hollywood knows, the **Walk of Fame** is a series of metallic stars inlaid into the sidewalk throughout the district, honoring various actual, quasi- and pseudo-celebrities of the past and present, from big-name actors to obscure radio commentators to people only famous for being famous. The laying of the stars began in 1960, instigated by the local **Chamber of Commerce**, which thought that by enshrining the big names in radio, television, movies, music, and theater, it could somehow restore the boulevard's past glamour and boost tourism. However, for every Laurence Olivier or Dustin Hoffman, plenty of dubious choices are also made; the Rolling Stones, for example, took decades to gain a star, long after they were past their prime, while such questionable picks as TV's *Rugrats* cartoon characters are enshrined frequently. Selected stars have to part with several thousand dollars for the privilege of being included: among them Marlon Brando (1717 Vine St), Marlene Dietrich (6400 Hollywood Blvd), Michael Jackson (6927 Hollywood Blvd), Elvis Presley (6777 Hollywood Blvd), and Ronald Reagan (6374 Hollywood Blvd). (For the full rundown, visit ⓦwww.hollywoodchamber.net.) Almost every month there's a ceremony for some new luminary, like Michelle Pfeiffer, or curiosity, like Donald Trump, to be "inducted" into the street; check the local newspapers for upcoming ceremonies. Strangely enough, the one major figure to actually die on the Walk of Fame was TV actor William Frawley – better known as Fred Mertz on *I Love Lucy* – who had a heart attack a short distance from his own star at 6322 Hollywood Blvd.

▲ Capitol Records Tower

appeared in countless movies, notable for its dynamic neon sign and interior mural of the stars drawn by the cartoonist Al Hirschfeld.

Around the corner, a bit of literary history can be found at 1817 Ivar Ave, the site of the fleabag rooming house where author and screenwriter **Nathanael West** lived during the 1930s after coming west in an unsuccessful attempt to revive his flagging finances. (The author vividly described Ivar Avenue as "Lysol Alley.") Gazing over the street's assortment of extras, hustlers, and make-believe cowboys, he penned the classic satirical portrait of Hollywood, *The Day of the Locust*, whose apocalyptic finale was inspired by West's witnessing of the Hollywood Hills wildfires in the summer of 1935 (and which, oddly enough, includes a character named Homer Simpson). Across the street, the former **Knickerbocker Hotel**, 1714 Ivar Ave, now a retirement center, was where the widow of legendary escapologist Harry Houdini conducted a rooftop seance in an attempt to assist her late spouse in his greatest escape of all. During the 1930s and 1940s, the hotel had a reputation for rooming some of Hollywood's more unstable characters, and a number of lesser names jumped from its high windows; in the 1950s the likes of Elvis Presley and Jerry Lee Lewis stayed here.

Further south on Ivar, between Sunset and Hollywood boulevards, the popular **Hollywood Farmers Market** (Sun 8am–1pm; ☏323/463-3171, ⓦwww .farmernet.com) has been doling out agrarian goodies for more than a decade, its hundred vendors selling their wares to locals and tourists alike. At 1623 Ivar Ave, the **Francis Howard Library** (Mon–Sat 10am–8pm, Sun 1–5pm; ☏323/856-8260) – named after the socialite wife of movie pioneer Sam Goldwyn – is a branch of LA's library system designed by Frank Gehry, and one of the master's less inspired works: fortress architecture with blank walls, a faceless facade, and maximum security above all. More inviting is the **Janes House**, back up on 6541 Hollywood Blvd, a 1903 Queen Anne dwelling that is now the last remaining residential site on central Hollywood Boulevard, though it's surrounded by a bland retail complex; the structure and its surroundings were renovated in 2006 to make way for a splashy eatery. A block west, you can find the well-worn dining booths of the **Musso and Frank Grill**, no. 6667 (see p.272), a 1919 restaurant that has been a fixture since the days of silent cinema. Here, writers, actors, and studio bosses would meet (and still do, occasionally) to slap backs, cut deals, and drink potent lunches. It's no accident that this was the place where, in Tim Burton's *Ed Wood*, the title character goes to drown his sorrows, only to encounter a loaded Orson Welles doing the same thing.

Across from the Grill, the **Egyptian Theatre**, 6708 Hollywood Blvd, is a unique, essential Hollywood icon: the very first Hollywood premiere (*Robin Hood*, an epic swashbuckler starring Douglas Fairbanks Sr), took place here in 1922. Financed by impresario Sid Grauman, in its heyday the Egyptian was a glorious fantasy, modestly seeking to re-create the Temple of Thebes, with usherettes dressed as Cleopatra. This great, restored building is managed by the American Cinematheque film foundation, and now plays an assortment of Hollywood classics, avant-garde flicks, and foreign films to small but appreciative crowds (typical ticket $10). Tourists, however, are encouraged to check out a short documentary, presented hourly, chronicling the rise of Hollywood as America's movie capital (Sat & Sun 11.40am; $7; ☎323/466-FILM, Ⓦegyptiantheatre.com). Alternatively, take a basic, 60min tour of the facility (Tues–Sun 10.30am–4pm; $7; by reservation only at ☎323/461-2020 ext 121) or get the grand tour of the theater itself in hour-long visits to sights like the backstage dressing rooms and projection booth, usually presented twice monthly (10.30am only; $10; call for details at ☎323/461-2020 ext 3). Much less appealing, the eastern corners of the Hollywood and Highland intersection feature a handful of dreary tourist traps – wax museum, oddities gallery, world-record exhibit – that are worthwhile only if you're very easily amused.

The Hollywood Heritage and Hollywood History museums

A five-minute walk north of the Hollywood and Highland intersection, the **Hollywood Heritage Museum**, 2100 N Highland Ave (Sat & Sun 11am–4pm; $5; ☎323/874-4005, Ⓦwww.hollywoodheritage.org), occupies a historic horse barn that originally stood at the corner of Selma and Vine streets. In 1913, Cecil B. DeMille, Jesse Lasky, and Sam Goldfish (later Goldwyn) rented one half of the structure while the barn's owner continued to stable horses in the other. From this base, the three collaborated to make *The Squaw Man*, Hollywood's first true feature film, whose success propelled them to move their operation – including the barn itself – to the current Paramount lot at Marathon Street and Van Ness Avenue. The barn was eventually brought to its present location as a monument to Hollywood history, and now exhibits memorabilia from the early days.

Just south of the Hollywood and Highland crossing, the **Hollywood History Museum**, 1660 Highland Blvd (Thurs–Sun 10am–5pm; $15; Ⓦthehollywoodmuseum.com), exhibits on its four levels the fashion, sets, make-up, and other artifacts taken from a broad swath of movie history, with particular focus on clothing, art design, models, special effects and props, including some from the latest Hollywood spectaculars. However, even though located in America's film capital, the museum has the feel of an overstuffed attic and pales in comparison to the much more comprehensive and informative Museum of Television and Radio in Beverly Hills. In the coming years, though, the Academy of Motion Picture Arts and Sciences (see p.116) will be building what promises to be a truly comprehensive film museum near Sunset Boulevard just south of Arclight Cinemas, with acclaimed French architect Christian de Portzamparc designing this showpiece (see Ⓦwww.moviemuseum.org for updates).

West of Highland Avenue

Looming on the west side of its eponymous intersection, the **Hollywood and Highland** complex (T 323/467-6412, W www.hollywoodandhighland.com) must rank as one of LA's most frustrating attractions. After nearly a billion dollars of public and private investment, the commitment of a major hotel, boutiques, and restaurants, and the relocation of the Oscars to the specially designed **Kodak Theater** on site, this towering beacon of commerce – which was supposed to revitalize Hollywood and give the district a cultural renaissance – is no better than your average suburban shopping mall. Its chosen, and perhaps unintentionally ironic, theme is the Babylonian set from the 1916 D.W. Griffith film *Intolerance*, from which the mall borrows heavily in its supersized columns, elephant statues poised atop massive pillars, and colossal, pseudo-Babylonian archway. Unrivaled in film history for almost fifty years (until the similarly ancient-themed *Cleopatra*), the movie was Hollywood's first real financial disaster.

One site that the mall has nearly swallowed up is the **Chinese Theatre** (T 323/464-8111, W www.manntheatres.com/chinese), 6925 Hollywood Blvd, now enveloped by a curving stucco wall and expanded into a multiplex, though the original auditorium is more or less intact. As for what remains of the building, it's an odd version of a classical Chinese temple, replete with dubious Chinese motifs and upturned dragontail flanks, and the lobby's Art Deco splendor and the grand chinoiserie of the auditorium make for interesting viewing. For $5 you can take in a **tour** of the theatre, complete with a look at VIP seating, a lounge, and balconies for the glitterati who attend premieres of big-budget spectaculars. Afterward, on the street outside, hop aboard a tour for a look at the "homes of the stars" (see box, p.31), or linger in the theater's forecourt to see the handprints and footprints left in cement by Hollywood's big names (see box below). You'll probably encounter hundreds of other sightseers as well as celebrity impersonators – Elvis, Marilyn, and Star Wars characters among them – low-rent magicians, and assorted oddballs vying for your amusement and money.

Across the street, the similarly impressive **El Capitan Theater**, no. 6834 (see p.317), is a colorful 1926 movie palace, with Baroque and Moorish details and

Hollywood impressions at the Chinese Theatre

Opened in 1927 as a lavish setting for premieres of swanky new productions, the **Chinese Theatre** was for many decades *the* spot for movie premieres, and the public crowded behind the rope barriers in the thousands to watch the movie aristocrats arriving for the screenings – a familiar scene memorably satirized in the classic musical *Singin' in the Rain*. The main draw has always been the array of cement **handprints** and **footprints** embedded in the theater's forecourt. The idea came about when actress Norma Talmadge "accidentally" stepped in wet cement (some say it was a deliberate publicity stunt) while visiting the construction site with owner **Sid Grauman**, a local P.T. Barnum of movie exhibitors who, with the Egyptian Theatre down the block and other such properties, established a reputation for creating movie palaces with gloriously vulgar designs based on exotic themes. The first formally to leave their marks were Mary Pickford and Douglas Fairbanks Sr, who ceremoniously dipped their hands when arriving for the opening of *King of Kings*, and the practice continues today, with celebrity hands, feet, cowboy guns, movie props, and assorted other images making impressions in the cement, along with various heartfelt odes to the glories of Sid Grauman. It's certainly fun to work out the actual dimensions of your favorite film stars, and to discover if your hands are smaller than Julie Andrews' or your feet are bigger than Rock Hudson's (or both).

a wild South Seas–themed interior of sculpted angels and garlands, plus grotesque sculptures of strange faces and creatures. Twice restored in recent years, the theater also has one of LA's great marquees, a multicolored profusion of flashing bulbs and neon tubes. Admission to the Disney-owned theater, which mostly shows cartoons and comedies, is worth the price to glimpse the eye-popping old Hollywood architecture. You can also drop in to sample the frat-house comedy stylings of ABC's *Jimmy Kimmel Live* talk show (TV tickets at ☎866/546-6984, movie tickets at ⓦwww.elcapitantickets.com).

A few doors down, at no. 7000, the **Hollywood Roosevelt** was movieland's first luxury hotel (see p.245). Opened in the same year as the Chinese Theatre, it fast became the meeting place of top actors and screenwriters, its Cinegrill restaurant feeding and watering the likes of W.C. Fields and F. Scott Fitzgerald. In 1929 the first Oscars were presented here, too. Look inside for a view of the fountains and elegantly weighty wrought-iron chandeliers of its marble-floored lobby. The place is thick with legend: on the staircase from the lobby to the mezzanine, Bill "Bojangles" Robinson taught Shirley Temple to dance; and the ghost of Montgomery Clift (who stayed here while filming *From Here to Eternity*) reputedly haunts the place. Moreover, the hotel is the starting point of in-depth, three-hour **walking tours** led by docents from the Hollywood Heritage organization, who take you around some of the area's historic old piles and point out where various famed and forgotten celebrities did their bidding (once a month, Sun 9am; $10; reserve at ☎323/465-6716, ⓦwww.hollywoodheritage.org).

The Hollywood Gateway and around

Hollywood Boulevard's historic stretch largely ends where it hits La Brea Avenue, on the corner of which stands Karl West's **Hollywood Gateway**. This iconic 1993 sculpture features a towering pylon and metallic Art Deco–styled roof supported by caryatids of movie goddesses Dorothy Dandridge, Dolores del Rio, Anna May Wong, and Mae West – supposedly an homage to diversity in Tinseltown history, though all four were imprisoned by the stereotypes of the era, making the sculpture strangely resemble a shiny cage. One long block north, at 7001 Franklin Ave, the **Magic Castle** is a spooky Victorian mansion and private club that puts on magic shows and other spectacles; the only nonmembers allowed a look inside are guests at the adjacent *Magic Castle Hotel*.

For a respite from the Hollywood scene, the **Wattles House and Park**, further west at 1824 N Curson Ave (tours by appointment only; ☎323/874-4005, ⓦwww.hollywoodheritage.org), is a relaxing spot at the edge of the Hollywood Hills. This 1907 estate contains an expansive park with picturesque grounds, several gardens with Japanese, Italian, and native-plant themes, and a palm court. The park is usually accessible if you call ahead; the house is more difficult to visit, though no less interesting, with its Mission Revival design, impressive arcade, and Craftsman detail.

Lower Hollywood

Although Hollywood Boulevard is the undisputed hub of Tinseltown legend, the actual focus of the early film industry was in **Lower Hollywood** around **Sunset and Santa Monica boulevards**, where the streets parallel the slightly lower slope further south. In the 1910s and 20s, these streets hosted five of the seven major film studios, but a decade later, four had left for more spacious lots in cities like Burbank, which offered huge parcels of land to these studios, with lower taxes than LA. Ultimately, only **Paramount** stayed in its Hollywood location, parked right on **Melrose Avenue**; farther west the street has now become best known for its many independent businesses, mostly boutiques these days.

Aside from this area, these streets are less touristy than Hollywood Boulevard, and their attractions are more modest and intermittent, aimed at those with a real yen to see the full spectrum of Hollywood. Aside from the west part of Melrose, most of the interesting spots should be explored by car, not on foot, as the strips can get dicey at night.

Sunset Boulevard

Famous as the title of the classic 1950 movie that featured Gloria Swanson as an aging, predatory silent-film star, **Sunset Boulevard** runs all the way from Downtown through Hollywood and into West Hollywood, where it becomes the colorful Sunset Strip (and beyond that runs on to the Pacific Ocean). Apart from **RKO Studios** to the south (which went under in 1955) and then-tiny **Universal** (which left in 1915), three filmmaking giants left sizable holes in the landscape when they departed more than six decades ago. **Warner Bros** (1918–29), **Columbia** (1920–1934), and **William Fox Studios** (1924–35) were located within twelve blocks of each other, but all their studio buildings have been changed or destroyed – the remodeled former Warner facility, 5858 Sunset Blvd, has been the filming site for everything from the original *The Jazz Singer* to Jimmy Cagney's *The Public Enemy* to the *Donny and Marie Show*; it's now a TV station, and no tours are offered.

Other, smaller, studios also occupied space along Sunset, and many actors would frequently try to get the attention of movie producers or casting directors by loitering around the corner of Sunset and Gower Street, the so-called **Gower Gulch**. Here, film extras in need of a few days' work would show up in the hope of being hired for the latest B-grade Western, as extras or emergency stuntmen. The gulch's air of desperation earned it the moniker "**Poverty Row**," which also collectively described the town's smaller studios, such as nearby Columbia, which Harry Cohn founded (along with Universal), before it grew to become one of the majors – after it left the area.

Down the street from the old Warner Bros studios, the recently refurbished **Hollywood Palladium**, 6215 Sunset Blvd, was best known for hosting the big names in swing, jazz, and big-band music, notably Glenn Miller and Lawrence Welk, who played here for a solid fifteen years, and the place still puts on concerts today, though of the rock, punk, and rap variety (see p.302). Across the street, at no. 6360, the white concrete **Cinerama Dome** (T 323/464-1478, W www.arclightcinemas.com) is an unmistakable sight, its hemispheric auditorium now part of a larger retail complex of theaters, shops, and eateries; the AFI organization also has regular screenings of Hollywood classics and art films here (tickets at T 323/464-4226, W www.afi.com). The dome was originally built to screen the three-projector films sweeping Hollywood at the end of the 1950s, but the movie fad faded even before the theater was completed. You can still see blockbusters in the dome on its central large, curved screen. Park in the lot for the adjacent **Amoeba Music** (see p.359), hands down LA's best music "shop," though indie clearinghouse or supermarket would be a better description of this massive vendor of vinyl, CDs and more. Nearby, the delectable Spanish Revival building at no. 6525, was, from the 1920s until the 1950s, known as the **Hollywood Athletic Club**, another of Hollywood's legendary watering holes. The likes of Charlie Chaplin, Clark Gable, and Tarzan himself (Johnny Weismuller) lounged beside its Olympic-sized pool, while Johns Barrymore and Wayne held Olympic drinking parties in the apartment levels above, with the Duke himself prone to chucking billiard balls at passing cars below. After standing empty for 25 years, the building reopened in the 1990s as a pool hall and restaurant, only to close again to the public; it now hosts special parties and private events.

Continuing west, the business complex at **Crossroads of the World**, 6672 Sunset Blvd, was, when finished in 1936, one of LA's major tourist attractions: its very first mall. The central plaza supposedly resembles a ship, surrounded by shops designed with Tudor, French, Italian, and Spanish motifs – the idea being that the shops are the ports into which the shopper would sail. Time has been kind to this place, and it has a definite, if muted, charm as the headquarters of the iconoclastic publisher Taschen (whose appealing Beverly Hills bookstore is also worth a visit; see p.359).

Further along, **Charlie Chaplin Studios**, just south of Sunset at 1416 N La Brea Ave, was a 1918 creation, built a year before the Little Tramp teamed with other celebrities to create the United Artists studio. Now owned by the Jim Henson Company, the complex is not open to the public but does exhibit a bit of whimsical, Tudor-flavored architecture from the street, especially as one of its little entry towers is topped with a statue of Kermit the Frog. A few blocks to the west, the **Guitar Center**, 7425 Sunset Blvd (℡323/874-1060, ⓦwww .rockwalk.com), a musical-instrument store, features handprints of your favorite guitar gods – Eddie Van Halen, Slash, and so on – embedded in the manner of the movie stars' handprints at the Chinese Theatre.

Santa Monica Boulevard

For a street with such a familiar name, **Santa Monica Boulevard** has few noteworthy attractions, at least in Hollywood proper. Often plied by prostitutes and drug dealers, the boulevard is home to a mix of Russian immigrants, pensioners, and middle-class gays. For excitement, you're better off heading further west into West Hollywood, where the street becomes a bit more lively – and safer. Still, despite its seediness, this stretch does have the distinction of bordering Hollywood's most famous graveyard.

Hollywood Forever cemetery

Not surprisingly for a town obsessed with marketing and PR, even the cemeteries in LA – and not just the actors – are renamed to draw the crowds. Thus the former Hollywood Memorial Park is now **Hollywood Forever**, 6000 Santa Monica Blvd (daily dawn–dusk; free; ℡323/469-1181, ⓦwww .hollywoodforever.com), though at least the graves have been kept in the same places. Close to the junction of Santa Monica and Gower and overlooked by the famous water tower of neighboring Paramount Studios, the cemetery displays myriad resting places of dead celebrities, most notably in its southeastern corner, a cathedral mausoleum that includes, at no. 1205, the resting place of **Rudolph Valentino**. In 1926, 10,000 people packed the cemetery when the celebrated screen lover died aged just 31, and to this day on each anniversary of his passing (August 23), at least one "**Lady in Black**" will likely be found mourning – a tradition that started as a publicity stunt in 1931 and has continued ever since. While here, spare a thought for the more contemporary screen star, Peter Finch, who died in 1977 before being awarded a Best Actor Oscar for his role in the film *Network* ("I'm as mad as hell, and I'm not going to take it anymore!"). His crypt is opposite Valentino's and tourists often lean their butts against it while photographing the marker for the "White Sheik."

Fittingly, outside the mausoleum, the most pompous grave belongs to **Douglas Fairbanks Sr**, who, with his wife Mary Pickford (herself buried at Forest Lawn Glendale), did much to introduce social snobbery to Hollywood. Even in death Fairbanks keeps a snooty distance from the pack, his ostentatious memorial (complete with sculptured pond), only reachable by a shrubbery-lined path from the mausoleum. If you revel in Tinseltown's postmortem pretensions, there are countless self-important obelisks and grandiose grave-markers throughout the park. More visually appealing, on the south side of Fairbanks' memorial lake, stands the appropriately black bust of **Johnny Ramone**, erected in 2004 following his death, and showing the seminal punk pioneer rocking out with dark, mop-top intensity. Further west, one of the cemetery's more animated residents is **Mel Blanc**, "the man of a thousand voices" – among them Bugs Bunny, Porky Pig, Tweety Pie, and Sylvester – whose epitaph simply reads "That's All, Folks."

Despite its morbid glamour, the cemetery also has a contemporary function. As you'll see around the Blanc memorial, there are many tightly packed rows of glossy black headstones with Orthodox crosses and Cyrillic lettering. These mark the resting places of **Russian and Armenian immigrants**, who increasingly populate the graveyard just as their living counterparts populate Central and West Hollywood.

Further along

There are only two other interesting sights along this stretch of Santa Monica Boulevard, the first of which is the **Formosa Café**, no. 7156 (see p.292 or Ⓦformosacafe.com), built around an old, remodeled trolley car, where celebrities from Humphrey Bogart to Marilyn Monroe came to drown their sorrows. It's still open, and its colorful ambience, though faded, makes it an excellent spot to savour authentic Hollywood spirits. Nearby, at 1041 Formosa Ave, is the independent production facility now known as **The Lot**, which used to be owned by Warner Bros, and before that housed **United Artists Studios** (starting in 1928), the production company of Charlie Chaplin (his second), Douglas Fairbanks Sr, Mary Pickford, and D.W. Griffith. With their studio as the symbol of the **star system** in the silent era, these four artists controlled their careers through the company, at least for a while, and helped craft the Hollywood marketing machine that sold movies by celebrity appeal, a system that endures to this day, for better or worse. The studio itself, however, was functionally dead by World War II, and has been periodically resurrected (with digs elsewhere) by financiers hoping to cash in

Laughing on cue

For many visitors, there's no greater highlight of a trip to LA than sitting in a **studio audience** and chuckling or applauding on cue to the would-be laughs generated by a TV sitcom. While not for everyone, such visits are required viewing for any proper television fanatic or old-movie buff – many production facilities are based in movie studios like Disney and Fox that would otherwise be off-limits to interlopers. Unless stated otherwise in the text, the main agency that handles the business of drumming up eager crowds for (live) laugh tracks is **Audiences Unlimited**. To be a member of an audience and experience the up-close taping of shows such as *According to Jim* and others, call Ⓣ818/753-3470 or visit Ⓦwww.tvtickets.com.

on the familiar studio name. If you want to venture inside the historic confines, you'll have to reserve space in the audience for whatever TV show might be taping there at the time you arrive; for information, call Audiences Unlimited (see box, p.105).

Melrose Avenue

The unofficial line between Mid-Wilshire and Hollywood, but included in the state's rendering of Hollywood's official borders, **Melrose Avenue** is home to the district's last major film studio and, further west, offers LA's most famous shopping strip outside of Rodeo Drive.

Paramount Studios

Standing at 5555 Melrose Ave are the grand gates of **Paramount Studios** (2hr tour Mon–Fri 10am & 2pm; $35; by reservation at ☎323/956-1777, ⊛www .paramount.com/studio), for many one of the essential icons of old Hollywood, though the original entrance – which Gloria Swanson rode through in *Sunset Boulevard* – is now inaccessible. The movie company, despite its many changes of ownership over the decades, is still located here and hosts assorted film and TV production facilities, and offers a **tour** as well. It isn't quite up to the standard of Universal's theme-park madness or Warner Bros's close-up visit, but if you want to poke around soundstages and a mildly interesting backlot (and have plenty of cash to spare), it may be worth it. However, fans of drawling TV shrink Dr Phil don't need to shell out to watch their hero in action: the lot is readily open to those who've reserved space in the audience for his and other, less familiar, programs (visit ⊛www.drphil.com or call the studio for details).

The shopping strip

For many, Melrose becomes worthwhile only between La Brea and Fairfax avenues, where it shifts from being a grimy traffic corridor to a busy **shopping strip** with a wide range of retailers and chains. In its heyday, Melrose was an eccentric world of its own, but since the 1990s a crush of designer boutiques and salons has been gaining ground at the expense of the older, quirkier tenants, diluting the strip's funky allure. Nowadays, you might drop a wad for a fancy

---

The rise and fall of bohemian Melrose

Synonymous to many with Los Angeles itself – splashy, anarchic, vulgar – **Melrose Avenue** came to national prominence in the 1980s for stores with edgy veneers and irreverent attitudes, the garish duds at Retail Slut, no. 7308, being only one of many such examples (see "Shopping," p.349). And although the exteriors of the 1990s soap opera *Melrose Place* were shot at an actual apartment complex in the area – further east in Los Feliz (see p.91) – that program's blow-dried beautiful people were a world away from the black-clad Gen-Xers and grungy hipsters of the real Melrose. More than anything else, though, what really defined the Melrose experience in its heyday was its widely eclectic selection of shops – junk emporia, perverse novelty stores, tarot-card readers, fetish lingerie dealers, etc – and colorful, eye-popping decor, making a stroll along the strip a truly odd and invigorating experience. Unfortunately, in the last decade, many of the shops that once defined the avenue have been edged out by steep rents and forced to move to newer digs in zones like Silver Lake, Venice, and Downtown's northeastern fringe. Predictably enough, they've been replaced by the types of chain-clothing dealers, pricey boutiques, pretentious salons, and other overpriced merchants you can find practically everywhere on the Westside.

dress or pick up a sleek pair of chic boots, but you won't see much in the way of antique dealers, toy shops, booksellers, or taverns; most of these have relocated to points east around Downtown or East Hollywood (including one of Melrose's greatest stores, Wacko; see p.361). As for **parking**, you won't find it easily on the avenue itself, but free spots exist on the side streets a block or two north and south of Melrose – as always, though, check the signs for parking restrictions.

The west end of Melrose is rather dull and mainstream: beyond Fairfax Avenue the street turns self-consciously chic and pricey until it reaches West Hollywood, where its color and vitality dissolve into an uninspiring stretch of elite boutiques, and most of the window-shoppers also vanish.

The Hollywood Hills

Once the exclusive domain of Hollywood's glitterati, and still a lofty location for the city's up-and-comers, the **HOLLYWOOD HILLS** are perhaps the best-known urban mountains in the US, synonymous with the legendary LA image of celebrities sipping champagne high above the common folk toiling in the urban sprawl. Roughly paralleling Hollywood itself, and forming the eastern end of the Santa Monica Mountains chain, these canyons and slopes offer truly striking views of the basin at night, when LA spreads out like a huge illuminated grid in all directions, seemingly without end. Beyond the stunning views, most of the appealing sights in this area are located just north of Hollywood Boulevard, on narrow, snaking roads that are easy to get lost on. If you want to do serious exploring in these hills, bring a subcompact car, lots of patience, and a detailed map, such as a *Thomas Guide*, or prepare to be befuddled.

The eastern Hollywood Hills

On the eastern side of the area, Beachwood Drive heads into the hills north of Franklin Avenue and was the axis of the **Hollywoodland** residential development, a 1920's product of *Los Angeles Times* news baron **Harry Chandler**, who found ample time for real-estate speculation when he wasn't strong-arming city politicians. The pretentious **stone gates** of the development sit at Beachwood's intersection with Westshire and Belden drives; the chief reason most people come to the area is for the view of the **Hollywood sign** at the top of Mount Lee above (see box, p.108). Unfortunately, there's no public road to the sign (Beachwood comes nearest, but ends at a closed gate) and you'll incur minor cuts and bruises while scrambling to get anywhere near. In any case, infrared cameras and radar-activated zoom lenses have been installed to catch trespassers, and innocent tourists who can't resist a close look are liable for a steep fine. For a much simpler look, check out Ⓦ www.hollywoodsign.org, where the letters are visible day or night, along with a virtual-reality tour of it.

If you've seen the disaster epic *Earthquake*, you may remember **Lake Hollywood**'s Mulholland Dam bursting and flooding the LA basin; however, this man-made, 2.5-billion-gallon body of water is anything but apocalyptic – just a pleasant, rustic refuge in the heart of the city. The clear, calm waters, actually a reservoir intended for drought relief, are surrounded by clumps of pines in which squirrels, lizards, and a few scurrying skunks and coyotes easily outnumber humans. You can't get too near the water, as metal fences protect it

Tales of the Hollywood sign

The **Hollywood sign** began life in 1923 as a billboard for the Hollywoodland development and originally contained its full name; however, in 1949 when a storm knocked down the "H" and damaged the rest of the sign, the "land" part was removed and the rest became the familiar icon of the district. The sign, however, saw plenty of rough times, including during 1960s and 70s when the weatherbeaten letters and one missing "O" of the crumbling sign mirrored the district's own ramshackle condition.

Despite its regular renovations (the first in 1978, the latest in 2005), the current incarnation has literally lost its radiance: it once featured four thousand light bulbs that beamed the district's name as far away as LA Harbor, but a lack of maintenance and frequent theft put an end to that practice. The public's easy access to the sign is also a distant memory, for it has gained a reputation as a suicide spot, ever since would-be movie star Peg Entwhistle terminated her career and life here in 1932, aged 24. It was no mean feat: from the end of Beachwood Drive she picked a path slowly upward through the thick brush and climbed the fifty-foot-high "H," eventually leaping from it to her death. However, stories that this act led a line of failed starlets to make their final exit from Tinseltown's best-known marker are untrue – though many troubled souls have tried and failed end it all here. Less fatal mischief has been practiced by students of nearby Cal Tech, who on one occasion took to renaming the sign for their school, and by other defacers representing USC, UCLA, the US Navy, and Fox Television.

from the general public, but the three-mile-long footpath that encircles it and crosses the dam makes for a relaxed stroll, especially for a glimpse of the stone **bear heads** that decorate the reservoir's curving front wall.

You can only reach the lake by car. To get to the **lake access road** (usually daily 6.30am–8pm; information at ☎323/463-0830, ⓦwww.hollywoodknolls .org/hollywood_reservoir.htm), go north on Cahuenga Boulevard past Franklin Avenue, turn right onto Dix Street and left to Holly Drive and climb up to Deep Dell Place; from there it's a sharp left on Weidlake Drive. Follow the winding street to the main gate.

Whitley Heights

West across Cahuenga Boulevard, pristine **Whitley Heights** is a small pocket of Spanish Colonial architecture, worth a look for its well-maintained houses and great city views. The district, accessible from Milner Road off Highland Avenue, was laid out in 1918 by business tycoon **Hobart J. Whitley**, an Owens Valley water conspirator who engineered the sale of San Fernando Valley real estate (under his aptly named corporation, "Suburban Homes"). He was also known as the "Father of Hollywood," as his Whitley Heights soon became a movie-star subdivision for such silent-screen greats as Marie Dressler, Gloria Swanson, Rudolph Valentino, and the first "Ben Hur," Francis X. Bushman. The area is fairly well protected from development, and while tours of some homes are occasionally offered by preservation groups such as the LA Conservancy (see p.55), you won't find any tourist brochures available. Still, it's worth taking a revealing look at an elegant, ungated "Old Hollywood" neighborhood – a far cry from modern celebrity enclaves like the well-guarded Malibu Colony.

The Hollywood Bowl and around

Near the Hollywood Freeway at 2301 N Highland Avenue, the **Hollywood Bowl** is an open-air auditorium that opened in 1921 and has since become something of an icon among outdoor band. The Beatles played here in the mid-1960s, but the Bowl's principal function is as the occasional summer home of the Los Angeles Philharmonic, which gives evening concerts from July to September (℡323/850-2000, ⓦwww.hollywoodbowl.org). These events are less highbrow than you might imagine, many of them featuring fist-pumping crowd-pleasers like *Victory at Sea* and the *1812 Overture*, as well as selections of smooth jazz, film music, and other inoffensive fare. More about the Bowl's history can be gleaned from the video inside the **Hollywood Bowl Museum** near the entrance (July–mid-Sept Tues–Sat 10am to showtime, Sun 4pm–showtime; mid-Sept–June Tues–Sat 10am–5pm; free; ℡323/850-2000). It's not an essential stop by any means, but is worth a visit if you have any affection for the grand old concrete structure. With a collection of musical instruments from around the world, the museum also features recordings of notable symphonic moments in the Bowl's history and architectural drawings by Lloyd Wright, Frank's son (more famous for his Wayfarer's Chapel, p.175, and spooky Sowden House, p.92), who contributed a design for one of the Bowl's many shells. The fifth and newest of these dates from the summer of 2004.

One of the elder Wright's memorable 1920s residences, the **Freeman House**, is just south of the Bowl at 1962 Glencoe Way (information at ℡323/851-0671): a squat, Mayan-modern hybrid made of concrete "knit-blocks," which doesn't actually seem like much from the outside, but inside you'll get an outstanding panoramic view of Hollywood, and a close-up look at Wright's geometric decorations and motifs. Like Wright's other major pre-Columbian experiment, the Ennis House (p.92), this one is in pretty bad shape due to earthquake damage. It's now owned by USC, which is overseeing a slow restoration; call for information on the latest progress. Another early 1920s design, the **High Tower**, is notable for a different reason. Inaccessible to the public, though viewable at the end of High Tower Drive, the Italian-styled campanile is the literary home of Raymond Chandler's Philip Marlowe – and Elliott Gould, playing Marlowe, lived in a dumpy apartment at the tower's apex in Robert Altman's 1973 film *The Long Goodbye* (see Review, p.416). The surrounding neighborhood is pleasant for walking, as many of its streets are pedestrian-only, tree-lined walkways.

The western Hollywood Hills

When he was directing *Chinatown*, Roman Polanski spent many hours in Jack Nicholson's house on **Mulholland Drive**, and later remarked of LA, "[t]here's no more beautiful city in the world … provided it's seen at night and from a distance." With its striking panorama after dark of the illuminated city-grid, stretching nearly to the horizon, Mulholland easily justifies the director's wry comment – and makes the **western Hollywood Hills** a good place to get a glimpse of the LA good life.

From its starting point near the 101 freeway to its terminus at LA County's beachside boundary, the road travels 21 miles through winding mountain passes and steep canyons, and offers a stunning overview of the region's size and character. The stretch between the 101 and 405 freeways is the best, especially at night, when alternating views of brightly lit LA and the San Fernando Valley, to the north, keep drivers dangerously distracted. Although parking is forbidden at night, daytime views are best experienced at a **roadside park**, at 7320 Mulholland Drive just west of Hillside Drive. Here, telescopes allow you to peek at Hollywood, Downtown, and the many palatial homes.

Further west lies the northern edge of 130-acre **Runyon Canyon Park** (daily dawn–dusk; ⓦ www.runyon-canyon.com), which actually improves on the views from Mulholland's crest. Park your car in the dirt near its chained gate and wander inside to a rocky outcrop that overlooks the city. Below, a path winds down to closer views of Hollywood until it eventually reaches the base of the hills themselves. If you have the stamina, take the long hike back up the hill to Mulholland, and keep a look out for B-list celebrities walking their dogs or burning off a few pounds for their next roles; otherwise, leave the park at Fuller Street (the only southern exit) and call a cab to take you back up to the top. From here, follow Mulholland west past the Woodrow Wilson Drive entrance to the elite subdivision of **Mount Olympus**, a residential exercise in 1970s vulgarity that is to Neoclassical architecture what a toga party is to ancient drama, with faux palazzos, pseudo-Roman statuary, goofy marble urns, and snarling stone lions added pell-mell to charmless stucco boxes. Much more appealing is the **Chemosphere**, 776 Torreyson Drive, architect John Lautner's

The Case Study Program

Of all the popular architectural images to appear in the decades after World War II, perhaps none has been as recognizable or influential as the one of two women reclining in their evening gowns inside a glass-enclosed home overlooking the illuminated grid of Los Angeles. The photograph was of Case Study House #22, at 1635 Woods Drive in the Hollywood Hills, one of the 36 **Case Study Houses** planned in the LA area in the two decades after the war.

Created by the editor of the influential *Arts and Architecture* magazine, **John Entenza**, the **Case Study Program** was designed to show how industrial materials like glass and steel could be used for elegant, affordably modern homes, using "open-floor" plans to eliminate dining rooms and unnecessary walls – all revolutionary concepts at the time. Surprisingly, for a program that showcased what were then rather avant-garde structures, it was quite popular locally, selected homes were displayed for the public, and nearly 400,000 visitors took a walk through the first six of these open houses. Especially influential in design circles, the low-cost houses used construction materials that were often donated for free by various building-supply companies, with a free plug in the magazine as an incentive. However, despite its popularity and influence, the program never really came close to its goal of converting the broader American public to the modern mindset, though it did create some pretty impressive works (check out Elizabeth A.T. Smith's *Blueprints for Modern Living* for more details; see "Books," p.425).

With designs chosen by Entenza and his staff at the magazine, the houses were numbered in the order they were planned, irrespective of when, or if, they were ever built (23 eventually was, all but two in LA). The eighth house in the series was its first masterpiece, Charles and Ray Eames' colorful 1949 steel-and-glass complex, the **Eames House and Studio**, a modular construction on the bluffs of Pacific Palisades that's a National Historic Landmark and perhaps the most famous of all the Case Study houses, despite only being assembled in a few days. Eventually, many of the biggest names in LA architecture – Richard Neutra, Raphael Soriano, Gregory Ain, among 27 others – took a stab at the program, with Craig Ellwood's **#16 house**, 1811 Bel Air Rd – a rigid exercise in steel, glass, and stone – and Neutra's wood-and-brick **Bailey House**, near the Eames House at 219 Chautauqua Blvd, among the finest examples. Unfortunately, for a program that was designed to have a great public impact, almost all these houses are now closed to the public, so a drive-by look will have to suffice if you're interested in seeing them. The only exception is the prominent Eames House, which offers lectures, seminars, and tours of the grounds by appointment (☎310/459-9663, ⓦ www.eamesfoundation.org).

giant UFO-like house, balanced on a huge space-age pedestal and overlooking the San Fernando Valley to the north. Today it's home to Benedikt Taschen, publisher of stylish art and architecture books.

Other architectural treats can be found with sufficient effort as well, notably the stunning **Case Study House #21**, 9038 Wonderland Park Ave, Pierre Koenig's modern hillside box, part of the influential Case Study Program (see box opposite). Despite its elemental glass-and-steel construction, the house is a design icon that recently sold for $3 million. Unfortunately, most of the area's other houses are hidden away, and there's no real way to explore in depth without your own car, a copy of the latest *Thomas Guide* map and, if possible, a detailed guide to LA architecture, such as *Los Angeles: An Architectural Guide* (see p.425). If you're more interested in peeking at the homes of the stars, check out one of the many tours designed expressly for celebrity gazing (see box, p.31), or look up a master list on the Internet (ⓦwww.seeing-stars.com is a good place to start). Notable movie-star houses include Rudolph Valentino's extravagant **Falcon Lair** (1436 Bella Drive), Errol Flynn's **Mulholland House** (7740 Mulholland Drive), and the former home of actress Sharon Tate – and studio of Trent Reznor of Nine Inch Nails – at **10066 Cielo Drive**, where some of the Manson killings took place.

Mulholland Drive continues past a series of enjoyable parks, including **Fryman Canyon Overlook**, a good place for a hike in the Santa Monica Mountains, and **Coldwater Canyon Park**.

West Hollywood

Between Hollywood proper and Beverly Hills, **WEST HOLLYWOOD** was for many years the vice capital of LA, with prostitution, gambling, and drugs all occupying prominent places on the debauched **Sunset Strip**. The area was incorporated in 1984, a move meant partly to clean up the place and partly to represent the interests of gays, seniors, and renters. West Hollywood has since gone on to become one of the most dynamic parts of the region, especially notable for its freewheeling bars and clubs, and housing prices have skyrocketed on many streets. However, this success has not entirely eliminated strife, and the new waves of Russian and Armenian immigrants making their homes near Santa Monica Boulevard are an uneasy mix with the city's long-standing residents. Not surprisingly, West Hollywood is in many ways more akin to Hollywood, in its progressive character and attitudes, than it is to the prosaic wealth of Beverly Hills.

Except for the Sunset Strip – the well-known asphalt artery that features LA's best nightlife and billboards – West Hollywood's principal attractions lie west of **La Cienega Boulevard** around the colossal **Pacific Design Center**. The area east of Crescent Heights Boulevard generally blends with the less inviting parts of lower Hollywood and has little appeal beyond a few clubs and restaurants.

The Sunset Strip

Sunset Boulevard from Crescent Heights Boulevard to Doheny Drive, long known as the **Sunset Strip**, is a roughly two-mile-long assortment of chic restaurants, plush hotels, and swinging nightclubs. These establishments first appeared during the 1920s, along what was then a dirt road serving as the main route between the Hollywood movie studios and the early Westside "homes of

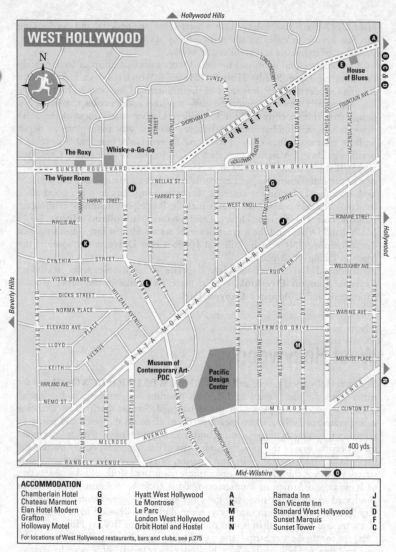

WEST HOLLYWOOD

Hollywood Hills

N

House of Blues

SUNSET PLAZA
SUNSET BOULEVARD
SUNSET STRIP
LONDONDERRY PL.

The Roxy   Whisky-a-Go-Go

SUNSET BOULEVARD

HOLLOWAY DRIVE

The Viper Room

HOLLOWAY PLAZA DR.

Beverly Hills

Hollywood

SHOREHAM DR.
LARRABEE STREET
HORN AVENUE
ALTA LOMA ROAD
LA CIENEGA BOULEVARD
FOUNTAIN AVE.
HACIENDA PLACE

NELLAS ST.
HARRATT ST.
WEST KNOLL
ROMAINE STREET
HAMMOND ST.
HARRATT STREET
SAN VICENTE
PALM AVENUE
HANCOCK AVENUE
WESTMOUNT DR.
DRIVE
STREET
WILLOUGHBY AVE.
PHYLLIS AVE.
LARRABEE STREET
BOULEVARD
ALFRED STREET
WARING AVE.
CYNTHIA STREET
VISTA GRANDE
RUGBY DR.
DICKS STREET
HILLDALE AVENUE
AVENUE
SANTA MONICA BOULEVARD
MELROSE PLACE
NORMA PLACE
DOHENY DRIVE
HUNTLEY DRIVE
WESTBOURNE DRIVE
SHERWOOD DRIVE
WESTMOUNT DRIVE
WEST KNOLL DRIVE
LA CIENEGA BOULEVARD
CROFT AVENUE
ELEVADO AVE.
LLOYD
KEITH
PLACE
Museum of Contemporary Art–PDC
Pacific Design Center
SAN VICENTE BOULEVARD
AVENUE
CLINTON ST.
HARLAND AVE.
MELROSE
NEMO ST.
ALMONT DR.
LA PEER DR.
ROBERTSON BLVD.
NORWICH DRIVE
MELROSE
AVENUE

0   400 yds

RANGELY AVENUE

Mid-Wilshire

ACCOMMODATION					
Chamberlain Hotel	G	Hyatt West Hollywood	A	Ramada Inn	J
Chateau Marmont	B	Le Montrose	K	San Vicente Inn	D
Elan Hotel Modern	O	Le Parc	M	Standard West Hollywood	F
Grafton	I	London West Hollywood	H	Sunset Marquis	L
Holloway Motel	I	Orbit Hotel and Hostel	N	Sunset Tower	C

For locations of West Hollywood restaurants, bars and clubs, see p.275

the stars." F. Scott Fitzgerald and friends spent many leisurely afternoons over drinks here, around the swimming pool of the long-demolished *Garden of Allah* hotel, and the nearby *Ciro's* nightclub was *the* place to be seen in the 1940s, surviving today as the *Comedy Store* (see p.314). With the demise of the studio system, the Strip declined, only reviving in the 1960s when a happening scene developed around the landmark *Whisky-a-Go-Go* club, which featured seminal rock bands such as Love, The Doors, and Buffalo Springfield, whose anthem "For What It's Worth" alludes to the riot that took place on the Strip after the police closed down a popular club called *Pandora's Box*. Since the incorporation of West Hollywood, the striptease clubs and head shops have been phased out and this fashionable area now rivals Beverly Hills for movie-industry executives per square foot, though there's plenty of chic grunge to keep you occupied, as well as a decent club and live-music scene.

Some tourists come to the Strip just to see the enormous **billboards**, which take advantage of a very permissive, longstanding municipal policy that allows all kinds of gargantuan signs to pop up along the road. The ruddy-faced Marlboro Man is now gone, but there are many more along the Strip to attract your eye: fantastic commercial murals animated with bright colors, movie ads with stars' names in massive letters, and self-promotions for mysterious actresses – note the amply bosomed "Angelyne" looming in Day-Glo splendor.

The Strip starts in earnest at the huge Norman castle of the **Chateau Marmont Hotel**, towering over the east end of Sunset Strip at no. 8221. Built in 1927 as luxury apartments, this stodgy block of concrete has long been a Hollywood favorite for its elegant private suites and bungalows, and you'll pay plenty for the privilege of staying here (see p.246). Howard Hughes used to rent the entire penthouse so he could keep an eye on the bathing beauties around the pool below, and the hotel made headlines in 1982 when comedian John Belushi died of a heroin overdose in the hotel bungalow that he used as his LA home. Across the street, the **House of Blues**, no. 8430, is a corrugated tin shack, with an imported dirt floor from the Deep South, that is one of the area's chief tourist attractions (and the flagship branch of an international chain), although it pales in comparison with the more authentic scene found around the **Whisky-a-Go-Go**, no. 8901, and the **Roxy**, no. 9009, both famed for their 1960s pedigree. Other spots, like the **Viper Room**, no. 8852, and the **Sunset Hyatt**, no. 8401, have their own notorious histories – the former being Johnny Depp's trendy lair for rockers where River Phoenix fatally overdosed, and the upscale hotel (known in the 1970s as the "Riot House") was the staging ground for the antics of The Who and Led Zeppelin, who took to racing motorcycles down its hallways and engaging in carnal acts with a fish (cited as the "Sleaziest Moment in Rock History," according to *Spin* magazine).

La Cienega Boulevard

La Cienega Boulevard divides West Hollywood roughly down the middle, separating the funky seediness to the east and the snooty affluence to the west. The street holds a mixture of excellent hotels, clubs, and restaurants, along with Cesar Pelli's **Pacific Design Center**, 8687 Melrose Ave (Mon–Fri 9.30am–5pm; ☎310/657-0800, ⓦ www.thepacificdesigncenter.com), a hulking complex known as the "Blue Whale," loaded with interior-design boutiques and furniture dealers. Completely out of scale to the low-slung neighborhood around it, the entire Center is open to the public for viewing, but purchasing anything inside requires the assistance of a professional designer. Still, you're likely to be satisfied just snooping around, not so much in the octagonal **Center Green** – also called the "Green Apple" – but in **Center Blue**, a massive barn with a mix of showrooms and boutiques. The center also features a Westside branch of the **Museum of Contemporary Art** (Tues–Fri 11am–5pm, Thurs closes 8pm, Sat & Sun 11am–6pm; free; ☎310/289-5223, ⓦ www.moca.org /museum/moca_pdc.php), focusing on architecture and industrial and graphic design with a sleek, modern bent, and often participating in shows with the two Downtown branches (see p.58 and p.65).

If you have a taste for contemporary architecture and design, there's even more to be found on the streets around the area, which are home to any number of fancy designers, art galleries, and trendy boutiques.

Schindler House

Back east of La Cienega Boulevard, the **Schindler House**, 835 N Kings Rd (Wed–Sun 11am–6pm; $7), was for years the blueprint of California modernist architecture, with sliding canvas panels designed to be removed in summer, exposed roof rafters, and open-plan rooms facing onto outdoor terraces. Coming from his native Austria via Frank Lloyd Wright's studio to work on the Hollyhock House (see p.91), R.M. Schindler was so pleased with the California climate that he built this house without any bedrooms, romantically planning to sleep outdoors year-round in covered sleeping baskets on the roof. However, like other newcomers unfamiliar with the region's erratic climate, he misjudged the weather and soon moved inside. Now functioning as the **MAK Center for Art and Architecture**, the house plays host to a range of avant-garde music, art, film, and design exhibitions, from the work of famous modernists like John Cage and Eric Owen Moss to lesser known photographers, artists, and architects (program information at ☏323/651-1510, ⓦwww.makcenter.com).

▲ Schindler House

Beverly Hills and West LA

Although Downtown and Hollywood are richer in historic and cultural attractions, **Beverly Hills** and **West LA** are ground zero for tourism in LA (at least outside of Disneyland). Along with neighboring West Hollywood, they boast the best hotels and restaurants, and relentlessly market themselves as the height of fashion – with an ersatz European flair. With its diverse architecture and plentiful gardens, there's more to Beverly Hills than just the elite boutiques of **Rodeo Drive**, but for most visitors, the focus lies within the three sides of the shopping zone known as the **Golden Triangle**. Above Beverly Hills, the canyon roads beyond Sunset Boulevard lead into the well-guarded enclaves of rich celebrities, while to the west, the bleak modern towers of **Century City** rise in the distance, with the district's main attraction being its large, eponymous mall.

As with the similar term "Westside," West LA has an amorphous definition, anything from the vaguely defined area between Beverly Hills and Santa Monica to everything west of Hollywood. Whatever the case, it's definitely crossed by the 405 freeway and extends from the mountain foothills to the I-10 freeway. One of West LA's main districts, **Westwood**, is a sunless corridor of towering office blocks along Wilshire Boulevard, but closer to **UCLA** Westwood becomes pedestrian-friendly in the so-called "Village," and the university itself is full of resplendent buildings and gardens. To the west, along the **Sepulveda Pass**, the residents hiding in the wooded wealth of **Bel Air** and **Brentwood** are less than welcoming, but the hilltop **Getty Center** is a travertine icon of monumental proportions that's one of LA's crown jewels of art and architecture. West LA's southern neighbor, **Culver City**, is far less conspicuous than other areas, even though it contains several historic movie studios, a clean and renovated downtown area, and a trove of eye-catching, experimental buildings.

Beverly Hills

The world over, **BEVERLY HILLS** is synonymous with suntanned Mercedes-drivers, fur-clad poodle-walkers, and outrageously priced designer clothes, illustrating how successful this city has been in marketing itself to the

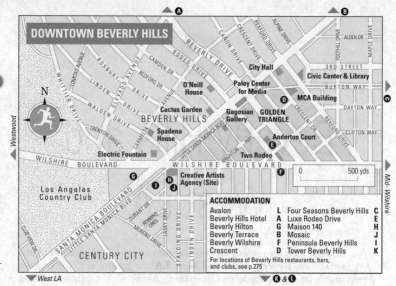

DOWNTOWN BEVERLY HILLS

City Hall
3RD STREET
Civic Center & Library
BURTON WAY
O'Neill House
Paley Center for Media
MCA Building
DAYTON WAY
Cactus Garden
Gagosian Gallery
GOLDEN TRIANGLE
BEVERLY HILLS
CLIFTON WAY
Spadena House
Anderton Court
Electric Fountain
Two Rodeo
WILSHIRE BOULEVARD
WILSHIRE BOULEVARD
0   500 yds
Creative Artists Agency (Site)
Los Angeles Country Club

ACCOMMODATION

Avalon	**L**	Four Seasons Beverly Hills	**C**
Beverly Hills Hotel	**A**	Luxe Rodeo Drive	**E**
Beverly Hilton	**G**	Maison 140	**H**
Beverly Terrace	**B**	Mosaic	**J**
Beverly Wilshire	**F**	Peninsula Beverly Hills	**I**
Crescent	**D**	Tower Beverly Hills	**K**

For locations of Beverly Hills restaurants, bars, and clubs, see p.275

CENTURY CITY

West LA

rest of the world. Inevitably, this self-promotion is more booster hype than reality, but if you've come here to fawn over celebrities and press your nose against the display windows, you won't leave disappointed. Beverly Hills's sparkling image is also kept up in part by a formidable local police force – with more cops per capita than any other city in the world – that keeps the streets free of panhandlers and others it deems undesirable. The glossy heart of Beverly Hills is **Rodeo Drive**, which slices through downtown with much pomp and circumstance, though it's not more than a few blocks long and there's little of interest beyond shopping. More picturesque sights are tucked away in the slopes and canyons north of here, but even there you'll find gated-off mansions to match the area's super-exclusive stores.

Wilshire Boulevard

The linear city of **Wilshire Boulevard** picks up west of the Miracle Mile (see p.78) to lead into Beverly Hills in grand style. The first sight of note is the **Academy of Motion Picture Arts and Sciences (AMPAS)**, 8949 Wilshire Blvd, the headquarters of the organization that puts on the Oscars each year (see box opposite) and has historically established standards for technical movie craft and style. The Academy also offers regular screenings of classics in its excellent Samuel Goldwyn Theater (and its newer Linwood Dunn Theater in Hollywood, 1313 Vine St), along with exhibits in its **galleries** showcasing items from classic and contemporary American films, from scripts and storyboards to still photographs and animation cels (box office Mon–Fri 9am–5pm, tickets $5; galleries Tues–Fri 10am–5pm, Sat & Sun noon–6pm; free; ☎310/247-3000, ⊛www.oscars.org/foundation). This stretch of Wilshire features other classic venues for movies, including the Zigzag Moderne **Wilshire Theater**, no. 8440 (☎323/655-0111), built in 1930, and nowadays a home to traveling stage productions; the exuberant neon of the **Fine Arts Theater**, no. 8556 (☎310/360-0455), a theatrical stage built in 1936, and now a well-restored, Art Deco–flavored spot

to catch a film; and the once–grand, now subdivided, **Music Hall Theater**, no.
9036 (☎310/274-6869).

The Golden Triangle

Downtown Beverly Hills, successfully labeled the **Golden Triangle** by the
city's PR department, is a ritzy wedge between Rexford Drive and Wilshire
and Santa Monica boulevards, dotted with some of LA's top retailers, hotels, and
eateries — all charging the premium you would expect for such prime real
estate. Street parking is tough to come by in the area, though there are a few
scattered public lots, two of them just off Beverly Drive, north of Brighton Way
and Dayton Way, respectively.

"I'd like to thank the Academy…"

The **Academy of Motion Picture Arts and Sciences** was formed in 1927 by titans
of the film industry such as Louis B. Mayer, Cecil B. DeMille, Mary Pickford, and
Douglas Fairbanks Sr. Officially created to advance the cause of filmmaking, it was
actually intended to combat trade-union expansion in Hollywood, which it tried to do,
unsuccessfully, for ten years. After that, the Academy concentrated instead on stand-
ardizing the **technical specifications** of moviemaking – including everything from
screenwriting to sound and lighting. To expand its membership and appeal, the
Academy began to include notable artists and craftworkers from most segments of
the business and to promote its award show as an event of national significance – if
not quite an arts festival on the level of Cannes or Venice, at least an opportunity for
starlets to parade past the footlights in the latest haute couture.

This show was, of course, the **Academy Awards**, which began two years after the
organization's creation and was designed to give the industry's stamp of approval to
its own film product. Called the **Oscar**, an award with many dubious explanations for
its name – everything from its being a forgotten acronym to the name of Academy
librarian Margaret Herrick's uncle – the Academy's official blessing was a much
sought-after honor even in its early years. From their infancy, however, the Oscars
have generally recognized the most well-crafted work produced by the **studio
system**, not necessarily the best films overall, so as not to bite the hand that feeds
it. This is why landmark works of cinema such as *Citizen Kane*, *Vertigo*, and *Taxi
Driver* have typically been ignored and tub-thumping "event" films like *The Greatest
Show on Earth*, *Cavalcade*, *Titanic*, and *Gladiator* have grabbed the accolades. Even
in recent years, despite the renowned strength of independent studios (most of them
subsidiaries of the majors), the top awards have gone to old-fashioned crowd-
pleasers and tearjerkers like *Million Dollar Baby* and *A Beautiful Mind*, leaving the
lower-budgeted films to clean up in "minor" categories like screenwriting and
cinematography.

The awards are not above the occasional debacle, though. The appearance
of a **streaker** during the 1974 show is the most notorious example, and actors
Marlon Brando and George C. Scott publicly refused their awards in the early
1970s, with Scott describing the awards as a "meat parade." More recently, the
awards ceremony has moved to a seemingly permanent home at the **Kodak
Theater**, inside the colossal Hollywood and Highland mall (see p.101). Ironically,
at a time when movie grosses seem to be breaking box-office records with each
passing year, the **TV ratings** of the awards show have nose-dived, and efforts to
hasten the interminable ceremony have had little success. You're still apt to see
award-winning actors blurting out cringe-inducing hosannas (Sally Field's "You
really, really like me!" or Cuba Gooding Jr's histrionics) or, more frequently, reading
laundry-list thank-yous to all the people in town who *really* matter: executives,
agents, managers, publicists, lawyers, ad infinitum.

Rodeo Drive

Most people's chief reason for visiting Beverly Hills is, of course, **Rodeo Drive**, which cuts right through a three-block area boasting the most exclusive names in international fashion. Some of the bigger names include Barney's, 9570 Wilshire Blvd, and, all on Rodeo itself, Chanel, no. 400; Giorgio Armani, no. 436; Gucci, no. 347; Christian Dior, no. 309; and Prada, no. 343. As yet, none of the stores charges for admission, though some do require an invitation. (For details on each store, see "Shopping," Chapter 20.) However, Rodeo Drive wouldn't be quite so successful if it didn't appeal to the masses and offer at least something affordable: to wit, a Niketown, 9560 Wilshire Blvd; Cheesecake Factory, 364 N Beverly Drive; Crate & Barrel, 438 N Beverly Drive, and countless other chain stores of the sort you can find in most American malls these days.

Adjacent to Rodeo Drive and Wilshire Boulevard, **Two Rodeo** (Ⓦwww .tworodeo.com) is the area's mock-European tourist corridor, where a cobble-stoned street leads visitors up into a curving path through what is designed to resemble a vaguely French or Italian village, or at least a Disney version of one. However, while the odd big name like Versace or Gianfranco Ferre finds residence here, half of the storefronts seem to be closed much of the time, and in any case no one does much shopping – snapshots of friends and family are the main draw, taken in front of buildings that more resemble a film set than a shopping zone. True to its LA identity, the Continental fantasy is built on top of a parking garage.

Just to the north of these snooty shops is Frank Lloyd Wright's decidedly unstodgy **Anderton Court**, now called "Tallarico," at 328 N Rodeo Drive, which resembles a boxy, miniature version of New York's Guggenheim museum crowned by a jagged horn, and is home to a few cramped retailers who must contend with Wright's awkward experiment in space and light. For a complete overview Beverly Hills shopping and the area's art and architectural treasures, take a trip on the **Beverly Hills Trolley** (11am–4pm: Sat year-round, also July–Aug & Dec Tues–Fri & Sun 11am–4pm; $5; Ⓣ310/285-2442), which

▲ Rodeo Drive

offers a 40-minute glimpse of the town's highlights, departing hourly from the corner of Rodeo and Dayton Way.

The Paley Center for Media and around

A few more interesting sights lie in and around Rodeo's elite commercial zone, most prominently the former **Museum of Television and Radio**, now awkwardly renamed the **Paley Center for Media**, 465 N Beverly Drive (Wed–Sun noon–5pm; $10, kids $5; ☎310/786-1000, ⓦwww.mtr.org), featuring a collection of more than 140,000 TV and radio programs, sometimes put together in informative exhibits, on such subjects as political image-making, famous advertising characters, and the best of radio and TV sitcoms, dramas, and thrillers. The museum, LA's only real attempt at providing a media museum of scholarly value, has a well-designed theater for public screenings of old and recent shows, including programs celebrating the golden age of 1950s TV and examining the role of the electronic media in reporting, and creating, the news. The building itself is immaculate white geometry from the leading practitioner of this style, Richard Meier – more famous for his Getty Center (see p.129) – whose other noteworthy Beverly Hills work is his spartan, garage-like **Gagosian Gallery**, just two blocks west at 456 N Camden Drive (Tues–Sat 10am–5.30pm; free; ☎310/271-9400, ⓦwww.gagosian.com), which shows modern painting, photography, and sculpture by the likes of Cindy Sherman, Eric Fischl, David Salle, and Chris Burden.

A few blocks away at 360 Crescent Drive, and representing a very different sort of architecture, is the former **MCA Building**, a 1939 triumph of the Classical Revival style, which won an American Institute of Architects Award of Merit and whose open forecourt features a lovely Florentine fountain set around classical columns and foliage. This pleasant escape from the shopping hubbub was designed by the city's pioneering black architect, Paul R. Williams, also famed for designing a number of celebrity homes, including those for Frank Sinatra, Lucille Ball, and Lon Chaney. Appropriately for LA, the building's classical glory is in the service of a Hollywood talent agency. Another architectural gem is the adjacent **Beverly Hills City Hall**, a 1932 concoction of Spanish Revival and Art Deco architecture that resembles a squat version of LA's City Hall (see p.55), except for the ornate dome dripping with Baroque details and vivid colors. Within the complex, the **Beverly Hills Municipal Gallery**, 450 N Crescent Drive (Mon–Fri 10am–4pm, Sun 11am-4pm; free; ☎310/550-4796), regularly offers programs of some interest, focusing on arts and crafts, furniture, antiques, and photography. On Rexford Drive, the **Civic Center and Library** complex is a postmodern Charles Moore confection with Art Deco elements, intended to give a contemporary design nod in City Hall's direction, though it remains much less appealing compared to its neighbor.

Outside the triangle

Just west of the triangle is the **Electric Fountain**, created in 1930 by the Beverly Hills Women's Club, through the efforts of comedian Harold Lloyd's mother. Depicting the history of the West on a circular frieze running along its base, the fountain spews water from the hands of a nameless Tongva native sitting atop its central column, deep in a rain prayer. Across from here, at the intersection of Wilshire and Santa Monica boulevards, sits the former headquarters of **Creative Artists Agency**, where powerbrokers, led by Mike Ovitz, made their company into one of the most feared institutions in town in the 1980s and early 90s. With its white-marble curtain wall and curved glass, the imperious I.M. Pei design befits the attitude of the company, but agents don't reign quite as supreme these days, and CAA sold the behemoth and moved to Century City in 2007.

Meanwhile, along Santa Monica Boulevard, the entire north side of the road in Beverly Hills is lined with a continuous two-mile strip of green known as **Beverly Gardens**. The most appealing stretch, between Camden and Bedford drives, is home to one of the largest municipal collections of cacti in the world and some fetching rose beds, and is a tranquil setting amid the abundance of prickly plants, littered here and there with a few middling sculptures.

Further north is the residential side of Beverly Hills, with its winding, palm-lined streets and Mercedes- and Bentley-filled driveways. Although a number of has-been and lesser-known stars live on these streets, the real interest is the fanciful architecture. Without a doubt the most peculiar item is the **Spadena House**, Carmelita Drive at Walden Avenue, whose sagging roof, gnarled windows, and pointed wooden fence have earned it the nickname the "Witch's House." Built as the headquarters for a Culver City movie company in the 1920s, the house was later moved here and is now a private home. Also outlandish and private, the **O'Neill House**, 507 N Rodeo Drive, looks like a melting birthday cake, with its undulating lines and lopsided, vaguely Art Nouveau shape. The increasingly curvaceous roads head into the hills and become more upmarket, converging on the pink-plaster **Beverly Hills Hotel**, on Sunset and Rodeo (see p.246), constructed in 1912 to attract wealthy settlers to what was then a town of just five hundred people. Much has changed in the intervening years, and the hotel's Mission style has been updated by a slew of renovations, though the core design of the building and its attendant gardens remain intact. Will Rogers, W.C. Fields, and John Barrymore were but a few of the celebrities known to frequent the bar here, and the hotel's social cachet still makes its *Polo Lounge* a prime spot for movie execs to power-lunch.

The northern hills and canyons

Above the *Beverly Hills Hotel*, in the **northern hills and canyons**, a number of well-concealed gardens and parks offer a respite from the shopping frenzy below. One such place, the wooded **Virginia Robinson Gardens**, 1008 Elden Way (tours Tues–Fri 10am & 1pm; $10, students $5; by appointment only at ☎310/276-5367), spreads across six acres of flora, with more than a thousand varieties, including some impressive Australian King Palm trees. The heiress to the Robinson's department-store chain bequeathed the land and the attached Mediterranean-style estate (not open to the public) to LA County. To the east, the grounds of the biggest house in Beverly Hills, **Greystone Mansion**, 905 Loma Vista Drive, are now maintained as a public **park** by the city (daily 10am–5pm; free), which uses it to disguise a massive underground reservoir. The fifty-thousand-square-foot manor somewhat resembles an imperious English Norman castle and was once the property of oil titan Edward Doheny, who was not only a huge figure in LA history, but also a major player in the Teapot Dome scandal of the 1920s (see box opposite) – the manor was built right after, in 1929. The house itself is rarely open to the public, except for periodic **Music in the Mansion** classical-music and jazz concerts ($25; ☎310/550-4796). At other times, you can admire the mansion's limestone facade, genteel courtyard (a car turnaround) and intricately designed chimneys, then stroll through the sixteen-acre park, with its ponds filled with koi and turtles, lovely gardens that are the frequent site of weddings and TV commercials, and expansive views of the LA sprawl below.

The Beverly Hills oil baron

The 1920s were a busy time for millionaire oil magnate **Edward L. Doheny**. Not only did the former mining prospector build the mansion of his dreams, **Greystone**, at the end of the Beverly Hills street that would one day bear his name, but he was also granted the title of Knight of the Equestrian Order of the Holy Sepulchre by the Roman Catholic Church and later had the main library at USC named after him, thanks to a million-dollar donation. Unfortunately, he was also involved in one of the biggest political scandals in US history.

Some three decades before, in 1892, Doheny and partner Charles Canfield struck **black gold** in the Temple-Beaudry district west of Downtown – a spot that quickly became the city's most lucrative terrain and which is now, ironically, one of its most desperate slums. But around 1909, petro-dollars made Doheny wealthy beyond all imagining, and he put some of his fortune into his elegant mansion in the Exposition Park district (which is still a marvel; see p.163) and invested even more into new wells throughout the city.

By 1921, the one-time miner was a formidable force in both the local and national economy, and he probably didn't need to offer a bribe to the newly installed Interior Secretary, **Albert Fall**, one of President Warren Harding's many corrupt minions, in exchange for preferential drilling leases in the Elk Hills region of Southern California. But he did just that, putting $100,000 in the secretary's wallet. Three years later, after Harding's untimely death, a national scandal was unearthed in Wyoming, where another bribery deal – this one engineered by oil titan Harry Sinclair – had been made over the lucrative **Teapot Dome** lease. Soon enough, the corrupt bargain for the Elk Hills property was uncovered, and Doheny was prosecuted. Over the next six years until 1930, the government tried to put him in prison, but two trials only resulted in acquittals on technicalities. Although the legal result was favorable for Doheny – though not for Fall, who served time – the damage was significant, and the scandal forever blackened his reputation. In a tragic coda to the story, Doheny's son, whom he had originally used to deliver Fall's bribe, died in a mysterious murder-suicide shooting inside the mansion in 1929.

There's also a rambling **Doheny Ranch**, formerly the oil baron's summer retreat, that's good for picnicking and idling two miles northwest, part of 600-acre **Franklin Canyon Park**, an isolated niche of the Santa Monica Mountains National Recreation Area. The canyon is a broad public preserve that also contains two idyllic reservoirs, and the ranch routinely sees plenty of local families, school kids, and even wedding parties. Although reaching the area may require a detailed map (or a visit to Ⓦlamountains.com), you can make the attempt by following Franklin Canyon Drive north into the parkland until you hit a fork in the road. The lake route, to the left, takes you to the upper reservoir, around which you can take a gentle walk amid ducks and old concrete abutments; the ranch route, to the right, leads to short hiking trails and a central lawn, popular throughout the year. This side of the park also contains several amphitheaters and the **Sooky Goldman Nature Center**, 2600 Franklin Canyon Drive (Ⓣ310/858-7272 ext 131), where you can learn all about the park's ecosystem and geology.

Further west, in the verdant canyons and foothills above Sunset Boulevard, a number of palatial estates lie hidden away behind security gates. **Benedict Canyon Drive** climbs from the *Beverly Hills Hotel* past many of them, including Harold Lloyd's 1928 **Green Acres**, 1040 Angelo Drive, where he lived for forty years. Although the secret passageways and a large private screening room are still intact (and off-limits to the public), the grounds, which once contained a waterfall and a nine-hole golf course, have since been broken up into smaller lots. Apart from the period-revival houses that dominate the area, a smattering of other styles can be found off Benedict Canyon, best among them the **Anthony House**, 910 Bedford Drive, a terrific Craftsman work by Charles and Henry Greene designed for the head of Packard Automobiles, which was originally sited in Hollywood until a later owner moved it here. The house, with its rugged wooden frame and elegant garden, bears more than passing resemblance to the brothers' larger and better-known Gamble House in Pasadena – though this one isn't open to the public.

Century City and around

CENTURY CITY, along with Bunker Hill, is LA's most egregious example of building for the automobile, and one of its least pedestrian-friendly areas, overrun by giant boulevards and dominated by bland, boxy skyscrapers. It is, however, something of a landmark for West LA, its huge, triangular **Century Plaza Towers** visible from far across the Westside, as well as from the air as you approach LAX. Originally part of the 20th Century-Fox studio lot, Century City began taking shape in the early 1960s when the studio sold off much of its acreage, during the height of glass-and-steel corporate modernism. The district remains flash-frozen in that era, with the exception of the splashy new building for Creative Artists Agency, 2000 Avenue of the Stars, which gleams as a proper glass box should, and features an odd rectangular cutout in the center to enliven the familiar geometry. If you're not here to power-lunch with agents and lawyers or to stay at the grand *Century Plaza* hotel (see p.247) across the street, the only real reason to visit is the **Century City Shopping Center**, 10250 Santa Monica Blvd (see p.346), a single-level, open-air mall loaded with pricey boutiques and department stores.

Perhaps due to its overall lack of charm, Century City has appeared in several dystopic Hollywood movies, most memorably in *Conquest of the Planet of the Apes* and in *Die Hard*, where Bruce Willis saved the day while holed up in the postmodern **Fox Plaza**, 2121 Avenue of the Stars. Just south at 10201 Pico Blvd, the current home of **20th Century-Fox** occupies much smaller digs than it used to, with much of its former 225 acres having been sold. Now owned by Rupert Murdoch's News Corporation, the company still has plenty of offices and movie sets on the premises, but the public is kept firmly out.

Around Century City

East of Century City, below Beverly Hills, an unassuming building houses the **Simon Wiesenthal Center for Holocaust Studies**, 9786 Pico Blvd. The US headquarters of the organization dedicated to prosecuting former Nazis, the center has an extensive library of Holocaust-related documents and photographs. The main draw for visitors, however, is the affecting **Beit HaShoa Museum of Tolerance** (April–Oct Mon–Thurs 11am–6.30pm, Fri 11am–5pm, Sun 11am–7.30pm; Nov–March Fri 11am–3pm; $10, students $7; ☎310/553-8403, ⓦwww.museumoftolerance.com), an extraordinary interactive resource center and one of the most technologically advanced institutions of its kind. Among other exhibits, it leads the visitor through multimedia re-enactments outlining the rise of Nazism to a harrowing conclusion in a replica gas chamber.

Further west, apart from the **Westside Pavilion**, another of LA's multilevel shopping mall complexes, at Pico and Westwood boulevards, the area's only other sight of note is the colossal **Mormon Temple**, the largest such building outside of Salt Lake City, located on a hilltop some blocks to the north at 10777 Santa Monica Blvd. Visible throughout the mostly flat Westside, the local headquarters of the church is easily recognized by its 257-foot tower crowned by the 15-ft-tall angel Moroni. Although the main part of the building isn't open to non-Mormons, you can enter the **visitor center** (daily 9am–9pm; free; ☏310/474-1549), and steal a peek at a 12ft marble sculpture of Jesus. Plus, if for some reason you've come to LA to hunt down long-lost family members, the LDS Church also has an on-site **Family History Center** (Tues–Thurs 10am–9pm, Fri–Sat 9am–5pm; free; ☏310/474-9990, ⓦwww.larfhc.org) that holds some 2.5 million microfilm documents for genealogy research, including links to British, Polish, Jewish, and African-American databases; the majority of visitors here, perhaps not surprisingly, are not Mormon.

Westwood and UCLA

Just west of Beverly Hills and Century City along Wilshire Boulevard, **WESTWOOD** is divided between the pleasant, low-rise neighborhood of **Westwood Village** – crowded with students, shoppers, and theater-goers – and the adjacent traffic corridor loaded with some of LA's tallest buildings. In earlier days, nearly all of Westwood resembled the Village, but during the 1970s and 1980s, the zone around Wilshire exploded with high-rises, where penthouse condos with private heliports sold for upwards of $12 million. Even now, after the boom has faded somewhat, the intersection of Wilshire and Westwood boulevards continues to be choked with overflowing traffic, with some of LA's longest and most aggravating waits for a green light.

At this corner, the **UCLA Hammer Museum**, 10899 Wilshire Blvd (Tues–Sat 11am–7pm, Thurs 11am–9pm, Sun 11am–5pm; $5, kids free, Thurs free to all; ☏310/443-7000, ⓦwww.hammer.ucla.edu), comprises a sizable art stash amassed over seven decades by the flamboyant oil tycoon **Armand Hammer**. Art critic Robert Hughes called the paintings here "a mishmash of second- or third-rate works by famous names," but while the Rembrandts and Rubenses may be less than stunning, the nineteenth-century pieces like Van Gogh's intense and radiant *Hospital at Saint Remy* more than make amends. There are some impressive American works as well, such as a Gilbert Stuart regal portrait of George Washington; Thomas Eakins' painting of *Sebastiano Cardinal Martinelli*, depicted with blunt, penetrating realism; and John Singer Sargent's *Dr Pozzi at Home*, one of the artist's skilled character studies. Just as compelling, some of the museum's exhibitions are drawn from the marvelous **Grunwald Center for the Graphic Arts** (by appointment at ☏310/443-7078), which has some 45,000 drawings, photographs, and prints from the Renaissance on, with some exceptional Expressionist works by Emil Nolde and Käthe Kollwitz, Impressionist etchings from Paul Cezanne, and more current drawings and prints by Jasper Johns. Now under the management of neighboring UCLA, the Hammer has become acclaimed for its insightful, sometimes risk-taking contemporary

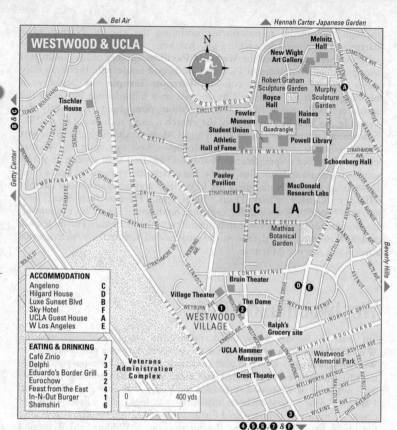

▲ Bel Air   ▲ Hannah Carter Japanese Garden

WESTWOOD & UCLA

ACCOMMODATION

Angeleno	C
Hilgard House	D
Luxe Sunset Blvd	B
Sky Hotel	F
UCLA Guest House	A
W Los Angeles	E

EATING & DRINKING

Café Zinio	7
Delphi	3
Eduardo's Border Grill	5
Eurochow	2
Feast from the East	4
In-N-Out Burger	1
Shamshiri	6

0 ——— 400 yds

and avant-garde exhibits – quite a leap from what the conservative Hammer had in mind when he built the art enclave.

Across from the museum, at the end of the driveway behind the Avco cinema, 1218 Glendon Ave, you'll find Armand Hammer's speckled marble tomb, sharing the cemetery of **Westwood Memorial Park** (daily 8am–5pm; ☎310/474-1579) with the likes of movie stars Peter Lorre and Natalie Wood, Truman Capote, Dean Martin, wildman jazz drummer Buddy Rich, and the alleged (unmarked) graves of Roy Orbison and Frank Zappa. To the left of the entrance in the far northeast corner, a lipstick-covered plaque marks the resting place of **Marilyn Monroe**. You can also spot some of these stars on the radiant mural inside the **Crest Theater** (☎310/474-7866), 1262 Westwood Blvd, also notable for its brash neon marquee.

Westwood Village

North of Wilshire, **Westwood Village** is one of LA's more walkable neighborhoods, a cluster of low-slung brick buildings that went up in the late 1920s, along with the campus of UCLA, which had just relocated from East Hollywood. Much of the original Spanish Colonial Revival design has survived the years, though most of the neighborhood businesses have been replaced by fancy boutiques and fast-food joints. It's an area that's easily explored on foot – street **parking** is nightmarish, so take public transit or, if you're driving, leave your car at one of the parking lots before beginning your wanderings. Even if you find a spot, keep in mind that the area boasts some of LA's most zealous and meticulous parking enforcement, and you'll pay $35 or more if you're even a minute overtime.

Broxton Avenue, the Village's main strip, is crowded with moviehouses and diners, but its focal point is the great Zigzag spire atop the 1931 **Fox Westwood Village** at 961 Broxton Ave, which, together with the neon-signed **Bruin** across the street, are impressive Moderne designs. Both are used occasionally by movie studios for flashy movie premieres, as well as sneak previews for test audiences; this is a big movie-going district, with thirty or so cinema screens within a quarter-mile radius. Another familiar Westwood image is **The Dome**, 1099 Westwood Blvd, the Spanish Colonial former offices of the developer who created the surrounding Westwood tract and many other districts. Nowhere is the developer's design signature more evident than at the one-time **Ralph's Grocery Store**, 1150 Westwood Blvd, a Spanish Romanesque structure with a red-tile roof and cylindrical corner tower. Among several historic structures west of UCLA, the best is R.M. Schindler's private **Tischler House**, 175 Greenfield Ave, which resembles a highly abstract boat: thick white rectangles jut out from the house's base, while the wooden-gabled living space on top recalls a ship's upper deck.

UCLA

The University of California at Los Angeles, or **UCLA**, is Westwood's dominant feature and one of the country's most prominent academic and athletic institutions, its group of lovely Romanesque buildings spread generously over well-landscaped grounds. It's worth a wander if you've time to kill, particularly for a couple of good exhibition spaces.

The campus originally occupied the site of the Downtown Library, later moving to Los Feliz, and by the mid-1920s relocated to Westwood, where it became a model of Northern Italian–styled Romanesque design: intended by architect **George Kelham** to resemble the redbrick structures of Milan and Genoa, the buildings around the central quadrangle, such as the library and science halls, seem to be plucked straight from a Lombard blueprint, giving the campus a classic "collegiate" look. This pristine quality was, however, diminished by the concrete and steel additions of the 1960s and 70s, and recent years have seen creative experimentation by the likes of Frank Gehry and Robert Venturi, though the Italian design thumbprint still remains.

The campus and around

A good place to start touring the campus is the **Mathias Botanical Garden**, 405 Hilgard Ave (daily 8am–4pm, summer Mon–Fri closes at 5pm; free; ☏310/825-1260, ⓦwww.botgard.ucla.edu), a bucolic glade on the east side of the university where you can pick your way along sloping paths through the redwoods and fern groves, past small waterfalls splashing into lily-covered ponds; it's a humble, agreeable spot to relax, and not often visited by anyone but the odd professor or student.

Around the corner is the campus hub of the central **quadrangle**, a greenspace bordered by UCLA's most graceful buildings, a terrific place for reading, socializing or frisbee-throwing. The most visually appealing structures here include **Royce Hall**, modeled on Milan's Church of St Ambrosio, with high

▲ Fox Westwood Village movie theatre

bell-towers, rib vaulting, and grand archways; and the **Powell Library** (Mon–Thurs 7.30am–11pm, Fri 7.30am–6pm, Sat 9am–5pm, Sun 1–10pm; ⓦwww .library.ucla.edu), featuring a spellbinding interior with lovely Romanesque arches, columns, and stairwell. The highlight is the dome above the **reading room**, where Renaissance printers' marks are inscribed, among them icons representing such pioneers as Johann Fust and William Caxton. (Ask at the reference desk for a guide to the art and architecture of the library.) Further south, Robert Venturi's 1991 **MacDonald Research Labs**, Westwood Blvd at Young Dr S, is worth seeking out for its postmodern take on the greatest hits of classical architecture, featuring off-color, brick upper stories with irregular windows, a concrete base, and quasi-Egyptian colonnade.

Further north, the **Fowler Museum of Cultural History**, Bruin Walk at Westwood Plaza (Wed–Sun noon–5pm, Thurs closes 8pm; free; ☎310/825-4361, ⓦwww.fowler.ucla.edu), offers an immense range of multicultural art – including ceramics, religious icons, paintings, and musical instruments. The museum's highlights include a worldwide selection of native masks, more than ten thousand textile pieces from different cultures an extensive collection of African and Polynesian art and various folk designs, from simple household implements to elaborate ritual costumes and ceremonial icons. To the northeast, just west of Hilgard Ave before it meets Sunset Blvd, the **Franklin Murphy Sculpture Garden** (always open; free) is LA's best outdoor display of modern sculpture, including pieces by such big names as Jean Arp, Henry Moore, Joan Miró, Henri Matisse, and Isamu Noguchi. Other notable works include Auguste Rodin's *Walking Man*, a stark nude composed of only a torso and legs, and George Tsutakawa's *OBOS-69*, a fountain resembling a stack of TV sets. If you really like the pieces on display here, you can take an informative free **tour** of the garden as well (check times and reserve at ☎310/443-7040).

Just north of the Murphy Garden, the **New Wight Art Gallery**, 11000 Kinross Ave (Mon–Fri 9am–4.30pm; free; ☎310/825-0557, ⓦwww.art.ucla .edu/gallery.html), has a less intriguing collection of contemporary art on display, and houses the **Center for Digital Arts**, which occasionally shows interesting multimedia works. Just east of the Wight Gallery and northeast of the garden, in **Melnitz Hall**, UCLA's **film school** has produced filmmakers like Francis Ford Coppola, Alison Anders, and Alex Cox, the more independent-oriented rival to USC's studio-dominated industry school. The school oversees the massive store-house of the **UCLA Film and Television Archive**, a treasure-trove of more than 200,000 items, among them classic, foreign, and art movies, and a wide range of old TV shows, state journalism footage, and even an assortment of Hearst newsreels from the turn of the twentieth century. To check out the collection, make an appointment at 46 Powell Library (where the archive's items are kept), or by calling ☎310/206-5388 (Mon–Fri 9am–5pm). Melnitz Hall also presents regular screenings of films, many drawn from the archives, in its **James Bridges Theater** (tickets $10; ☎310/206-FILM, ⓦwww.cinema.ucla.edu).

UCLA is well known for its athletic prowess, winning more NCAA basketball championships – eleven – than any other team. Some of this history is on display at the **Athletic Hall of Fame** (Mon–Fri 8am–5pm; free; ⓦuclabruins .cstv.com/ot/hof.html) near the center of campus along Bruin Walk east of Young Dr W, where you can check out the school's awards in basketball, football, and volleyball, among other sports. UCLA's basketball team plays just west of here, at **Pauley Pavilion**, along with its volleyball and gymnastics squads, while the football team's home is the Rose Bowl (see p.197).

For a more contemplative experience, travel just north of campus to UCLA's **Hannah Carter Japanese Garden**, 10619 Bellagio Rd (Tues, Wed & Fri 10am–3pm; free; by appointment only at ☎310/794-0320 or ⓦwww.japanesegarden .ucla.edu), an idyllic spot featuring magnolias and Japanese maples, and traditional structures and river rocks brought directly from Japan – though four hundred tons of dark-brown rocks were also hauled in from Ventura County to lend the right aesthetic touch. Adding to the calming Zen feel are a pagoda, teahouse, quaint bridges, and assorted gold and stone Buddhas.

The Sepulveda Pass and around

The gap through the Santa Monica Mountains known as the **Sepulveda Pass** runs alongside some of LA's most exclusive residential neighborhoods, dividing Brentwood from Bel Air and some of the exclusive areas further north, where you'll find the **Getty Center**, the city's art showpiece. The pass often gives tourists their first views of central LA as they travel south on the 405 freeway into town and was, like the eponymous boulevard and district, named for Mexican soldier **Francisco Sepúlveda**, whose family controlled over fifty thousand acres of land in the LA region, and who gained ownership in 1839 of the Rancho San Vicente y Santa Monica, which once encompassed the surrounding area. The former rancho contains both the freeway and part of Sepulveda Boulevard – the longest road in LA County, leading from Long Beach into the north San Fernando Valley — which acts as an alternative route, meandering through the hills, if you have plenty of time to kill.

Bel Air and Brentwood

BEL AIR, just northwest of UCLA and east of the 405 freeway, is an elite subdivision – home to just under eight thousand swells – with opulent black gates fronting Sunset Boulevard and security guards driving about to catch interlopers. For many, this district and Rodeo Drive seem to be the very definition of wealth in the city, though despite its famous name and reputation, very little goes on here, as the only business is the well-known, luxurious **Bel Air Hotel** (see p.247) and the residential architecture is near impossible to see, typically hidden behind thick foliage. If you'd like to make an attempt, though, you're free to wander, as long as you don't linger: the neighborhood security guards are always on the lookout for miscreants, real and imagined.

For a closer look at the well-heeled, **BRENTWOOD** to the west is a better bet. Known for its most famous former resident, O.J. Simpson (his Tudor mansion has since been razed), Brentwood also has an upscale shopping strip along **San Vicente Boulevard**, with a good range of boutiques and restaurants, as well as one of LA's best booksellers, Dutton's (see p.357). The neighborhood also contains several residences of architectural interest, such as Frank Gehry's **Schnabel House**, 526 N Carmelina Ave, a chunky collection of metal cubes connected to an incongruous Moorish dome, partially visible from the sidewalk, and Frank Lloyd Wright's **Sturges House**, 449 Skyeway Rd, looking like a giant wooden shingle cantilevered off a hillside and hovering over the street below it, one of Wright's few LA experiments in contemporary, rather than pre-Columbian, housing design. Further north at 16221 Mulholland Drive, Charles Moore's exercise in ecclesiastical postmodernism, the **Bel Air Presbyterian Church** (T818/788-4200, Wwww.belairpres.org), contains playful Gothic touches amid its asymmetrical contemporary style, and is one of several of the architect's churches in LA.

Skirball Cultural Center

Back along Sepulveda Boulevard, near the crest of the Santa Monica Mountains, the compelling **Skirball Cultural Center**, 2701 N Sepulveda Blvd (Tues–Sat noon–5pm, Sun 11am–5pm; $10, students $7; T310/440-4500, Wwww.skirball.org), housed in a striking modern complex by architect Moshe Safdie, is an institution with several missions. One, its original purpose, is to focus on the history, beliefs, and rituals of Judaism, concentrating on the more mystical elements of the faith and offering a broad overview of Judaic treasures, from Hanukkah lamps to a Holy Ark (a cabinet for Torah scrolls) from a German synagogue. The second goal of the Skirball is to be a modern center for Jewish expression in science, art, philosophy, and popular culture – including occasional musical and comedy performances. Thus, you may see a wide range of events and exhibits in its galleries, everything from the illustrated theories of Albert Einstein to dramatic photography shot in Israel. Finally, the center looks at the American diaspora in stark photographs of c.1900 immigrants and written mementos of their arduous travel and assimilation (or not); among assorted other historic American artifacts are an early copy of the Declaration of Independence and one of Abe Lincoln's stovepipe hats.

The Getty Center

Off Sepulveda and west of the 405 freeway, Getty Center Drive leads up to the monumental **Getty Center** (Tues–Thurs & Sun 10am–6pm, Fri & Sat 10am–9pm; free, parking $8; ☎310/440-7300, ⓦwww.getty.edu). The grand 110-acre museum and research complex towering over the city was built over fifteen years at a cost of $1 billion to hold the vast art holdings of oil mogul **J. Paul Getty**. To rise up to this gleaming city on a hill by bus, you'll need to take MTA line #761 from UCLA after taking line #2 or #302 from Downtown; if you come by car, there's a parking lot at the base of the hill; either way, a tram ride can get you up to the complex – a slow, enchanting ride that features fine vistas of the metropolis, which you can also get by hoofing it up the slope.

Construction of the Center took eight years, from 1989 to 1997. Its architect, **Richard Meier**, originally planned for the whole complex to be wrapped in white metallic panels – his signature modern style – but protests from the Brentwood neighbors over sun glare forced him to redesign part of the Center in travertine: a good choice, since it combines the ancient roughness of fossil-bearing sandstone with the austere geometry of high-modernism, ultimately

▲ Getty Center

leading some to dub the site the "American Acropolis." However, even the museum curators acknowledge that Getty himself would have been horrified to see such a modernist creation, no matter how brilliant, built in his name, since he was a staunch art and architectural reactionary – preferring the figurative, ornamental, and historical to the abstract, severe, and contemporary. Except for the photography collection and a handful of twentieth-century works, the building itself is the only thing modern about the place.

Getty started building his massive collection in the 1930s, storing much of it in his own house until the first **Getty Museum** opened in 1974 on an ocean bluff near Malibu. That site, which had been closed for years, reopened as a showcase for the foundation's antiquities in 2007 (see p.216). The **museum** itself is now on the grounds of the Center, which also includes facilities for art research, conservation, and acquisition, though none of these are open to the public. Despite the huge investment, the Getty Foundation still has billions in reserve and must, by law, spend hundreds of millions each year from its endowment. Thus, it plays an elephantine role on the international art scene and can freely outbid its competitors for anything it wants. However, it's not immune from outside pressure, as in the recent indictment in Italy of a Getty director for alleged illegal removal of that country's antiquities. Although the institution didn't explicitly admit fault, it did return forty ancient works with dubious provenance – from Pompeiian frescos to Greek limestone and marble statues to various bronzes and vases – in an effort to ensure cooperation with the country's art officials should the need arise to secure more (non-ancient) treasures from that part of the Old World.

Gardens

A good place to begin exploring the museum is outside in its **Central Garden**, a concentric array of leafy terraces designed by conceptual artist Robert Irwin. Occupying the middle ground of the complex, the garden is a stunning arrangement, leading crowds along sloping paths through azaleas, bougainvilleas, and other plants and flowers, while the austere pavilions loom imperiously in the background. Though the garden provides a glorious centerpiece, Meier didn't much care for it and fought a number of public battles with its designer, though in this case he lost – luckily – and the garden is a pleasant multicolored oasis in a sea of white. More in the style of Meier, perhaps, is the topiary formalism of the **Desert Garden**, on the south end of the complex, where a low-scaled set of hardy plants sits in tight, circular confinement above a cliff of the Santa Monica Mountains, the plants assuming their role as a rigid natural component of Meier's spartan design scheme.

Taking a break at the Getty

If you spend a full day here – and many do – you'll want to grab a bite in one of the Getty's two central eateries. The **restaurant** (Tues–Sat 11.30am–2.30pm, Fri & Sat also 5–9pm, Sun 11am–3pm; reservations suggested at ⓣ310/440-6810) serves California cuisine and attracts locals who don't mind dropping a few extra dollars for an elegant setting and salads, pasta, crab cakes, and the like. Most visitors, however, head to the lower level for the massive **café** (Tues–Thurs 11.30am–5.30pm, Fri & Sat 11.30am–8.30pm, Sun 11.30am–3pm), which has a broad and adequate sampling of international cuisines laid out in the style of a cafeteria, and not much tastier, though a bit pricier. There are also **seasonal cafés** around the terrace and courtyard, oriented more toward providing simple snacks and coffee.

GETTY MUSEUM

COURTYARD LEVEL

Stairs
Lift

SOUTH PAVILION

WEST PAVILION

Sculpture

Photographs

Decorative Arts

Decorative Arts

Boulder Fountain

Rotating Exhibits

Central Garden

◀ Cactus Garden

Drawings

Sculpture

EAST PAVILION

Museum Courtyard

Rotating Exhibits

Illuminated Manuscripts

Decorative Arts

Sculpture

NORTH PAVILION

▶ Restaurant & Café

UPPER LEVEL

SOUTH PAVILION

WEST PAVILION

Paintings (after 1800)

Paintings (1600-1800)

Rotating Exhibits

EXHIBITIONS PAVILION

Temporary Exhibits

◀ Cactus Garden

Paintings (1600-1800)

Paintings (1600-1800)

EAST PAVILION

Paintings (before 1600)

NORTH PAVILION

Furniture and decorative arts

The museum itself consists of five two-story structures that are landscaped around open plazas and shallow fountains, with the collection spread throughout buildings that are linked by bridges and walkways. No matter where you start, you'll find the artworks still heavily influenced by Getty's tastes, long after the oil baron's death. One of his greatest enthusiasms was his formidable array of ornate **furniture** and **decorative arts**, with clocks, chandeliers, tapestries, and gilt-edged commodes, designed for the French nobility from the reign of Louis XIV, filling several overwhelmingly opulent rooms and dripping with all the gold, silver, silk, and velvet you might expect. The museum even stages an ongoing presentation of video and on-site **reproductions** of classic items of furniture, showing in full detail the painstaking steps that went into creating cabinets, bureaus, and commodes for the elite. This collection is certainly fascinating, perhaps more so to design historians, but it's the museum's paintings, sculpture, and photographs that will really overwhelm you.

Painting

In **painting**, the European art is principally from the post-Renaissance era, but there are a few notable exceptions, including several from the **early to high Renaissance**. Among these are Andrea Mantegna's stoic but affecting *Adoration of the Magi*, Correggio's *Head of Christ*, a rich portrait that rivals Rembrandt's work for emotional expression, and Titian's *Venus and Adonis*, depicting in muted colors the last moments between the lovers before the latter is gored by a wild boar. Notable **Mannerist** works include Pontormo's *Portrait of a Halberdier*, in which the subject's almost-blank expression has been variously interpreted as arrogant, morose, or contemplative, and Veronese's richly detailed *Portrait of a Man*, perhaps of the painter himself – a sword-bearing nobleman gazing proudly down at the viewer.

The finest works from the seventeenth century are **Flemish** and **Dutch**. Among the highlights are Rubens' *Entombment*, a pictorial essay supporting the Catholic doctrine of transubstantiation; Hendrik ter Brugghen's *Bacchante with an Ape*, showing a pathetic drunken libertine clutching a handful of grapes, an action mirrored by his pet monkey; and a trio of Rembrandts that emphasize the artist's interest in character and form: *Daniel and Cyrus before the Idol Bel*, in which the Persian king tries foolishly to feed the bronze statue he worships; *An Old Man in Military Costume*, the exhausted, uncertain face of an old soldier; and the great portrait of *Saint Bartholomew*, showing the martyred saint as a quiet, thoughtful Dutchman – the knife that will soon kill him visible in the corner of the frame.

While some lesser **French Neoclassical** works are included, notably David's overly slick and unaffecting *Farewell of Telemachus and Eucharis*, one of the best works from the period is Gericault's later *Portrait Study*, a sensitive portrait of an African man. The Getty Center is also known for bidding on **Impressionist** works; as such, these acquisitions read like a laundry list of late nineteenth-century French art: a portrait of *Albert Cahen d'Anvers* by Renoir, the inevitable Monet haystacks, and one of Degas' ballet dancers. Van Gogh's *Irises* was the object of a bruising 1980s bidding war, in which an Australian financier beat out other competitors (at a price of more than $50 million), but later defaulted on his payments; the painting languished in legal limbo before the Getty Trust snatched it up for an unknown price.

Other significant works from the **nineteenth century** include *Bullfight* by Goya, in which the bull stares triumphantly at a group of unsuccessful matadors;

J.M.W. Turner's frenzied *Ships at Sea, Getting a Good Wetting*, all hazy colors and soft lines that look surprisingly modern and abstract; and Caspar David Friedrich's elegant and understated *A Walk at Dusk*, a Romantic painting of a lone man bowing before a stone cairn during twilight.

Drawings and manuscripts

The museum also boasts a wide collection of **drawings**, among the best of which are Albrecht Dürer's meticulous *Study of the Good Thief*, a portrait of the crucified criminal who was converted on the cross; his *Stag Beetle*, precise enough to look as if the bug were crawling on the page itself; Piranesi's dramatic image of a ruined, but still monumental, *Ancient Port*; and William Blake's bizarre watercolor of *Satan Exalting over Eve*, an expressionless devil hovering over his prone captive.

Also fascinating is the museum's excellent collection of medieval **illuminated manuscripts**, depicting Biblical scenes such as the Passion cycle, as well as notable saints. Exquisitely drawn letters introduce chapters from Scripture and maintain their radiance to this day, especially when lit from behind in a dark, dramatic gallery. One of the most interesting volumes is the *Apocalypse with Commentary by Berengaudus*, an English Gothic tome that shows the Book of Revelation in all its fiery detail, including an image of the Four Horsemen of the Apocalypse looking more like medieval knights.

Sculpture, photography, and other arts

As for **sculpture**, the most memorable are Benvenuto Cellini's *Hercules Pendant*, a small, finely rendered piece of jewelry that shows the ancient hero in shock, mouth agape; Antonio Canova's gracefully Neoclassical rendering of the god *Apollo*; and Gian Lorenzo Bernini's much smaller *Boy with a Dragon* – done when he was only 16 – depicting a plump toddler bending back the jaw of a dragon with surprising ease, either a playful putto or Jesus himself, depending on your view. The work of the great French classical sculptor Jean-Antoine Houdon also makes a few appearances, the most notable a bust of stately, proud royal bureaucrat *Marie-Sebastien-Charles-Francois Fontaine de Bire*.

Some of the Getty's excellent array of **photographs** include renowned works by Stieglitz, Strand, Weston, Adams, Arbus, and others, but again, it's the museum's less familiar works that are the most intriguing: an 1849 *Portrait of Edgar Allan Poe*, by an unknown photographer, has the writer staring at the camera with manic intensity; Thomas Eakins's photo study *Students at the Site for "The Swimming Hole"*, which the painter used as a dry run for his famous painting, showing his pupils jumping naked from a flat rock into a muddy pond; Civil War photographer Timothy O'Sullivan's seemingly doomed wagon train grinding on through the *Desert Sand Hills*; and August Sander's feral *Frau Peter Abelen*, an androgynous woman with slicked-back hair, white culottes, business shirt and tie, holding an unlit cigarette between gritted teeth.

Beyond all this, the museum hosts **temporary exhibitions** of classical and modern work (often with accompanying art films on the same themes, in the Williams Auditorium), everything from medieval tapestries and religious icons to old-fashioned lithographs and avant-garde photography. Displays that relate to recently conserved works are also on view in the lobby of the neighboring **Getty Research Institute**, just west of the main museum entrance (also free; same hours), which allows a brief glimpse into the workings of the rest of this sizable organization – though unfortunately, no tours are offered.

Culver City

Several miles south of Beverly Hills and Westwood, triangular **CULVER CITY** is one of the Westside's lesser-known points of interest, its past rich with movie lore and its current face shaped by groundbreaking architectural experiments. An extensive facelift since the 1990s has resulted in more parks and footpaths, streets lined with old-fashioned lampposts and jacaranda trees, and fewer drab streets and buildings. Wedged between unappealing Venice Boulevard and the 405 freeway, it's one of LA's most ethnically diverse cities, with a harmonious mix of whites, blacks, Hispanics, and Asians. The city center is around the redesigned intersection of Washington and Culver boulevards, which hosts a weekly **farmers' market** (Tues 4–9pm; free) on a block-long stretch, a good bet for assorted snacks and produce from tomatoes and lettuce to peaches and plums, depending on the season. Looming over the intersection is the early-twentieth-century **Culver Hotel** (see "Accommodation," p.248), which has partially been restored to its original splendor, replete with checkered marble flooring and iron railings. Plenty of Hollywood history took place inside the hotel, which started as Harry Culver's office space, was later purchased by John Wayne, and was often a favorite spot to stay for stars like Greta Garbo and Clark Gable. However, stories of drunken debauchery by the midget cast of the *Wizard of Oz* – who apparently stayed here during the filming – are more Hollywood myth than reality.

Just east, one of the first classic Culver City buildings you'll see on your way into town is the **Ivy Substation**, at Culver and Venice boulevards, a 1907 power station for the old Red Car public transit line, which ended service in 1953, dismantled by a combination of oil and gas company subterfuge and local neglect. Located in a palm-tree-filled park, the Mission Revival building has been reborn as a 99-seat performing arts venue, though one that's irregularly open (call for details at ☎310/253-5762). Other major structures can be found nearby, including the **Helms Bakery**, 8800 Venice Blvd, a WPA landmark with

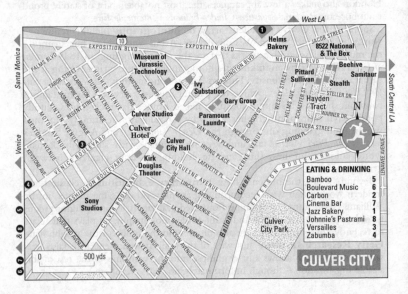

its original iron lamps, grand sign and fixtures, which is now home to a range of furniture dealers and design showrooms, as well as the *Jazz Bakery* (a music venue reviewed on p.305).

West of the Culver Hotel, the old Culver Theater, 9820 Washington Blvd at Duquesne Ave, is a striking 1947 moviehouse with a streamlined marquee and sparkling neon pylon; it has been reborn as the **Kirk Douglas Theater** (℡213/628-2772, Ⓦwww.taperahmanson.com), named after the star of *Paths of Glory* and *Spartacus*. Not far away, **City Hall**, 9770 Culver Blvd (Mon–Fri 8am–5pm), is notable for its huge, detached facade – a re-creation of the entryway to the previous City Hall. Between the facade's freestanding archway and the actual building, you'll find a pleasant park with a peek-through movie camera detailing the city's film history. For more eye-catching architecture, head a mile east to the **Hayden Tract**, a stretch of Hayden Avenue that, apart from being a city business district, is also one of LA's most fertile spots for wild modern building designs (see box, p.136).

Culver City movie studios

Without a doubt, Culver City's most significant historic structures are its movie studios, many of which still function, though in different guises. The man responsible for creating the two greatest studio complexes was **Thomas Ince**, a film pioneer and producer who essentially created the mechanized modern industry, with specialized roles for craftspeople and assigned roles for producers, directors, screenwriters, and so on, a rigid hierarchy that persists to this day and is still synonymous with the Hollywood "industry" of moviemaking. He was a major film-industry figure until he was mysteriously killed on William Randolph Hearst's yacht. Fans of *Gone With the Wind* may recognize the producer's Ince Studios, now **Culver Studios**, at 9336 Washington Blvd – predictably, this Colonial Revival "mansion" is no more than a facade.

Ince's later, bigger creation was **Triangle Pictures**, 10202 Washington Blvd, which he helped build with the financial aid of Harry Culver, a journalist and realtor who founded the city specifically for the movie business. Triangle became **MGM** by the 1920s, helmed by legend Louis B. Mayer, who held on as the studio's tough-as-nails boss for three decades and oversaw the site, creating some of Hollywood's biggest productions during the Golden Age of Movies. The bloom faded in the 1950s and 60s, though, and sections of the lot were sold off to developers and what was left was swallowed up by **Sony** in the 1980s. You can still stroll past the fine old colonnade, but unfortunately, most of the glorious MGM backlot was torn down, so if you go on a **tour** of the Sony facility (Mon–Fri 9.30am, 10.30am, 1.30pm & 2.30pm; $25; ℡323/520-TOUR) you'll have to be content with sauntering by massive, often empty soundstages and sets for TV shows you may or may not have heard of.

The Museum of Jurassic Technology

If movie history and weird architecture aren't enough for you, top off your trip with a visit to the bizarre **Museum of Jurassic Technology**, 9341 Venice Blvd (Thurs 2–8pm, Fri–Sun noon–6pm; $5; Ⓦwww.mjt.org), on the northern edge of Culver City. As much an art museum as a science center, this institution has little to do with distant history or roving dinosaurs. Rather, it tries to find the intersection between the scientifically possible, the culturally mythical, and the artistically absurd. In practice, this means it features a great range of oddities from the pseudo-factual to the paranormal to the just plain creepy. Examples

Eric Owen Moss and the Hayden Tract

Most small towns, even in LA, are known for their conservatism in design and architecture. Culver City is a major exception. With architect/artist **Eric Owen Moss** (director of Downtown's trailblazing SCI-Arc school; see p.58), this city has not only welcomed some bizarre buildings, it has also helped subsidize the business sites for many of his clients and prominently advertised his groundbreaking work. The **Hayden Tract**, one such city-subsidized business strip, has excellent examples of contemporary architecture ranging from austere modernism to cockeyed deconstructivism – indeed, Moss has tagged the entire area, a former industrial zone, as **The New City**, and the city has charged him with the task of redesigning it over the course of many years.

In the Tract, you can find a whole series of Moss's designs, including the 1997 **Pittard Sullivan** building, 3535 Hayden Ave, a giant gray box with massive wooden ribs poking out of its sides, somewhat like flying buttresses. Thanks to its architect, the company even got around a Culver City building code – that one percent of any structure's budget must be used for public art – when the building itself was declared art. Nearby, **8522 National**, also known as the IRS Building (1990), features a jangled-up facade with a white staircase leading to nowhere. Adjacent to this is **The Box**, with a cubic window riveted to one of its corners and seeming ready to come off its hinges and tumble down onto the street below. One of the best Moss works in the Tract is the 1995 **Samitaur**, 3457 S La Cienega Ave, massive, gray warehouse-like offices with skewed lines, sharp points, and a freakish sense of proportion. The eye-popping jumble of **The Pterodactyl** (2002), unfortunately lies hidden in a private parking lot, but another, the overwhelming **Stealth** (2001), 3530 Hayden Ave, is fronted by a massive, dark wall of projecting angles that seems more like the setting for a science-fiction film than a business complex, and with its arch geometry even suggests the sleek design of the eponymous bomber. Perhaps strangest of all, the **Beehive** (2001), 8520 National Blvd, is a bulbous take on the concept of the (business) hive, with curving bands and a rooftop stairway.

A pocket of Moss's earlier works, from 1987 to 1989, sits near Ince Boulevard and Lindblade Street. The **Gary Group** building offers a fragmented white-and-red sign with – again – a ladder leading to nowhere, while the side of the structure is a concrete wall ornamented with jutting brick cubes and an array of metal chains. The adjoining **Paramount Laundry** is no more conventional: a series of fat red columns supports a metal awning, with one column sitting several feet out of place, but leaning desperately to give a hand to the others.

Moss isn't done yet with Culver City, and future years have the architect planning all manner of curious retrofits, additions, and transformations, among them the twisting, churning Gateway Art Tower; the curved, writhing Conjunctive Points Theater Complex; and a series of expressive, daring projects at the corner of National Boulevard and Hayden Avenue. To learn more about the plans of this pioneering modern architect, head to ⓦ www.ericowenmoss.com.

include trailer-park artworks, showing junk collections next to tiny model RVs and mobile homes about to be swallowed up by the earth; exhibitions of folk superstitions, most memorably the image of dead mice on toast used as a cure for bedwetting; written and oral narratives of crank scientists and researchers, many of whom have reputedly disappeared under strange circumstances or gone mad; a strange re-creation of a Baroque-era museum run by a Jesuit scholar; and a collection of unearthly insects, such as an Amazonian bug that kills its prey through the use of a giant head-spike. The ultimate effect is quite unnerving, as these vivid exhibits are shown in dark rooms without windows or sunlight. For his curious efforts shown here, museum creator David Wilson was the winner of a MacArthur Fellowship in 2001.

5

Santa Monica and Venice

L ocated on the western edge of LA, the contiguous beach districts of **SANTA MONICA** and **VENICE** supposedly represent two different sides of LA: Santa Monica, the trendy, well-heeled liberal enclave with chic galleries, shops, and coffeehouses; and Venice, the offbeat, anarchic focus of dive bars, junk emporia, and fringe galleries. This is more of a myth than reality, since the beachside blocks of each city are increasingly similar, lined as they are with upscale condos and expensive hotels. Driving north on Main Street, it can be hard to discern exactly where Venice stops and Santa Monica starts. Both places also have in common moderate temperatures – they're cooler than the rest of the basin, with average midsummer temperatures sitting comfortably around 66°F. Perhaps for this reason, these areas have become home to at least one-quarter of LA's population of British and Irish expatriates, many of whom can be spotted in the local Euro-friendly pubs, clubs, and diners.

As the epitome of Southern California's laid-back sun-and-surf culture, the two cities contain some of the region's most enjoyable spots, with little of the pretension of Beverly Hills and West LA, and much in the way of easygoing attitudes and pleasantly low-scale development. Santa Monica's population is relatively stagnant due to the steep price of new housing and, like other parts of the Westside, is still fairly WASPy. Multiculturalism, however, has been long established in Venice, which was one of the few coastal cities not to use restrictive covenants to keep blacks from living there. It was also an alternative melting pot of sorts in the 1960s, when the place was really shambling, attracting a number of up-and-coming artists and musicians inspired by the mix. Still, the district continues to be home to a much wider range of classes and races than Santa Monica, and nowhere are these contrasts more apparent than near **Abbot Kinney Boulevard**, where upscale boutiques sit just a few short blocks from one of LA's grimmer ghettos, Oakwood.

Further south, the colorless real-estate tract of **Marina del Rey** offers few spots of interest, but the adjacent **Ballona Wetlands** have much natural appeal and **Playa del Rey** maintains a certain faded charm, which takes an eerie turn near the airport, around the site of LA's only urban ghost town.

Santa Monica

A low-slung, oceanside burg with rent-controlled apartments, a relaxed air, and easy access to the rest of the city, **Santa Monica** is for the most part an exclusive mix of expensive historic-revival bungalows and out-of-reach "apartments-for-life," coveted zealously by their lucky tenants. However frustrating the place is to move into, Santa Monica is a great spot to visit, a compact and friendly bastion of breezy charm. The entire area is well served by public transit and near enough to the airport, plus there's a wide array of accommodation, making it a good base for seeing the rest of LA.

As little as a century ago, most of the land between Santa Monica and what was then Los Angeles was covered by ranch lands and citrus groves, interrupted by the outposts of Hollywood and Beverly Hills. Like so much of the state, the land was owned by the **Southern Pacific Railroad**, whose chief Collis Huntington tried to make Santa Monica into the port of Los Angeles, losing out to Phineas Banning and other established interests in San Pedro and Wilmington – a blessing in disguise for Santa Monica. The linking of the beachfront with the rest of Los Angeles by the suburban streetcar system, known as the **Red Cars**, meant the town grew into one of LA's premier getaways – a giant funfair city that was the inspiration for Raymond Chandler's anything-goes "Bay City," memorably described in *Farewell My Lovely*. While working- and middle-class

Healing the Bay

Although Los Angeles has a well-deserved reputation for its noxious air, its **water pollution** is less well-known to the nation, though is in many ways worse: while the city's air pollution has actually tailed off in recent decades, the **Santa Monica Bay** continues to suffer from all kinds of problems, only slowly getting better.

Cities and districts from Santa Monica to Palos Verdes have the bad luck of being trapped next to nearly all of LA's outlets for wastewater and sewage, with streetside **storm drains** emptying the runoff of a 5000-mile network of LA urban sprawl and a single treatment center – **Hyperion**, near LAX – handling the task of cleaning up the collective filth. The periodic storms that LA receives, often driven by El Niño currents in the Pacific Ocean, make matters exponentially worse, forcing torrents of raw, untreated sewage directly into the bay and making any bodily contact with the seawater potentially hazardous, leading to anything from conjunctivitis to skin rashes.

You can see the pollution problem in full color just by walking past one of Santa Monica's storm drains, and seeing the rainbow slick of detritus floating along with the flecks of garbage. Just one look, or a sniff of the air, should be more than enough to keep you from bathing in Santa Monica Bay or from eating anything you might catch while fishing off the pier.

Still, there have been improvements to the bay in the last fifteen years since **Heal the Bay** and other such environmental groups were formed: Hyperion no longer freely dumps sewage as it once did, and chemical companies have stopped flushing DDT offshore. If you really feel the need to catch the California waves, make sure to do so well away from city piers – often the most polluted zones – and don't wade within one hundred yards of a beachside drain or venture into the water within three days after a storm, when runoff, sewage, bacteria, and algae combine to form a repellent aquatic poison.

To check out the sands beforehand, visit the Heal the Bay website at ⓦwww .healthebay.org, which also provides updates on the latest progress in the uphill fight against water pollution, and click on the color-coded beach map detailing which areas are fine for swimming or fishing.

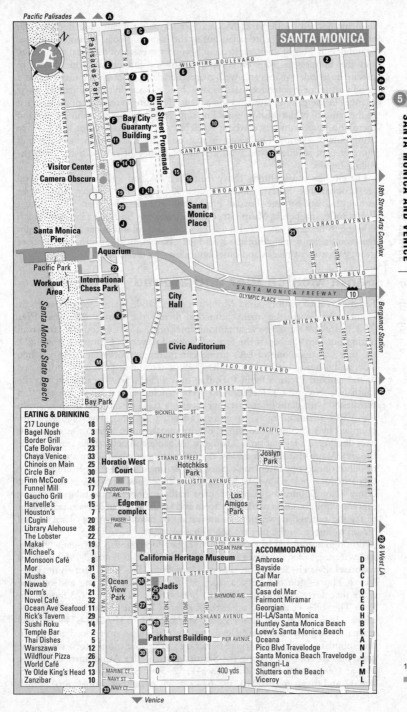

SANTA MONICA

Pacific Palisades ▲ ▲ (A)

WILSHIRE BOULEVARD

ARIZONA AVENUE

Third Street Promenade

Bay City Guaranty Building

SANTA MONICA BOULEVARD

Visitor Center
Camera Obscura

BROADWAY

Santa Monica Place

COLORADO AVENUE

Santa Monica Pier

Aquarium

Pacific Park

Workout Area

International Chess Park

OLYMPIC BLVD

SANTA MONICA FREEWAY
OLYMPIC PLACE

Santa Monica State Beach

City Hall

MICHIGAN AVENUE

Civic Auditorium

PICO BOULEVARD

Bay Park

BAY STREET

BICKNELL ST

PACIFIC STREET

Horatio West Court

Hotchkiss Park

STRAND STREET

HOLLISTER AVENUE

Joslyn Park

Edgemar complex

WADSWORTH AVE.

FRASER AVE.

Los Amigos Park

OCEAN PARK BOULEVARD

OCEAN PARK

California Heritage Museum

HILL STREET

Ocean View Park

RAYMOND AVE.

Jadis

ASHLAND AVENUE

Parkhurst Building

PIER AVENUE

MARINE CT.
NAVY ST.
NAVY CT.

0   400 yds

▼ Venice

EATING & DRINKING

217 Lounge	18
Bagel Nosh	3
Border Grill	16
Cafe Bolivar	23
Chaya Venice	33
Chinois on Main	25
Circle Bar	30
Finn McCool's	24
Funnel Mill	17
Gaucho Grill	9
Harvelle's	15
Houston's	7
I Cugini	20
Library Alehouse	28
The Lobster	22
Makai	19
Michael's	1
Monsoon Café	8
Mor	31
Musha	6
Nawab	4
Norm's	21
Novel Café	32
Ocean Ave Seafood	11
Rick's Tavern	29
Sushi Roku	14
Temple Bar	2
Thai Dishes	5
Warszawa	12
Wildflour Pizza	26
World Café	27
Ye Olde King's Head	13
Zanzibar	10

ACCOMMODATION

Ambrose	D
Bayside	P
Cal Mar	C
Carmel	I
Casa del Mar	O
Fairmont Miramar	E
Georgian	G
HI-LA/Santa Monica	H
Huntley Santa Monica Beach	B
Loew's Santa Monica Beach	K
Oceana	A
Pico Blvd Travelodge	N
Santa Monica Beach Travelodge	J
Shangri-La	F
Shutters on the Beach	M
Viceroy	L

residents flocked to the Santa Monica Pier for its thrill rides and freewheeling atmosphere, the town's elite sailed out to the gambling boats anchored offshore to indulge in a bit of illicit excitement beyond the reach of the local authorities, and the business bigwigs entertained mistresses and underworld cronies in private beachside cabanas and well-guarded enclaves. Though the mix created a good setting for a detective yarn, today Chandler wouldn't recognize the place: changes in the gaming laws and the advent of private swimming pools have led to the removal of the offshore gambling ships and many of the bathing clubs, and there's no longer any place where a celebrity or business hotshot is really free from public scrutiny. The result is that Santa Monica is now among LA's more elegant seaside towns, with a relative absence of seamy drama or high-rolling hijinks.

The city lies across Bundy Drive from West LA, and splits into three general areas: **oceanside** Santa Monica, holding a fair bit of its history and tourist attractions, sits on the coastal bluffs and includes the pier, Third Street Promenade, and beach; **Main Street**, running south from the pier into Venice, is home to designer eateries and quirky shops; and **inland** Santa Monica is split between exclusive neighborhoods and art galleries, to the north, and acres of grungy apartment blocks and quiet bungalows, to the south.

Santa Monica Pier and around

For most casual visitors Santa Monica is worthwhile mainly for its oceanside amusements, with the main attraction being the **Santa Monica Pier** (℡310/458-8900, Ⓦwww.santamonicapier.org), a busy tourist attraction jutting out into the bay at the foot of Colorado Avenue. Constructed in 1874, the pier was once one of LA's prime entertainments, offering nerve-jangling rides and a heady carnival atmosphere, while remaining fairly tame compared to the raucous Pacific Ocean Park that took shape a few decades later to the south (see box, p.142). Rebuilt and reconstructed several times, it was often threatened with demolition, narrowly averting this fate on several occasions in the 1970s (thanks largely to citizen advocacy groups). The pier was also pounded by merciless storms in 1982 that nearly drove it into the sea, and it later developed a reputation as a hangout for gangs and petty thugs from outside the area. Many visitors stayed away, especially at night when skirmishes between hoodlums and cops often took place, and business suffered accordingly. Since then, the local police have made their presence felt and nearly all of the violent crime is long gone, and nightly tourist traffic is once again visible, attracting everyone from business workers to teens and families. But unless you really want to try the watered-down rides or are eating or drinking here, it's hard to find reason to linger on the pier for more than an hour.

Although dominated by an assortment of fast-food stands, video-game parlors, and watering holes, the pier's most obvious appeal is its restored 1922 wooden **carousel** (March–Sept Mon–Thurs 11am–5pm, Fri–Sun 11am–7pm; Oct–March Thurs–Mon only; 50¢ a ride), in its own squat building and offering more than forty colorful hand-carved horses, featured in the 1973 movie *The Sting*. The roller coaster and other thrill rides of **Pacific Park** (June–Aug daily 11am–11pm, Sat & Sun closes 12am; $17, kids $9; ℡310/260-8744, Ⓦwww .pacpark.com) may catch your eye, but the place is an overpriced attempt to lure suburban families, and you're better off saving your money for a real theme park. Instead, consider visiting the **Santa Monica Pier Aquarium**, below the pier at 1600 Ocean Front Walk (Tues–Fri 2–5pm, Sat & Sun 12.30–6pm; $5, kids 12 and under free; ℡310/393-6149, Ⓦwww.healthebay.org/smpa), which

▲ Santa Monica Beach

is run by the Heal the Bay environmental group; here you can find out about marine biology and get your fingers wet touching sea anemones and starfish.

To the south, kids can clamber about on the chunky stone sculptures of a **children's park**, and near the end of the pier, anglers cast their lines into the murky depths of Santa Monica Bay, while below the pier, **Santa Monica State Beach** is a popular strip of sand, tightly packed with visitors on summer weekends. Swimming (or fishing) here is a gamble due to contaminants from nearby storm drains (see box, "Healing the Bay," p.138), but the threat of water-borne infections doesn't keep some locals from venturing out into the waters.

Just south of the pier, Santa Monica features LA's original "Muscle Beach," which predates Venice's own, more famous version, though it's a bit on the small side. Still, there are enough rings, bars, and other athletic equipment here to make it suitable for would-be bodybuilders and fitness fans. If you'd rather match wits than compare biceps, visit the adjacent **International Chess Park**, a fancy name for a serviceable collection of chessboards that attracts a range of players from rank amateurs to slumming pros. Finally, a **bike path** begins at the pier and heads twenty miles south to Palos Verdes, a stretch that ranks as one of the area's top choices for cycling. You can rent bicycles, surfboards, or rollerblades at equipment-rental shacks by the pier, or just stroll along taking in the local color.

Palisades Park

North of the pier across Ocean Avenue, **Palisades Park** is a palm- and cypress-tree-lined strip that affords stunning views stretching from Malibu to Palos Verdes – all the while sitting precariously atop high bluffs that are constantly being eroded. At least half of the **cliffside sidewalk** around the edge is usually fenced off, as it has a tendency to tumble down the bluffs, especially after heavy rains. Inside the park, you may want to stop by the **visitors information office** (daily 10am–4pm, summer 9am–5pm;

141

Swept away with the tide

As with so much of LA, the **early days** of Santa Monica are visible here and there in pieces, but old construction has in large measure been razed to make way for new development. The strip of sand around the Santa Monica Pier was once the site of some of LA's swankiest hotels, none more impressive than the Queen Anne colossus of the **Arcadia**, named after the wife of sheep-rancher and real-estate bigwig Robert S. Baker. He purchased much of the land that would become Santa Monica from the Sepulveda family, one of LA's old Spanish landowners (who also had dealings in West LA; see p.128), and the huge hotel, finished in 1887, became an icon of the Southern California coast.

Pumped up by the burgeoning development symbolized by the Arcadia, realtors of the era tried to call the town the "**Zenith City by the Sunset Sea**," which predictably didn't catch on – though the 1890s brought more people as Santa Monica continued to grow as a resort town. In later decades the boom continued and the great beach houses just north of the pier were known as the "**Gold Coast**," because of the Hollywood personalities who lived there. The largest still standing, the **North Guest House**, 415 Palisades Beach Rd, was built as the servants' quarters of a massive 120-room house, now demolished, which William Randolph Hearst built for his mistress, actress Marion Davies. MGM boss Louis B. Mayer owned the adjacent Mediterranean-style villa, which was later rumored to be the place where the Kennedy brothers had their secret liaisons with Marilyn Monroe. Later rechristened as the **Sand and Sea** beach club, the old Hearst complex was closed after the 1994 Northridge earthquake, but the state has been working to redevelop the five-acre site for public use.

Further south, **Ocean Park Boulevard** was one of the main routes to the coast via the old streetcars of the **Pacific Electric**, and the entire beachfront between here and the Venice border, now overshadowed by massive condominiums, used to be the site of a resort community developed by Abbot Kinney, the man behind the design of Venice itself. Along with vacation bungalows, a wharf, and a colorful boardwalk, the neighborhood also featured the largest and wildest of the old amusement piers: the fantastic **Pacific Ocean Park**, or "P-O-P" as it was known, with a huge roller-coaster, a giant funhouse, and a boisterous midway arcade. Architectural historian Reyner Banham once described as a "fantasy in stucco and every known style of architecture and human ecology." Against the sanitized fun zones like Disneyland, though, the old piers began to look faded and depressing, and despite a late-1950s refurbishment, P-O-P went steadily downhill, languishing for a time as a makeshift obstacle course for daredevil surfers (best seen in the film *Dogtown and Z-Boys*; see p.417) before being demolished in the mid-1970s.

ⓣ310/393-7593, ⓦwww.santamonica.com), in a kiosk just south of Santa Monica Boulevard, at 1400 Ocean Ave. The center's handy map shows the layout of the town and the routes of the Santa Monica Big Blue Bus transit system, a useful Westside complement to the MTA network (ⓣ310/451-5444, ⓦwww.bigbluebus.com). There's another visitor center in the nearby mall (see opposite), but this one's a bit more central.

Nearby, the **Camera Obscura**, 1450 Ocean Ave (Mon–Fri 9am–4pm, Sat & Sun 11am–4pm; free; ⓣ310/458-8644), provides unique entertainment by way of an old-fashioned device that prefigures modern photography. Inside a darkened room, you can view images of the outside world projected onto a circular screen by a rotating mirror on the roof – the sort of tool artists like Jan Vermeer once used as a visual aid for painting. On clear days, the clarity of the images can be startling. The camera is located within a social center for the elderly (with "Camera Obscura" clearly written on the facade), so make sure to ask someone inside for access to this upstairs room.

The Third Street Promenade

Two blocks east of Ocean Boulevard, between Wilshire and Broadway, the **Third Street Promenade** is a pedestrian stretch that must rank as one of LA's most densely touristed, especially on summer weekends, when trudging from one end of the area to the other can be an exhausting experience. Although it's sometimes fun to hang out in the cafés, bars, and nightclubs, or play a game of pool, chain retailers have virtually conquered the strip. As with Melrose Avenue (see p.106), what used to be an array of independent booksellers, boutiques, and novelty shops has transformed into the sort of showcase for corporate America's products that you can find in almost any suburban mall.

Still, there are flashes of originality amid the familiar names, and the promenade can be really busy at night, when huge numbers of tourists and locals jostle for space with sidewalk poets, swinging jazz bands, and street lunatics, under the watchful eyes of water-spewing **dinosaur sculptures** draped in ivy. The mall is anchored at its southern end by the drab **Santa Monica Place**, a white stucco pile that's among architect Frank Gehry's less inspired work, with the usual assortment of chain stores and a mandatory food court. Just to the north, towering over the shopping strip, is the recently restored **Bay City Guaranty Building**, Third Street at Santa Monica Boulevard, a Zigzag Moderne marvel topped by a colorful clock that was for years Santa Monica's tallest building.

A little further north, the 1939 **Shangri-La apartments**, now a hotel at Ocean and Arizona avenues (see "Accommodation," p.250), are perhaps Santa Monica's finest example of the 1930s Streamline Moderne style, which used nautical motifs to great effect, making this structure look like a giant, landlocked ocean liner. Finally, just one block away on Ocean Avenue in Palisades Park, stands the austere statue of the city's namesake, **Santa Monica**, the mother of St Augustine, a serene white pillar at the edge of the Pacific Ocean.

Main Street

The completion of the Santa Monica Freeway in 1965 bridged a deep arroyo and brought the city's beachfront homes within a fifteen-minute drive of Downtown (barring traffic gridlock), while isolating the north side of town from **Main Street**, five minutes' walk from the pier. Here, the collection of classy boutiques, bars, and restaurants makes it one of the most popular shopping districts on the Westside. Beyond shopping, eating, and drinking, though, there's not much to do.

The big chain stores have arrived on the street, but there are still enough quirky local operations to make a visit here worthwhile, notably **Jadis**, 2701 Main St (℡310/396-3477), a prop-rental operation that, while not open to the general public, does offer LA's best display window: a collection of mannequins posed in various demented dioramas from 1930s horror films, such as a mad scientist's lab, and surrounded by all sorts of antiquated technical junk and contraptions. To make for a more comprehensive day of consumerism, you can travel between Main Street and the Third Street Promenade on the **Tide Shuttle** (every 15min; Sun–Thurs noon–8pm, Fri & Sat noon–10pm; ℡310/451-5444), ponying up a mere quarter to hit all the shopping highlights, as well as travel along the sands south of the pier.

One of the few actual sights, the **California Heritage Museum**, no. 2612 (Wed–Sun 11am–4pm; $5; ℡310/392-8537, Ⓦwww.californiaheritagemuseum .org), is the city's effort to preserve some of its architectural past. Two houses were moved here to escape demolition: one house – the museum itself – hosts temporary displays on California cultural topics, and has permanent exhibits on regional pottery, furniture, quilts and decorative arts, while the other house is known as the *The Victorian* (☎310/392-4956, ⓦwww.thevictorian.com), now a special-event venue. There are also several noteworthy buildings on and around Main Street, including the angular gray volumes and strange geometry of Frank Gehry's **Edgemar** shopping development, no. 2415, a deliberately awkward construction that rewards closer inspection, especially on its second floor, where the sheet-metal design brings to mind an abstract sculpture. The more traditional **Parkhurst Building**, south on Main Street at Pier Avenue, is a 1927 Spanish Colonial Revival gem; while the cool white arches and simple boxlike shapes of Irving Gill's **Horatio West Court** (1919), north of Edgemar at 140 Hollister Ave, prefigured the rise of local modernism by about twenty years, with a generous helping of austere Mission Revival. It's one of the few surviving works by the under-appreciated architectural pioneer.

Inland Santa Monica

Although **inland Santa Monica** is generally marked by quiet, cozy neighborhoods, fast-food diners, and entertainment-industry office parks, there are a handful of interesting attractions that make a visit here worthwhile.

Wilshire Boulevard is the main commercial axis of this area – less engaging than elsewhere in town – but further north, near the city border, **San Vicente Boulevard** is a more appealing diversion, a grassy tree-lined strip and a joggers' freeway that leads east to the wealthier confines of Brentwood. LA's true health mania is visible just two blocks north of San Vicente, along Adelaide Drive between First and Seventh streets. Here an entire stair-climbing culture has evolved along the giant **Santa Monica Stairs** that connect Santa Monica with the Pacific Palisades stretch of Entrada Drive. On any given morning, crowds of locals trot up and down the street, just waiting for a chance to descend down the bluffs and charge back up again, red-faced and gasping for air. You, too, may wish to descend the steps, to get a glimpse of the tonier confines of Pacific Palisades, Santa Monica's even more well-heeled neighbor to the north (see p.213).

Two blocks south of San Vicente, the pricey restaurants and boutiques of **Montana Avenue** mark the upward mobility of the area, but offer little you haven't seen elsewhere in West LA. The area does have one piece of world-class architecture in the wild **Gehry House**, 22nd St at Washington Ave, a fitting reflection of architect Frank Gehry's early taste for the perverse and unusual. Now partially hidden by foliage and remodeled for the worse, the house shattered conventional notions of architecture upon its completion in 1978: not a unified design at all, but what appears to be random ideas thrown together helter-skelter and bundled up with concrete walls and metal fencing.

Bergamot Station and around

Inland Santa Monica has many fine **galleries** with works by emerging local and international artists. **Bergamot Station**, the city's aesthetic hub, is a collection of former tramcar sheds at 2525 Michigan Ave, near the intersection of 26th and Cloverfield, which houses a multitude of small art galleries (most open Tues–Fri 10am–6pm; free). Many of LA's latest generation of artists have shown here, and the highlight is the **Santa Monica Museum of Art**, in Building G-1 (Tues–Sat 11am–6pm; $5; ☎310/586-6488, ⓦwww.smmoa.org). This is a good space to see some of the most engaging and curious work on the local scene, in temporary

Sun, sand, and surf

From San Diego to Santa Barbara, Southern California is synonymous with American beach culture and its attendant body worship, sporting enthusiasm, and after-hours debauchery. The stereotype has been refined and perpetuated by decades worth of pop music and Hollywood movies that identify the region with the good life by the sea — the fame of celebrity colonies like Malibu doesn't hurt, either. Indeed, the image is a potent one, and has been carefully cultivated since LA started promoting itself as a mecca for sunshine and healthy living in the late nineteenth century.

Santa Monica beach-goers, circa 1890 ▲

Gidget and friends at the beach ▼

Golden sands

During LA's Victorian-era reign as a land of clean air and citrus groves, salt-water bathing natatoriums, open-air **board-walks**, and carnivals peppered the coast. In 1907 surfing arrived from Hawaii, but the sport had not yet developed a national following, and most Southern Californians were content to enjoy the beach as a backdrop for **pleasure piers** like Venice and Pacific Ocean Park. In later decades, changing demographics and oil-drilling pollution shut down the funfairs, leaving the local beach scene in need of reinvention.

The **1960s** changed everything: The *Gidget* movies popularized the surf scene throughout the world, while more serious adventurers saw the thrills awaiting them in the *Endless Summer*

So Cal surfers ▼

Surf's up

Although a sport as challenging as **surfing** is not something you can pick up on a single trip to California, there are many good resources once you get here. We've listed sport-rental vendors throughout the guide (see "Sports and Outdoor Activities" for more info; p.322), some of which run their own training sessions or camps.

Each beach in Southern California has its own vibe: some are friendly; others give off a hostile, "locals only" attitude; some are popular with a wide range of people, such as Zuma Beach north of Malibu, while more daunting places, like Rincon Point between Santa Barbara and LA, are best suited for pros who know what they're doing. A good bet for information is to pick up a book like the *Guide to Southern California Surf Spots* (see p.422); for weather reports, try calling or visiting Watch the Water (☎310/457-9701, ⓦwww.watchthewater.org).

documentaries. The Beach Boys, Jan and Dean, and other pop artists sang of the glories of California beach life, while Venice became a home for up-and-coming artists and musicians, like Billy Al Bengston, Robert Williams, and Ed "Big Daddy" Roth raising the area's profile by shaking up the staid LA cultural scene and making fortunes in the art world. Soon, **Venice Beach** would be famed for its boardwalk and Muscle Beach, and beach cities named Huntington, Manhattan, Hermosa, and Laguna would promote their own indigenous beach scenes.

▲ Blading and biking on the Venice Boardwalk
▼ Sunbathers in Santa Monica

Oceanside pursuits

Southern California's beach culture hasn't looked back in the last four decades. Developers have plunked down the predictable condos and made once-funky places like Venice affordable only to millionaires, but there are still countless **oceanside pursuits** worth a try, many of which don't require a lot of money. The beach boardwalk extends from Santa Monica down to Redondo Beach, and is a great place to jog, bike, rollerblade, or stroll, divided down the middle just like a miniature LA freeway. Closer to the waves, activities from bronzing to basketball, pumping iron to paragliding, water skiing to windsurfing, are available for your amusement, while music fans can duck into a club for a seaside nightcap – you can even camp in some places. But more than anything else, it's the mix of people that defines the beach's appeal. The sand and surf bring together everyone from Hollywood hipsters to working-class immigrant families to Westside jet-setters. And in class- and culture-stratified LA, that's a rarity.

▼ Venice bike path

Huntington Beach ▲

Zuma Beach ▼

The best LA beaches

These sandy stretches are among the best the Los Angeles region has to offer.

Abalone Cove – Fascinating scenery on the south side of the Palos Verdes Peninsula, where the cove offers tide pools and kelp beds rich with sealife.

Carbon Beach – South of Malibu Pier, this is celebrity-watching central on the sands, where actors, agents, and lawyers talk shop and negotiate on the famous "Dealmaker's Rock."

Crystal Cove State Park – This marvelous beach, in a park spread over two thousand acres along the Pacific Coast Highway, is great for diving, snorkeling, and poking around tide pools; you can stay in one of 46 historic bungalows and cottages.

Huntington Beach – Beach culture Orange County-style, with regular surfing competitions, and a buzzing, friendly vibe.

Leo Carrillo State Beach – At the northern edge of LA county, a favorite spot for surfing as well as camping, with kayaking and fishing also drawing locals in the know.

San Clemente – Known to most of the country as the place where "Tricky Dick" Nixon retired, but to surfers as one of the top places in the region to catch a wave.

Surfrider Beach – If you've seen *Gidget* or *Beach Blanket Bingo*, you know this longstanding, prime-time surf spot.

Victoria Beach – Wonderfully secluded alcove of sand that appeals to Laguna Beach residents for its clean water, pristine environs, and relative lack of tourists.

Zuma Beach – A popular beach with a range of fun activities and close proximity to the great arcing hump of Point Dume.

exhibitions ranging from simple painting shows to complex, space-demanding installations and career-spanning retrospectives of California art pioneers. Among the regular displays, don't miss the **Gallery of Functional Art**, Building E-3 (free; ☎310/829-6990, ⓦwww.galleryoffunctionalart.com), offering an array of mechanical gizmos and eccentric furniture like cubist lamps and neon-lit chairs. If you want to check out more art, the **18th Street Arts Complex**, further inland at 1639 18th Street (Mon–Fri 11am–5.30pm; ☎310/453-3711, ⓦwww.18thstreet.org), is a hip and modern center for various types of art, much of it experimental. The performance space **Highways**, 1651 18th Street (☎310/315-1459, ⓦwww.highwaysperformance.org), is one such example in the complex (see p.312), showcasing edgy political and gender-based work.

Venice

South of Santa Monica, **Venice** was laid out in the marshes of Ballona Creek in 1905 by developer Abbot Kinney as a fantasy replica of the northern Italian city (see box, p.146). While most of the architecture and canals have long since disappeared, the lingering pseudo-European atmosphere has since proved just right for pulling in the artsy crowd he was aiming at, making Venice a nice spot to check out what remains of its underground arts scene and bohemian charm. Even the mainstream commercial enterprises get into the spirit. Main Street, for instance, is the former home of the offices of advertising firm **Chiat/Day**, just south of Rose Street. Marked by Claes Oldenburg's huge pair of binoculars that overshadow the entrance, the Frank Gehry–designed offices are one of LA's visual icons. A block north is the grotesque **Ballerina Clown**, an enormous sculpture by Jonathan Borofsky perched above the intersection of Rose Avenue and Main Street, its lithe body and stubbly clown mask making for a disturbing combination. Elsewhere, a strong alternative arts scene centers around the **Beyond Baroque** literary center in the old City Hall, 681 Venice Blvd ($7 per event; ☎310/822-3006, ⓦwww.beyondbaroque.org), a good place to get a flavor of the work of local artists and the city's latest cultural trends, catch one of the regular book readings, or sign up for a workshop in poetry, prose, or drama. Next door, SPARC offers pricey tours of some of the more remarkable murals around town (see box, p.31).

Venice Beach and Boardwalk

It's **Venice Beach** that draws most people to the district, and nowhere else does LA parade itself quite so openly, colourfully, and aggressively as it does along the **Venice Boardwalk**, a wide pathway tracking alongside the sands that's packed on weekends and all summer long with jugglers, fire-eaters, Hare Krishnas, and roller-skating guitar players. You'll have no difficulty picking up your choice of cheap sunglasses, T-shirts, personal stereos, sandals, and whatever else you need for a day at the beach. In the sands beyond are several squat concrete walls and towers that make up an officially sanctioned **graffiti park**, where the (usually temporary) designs might include anything from the Virgin of Guadelupe to abstract tagger self-portraits to cryptic letters spelling out mysterious, indecipherable phrases. South of Windward Avenue along the Boardwalk is **Muscle Beach**, a legendary outdoor weight-lifting center where stern-looking, would-be Schwarzeneggers pump serious iron, high-flying gymnasts swing on the adjacent rings and bars, and serious

American Venice

As with various other parts of LA, such as Beverly Hills and San Marino, the development of **Venice** owed much to the desire to copy European models; however, if it weren't for a lucky coin flip, this Old World simulation would never have existed. When **Abbot Kinney**, winner of a fabled toss with his former real-estate partners, gained control of the area in 1904, he set about on a quixotic quest to build a paragon of learning, art, and culture from scratch. After deciding to base his ideal burg on the great Renaissance city-state, and once this area was linked up to the rest of LA by the Red Car mass transit line, Kinney began construction of the town, then labeled **"Venice-by-the-Sea."** He first drained the land's marshes and developed an extensive network of canals and roads, then created theaters, performance venues, and sites for restaurants and cafés, and even a think-tank for the liberal arts. He put much of his own money into the effort, investing about $1.5 million, and the initial payoff seemed great. Visitors were smitten by the new arts center's bungalows and hotel rooms, its gondoliers (some from Italy) navigating the waterways, and its pleasant pier for seaside relaxation.

Culture alone, however, did not pay the bills, and soon the crowds were demanding more thrills and less thinking. In response, Venice shifted its focus to providing amusement for its seasonal vacationers and daily visitors, and Kinney oversaw the formation of what would become LA's greatest **boardwalk**. Minaret-topped palaces, rollercoasters, a Ferris wheel, giant balloons, freak shows, and all manner of carnival attractions were soon found along Venice's once-austere oceanfront, and by 1911, against competition from his Pacific Ocean Park neighbors to the north, Kinney engineered the town's incorporation, even though it scarcely resembled his original notion for the community (aside from certain visual motifs like the canals). The city thrived for about a decade, until the **oil industry** moved in next door: when the derricks started their crude production, water pollution became a major threat to the beloved canals, and before long the central lagoon and outlying channels became fetid sites for waste disposal and seeping filth. Although the boardwalk was still attracting tourists, the decaying canals sullied the town's image, leading to a significant fall-off in visitors. Without any solution in sight, Venice's city leaders (which at that point did not include Kinney, who died in 1920) allowed the growing metropolis of LA to take over. Before long, the larger city paved over most of the canals and the main lagoon around Windward Circle. Later decades would bring Depression-era economic convulsions, more oil wells, the demise of the boardwalk, and the severing of the Red Car line, all of which turned Venice into a shadow of its former self. The town's nadir may have come in 1958, when Orson Welles used it as a location in his film *Touch of Evil*, plausibly remaking it into a shabby Mexican border town rife with corruption and murder.

In the 1960s and 70s, Venice witnessed a renewed **arts scene,** with painters and poets moving into the cheaper apartments on Venice's oceanside blocks, and a redesigned boardwalk offering a hint of the old carnival atmosphere. The rock music scene also flourished in spots — Jim Morrison met Ray Manzerak here to form the nucleus of The Doors, who played at the district's Cheetah Club (which burned a few years later) — and the area made appearances in cult movies like the Peter Fonda biker flick *The Wild Angels*. But as soon as Venice re-established its bohemian bona fides, the rest of the city and the property developers began paying attention. By the 1980s many of the old residents of the quaint seaside buildings were driven out by gentrification, rents went up accordingly, and the place began to resemble just another funky but pricey LA arts zone. These days, little remains of Kinney's original plan, although vestiges, such as the fading colonnade and five renovated canals, are still visible here and there.

games of basketball take place on the concrete courts – don't come if you can't hit the rim. Contact the Venice Beach Recreation Center, 1800 Ocean Front Walk (℡310/399-2775; ⓦwww.laparks.org/venice), for information on the various activities and contests that occur here, including the Bench

Press Championships held in July. Rollerbladers, skateboarders, volleyball players, and bicyclists are ubiquitous throughout the year, and there are **rental shacks** along the beach for picking up skates, surfboards, or bikes.

Beyond the beach, the rather basic **Venice Pier** stretches into the ocean off of Washington Street, but don't expect much in the way of carnival fun or thrill rides – the pier doesn't offer a great deal of entertainment value these days, since it's used mostly for fishing in the often-polluted bay, and is a far cry from the wild amusement of old. Incidentally, be warned that Venice Beach at night can be a **dangerous** place. Walking on the beach after dark is illegal, but you should have no problem supping at a beachside café or browsing at a record store.

Windward Avenue and around

Windward Avenue is Venice's main artery, running from the beach into what was the Grand Circle of the canal system, now paved over and ringed by a number of galleries and the Venice **post office**, Windward Ave at Grand Ave, where you can peek at a mural of the early city layout. On the west side of the circle, the curvaceous roller-coaster facade of the postmodern 1987 **Race Through the Clouds** building pays tribute to the old theme park with a sweeping neon track and metal gridwork. Closer to the beach, colorful giant **murals** – depicting everything from a shirtless Jim Morrison (1811 Ocean Front Walk) to Botticelli's Venus on rollerskates (Windward at Speedway Avenue) – cover the walls of the original structures; while a Renaissance-style **arcade**, around Windward's intersection with Pacific Avenue, is alive with health-food shops, used-record stores, and rollerblade-rental stands. Left over from the district's high-art phase a hundred years ago, a handful of **classical columns** are painted in Day-Glo colors that Kinney would no doubt have gasped at, while others retain their original black-and-white coloring. Look closely at some of the columns and you'll see an odd touch: on their Ionic capitals are engraved the faces of local businessmen – a pointed reminder of Venice's entrepreneurial roots, and its early hubris.

This area has also become home to some of LA's most inventive artists and designers, whose offices are scattered around Windward Avenue and the traffic circle. You'll see the fruits of their labors in the small boutiques and far-out houses throughout the district, but especially to the south, along Ocean Front Walk (see opposite). Lovers of **experimental architecture** may also want to visit the section of town between California Avenue and Venice Boulevard, around Superba and Amorosa courts, where Thom Mayne's **Morphosis** architecture firm has created numerous colorful, bizarre structures around several notoriously narrow and hard-to-navigate streets.

Just a few blocks south from Windward, the five remaining **canals** are still crossed by their original 1904 bridges – quaint wooden structures that are among LA's few touches of Americana – and you can also sit and watch ducks paddle around in the still waters. It's a great place to walk around, though if you're in a car and wish to avoid the tiny, mazelike streets between the canals, there's only one way to see the area. Head north on Dell Avenue between Washington and Venice boulevards – a route that often draws a procession of slow-moving motorized gawkers. Whether you walk or drive, you'll get an eyeful of eclectic residential styles, modernist cubes and Tudor piles mixed in with Colonial bungalows and postmodern sheds, all of them now worth millions. Keep in mind there's no organized way to take a boat trip through the canals; if you happen to get friendly with a resident, you may be able to talk him or her into giving you a **rowboat ride** around the canals – many homes have the skiffs docked right next to their back yards.

To the north, running diagonally between Venice Boulevard and Main Street, the shopping strip of **Abbot Kinney Boulevard** features a range of fine restaurants, funky clothing stores, and arty boutiques, and makes a handy shortcut to get through the district. However, wandering away from the strip at night is strongly discouraged, as this street is the southern border of Venice's notorious Oakwood ghetto. Even here, however, you can find the home of the odd celebrity – Dennis Hopper's **Hopper Studio**, 326 Indiana Ave, the ultimate in maximum-security architecture: a slanted, corrugated-steel box with no windows, incongruously surrounded by a quaint, white picket fence.

▲ A canal in Venice

Ocean Front Walk

Between Marina del Rey and the ocean lies narrow Pacific Avenue, home to some of LA's better contemporary residential architecture. Park either at the channel-side lot on the south side, near Via Marina street, or along the curb on the north side, and follow **Ocean Front Walk** (actually the same route as the Venice Boardwalk further north) for a pleasant stroll by the sands and the colorful modern houses. From Venice Pier, the intersecting streets are named alphabetically – from Anchorage Street to Yawl Court – in keeping with the nautical theme.

From the north, you'll first hit Antoine Predock's groundbreaking **Douroux House**, 2315 Ocean Front Walk, frequently captured in TV commercials. Atop the heavy concrete frame are rooftop bleachers and a big red window that pivots toward the sea, allowing the ocean breezes to easily sweep through the cubic structure. Not far away is Frank Gehry's **Norton House**, 2509 Ocean Front Walk, which features a curious boxy room projecting above the rest of the structure like an off-kilter crow's nest on a boat. Further south is the blue-and-white **Yacht House**, 3900 Pacific Ave, just a block east of Ocean Front Walk, an Art Deco–inspired "boat" whose bow is firmly stuck in the concrete sidewalk. Since new and off-kilter houses are being built here all the time (often by movie-industry moguls), bring a copy of the latest LA architecture guide to find out which big name designed which eye-opening curiosity.

South of Venice

At its nadir in the 1950s and 1960s, Venice was confronted with a new and unwelcome neighbor to the south: **Marina del Rey**, a massive real-estate tract that blotted out the old city's coastal views with high-rises. As with the colossal towers plunked down along Wilshire Boulevard in Westwood, investment capital proved irresistible to the indifferent county commissioners who controlled the unincorporated land, and Marina del Rey has since grown up in big, ugly spasms. Unless you own a yacht and are free to tool around the area's upscale marina (or stay in one of its handful of fancy hotels), you're unlikely to get very close to the water; the whole area is ringed by dreary chain restaurants, giant office complexes, and ugly apartment superstructures – more closely resembling the tenements of the East Coast than any notion of luxury living.

Still, despite its utter lack of charm, many visitors often find themselves in Marina del Rey for one reason or another: the nearness of LAX, an attempted shortcut past the congestion of Lincoln Boulevard, or just plain bad luck. Along the south end of the area, at the end of Fiji Way, **Fishermen's Village** is Marina del Rey's top visitor attraction, though it's hard to see why, consisting as it does of low-end seafood joints and endless trinket and T-shirt shops. More appealing is the channel-side walking and biking **path** that stretches from the end of Fiji Way out to the end of the spit. Not only is this the place where the Christmas **regatta** takes place, but it's also a good spot to watch everyday yachts and speedboats make a leisurely sail into the marina. On the south side of the channel, Fiji Way dead-ends near a path that can take you to the end of the jetty, from where it's a short jog south over a channel **bridge** crossing Ballona Creek, really a storm drain, into the marginally more interesting district of **Playa del Rey**.

Ballona Wetlands

Further south down Lincoln Boulevard, Marina del Rey gives way to the wide expanse of the six-hundred-acre **Ballona** (pronounced *BY-oh-na*) **Wetlands**, encompassing bodies of fresh and salt water that are home to two hundred major bird species and a host of other creatures, though their ecosystem has been disrupted in recent years by a rising number of foxes, which roam freely. Although off limits to humans, this natural preserve can be toured at a distance, starting by heading west on Jefferson Boulevard (off Lincoln) and taking a left onto Culver Boulevard. While you might not see conspicuous wildlife, you will get a sense of the uniqueness of this terrain in the heavily urbanized LA basin.

Before Abbot Kinney created what is now Venice, the wetlands of this mid-coastal area stretched all the way to the border of the community of Ocean Park. Because of the area's proximity to the LA airport (then called "Mines Field"), **Howard Hughes** in the 1940s located his airplane-manufacturing facility on its eastern side, and at its peak the plant had countless huge hangars and engineering facilities, as well as the nation's longest private runway; it was also the place where the notorious **Spruce Goose** was built. Hughes Aviation lasted a half-century here, until several decades after its founder's death, but in 1994 relocated elsewhere. That's when the preservation battles for the wetlands began in earnest.

For well over 15 years developers and environmentalists have battled for permanent control of this prime real estate, with the old aviation site (and parcels around it) turning into an 1100-acre tract of new condos and commercial structures called **Playa Vista**, and activists putting up a fierce rearguard action to protect what's left over. Although plans to build the Dreamworks SKG movie studio here were successfully scuttled after adverse publicity, part of "Phase Two" of the monumental development has proceeded apace, building over an ancient Indian burial ground and putting the exhumed bodies in cold storage. However, on some matters the city has ruled against the developers and slowed down the project, and ecologists aren't yet done: they continue to battle on a number of fronts, from methane-gas leakage issues to cultural preservation to ensuring the survival of a remaining, 200-acre wetland parcel. In fact, in the last twenty years there have been no fewer than twenty lawsuits to stop "progress" in the wetlands, and the jury (or at least the judge) is still out on what the final shape of the wetlands will be. Several hundred acres have been preserved as a concession (most west of Lincoln Blvd), but the conflict shows no sign of abating; for the latest news on the seemingly endless saga, check out Ⓦ www.ballona.org.

Playa del Rey

To the west from the wetlands, Culver Boulevard leads to the former resort community of **Playa del Rey**, once an essential link in the Red Car transit line and the site of grand hotels, restaurants, and a funicular railway, but since reduced to a faded collection of commercial shacks and unattractive condos. The **lagoon**, nestled near the beach along Pacific Street, is a popular spot for dog-walking, but you're better off heading up to a high bluff above the main part of Playa del Rey, to the neighborhood of **Palisades del Rey**, which makes for a pleasant, hilly hike past some fine views of the ocean. There used to be more to this neighborhood (including historic houses by the likes of R.M. Schindler), and to Playa del Rey overall, but the need for a sound barrier between LAX and the ocean did much to ruin its idyllic setting. When the county condemned the property here in the 1960s, hundreds of homes were destroyed and an entire neighborhood all but disappeared. The result was one of LA's strangest attractions: a modern-day **ghost town** stretching for several miles from Waterview Street to Imperial Highway along Vista del Mar. Chain-link fences guard the empty streets, now lined by crumbling housing foundations and defunct street lights. The only residents these days are some 50,000 **El Segundo blue butterflies** that have moved in since the south end of the area was turned into an ecological preserve. Head to Sandpiper Street to survey the surreal scene close up, or at least until the next blaring takeoff of a jumbo jet makes you jump back in your car.

6

South Central and East LA

D espite their familiarity from LA-based movies, **South Central** and **East LA** are far removed from the tourist circuit, and avoided by most visitors and almost all Westsiders, many of them believing any venture south of the I-10 freeway to be an open invitation to murder, mugging, or some other threat. In truth, while these places can be dicey and should be avoided at night, the ghetto stereotypes are blown out of proportion in selected districts, and a number of interesting museums and historic-revival homes can be found here, especially on the northern side of South Central around Exposition Park and West Adams.

Contained mostly within the boundaries of the 405, 605, and 10 freeways, South Central and East LA make up a large portion of the LA basin, encompassing diverse cultures, with neighboring communities often separated by major differences in language, ethnicity, and religion. Hispanic population growth is a constant throughout these areas, as it is throughout the rest of LA: as late as the 1980s, the racial makeup was 75 percent black; twenty years later, it's 60 percent Latino, and increasing yearly.

South Central LA

Without doubt, **SOUTH CENTRAL LA** does not rank on the city's list of prime attractions, and most of the city's tourist authorities act as if the district simply doesn't exist, aside from the Watts Towers. However, it does make up a considerable part of the metropolis: a big oval chunk bordered by Alameda Street and the 10 and 405 freeways (the latter forming the western and curving southern border of the area). Typically made up of detached bungalows enjoying their own patch of palm-shaded lawn, South Central nevertheless has some of the worst poverty in the area, especially the closer you go toward districts like Watts and Compton. Most residents have little chance to move up the social ladder – a situation that fosters large, pervasive youth gangs, which have only been getting bigger and more violent in recent years.

Not surprisingly, throughout much of the district, every block for miles looks much like the last, peppered with fast-food outlets, dingy liquor stores, swap meets, and abandoned industrial buildings, with the occasional outdoor market to brighten the gloom. Most out-of-area commuters obliviously zip through the area on the Harbor Freeway (I-110), which is largely confined to its own walled-off channel. Nonetheless, if you have the time and aren't put off by fears of crime, there are compelling sights to be found, including the historic homes of **West Adams**, several museums in **Exposition Park**, and the folk-art masterpiece of the **Watts Towers** – which should all be seen in daylight.

Some history

Like other parts of the city, much of South Central LA was settled in the nineteenth century by **Mexican immigrants** when the area was still governed by Mexico, and its large land tracts divided up as ranchos. Later, after the US took control of the land and California became the 31st state in 1850, **white Protestants** began migrating from the Midwest, drawn by the sunny weather, low cost of living, and favorable job market, continuing into the early twentieth century. By the time of World War II, West Adams was still among the chicest neighborhoods of LA, universities like USC and Pepperdine had taken root in the area, and a young George Bush (the elder) moved his family to work in the burgeoning oil town of Compton.

Although LA had the largest African-American settlement on the West Coast at the time, it was the war that brought blacks in great numbers from the South and the East Coast to work in defense-related industries, especially aerospace (the era has been vividly detailed in the murder-mystery prose of Walter Mosley; see p.429). Born or raised in LA were such notables as jazz musicians Dexter Gordon, Charles Mingus, and Eric Dolphy, United Nations undersecretary Ralph Bunche, dance choreographer Alvin Ailey, and Hollywood actress Dorothy Dandridge. (Even in the nineteenth century, when their population was significantly lower,

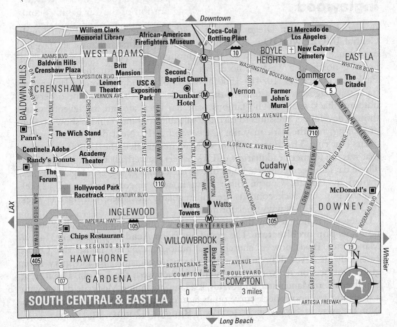

black Angelenos were visible throughout the city, including such prominent figures as Robert Owens, a former slave who became the wealthiest and most prominent African-American in Southern California in the 1850s.)

Most of the new residents were unpleasantly surprised to experience a taste of the Old South in new LA. The rampant, blatant discrimination of the time ensured the widespread presence of **color bars** and **restrictive covenants** – social codes and housing bylaws that kept blacks out of white neighborhoods. African-Americans were hemmed in by avenues like Western and Slauson for their home-buying, and faced extreme hostility from whites whenever they ventured out of their neighborhoods to buy groceries, meet with friends, or watch movies. Because of this, areas like Central Avenue and West Adams became segregated, though culturally rich, enclaves for blacks, with a thriving entertainment scene in the former and excellent architecture in the latter.

The **Civil Rights Era** and changing demographics put an official end to the old ways of segregation in the 1950s and 60s, and LA's southern neighborhoods have become a diverse blend of blacks, Hispanics, and Asians, with many districts changing character in just a few decades. However, many problems persist, and what was formerly political and social apartheid has instead become de facto **economic segregation**. Poor and working-class blacks, even up to the middle class, are still stuck in South Central LA – largely to the western side – with Latinos increasingly settling in Watts and many other neighborhoods across the southern and eastern side. City authorities have tried to brighten things up, at least superficially, by renaming the district "South Los Angeles," hoping the name change will somehow alleviate the desperate conditions, but aside from confusing visitors (since "South LA" generally refers to the harbor area), the bureaucratic legerdemain seems to have fooled no one.

Inglewood

Bordered by the San Diego Freeway (I-405) on the western edge of South Central, **INGLEWOOD** is, as the home to LAX, the first area most air travelers experience in LA – mainly to fight through the traffic congestion when heading north to a Westside hotel. It's also well known for the **Hollywood Park Racetrack** (Ⓣ310/419-1500, Ⓦwww.hollywoodpark.com), a landscaped track with lagoons and a state-of-the-art widescreen that shows the otherwise obscured back straight. The famous park has been around for seventy years, though developers' pressures to turn the valuable land into condos show no sign of abating, and the park may not last beyond 2010. Next door are the white pillars that ring **The Forum**, 3000 W Manchester Blvd, the 17,000-seat arena that was the former headquarters of LA's Lakers (basketball) and Kings (hockey). These days it's been converted into one of the country's biggest mega-churches, owned by Faithful Central Bible Church, with a congregation of 12,000, though pop and rock concerts are still regularly held here during the week (Ⓣ310/330-7300, Ⓦwww.thelaforum.com).

Unless you're here to play the horses or hear a concert, Inglewood's best attraction is its **pop architecture**. The grand but faded **Academy Theater**, 3141 W Manchester Blvd, now a church, was built in 1939 to house the Oscars ceremony (it never did), and features a giant Moderne spire and spiky neon globe that beckon to worshippers, while further west, the **Loyola Theater**, at Sepulveda and Manchester boulevards, is a late Streamline Moderne design with a sweeping, red goose-neck curve on its facade, which now serves as office space. Not far away at 805 Manchester Blvd, **Randy's Donuts** (Ⓣ310/645-4707,

@randys-donuts.com) is one of LA's more surreal icons, a 1954 fast-food shack topped by a giant brown donut, easily visible on your way to and from LAX; while **Pann's** (☎323/776-3770, @www.panns.com), a mile north at La Tijera Boulevard and Centinela Avenue, still serves comfort food in what is perhaps the greatest 1950s "Googie"-style diner of all, with a big neon sign, pitched and gabled roof, exotic plants, gravel roof, and a wealth of primary colors. Other classic diners are in fairly shopworn condition, except for the striking **Chips Restaurant**, a few miles south at 11908 Hawthorne Blvd (☎310/679-2947), showcasing one of LA's great signs, three aquamarine columns supporting a sparkling set of letters (plus cheap comfort food to boot, including eggs, grits and toast), and the zesty **Wich Stand**, 4508 Slauson Ave, graced with a towering, neon-lit pylon, though it no longer serves "De Luxe" hamburgers and deviled-egg sandwiches – it's now a health-food store, *Simply Wholesome* (☎323/294-2144).

Centinela Adobe

Just south of *Pann's*, the historic **Centinela Adobe**, 7643 Midfield Ave (Wed & Sun 2–4pm; free; private tours by appointment at ☎310/671-2075), was once home to Ignacio Machado, an heir to one of the Mexican founders of Los Angeles. It's the oldest building in the area, dating from 1834 and furnished with antiques and replicas, including a good array of Victorian clothing and furniture, and offering details on Machado's life and his surrounding Aguaje de Centinela rancho, a 2200-acre land parcel granted him by the Mexican government. Also on site is the **Daniel Freeman Land Office**, built in 1887, a center for historic preservation, and a storehouse of curios and memorabilia recalling Inglewood city history and culture, from the town's origins as the site of LA's first chicken and chinchilla farms to its rise as a center for brick production and, later, as a home to the aerospace and defense industries.

Crenshaw, Leimert Park, and Baldwin Hills

Just to the north, **CRENSHAW** and adjacent **Leimert Park** form the contemporary hub of African-American social activity in LA. Where once the nucleus of black culture was along Central Avenue, south of Downtown, it's now along **Crenshaw Boulevard**, a busy stretch of restaurants and book and record stores, as well as the **Baldwin Hills Crenshaw Plaza**, 3650 W Martin Luther King Jr Blvd (Mon–Fri 10am–9pm, Sat 10am–8pm, Sun 11am–6pm; ☎323/290/6636, @www.crenshawplaza.com), a multimillion-dollar shopping mall. The stunning **Leimert Theater**, 3314 43rd Place, an Art Deco gem by architects Morgan, Walls and Clements (see box, p.78), features a towering oil-derrick sign with neon accents. For a time it was a performing-arts complex owned by Marla Gibbs, best known as Florence from the TV show *The Jeffersons*, but it has remained closed for about a decade while the state tries to reopen it for local artistic purposes. The theater stands in the heart of **Leimert Park Village**, several blocks of lively shops and decent restaurants. There are also a few solid jazz, R&B, and blues **clubs** here, notably the *World Stage*, 4344 Degnan Blvd (concerts Fri & Sat; $10; ☎323/293-2451, @www.theworldstage .org), which doubles as an arts center with creative workshops for up-and-coming writers, musicians, and poets. Also here is the redoubtable *Babe & Ricky's Inn*, 4339 Leimert Blvd (Mon & Wed–Sat; $8–15; ☎323/295-9112, @www.bluesbar.com), which serves up solid helpings of soul food as well as a range of blues five nights a week; this is the legendary institution's most recent of various locations since the 1960s.

Above Crenshaw and Leimert Park, the black upper-middle class resides in pleasant **Baldwin Hills**, named after Wall Street gambler and Santa Anita racetrack-builder E.J. "Lucky" Baldwin. Just before he died in 1909, Baldwin acquired the old Rancho La Cienega, which encompassed the hills and was named after the misspelled Spanish word for "marsh." (He also built an estate east of Pasadena that's now home to the LA County Arboretum; see p.202.) Later, the area would host the Olympic Village for LA's 1932 summer games and become the site of a catastrophic 1963 dam-burst and flood. This was due in no small part to environmental damage from oil drilling, which continues to this day and is most visible here along La Cienega Boulevard, giving a hint of what much of petroleum-obsessed LA looked like in the 1920s. If for some reason you feel like getting a closer look at the pumps while relaxing or burning off some calories, **Kenneth Hahn State Recreation Area**, 4100 S La Cienega Blvd (daily 6am–dusk; ☎323/298-3660), is strangely placed right in the middle of it all, with seven miles of trails, a lake for fishing, baseball diamonds, picnic tables, and a sandy volleyball court.

West Adams

The charming, but faded, **West Adams** neighborhood, along Adams Boulevard from Crenshaw Boulevard to Hoover Street, was one of LA's few racially mixed neighborhoods in the early part of the twentieth century. It was also one of the spots where movie stars tended to live, known in the 1920s and 30s as "**Sugar Hill**" and full of notable celebrities such as movie-musical director Busby Berkeley, and (literal) silent-film heavyweights Fatty Arbuckle and Theda Bara. After World War II and the demise of racist restrictive property covenants, many wealthy blacks began moving in as well, including Ray Charles, Little Richard, and Joe Louis. Unfortunately, the politics of the 1950s and 60s took their toll on the neighborhood, partly because of the construction of the **Santa Monica Freeway** (I-10), which slashed the area in half; much of this effect was intentional, as political leaders sought to prevent black settlement further north, and cleaving the area seemed like a handy, if nefarious, way of going about it. Despite the subsequent decay, the neighborhood retained many of its classic houses – unusual for LA – in styles from Victorian to Craftsman to all manner of historic revivals, some homes mixing all of them together. In the last decade, the district has even experienced a small revival, with new homeowners of all colors arriving to renovate the grand old properties, raising the specter of gentrification in future years.

These days, West Adams hosts no fewer than three different historic-preservation zones, though many of the grand houses and mansions have become religious institutions. The bulk of the most notable structures can be found near Adams' intersection with Arlington Avenue. In this vicinity, Berkeley's estate, the 1910 **Guasti Villa**, 3500 W Adams Blvd, is a graceful Renaissance Revival creation that might fit nicely in Italy but is now home to a New Age spiritual institute. However, you can still pop in at least once a year to experience the Da Camera Society's chamber music (see p.307). Nearby, the **Lindsay House**, no. 3424, a terracotta curiosity with a heavy stone facade and unique tilework (the first owner was a tile manufacturer), has become Our Lady of Bright Mount, a Polish Catholic church (☎323/734-5249); and the **Walker House**, no. 3300 (☎323/733-6260), a mishmash of Craftsman bulk, Tudor half-timbering, and a Mission-style tile roof, has turned into a Korean Seventh-Day Adventist church. Just north, the **Marquis House**, 2302 W 25th St, is a jumble of eclectic Victorian touches from 1904 whose main claim to fame is its role as the Fisher funeral home in the TV series *Six Feet Under*, and the **South Seas House**, 2301 W 24th St (Mon–Fri 8am-10pm, Sat 10am-4pm; ☎323/373-9483), is a community center that you can visit to sample the place's odd 1902 blend of Victorian and Polynesian architecture. Further east, the **Britt Mansion**, 2115 W Adams, is a 1910 Neoclassical gem with grand white columns and adjoining gardens. To take a closer peek at one section of the neighborhood, Western Heights, you can sign up for a **tour** that encompasses eight historic homes (occasionally Sun 11am–4pm; $35; ⓦwww.westernheightsonline.com).

The finest building in West Adams is not a home but the striking French Renaissance **William Clark Memorial Library**, 2520 Cimarron St (Mon–Fri 9am–4.45pm; free; ☎323/735-7605, ⓦwww.humnet.ucla.edu/humnet /clarklib), with its elegant symmetry, yellow-brick walls, formal gardens, and grand entrance hall – a splash of Continental elegance in an unexpected LA setting. As millionaire heir to a copper fortune, founder of the LA Philharmonic, and a US Senator from Montana, Clark amassed this great collection before donating it to UCLA, which continues to oversee it. Besides rare volumes by Pope, Fielding, Dryden, Swift, and Milton, plus a huge set of letters and manuscripts by Oscar Wilde, the library includes four Shakespeare folios, a group of works by Chaucer, and copies of key documents in American history pertaining to the Louisiana Purchase and the like. Four annual **exhibitions** are given of selected works from the collection.

USC

The **USC** (University of Southern California) campus, a few miles south of Downtown and east of West Adams, and easily accessed along Jefferson or Exposition boulevards, is a wealthy enclave in one of the city's poorer neighborhoods. For many years a breeding ground for political and economic fat cats, the university was well known for hatching LA's shadow rulers for the secretive "**Committee of 25**," supplying Richard Nixon with gung-ho advisers like H.R. Haldeman, and generally acting as the reactionary force in the local academic scene.

Today, USC, or to wags, the "University of Spoiled Children," is among the most expensive universities in the country, its undergraduates thought of as more likely to have rich parents than fertile brains. Indeed, the stereotype often seems borne out, both by their easygoing, beach-bumming image, and by USC's being more famous for its sporting prowess than its academic achievements. Within fifteen years of the school's 1874 founding, it already had a **football** team, becoming the first university in Southern California to play the game. They remain a dominant force today, having won back-to-back national championships in 2003–4, and famous alumni include O.J. Simpson, who, before his courthouse escapades, collected college football's highest honor, the Heisman Trophy, when he played here.

Though largely white and conservative, the university hasn't escaped to the suburbs (unlike its right-wing counterpart, Pepperdine), and there have even been a few small steps to integrate the **campus** more closely with the local, mainly black and Hispanic, community. Based on an Italian Romanesque style similar to that of UCLA, USC's 1920s buildings are much more forbidding, though they exhibit nice detail and ornament. The lack of greenspace at times gives the campus the appearance of a concrete desert, and the austere character of its modern buildings can, in places, look like something out of a desolate de Chirico painting. Unlike UCLA, where you can visit to idle away the time, you go to USC strictly to get something done.

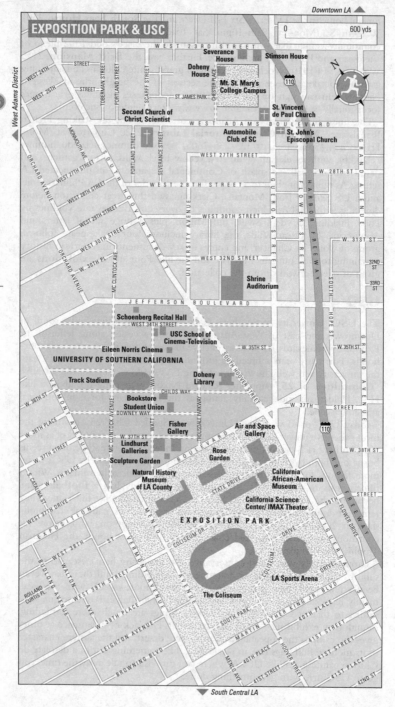

EXPOSITION PARK & USC

0   600 yds

N

◀ West Adams District

WEST 23RD STREET

STREET

WEST 24TH STREET

WEST 25TH STREET

TOBERMAN STREET

PORTLAND STREET

PORTLAND STREET

SCARFF STREET

CHESTER PLACE

ST. JAMES PARK

Severance House

Doheny House

Stimson House

Mt. St. Mary's College Campus

110

Second Church of Christ, Scientist

St. Vincent de Paul Church

WEST ADAMS BOULEVARD

Automobile Club of SC

St. John's Episcopal Church

WEST 27TH STREET

MONMOUTH AVE

ORCHARD AVENUE

WEST 27TH STREET

SOUTH HOOVER STREET

PORTLAND STREET

SEVERANCE STREET

UNIVERSITY AVENUE

FIGUEROA STREET

FLOWER STREET

HARBOR FREEWAY

GRAND AVENUE

W. 28TH ST

WEST 28TH STREET

WEST 28TH STREET

WEST 29TH STREET

WEST 30TH STREET

WEST 30TH STREET

MC CLINTOCK AVE

WEST 30TH PL.

WEST 32ND STREET

Shrine Auditorium

W. 31ST ST

HOPE ST

32ND ST

33RD ST

SOUTH

JEFFERSON BOULEVARD

Schoenberg Recital Hall

WEST 34TH STREET

USC School of Cinema-Television

Eileen Norris Cinema

UNIVERSITY OF SOUTHERN CALIFORNIA

Track Stadium

W. 35TH ST

SOUTH HOOVER STREET

W. 35TH ST

GRAND AVENUE

Doheny Library

WAY

VERMONT AVENUE

W. 36TH ST

Bookstore

Student Union

CHILDS WAY

DOWNEY WAY

W. 37TH

Fisher Gallery

MC CLINTOCK AVENUE

WATT

TROUSDALE PARKWAY

Air and Space Gallery

110

W. 38TH ST

W. 36TH PLACE

W. 37TH ST

WEST 37TH STREET

Lindhurst Galleries

Sculpture Garden

Rose Garden

S. CATALINA ST

WEST 37TH PLACE

Natural History Museum of LA County

MENLO

BOULEVARD

STATE DRIVE

California African-American Museum

California Science Center/ IMAX Theater

HARBOR FREEWAY

STREET

38TH STREET

FIGUEROA DRIVE

EXPOSITION

EXPOSITION PARK

VERMONT AVENUE

WEST 37TH DRIVE

WEST 38TH

ST

COLISEUM DR.

COLISEUM

DRIVE

WALTON AVE.

BUDLONG AVENUE

WEST 39TH STREET

ROLLAND CURTIS PL.

LA Sports Arena

COLISEUM

DRIVE

The Coliseum

S. HOOVER STREET

40TH PLACE

41ST STREET

41ST STREET

W. 39TH PLACE

LEIGHTON AVENUE

BROWNING BLVD.

SOUTH PARK

DRIVE

MENLO AVE.

MARTIN LUTHER KING JR BLVD

40TH PLACE

41ST STREET

41ST STREET

41ST PLACE

42ND ST

The campus

While sizable, USC's campus is reasonably easy to get around. You might find it easiest, however, to take the free fifty-minute **walking tour** (leaving on the hour Mon–Fri 10am–3pm; by reservation at ☎213/740-6605, ⓦwww.usc.edu), which departs from the Admission Center, reachable off McCarthy Way west of Figueroa Street. Without a guide, a good place to start is the **Doheny Library**, between Childs Way and Trousdale Pkwy (hours vary, often Mon–Thurs 8am–midnight, Fri 8am–5pm, Sat 9am–5pm, Sun 1–10pm; ☎213/740-2924), an inviting Romanesque pile named after the famous LA oil baron, where you can pick up a campus map and investigate a large stock of overseas newspapers and magazines. Another good place for information is the **Student Union** building, just across from the library.

Of things to see, USC's art collection is housed in the **Fisher Gallery**, 823 Exposition Blvd (Tues–Sat noon–5pm; free; ☎213/740-4561, ⓦwww.fishergallery.org), showing a wide range of art, from international and multicultural to avant-garde and contemporary. It stages several major international exhibitions each year and has a broad permanent collection, best for its nineteenth-century American works, including Thomas Cole's *The Woodchopper*, a Hudson River School painting, and Albert Bierstadt's landscape of *A Stream in the Rocky Mountains*, a grand Romantic vista. Elsewhere, you can see smaller shows of students' creative efforts, as well as retrospective shows featuring the models, blueprints, and sketches of internationally famous architects, in the **Helen Lindhurst Architecture Gallery**, in the USC School of Architecture, 850 W 37th St (Mon–Fri 10am–6pm, Sat noon–5pm; free; ☎213/740-2723). The **Helen Lindhurst Fine Arts Gallery**, room 103 in the same complex (Mon–Fri 9am–4pm; free; ☎213/740-2787, ⓦfinearts.usc.edu/lindhurst), focuses on contemporary and experimental works from student and regional artists. If music is more to your interest, the **Arnold Schoenberg Institute Recital Hall**, near the middle of campus at 3443 Watt Way (concert line ☎213/740-2584), is one of five concert venues on campus that hosts regular performances by students, faculty, and guest performers, and not necessarily strictly of the craggy modernism that the hall's namesake championed when he taught at the university during the mid-1930s. Although the composer's treasure trove of archives was lodged at USC for decades, his heirs removed them to Vienna after a public dispute with the school in 1995.

There's plenty of bad public art on campus; one of the few compelling pieces is Jenny Holzer's **First Amendment**, in the **sculpture garden** around Harris Hall, Bloom Walk east of Watt Way – a work commemorating the Hollywood Ten, those writers and directors blacklisted for refusing to rat out their colleagues as Communists in the McCarthy era. Steps of stone slabs lead to ten circular benches, all of which are inscribed with the names and writings of the persecuted filmmakers.

Finally, the campus is also home to the **School of Cinema–Television**, a mainstream rival to the UCLA film school in Westwood. Ironically, **Steven Spielberg** couldn't get in to USC when he applied, but nowadays his name is hallowed here, and writ large on the wall of the large and expensive sound-mixing center he later funded. You can sometimes catch a good classic or foreign flick at the nearby **Eileen Norris Cinema**, just south of the Cinema School at 3507 Trousdale Parkway; drop by for a look at the monthly schedule of screenings (or call ☎213/740-3332 for information).

Exposition Park

Once known as Agricultural Park because of its produce vendors and farming exhibits, **Exposition Park**, just south of USC with its main entrance near 3800 S Figueroa St (Ⓣ213/763-0114), is, given the bleak nature of the surrounding area, one of the better parks in LA, incorporating lush gardens and several modest museums. Although this area just south of USC – along with the residential neighborhoods north of the school – was once home to LA's elite, subsequent white flight and economic downturns have taken their toll, an effect visible in the countless drab strip malls and liquor stores that have set up shop on the surrounding blocks.

Along with being a favorite lunchtime picnic spot for school kids, the park's big draw is the **California Science Center**, one of a cluster of **museums** off Figueroa Street at 700 State Drive (daily 10am–5pm; free, parking $6; Ⓣ213/744-7400, Ⓦwww.californiasciencecenter.org), a multimillion-dollar showcase for scientific education. The museum's highlights include scores of working models and thousands of pressable buttons. Displays include a walk-in periscope, imitation earthquake, and a demonstration wind tunnel. Three of the museum's attractions – a "high-wire" bicycle, motion simulator, and rock-climbing wall – cost $7 jointly. In the same complex, an **IMAX Theater** (tickets $8, kids $4.75; information at Ⓣ213/744-2015) plays a range of eye-popping documentaries on a gigantic curved screen. Nearby, the **Air and Space Gallery** (free; same hours and info as the Science Center), marked by a jet stuck to its facade, offers a series of satellites and telescopes and a slew of airplanes and rockets. The menacing presence of an LAPD helicopter "air ship" complements their constant drone in the skies above the neighborhood. The building itself is a white cubic mass designed by Frank Gehry, prefiguring some of his later, better work. Close by, the **California African-American Museum**, 600 State Drive (Tues–Sat 10am–5pm, Sun 11am–5pm; free, parking $6; Ⓣ213/744-7432, Ⓦwww.caamuseum.org), has diverse temporary exhibitions on the history and culture of black people in the Americas, including musical instruments from Africa and the Caribbean, shows devoted to the life and legacy of performers like Ella Fitzgerald, and painting and sculpture by local artists.

On a sunny day, take a stroll through Exposition Park's **Rose Garden**, 701 State Drive (mid-Mar to Dec daily 9am–dusk; free; Ⓣ213/765-5397). The flowers are at their most fragrant in April and May, which is when the bulk of the visitors come by to admire the 16,000 rose bushes and the charm of their setting. Finally, near the center of the park, the grand **Coliseum**, 3939 S Figueroa St, was the site of the 1932 and 1984 Olympic Games. Since then, though, it's seen its glory days fade, with the Raiders pro-football team long gone and possible deals to land a new NFL franchise repeatedly failing. However, stiff demand for home games for the dominant USC football team, one of the top squads in the country, allows them to charge a minimum of $75–87 per game for nosebleed seats, and much more for anything better (Ⓣ213/740-GOSC, Ⓦusctrojans.cstv.com). Otherwise, the imposing grand arch on the facade and muscular, headless commemorative statues create enough interest to make the place worth a quick look.

Natural History Museum of Los Angeles County

In the northwest corner of Exposition Park, the **Natural History Museum of Los Angeles County**, 900 Exposition Blvd (Mon–Fri 9.30am–5pm, Sat & Sun 10am–5pm; $9; Ⓣ213/763-3466, Ⓦwww.nhm.org), is an explosion of Spanish Revival architecture with echoing domes, travertine columns, and

▲ Dinosaur skeletons in the Natural History Museum of Los Angeles County

a marble floor. It's the park's most striking building and its best museum, with the biggest collection. Foremost among the exhibits is a tremendous stock of dinosaur bones and fossils, and some imposing skeletons (usually casts), including the crested "duck-billed" dinosaur, the skull of a Tyrannosaurus rex, and the astonishing frame of a Diatryma – a huge, flightless prehistoric bird. Exhibits on rare sharks, the combustible native plant chaparral, and a spellbinding insect zoo – centered around a sizable ant farm – add to the appeal, but there's a lot here beyond strict natural history, so you should allow several hours at least for a comprehensive look around. In the fascinating Pre-Columbian Hall, you'll find Mayan pyramid murals and the complete, reconstructed contents of a Mexican tomb, while the Californian history sections document the early (white) settlement of the region during the Gold Rush era and after, with some evocative photos of LA in the 1920s. Topping everything off is the breathtaking gem collection: several roomfuls of crystals, and a tempting display of three hundred pounds of gold, safely off-limits to prying fingers.

University Park

Just to the **north of USC** and Exposition Park, around Adams Boulevard and Figueroa Street, is **University Park**, a pocket of some of LA's most important early twentieth-century architecture. Much of it reflects the power of the district's most famous resident, oil magnate **Edward Doheny** (see box, p.121), and most of it is now given over to religious purposes. The intersection of Adams and Figueroa itself features three of LA's best period-revival designs from the 1920s: **St John's Episcopal Church**, 514 W Adams Blvd (℡213/747-6285), an Italian Romanesque showpiece that features plenty of Venetian glass and Italian marble and mosaics, as well as the modern image of Martin Luther King Jr in stained glass; the church-like **Automobile Club of Southern California**, 2601 S Figueroa St (213/741-3686), a Spanish Baroque structure with a high octagonal tower and Mexican terrazzo tile; and the grand **St Vincent de Paul Church** (℡213/749-8950), catercorner to St John's, Doheny's own donation to the faith, an even more ornamental Spanish Baroque

Cops and riots

Los Angeles has had a longstanding reputation as having one of the most brutal police forces in the nation – the **LAPD** – whose paramilitary tactics were developed under 1950s super-cop **William Parker**. In reaction to its longstanding mistreatment of local blacks, the district of Watts first achieved notoriety as the scene of the six-day **Watts Riots** of August 1965. The arrest of a 21-year-old African-American man, **Marquette Frye**, on suspicion of drunken driving, gave rise to charges of police brutality and led to bricks, bottles, and slabs of concrete being hurled at police and passing motorists during the night of the 11th. The situation had calmed by the next morning, but by the following evening both young and old were on the streets, venting an anger generated by years of abuse by the police force and other white-dominated institutions. Weapons were looted from stores and many buildings set afire (though few residential buildings, black-owned businesses, or community services, such as libraries and schools, were torched); street barricades were erected, and the events then took a more serious turn. By the fifth day the insurgents were approaching Downtown, which led to the callout of the **National Guard**: 13,000 troops arrived, set up machine-gun placements and road blocks, and imposed a curfew, causing the rebellion to subside. In the aftermath of the uprising, which left 36 dead, one German reporter said of Watts, "It looks like Germany during the last months of World War II."

Watts hit the headlines for a second time in 1975, when members of the **Symbionese Liberation Army** (SLA), who had kidnapped publishing heiress Patty Hearst, fought a lengthy – and televised – gun battle with police until the house they were trapped in burned to the ground. The site of the battle, at 1466 E 54th St, is now a vacant lot, though the surrounding houses are still riddled with bullet holes.

Despite all the violence, nothing had changed by the 1980s when chief **Daryl Gates** hit the headlines for his new and disturbing LAPD tactics: the department's own tank bashed down the walls of alleged (often innocent) drug suspects, its helicopter gunships were thick in the skies over South Central LA, and the chief himself proudly argued, in front of Congress, that casual drug-users should be taken out and shot. Gates was allowed to get away with these quasi-fascist antics only for so long, though, before he was forced out. In the **riots of 1992**, three white Los Angeles police officers were unexpectedly acquitted of using excessive force after they were videotaped kicking and beating African-American motorist **Rodney King**. What few predicted was the scale and intensity of the response to the verdict, which was partly fueled, ironically enough, by the almost total lack of a police presence during the first evening's bloodshed. Beginning in South Central LA, where motorists were pulled from their cars and attacked, the situation quickly escalated into a tumult of arson, shooting, and looting that spread from Long Beach to Hollywood. It took the imposition of a four-day dusk-to-dawn curfew, and the presence on LA's streets of several thousand well-armed National Guard troops, to restore calm – whereupon the full extent of the rioting became known. The **worst urban violence** seen in the US since the bloody, Civil War–era New York draft riots had left 58 dead, nearly 2000 injured, and caused an estimated $1 billion worth of damage.

Prompted by the Rodney King case, the **Christopher Commission** was set up to investigate racial prejudice within the LAPD, but its recommendations were blatantly ignored. The **Rampart police scandal** in 2000 revealed evidence of possible hit-squad tactics and other vigilante actions by members of the LAPD, confirming people's worst fears that the cops were beyond civilian, or even anyone's, control. While politicians and Westsiders expressed shock at such charges, no one in South Central was very surprised. Since then, even though New York's trailblazing former police chief **William Bratton** has been brought in to turn things around, almost nothing has changed. **Gang violence** in 2008 is a regular occurence, with more Latino suspects than before. However, since much of South Central is well off the radar screen of upscale white Los Angeles, the problems continue to fester and worsen – waiting for the next spark to send LA up in flames once more.

creation with a sparkling, tiled dome and richly detailed steeple. Nearby, the **Stimson House**, 2421 S Figueroa St, is a Romanesque castle-home, made in 1891 of red sandstone, that appears ready for a Crusader battle and is, fittingly enough, now a Christian religious institution.

One long block to the west, **Chester Place** and **St James Park** are pedestrian-friendly zones loaded with the opulent residences of some of LA's most prominent citizens of the early twentieth century. The area's centerpiece is the palatial **Doheny House**, 10 Chester Place (Mon–Fri 8am–5pm; ℡213/477-2767), a triumph of the Spanish Gothic style, where you can dawdle in the palm conservatory and immense dining hall built to seat one hundred guests. After the 1958 death of Edward Doheny's wife Estelle, this and the surrounding property were given to **Mount St Mary's College**, and the house is now one of several elegant buildings on campus. Periodically, the Da Camera Society offers "Doheny Soirees" (Oct–May, days vary; see p.307), in which chamber music is played under the mansion's beautiful, reverberant dome. Right by here are more intriguing period-revival creations, including the **Severance House**, 650 W 23rd St, a 1904 Mission Revival structure with some Victorian detailing in back (and now a resource center for Vincentian Catholic priests); and the **Second Church of Christ, Scientist**, 948 W Adams Blvd (℡213/749-3761), a Neoclassical jewel with forty-foot-high Corinthian columns and a copper dome that shelters a thousand souls.

Just across the street from USC lies the most exotic piece of architecture in the area, the **Shrine Auditorium**, 665 W Jefferson Blvd (tickets and info at ℡213/748-5116, Ⓦwww.shrinela.com), best known as the former venue of the Oscars ceremony, which was presented here biannually from 1986 to 2001, before moving on to the Kodak Theater in Hollywood. Looking like a vestige of an *Arabian Nights* set in Hollywood, this 1926 Islamic-inspired fantasy, with its onion domes and streetside colonnade, is frequently a venue for traveling religious revival meetings, pop concerts, circuses, pageants, and award shows.

Central Avenue

The focus of African-American commerce and culture during the interwar years, **Central Avenue** had a vigor that has never been recaptured. With pre-1960's segregation and restrictive housing covenants prohibiting blacks from living in most of LA, this avenue from Eighth Street to Vernon Avenue became the hub for numerous restaurants, nightclubs, and jazz halls. Such hot spots as the *Down Beat Club* and *Last Word* attracted a broad mix of blacks, from blue-collar workers to celebrities, and a few whites from the Westside as well.

With the end of official segregation, Central Avenue inevitably declined, but there are still several appealing sights amid the abandoned lots and strip malls. A superb example of Streamline Moderne architecture lies at the north end of the street: the **Coca-Cola Bottling Plant**, 1334 S Central Ave, looking like a huge, landlocked ocean liner, complete with rounded corners (with oversized Coke-bottle sculptures), porthole windows, and ships' doors. Besides being in excellent condition, the plant is still churning out bottles for the soft-drink giant. Built in 1937, this was the second groundbreaking building in LA created by Robert Derrah, after his Crossroads of the World (see p.104). Nearby at 1401 S Central Ave, the **African-American Firefighters Museum** (Tues & Thurs 10am–2pm, Sun 1–4pm; donation; ℡213/744-1730, Ⓦwww.aaffmuseum.org) is housed in Engine Company #30, LA's first all-black fire station, which protected the area from 1913 to 1980, and now displays a modest collection of historic equipment and memorabilia.

Eleven blocks south, pioneering black architect Paul R. Williams' first major building, the **Second Baptist Church**, 2412 Griffith Ave (T 213/748-0318, W www.sbcla.org), is a striking Romanesque Revival church built in 1924 for a congregation dating from 1885, making it LA's oldest black religious institution. Further south, the **Dunbar Hotel**, 4225 S Central Ave, was the first US hotel built specifically for blacks and patronized by many prominent African-Americans – W.E.B. DuBois and Duke Ellington among them – during the 1930s through the 1950s. The hotel is only visible in its restored lobby and facade, as it is now a home for the elderly. It does, however, host the **Central Avenue Jazz Festival** in late July (more details at T 213/485-2437, W www.centralavenuejazzfestival.com), which gives a hint of the area's swing and vigor in the old days.

Watts and Compton

Few neighborhoods inspire more fear in white LA than Watts and Compton, known mostly for their street crime and rap music. It is true that these spots can be dangerous, especially at night; Watts is best explored by those familiar with the area or in the company of a local, while Compton shouldn't be explored at all, at least beyond the fringes.

The abandoned Art Deco campus of **Pepperdine University**, Vermont Avenue and 80th Street, is one of LA's most visible emblems of white flight,

---

The gangs of LA

South Central LA is the heartland of the city's infamous **gangs**, said to number 26,000 members (or more) among them and responsible for up to 800 murders in the last year. They've existed for more than fifty years and often encompass several generations of a family. The black gangs known as **Crips** and **Bloods** are the most famous, but there are many huge Hispanic gangs as well, most prominently the **18th Street Gang** who, despite their name, operate all over the LA basin, as well as the US, Mexico, and beyond. The characteristic violence associated with these groups often stems from territorial fights over drug dealing, with many gangs staking claim to certain neighborhoods in their monikers. The larger gangs employ rather sophisticated schemes involving protection rackets, money laundering, and expansion into legitimate businesses from small retail operations to, it is rumored, the music industry – all tactics reminiscent not of common street thugs, but of old-style mobsters.

The old stereotype of LA gangs is increasingly outdated, though. Gang life used to be fairly contained within the city, and could be broken down into simple black-on-black violence, which occasionally spilled into other neighborhoods (such as Westwood in the 1980s), making white Westsiders paranoid and supportive of all manner of hamfisted police tactics. Nowadays, though, local gangs are increasingly **international**, with chapters not only reaching other cities throughout the western US, but also strongly linked to Mexican gangs and organized-crime syndicates. Indeed, LA serves as a training ground for budding gangsters from Central America who, after their deportation, return to their home countries schooled in the high-tech ways of first-world killing, inflicting more misery on a region already awash in violence and poverty.

That said, with all the different ethnic gangs in the city, don't try to decipher the **graffiti** you see on the wall of an inner-city liquor store, or wrongly assume that a gang member must be an obvious hoodlum in the "bad part of town." This sort of crime is intrinsic to the city as a whole, and is only at its most violent and visible in ghettos like South Central or Pico Union. However, by sticking to familiar areas in the day and well-policed districts at night, tourists should have few problems with gangs.

marking the spot where the Church of Christ–affiliated school was located from 1937 to 1972, after which it left for a bluff in Malibu. Further south from here, South Central becomes much grittier.

Watts

Now more Hispanic than black, **WATTS** provides only one (very) compelling reason to visit, and only during the day: the Gaudí-esque **Watts Towers**, sometimes called the Rodia Towers, at 1765 E 107th St (30-minute tours Fri 11am–3pm, Sat 10.30am–3pm, Sun 12.30–3pm; $7; ☎213/847-4646), a half-mile north off the 105 freeway on Wilmington Avenue. Constructed from iron, stainless steel, old bedframes, and cement, and adorned with bottle fragments and some 70,000 crushed seashells, these striking pieces of folk art are shrouded in mystery. Their maker, Italian immigrant **Simon Rodia**, had no artistic background or training, but labored over the towers' construction from 1921 to 1954, refusing offers of help and unable to explain their meaning or why he was building them. Once finished, Rodia left the area, refused to talk about them, and faded into obscurity. The towers, the tallest standing at almost 100 feet, managed to stave off bureaucratic hostility and structural condemnation for many decades, and at least one close encounter with the wrecking ball, before finally being declared a cultural landmark. One especially good time to come is during the late-September weekend that hosts the Saturday Day of the Drums Festival and Sunday Watts Towers Jazz Festival, both signature events in the city. Both take place at the adjoining **Cultural Crescent Amphitheater**; call the Watts Tower Arts Center, 1727 E 107th Street (☎213/847-4646, ⓦwww .wattstowers.org), for details and program listings.

Compton

Between Watts and the LA Harbor, the few districts are of passing interest. Despite its fame as the home of many of LA's rappers, as well as tennis champs Serena and Venus Williams, **COMPTON** is not a place where strangers should attempt to sniff out the local music scene. Oddly enough, the town's most famous resident was none other than former president George Bush (Sr), who lived here when the city was still known for its oil wells, and when whites were still in power. With the white flight of the 1950s and 1960s, though, investment capital dried up and Compton hasn't recovered – the city has the nation's highest murder rate for any municipality its size. At the edge of town, though, history buffs secure in their cars can stop at the **Dominguez Ranch Adobe**, just off the 91 freeway at 18127 S Alameda St (Sun & Wed 1, 2 & 3pm; ☎310/603-0088), which chronicles the social ascent of the adobe's founder, Juan Jose Domínguez. One of the soldiers who left Mexico with Padre Junípero Serra's expedition to found the California missions, he was rewarded for his long military service in 1782 by the granting of 75,000 acres of surrounding land. The six main rooms of the 1826 adobe are on display and are worth a look for anyone intrigued by pre-American California.

East LA

You can't visit LA without being aware of the Hispanic influence on the city's demography and culture, whether through the thousands of Mexican restaurants, the innumerable street names in Español or, most obviously, the preponderance of Spanish spoken on the streets in dialects from Tijuana to Oaxaca, from Guatemala to Peru. Of the many Hispanic neighborhoods all over the city, the most long-standing is **EAST LA**, which begins two miles east of Downtown, across the concrete flood-control channel of the LA River.

There was a Mexican population here long before the white settlers came, and from the late nineteenth century onward millions more arrived, chiefly to work as agricultural laborers in orchards and citrus groves. As the white inhabitants gradually moved west towards the coast, the Mexicans stayed, creating a vast Spanish-speaking community that's one of the most historic in the country, as well as one of the most insular and unfamiliar to outsiders.

Activity in East LA (commonly abbreviated to "ELA" or "East Los") tends to be outdoors, in cluttered markets and busy shopping pavilions. Non-Hispanic visitors are thin on the ground, but you are unlikely to meet any hostility on the streets during the day – though you should steer clear of the rough and very male-dominated bars, and avoid the whole area after dark. **Guadalupe**, the Mexican depiction of the Virgin Mary, appears in mural art all over East LA, nowhere more strikingly than at the junction of Mednik and Cesar Chavez avenues. Lined with blue tile, the mural serves as an unofficial shrine where worshippers place fresh flowers and candles.

Other than the street life and murals, there are few specific "sights" in East LA other than the mausoleum of **New Calvary Cemetery**, 4201 E Whittier Ave (daily 8am–5pm, spring & summer closes 6pm; ☎323/261-3106). Rivaling City Hall for sheer audacity, the monumental tomb piles on the styles, with Corinthian columns and pilasters, an Egyptian-pyramid roof and a few Byzantine domes, plus some sculpted angels thrown in for good measure. Beyond its exterior panache, the mausoleum is also the resting place of rich, old-time Angelenos like Edward Doheny, jazz great Jelly Roll Morton, and movie stars like Lionel and Ethel Barrymore, and Lou Costello.

For a more animated scene, stroll along **Cesar Chavez Avenue**, preferably on a Saturday afternoon – the liveliest part of the week – going eastward from Indiana Street, and check out the wild-pet shops for their free-roaming parrots

▲ El Mercado de Los Angeles

and cases of boa constrictors. In the **botánicas**, which cater to practitioners of santéria – a religion that is equal parts voodoo and Catholicism – browse among the shark's teeth, dried devilfish, and plastic statuettes of Catholic saints, or explain to the shopkeeper (in Spanish) what ails you, then pick out remedies from a wide selection of magical herbs, ointments, and candles. Only slightly less exotic fare can be found in **El Mercado de Los Angeles**, 3425 E First St (daily 10am–8pm; ☎323/268-3451), an indoor market somewhat similar to Olvera Street (see p.52), but much more authentic. Outdoor murals depict a Maya god and warrior, as well as actor Edward James Olmos, and an indoor warren of shops called *botanicas* sell clothing, Latin American food, and arts-and-crafts pieces; the top floor, where the restaurants are located, is the most musical, with mariachi bands playing well after midnight every day.

Of the nearby districts, the only one of conceivable interest is **MONTEREY PARK**, northeast of East LA, a reasonably safe area that has the highest

The dirty heart of Southeast LA

Following the path of Interstate 5 between South Central and East LA, **Southeast LA** is generally made up of low-grade industrial sites and their dingy bedroom communities, along with large expanses of postindustrial concrete desert. In the years following World War II, Southeast LA was a center for auto manufacture and tire-making, but the subsequent loss of blue-collar jobs led to the disappearance of much of the white and black population. They were replaced by Mexican and Central American immigrant laborers, many of whom would work at or below the minimum wage in sweatshops. Because this is one of the main US centers for (often illicit) new arrivals, population density in some places has become overwhelming – the tiny town of **Cudahy** packs nearly 25,000 people on one square mile of land, and not surprisingly has one of the country's highest poverty rates – while in other industrial towns, residential zones are practically forbidden, sweatshops evade labor laws through intentional lack of local oversight, and drug and contraband smuggling are major underground industries.

If, for some reason, you should wind up here, there are a few things worth checking out, starting in **Vernon**, an inhospitable burg whose only highlight is the **Farmer John's Mural**, 3049 E Vernon Ave, a bucolic idyll on a meat-packing plant, painted by a Hollywood set designer in the 1960s. It depicts a team of little pigs scampering about a farm, cavorting with a family, and managing to scale the building walls – an amusing scene that almost makes you forget the ugly business inside. Further east, in Commerce, is **The Citadel**, right off I-5 at 5675 Telegraph Rd (daily 10am–8pm; ☎323/888-1724, ❀www.citadeloutlets.com), modeled on the ancient Assyrian architecture of Khorsabad in the Middle East; note the massive battlements and carvings of priests and warriors on the huge facade. Built by the architecture firm of Morgan, Walls, and Clements (see box, p.78), this structure started life as the Samson Tyre and Rubber Company, was a backdrop for the 1950s spectacular *Ben Hur*, then abandoned, and finally restored and turned into a fashion outlet.

To the south, the community of **Downey** is unremarkable in itself, but does feature a true pop-architecture icon – the country's original **McDonald's** fast-food restaurant, 10207 Lakewood Blvd (☎562/622-9248), opened in 1953, a year before the chain officially started. Boasting a much more exuberant, colorful design than the mansard-roofed clones of today, this *McDonald's* also features big yellow-neon arches that stretch over, and into, the building itself, plus a winking chef named "Speedee" atop its 60-foot-high sign. More than just an old burger joint, the restaurant is also listed as a cultural monument by the National Trust for Historic Preservation and even has its own museum and gift shop.

percentage of Asian residents of any city in the nation (62 percent) and is a major gateway for Taiwanese and mainland Chinese immigrants arriving in the US. It's also home to a number of excellent authentic Chinese restaurants, as well as many nightclubs, ethnic grocers, and theaters, on its main drag, **Atlantic Boulevard**.

Whittier and around

Well to the south of East LA, and almost to the border of Orange County, the small town of **WHITTIER**, originally founded by Quakers and named after Quaker poet John Greenleaf Whittier, offers a handful of interesting sights. It was here that **Richard Nixon** – a Quaker himself – was raised, went to law school, and started his first law office. (His birthplace and library is in the Orange County town of Yorba Linda; see p.231.) You can find out more at the engaging **Whittier Museum**, 6755 Newlin Ave (Sat & Sun 1–4pm; $4; ℡562/945-3871, Ⓦwww.whittiermuseum.org), where docents lead a tour past a treasure-trove of historic city artifacts and assorted gizmos ranging from a working-model of an oil derrick to replicas of a Pacific Electric Red Car. Other highlights include an old-fashioned barn and Victorian cottage, a rebuilt version of a Quaker meeting hall, and the desk Tricky Dick used in his first law office.

For a look at another politician who had an even harder time of it, there's the engaging **Pio Pico State Historic Park**, 6003 Pioneer Blvd (Wed–Sun 10am–5pm; free; ℡562/695-1217 ext 102, Ⓦwww.piopico.org), a nine-thousand-acre tract that used to be the ranch of **Pio Pico**, the last Mexican governor of California, and centered around an **adobe** full of Victorian furnishings and artifacts tracing his life. Constructed in 1853, the house saw Pico lose his governorship, re-emerge on the LA City Council, make a fortune in real estate and finally go bankrupt, eventually dying penniless. All this history is on display during one of the regular adobe tours (on the hour Wed–Sun 1–3pm, also Sat & Sun 10–11am).

Several miles south, at 10211 Pioneer Blvd, the **Clarke Estate** (Tues & Fri 11am–2pm; free; ℡562/868-3876) is a popular wedding spot, with elegantly landscaped grounds. It's also one of Irving Gill's Mission Revival and early-modern melds (see p.144). Spartan white arches give way to Mediterranean balconies, and Tuscan columns are used to offset a number of pre-Columbian reliefs and icons – giving a hint of what LA would have looked like if it had been colonized by Italians and Mayans, instead of Spaniards. Neighboring **Heritage Park**, 12100 Mora Drive (daily 7am–9pm; free), is also worth a look for its collection of re-created, local historic buildings, including a windmill, conservatory, and carriage barn from the 1870s and 80s, accompanied by a pretty English garden and an eighty-ton locomotive that sits on railroad lines dating back to the 1870s as well. Less refined is the **LA County Sheriff's Museum**, 11515 S Colima Rd (Mon–Fri 9am–4pm; free; ℡562/946-7859), where you can examine a replica of an early jail and a sizable set of law-enforcement antiques – from classic tommy-guns to razor-sharp ice picks. Look, too, for the menacing meat hooks and crude knives that were popular tools in LA's mid-nineteenth-century "Hell Town" days.

Workman-Temple Homestead Museum

If you've already ventured this far for historic attractions, you might as well head north to the **Workman–Temple Homestead Museum**, 15415 E Don Julian Rd (tours on the hour Wed–Sun 1–4pm; free; ℡626/968-8492, Ⓦwww .homesteadmuseum.org), a historic estate that's the lone point of interest in the drab **CITY OF INDUSTRY**. Here, docents will lead you around the place where an early emigrant party first staked a regional land claim and constructed this historic Spanish Colonial house around an 1840 adobe, complete with expansive grounds. There's a smokehouse and water tower, as well as a cemetery that contains the graves of many figures from regional history, including that of Pio Pico. The house itself is striking, full of carved wooden details, wrought-iron railings, and tiled stairways, and the glimmering centerpiece – stained-glass windows depicting steadfast family members on their westward trek to Southern California.

7

The South Bay and LA Harbor

S tretching south of LAX and South Central all the way to the edge of Orange County, the oceanside cities of the **South Bay** and the **LA Harbor** share little in common except their proximity to the sea and insularity from the rest of the metropolis. While the bluffs around the beaches are the province of wealthy whites, poor and working–class whites, blacks and Latinos reside many miles inland, in bland suburbs like Carson and Hawthorne, and in bleak districts like North Long Beach. Overall, though, the area's balmy climate and windswept scenery make this one of the city's most visually appealing regions, at least by the shoreline.

The South Bay begins south of the airport, with three **south beach cities** that are smaller and more suburban than LA's other seaside towns, and worth a brief idyll. Further south, and visible all along this stretch of the coast, the **Palos Verdes Peninsula** occupies a wild, craggy stretch of coastline, with some rustic parks and pricey real estate – much of it behind locked gates – while rough-hewn **San Pedro** is a gritty working town that forms part of the site for the LA Harbor. Its counterpart, **Long Beach**, is best known as the home of the *Queen Mary*, even though it is also the region's second-largest city, with nearly half-a-million people. Hardly a major draw for visitors, **LA harbor** itself is a massive complex divided between San Pedro and Long Beach, consisting of so many ship passages, trucking routes, and artificial islands that the huge Vincent Thomas Bridge had to be built to carry travelers over the entire works.

Perhaps the most enticing place in the area is **Santa Catalina Island**, located twenty miles offshore and easily reached by ferry. Little visited, the interior of the island remains largely a wilderness, with many unique forms of plant and animal life, and there's just one significant center of population, **Avalon**, a charming city in which the main form of motorized transport is the golf cart.

South beach cities

South of LAX along the coast, you'll find few interesting sights, just the candy-striped stacks of the Scattergood steam plant, a few oil refineries, and LA's only

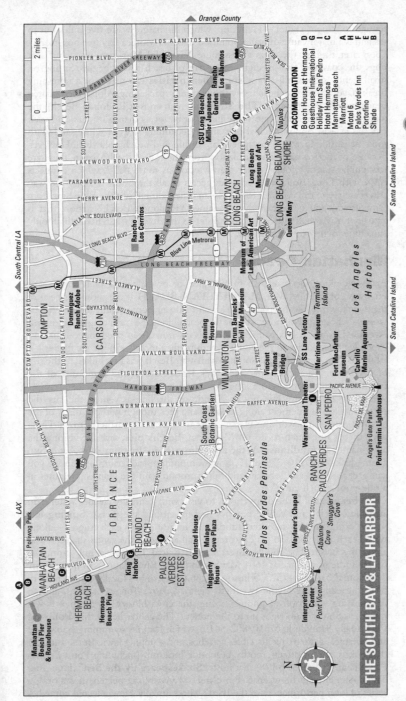

▲ Orange County

LOS ALAMITOS BLVD

PIONEER BLVD

SAN GABRIEL RIVER FREEWAY

605

405

SEAL BEACH BLVD

WESTMINSTER AVE

Rancho
Los Alamitos

CSI Long Beach/
Miller Japanese
Garden

Naples

DOWNTOWN
LONG BEACH

Long Beach
Museum of Art

LONG BEACH

BELMONT
SHORE

Museum of
Latin American Art

Queen Mary

Blue Line Metrorail

LONG BEACH FREEWAY

Los Angeles
Harbor

▼ Santa Catalina Island

Rancho
Los Cerritos

Dominguez
Ranch Adobe

COMPTON

CARSON

WILMINGTON

Banning
House

Drum Barracks
Civil War Museum

Vincent
Thomas
Bridge

SS Lane Victory

Maritime Museum

Fort MacArthur
Museum

Cabrillo
Marine Aquarium

Terminal
Island

▼ Santa Catalina Island

South Central LA ►

LAX ►

Polliwog Park

MANHATTAN
BEACH

Manhattan
Beach Pier
& Roundhouse

HERMOSA
BEACH

Hermosa
Beach Pier

TORRANCE

King Harbor

REDONDO
BEACH

PALOS
VERDES
ESTATES

Malaga
Cove Plaza

Haggerty
House

Olmsted House

South Coast
Botanic Garden

Warner Grand Theater

SAN PEDRO

PACIFIC AVENUE

Angel's Gate Park

Point Fermin Lighthouse

RANCHO
PALOS
VERDES

Palos Verdes Peninsula

Wayfarer's Chapel

Interpretive
Center
Point Vicente

Abalone
Cove Smuggler's
Cove

ACCOMMODATION

Beach House at Hermosa	D
Guesthouse International	G
Holiday Inn San Pedro	I
Hotel Hermosa	C
Manhattan Beach Marriott	A
Motel 6	H
Palos Verdes Inn	F
Portofino	E
Shade	B

0   2 miles

N

sewage-treatment center – Hyperion, which discharges waste five miles out to sea and is a major cause of water pollution in Santa Monica Bay (see box, p.138). Soon after, though, the main access route, **Vista del Mar**, rises up a bluff as it hugs the coastline, and an eight-mile strip of beach towns begins. Sitting on small, gently sloped hills, these **south beach cities** can make for a refreshing break if you like your beaches without trendy packaging. Along their shared beach boardwalk known as **The Strand** (which ends at Redondo Beach), the joggers and roller skaters are more likely to be locals than outsiders, and each city has at least one municipal pier and a beckoning strip of white sand, with most oceanside locations equipped for surfing and beach volleyball. However, because of the towns' relative isolation from the rest of the LA basin, there are few public transit choices, other than Metro bus route #232, which connects LAX with Long Beach and provides access to all three towns along the way. Alternately, you can connect to the Green Line light rail (via the Blue Line from Downtown) and get off at the misnamed "Redondo Beach" station, that is actually for Manhattan Beach, and transfer to that town's #126 line, which only runs infrequently during the day.

Manhattan Beach

Accessible along the bike path from Venice, or by car via PCH (Pacific Coast Highway) or Vista del Mar, **MANHATTAN BEACH** is the most northern of the three towns, a likeable place with a well-to-do air, home mainly to white-collar workers whose stucco houses sit near the beach, along the main drag of **Highland Avenue**. Despite its lack of pretension, this town has been rated the fourth-most expensive place to live in the country, with median incomes in the six figures.

Like its counterparts to the south, Manhattan Beach was first linked to the rest of LA by the Pacific Electric Railway's **Red Cars** at the beginning of the twentieth century, and before long this stretch was a favorite spot for pleasure-seekers of all types. While not as chaotic or thrilling as Venice, the city did provide a day's amusement along its sands and pier, though without many of the carnival games and working-class visitors of that more northerly town. These days, there's not much to do on Manhattan Beach's **pier**, save for visiting the aptly named **Roundhouse**. At the **aquarium** (Mon–Fri 3pm–dusk, Sat & Sun 10am–dusk; $2; ☎310/379-8117, ⊛www.roundhouseaquarium.org) inside you can peer at sharks and lobsters, and fiddle around with the helpless creatures in a tide-pool "touch tank."

The **beach** itself is the main reason to visit, with generally cleaner water than at Santa Monica and Venice beaches (except around the piers). **Surfing** is a major local pastime – an international surf festival occurs each August – along with beach volleyball. To play, just rent a ball at one of the rental shacks found along the beach. The mildly diverting **Historical Center**, a mile from the beach in the post office at 1601 Manhattan Beach Blvd (Sat & Sun noon–3pm; donation; ☎310/374-7575, ⊛history90266.org), exhibits locally crafted pottery from the early part of the twentieth century, native Tongva artifacts, and an illuminating collection of photos, tracing the city's history, from when it was known as Shore Acres right up to the present. The center lies within **Polliwog Park** (daily 8am–dusk; ☎310/802-5410), which features swimming pools, rose and botanical gardens, picnic tables, gazebos, and a sloping lawn. In the summer the park is one of fifteen, mostly beachside locations (including Point Fermin Park in San Pedro; see p.178) that hosts "**Shakespeare by the Sea**" (June–Aug Thurs–Sun usually between 7–8pm; free; ⊛www.shakespearebythesea.org), a series of local performances of the Bard's works, usually a few selected comedies that rotate between the sites. It's better than you might expect since, this being LA, there's always a large pool of actors to draw from.

Hermosa Beach and Redondo Beach

To the south, **HERMOSA BEACH**, across Longfellow Avenue, is smaller and less showy than Manhattan Beach, but the town is in many ways more enjoyable, with a hint of a bohemian feel — or as much of one as is possible in a town with scads of million-dollar homes. It also has a lively beachside strip, which is most energetic near the foot of the **pier** on Twelfth Street. The place is packed with restaurants and clubs, among them one of the South Bay's best-known nightspots, *The Lighthouse Cafe* (☎310/376-9833, ⓦwww.thelighthousecafe .net; see p.304). The area has long been a major hangout for revelers of all stripes, and a good time to come is during the **Fiesta Hermosa** (ⓦwww .fiestahermosa.com), a three-day event held twice a year, over Memorial Day and Labor Day, when you'll find music (including surf rock), tasty food, and displays of regional arts and crafts. Apart from ocean-based activities, the town boasts the lush **Hermosa Valley Greenbelt** – a former railroad easement that's now been turned into a long, grassy strip running between Valley Drive and Ardmore Avenue, which connects to Manhattan Beach and makes a good place to relax or to work out on any of several bike and jogging paths.

Further south, despite its familiar name and fine views of Palos Verdes' stunning greenery, **REDONDO BEACH**, across Herondo Street, is less inviting than its relaxed neighbor, with hardly any noteworthy sights. Condos and hotels line the beachfront, and the yacht-lined King's Harbor is off limits to curious visitors.

The Palos Verdes Peninsula

South of the beach cities, the **PALOS VERDES PENINSULA**, a great green mound marking LA's southwest corner, is known for its rugged beaches and secluded coves, sweeping views of the coastline, and some of the most expensive real estate in Southern California, or the nation for that matter. Originally intended as a "millionaires' colony" by 1920s developers, Palos Verdes has more or less worked out according to plan, with several gated communities like **Rolling Hills**, numerous multimillion-dollar estates, and an armada of private security guards making sure the place stays as exclusive as it looks. Despite this, the Palos Verdes Peninsula is one of the best spots for experiencing nature in the area (especially along Palos Verdes Drive), with sea cliffs and tide pools, and its oceanside scenery is nothing less than awe-inspiring. Keep in mind, though, that it's assumed none of the residents need public transportation, so almost none is available.

North Palos Verdes

The northwest section of the peninsula is largely ungated and accessible, with most attractions located near the coast of **PALOS VERDES ESTATES**, the first city founded on the peninsula, in 1939, and the one with by far the most significant architecture and public greenspace. The area was first laid out by **John Olmsted** and **Frederick Law Olmsted Jr** – sons of the famed designer

Once a month, the Palos Verdes Peninsula Land Conservancy offers **hiking tours** of some of the most invigorating spots on Palos Verdes, from Malaga Dunes to Portuguese Bend, including marshes, canyons, cliffs, and other dramatic vistas. The treks typically take place the second Saturday of the month, are free, and last two to three hours, sometimes in rather rugged environs, and focus on the ecological, historical, or cultural value of a given area – information you're not likely to discover very easily otherwise (information at ☎310/541-7613, ⓦwww.pvplc.com).

of New York's Central Park – who came here in the early twentieth century to design upscale neighborhoods and advise on the future direction of urban planning in LA (suggestions that were ahead of their time and were, predictably, ignored). Palos Verdes Estates amounts to a small-scaled version of what might have been had the Olmsted brothers had their way. Nearly one-third of its space is preserved as parkland, on which you may come across a roaming herd of peacocks. The town itself has a pseudo-European air, with a complete absence of stop lights along circuitous streets that overlook the ocean, and tightly controlled commercial development. Indeed, the town's early overseers were so committed to the period-revival aesthetic that all new designs, housing or otherwise, had to be reviewed and approved by an officially sanctioned "**art jury**" – surely the only time this has ever happened in LA.

The best place to soak in this "Old World" atmosphere is at **Malaga Cove Plaza**, Palos Verdes Drive at Via Corta, a Spanish Revival–flavored commercial and civic center with a central plaza and arcaded buildings, which the Olmsteds planned as a prototype for four other such areas in the city, none of which was ever built. The main draw here is the **Neptune Fountain**, a smaller replica of a 1563 structure in Bologna, Italy, of the same name, featuring a bronze sculpture and mock-late-Renaissance design. Elsewhere, much of the city's seaside architecture has a strong Mediterranean flair. Some examples are the **Olmsted House**, Paseo del Mar at Via Arroyo, an elegant Spanish Colonial estate with a walled garden that was built for Frederick Law Olmsted Jr, and the **Haggerty House**, 415 Paseo del Mar, an Italian-style villa that was built by the Olmsteds themselves, since reincarnated as the Neighborhood Church (☎310/378-9353, ⓦwww.neighborhoodchurchpve.org). For a different sort of experience, you might try locating the **Malaga Dunes**, a small ten-acre pocket of what was once an extensive ancient sand-dune ecosystem that led all the way up to the Ballona wetlands (see p.150). Now, this sandy terrain is all that remains, though it's worth exploring for its rich variety of birdlife, eucalyptus grove, and unusual habitat. To get there, go just east of the intersection of Palos Verdes Drive North and Palos Verdes Drive West, where the dunes lie on the hillside across the ravine. For more information or to take one of its occasional tours, contact the Palos Verdes Peninsula Land Conservancy (see box above).

South Coast Botanic Garden

Inland on the north peninsula, there are few compelling sights save the **South Coast Botanic Garden**, 26300 Crenshaw Blvd (daily 9am–5pm; $7; ☎310/544-1948; ⓦwww.southcoastbotanicgarden.org), a relaxing spot that was first home to a diatomite pit for 37 years, mined for diatoms, or single-celled algae fossils, and then to a giant landfill. In the 1950s and 1960s, LA dumped 3.5 million tons of its trash here, creating one of the bigger eyesores in the region, but since 1961, the landfill has been covered by layers of soil and successfully reclaimed as a garden, filled with exotic bromeliads, an expansive cactus garden, various palm trees, ferns, fuchsias, dahlias, herbs, and flowering plants, and even a small French-style garden. The only sign of its former life is the terrain itself, which, thanks to the subsiding of the garbage below, has a weirdly undulating landscape, peppered here and there with "exhaust" pipes that allow for the release of carbon dioxide and methane from the chemical stew underground.

South Palos Verdes

South of Palos Verdes Estates along Palos Verdes Drive, the beaches are more easily visited, and worthwhile for their significant natural attractions, one of which is the promontory of **Point Vicente**, sitting on high cliff walls above the Pacific Ocean. An **interpretive center**, 31501 Palos Verdes Drive W (daily 10am–5pm; donation; ☎310/377-5370) here provides displays on the native and Spanish history of the region, the area's biology and geology, and especially the presence of **whales** – which you might see from the point during their seasonal migrations (heaviest Dec–Jan and March–April), when they occasionally get close enough to photograph. Nearby, a **lighthouse**, 31550 Palos Verdes Drive W (second Sat of month 10am–3pm; free; ☎310/541-0334, ⊛www .palosverdes.com/pvlight), dates from 1926 and towers nearly two hundred feet above sea level in a dramatic cliffside setting.

South on Palos Verdes Drive, **Abalone Cove**, reached from a parking lot on Barkentine Road via a quarter-mile walk, boasts a cobblestoned beach, rock and tide pools, and, offshore, kelp beds alive with sea urchins, rock scallops, and the increasingly rare abalone. Don't be tempted to make off with any, though, since the place is an **ecological reserve** (Mon–Fri noon–4pm, Sat & Sun 9am–4pm; parking $5; ☎310/377-1222), and the authorities take a dim view of anyone stealing the cove's namesake.

The Wayfarer's Chapel and Portuguese Bend

While you're in the area, don't miss one of the peninsula's signature sights, **Wayfarer's Chapel**, 5755 Palos Verdes Drive, a masterpiece of pitched glass and

▲ Wayfarer's Chapel

wood that was designed by Frank Lloyd Wright's son, Lloyd. A tribute to the eighteenth-century Swedish scientist and mystic Emanuel Swedenborg, and funded by the Swedenborgian Church, the ultimate aim is for the redwood grove around the chapel to grow and entangle itself in the glass-framed structure – a symbolic fusing of human handiwork with the forces of nature. Unsurprisingly, the place is one of LA's top choices for weddings. The **visitor center** (daily 8am–5pm; ☎310/377-7919; ⓦwww.wayfarerschapel.org) lays out the history and architecture of the chapel, and can send you on your way with a self-guided walk through the dramatic site. A half-mile south, the coast at **Portuguese Bend** provides another striking ocean vista (though it's also prone to landslides), and was once the place where Portuguese whalers hunted gray whales for their blubber, which was harvested for its oil. Their trade came to an end due to a lack of firewood to run their operation, and the only trace of their activity is the place name they inspired. Still, the Bend occupies a thousand-acre preserve that, while ill-suited for home building and road construction (given the geological "slippage"), is great for hiking and biking in inspired surroundings.

San Pedro

Forming part of the site of the LA Harbor – or, as it likes to call itself, **Worldport LA** (ⓦwww.portoflosangeles.org) – scruffy **SAN PEDRO**, at the southeastern edge of the Palos Verdes Peninsula, is a diverse blue-collar town settled by immigrants from Portugal, Greece, Mexico, and Yugoslavia. As one of several places along the West Coast where labor strife erupted during the Depression, the city has a long tradition of populism and a nagging antipathy toward the city of Los Angeles, which annexed it in 1909, despite local opposition. And indeed, except for a thin, narrow strip that connects it to the rest of LA, San Pedro is very isolated from the goings on of its municipal landlord. For better or worse, everything about San Pedro, from its low-rise, old-time buildings to its maritime atmosphere, gives it a unique flavor that bears little in common with any place else in the metropolis. Locals use the American pronunciation (PEE-dro) for the town name, rather than the Spanish one.

Downtown San Pedro

San Pedro's harbor abuts the district's **downtown** and forms part of the massive Port of Los Angeles – with Long Beach, the biggest in the world outside of China and Singapore. The focus of all shipping activity is an industrial zone known as **Terminal Island**, a man-made island across the harbor's main channel that offers nothing but bleak industrial vistas of endless stacks of shipping containers. While you'll have to keep your distance from the docks and machinery, there are some points along the channel worth investigating.

Although it's heavily promoted, don't bother with downtown's overrated **Ports o' Call Village** – a dismal batch of wooden and corrugated-iron huts supposedly capturing the flavor of seaports around the world by way of its T-shirt and junk-food vendors.

To get a better sense of the harbor's history, a good place to start is the **SS Lane Victory**, in Berth 94, off Swinford Street, across from the shipyard (daily

The Port of San Pedro

First called the **"Bay of Smokes"** for the many fires set by Tongva natives along its shoreline, this formerly Spanish-controlled area was named in 1603 after **St Peter** and consolidated in 1784 into the territory owned by **Juan Domínguez**, whose ranch house is still standing in Compton (see p.165). Later, around the time it was usurped by the US in the Mexican–American War, San Pedro became a major center for the maritime trade of animal skins and beef tallow, and, by taking advantage of the Wilmington-to-Downtown LA **rail lines** of entrepreneur **Phineas Banning**, was linked to cities throughout the region in the 1870s. A decade later, the city was incorporated and began maturing as a port, with the action centered on **Timms Landing**. Although little physical evidence remains, you can get a sense of the place during this period by reading Richard Henry Dana's classic maritime book *Two Years Before the Mast*.

Around this time, **Collis Huntington** of the Southern Pacific Railroad was threatening to develop Santa Monica as the chief harbor of the region, clashing with many LA bigwigs as he did so, especially Harrison Gray Otis of the *Los Angeles Times*, whose newspaper did much to excite passions for a "free" harbor. In the end, Huntington's battle was unsuccessful, and by the end of the century, construction on a massive two-mile breakwater had begun in San Pedro and was completed a decade later. Shortly thereafter, Los Angeles mounted its annexation drive, and the military base **Fort MacArthur** was built next to the harbor. The world wars and a booming maritime economy further helped San Pedro to attract shipbuilding industries and commercial canneries, and by the 1950s, despite occasional labor conflicts, the district hit its peak.

The industrialization of the harbor took its toll on the environment, however, resulting on one occasion in smog so thick that the airport had to be shut down. Even worse, for many decades corporations pumped **DDT** directly into the sea near Palos Verdes, and today the contaminant sits in a giant deadly puddle on an offshore seabed. Along with this, economic **recessions** and industrial retrenchment contributed to San Pedro's decline, and by the 1980s the city was decayed, full of boarded-up businesses and postindustrial eyesores. In the last fifteen years, though, redevelopment money, some ecological clean-up, and the opening of new museums have helped revitalize the city, though it's still well off the itinerary of most casual LA visitors.

9am–3pm; $3; ☎310/519-9545, ⓦwww.lanevictory.org). The huge, ten-thousand-ton cargo ship was built in the shipyard in 1945 for World War II, also operated in Korea and Vietnam, and today is maintained by the Merchant Marine. Tours lead through its many cramped spaces, including the engine and radio rooms, crew quarters, galley, and bridge. If you're after a ride, the ship offers all-day summertime **cruises** to Santa Catalina Island (one weekend per month July–Sept; $125, kids $75; ☎310/519-9545), involving onboard meals, historical re-enactments with captured stowaway spies, and dogfights with old-fashioned biplanes and Japanese and American air squadrons. Overhead is the towering **Vincent Thomas Bridge**, California's third-longest suspension bridge, completed in 1963 to take over the work of transporting sailors and fishermen to and from Terminal Island.

There's more nautical history at the **Maritime Museum**, further south at Sampson Way at Sixth Street (Tues–Sat 10am–5pm, Sun noon–5pm; $3; ☎310/548-7618, ⓦwww.lamaritimemuseum.org). Occupying the old ferry tower, the museum is a storehouse for artifacts from the glory days of San Pedro's fishing industries, focusing on everything from old-fashioned clipper-ship voyages to contemporary diving expeditions. Besides plenty of model ships, the museum has interesting exhibits on Native American seacraft, navigation devices, and artful scrimshaw from the whaling era. Behind the museum, full-sized boats are displayed, including an old-fashioned schooner and a racing yacht. Next door, at Berth 86, the museum houses **Fireboat 2** in its own large, red building. Nearly one hundred feet long, this restored 1925 floating fire station served the LA Fire Department until 2003, spraying over ten thousand gallons a minute to put out naval fires around the harbor. Just west, the austere **Bloody Thursday Monument**, S Harbor Blvd at E 5th Street, is another reminder of the city's gritty past. Marking the 1934 strike by waterfront workers, many of them new immigrants, it commemorates the two who were killed when police and guards opened fire. It took more than fifty years for the authorities to officially acknowledge the event with this marker. Four blocks west of the Maritime Museum, old downtown San Pedro has been refurbished in recent years, thanks in part to the restoration of the opulent **Warner Grand Theater**, 478 W Sixth St (℡310/548-7672, ⓦwww.warnergrand.org), a terrific 1931 Zigzag Moderne moviehouse and performing-arts center with dark geometric details, grand columns, and sunburst motifs, a style that almost looks pre-Columbian. Also part of the clean-up effort is the **San Pedro Trolley** (Fri–Mon 10am–6pm; $1), a collection of three classic 1908 Pacific Electric Red Cars (two replicas, one restored) linking most of the city's major attractions, running alongside Harbor Boulevard and connecting the SS *Lane Victory* with the Cabrillo Marina at 22nd Street.

Fort MacArthur Museum

To the south, the **Fort MacArthur Museum, 3601 S Gaffey St** (Tues, Thurs, Sat & Sun noon–5pm; free; ℡310/548-2631, ⓦwww.ftmac.org) is sited on the former Battery Osgood, a gun emplacement at the original **Fort MacArthur**, a military post built in the late nineteenth century and named after General Arthur MacArthur – Douglas's dad. During the Cold War, the fort became a launch site for the early Nike-Ajax and later nuclear-warhead-equipped Hercules missiles, one of sixteen such sites in LA (the only other one now open to the public can be found in the Santa Monica Mountains; see "San Vicente Mountain Park," p.222). Reflecting its history, the fort's museum displays a clutch of military uniforms and old photographs, scads of antique radio equipment, as well as assorted disarmed bombs, mines, and missiles.

Point Fermin

At the tip of San Pedro, about a mile south of the trolley terminus, is **Point Fermin**, a cape that, at the end of the eighteenth century, explorer George Vancouver named for an early Franciscan missionary, Padre Fermín Lasuén. On the cape's far end, across Paseo del Mar, **Point Fermin Park** is a verdant, palm-laden strip of land sitting atop ocean bluffs that mark LA's southernmost point, as well as a Monarch butterfly wintering location. Hidden on the seaward edge of the bluffs, blocked off by chain-link fences, sits what's left of an early twentieth-century resort known as **Sunken City**, where the crumbling streets and housing foundations, much of them covered in graffiti, are officially off-limits to the public. Fans of *The Big Lebowski* will recognize this as the spot where Walter and the Dude try to dispose of their friend's ashes, to little avail. If you'd like to visit without trespassing, the Palos Verdes Peninsula Land Conservancy offers periodic **tours** of this and other interesting spots on the peninsula (see box, p.174).

Inland, **Point Fermin Lighthouse**, 807 Paseo del Mar (tours usually on the hour Tues–Sun 1–4pm; donation; ℡310/241-0684), once contained a 6600-candlepower light and beamed it 22 miles out to sea. Ending its service during World War II, the lighthouse fell into disrepair until it was renovated in the

1970s; in 2004, it was spruced up again and reopened to the public. Now you can get a sense of its quaint old Victorian style and take a peek from the chamber where the light used to beam; there's also an outdoor whale-watching station where you can read up on the winter migrations. Bottle-nosed dolphins can often be seen during their fall departure and spring return as well.

Just north is **Angel's Gate Park**, at 3601 Gaffey St, on a windswept hill overlooking the Pacific. At the top of the hill, a central pagoda contains the **Korean Bell of Friendship** (daily 10am–6pm), a 17-ton copper-and-tin gift to the city from South Korea. Inscribed with Korean characters and twelve lines representing the signs of the zodiac, the bell has no clapper; instead, a hefty log strikes the instrument only on three key days of the year: Korean and American independence days, and New Year's Eve. It's a fine spot for photos and, not surprisingly, a regular backdrop for weddings.

Cabrillo Marine Aquarium and beyond

Below the bluffs, a beachside path winds around the cape and reaches the excellent **Cabrillo Marine Aquarium**, 3720 Stephen White Drive (Tues–Fri noon–5pm, Sat & Sun 10am–5pm; $5, parking $1/hr; ☎310/548-7562, ⓦ www .cabrilloaq.org), where a diverse collection of marine life has been assembled into tanks and assorted displays: everything from predator snails and sea urchins to larger displays on otters, seals, and whales, plus the rare "sarcastic fringehead" (a peculiar fish whose name makes sense once you see it). Fully visible from the aquarium, a short jetty extends to a 1913 **breakwater** that is over 9200 feet long, constructed from three million tons of rock hauled over from Santa Catalina Island, and marks the harbor entrance. At the end of it sits the **Angel's Gate Lighthouse**, a 75-foot-tall Romanesque-styled monolith that blasts its automated foghorn twice per minute, using a rotating green light to direct ships into the protected harbor and helping them avoid the rock seawall.

Wilmington

North of San Pedro, **WILMINGTON** is the center of LA's petroleum industry, and holds the third-largest oil field in the entire US, extending from the Palos Verdes Peninsula to the bay outside Long Beach. The city's stark industrial landscape, dotted with derricks and refineries, massive towers spurting jets of flame, and cargo trucks barreling down the bleak Terminal Island Expressway, was used to great effect as the dystopic backdrop for the *Terminator* movies.

It's startling that such a grim setting could be the home of several key struc-tures from LA history, but it is the bleakness that protects them from zealous LA developers. The first, the grand **Banning House**, 401 East M St (guided tours at the bottom of the hour Tues–Thurs 12.30–2.30pm, Sat & Sun 12.30–3.30pm; $5; ☎310/548-7777, ⓦ www.banningmuseum.org), is an 1864 Greek Revival estate that was the residence of mid-nineteenth-century entrepreneur **Phineas Banning**, who made his fortune when the value of his land increased astro-nomically as the harbor was developed. Through his promotion of the rail link between Wilmington and Downtown LA, he also became known as "the father of Los Angeles transportation" (at a time when the local transit system was one of the best in the world), and helped push for the creation of a breakwater and lighthouse as well. However, in his final years, he argued against extending the rail line to San Pedro, which ultimately led to his own city's gradual decline, which was reversed only in the 1930s with the discovery of oil. The 23-room house remains an engaging spot to visit, full of opulent Victorian touches (chandeliers, elegant place settings, and the like) and several restored carriages and stagecoaches kept in an outside barn.

Also in town is the **Drum Barracks Civil War Museum**, 1052 Banning Blvd (hourly tours Tues–Thurs 10am–1pm, Sat & Sun 11.30am–2.30pm; $3; ☎310/548-7509, ⓦwww.drumbarracks.org), originally part of a military base called Camp Drum and named for its commander, Richard Drum. Today, the only building remaining is the rickety barracks, housing a hodgepodge of nineteenth-century military antiques and artifacts, notably a 34-star US flag and an early version of a machine gun, as well as a complement of guns and muskets. In the 1860s, this base was the Southwest headquarters for the US Army, which processed volunteers here before sending them to fight in the battles in the East, and a staging point for attacks on Confederate troops in neighboring Arizona and New Mexico. In later decades it became a base for federal soldiers fighting the native tribes of the Southwest.

Long Beach

Along with San Pedro, **LONG BEACH** is the home of the the Port of Long Beach and a sizable Southern California city in itself, with many acres of tract homes and flat, sprawling development. Not surprisingly, almost all of its interesting sights are grouped near the water, away from the port to the west, as are the tourist-oriented attractions around **Shoreline Drive** and the historic architecture of **downtown**. Long Beach Transit connects downtown with the major shoreline sights by shuttle bus (free), water taxi ($1), and catamaran ($3) (information at ☎562/591-2301, ⓦwww.lbtransit.org).

Once the stomping ground of off-duty naval personnel, Long Beach was packed with porn shops and sleazy bars until the 1980s, when a billion-dollar cash infusion spawned glossy office buildings and hotels, as well as a convention center, shopping mall, and the restoration of some of the best *c.*1900 buildings on the coast. Inland from downtown, however, it's a different story – bleak housing projects that run continuously north into impoverished South Central LA. The only real point of interest is **Rancho Los Cerritos**, 4600 Virginia Rd, northeast of the junction of the 405 and 710 freeways (Wed–Sun 1–5pm, tours Sat & Sun on the hour; free; ☎562/570-1755, ⓦwww.rancholoscerritos .org), the center of what was once a 27,000-acre tract that was part of a 1784 Spanish land grant of 300,000 acres. This U-shaped adobe dates from 1844 and sits on five leafy acres with a number of cypress and black locust trees, a delightful garden of roses, herbs, and exotic plants, and an antiquated water tower. The restored orchard features the kind of citrus fruits, avocados, macadamia nuts, and cherimoyas that once flourished here. Fortunately, the site is easily accessible, via the 710, to Long Beach's more prominent attractions near the harbor.

Shoreline Drive and around

Since the early 1900s, Long Beach has sold itself as a splashy resort and, while it's difficult to imagine a romantic getaway nestled behind an industrial port basin, the city keeps trying. Its major seaside amusements now sit close to the curving strip of **Shoreline Drive**, an area that was more of an entertainment center a century ago than it is today.

Around 1910, Long Beach developed its municipal pier, known as "**The Pike**," which teemed with street vendors and throngs of tourists queuing up for such thrilling rides as the Jack Rabbit Racer and Salt Water Plunge. The highlight was the legendary artwork of the **Looff Carousel**, designed in 1911 by master builder Charles Looff. After the carousel burned in 1943, the pier began its decline, and today it's long gone; these days, the focus of attention is **Shoreline Village**, just south of Shoreline Drive (Ⓦwww.shorelinevillage .com), a ragtag collection of middling shops and restaurants. Aside from the bikes and rollerblades for rent here, the only real draw is the **Tallship American Pride**, a 130ft cutter which is a simulation of an 1848 vessel, offering tourists three-hour whale-watching outings (Sat 10am–1pm & 1.30–4.30pm; $35) and brunch and dinner cruises around the harbor (Sat & Sun times and dates vary; $45–49; by reservation only at ℡714/970-8801, Ⓦwww.americanpride.org).

North of Shoreline Village, along Ocean Boulevard, a row dominated by upscale corporate hotels has become the most visible symbol of Long Beach's renovation. Among them stands the appealing 1926 **Breakers Hotel**, 200 E Ocean Blvd, twelve sandstone-clad stories of Spanish Baroque Revival design topped by a green copper roof. Although the hotel itself now serves as senior housing, the top-floor *Sky Room* bar and restaurant (℡562/983-2703) is still a good spot for a drink in Art Deco surroundings. Two blocks south, Seaside Way connects with Shoreline Drive to create the circuit used for the **Long Beach Grand Prix** (tickets at ℡1-888/82-SPEED, Ⓦwww.longbeachgp.com), an Indy car race that attracts several hundred thousand spectators in mid-April for a three-day event.

Around a lagoon south of Shoreline Drive, the intriguing, if pricey, **Aquarium of the Pacific** (daily 9am–6pm; $21, kids $12; ℡562/590-3100, Ⓦwww .aquariumofpacific.org) exhibits the aquatic flora and fauna of three distinct regions, namely the local Southern Pacific, Northern Pacific, and tropical zones. There are more than ten thousand species here, from the familiar sea lions and otters, tide-pool creatures and assorted ocean flora, to the more exotic leopard sharks and giant Japanese spider crabs. From behind the glass of the Shark Lagoon, you can get an up-close look at the pearly-white grins of these deadly predators. Outside, between November and March, more than fifteen thousand nemeses of the shark cruise the "**Whale Freeway**" past Long Beach on their annual migration to and from winter breeding and birthing grounds in Baja California. Of several tour operators in the area, Harbor Breeze, at Rainbow Harbor next to the aquarium (℡562/432-4900, Ⓦwww.longbeachcruises.com), operates good two-hour whale-watching trips for $20 per adult, $10 per child.

Along Ocean Boulevard, the four pastel "**islands**" visible offshore are not resort colonies, but rather oil-drilling platforms painted in soothing colors and each named, oddly enough, after a deceased NASA astronaut. This is Long Beach's attempt to beautify its harbor, which has over four hundred oil and gas wells operating at any one time.

The Queen Mary and Scorpion submarine

Long Beach's most famous attraction is the mighty ocean liner **Queen Mary**, moored on Pier H at the end of Queens Highway South (daily 10am–6pm; $23 self-guided tours, kids $12; combo tickets with Aquarium of the Pacific $35, kids $19; ℡562/435-3511, Ⓦwww.queenmary.com), acquired by the city in

1964 with the sole aim of boosting tourism, which it has succeeded in doing, well beyond expectations. The ship lies across the bay, opposite Shoreline Village, and is accessible either by a lengthy walk or Long Beach Transit (see p.180). Now a luxury hotel, the ship offers exhibits that suggest that all who sailed on the vessel – the flagship of the Cunard Line from the 1930s until the 1960s – enjoyed the extravagantly furnished lounges and luxurious cabins, all carefully restored and kept sparkling. But a glance at the spartan third-class cabins reveals the real story: the tough conditions experienced by the impoverished migrants who left Europe hoping to start a new life in the US. The red British telephone kiosks around the decks and the cheesy displays in the engine room and

▲ The Scorpion submarine

wheelhouse don't help, but it's nonetheless a marvelous ship. Apart from the wealth of gorgeous Art Deco details (glasswork, geometric decor, and stream-lining), there are also stores and restaurants, and even a wedding chapel, and the site hosts numerous festivals throughout the year, from a celebration of all things Scottish to a reggae fest. In addition, various lounges, clubs, and cabarets compete for your attention, and there are assorted "ghost" walks and Halloween events that try to make you believe the old boat is haunted.

A later addition to the *Queen Mary* site, the **Scorpion submarine** (same hours as Queen Mary; $11, or combo ticket $30; ⓦ www.russiansublongbeach .com), was used in the service of the Soviet, and then Russian, navy until 1994, carrying a payload of 22 nuclear weapons and powered by diesel engines – a rather creaky means of locomotion for a craft built in 1972. It's worth a look for its antiquated technology and cramped crew quarters, and makes for a bracing experience after taking a sanitized tour of the *Queen Mary*.

Downtown Long Beach

Running from Magnolia Avenue to Alamitos Boulevard and Ocean Boulevard to Tenth Street, **downtown Long Beach** offers a wide array of boutiques, antique dealers, and bookstores, many of them around a three-block strip known as **The Promenade**, lined with touristy restaurants that can get quite busy on weekend nights. The downtown core is easily reached from Downtown LA via the Blue Line light rail, which terminates two blocks west of the Promenade at **Pine Avenue**. This stretch has some of the city's best-preserved architecture – historic-revival buildings that have since been reborn as hotels, artists' lofts, galleries, and nightclubs. Highlights include the **First National Bank Building**, 115 Pine Ave, a 1900 Beaux Arts structure with a resplendent clock tower; the 1903 **Masonic Temple**, no. 230, a triple-gabled building with a brilliant sun mural inside on its second story; and the **Rowan Building**, no. 201, a vibrant 1931 Art Deco creation with detailed terracotta decor. In the vicinity, and not to be missed by readers, is one of the largest used booksellers in California, Acres of Books, 240 Long Beach Blvd (ⓣ 562/437-6980, ⓦ www .acresofbooks.com), located on this spot for nearly fifty years.

Further east is the striking **Villa Riviera**, 800 E Ocean Blvd (ⓦ www .villariviera.net), a fourteen-story Gothic Revival apartment block, recognizable by the high dormers on its pitched copper roof, pointed octagonal turret, and narrow ground-level archways. Curved to accommodate the bend in Ocean Boulevard, the Villa was the second-tallest building in all of LA when built in 1929, and still strikes many as one of its most impressive. Just down the block, the 1904 **Tichenor House**, 852 E Ocean Blvd, a private, U-shaped Craftsman residence with Japanese touches, was designed by the firm of Greene & Greene (see Pasadena's Gamble House, p.196) for an early Long Beach civic leader. It's the first house for which they also designed the interior furnishings, which would become their standard practice. Several blocks north, the **Museum of Latin American Art**, 628 Alamitos Ave (Tues–Fri 11.30am–7pm, Sat 11am–7pm, Sun 11am–6pm; $5; ⓣ 562/437-1689, ⓦ www.molaa.com), is devoted to the broad subject of Hispanic art. Showcasing artists from Mexico to South America, the absorbing collection includes big names like Diego Rivera and José Orozco, as well as lesser-known newcomers working in styles that range from high modernism to magical realism. Four blocks west, **St Anthony Roman Catholic Church**, 600 Olive Ave (ⓣ 562/590-9223), is one of LA's most colorful churches, an appealing mishmash of historic styles constructed in 1933 and remodeled two decades later. Note the eye-catching

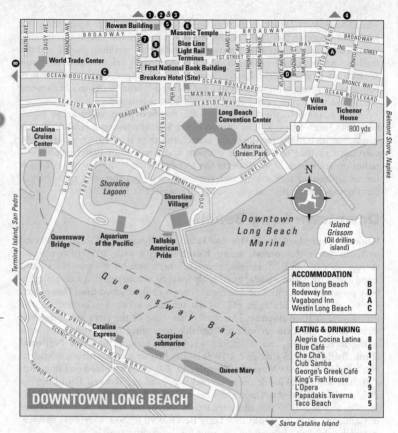

▲ ● ❶, ❷ & ❸

Rowan Building ⑤

⑥ Masonic Temple

BROADWAY

World Trade Center

⑦ Blue Line
Light Rail
Terminus

⑧ First National Bank Building

⑨ Breakers Hotel (Site)

OCEAN BOULEVARD

Villa
Riviera

Tichenor
House

0   800 yds

Catalina
Cruise
Center

Long Beach
Convention Center

Marina
Green Park

Shoreline
Lagoon

Shoreline
Village

Downtown
Long Beach
Marina

Island
Grissom
(Oil drilling
island)

N

Queensway
Bridge

Aquarium
of the Pacific

Tallship
American
Pride

Queensway Bay

Catalina
Express

Scorpion
submarine

Queen Mary

ACCOMMODATION

Hilton Long Beach	B
Rodeway Inn	D
Vagabond Inn	A
Westin Long Beach	C

EATING & DRINKING

Alegria Cocina Latina	8
Blue Café	6
Cha Cha's	1
Club Samba	4
George's Greek Café	2
King's Fish House	7
L'Opera	9
Papadakis Taverna	3
Taco Beach	5

DOWNTOWN LONG BEACH

▼ Santa Catalina Island

neo-Gothic stained glass and hexagonal turrets, along with the facade's sizable Byzantine golden mosaic, depicting the Virgin Mary amid flocks of angels.

East Long Beach

A mile east from the Villa Riviera, the **Long Beach Museum of Art**, 2300 E Ocean Blvd (Tues–Sun 11am–5pm, Thurs closes 8pm; $7; ☎562/439-2119, Ⓦ www.lbma.org), is housed in a stately 1912 Craftsman home, featuring a modest collection of early modernism, folk art, and Southern Californian art. The museum is notable for its hoard of video art – one of the country's biggest collections – some 3000 pieces in all. A mile further, the affluent **Belmont Shore** district is full of designer shops and yuppified cafés, though there's not much to see.

From here, Second Street crosses man-made Alamitos Bay to reach the island community of **Naples**, supposedly designed after the Italian city, if that city was loaded with rows of T-shirt and trinket vendors. While the thin, circular **canal** may give you a romantic thrill during hour-long boat rides with picnic meals and serenading gondoliers (daily 11am–11pm; $75 for two people; call Gondola Getaway for details ☎562/433-9595, Ⓦ www.gondolagetawayinc.com), the place is still little more than a tacky aquatic suburb thronged with tourists.

Two miles north, **Rancho Los Alamitos**, 6400 Bixby Hill Rd (Wed–Sun 1–4pm, tours every half-hour; free; ☎562/431-3541, ⓦwww.rancholosalamitos .com), is a grand version of the typical nineteenth-century adobe, with six historic buildings and plenty of antiques and relics from the Spanish and Mexican eras. Built in 1806, the renovated ranch house is noteworthy for its four acres of gardens, where you can wander amid herbs, roses, cacti, jacaranda, and oleander planted along the terraces and landscaped walks. Nearby, the campus of California State University at Long Beach is best known for its towering, dark-blue aluminum **Pyramid**, an athletic complex, but is mainly worth visiting for the **Earl Burns Miller Japanese Garden**, 1250 Bellflower Blvd (Tues–Fri 8am–3.30pm, Sun noon–4pm; free; ☎562/985-8885, ⓦwww .csulb.edu/~jgarden), a peaceful spot amid weeping willows, bamboo, and Japanese maples.

Santa Catalina Island

Overlooked by many visitors, **SANTA CATALINA ISLAND** is an inviting mix of uncluttered beaches and wild hills twenty miles off the coast. Claimed by the Portuguese in 1542 as San Salvador, and renamed by the Spanish in 1602, it has stayed firmly outside the historical mainstream. Since 1811, when the indigenous Tongva Indians were forced to resettle on the mainland, the island has been in private ownership, and has over the years grown to be something of a resort – a process hastened by businessman **William Wrigley Jr** (part of the chewing-gum dynasty), who financed the Art Deco–styled **Avalon Casino**, the island's major landmark, in the 1920s, and used the island as a spring-training site for his baseball team, the Chicago Cubs, until the early 1950s.

Since 1975 the island has been almost entirely owned by the **Catalina Island Conservancy**, which maintains a sizable nature preserve here, and in more recent years Catalina has become a popular destination for boaters and nature lovers, and its small marina swells with luxury yachts and cruise ships in summer. Even so, the elegant hotels are unobtrusive among the whimsical architecture, and cars are rare – there's a ten-year waiting list to ferry one over. Consequently, most of the three thousand islanders walk, ride bikes, or drive electrically powered golf carts. Note that the island's one town, Avalon, narrowly escaped devastation in the May 2007 **wildfires**, which damaged nearly 5000 acres of the more rural parts of the island. Much of the area west of Avalon remains burned over, so be sure to call ahead before scheduling anything in the hinterlands, due to rebuilding and habitat restoration efforts.

Avalon and Two Harbors

The main city on the island, **AVALON**, can be fully explored on foot in an hour or two; pick up a map from the **Chamber of Commerce** at the foot of the ferry pier (☎310/510-1520, ⓦwww.catalinachamber.com). The town itself offers the usual assortment of T-shirt vendors, restaurants, and boat operators, but the undeniable highlight is the resplendent **Avalon Casino**, on a promontory north of downtown at 1 Casino Way. Built as a dance hall and moviehouse, this 1920s structure still features an Art Deco ballroom and lavishly decorated auditorium: painted wild horses and unicorns roam through

One of the major challenges of **visiting Santa Catalina** is just getting to the island itself and making arrangements to stay. It's not difficult by any means, but does require planning to make sure you don't end up staying in an overpriced resort and paying top-dollar for a tour that you might otherwise take for cheap.

Arrival and transportation

Depending on the season, round-trip **ferry** trips run several times daily from Long Beach, and cost $50–60 round trip. Operators include Catalina Explorer (℗1-877/432-6276, ⓦwww.catalinaferry.com), Catalina Express (℗1-800/481-3470, ⓦwww.catalinaexpress.com), and, from Newport Beach, Catalina Flyer (℗949/673-5245, ⓦwww.catalina-flyer.com).

Santa Catalina Island Company (℗1-800/626-1496, ⓦwww.visitcatalinaisland .com) offers tours of the Avalon Casino ($16), bus trips through the outback ($69–99), and harbor cruises and glass-bottom-boat rides ($16–36), while **Catalina Adventure Tours** provides slightly cheaper versions of the same ($15–63; ℗310/510-2888, ⓦwww.catalinaadventuretours.com). **Golf carts**, for which you need a driver's license, and **bikes** (both banned from the rough roads outside Avalon) can be rented from stands in town. Bikes run $12–40 per day, depending on the model, while golf carts are much steeper, at $35–40 per hour only. Near the boat dock, Brown's Bikes is one of the more popular options (℗310/510-0986, ⓦwww.catalinabiking.com), with rentals from $12/day for a one-speed to $30/day for a six-speed.

Accommodation

The cost of the cheapest reasonable accommodation in Avalon hovers upwards of $100, and most beds are booked up throughout the summer and at weekends. The most interesting hotel is the *Zane Grey Pueblo*, 199 Chimes Tower Rd (℗310/510-0966 or 1-800/446-0271; ⓦwww.zanegreypueblohotel.com; $50), which has sixteen rooms overlooking the bay or mountains, with an enticing off-season (Nov–April) weekday rate of $65. The cheapest overall is usually the *Atwater*, 125 Sumner Ave (May–Oct only; ℗310/510-2500 or 1-800/626-1496; $85), though there are units here that reach $390. If you really have a bundle to spend, the *Inn on Mt. Ada*, 398 Wrigley Road (℗310/510-2030, ⓦwww.innonmtada.com; $390), is the final word in Catalina luxury. One interesting choice is the *Banning House Lodge*, near Two Harbors (℗310/510-4228), a rambling Craftsman home that has 11 bed-and-breakfast rooms with a courtyard, continental breakfast, and private baths ($119 weekdays, $159 weekends; rates jump by $80 in the summer). The only budget option is camping: Hermit Gulch is the closest site to Avalon and the busiest. Four other sites in Catalina's interior – Blackjack, Little Harbor, Parsons Landing, and Two Harbors (all $12 per person, kids $6) – are much more distant, but also roomier. Book at ℗310/510-8368 or ⓦwww.scico.com/camping.

Sports and outdoor activities

The waters around Catalina are rich in yellowtail, calico bass, barracuda, and sharks. On Green Pier, Joe's Rent-a-Boat (℗310/510-0455, ⓦwww.catalina.com/rent-a-boat.html) can get you started **fishing** with basic runabouts starting at $45/hour or $225/day, as well as kayaks ($15/hr) and pedal boats ($15/hr) for pleasure cruising using your own horsepower. On Descanso Beach beyond the Casino, Descanso Beach Ocean Sports (℗310/510-1226, ⓦwww.kayakcatalinaisland.com) has similar kayak-rental rates, as well as **snorkeling** packages ($64/four hrs) and guided kayak tours ($38–78). **Snorkel** and **scuba** gear is available for rent at Catalina Divers Supply, on the pier and at the Casino (℗310/510-0330 or 1-800/353-0330, ⓦwww .catalinadiverssupply.com), for $27 per day for a complete snorkel set, and $55 for the full scuba package.

a forest on the side wall, while a sleek superhero rides a wave on the front screen and, above it all, a waif-like Botticelli Venus stands atop a seashell over the heads of two thunderbolt-clutching gods. Perhaps not surprisingly, the muralist for the theater, John Beckman, also helped design the equally fanciful Chinese Theatre in Hollywood, and you can still see Hollywood movies here on evenings throughout the year – an absolute must for any movie buffs who venture out this far. You can **tour** this historic place (50min; $16; by reservation at ℡1-800/626-5440) and get a glimpse of the 1929 pipe organ and upper ballroom where the big bands used to play. Included in the tour price is admission to a small **museum** (daily 10am–4pm, Jan–Mar closed Thurs; $4; ℡310/510-2414 ⓦwww.catalinamuseum.com) on the casino premises, which displays Native American artifacts from Catalina's past, fishing and ranching stories, tiles from local potters, old photographs and exhibits on biology, and Hollywood's use of the island as a scenic backdrop.

To the south, the **Zane Grey Pueblo Hotel**, 199 Chimes Tower Rd, is the former home of the Western author, who visited Catalina with a film crew to shoot *The Vanishing American* and liked the place so much that he stayed, building for himself this "Hopi pueblo" house, complete with beamed ceiling, stark white walls, and thick wooden front door. The hotel rooms (see box opposite) are themed after his books, and the pool is shaped like an arrowhead. Similarly, the **Inn on Mt. Ada**, at 398 Wrigley Terrace Rd on the south hillside of Avalon, was the 1921 Colonial Revival home of William Wrigley and is now an elegant hotel (see box opposite), with sweeping ocean views and a fine garden. Also striking is the **Holly Hill House**, 718 Crescent Ave, an 1890 Queen Anne cottage on a high bluff overlooking the bay, with an elegant, striped conical tower, and wraparound verandas.

Several miles southwest of Avalon, the **Wrigley Memorial and Botanical Garden**, 1400 Avalon Canyon Rd (daily 8am–5pm; $5; ℡310/510-2595), administered by the Catalina Island Conservancy, displays all manner of natural delights on 38 acres, but is especially strong on native, endangered plants, such as indigenous varieties of manzanita, ironwood mahogany, and the wild tomato – a poisonous member of the nightshade family. Also fascinating is the Wrigley memorial, where a striking **cenotaph**, made from Georgia marble, blue flagstone, and red roof-tiles, honors the chewing-gum baron. A grand tiled staircase leads to an imposing Art Deco mausoleum, where Wrigley was to have been interred – though he's buried elsewhere. While you're in the vicinity, you can check out the **Nature Center at Avalon Canyon**, 1202 Avalon Canyon Rd (June–Aug daily 10am–4pm; free; ℡310/510-0954), which has displays on the endemic flora and fauna and the island, its unique ecosystem, and the importance of conservation to the area.

Northwest of Avalon, the small, isolated resort town of **TWO HARBORS** sits on a small strip of land that connects Cherry Cove and Catalina Harbor. With a large marina and campground, the town is suitable enough for outdoor activities like kayaking, snorkeling, and scuba diving, but otherwise there's little to see.

The island interior

If you have the opportunity and a few spare days to explore it, venture into the rugged **island interior**, comprising 42,000 acres of wilderness, untouched by anything but the occasional wildfire, and home to many indigenous creatures and plants, and more than one hundred types of native birds. You can take a **bus tour** if time is short (see box opposite); if it isn't, get a map and a free

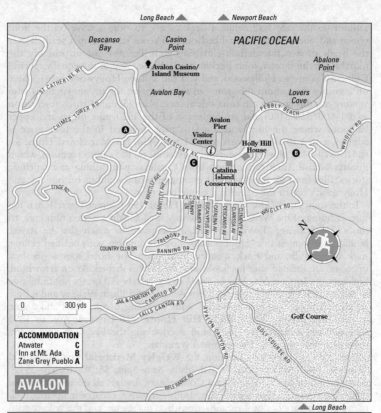

Long Beach ▲   ▲ Newport Beach

PACIFIC OCEAN

Descanso Bay

Casino Point

Avalon Casino/
Island Museum

Abalone Point

ST CATHERINE WY

CHIMES TOWER RD

Avalon Bay

Lovers Cove

PEBBLY BEACH

WRIGLEY RD

Ⓐ

STAGE RD

Avalon Pier

CRESCENT AV

Visitor Center

ⓘ

Holly Hill House

Ⓑ

Ⓒ

Catalina Island Conservancy

W WHITLEY AVE

E WHITLEY AVE

BEACON ST

SUMMER AV

SUNNY INN

EUCALYPTUS AV

CATALINA AV

DESCANSO AV

CLARISSA AV

CLEMENTE AV

WRIGLEY RD

N

TREMONT ST

COUNTRY CLUB DR

BANNING DR

JAIL & CEMETERY RD

CARRILLO DR

FALLS CANYON RD

AVALON CANYON RD

GOLF COURSE RD

Golf Course

0   300 yds

ACCOMMODATION
Atwater   C
Inn at Mt. Ada   B
Zane Grey Pueblo   A

RIFLE RANGE RD

AVALON

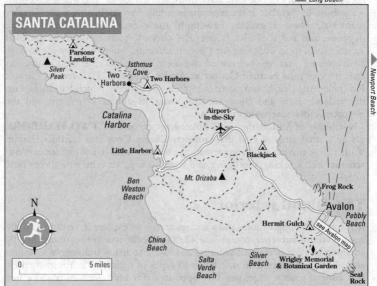

▲ Long Beach

SANTA CATALINA

Parsons Landing

Isthmus Cove

Silver Peak

Two Harbors

Two Harbors

▲ Newport Beach

Catalina Harbor

Airport-in-the-Sky

Little Harbor

Blackjack

Ben Weston Beach

Mt. Orizaba ▲

Frog Rock

Avalon

Pebbly Beach

Hermit Gulch

see Avalon map

N

China Beach

Salta Verde Beach

Silver Beach

Wrigley Memorial & Botanical Garden

Seal Rock

0   5 miles

wilderness permit, which allows you to hike and camp, from the Chamber of Commerce or from the **Catalina Island Conservancy**, 125 Claressa Ave (daily 8.30am–3.30pm; ☏310/510-2595, Ⓦwww.catalinaconservancy.org), which owns and manages 88 percent of the island's land; mountain biking (the only type allowed in the outback) requires a $65 permit, or $90 per family.

There are some unique **animals** roaming about the wildlands, among them the Catalina Shrew, so rare it's only been sighted twice, and the Catalina Mouse, bigger and healthier than its mainland counterpart thanks to abundant food and lack of natural enemies. There are also foxes, ground squirrels, pigs, bald eagles, and quail, along with **buffalo**, descended from a group of fourteen left behind by a Hollywood crew filming Zane Grey's *The Vanishing American*; there is now a sizable herd of 150 or more wandering about the island.

8

The San Gabriel and San Fernando valleys

R unning north of central LA, below the crests of their respective mountain ranges, lie the expansive **SAN GABRIEL** and **SAN FERNANDO VALLEYS**, which start close to one another a few miles north of Downtown and span outwards in opposite directions – east to the deserts around Palm Springs for the sloped foothills of the San Gabriel, west to Ventura on the California coast for the relatively flat San Fernando.

In the San Gabriel Valley, on the east side of the Verdugo Mountains, **Pasadena** is a cultural counterweight of sorts to the city of LA, a small,

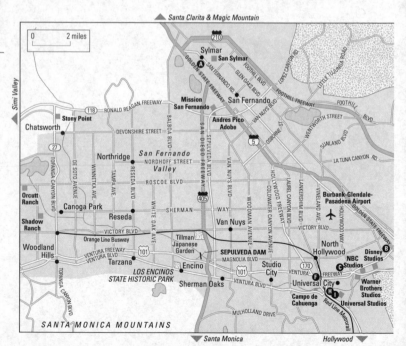

patrician town full of great architecture and diligent historic preservation, for years the province of old money but more recently enlivened by tourist shopping dollars. The neighboring cities of **South Pasadena** and **San Marino** also have their charms, particularly the latter's Huntington Library and Gardens, though the rest of the San Gabriel Valley holds much more dispersed pleasures – including the LA Arboretum and San Gabriel Mission – worth a look only if you're staying in the LA region for at least a week.

North of the Hollywood Hills, the San Fernando Valley offers a more sprawling landscape, stitched together by seemingly endless ribbons of asphalt under a boiling summer sun. The upper-middle-class suburb of **Glendale** is mainly home to the famous cemetery Forest Lawn; while **Burbank**, further west, is studio central, accommodating the likes of Disney, Warner Bros, NBC, and, in its own municipal enclave, Universal – all but Disney are tourable. Further west are the bulk of LA's suburbs, known collectively as "**the Valley**," with historic attractions here and there, but mostly known for their copious minimalls. At the apex of the triangular San Fernando Valley, places like **San Fernando** have a rich heritage, while further north, exciting **Magic Mountain** easily outdoes Disneyland for death-defying rides.

The San Gabriel Valley

Set at the foothills of the San Gabriel Mountains, the **San Gabriel Valley** escapes the derision that Angelenos pile upon the San Fernando Valley. However, though it has genuine cultural cachet in many places, it contains just as many dreary

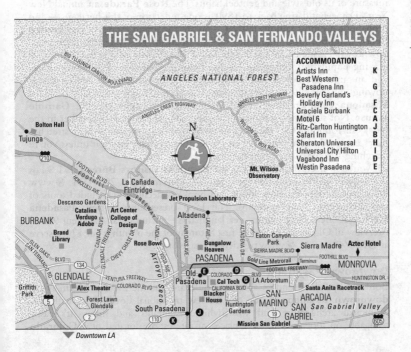

expanses as anywhere in the region – especially the eastern side, where you can breathe in some of the basin's worst smog, blown this way from central LA.

After its early settlement by native Tongva tribes and the later arrival of Spanish soldiers and missionaries, the San Gabriel Valley had become by the beginning of the twentieth century a choice region for American agriculture, growing predominantly grapes and citrus crops. Railroads brought new migrants, and by the 1950s, the foothills of the San Gabriel Mountains developed into another populous arm of LA, with suburban ranch houses and swimming pools taking the place of ranches and orange groves. One thing that has not changed, however, is the torrential flooding. Thanks to its specific climate and geography, the Valley has always been a prime spot for **winter deluges**: great cascades of water sweep down the hillsides, turning into mudslides by the time they reach the foothills, and then charging through the canyons and destroying all in their wake – including encroaching homes. This problem has been an occasional impediment to hillside growth, but with the creation of huge "**catch basins**" to contain the mudslides, real-estate developers have been able to push growth further up into the mountains.

Pasadena

At the western edge of the San Gabriel Valley, **PASADENA** is a mix of old-fashioned charm and contemporary appeal, no longer just the domain of the blue-haired mavens clichéd in *Little Old Lady from Pasadena*, the famous surf-pop song by Jan & Dean.

Located ten miles northeast of Downtown LA, and connected to it by the rickety Pasadena Freeway (110 north), Pasadena was, like much of LA, settled by Midwesterners (in this case from Indiana) and even today retains a measure of its old style and genteel habits. The **Rose Parade**, an annual New Year's Day event dating back to 1890, is one reflection of this heritage — and probably LA's most famous festival — as are the grand estates of the **Arroyo Seco** neighborhood and the stylish Spanish Revival architecture of downtown Pasadena. In the 1970s and 1980s, Pasadena was in a slump, its graying population dying and leaving behind a number of decaying estates and an unkempt downtown. However, once urban-renewal dollars began flowing in the 1990s, tourists rediscovered the town, especially its **Old Pasadena** commercial strip and architectural treasures like the **Gamble House**. Not surprisingly, most of the city's appeal can be found either in the blocks surrounding Old Pasadena or in Arroyo Seco; while the burg stretches miles eastward, there's little reason to venture in that direction unless you're searching for cheap accommodation.

If you're in need of information, the **Pasadena Visitors Bureau**, 171 S Los Robles Ave (Mon–Fri 8am–5pm, Sat 10am–4pm; ☎626/795-9311, ⊛www .pasadenacal.com), provides **maps** and booklets detailing self-guided tours of city architecture and museums. The local preservation society, **Pasadena Heritage**, offers regular tours area landmarks – including an excellent 90min overview of Old Pasadena on the first Saturday of the month (9am; $10; reserve at ☎626/441-6333, ⊛www.pasadenaheritage.org).

Downtown Pasadena

Bordered by Lake Avenue, California Boulevard, and the 210 and 710 freeways, **downtown Pasadena** is one of LA's few traditional downtowns, with fine municipal architecture and worthwhile restaurants and shops. It's easily navigable on foot as well: most places of interest are located near **Colorado**

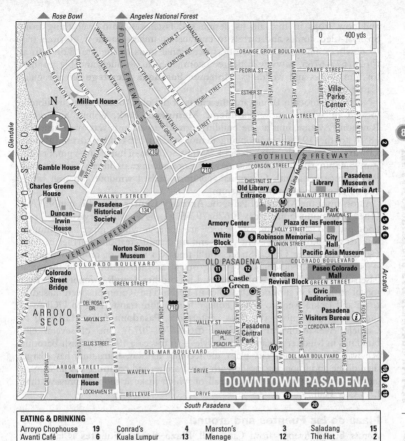

Rose Bowl ▲   Angeles National Forest ▲

DOWNTOWN PASADENA

0   400 yds

N

Millard House

Gamble House

Charles Greene House

Duncan-Irwin House

Pasadena Historical Society

Norton Simon Museum

Colorado Street Bridge

ARROYO SECO

Tournament House

Villa-Parke Center

Old Library Entrance ❸

Library

Pasadena Museum of California Art

Pasadena Memorial Park

Armory Center

White Block ❼ ❽ Robinson Memorial

❿

Plaza de las Fuentes

City Hall

Pacific Asia Museum

OLD PASADENA

⓫ ⓬

⓭ Castle Green

⓮

Venetian Revival Block

Paseo Colorado Mall

Civic Auditorium

Pasadena Visitors Bureau ℹ

Pasadena Central Park

⓯

⓳

⓴

South Pasadena ▼   ▼

❶

❷

EATING & DRINKING

Arroyo Chophouse	19	Conrad's	4	Marston's	3	Saladang	15
Avanti Café	6	Kuala Lumpur	13	Menage	12	The Hat	2
Azeen's	9	La Estrella	1	Old Towne Pub	7	Wolfe Burger	5
Burger Continental	18	La Luna Negra	14	Pie 'n' Burger	17	Xiomara	8
Café Santorini	10	Market City Caffé	11	Rose Tree Cottage	20	Zona Rosa	16

Boulevard, the city's commercial axis. On and around this boulevard, between Fair Oaks and Euclid avenues, is **Old Pasadena** (Ⓦ www.oldpasadena.org), a mix of antique sellers, used book and record stores, cafés, clothing boutiques, and theaters, which gets quite crowded on weekends. The handy **Gold Line** light rail (see p.29) links directly to Downtown LA, with the stop at Memorial Park being the most convenient for Old Pasadena. Although there are few official sights on the strip itself – other than elegant architecture, such as the Italianate **White Block**, Fair Oaks Avenue at Union Street, and the 1894 **Venetian Revival Building**, 17 S Raymond Ave – Old Pasadena does feature decent attractions within several blocks.

Just south of Colorado Boulevard is the fascinating **Castle Green**, also known as "Hotel Green," 99 S Raymond St, formerly a 1903 resort that centered around a now-demolished hotel across the street. Later additions included the apartments that remain today, plus a **bridge** that crossed Raymond Avenue to link the structures. Although the walkway, which was billed as the "Bridge of Sighs" after the Venetian version, has been sliced in half and now stops in mid-air, its design still fascinates, with everything from Spanish-tiled domes and turrets to curvaceous arches – a short, glorious trip to nowhere. The Castle itself offers occasional tours of the site ($20; info at ☎626/577-6765, ⓦwww.castlegreen.com), which is understandably popular for film shoots and weddings. Moreover, **Pasadena Heritage** offers regular Castle tours.

North of Colorado Boulevard, the **ruins** of the old Romanesque city library, located in what is now **Pasadena Memorial Park**, Walnut Street and Raymond Avenue, hint at the building's grandeur when it was open from the 1880s to the 1930s, before being demolished in 1954. The current **Public Library**, three blocks away at 285 E Walnut St (Mon–Thurs 9am–9pm, Fri–Sat 9am–5.45pm; ☎626/744-4066, ⓦwww.ci.pasadena.ca.us/library), is a Spanish Renaissance gem with Corinthian columns, arched windows, Spanish tiling, and an elegant courtyard and atrium.

Across from the Memorial Park, the **Armory Center**, 145 N Raymond Ave (Tues–Sun noon–5pm; free; ☎626/792-5101, ⓦwww.armoryarts.org), is a good place to get a glimpse of the local art scene, showing a mix of community folk art and professional avant-garde and modernist creations. Further east, on Garfield Avenue at Union Street, you'll find two nine-foot bronze sculptures — strange, disembodied heads gazing out at an intersection — of the great baseball pioneer **Jackie Robinson** and his brother, **Frank**, winner of a silver medal at the 1936 summer Olympics in Berlin. The Robinsons were raised in town and Jackie went to junior college here before transferring to UCLA. In the brothers' eyeline is the city's centerpiece, **Pasadena City Hall**, 100 N Garfield Ave (Mon–Fri 9am–5pm; ☎626/744-7073), one of several city buildings in Mediterranean Revival styles – in this case 1920's Spanish Baroque Revival. Set on a wide city plaza, the recently renovated structure has a large, tiled dome and imposing facade with grand arches and columns, and an elegant garden with a patio and fountain, all of which make it more impressive than LA's City Hall.

Plaza de las Fuentes and around

Across Euclid Avenue from City Hall, **Plaza de las Fuentes** is landscape architect Lawrence Halprin's postmodern public square, with colorful tile work and a blocky pastel design, that suffers in comparison to its elegant neighbor.

The engaging **Pacific Asia Museum**, diagonally southeast at 46 N Los Robles Ave (Wed–Sun 10am–6pm; $7; ☎626/449-2742, ⓦwww.pacificasiamuseum .org), is modeled after a Chinese imperial palace, with a sloping tiled roof topped with ceramic-dog decorations, inset balconies, and dragon-emblazoned front gates. For twenty-five years, until 1948, this was the home of collector Grace Nicholson, who came to Pasadena around the beginning of the twentieth century and started amassing the expansive collection, which now includes thousands of historical treasures and everyday objects from Korea, China, and Japan, including decorative jade and porcelain, various swords and spears, and a large cache of paintings and drawings. In the museum's peaceful **courtyard garden**, koi fish rest in pools beneath marble statues and a variety of trees native to the Far East. Just around the corner, the **Pasadena Museum of California Art**, 490 E Union St (Wed–Sun noon–5pm; $6; ☎626/568-3665, ⓦwww.pmcaonline.org), offers an eye-opening focus on the many aspects of the state's art since it became part of the Union in 1850, in all kinds of media from painting to photography to digital art. Kenny Scharf's colorful graffiti murals, which jump off the walls with lurid primary hues and comic-book-like characters, are unfortunately confined to the walls of the museum's parking garage.

▲The Spanish Baroque Revival Pasadena City Hall

Bungalow Heaven and CalTech

Two miles northeast of Old Pasadena, the **Bungalow Heaven** historic district, bordered by Washington and Orange Grove boulevards and Hill and Catalina avenues, features some 800 quaint Craftsman bungalows that offer a glimpse of what much of the city looked like in the early 1900s. For Arts and Crafts enthusiasts, the neighborhood association puts on a yearly **tour** on the last Sunday in April ($15–20; information at ☏626/585-2172, Ⓦwww.bungalowheaven.org), peeking into six to eight of the classic structures. Further south, the commercial strip of **South Lake Avenue** (Ⓦwww.southlakeavenue.com) pulls in its share of visitors for its seven hundred or so retailers, but should be avoided unless you're in the mood for a cheek-to-jowl encounter with hordes of shoppers.

More appealing is the **California Institute of Technology**, or **CalTech**, campus, a few blocks east of Lake Avenue on California Boulevard, best known for its "cool nerd" students and media-friendly seismologists who inevitably pop up on the local news every time a major temblor rumbles through the region. However, CalTech is worth visiting for its splendid assortment of pre-WWII architecture, notably the Spanish Baroque–inspired buildings of LA Central Library designer **Bertram Goodhue** and the Islamic-styled work of Edward Stone; the campus makes for a fascinating jaunt if you have even the slightest interest in historic buildings. **Architecture tours** depart from the Spanish Colonial–style Atheneum, 551 S Hill Ave (Sept–Oct & Jan–June fourth Thurs of month, Nov third Thurs; 11am only; free; reserve at ☏626/395-6327, Ⓦwww.caltech.edu), while for your own, self-guided campus tour, get a brochure from the visitor center at 315 S Hill Ave (Mon–Fri 9am–5pm).

The Norton Simon Museum

Just across the 710 freeway from downtown Pasadena, the collections of the **Norton Simon Museum**, 411 W Colorado Blvd (Wed–Mon noon–6pm, Fri closes 9pm; $8, students free; ☏626/449-6840, Ⓦwww.nortonsimon.org), merit at least an afternoon of wandering through its dramatic, intimate galleries, which host Southern California's best selection of Old World art.

The museum's focus is **Western European painting** from the Renaissance to early modernism. It's a massive collection, much of it rotated, but most of the major pieces are usually on view. Highlights include Dutch paintings of the seventeenth century – notably Rembrandt's vivacious *Titus, Portrait of a Boy* and Frans Hals's austerely aggressive *Portrait of a Man* – and Italian Renaissance work including Botticelli's tender *Madonna and Child with Adoring Angel*, Giorgione's leering *Bust Portrait of a Courtesan*, and Raphael's lovely modeling of the serene figures of the *Madonna and Child with Book*. There's a good sprinkling of French Impressionists and post-Impressionists: Monet's light-dappled *Mouth of the Seine at Honfleur*; Manet's plaintive *Ragpicker*; and Degas' *The Ironers*, capturing the extended yawn of a washerwoman; plus minor works by Cézanne, Gauguin, and Van Gogh. There are also some appealing, but less-heralded works from different eras, including Zurbaran's *Still Life with Lemons, Oranges and a Rose*; Jan Steen's *Wine is a Mocker*, an image of rural peasants assisting a drunken bourgeoise as she lies pitifully in the dirt; and Tiepolo's *The Triumph of Virtue and Nobility over Ignorance*, in which the winged, angelic victors gloat over their symbolic conquest of the wretched, troll-like figure of Ignorance.

Unlike the Getty Center (see p.129), the Norton Simon also boasts a solid collection of **modernist greats,** from Georges Braque and Pablo Picasso to Roy Lichtenstein and Andy Warhol. As a counterpoint to the Western art, the museum has a fine collection of **Asian art**, including highly polished Buddhist and Hindu figures, some inlaid with precious stones, and many drawings and prints—the highlight being Hiroshige's masterful series of colored woodblock prints, showing nature in quiet, dusky hues.

The Arroyo Seco

The isolated pocket northwest of the junction of the 134 and 210 freeways, known as **Arroyo Seco**, or "dry riverbed" in Spanish, is home to some of LA's best residential architecture. Orange Grove Avenue leads you into the neighborhood from central Pasadena and takes you to the **Pasadena Historical Society**, 470 W Walnut St at Orange Grove (Wed–Sun noon–5pm; $5, kids free; ☎626/577-1660, ⓦwww.pasadenahistory.org), which has fine displays on Pasadena's history and is surrounded by tasteful gardens. The museum is most interesting for the on-site **Feynes Mansion** (tours Wed–Fri 1pm, Sat & Sun 1.30 & 3pm; $4), designed by Robert Farquhar, also famous for his William Clark Memorial Library (see p.157) in South Central's West Adams neighborhood, and for Downtown LA's California Club (see p.66. Decorated with its original 1905 furnishings and paintings, this elegant Beaux Arts mansion was once the home of the Finnish Consulate, and much of the folk art on display comes from Pasadena's "twin town" of Jarvenpää in Finland.

But it's the **Gamble House**, 4 Westmoreland Place (60min tours on the hour Thurs–Sun noon–3pm; $10, students $5; reserve at ☎626/793-3333 ext 13, ⓦwww.gamblehouse.org), that's Pasadena's architectural centerpiece, the crown jewel in the rich architectural legacy of the brothers **Charles and Henry Greene**. Built in 1908 for David Gamble, of the consumer-products giant Proctor & Gamble, this masterpiece of Southern Californian Craftsman architecture helped give rise to a style that's replicated all over the state, freely combining elements from Swiss chalets and Japanese temples in a romantically sprawling, shingled mansion. Broad eaves shelter outdoor sleeping-porches, which in turn shade terraces on the ground floor, leading out to the spacious lawn. The interior was crafted with the same attention to detail, and all the carpets, cabinetry, and lighting fixtures were designed specifically for the house. The area around the Gamble House has at least eleven other private homes by

Arroyo culture

The neighborhood around the **Arroyo Seco** has shifted somewhat through the years. Orange Grove Boulevard, several blocks east of the Arroyo proper, was around the turn of the twentieth century lined with a series of grand estates, tagged "**Millionaires' Row**," with the local gentry using the Arroyo itself as a source of wood and a place to picnic. The palaces went into decline by the mid-twentieth century, to be replaced eventually by the apartment blocks visible today. At the time the Row was at its grandest, just after 1900, the Arroyo Seco was being built up by numerous **Arts-and-Crafts**-movement intellectuals, many from the East Coast. They were inspired by the English example of William Morris, and preached a return-to-nature philosophy that reacted against precious Victorian ornamentation as well as the early-modern design aesthetic then taking shape, along with industrialized culture in general. Built in the Arroyo's wooded lots amid craggy rocks and rugged cliffsides, the resulting Craftsman monuments were manifestations of a new **Arroyo Culture**, its artisan practitioners prized for working with wood, clay, and stone. Not surprisingly, one of their heroes was Charles Lummis, famed for his eponymous boulder house in Highland Park (see p.70), and an equally prominent intellectual of the time, as well as an ardent booster for the new style, working as the city librarian and the first city editor of the *Los Angeles Times* when it was especially powerful in local affairs. Architects Charles and Henry Greene and Frank Lloyd Wright were all attracted by the Arroyo too, if not full believers in its attendant ideology. The culture faded, however, as much of the area was bought up by wealthy Angelenos in 1910–1930. Fortunately, the architecture has been largely preserved – even as prices on the homes have predictably skyrocketed.

the two brothers, including **Charles Greene's own house**, 368 Arroyo Terrace, and the picturesque **Duncan–Irwin House**, around the corner at 240 N Grand Ave, a perfect two-story Craftsman with stone lanterns and a rustic stone wall out front. Also worth a look is San Marino's Blacker House (see p.199), considered their best home after this one.

A quarter of a mile north of here is Frank Lloyd Wright's "La Miniatura," also known as the private **Millard House**, which you can glimpse through the gate around 585 Rosemont Ave, a small, concrete-block house supposedly designed to look like a jungle ruin, with thick foliage growing over Mayan-style architecture. Also in the vicinity are works by noted architects Gregory Ain, Richard Neutra, and Craig Ellwood. The preservation organization Pasadena Heritage hosts occasional events that allow a look into some of these homes, in the Arroyo Seco and elsewhere (see p.192). Several miles north at 1700 Lida St, Craig Ellwood's **Art Center College of Design**, a monumental steel-and-glass span crossing a natural ravine, is home to one of the area's best schools for groundbreaking modern design. For a few examples, check out the eye-catching, often experimental modern sculptures and installations in the school's **Williamson Gallery** (Tues–Sun noon–5pm, Fri closes 9pm; free; ☎626/396-2446, ⓦwww.artcenter.edu/williamson).

The Rose Bowl and Tournament House

North of the arroyo, the historic 104,000-seat **Rose Bowl** was built in 1922, just off Arroyo Boulevard at Rose Bowl Drive and out of use most of the year. As a national historic landmark and, according to *Sports Illustrated*, the best venue for college sports in the country, it's where one of college football's four Bowl Championship Series games is played in early January, meaning every fourth year the Rose Bowl officially gets to decide the champion. It's also home to a popular monthly **flea market** (second Sun of month; $7, reserve tickets at

☎ 323/560-7469) and, in the autumn, the place where the UCLA football team plays its home games (☎ 310/825-2101, ⓦ uclabruins.cstv.com).

To the south on Arroyo Boulevard, pass under the monumental spans of the **Colorado Street Bridge**, one of the area's structural wonders – a 1486-foot monolith of curving concrete, built in 1913 – to reach the **Tournament House**, 391 S Orange Grove Blvd (tours Feb–Aug 2–4pm; free; ☎ 626/449-4100, ⓦ www.tournamentofroses.com), the administrative headquarters of the annual **Rose Parade**, which began in 1890 to publicize the mild Southern California winters, and now attracts over a million visitors every year to watch its marching bands and elaborate flower-emblazoned floats. The mansion itself is a pink 1914 Renaissance Revival gem, once owned by gum king William Wrigley, and well worth a look for its grand manor and surrounding gardens – containing up to 1500 types of roses.

South Pasadena

For all its historic architecture and small-town appeal, **SOUTH PASADENA** only exists as it is today because of a series of lawsuits over the past thirty years fighting the completion of the **710 freeway**, which would have divided the town in half and wiped out a thousand homes and seventy-odd historic sites. At the moment the town seems to have won the legal battle and forced the state transit authority, CalTrans, to devise a solution involving tunneling under nearly five miles of the town.

One reason for residents' concern is South Pasadena's wealth of fine buildings and architectural legacy. The city's main strip, **Fair Oaks Avenue**, used to be part of the famous **Route 66**, and it's here where you can find such eye-catching sights as the landmark **Rialto Theater**, no. 1023, a 1925 movie palace that's also been a theatrical stage and vaudeville venue. The place closed in 2007, and awaits rebirth, perhaps as a performing-arts house. **Meridian Avenue**, which parallels Fair Oaks Avenue several blocks west, takes you through the quaint Victorian-era homes south of the 110 freeway and into the larger residences north of it. On the southern end, the **Meridian Iron Works**, 913 Meridian Ave (Thurs 3–8pm, Sat 1–4pm; free; ☎ 626/799-9089, ⓦ www.sppreservation.org), is a sturdy old pile from 1887 that houses the South Pasadena Preservation Foundation Museum, where exhibits and photographs cover the history of the ironworks (and its former lives as a hotel, blacksmith, and bicycle dealer), as well as the city itself, including assorted curios from a local ostrich farm.

To the north, Meridian Avenue runs into posh **Buena Vista Street**, notable for two grand dwellings by Charles and Henry Greene: the **Garfield House**, no. 1001, a fairly well-preserved 1904 Swiss chalet with numerous Craftsman elements that was once the home of murdered US President James Garfield's widow; and the adjacent **Longley House**, no. 1005, the brothers' first commission, an eclectic 1897 mix of revival styles from Romanesque to Moorish to Georgian. A few blocks east, at the end of Oaklawn Avenue, the Greene's 1906 **Oaklawn Bridge**, a restored concrete relic with vine-draped river-rock portals, spans the railway gully of the former Southern Pacific and Santa Fe line, which has been recently reincarnated for use by the Metrorail **Gold Line**, connecting Pasadena with Downtown LA.

San Marino

East of South Pasadena, uneventful **SAN MARINO** is known for some of LA's most privileged residents and widest neighborhood streets. One of the most notable structures is the **Blacker House**, 1177 Hillcrest Ave, Charles and Henry Greene's 1907 Craftsman marvel, with dark wooden beams, horizontal layout, rustic appearance, and Asian-influenced details. Unlike the larger Gamble House, you can't get into this one for regular tours, but it is worth a stop just to admire the design from the street. Unfortunately, after the original owners died, the once-expansive grounds were subdivided and many of the interior furnishings – now collectively worth millions – were sold off at fire-sale prices.

Beyond architecture, there's little of interest in town beyond the legacy of railway and real-estate magnate **Henry Huntington**, preserved in his museum and gardens. Before hitting the museum, you may want to check out **El Molino Viejo**, 1120 Old Mill Rd (Tues–Sun 1–4pm; free; ☎626/449-5458, ⓦwww .old-mill.org), a weathered structure of brick, adobe stone, and wooden beams, and built as a flourmill in 1816 by Spanish missionaries from Mission San Gabriel. Nowadays the old mill presents a few historical exhibits and photographs, plus an art gallery and diagrams of how water generated the power to make flour; there's also a nice on-site garden featuring quince and citrus trees. Just to the west, the towering **Ritz-Carlton Huntington Hotel**, atop a hill at 1401 S Oak Knoll Ave (see "Accommodation," p.252), began life as the *Wentworth Hotel* in 1906, later to be taken over by Huntington. The very definition of palatial accommodation, the hotel's Mediterranean-style main building boasts attractive gardens out back, and, further away, small bungalow-style residences for its swankiest guests – the only part of the hotel off limits to the general public.

The Huntington Library and Gardens

The main reason any outsider visits San Marino is to check out the **Huntington Library, Art Collections and Botanical Gardens**, just off Huntington Drive at 1151 Oxford Rd (Tues–Fri noon–4.30pm, Sat & Sun 10.30am–4.30pm; $15, kids $6; ☎626/405-2100, ⓦwww.huntington.org). The cache of art is based on the collections of Henry Huntington, the nephew of childless multimillionaire Collis P. Huntington, who owned and operated the Southern Pacific Railroad – which in the late-nineteenth century had a virtual monopoly on transportation in California. Henry, groomed to take over the railroad from his uncle, was dethroned by the board of directors and took his sizable inheritance to LA. Once there, he bought up the existing streetcar routes and combined them as the Pacific Electric Railway Company, which in turn controlled the Red Car line that soon became the largest transit network in the world, and helped make Huntington the largest landowner in the state. He retired in 1910, moving to the manor house he had built in San Marino, devoting himself full time to buying rare books and manuscripts, and marrying his uncle's widow Arabella and acquiring her collection of English portraits.

You can pick up a self-guided **tour** of each of the three main sections from the bookstore and information desk in the entry pavilion. The **library**, right off the main entrance, is a good first stop, its two-story exhibition hall containing many manuscripts and rare books, among them a Gutenberg Bible, a folio of Shakespeare's plays, Thoreau's manuscript for *Walden*, Thomas Jefferson's architectural plans, and the **Ellesmere Chaucer**, a *c.*1410 illuminated version of *The Canterbury Tales*. Displays trace the history of printing and of the English language from medieval manuscripts to a King James Bible, from Milton's *Paradise Lost* and Blake's *Songs of Innocence and Experience* to first editions of Swift, Coleridge, Dickens, Woolf, and Joyce.

The recently renovated **Huntington Gallery**, a grand mansion done out in Louis XIV carpets and later French tapestries, has works by Van Dyck and Constable and the pop stars of the whole collection – Gainsborough's *Blue Boy* and Reynolds' *Mrs Siddons as the Tragic Muse*. More striking are Turner's *Grand Canal, Venice*, a vibrant, hazily sunlit image of gondolas on the water, and Blake's mystical *Satan Comes to the Gates of Hell*, the most stunning work in the collection, showing the ghostly, bearded figure of Death facing off with spears against a very human Satan and a serpentine Eve.

A short distance northwest of the Huntington Gallery, the **Scott Gallery for American Art** displays paintings by Edward Hopper and Mary Cassatt, and Wild West drawings and sculpture, and also features work by the architects Greene & Greene.

For all the art and literature, though, it's the grounds that make the Huntington truly worthwhile. The acres of beautiful themed **gardens** surrounding the buildings include a Zen Rock Garden, complete with an authentically constructed Buddhist Temple and Tea House, and a Desert Garden with the world's largest collection of desert plants, including twelve acres of cacti. Also here are two lush rose gardens, a sculpture garden full of Baroque statues, and a Japanese garden dotted with koi ponds, cherry trees, and "moon bridges." While strolling through these botanical splendors, you might also visit the Huntingtons themselves, buried in a neo-Palladian **mausoleum** at the northwest corner of the estate, beyond the rows of an orange grove, built as a marble Greek temple and claimed to be the inspiration for the later 1930s Jefferson Memorial in Washington, DC.

North of Pasadena

The cities and districts **north of Pasadena**, such as **Altadena** and **La Cañada Flintridge**, sit on hillsides that lead into the **Angeles National Forest**, a 650,000-acre wilderness in the San Gabriel Mountains that is a favorite weekend spot for locals. There are numerous activities in the forest, from fishing and hunting to water skiing, biking, and hiking. You can also **camp** (free–$12) at any one of some 50 locations; most have 5–20 campsites, but the larger ones, Chilao and Los Alamos, boast around 100 each. Keep in mind that some, but not all, parts of the forest require a $5 Northwest Forest Adventure Pass, which you can acquire from one of the three visitor centers or online. For locations, maps, and the full range of activities on offer, contact the Forest Center (☎626/796-5541, ⓦwww.fs.fed.us/r5/angeles).

Threatened by flood during heavy rains, the foothills of the forest are some of the more precarious places to live in LA, and you can see part of their elaborate flood-control system just off Oak Grove Drive and Foothill Boulevard in La Cañada Flintridge, where the 1300-acre **Hahamongna Watershed Park** (daily dawn–dusk; ☎626/744-7275) and Devils Gate Reservoir are dramatic testaments to the power of water: a huge green slope and massive catch basin designed to contain water, mud, rocks, housing debris, and assorted other elements in the event of catastrophic flooding.

The Jet Propulsion Laboratory and Descanso Gardens

Immediately north of the park and reservoir is one of the cornerstones of America's military-industrial complex: the **Jet Propulsion Laboratory** (JPL), 4800 Oak Grove Drive in La Cañada Flintridge (2hr tours alternate by week, Mon or Wed 1pm; free; by reservation at ☎818/354-9314, ⓦwww.jpl.nasa .gov), devoted to the development of space-related machinery such as orbiting satellites, long-range missiles and rockets, and secretive government projects. The tours are very popular, and you'll have to reserve well in advance and bring some form of ID – a visa or passport if you're a foreigner. Despite the JPL's obvious military mission, the lab chooses to focus on more PR-friendly displays, including replicas of the solar-system-exploring *Voyager* craft and the *Magellan* and *Galileo* vehicles that mapped Venus and Mars; photos from the Saturn-bound *Cassini* craft; and exhibits on the Hubble telescope, killer asteroids, and Hollywood's version of outer space.

West off Foothill Boulevard, **Descanso Gardens**, 1418 Descanso Drive, La Cañada Flintridge (daily 9am–5pm; $7, kids $2; ☏818/949-4200, ⑩www .descansogardens.org), squeezes all the plants you might see in the region's mountains into 155 acres of landscaped park, especially brilliant in spring when the wildflowers are in bloom. The centerpiece is a live-oak forest loaded with camellias, and there's also a Japanese tea house and garden, with a narrow red footbridge, and a tranquil bird sanctuary for migrating waterfowl.

Angeles National Forest and around

North from the 210 freeway, the **Angeles Crest Highway** (Hwy-2) heads into the mountains above Pasadena, through an area once dotted with resorts and wilderness camps; to park in many areas, you'll need a Northwest Forest Adventure Pass (see opposite). Today, a hike up any of the canyons will bring you past the ruins of old lodges that either burned down or were washed away toward the end of the 1930s, when automobiles became popular. One of the most scenic of these trails, a rugged five-mile round-trip, follows the route of the **Mount Lowe Scenic Railway**, once one of LA's biggest tourist attractions, a funicular that hauled tourists 1500 feet up to Echo Mountain, to the remains of "**White City**" – formerly a mountaintop resort of two hotels, a zoo, and an observatory. Today, you'll see little more than crumbling walls, but the trail's expansive views of the basin can be striking when smog isn't a problem. To follow the old route of the railway (that ended service in 1937), drive north on Lake Avenue in Altadena until it ends at the intersection of Loma Alta Drive. Find a parking spot and head east along the trailhead. The site's historical committee (☏562/868-8919, ⑩www.mtlowe.net) offers information on the background and topography of this special place, along with a number of current and antique trail maps. More fine hiking in Altadena can be found further east in **Eaton Canyon Park**, 1750 N Altadena Drive, a natural refuge on 190 acres, where the on-site **nature center** (daily 9am–5pm; free; ☏626/398-5420, ⑩www.ecnca.org) provides more information on the region's geology, flora, and fauna.

Further north, the Angeles Crest Highway heads up to Mount Wilson, high enough to be a major site for TV broadcast antennae. At the peak, the **Mount Wilson Observatory** has a small **museum** (April–Nov 10am–4pm; $1; ☏626/440-9016, ⑩www.mtwilson.edu) where you can browse astronomical displays detailing the work of Edwin Hubble, who, aside from having a famous telescope named after him, developed the theory of cosmological expansion. The observatory was built by the Carnegie Institution in 1904, and although the last century of growth has added much light pollution, Carnegie researchers still find it useful, even if most of their groundbreaking discoveries are made in the Andes mountains. For peering through the 60-inch **observatory telescope** itself, you'll either have to reserve a partial evening for one to 25 people for $650, or go through the Mount Wilson Observatory Association (⑩www.mwoa.org), which reserves blocks of time for its members ($20 fee) for viewing, and arranges regular group tours of the facility.

East of Pasadena

East of Pasadena, the San Gabriel Valley becomes a patchwork of small cities with a few appealing sights scattered across large distances. The one feature these places share is Foothill Boulevard, which before it was displaced by the Foothill Freeway (Hwy-210), was famously known as **Route 66**. Formerly the main route across the US, "from Chicago to LA, more than three thousand miles all the way," the strip has declined in recent decades, though sections of the road have been smartened up with fresh neon and retro-flavored building renovations. The Gold Line light rail runs from Downtown LA to Old Pasadena up to Sierra Madre, but isn't really convenient for accessing these far-flung sights.

Arcadia, Sierra Madre, and San Gabriel

If you follow Foothill Boulevard out of Pasadena, you'll come to **ARCADIA**, a colorless suburb whose **LA County Arboretum**, 310 N Baldwin Ave (daily 9am–4.30pm; $5; ☎626/821-3222, ⌨www.arboretum.org), contains many impressive gardens and waterfalls, flocks of peacocks and, of course, a great assortment of trees, arranged by their native continents. This was the 127-acre home of Elias "Lucky" Baldwin, who made his millions in the silver mines of Nevada's Comstock Lode in the 1870s, settled here in 1875, and built a fanciful white mansion along a palm-tree-lined lagoon (later used in the TV show *Fantasy Island*) on the site of the 1839 Rancho Santa Anita. Curiously, scenes in *Jurassic Park* were also filmed here, perhaps inspired by the park's own "Prehistoric and Jungle Garden" section. Nearby, Baldwin also bred horses and raced them on a track that has since grown into the **Santa Anita Racetrack**, W Colorado St at Huntington Dr (racing Oct to early Nov & late Dec to late April Wed–Sun, post time 12.30pm or 1pm; $5 admission; ☎626/574-RACE, ⌨www.santaanita.com), still the most famous racetrack in California, with a Depression-era steel Art Deco frieze along the grandstand.

The foothill district of **SIERRA MADRE**, on the northern edge of Arcadia, lies directly beneath Mount Wilson and is worth a visit if you're a hiker. A 15-mile round-trip trail up to the summit makes for an excellent, if tiring, trek; to find the route, take Baldwin Avenue north from the 210 freeway until it becomes Mount Wilson Trail and ends at the trailhead. Part of the trail follows the **Mount Wilson Toll Road**, a narrow, antique route that was open to horses and cars for 45 years (until 1936) and, amazingly, hosted the occasional auto race as well. South of Sierra Madre stands the valley's original settlement, the church and grounds of **Mission San Gabriel Arcangel**, 428 S Mission Drive (daily 9am–4pm; $5; ☎626/457-3035, ⌨sangabrielmission.org), in the heart of the small town of **SAN GABRIEL**. The mission was established here in 1771 by Junípero Serra and the current building finished in 1812. Despite decades of damage by earthquakes and the elements, the church and grounds have been repaired and reopened, their old winery, cistern, kitchens, gardens, and antique-filled rooms giving some sense of mission-era life.

Further east

The attractions further east are even more isolated. The lone draw out in **MONROVIA**, east of Sierra Madre, is the zany **Aztec Hotel**, 311 W Foothill Blvd (☎626/358-3231, ⌨aztechotel.com), a 1925 pre-Columbian creation from Mayan revivalist Robert Stacy-Judd that is still maintained as a hotel, bar, and restaurant. Its faux-ancient carvings and designs, monumental appearance, and stunning facade encase a lobby that displays antiques such as the original gas pumps found along Route 66. Beyond here, the only reason most Angelenos venture further east is to take a splash at **Raging Waters**, in the suburb of San Dimas at 111 Raging Waters Drive (May & early Sept Sat & Sun 10am–5pm; June–Aug Mon–Fri 10am–8pm; $35, kids $22; parking $8; ☎909/802-2200,

@www.ragingwaters.com). The aquatic theme park with plenty of tubes and slides for cooling off in the summer heat, and plenty of summer smog as well – the area suffers some of the region's worst air pollution, thanks to unfavorable winds blowing in from central LA.

The San Fernando Valley

Home to acres of asphalt, countless minimalls, and nonstop tract housing, the **San Fernando Valley** is often derided by LA Westsiders as the epitome of dull, faceless suburbia. The Valley has also become known for its rabid **secessionist movement**, which blames all difficulties – from crime to potholes to crummy schools – on Downtown LA bureaucrats, though so far the group has made little progress. Other than theme parks and movie-studio tours, the valley has pretty sparse attractions, but you may want to seek them out if you find yourself trapped here for some reason.

The Valley's 1769 Spanish discovery predated the settlement of Los Angeles, and it was first named after **St Catherine**, only later acquiring its present moniker with the development of Mission San Fernando at its northern tip. After the US took possession of California and the Southern Pacific Railroad cut through it, the Valley rapidly transformed, going from a nineteenth-century

Aqua in Los Angeles

Just beyond Mission San Fernando, I-5 runs past two of LA's main reservoirs, the water carried by the **California Aqueduct**, traveling from the Sacramento Delta, and the **LA Aqueduct**, coming from the Owens Valley and Mono Lake on the eastern slopes of the Sierra Nevada Mountains.

How LA came into the latter water source, however, is a shady matter indeed. Acting on behalf of water czar **William Mulholland**, agents of the city, masquerading as rich cattle-barons interested in establishing ranches in the Owens Valley, bought up most of the land along the Owens River in the first years of the twentieth century before selling it, at great personal profit, to the city of Los Angeles. Tellingly, when the first rush of water was brought to the city with great fanfare, Mulholland publicly pronounced his triumph with the memorable command, "There it is! Take it!" The Owens Valley farmers didn't take this subterfuge lying down, however, and resorted to **dynamiting** sections of the aqueduct in later years. The violent tactics proved of little use, though, for as soon as the water began flowing, LA's San Fernando Valley **suburbs** began to blossom, along with the profits of their new Downtown property owners. These were the region's major bigwigs, bankers, and real estate magnates who, with the *Los Angeles Times* as their propaganda organ, trumpeted the development as the height of civic duty, even as they were employing Mulholland's agents to trick the valley farmers into selling their land for a fraction of its potential value.

There is little doubt that the LA Aqueduct has served the interests of the city well, bringing water to two million people, but the morality and legality of such a distant supply of water is still disputed. After much controversy, even the state supreme court ruled that the endangered Mono Lake area – the salty home of fascinating tufa (gnarled limestone) columns – must finally be removed from the clutches of LA's water empire. This result (along with California's losing its grip on a generous portion of the Colorado River's water) has forced the city finally to get down to serious **water-management** policies, controlling the amount of the precious fluid used to water people's lawns and fill their swimming pools.

tract of wheat fields and ranchos to an early twentieth-century expanse of citrus groves to a post-World War II dynamo of industry, media, and, above all, suburban housing. The spark that made all this development possible was the 1913 construction of the LA Aqueduct (see box, p.203). Today, the agricultural ghosts are apparent only in streets with idyllic names like Orange Grove, Walnut, and Magnolia, and "bucolic" is the last word anyone would use to describe this sun-blasted desert of concrete and asphalt.

Glendale

West of Pasadena, beyond the Verdugo Mountains, **GLENDALE** is an upper-middle-class suburb that extends from Griffith Park all the way past the northern reaches of foothill cities like La Cañada Flintridge. At least its downtown is compact, south of the 134 freeway along Brand Boulevard. Apart from a handful of serviceable boutiques and restaurants (among them the terrific *Porto's Bakery*; see p.265), you'll find the **Alex Theater**, 268 N Brand Blvd, a striking piece of green-and-yellow Art Deco with a towering pylon; it now serves as a performing-arts venue and one of the sites for the annual Last Remaining Seats festival (see p.335 or ℡818/243-ALEX, ⓦwww.alextheatre.org).

North of the 134, the city has a smattering of noteworthy sites, such as the **Catalina Verdugo Adobe**, 2211 Bonita Drive (grounds daily 7am–dusk; free), dating from 1828 and retaining something of its original look, though a north wing was added later. Though the adobe itself is not open to the public, the gardens contain the knotty remains of the **Oak of Peace**, which, when it was alive, was said to be more than five hundred years old. It stood where in 1847 Mexican leaders agreed to surrender to US troops in the Mexican-American War, though the treaty signing occurred elsewhere two days later. To the northwest in Brand Park, the **Brand Library and Art Center**, or "El Miradero," 1601 W Mountain St (Tues & Thurs noon–9pm, Wed 10am–6pm, Fri & Sat 10am–5pm; free; ℡818/548-2051, ⓦwww.brandlibrary.org), looks nothing remotely like anything else in LA. This white oddity from 1902 is said to be modeled on the East India Pavilion at Chicago's 1893 Columbian Exposition, and features a striking quasi-Islamic Spanish design of domes and minarets containing art books from the main Glendale Library. The site also has an art gallery and hosts lectures, performances, and recitals, plus monthly talks by members of the LA Opera, when it's in season (Oct–June usually second Sat 2pm; free). Also located in Brand Park is the so-called **Doctors House** (tours Sun 2–4pm; $1; ⓦwww.glendalehistorical.org/doctors.html), a charming Eastlake residence from 1888, which was named for three physicians who lived there successively. You can take a look at period decor, a projecting roofline and dormers, latticed white porches, and gardens with a gazebo.

Forest Lawn Glendale

For most visitors, the main reason to come to Glendale is to visit the city's famous branch of **Forest Lawn Cemetery**, 1712 S Glendale Ave (daily 8am–5pm; free; ℡1-800/204-3131, ⓦwww.forestlawn.com), at the vanguard of the American way of death for nearly a century. Founded in 1917 by one Dr Hubert Eaton, this soon after became *the* place to be buried, its pompous landscaping and pious artworks attracting celebrities by the dozen to fill out the plots. The graveyard's success has allowed it to expand throughout the LA region, notably with a branch near Griffith Park, in the Hollywood Hills (see p.96), though the others – in distant places like Covina Hills, Cypress, and Cathedral City – are best avoided.

It's best to climb the hill and see the cemetery in reverse from the **Forest Lawn Museum** (open during park hours; free), whose hodgepodge of worldly artifacts includes coins from ancient Rome, Viking relics, medieval armor, and a mysterious, sculpted Easter Island figure, discovered being used as ballast in a fishing boat in the days when the statues could still be swiped from the island. How it ended up here is another mystery, but it is the only one on view in the US. The museum also hosts regular shows that may feature inoffensive modern art, stained glass, and funerary sculptures, among other things.

Next door to the museum, the **Hall of the Crucifixion-Resurrection** (daily 10am–noon & 2–4pm) houses the colossal *Crucifixion* by Jan Styka – an oil painting nearly 195 feet tall and 45 feet wide, showing Jesus standing by a fallen cross, not being crucified as the title would suggest. In any case, you're only allowed to see it during the ceremonial unveiling every hour on the hour. Besides this, Eaton owned a stained-glass "re-creation" of Leonardo da Vinci's *Last Supper* – housed in the Memorial Court of Honor and unveiled every half-hour (daily 9.30-4pm) – and, realizing that he only needed one piece to complete his trio of "the three greatest moments in the life of Christ," he commissioned Robert Clark to produce *The Resurrection* – which is also unveiled every half-hour, appropriate since it's only half the size of the Styka. If you can't stick around for the ceremonial showings (with both, in any case, the size is the only aspect that's impressive), you can check out the scaled-down replicas just inside the entrance.

Perversely, despite its ostentatious character, Forest Lawn chooses to coyly downplay the presence of so many Hollywood glitterati lying in its grounds. Therefore, you'll be met with cold stares should you inquire where your favorite celebrity might be buried or interred. Bring a cemetery tour booklet (found easily online or from a local bookseller) and, from the museum, walk down through the terrace gardens – loaded with sculptures modeled on the greats of classical European art, along with an ungainly 13-foot rendering of George Washington – to the **Freedom Mausoleum**, where you'll find a handful of the cemetery's better-known graves. Just outside the mausoleum's doors, Errol Flynn lies in an unspectacular plot (unmarked until 1979), rumored to have been buried with six bottles of whiskey at his side, while a few strides away is the grave of Walt Disney, who is not in the deep freeze as urban legend would have it. Inside the mausoleum you'll find Clara Bow, Nat King Cole, Jeanette MacDonald, and Alan Ladd placed close to each other on the first floor. Downstairs are Chico Marx and his brother Gummo, the Marx Brothers' agent and business manager. Back down the hill, the **Great Mausoleum** is chiefly noted for the tombs of Clark Gable (next to Carole Lombard, who died in a plane crash just three years after marrying him), and Jean Harlow, in a marble-lined room that cost over $25,000, paid for by fiancé William Powell. Amid all this morbid glamour, the cemetery has actually been the site of thousands of **weddings**, not least being Ronald Reagan's star-crossed wedlock with Jane Wyman in 1940.

Burbank

Although Hollywood's name is synonymous with the movies, in reality many of the big studios moved out of Tinseltown long ago, and much of the business of making films (and TV shows) is located west of Glendale in otherwise boring **BURBANK**. Hot, smoggy, and ugly, Burbank nonetheless has an official "Media District" bustling with activity. **Disney** is the most visible of the studios, with Robert A.M. Stern's starry wizard-hat building, Riverside Dr

North Hollywood

Glendale

BURBANK STUDIOS

N

0   800 yds

▼ *Universal Studios & Hollywood*

at Keystone St, visible from the 101 freeway just east of the Buena Vista St exit, housing over seven hundred animators. Less appealing is Disney's other public face, its **Studio Office Building**, 500 S Buena Vista St, a clumsy effort from Michael Graves that has five of the Seven Dwarfs propping up the building's roof. As for touring the studio, forget it – the secretive company would rather have you plunk down your cash in Disneyland.

Nearby, **NBC**, 3000 W Alameda St (box office open Mon–Fri 9am–4pm; $8; reserve at ☎818/840-3537), offers an engaging 75min tour of its production facility, even though only a handful of shows currently tape there. The studio also gives you the chance to be in the audience for the taping of a TV program (phone ahead for free tickets), such as Jay Leno's *Tonight Show*. **Warner Brothers**, 4000 Warner Blvd at Hollywood Way, offers a tour (Mon–Fri 8.30am–4pm; $45; ☎818/972-TOUR; ⓦwww2.warnerbros.com/vipstudio tour) that takes you past the sound stages, around the production offices, and to the outdoor sets for movies and TV shows. Ultimately, you won't get to see any actual filming, but if you want to see a working environment of a studio, it's worth the money.

Beyond the studios, Burbank's greatest attraction is the oldest **Bob's Big Boy** in existence, 4211 Riverside Drive (☎818/843-9334, ⓦwww.bobs.net), a well-preserved "Googie"-style coffee shop from 1949, and home of the "Double Deck" hamburger. It's been used for a host of Hollywood flicks, including an Austin Powers sequel, and for good reason: the 70-foot-tall pink-and-white neon sign is a knockout. Occasionally on Friday nights, the restaurant hosts stylish hot-rod shows in the parking lot (5–10pm), and every Saturday and Sunday night, you can chow down on your burgers and fries with old-fashioned car-hop service (5–10pm).

▲ Bob's Big Boy in Burbank

Universal Studios and CityWalk

Just to the south along the 101 freeway, the largest of the backlots belongs to **Universal Studios** (hours vary, often summer daily 8am–10pm; rest of year daily 10am–6pm; $61, kids $51; ☎818/508-9600, ⓦwww.universalstudioshollywood.com), where the four-hour-long "tours" are more like a trip around an amusement park than a visit to a film studio, with the first half featuring a tram ride through a make-believe set where you can experience the fading magic of the Red Sea parting. Inside the corny Entertainment Center, where unemployed actors engage in Wild West shootouts and stunt shows based on the studio's movies, there's also a "collapsing" bridge. The theme rides are based on the studio's more popular films, including *Back to the Future* (a jerky trip on a motion simulator), *Jurassic Park* (close encounters with prehistoric plastic), *Terminator 2* (a 3-D movie with robot stuntmen), and *Shrek 4-D* (another motion simulator, plus another 3-D movie). You never actually get to see any filming, though.

Also part of the complex is **Universal CityWalk** (ⓦwww.citywalk hollywood.com), an outdoor mall that's free to all who pay the parking fee, where chain diners draw masses of families, chain boutiques draw gaggles of teenagers, and giant TV screens run ads for the latest Universal releases. The place was designed by shopping-mall architect extraordinaire Jon Jerde, and while mildly diverting for its pint-sized reproductions of LA landmarks, it's not much better than the usual massive mall; try Jerde's Horton Plaza (see p.370) in San Diego for a more immersive retail experience.

Tujunga

Seven miles north of Glendale and Burbank on Foothill Blvd, **TUJUNGA** (tah-HUNG-ah) is mainly notable for its remarkable collection of boulder houses and bungalows built in the 1910s and 1920s, the inspiration of a small community of Socialists who, like the dwellers in Pasadena's Arroyo Seco, believed earthy materials like wood and stone made for the best, and most moral, forms of construction. Their restored 1913 clubhouse, **Bolton Hall**, 10106 Commerce Ave (Tues & Sun 1–4pm; free; ☎818/352-3420), hints at their aims, with a rocky central tower and interior with exposed wooden beams. This striking creation was LA's second historic monument (after the Avila Adobe, which no longer exists in its original form; see p.52), and displays a good selection of antiques from its rich and varied history – it has also doubled as the town's city hall, and its jail. Curiously enough, the structure's name actually honors an author named "Bolton Hall," a friend of the developer who gave rise to the surrounding town.

The western San Fernando Valley

Beyond Burbank, the **western San Fernando Valley** suburbs of Los Angeles – some of the more well-known of which are **North Hollywood**, **Sherman Oaks**, **Van Nuys**, and **Reseda** – are often collectively called "the Valley," immediately bringing to mind strip malls, fast-food joints, and endless asphalt. The Valley is also the capital of America's **porn industry**, with CD sales and Internet demand making the low-rent video studios and distribution warehouses here an integral part of the local economy – cranking out more acres of photographed flesh than just about any spot on the planet. However, this is one aspect of the Valley's movie industry that, not surprisingly, is kept discreetly behind the closed doors of unmarked concrete warehouses and strip-mall office suites.

The first of the Valley's official points of interest is **Campo de Cahuenga**, across from Universal Studios – and a Red Line subway stop – at 3919 Lankershim Blvd, in North Hollywood (Sat & Sun 10am–2pm; donation; ℡818/762-3998 ext 2, ⓦwww.campodecahuenga.com). Perhaps LA's most important historical site, this is where generals John Frémont and Andres Pico signed the 1847 Treaty of Cahuenga between the US and Mexico – which led to the more famous Treaty of Guadalupe Hidalgo – thus ending the Mexican-American War, and later allowing the US to officially acquire California and the rest of the Southwest. The adobe on the grounds is only a replica of an original 1840s structure, but every January you can watch a historical re-enactment of the events that made the site famous.

Several miles north on Lankershim Boulevard, the **North Hollywood Arts District** (ⓦwww.nohoartsdistrict.com), located around Magnolia Boulevard between Burbank and the western San Fernando Valley (and accessible by the Metrorail Red Line), was named "NoHo" by county bureaucrats as a play on New York's SoHo. Otherwise it has little in common with that fabled place, its performing-arts centers, theatres, and restaurants too spread out to make for any sort of pleasurable strolling.

About six miles west off Burbank Blvd in Van Nuys, the 6.5-acre **Tillman Japanese Garden**, 6100 Woodley Ave, near the 405 freeway (grounds Mon–Thurs noon–4pm, Sun 10am–3.30pm, tours by reservation only Mon–Thurs; $3; ℡818/751-8166, ⓦwww.thejapanesegarden.com), is a pleasant spot adorned with stone lanterns, bonsai trees, low bridges, a tea house, and artful streams and pools; the site uses reclaimed water from a nearby treatment plant and sits in the giant flood plain behind the **Sepulveda Dam**, visible along Burbank Blvd west of the 405 freeway. Thanks to Hollywood, the dam is perhaps the most famous sight in this part of the Valley, a monolithic, futuristic wall of concrete towers and abutments that's appeared in everything from *Escape from New York* to *Gattaca*.

Due southwest off Ventura Boulevard, the district of **Encino** sits near **Los Encinos State Historic Park**, 16756 Moorpark St (Wed–Sun 10am–5pm; free; ℡818/784-4849, ⓦlos-encinos.org), which includes all that remains of an original Native American settlement and later Mexican hacienda, along with an extensive cattle and sheep farm. In addition to a blacksmith's shop and lake fed by a natural spring, the main attraction is an 1849 adobe house, featuring high-ceilinged rooms that open out onto porches, shaded by oak trees (in Spanish, *encinos*), and kept cool by the two-foot-thick walls.

The Shadow and Orcutt ranches

At the western end of the Valley on Vanowen St, in **West Hills**, are a few minor historic points of interest, including the **Shadow Ranch**, 22633 Vanowen St (grounds Mon–Fri 9am–10pm, Sat & Sun 9am–5pm; free; ℡818/883-3637), the center of a 23,000-acre rancho that was controlled by land moguls I.N. Van Nuys and Isaac Lankershim, with some seventy barns and a thousand head of cattle. These days, the once-huge rancho has been subdivided and sold off, and the property is mainly notable for its great stand of eucalyptus trees imported from Australia over 120 years ago, along with a main ranch home that retains its historic allure and hosts occasional arts-and-crafts shows. To the northwest is the **Orcutt Ranch**, 23600 Roscoe Blvd (daily 8am–5pm; free; ℡818/346-7449), also known as "Rancho Sombre del Roble," or Ranch Shaded by the Oak. Indeed, there's an impressive plot of ancient oaks here, some five hundred rose bushes, and citrus trees and bamboo too, alongside a traditional Spanish Colonial ranch house with a romantic grotto and a large sundial. Dating from

1921, the ranch originally belonged to William Orcutt, the oil geologist who first found fossils in the La Brea Tar Pits, and initially spread out over two hundred acres – about ten times its current size.

The northern San Fernando Valley

A few miles east of Orcutt Ranch, Topanga Canyon Boulevard heads into the far northwest reaches of the Valley to **Stony Point**, just off Hwy-118, a bizarre sandstone outcrop that has been used for countless Westerns, usually for a climactic gun battle, and in recent decades as a venue for LA's contingent of rock climbers (for more information, check out ⓦ www.sowr.com). The area, though crossed by both Amtrak and Metrorail trains, has a desolate spookiness about it. The terrain was used as a hideout by the legendary late-nineteenth-century bandit Joaquin Murrieta, as a shooting location for episodes of *Bonanza* and *The Lone Ranger*, and during the late 1960s, as a hangout for the Manson family, who lived for a time at the **Spahn Ranch**, just west at 1200 Santa Susana Pass, but off-limits to the public.

West of Stony Point, at the end of Santa Susana Pass Rd, the little town of **Simi Valley** is the home of the **Ronald Reagan Presidential Library** (daily 10am–5pm; $7; ⓣ 805/522-2977, ⓦ www.reaganlibrary.com/pma), containing all the papers pertaining to the eight-year reign of the Gipper, as well as his memorial site. More captivating is the bizarre folk-art shrine of **Grandma Prisbrey's Bottle Village**, 4595 Cochran St (by appointment only; ⓣ 805/584-0572, ⓦ www.bottlevillage.com), where 13 buildings and 20 sculptures – from the Leaning Tower of Pisa to simple shacks – are constructed from colorful bits of junk. Auto parts, broken lightbulbs, pencils, glass bottles, and other detritus all show up in the design, the highlight of which is the "Doll Head Shrine," a thoroughly disturbing array of antique plastic doll-heads stuck on poles. Although the site was damaged in the Northridge earthquake (and nearly torn down), slow work is being done to restore it.

Earthquake central: the San Fernando Valley

The devastating 6.7 magnitude **earthquake** that shook LA on the morning of January 17, 1994, was one of the most destructive disasters in US history. Fifty-five people were killed, two hundred more suffered critical injuries, and the economic cost was estimated at $8 billion. The tremor toppled chimneys and shattered windows all over Southern California, with the worst damage concentrated at the epicenter in the San Fernando Valley community of **Northridge**, where a dozen people were killed when an apartment building collapsed. At the northern edge of the Valley, the I-5/Hwy-14 interchange was destroyed, killing one motorist and snarling traffic for at least a year; while in West LA, the Santa Monica Freeway overpass collapsed onto La Cienega Boulevard at one of LA's busiest intersections. The Northridge event followed a quake in the eastern desert around **Landers** a few years earlier, and just eclipsed LA's previous worst earthquake in modern times, the 6.6 magnitude temblor of February 9, 1971, which had its epicenter in **Sylmar** – also in the Valley.

Small earthquakes happen all the time in LA, but in the unlikely event a sizable one strikes when you're in LA, protect yourself under something sturdy, such as a heavy table or a door frame, and well away from windows or anything made of glass. In theory, all the city's new buildings are "quake-safe;" the extent of the crisis in January 1994, however, forced the city to re-examine and reinforce buildings – though as the quake recedes in memory, the job seems to diminish in perceived importance. So when the inevitable "**Big One**," a quake in the 8+ range, arrives, no one knows exactly what will be left standing.

San Fernando and Sylmar

At the northern tip of the Valley, the San Diego, Golden State, and Foothill freeways join together at I-5, the quickest route north to San Francisco. Standing near the junction, at 15151 San Fernando Mission Blvd in the small town of **SAN FERNANDO**, the church and many of the historic buildings of **Mission San Fernando Rey de España** (daily 9am–4.30pm; $5; T818/361-0186) had to be completely rebuilt following the 1971 Sylmar earthquake. It's hard to imagine now, walking through the nicely landscaped courtyards and gardens, but eighty-odd years ago, director D.W. Griffith used the then-dilapidated mission as a film site for *Our Silent Paths*, his tale of the Gold Rush. Nowadays, there's a good collection of pottery, furniture, and saddles, along with an old-time blacksmith's shop. As an unexpected touch, in 2005 comedian Bob Hope was interred at the site, in his own memorial garden underneath a red hemispheric shell.

Also in the vicinity, another key nineteenth-century site can be found at 10940 Sepulveda Blvd, the **Andres Pico Adobe** (Mon 10am–3pm & third Sun of month 1–4pm; free; T818/365-7810, Wwww.sfvhs.com), the well-preserved estate and grounds of the eponymous Mexican general who fought off American troops, at least for a while, in the 1840s. This lovely, two-story brick adobe was built in 1834, with an upper story added in 1873 – which is the year to which the adobe has been restored. It's crammed with period furnishings and historical bric-a-brac, and makes a good spot for a stroll in an idyllic setting.

Up the road in nearby **SYLMAR** – famous mainly as the site of the 1971 earthquake – the wondrous **San Sylmar**, 15180 Bledsoe St (Tues–Sat 9am–4.30pm; tours by reservation 10am & 1.30pm; free; T818/367-2251, Wwww.nethercuttcollection.org), is a storehouse for all kinds of Wurlitzer organs, antique player-pianos, cosmetic paraphernalia, Tiffany stained glass, and classic French furniture, collected by J.H. Nethercutt, the chairman of Merle Norman Cosmetics, and his wife Dorothy. Most worthwhile, however, is its **Nethercutt Collection**, a stunning showroom filled with collectors' vintage automobiles such as Packards, Mercedes, and Bugatti. The eye-popping highlights, though, are the Duesenbergs, splendid machines driven by movie stars in the Jazz Age, including a silver 1933 Arlington Torpedo with curvaceous lines, sinuous bumpers, and an array of exposed chrome pipes.

North of the valleys

The expanding communities **north of the valleys** offer several compelling historical and cultural sights along or near the I-14 freeway, which leaves the San Fernando Valley to make a harsh trek into the periphery of the Mojave Desert – still part of the huge County of Los Angeles. To the far north of San Fernando, the remains of the former company town of **Mentryville**, three miles west of I-5 at 27201 W Pico Canyon Rd (grounds daily 9am–dusk; guided tours noon–4pm first & third Sun of month; donation; Wwww .mentryville.org), are where California's very first oil well was dug, in 1876. The boom only lasted a few decades and, although the original well – Pico no. 4 – pumped until 1990 (making it the longest-operating oil well in history, at 114 years), the site was a ghost town for many years, until the state bought it from Chevron Oil. Saved from further decay, the preserved red-and-white barn, one-room 1880s schoolhouse, and 13-room Victorian mansion of town-founder Charles Alexander Mentry evoke some of the city's old character. For the more adventurous, trails lead away from the townsite into the hills of surrounding **Pico Canyon**, which is a popular summer site for hiking, mountain biking, and horseback riding.

To the east, in the town of **SANTA CLARITA**, the **William S. Hart Ranch and Museum**, 24151 San Fernando Rd (Wed–Fri 10am–1pm, Sat & Sun 11am–4pm; June–Aug Wed–Sun 11am–4pm; free; ☎661/254-4584, ⓦ www.hartmuseum.org), holds a fine assemblage of native artworks, Remington sculptures, displays of spurs, guns, and lariats, Hollywood costumes, and authentic cowhand duds, housed in a Spanish Colonial mansion on a sizable 265-acre ranch. The estate was constructed by silent-movie star Hart, who made 65 westerns and is still considered one of the all-time cowboy greats – playing many more complex and often troubled heroes, as well as anti-heroes, than his main cinematic rival, the smiling, white-hatted Tom Mix.

Nearby **Six Flags Magic Mountain**, Magic Mountain Parkway at I-5 (hours vary, often summer daily 10am–10pm; rest of year Sat & Sun 10am–8pm; $60, kids $30, $15 parking; ⓦ www.sixflags.com/parks/magicmountain), is a three-hundred-acre complex that has some of the wildest roller coasters and rides in the world – a hundred times more thrilling than anything at Disneyland. Highlights include the Viper, a huge orange monster with seven loops; the appropriately named Goliath, full of harrowing 85mph dips; and Déjà Vu, a high-speed gut-wrencher that twists and jerks you in several different directions at once. The latest coaster, Tatsu, might be the biggest white-knuckler of all, sending you through the requisite loops while strapped in face-down at a 90-degree angle. The adjacent water park, **Hurricane Harbor** (same hours; $30, kids $21, or $70 for both parks; ⓦ www.sixflags.com/parks/hurricaneharborla), provides aquatic fun if you don't mind getting splashed by throngs of giddy pre-adolescents.

The I-14 freeway, also called the Antelope Valley Freeway, branches off from I-5 into an extension of the Mojave Desert and takes you to 745-acre **Vasquez Rocks Park**, off Agua Dulce Canyon Road at 10700 W Escondido Canyon Rd (☎661/268-0840), where acres of jagged, rocky outcroppings and an undulating terrain make for one of Hollywood's favorite film locations: everything from *The Flintstones* to *Dracula* to *Star Trek* has been shot here. Even more mythically, the illicit treasure of bandit Tiburcio Vásquez – one of LA's legendary figures, something like a Hispanic Jesse James – is supposedly buried in the vicinity. Further up I-14, near the remote desert burg of **LANCASTER**, the awe-inspiring **Antelope Valley Poppy Reserve**, on Lancaster Drive, spreads over 1800 acres. The reserve comes alive in late April as the site of the annual **California Poppy Festival** (during event, 10am–6pm; tickets $7; ☎661/723-6075, ⓦ www.poppyfestival.com), when the eye-blinding, fiery blooms appear in a sea of fluorescent orange.

9

Malibu and the Santa Monica Mountains

H ome to some of LA's most expensive real estate, **MALIBU** and the **SANTA MONICA MOUNTAINS** comprise a sweeping terrain relatively free from smog and crime, representing the contemporary good life in Southern California. Any Angeleno lucky enough to make it almost immediately tries to move here. The area features some of LA's most picturesque scenery, its rambling canyons, striking valleys, and dense forests making up a surprisingly large, pristine wilderness amid the metropolis.

Ironically, the town and mountains are also under constant threat from natural dangers, built on eroding cliffs forever sliding into the ocean and blackened by summer hillside fires, which leave a slick residue of burnt chaparral – a perfect surface for the catastrophic floods and mudslides that come just a few months later. The periodic arrival of El Niño–driven wet weather only makes the situation more dire, with watery calamities a constant, inescapable threat, sometimes with whole neighborhoods being washed away.

From **Pacific Palisades**, a chic district just northwest of Santa Monica, to rustic **Topanga Canyon**, a wooded neighborhood with an artistic flair, to beautiful **Point Dume**, a whale-watching promontory, these areas are best navigated by car on the popular beachside motorway, the Pacific Coast Highway (also known as "PCH" or Highway 1). North of PCH, **Mulholland Highway** provides an alternative trip through the area, winding through the Santa Monica Mountains and skipping Malibu entirely, instead reaching the ocean less than a mile from LA County's distant northwest boundary – at one of its prime spots for surfing.

Pacific Palisades

Driving north on PCH beyond the bluffs of Santa Monica, you reach the sandy crescent of **Will Rogers State Beach** and, on the other side of the road, **PACIFIC PALISADES**, once an upper-crust community of artists and writers, but now the home of media-industry millionaires. No amount of wealth, however, has been able to keep the district's hillsides from slowly falling into the ocean. With each winter's storms, more of the place gets washed away

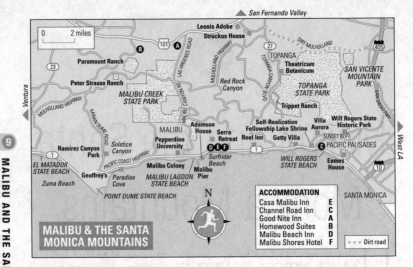

ACCOMMODATION
Casa Malibu Inn	E
Channel Road Inn	C
Good Nite Inn	A
Homewood Suites	B
Malibu Beach Inn	D
Malibu Shores Hotel	F

= = = Dirt road

MALIBU & THE SANTA MONICA MOUNTAINS

by simple erosion or mudslides, blocking traffic on PCH and shrinking the backyards of the clifftop homes.

The Eames House and around

You can't visit most of the homes of the elite, with the notable exception of the **Eames House**, also known as Case Study House #8, just off PCH at 203 Chautauqua Blvd, perhaps the most influential house of post-war LA. Fashioned out of prefabricated industrial parts in 1947 as part of the renowned Case Study Program (see box, p.110), the compound boasts a main residential unit and an adjacent studio building, both resembling large, colored metal-and-glass boxes, or a Mondrian painting in 3D, and surrounded by a grove of eucalyptus trees. The house's builders, Charles and Ray Eames (his wife), were one of the city's most creative couples in the 1950s, contributing thoughtful designs for art and architecture, furniture (especially the famous molded bucket chairs), and cinema – their short film *House: after 5 years* celebrates their residence with no less than three hundred evocative photographs. For modern architecture fans, this is probably the most beloved spot in LA; the Eames family still owns and uses the structure, and in 2006 the site was declared a National Historic Landmark. However, only the grounds and exterior are viewable (Mon–Fri 10am–4pm, Sat 10am–3pm; free; by appointment only at ☏310/459-9663, ⊛www.eamesfoundation.org).

The neighboring **Entenza House**, at no. 205, which was #9 in the Case Study Program, isn't quite up to the standard of the landmark next door, but this steel-framed structure was nonetheless built by the same architect, Charles Eames, with help from Eero Saarinen (best known for New York's TWA Terminal); also in this glorious pocket of modern architecture is Richard Neutra's wood, glass, and steel marvel, the **Bailey House**, no. 219, which was #20 in the Program and sold a few years ago for $4 million — a steal, given that some Neutra houses, which are treated like huge pieces of modernist art, have recently been on the market for as much as $20 million. Best of the more contemporary buildings in Pacific Palisades is the **Schwartz House**, just north, off W Channel Rd at 444 Sycamore St, designed in 1994 by Pierre

Koenig, more famous for his late-1950s Case Study House #22 (see box, p.110). His unique design includes a black-steel frame and foundation pivoted at a 30-degree angle from the rest of the boxy gray house, making for an unusual Rubik's Cube effect, which also has the function of keeping the living room and bedrooms out of the full glare of the rising sun.

Will Rogers State Historic Park

Continue north on Chautauqua Blvd, then east on Sunset Boulevard to **Will Rogers State Historic Park** (summer daily 8am–dusk; rest of year daily 8am–6pm; free; T 310/454-8212), a steep climb from the MTA bus (#2, #302) stop. This was the home and ranch of Depression-era cowboy philosopher and journalist **Will Rogers**, one of America's most popular figures of the time, and renowned for saying that he "never met a man he didn't like" – though it's less well-known that he was a socialist who was also, ironically, mayor of Beverly Hills. His isolated Pacific Palisades estate did much to attract Hollywood celebrities, many of whom were his friends, away from central LA, which at the time was quite a trip. After his death in a plane crash in 1935, there was a nationwide thirty-minute silence. The overgrown ranch-style house serves as an informal **museum**, filled with cowboy gear and Native American art. Though the house has been renovated recently, the state is still working on restoring the grounds to something resembling their appearance in Rogers' time. The surrounding 200-acre park has miles of foot and bridle paths, including **polo grounds** where matches take place during the spring and summer (April–Oct Sat 2–5pm, Sun 10am–1pm; free).

Castellammare

The western side of Pacific Palisades, **Castellammare** was named after a Latin port known as the "castle by the sea," its 1920s design mimicking Italian villas and Spanish Colonial estates. Although it's now just another rich suburb, it does hold some appeal, mainly in structures whose settings are just as dramatic as their architecture.

Just before the street reaches PCH, Sunset Boulevard takes a large, curving descent around the **Self-Realization Fellowship Lake Shrine**, 17190 Sunset Blvd (Tues–Sat 9am–4.30pm, Sun 12.30–4.30pm; free; T 310/454-4114, Ⓦ www.yogananda-srf.org/temples/lakeshrine), a religious monument created in 1950 by Paramahansa Yogananda, whose life and works are recounted in an on-site **museum** (Tues–Sat 11am–4pm, Sun 10–10.30am & noon–4pm; free), detailing the spiritual leader's progressive thoughts on ecumenism, global peace, and the like. The ten-acre lake shrine is an ode to world faiths, featuring symbols and credos of the major religions. Visitors are invited to circle the lake on a literal path of spiritual enlightenment, pausing to view such sights as the **windmill chapel** (Tues–Sun 1–4.30pm; free), a church built as a replica of a sixteenth-century Dutch windmill, along with a massive archway topped with copper lotus flowers, a houseboat that the shrine's Indian founder once used, a bird refuge, gardens with religious symbols, and plaques and signs quoting the Bible, the Koran, and such. The giant, gold-domed **temple** looming above on the hilltop at 17080 Sunset Blvd is usually off-limits, except on Sunday mornings (9am & 11am, also Thurs 8pm) when lectures are given on such New Age topics as finding your soul and experiencing "Life – A Cosmic Motion Picture." With any luck, you might even spot a few earthly motion-picture stars in the crowd, getting their spiritual sustenance.

Up the bluffs from Sunset, the **Villa Aurora**, 520 Paseo Miramar, is an idyllic 1927 Spanish Colonial structure that was conceived as a public-relations project by the *LA Times*, which devoted a series of articles to the construction of the house and all its modern amenities – dishwasher, electric fridge, gas range, three-car garage – and stunning Mediterranean style, carried through in the Spanish tile, wrought-iron balconies, and alluring gardens. Readers were encouraged to tour the house and, it was hoped, be inspired to buy their own suburban dream home. Later, as the home of writer Lion Feuchtwanger, it became the focus of German emigres, hosting salons attended by Bertolt Brecht, Thomas Mann, Kurt Weill, Arnold Schoenberg, and Fritz Lang, as well as Charlie Chaplin, and has since been reborn as a nonprofit organization that presents lectures, poetry readings, film screenings, and music recitals of contemporary artists from Europe (usually free; ☏310/454-4231, ⓦ www.villa-aurora.org).

The Getty Villa

Just west of Sunset Boulevard's intersection with PCH, the **Getty Villa,** 17985 PCH (Thurs–Mon 10am–5pm; free, parking $8 or take Metro Bus #534; by reservation only at ☏310/440-7300, ⓦ www.getty.edu), was originally the site of the full Getty Museum, until that site was reconstructed on a West LA hilltop (see p.129) and this one underwent significant renovation. It reopened in 2006 and now serves as the Getty Foundation's spectacular showcase for its wide array of Greek and Roman antiquities. If classical art is your forte, this should be your one essential stop in Southern California. Modeled after a Roman country house buried by Mount Vesuvius in 79 AD, the villa is built around its own fetching gardens, one an expansive courtyard complex surrounding a long, shallow pool and peppered with black, faintly menacing replicas of stern-looking Roman heads, the other a pleasant herb garden that shows the kinds of plants used for cooking two millennia ago.

Inside, the museum is based around a two-story peristyle and courtyard, where a quaint pool is surrounded by more austere black statues. The rooms are grouped in themes ranging from religious and mythic to theatrical to martial. Highlights include the *Getty Kouros*, a rigidly posed figure of a boy that conservators openly state could be a later forgery, a *Cult Statue of Aphrodite* from the Golden Age of Greece (fifth century BC), with flowing robe and

▲ Getty Villa

voluptuous limestone figure, and a Hellenistic *Statue of a Victorious Youth*, wearing only an olive wreath, which was carefully restored after having been recovered from the sea floor. Athenian vases are also well represented, many of them the red-ground variety, as are ancient kylikes, or drinking vessels, and ceremonial amphorae, or vases given as prizes in athletic contests. Not to be missed is a wondrous Roman skyphos, a fragile-looking blue vase decorated with white cameos of Bacchus and his friends, properly preparing for a bacchanalia. Keep in mind that forty of these items will soon be returning to their ancient home: the Italian government made an agreement with the Getty to send them back after doubts were raised about the legality of their provenance. Still, there's more than enough here to keep you interested, and the site easily merits a full afternoon of exploration.

Topanga Canyon

Around Topanga Canyon Boulevard north of PCH, **Topanga Canyon** is a stunning natural preserve. With hillsides covered in golden poppies and wildflowers, one hundred and fifty thousand acres of these mountains and adjacent seashore have been protected as the **Santa Monica Mountains National Recreation Area** (ⓦwww.lamountains.org). Boasting fine views and fresh air, the area is wilderness in many places, and you can still spot a variety of deer, coyote, and even the odd mountain lion. Like LA itself, the mountains are not without an element of danger, especially in winter and early spring, when mudslides cause damage that can prevent you from traversing certain trails. Otherwise, rangers offer free guided hikes throughout the mountains most weekends (information and reservations at ⓣ818/597-9192). Also, there are self-guided trails through the canyon's **Topanga State Park**, off Old Topanga Canyon Boulevard at the crest of the mountains, with spectacular views over the Pacific. A good starting point for visitors is **Trippet Ranch**, east of the boulevard on Entrada Road, where trails like the Musch Trail - an easygoing trek through prime wildflower country-thread through terrain less rugged than other parts of the park. The local Audubon Society offers monthly birdwatching hikes through this and other LA-area nature zones (reserve at ⓣ323/874-1318, ⓦwww.laaudubon.org). If you'd like to find out more, the Santa Monica Mountains **visitor center** in neighboring Thousand Oaks, 401 W Hillcrest Drive (daily 9am–5pm; ⓣ805/370-2301, ⓦwww.nps.gov/samo), has maps and information.

The nearby community of **TOPANGA**, further up Topanga Canyon Boulevard, was a proving ground for West Coast rock music in the 1960s and 70s, when Neil Young, the Byrds, Canned Heat, Emmylou Harris, Joni Mitchell, Jim (and Van) Morrison, and many other artists moved here and held all-night jam sessions in the fabled Topanga Corral nightclub (burned in 1986) or in sycamore groves along Topanga Creek; a less salubrious arrival was Charles Manson, whose followers managed to kill a resident in 1969. The neighborhood still has an air of history, although many musicians have left, making way for richer folk without an ounce of musical talent. One of the few conventional attractions is the **Will Geer Theatricum Botanicum**, 1419 Topanga Canyon Blvd, a wooded outdoor amphitheater that usually runs a pair of good summer performances of Shakespeare, and another pair of more modern works (June–Oct Fri–Sun; $20–25, kids $8; information and tickets at ⓣ310/455-3723,

@www.theatricum.com). Named after and founded by Will Geer, TV's Grandpa Walton, who moved here to get away from the Hollywood blacklist in the 1950s, the theater is still very much a family affair, with daughter Ellen now directing the plays. If you're around for Memorial Day weekend, drop by the area for **Topanga Days** (at the **Topanga Community House**, 1440 Topanga Canyon Blvd; $15; info at T 310/455-1980, @www.topangacommunityclub .org), a country-flavored fair with art-and-craft booths, belly-dancing, music, and vegetarian-oriented cuisine.

Before leaving the area, don't miss **Red Rock Canyon**, off Old Topanga Canyon Road at 23601 Red Rock Road, a stunning red-banded sandstone gorge that was formerly a Boy Scout retreat and is now a state park. The colorful rock formations, surrounding gardens, and riparian wildlife give you a good reason to leave your car behind and go exploring on foot.

Malibu

Further up PCH, past a long stretch of gated beachfront homes, lies **MALIBU**, the very name of which conjures up images of beautiful people sunbathing on palm-fringed beaches and lazily consuming cocktails. However, getting to the beach itself is a notorious problem for the public here (see box opposite). As you enter the small town, the succession of tourist-oriented surf shops and unassuming restaurants around **Malibu Pier** (primarily for fishing, at 23000 PCH), don't exactly reek of big money, but the secluded estates just inland are as valuable as any in the entire US.

Malibu Lagoon State Beach and around

Adjacent to the pier, **Surfrider Beach** is a major surfing nexus, first gaining notice when the sport was brought over from Hawaii and mastered by Southern California pioneers. The waves are best in late summer, when storms off Mexico cause them to reach upwards of eight feet – not huge for serious pros, but big enough for you. This was the surfing capital of the world in the early 1960s, with the *Gidget* and *Beach Blanket Bingo* movies (starring the likes of Sandra Dee, Annette Funicello, and Frankie Avalon) helping draw the masses. Just to the west of Surfrider is **Malibu Lagoon State Beach** (daily 8am–dusk; T 818/880-0350), a nature reserve where birdwatching walks around the lagoon are offered on occasional weekends, along with seasonal guided tours that showcase, among other things, the sea life in the marshes and tide pools. A small **museum**, 23200 PCH (Wed–Sat 11am–3pm; donation), gives you the historical rundown, from the Chumash era up to the arrival of Hollywood movie stars, with special emphasis on the long-running "Rindge saga" that informs much of Malibu's modern history.

The story involves one **May K. Rindge** (widow of entrepreneur Frederick Rindge), who, up until the 1920s, owned all of Malibu – considered at the time to be the single most valuable real-estate parcel in the US. Employing armed guards and dynamiting roads to keep travelers from crossing her land on their way to and from Santa Monica, Rindge operated her own roads and private railroad and fought for years to prevent the Southern Pacific Railroad from laying down track through her property, as well as the state of California from building the Pacific Coast Highway across her land. She ultimately lost her legal battle in the state supreme court, and her money in the Depression; the road was built in 1928.

Visitors to Malibu commonly believe that all **beaches** in the area, aside from the officially marked state or county variety, are off-limits to interlopers – not surprising considering the sands are located in the very backyards of the gated communities that hug the Malibu shoreline. In reality, the sand along Santa Monica Bay is **open to visitors** below the high-tide mark, which means that as long as you stay off the private beachside territory above that mark (ie sticking to where the sand is wet and/or matted, instead of dry and hilly), you can go anywhere you please, peering into the guarded domains of the rich and famous – of which there are many, as any guide to stars' homes will tell you. The challenge, however, is in finding the **pedestrian rights-of-way** that give access to the beach. To begin with, there are no rights-of-way around the Malibu Colony, that gated and well-guarded celebrity province in the center of town, but if you don't mind walking a mile and a half along the ocean to get to the beaches behind these homes, you can park your car along the 22700 block of PCH (public parking lots are rare around here) and then take the unmarked stairway down to the sands. If for some reason you're thwarted at that entrance, or your *Map to the Stars' Oceanside Houses* simply directs you elsewhere, other access points can be found at 19900, 20300, and several between 24300 and 25100 PCH – admittedly farther from where the glitzy action is. Keep in mind also that these public-access points have been the subject of a number of **lawsuits** in recent years, with the wealthy sometimes putting up barriers — or misleading "Private Property" signs — to the less well-heeled, and aggrieved beach lovers seeking their revenge in court. If possible, don't let these things deter you, for the above access points are all legally protected and well established. Make sure to report any illegal obstructions to public access to the state coastal commission (⊕805/585-1800), which tries to rigorously enforce the rules and can provide additional information on any public easement in the area.

For a much simpler approach, drop by the Malibu Pier and then go north a half-mile to a mile east to Carbon Beach, also known as "Billionaire's Beach," which lines many of the back doors of the elite, and even features a prominent, legendary **"Dealmaker's Rock,"** where the rich and famous, or at least their producers, lawyers, and agents, cut deals in bathing suits and jogging sweats. Even better, what decent works of architecture there are in Malibu can be spotted in full glory along this beach. There are few better than Richard Meier's stunning **Ackerberg House**, 22466 PCH, which looks like a nondescript wall of cement and white tile from the street, but from the beach looks exactly as its architect intended: a 1986 practice run for the Getty Center, rendered small, with the same rigidly geometric form clad in white-steel paneling and wraparound windows.

Before her mother went broke, Rindge's daughter and her husband hired architect Stiles O. Clements, of the legendary firm of Morgan, Walls and Clements (see box, p.78), to design the magnificent **Adamson House** (grounds 8am–sunset, house Wed–Sat 11am–3pm; $5; ⊕310/456-8432, ⓦwww.adamsonhouse .org), on the grounds of the Malibu Lagoon museum at 23200 PCH. One of LA's finest pieces of Spanish Colonial architecture, the opulent house features Mission Revival and Moorish elements, such as individually carved teak doors, glazed ceramic tiles, detailed ironwork, and Spanish and Middle Eastern furnishings, as well as expansive gardens and a pool and fountain.

The Malibu Colony and downtown

After May Rindge's mischief finally ceased, her son took over the ranch and quickly sold much of the land, establishing the **Malibu Colony**, along Malibu Colony Drive off of Malibu Road, as a haven for movie stars. Unless you take a long oceanside trek (see box, p.219) to see the estates of the glitterati from the sands, there's very little to see here because the public is barred admittance. For a celluloid look inside, check out Robert Altman's *The Long Goodbye*, in which the colony, and Altman's own house, plays home to washed-up artists and blasé murder suspects. If you're after a glimpse of the stars, visit the **Malibu Colony Plaza**, near the area's gated entrance, good for starspotting and stocking up on food and drink before a day on the sands, or **Malibu Country Mart**, 3835 Cross Creek Rd, where celebrities are regularly seen munching on veggies or sipping espressos.

To the north, spiritual relaxation can be found at the **Serra Retreat**, 3401 Serra Rd (☎310/456-6631, ⓦwww.serraretreat.com), a nondenominational religious haven named for Franciscan friar and missionary Junípero Serra, one of several such retreats operated by the friars throughout the West. You can enjoy a weekend getaway here in one of the hundred rooms, wander the flower gardens or get a fantastic hilltop view of the Pacific. The retreat was originally meant to be the **Rindge Mansion**, but construction was mothballed during the Depression and the half-built property given over to the Franciscans, who finished the mansion and established their retreat here in 1943, only to see it burn down in 1970 and rebuilt after the missions of old.

North of downtown

Pepperdine University, 24255 PCH, moved north of downtown Malibu after hastily abandoning its Art Deco digs in South Central LA in 1971, and is mainly notable for its sloping green lawns and gigantic white cross. The campus's **Frederick R. Weisman Museum of Art** (Tues–Sun 11am–5pm; free; ⓦwww .pepperdine.edu/arts/museum) sometimes puts on good shows of modern abstraction and California art.

Across from Pepperdine, the six-acre, hilltop **Malibu Bluffs State Park**, at the intersection of Malibu Canyon Rd at 24250 PCH, is a prime local spot for whale watching in the winter months (November through March), when you may spot orcas or baleen whales, depending on the time and weather. Further up, the less-crowded shoreline of **Dan Blocker County Beach**, 26000 PCH – dedicated to the actor who played Hoss in TV's *Bonanza* – is the most appealing sight before you get to Corral Canyon Road, which leads you into **Solstice Canyon Park**, one of LA's hidden treasures and also one of its most peculiar. A mile down placid Solstice Canyon Creek on the Solstice Canyon Trail is a rustic **cabin** from 1865 sitting in a state of arrested dilapidation – supposedly the oldest stone structure in Malibu. Past the cabin are the atmospheric remains of a modern estate known as **Tropical Terrace**, built in 1952 by master architect Paul R. Williams (more famous for the MCA Building in Beverly Hills, p.119), which was once surrounded by a ranch stocked with buffalo, camels, giraffes, and African deer. Burned in 1982, the basic structure of the house is still standing, as are its surrounding brick steps, garden terraces – with inlaid horseshoes and bits of colored glass – and a partially visible bomb shelter, with trees sprouting through the concrete and vines covering the brickwork. Beyond this, part of the estate was also leased by the technology firm TRW to test satellite and medical equipment, and you can still spot several structures for this research (done here because of the acoustic quirks of the canyon) along the 1.5-mile TRW Loop Trail. Several other trails here are worth the jaunt, ranging from one-to-two miles and taking you past assorted small seasonal waterfalls, oak groves, wildlife such as deer and bobcat, and some fine views out to the Pacific.

Point Dume and beyond

Several miles northwards up the coast from downtown Malibu, **Point Dume**, named after the Franciscan padre Francisco Dumetz in 1793, is the tip of a great seaward promontory of lava from an ancient volcano, offering stunning vistas of Santa Monica Bay. Along with being a popular whale-watching spot from November to March, it also features some excellent strips of sand. **Zuma Beach** (most beaches in the area daily 7am–10pm; parking $7-8), north at 30000 PCH, the largest of the LA County beaches, is popular for its surfing, scuba diving and fishing; it's also where the surprise ending of the original *Planet of the Apes* was filmed. On the east side of the point, at 28128 PCH, **Paradise Cove** is a private beach that makes for a fine walk, with superb views of fancy houses getting ready to fall into the surf from their high perches. Parking, unfortunately, is $25, so you're best off hoofing it for a mile heading east from Point Dume County Beach, at the tip of the promontory.

North of Point Dume and PCH, **Ramirez Canyon Park**, at 5750 Ramirez Canyon Rd, in Ramirez Canyon Park (tours $35; by reservation only at ⊤310/589-2850, ⊚www.lamountains.com), is a 22-acre complex of houses and gardens that Barbra Streisand donated to the Santa Monica Mountains Conservancy in 1993. Amid extensive flower, herb, and fruit gardens, you can get a glimpse into her former properties: the stained-glass windows and river-rock fireplace of the quaint "Barn," the Mediterranean and Art Nouveau stylings of the "Peach House," and the Craftsman splendor of the singer's one-time production company building, the "Barwood." The finest building on the site is the "Deco House," with its red-and-black colors, geometric decor, and stainless-steel panels taken from Downtown's Richfield Building, before that Art Deco monument was destroyed in 1968.

Several miles up the coast from Point Dume, at 32100 PCH, **El Matador State Beach** was where the opening shots of the movie musical *Grease* were filmed, and still has the flair of a secluded private beach, because its entrance is an easily missable turn off PCH – look for it on the south side of the road about a half-mile east of the junction with Encinal Canyon Drive. Another five miles north, where Mulholland Drive reaches the ocean, **Leo Carrillo** ("ca-REE-oh") **State Beach Park**, 35000 PCH, marks the northwestern border of LA County. The mile-long sandy beach is divided by Sequit Point, a bluff with underwater caves and a tunnel you can pass through at low tide, and is also one of LA's best campgrounds (see p.256). The beach has starred in quite a few Hollywood flicks (including several in the *Gidget* series), much like its namesake: Carrillo was an actor who appeared in nearly one hundred films and was best known as Pancho in the 1950s TV show *The Cisco Kid*. Today, his surname is synonymous with some of LA's best surf.

Mulholland Highway

Most familiar as the road running along the crest of the Hollywood Hills, Mulholland Drive continues a mile west of the 405 freeway as **Mulholland Highway**, taking drivers through the heart of the Santa Monica Mountains. For most of its first seven miles westward, from Encino Hills Drive to Topanga

Canyon Boulevard, Mulholland is a bumpy, winding dirt road that's closed to auto traffic, strewn with broken rocks, fallen trees, and sizable mudholes, truly earning its nickname, "**Dirt Mulholland**" – though the awe-inspiring vistas and abundant greenery are reward enough for hikers and mountain bikers. While in the area, don't miss the towering hilltop of the 10-acre **San Vicente Mountain Park**, 17500 Mulholland Hwy, less than three miles west of the 405 freeway. A decommissioned military site. it was used between 1956 and 1968 as a radar center and launching pad for Nike anti-aircraft missiles, to be fired in the event of a Soviet bomber run over LA. This unusual state park offers you the chance to climb a zigzagging stairway up to a hexagonal viewing platform on top of the command tower, where you can ponder the Cold War while staring down at striking vistas of the San Fernando Valley.

The Struckus House and Leonis Adobe

The paved, auto-friendly portion of Mulholland Highway can be picked up roughly around Canoga Avenue in the suburb of Woodland Hills, or from the Mulholland Drive exit off the 101 freeway. Just to the north, the **Struckus House**, Canoga Avenue at Saltillo Street, is one of LA's most unusual homes, designed by quirky architect Bruce Goff (see also LACMA's Pavilion for Japanese Art, p.84). Looking somewhat like an alien landing pod, it features a four-story redwood cylinder decorated with four vertically stacked, convex "eyes," a wooden roof with flywheel spokes, and a square door that pivots on a single ball-bearing. For a close-up look at another of the area's notable buildings, head north toward the 101, west of Mulholland Drive, to the **Leonis Adobe**, 23537 Calabasas Rd (Wed–Sun 1–4pm, Sat opens 10am; $4; ☏818/222-6511, ⓦ www.leonisadobemuseum.com), an 1844 ranch and adobe, which was remodeled in 1880. The grounds of this lovely Spanish estate include a black-smith, windmill, barn, and restored carriage, as well as the engaging **Plummer House**, a Victorian-era home relocated from Hollywood and now the rancho's visitor center, where you can see exhibits on the estate's history.

Malibu Creek State Park and Paramount Ranch

To the south, Mulholland Highway takes you through the forest, brush, and scattered dwellings of the Santa Monica Mountains, at times via dizzying switchbacks and narrow cliffside passages. There are many excellent state and regional parks here (get a sense of their size and splendor at ⓦ lamonica.com) and plenty of movie history, too. Perhaps the most notable site is **Malibu Creek State Park**, just south of Mulholland Highway on Las Virgenes Road (daily dawn–dusk; ☏818/880-0367), a scenic 4000-acre park that was once home to early Chumash tribes. It much later belonged to 20th Century-Fox studios, which filmed many Tarzan pictures here, as well as the original *Planet of the Apes*, and used the chaparral-covered hillsides to simulate South Korea for the film and TV show *M*A*S*H*. The park features countless gorgeous vistas, lagoons, buttes, and canyons, as well as sheer cliffs and the lovely watercourse of Malibu Creek itself; there's also the odd sight of Malibu Dam, a 1926 creation of onetime Malibu land baron May K. Rindge, which was been filled in with sediment and now acts as a 100-foot-tall waterfall. The park is known for its fishing, rock climbing, and bird watching – and wildlife viewing in general, since it's rich with eagles, mule deer, bobcats, and cougars, among many gentler creatures. Pick up a map at the visitor center or at a kiosk to avoid getting lost on its nearly fifteen miles of hiking trails, or make a reservation beforehand to pitch your tent and camp (see p.256).

▲ Filming a Western at Paramount Ranch

Further west on Mulholland, **Paramount Ranch**, 2813 Cornell Rd (daily 8am–5pm; 818/222-6511, ⓦwww.nps.gov/samo/maps/para.htm), is another old studio lot dating from 1927, with a few short trails and an intact Western movie set used in films starring Gary Cooper, W.C. Fields, and Hopalong Cassidy, and TV programs like *The Rifleman*, *The Cisco Kid*, and *Dr. Quinn Medicine Woman*. Film and TV crews still occasionally shoot here on weekdays, though generally without public notice. Oddly, visitors often mistake the phony rail station and tracks behind the set and the dummy cemetery for the real things.

West to the ocean

A few miles west of Cornell Road, at 30000 Mulholland Hwy, the charming **Peter Strauss Ranch** (ⓣ805/370-2301, ⓦwww.nps.gov/samo/maps/peter .htm) was once the site of the **Lake Enchanto Resort**, a top LA amusement spot from the 1930s through the 1950s, until a nearby dam burst and washed it away. Resurrected variously as a resort and a nudist colony, the property passed into the hands of actor and producer Peter Strauss, who, after yet another dam burst, turned it over to the Santa Monica Mountains Conservancy. Although a few hints of the old days remain – such as a disused swimming pool and terrazzo patio – the park is a pretty low-key attraction, with a short walking trail, aviary and cactus garden.

Mulholland continues westward until it reaches the Pacific Ocean near Leo Carrillo State Beach Park (see p.221), passing a number of excellent parks and striking vistas along the way, most of them controlled and protected by the Santa Monica Mountains Conservancy. Other than these natural delights, the last point of interest on Mulholland is the **Arch Oboler House**, a little-known Frank Lloyd Wright structure near Westlake Boulevard and the LA County line at 32436 Mulholland Hwy. The unfinished studio and gatehouse, angular curiosities built of wood and stone, were meant to be part of an expansive hillside complex for the now-forgotten director Oboler, creator of such works as the radio horror classic *Lights Out*, the first movie in 3D, *Bwana Devil*, and *Five*, about the survivors of a nuclear holocaust – which the director filmed here at his own residence.

Orange County

N ow that the abundant citrus groves that inspired its name are long gone, **ORANGE COUNTY** has more of a reputation for insular, suburban conservatism than it does for fruit. The long-standing stereotype painted the place as a West Coast version of Levittown – where tract homes and asphalt stretched to the horizon and anyone not conforming to bourgeois propriety was shunned or forced into exile in LA proper. These days, though, Orange County is no more bland and homogenous than any other part of metropolitan LA. In fact, the county has since the 1980s become multi-cultural, with rising numbers of Latino immigrants transforming cities like Santa Ana, and other newcomers from Southeast Asia, India, and Eastern Europe developing their own urban communities as well. The fractured social landscape of libertarian beach cities, reactionary old-line suburbs, burgeoning immigrant districts, and hordes of itinerant tourists is bound together by the ubiquitous freeway system.

The original heart of the 1940s and 1950s suburbs, **inland Orange County** is famous as the domain of Mickey Mouse and Knott's Berry Farm, with the other handful of diversions too spread out to be handily seen by public transit. More appealing, the **Orange County coast** is a collection of relaxed seaside towns with both easygoing "surfer-dude" attitudes and upscale, beach-condo snootiness. It's hard to identify the southern limit of the coastal cities: they just blend into even more housing colonies as you head further south – a seemingly endless exurban stretch between LA and San Diego.

Inland Orange County

Located in the heart of **INLAND ORANGE COUNTY**, the first modern theme park, **Disneyland**, was opened in 1955 by Walt Disney, who correctly divined that the area around the seminal playland – the bland burg of **Anaheim** – would become the next great population center in Southern California. It did, but not as he intended: for miles around the park stretch nothing but tacky strip malls, chain motels, and knick-knack shops. Nonetheless, this suburb and those around it continue to grow rapidly, drawing immigrants by the thousands. **Westminster**, for example, is now the site of Little Saigon, a center for Vietnamese expatriates, and is the most fervent bastion of anti-Communism in Southern California, long after the end of the Cold War.

One thing hasn't changed: Disneyland still dominates the area. Elsewhere, the thrill rides at **Knott's Berry Farm** go some way to restoring antique notions

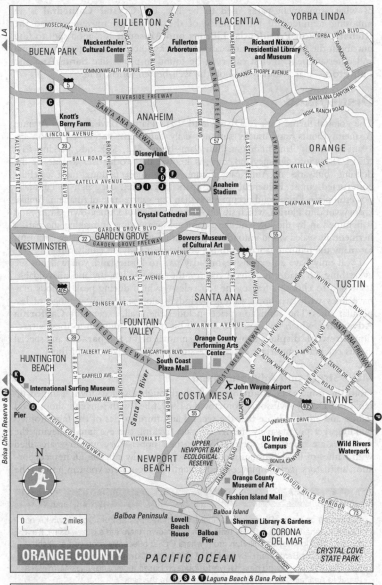

ORANGE COUNTY

10

ORANGE COUNTY

225

ACCOMMODATION

Best Western Huntington Beach	K	Fairmont Newport Beach	N
Comfort Inn	F	HI-Anaheim/Fullerton	A
Courtyard by Marriott	C	Hilton Waterfront Beach Resort	O
Desert Palms	J	Holiday Inn Buena Park	B
Disneyland Hotel	D	Inn at Laguna Beach	T
Mission Inn	P	Pavilions	H
Motel 6	G	Ritz-Carlton Laguna Niguel	R
Newport Coast Villas	Q	Stovall's Inn	I
Pacific Inn	M	Sun 'n Sands Motel	L
Park Place Inn	E	Surf and Sand Resort	S

of what amusement parks used to be like, the **Crystal Cathedral** is an imposing reminder of the potency of the evangelical movement, and the **Richard Nixon Presidential Library and Museum** is a good spot to find out about the illustrious life and career of Tricky Dick. Isolated spots of cultural and entertainment interest can even be found in places like **Santa Ana** and **Fullerton** – places usually well off the well-beaten tourist trail.

Disneyland

The colossal theme park of **Disneyland**, 1313 Harbor Blvd at Katella Avenue, Anaheim (hours vary, usually summer daily 8am–1am; rest of year Mon–Fri 10am–6pm, Sat 9am–midnight, Sun 9am–10pm; $63, $53 kids, parking $11; ☎714/781-4565, ⓦdisneyland.com), is known the world over as one of the defining bulwarks of American culture – the most famous, most carefully constructed, most influential theme park anywhere. For such a culturally powerful place, Disneyland occupies less than one square mile of Anaheim (unlike Disneyworld in Florida, which sits on 46 square miles of Disney-owned turf), and is hemmed in by the low-end developments surrounding it, making the park a hermetically sealed world unto itself. Even within such rigid boundaries, it remains for many the ultimate fantasy, with the emphasis strongly on family fun.

If you only have an expensive, one-day pass to Disneyland, you will not see everything, no matter how hard you try: the lines are lengthy and unavoidable. It's wisest to choose a few of the top rides – which during peak periods may have lines with two-hour waiting periods – alongside a larger range of less popular ones. The admission price includes them all, except for **California Adventure**, which will cost you quite a bit more. In addition to these attractions, **firework displays** explode every summer night, and **parades** and special events celebrate important occasions – such as Mickey Mouse's birthday.

Main Street and Adventureland

From the front gates, **Main Street** leads through a scaled-down, camped-up replica of Disney's Missouri hometown *c*.1900, filled with souvenir shops, food stands, and arcades. Note that the second and third stories of the false-fronted buildings get progressively smaller in scale, tricking the eye into believing the structures are taller than they really are; their upper-story windows are filled with names of local "businessmen" who were actually notable Disney corporation animators, park employees, and executives. From here you can hop on the

Planning a trip to Disneyland

Depending on traffic, Disneyland is about 45 minutes by **car** from Downtown LA on the Santa Ana Freeway (I-5). By **train** from Downtown (there are a dozen daily), it's a thirty-minute journey to Fullerton, from where OCTD buses will drop you at Disneyland or Knott's Berry Farm. By **bus**, MTA #460 from Downtown takes about ninety minutes, and Greyhound runs twelve-to-fourteen buses a day and takes 45 minutes to get to Anaheim, from where it's an easy walk to the park.

As for **accommodation**, most people try to visit Disneyland just for the day and spend the night somewhere else, or at home. If you must stay in this rather drab and often overpriced area, we've listed some reasonable options on p.253; alternately, the *HI-Anaheim/Fullerton* hostel is the cheapest bet in the area (see p.255). If you don't want to eat the park's greasy fast food or its overpriced "fine dining," you'll need to leave the place and travel a fair way. The "Eating" listings on p.265 and p.288 suggest some of the more palatable options.

pint-sized Disneyland Railroad (usually two or three run at one time) that encircles the park **for a scenic tour**, or hail a horse-drawn streetcar. Most people just plow directly to **Sleeping Beauty's Castle**, a pseudo-Rhineland palace that employs the same progressive-scale technique as the windows on Main Street. Familiar from the Disney company logo, it certainly looks inviting, but in reality isn't much more than a giant prop - you can't go inside.

Radiating out clockwise from Main Street, **Adventureland** was built near the height of the Tiki craze in the 1950s, and could make for a swinging, retro-kitsch experience, if Disneyland ever bothered to fully renovate it. As it is, the old-time centerpiece, the Jungle Cruise, looks pretty antiquated these days, offering "tour guides" making crude puns about the fake animatronic beasts creaking amid the trees, and a few fake piranhas thrown in recently to provide more (tame) thrills. Tarzan's Treehouse isn't much better, little more than a movie tie-in taking up the space once occupied by the Swiss Family Robinson Treehouse. Now, catwalks in the branches of the huge artificial tree and rustic rooms with assorted playthings target an eight-year-old audience. Ultimately, if you're going to spend any time at all in this section, get in line for the **Indiana Jones Adventure**. Two hours of waiting in line are built into the ride, with an interactive archeological dig and 1930s-style newsreel show leading up to the main feature – a speedy journey along 2500ft of skull-encrusted corridors, loosely based on the *Indiana Jones* movie trilogy, in which you face fireballs, burning rubble, venomous snakes, and a rolling-boulder finale.

The nearby **New Orleans Square**, clockwise to the northwest of Adventureland, is the site of **Club 33**, Walt's ultra-exclusive dinner club for his chums in the corporate and political elite, which even today offers membership by invitation at a (last-reported) entry cost of $10,000. Still, there's a 14-year waiting list to get into the club, where microphones were once hidden in the chandeliers to record the comments of dinner guests. It's also the only place in the park where alcohol is served. Although you definitely can't get in, you can spot the club's door, marked with a "33." The door is located next to the facade of the *Blue Bayou* restaurant, which, despite its jaw-dropping prices for steak and seafood, has some of the best dining ambience in Orange County: a darkly romantic waterfront scene with dim lighting, old-fashioned Southern decor, and imitation crickets chirping in the distance. (Reserve early at ☎714/956-6755, the reservation line for all Disneyland restaurants, or ☎714/781-3463 for priority seating.)

From your table, you'll be able to see crowds lining up for the square's signature ride, the **Pirates of the Caribbean**, a renowned boat-trip through underground caverns, with drunken pirates singing, laughing skeletons, and all manner of ruddy-cheeked yokels hooting and bellowing for your amusement. The ride has, however, been significantly neutered in recent years, as the evil blokes no longer chase women and assorted blatant movie tie-ins have been included to cash in on the film franchise, which was itself based on the ride. Nearby, another of Disneyland's legendary rides, the **Haunted Mansion**, features a riotous "doom buggy" tour in the company of the house ghouls, with a nightmarish elevator ride to start the trip off in skin-crawling fashion and plenty of creepy portraits to stare at along the way, culminating with a ghost hitching a ride in your buggy.

Frontierland and Fantasyland

Less fun is **Frontierland**, the smallest of the various themelands, located further clockwise around the park. Supposedly the area takes its cues from the Wild West and the tales of Mark Twain, but any unsavory and complex elements have been carefully deleted; still, Tom Sawyer Island offers an elaborate playground for tots, with treehouses, caves, and canoes. It's in the process of being "updated" with animatronic pirates and a Dead Man's Grotto to tie in with Disney's movie franchise, *Pirates of the Caribbean*. The centerpiece of Frontierland, Thunder Mountain Railroad, is a slow-moving roller coaster that plods through a rocky landscape resembling a cartoon version of a Hollywood Western. Nearby, the focus of **Critter Country** is Splash Mountain, a fun log-flume ride in which you can expect to get drenched. Young children and those with a flair for the surreal will find amusement in adjacent The Many Adventures of Winnie the Pooh, in which you follow Pooh Bear as he has bizarre dreams and encounters strange creatures in the Hundred Acre Wood.

Across the drawbridge from Main Street, **Fantasyland** shows off the cleverest and most sentimental aspects of the Disney mindset. The highlight, Mr Toad's Wild Ride, is a jerky funhouse trip through Victorian England featuring a trip into hell. The other rides are much tamer, such as those involving Peter Pan flying over London, Snow White being tormented by the wicked witch, and Alice in Wonderland descending down the rabbit hole. It's a Small World gets the most extreme reactions, with children delighting in this boat tour of the world's continents – in which 400 animated dolls sing the same cloying song over and over again – and adults finding it a slow, gurgling torture test. Distract yourself by trying to spot the sole non-smiling character on the entire ride, a frowning clown in the final room. Lastly, the one Fantasyland roller coaster, the Matterhorn, is somewhat entertaining for its phony cement mountain and goofy abominable snowman appearing when you round a corner, though the dips and curves are rather bland compared with most coasters these days.

Tomorrowland and Toontown

On the park's northern end, **Toontown**, a cartoon village with goofy sound effects and Day-Glo colors, is aimed only for the under-10 set and generally unbearable for older, thrill-seeking visitors, with the exception of Roger

Rabbit's Car Toon Spin, which jerks you around in a cartoon taxi through a goofy landscape based on scenes from the 1988 movie.

On the eastern side of the park, **Tomorrowland** is Disney's vision of the future, where theme-park regulars know to go first when the place opens. Here, the Space Mountain roller coaster zips through the pitch-blackness of "outer space," bumbling scientists dabble with 3D trickery in Honey, I Shrunk the Audience, and a runaway space cruiser blasts through the Moon of Endor (home of the Ewoks) in George Lucas's Star Tours. This idea of the future occasionally looks like a hangover from the past – note rides such as Autopia, where you drive a miniature car at a glacial pace – but

▲ Entrance to Tomorrowland in Disneyland

this fun zone has been updated somewhat in recent years, with new rides like the Jules Verne–inspired Astro Orbiter taking the place of old ones like the torpid PeopleMover and its failed replacement, Rocket Rods. The Finding Nemo Submarine Voyage picks up where its predecessor, 20,000 Leagues Under the Sea, left off, giving you a quick underwater tour of notable aquatic scenes from a hit movie. One of the more interesting additions is Innoventions, which comes with a lot of futurist babble but is really a fun opportunity to look at, and play with, the latest special effects.

California Adventure

The newest part of Disneyland is **California Adventure**, technically a separate park but connected to the main one in architecture, style, and spirit. Aside from its slightly better food, California Adventure is really just another "land" to visit, albeit a much more expensive one. You cannot get access to both parks with a single-day admission ticket, so if you want to visit, you'll instead have to shell out another $63 or plunk down $83 for a two-day pass that covers both. Such high prices and the comparative lack of thrills have really punctured the hype that Disneyland built up for this park, so unless you're hopelessly obsessed by all things Disney, you're better off avoiding the place.

There are a handful of highlights if you do visit: Grizzly River Run is a fun giant-inner-tube ride, splashing through plunges and "caverns"; Soarin' Over California is an exciting trip on a mock-experimental aircraft that buzzes through hairpin turns and steep dives; and the **Pacific Pier** zone has a slew of old-fashioned carnival rides – from California Screamin', a sizable roller coaster, to the Ferris-like Sun Wheel – that only faintly recall the wilder, harder-edged midways of California's past. There's also a rather tame zone devoted to Tinseltown, the **Hollywood Pictures Backlot** which, aside from a few theaters, special-effects displays, and the Twilight Zone Tower of Terror (a shock-drop ride in a haunted hotel), is mainly notable for its design, which loosely borrows from the movie set of D.W. Griffith's 1916 failure *Intolerance* – exotic columns, squatting elephants, and so on (a design also used in the Hollywood and Highland mall; see p.101). Perhaps most problematic for families visiting California Adventure is the relative lack of kid-oriented attractions, which are basically confined to the colorful, slow-moving rides of **A Bug's Land** and the 3D arcade-style ride Toy Story Mania, opening in summer 2008.

Knott's Berry Farm

Though making up a distinct minority, partisans of **Knott's Berry Farm**, four miles northwest of Disneyland, off the Santa Ana Freeway at 8039 Beach Blvd (hours vary, usually summer Sun–Thurs 9am–11pm, Fri & Sat 9am–midnight; rest of year Mon–Fri 10am–6pm, Sat 10am–10pm, Sun 10am–7pm; $50, kids $19; ☎714/220-5200, ⓦwww.knotts.com), claims it's every bit as good, if not better, than Disneyland—at least for thrill rides. This relaxed, though still pricey, park was born during the Depression, when people began lining up for the fried-chicken dinners prepared by Mrs Knott, a local farmer's wife. To amuse the children while they waited for their food, Mr Knott reconstructed a Wild West ghost town and added amusements until the park had grown into the sprawling sideshow of roller coasters and carnival rides standing today.

Unlike Disneyland, this park can easily be seen in one day, as long as you concentrate on the roller coasters. Although there are ostensibly six themed lands here, several of them consist only of familiar carnival rides, fast-food stands, and dodgy versions of history. **Camp Snoopy** is the Knott's version of

Disney's Toontown, enlivened by the presence of the Sierra Sidewinder roller coaster, while the **Wild Water Wilderness** isn't really a theme area at all, but simply the site of the moderately exciting Bigfoot Rapids giant-inner-tube ride. Recently opened in the formerly tame **Ghost Town** part of the park, the GhostRider roller coaster delivers excellent thrills with its old-fashioned wooden design and "haunted mine train" theme. The gut-wrenching, inverted Silver Bullet has also debuted, sending you around multiple loops and rolls that can easily, and happily, induce nausea.

Beyond this, **Fiesta Village** is home to Montezooma's Revenge, the original one-loop coaster, and Jaguar, a high-flying coaster that spins you around the park concourse. The **Boardwalk** is all about heart-thumping thrill rides: the Boomerang, a forward-and-back coaster that spends a lot of time upside-down; Supreme Scream, a delightfully terrifying freefall drop; Xcelerator, a coaster with a stomach-churning catapult mechanism; and the Perilous Plunge, a hellish drop at a 75-degree angle that's far more exciting than any old log-flume ride. This Boardwalk, Knott's version of a carnival midway, with its death-defying rides and vomit-inducing thrills, easily puts Disney's Pacific Pier to shame. The adjacent Knott's water park, **Soak City U.S.A.** (June–Sept only, hours vary but generally daily 10am–5pm or 6pm; $28, $17 for children or adult entry after 3pm; ⊛www.knotts.com/soakcity), offers 21 rides of various heights and speeds, almost all of them involving the familiar water slides – either with or without an inner tube – which can really bring out the sweltering masses on a hot summer day.

Around Disneyland

South of Disneyland just off the Santa Ana Freeway, in otherwise uneventful **GARDEN GROVE**, the giant **Crystal Cathedral**, 12141 Lewis St (tours Mon–Sat 9am–3.30pm; free; ☎714/971-4013, ⊛www.crystalcathedral.org) is a hugely garish Philip Johnson design of tubular space-frames and plate-glass walls that forms part of the vision of televangelist Robert Schuller. Not content with owning the world's first drive-in church next door, Schuller commissioned this dramatic prop to boost the ratings of his Sunday sermons, raising $1.5 million for its construction during one service alone. These sermon-spectacles reach their climax with the special **Christmas production** (late-Nov to early Jan; $35-55; reserve at ☎714/544-5679), using live animals in biblical roles and people disguised as angels suspended on ropes.

A more worthwhile attraction lies in the nearby burg of **SANTA ANA**, where the splendid **Bowers Museum of Cultural Art**, 2002 N Main St (Tues–Sun 11am–4pm; $17 weekdays $19 weekends; ☎714/567-3600, ⊛www .bowers.org), features anthropological treasures from early Asian, African, Native-American, and pre-Columbian civilizations. Showcasing artifacts as diverse as ceramic Mayan icons, hand-crafted baskets from native Californians, and highly detailed Chinese funerary sculpture, the museum is an essential stop for anyone interested in the art and history of non-Western civilizations.

Fullerton

North of Disneyland, unimposing **FULLERTON** also has a few interesting sights, among them the 26-acre **Fullerton Arboretum**, in the northeast corner of the California State campus at 1900 Associated Rd (daily 8am–4.45pm; donation; ☎714/278-3579, ⊛www.arboretum.fullerton.edu). Its series of themed gardens, ranges from desert succulents to Mediterranean plantings to forested groves, and includes cycads, palms, cacti, rare fruits, and even the kind of citrus groves that used to grow in abundance in Orange County. In the middle of the arboretum stands the **Heritage House** (tours Sat & Sun 2–4pm; $2), an 1894 Eastlake Victorian that, with its historic displays and vintage decor, harkens back to a more bucolic time.

Much more surprising is the presence of an esteemed institution in such a little-known hamlet like Fullerton, the **Muckenthaler Cultural Center**, 1201 W Malvern Ave (Wed–Sun noon–4pm; free; ☏714/738-6595, ⓦwww .muckenthaler.org), located in an attractive 1924 Renaissance Revival mansion and hosting a wide range of cultural events and exhibits. The specialties here are ceramics and international art, with Native-American art and textiles, African craftwork and jewelry, and contemporary Korean ceramics only a few of the highlights. There are also countless examples of decorative arts, drawings, and textiles from around the world – not to mention displays of work by local artists, and, this being Southern California, an annual display of "automotive art" in the spring, with many colorful car-related illustrations and designs.

The Richard Nixon Presidential Library and Museum

Mickey Mouse may be its most famous resident, but Orange County's most infamous was 37th US president Richard Milhous Nixon, born in 1913 in what is now freeway-caged **YORBA LINDA**, eight miles northeast of Disneyland. Here, off Imperial Hwy, the **Richard Nixon Presidential Library and Museum**, 18001 Yorba Linda Blvd (Mon–Sat 10am–5pm, Sun 11am–5pm; $10; ☏714/993-5075, ⓦwww.nixonlibrary.gov), exhibits items like the presidential limousine, campaign relics, and the little house where the future president was born. In the works is what promises to be a substantial research facility. Only in July 2007 was control over the site handed over to the federal government, making it one of the nation's officially approved presidential libraries. The change promises to improve the scope of exhibits and critical analysis of Nixon's administration, and provide less of the sugar-coated view of Watergate for which the memorial was once notorious.

In coming years, the new federal overseers promise easier access to the Watergate tapes (some of which are accessible online) and other crucial documents from the time. Still on view, most likely, will be showings of the famous "Checkers" speech (see box, p.232); the **World Leaders Gallery** of Nixon's heyday, with Mao, Brezhnev, and de Gaulle among them, cast in metal and arranged in rigid, pompous poses; and the **Presidential Auditorium,** where you get the chance to ask "Tricky Dick" a question. After making your selection, Nixon's gaunt features fill the overlarge screen and provide the stock reply – though "I am not a crook" is never one of the correct answers. More telling, out on the lawn is the very **helicopter** he used as president, and when he was whisked away from the White House after resigning in disgrace.

There's also a re-creation of the **East Room** of the executive mansion, replicated in architecture and decor. It's an odd tribute, given that Nixon was always uncomfortable in Washington and did all he could to escape it. Even in death, he avoided lying in state and made provision for his memorial service to take place here, where he's buried.

On your way out, stop by the **gift shop** to see its most popular item, a picture of Nixon greeting a zonked-out Elvis in the Oval Office, on the occasion of the president's granting the King – ironically, as it turned out – honorary status as a federal agent in the war on drugs.

The only president ever to resign from office, as well as the only president raised as a Quaker, **Richard Nixon** was unique in many ways. And although historians continue to assess the strengths and weaknesses of his foreign and domestic policies, the man easily qualified as one of the most dangerous and unstable figures to hold the office of president.

A lawyer from the sleepy town of Whittier (see p.168) and fresh from wartime, non-combat service in the Navy, **Richard Milhous Nixon** entered politics as a Republican congressman in 1946, quickly smearing his incumbent rival Jerry Voorhees as a closet Communist and later running for the Senate, calling his opponent Helen Gahagan Douglas the "Pink Lady... right down to her underwear." For all his venom, Douglas gave him the name that stuck throughout his career – **Tricky Dick**.

Shortly after arriving in Washington, Nixon joined the **House Un-American Activities Committee (HUAC)**, a legendary group of red-baiters led by the infamous Joseph McCarthy, which wrecked the lives and careers of many Americans. Although these hearings eventually backfired on McCarthy (he was later censured by Congress), they launched Nixon to national prominence, and he became Dwight Eisenhower's **vice-president** in 1953, at only 39 years old. It almost didn't happen, though: just before the election, the discovery of undeclared income precipitated the "funds crisis," which cast doubts over Nixon's honesty. Incredibly, his **"Checkers speech"** convinced 58 million TV viewers of his integrity, his performance climaxing with the statement that, regardless of the damage it may do to his career, he would not be returning the cocker spaniel (Checkers) given to him as a gift and now a family pet.

Eight years later, Nixon was defeated in his own bid for the presidency by John F. Kennedy, due in no small part to his sweaty, nervous appearance during their 1960s live **TV debates** (some allege he went down as a result of voting by cattle in Texas and the dead in Chicago). This loss led him into his **"wilderness years"**: avoiding the spotlight, except to raise money for fellow Republicans, he took several lucrative corporate posts and wrote *Six Crises*, a book of deep introspection and some degree of paranoia. Seeking a power base for the next presidential campaign, Nixon ran for the governorship of California in 1962. His humiliating defeat to Pat Brown ended with a memorable jibe at the press ("You won't have Nixon to kick around anymore") and prompted a short-lived "retirement," which did nothing to suggest that six years later he would beat Ronald Reagan to the Republican nomination and be **elected president** in 1968.

The country Nixon inherited was more divided than at any time since the Civil War. The **Vietnam War** was at its height, and in time his large-scale illegal bombing of Cambodia earned him worldwide opprobrium. Nonetheless, facing a weak opponent in George McGovern, Nixon was decisively re-elected in 1972, winning 49 states, and he managed to achieve groundbreaking deals with China and the USSR over official recognition and trade, and nuclear-arms arsenals, respectively.

Despite his victory, Nixon's second term ended prematurely over the **Watergate Scandal**. In January 1973, seven men were tried for breaking into and bugging the headquarters of the Democratic Party in Washington's Watergate building, an act discovered to have been financed with money allocated to the Committee to Re-elect the President (CREEP). Ironically, Nixon's insistence on taping all White House conversations in order to ease the future writing of his memoirs was to be his undoing in the crisis. Upon the revelation of a "smoking gun" tape proving his complicity in obstructing justice, Nixon **resigned** in 1974 under threat of impeachment.

The full **pardon** granted to Nixon by his successor, Gerald Ford, did little to arrest widespread public disillusionment with the country's political machine. Remarkably, Nixon's post-presidency saw him quietly seek to establish elder-statesman credentials, opining on world affairs through books and newspaper columns, and waging a seemingly endless legal battle to keep control of the notorious audiotapes. He died in 1994 and was buried at Yorba Linda.

The Orange County coast

A string of upscale towns stretching from the edge of the LA Harbor to San Diego County 35 miles south, the **ORANGE COUNTY COAST** is suburbia with a shoreline: swanky beachside houses line the sands, and the general ambience is easygoing, affluent, and conservative or libertarian, depending on the area. As the names of the main towns suggest – **Huntington Beach**, **Newport Beach**, and **Laguna Beach** – most of the good reasons to come here involve sea and sand, though a handful of museums and festivals can also make for an interesting excursion as well. To the far south, **San Juan Capist-rano** merits a stop as the site of the best-kept of all the Californian missions, and **San Clemente** is a surfing hotspot and one-time stomping ground for Richard Nixon.

The fastest way to **travel** from LA to San Diego skips the coast by passing through Orange County on the inland San Diego Freeway, the 405. The coastal cities, though, are linked by the more appealing **Pacific Coast Highway (PCH)**, part of Hwy-1, which you can pick up from Long Beach (or from the end of Beach Boulevard in Anaheim). OCTD bus #1 rumbles along PCH roughly hourly during the day, though Greyhound connections aren't so good: San Clemente and San Juan Capistrano are on the regular transit route, but there are no buses to Huntington, Laguna, or Newport beaches. **Amtrak** connects Downtown LA (or Disneyland) to San Juan Capistrano, though you can travel all the way along the coast from LA to San Diego using local buses for about $6 – but allow a full day for the trip. A pricier, but more worthwhile, transit option is the Metrolink commuter train line (see p.29), which not only connects Downtown LA with Orange County down to San Clemente, but continues on to Oceanside in San Diego County, from where you can pick up that region's Coaster and connect to downtown San Diego.

Huntington Beach

Starting on the north coast, **HUNTINGTON BEACH**, or **"Surf City,"** is the most free-spirited of the beach communities and one that you don't need a fortune to enjoy. It's a compact place composed of cafés and shops grouped around the foot of a long **pier**, off PCH at Main Street. Here, you can find the **Surfers Walk of Fame**, appropriately honoring the greats of the sport – this is where California **surfing** began in 1907, imported from Hawaii to encourage curious day-trippers to visit on the Pacific Electric Railway (whose chief, Henry Huntington, the town was named after). Top surfers still flock here to take a crack at notable stretches like Bolsa Chica, Dog, and Huntington State beaches, and there are also regular lifeguarding, kite-flying, and, especially, surfing competitions (see Ⓦwww.hbsurfseries.com). Even more of this culture can be found at the **International Surfing Museum**, 411 Olive Ave (Oct–May Thurs–Mon noon–5pm; June–Sept open daily; $3; ☎714/960-3483, Ⓦwww.surfingmuseum.org), which features exhibits on such legends as Corky Carroll and Duke Kahanamoku, historic posters from various world surfing contests, and an array of traditional, contemporary, and far-out boards, including one shaped like a Swiss Army Knife.

From mid-September through October, the largely blond and suntanned locals celebrate a fun **Oktoberfest**, with German food and music (see Ⓦwww .surfcityusa.com for information on this and other events). Otherwise, there's not much else to see, though several miles north, nature lovers won't want to

▲ Surfers at Huntington Beach

miss the **Bolsa Chica State Ecological Reserve**, PCH at Warner Avenue, a sizable wetland preserve that's been kept out of the hands of local developers by state regulation. Taking a one-and-a-half-mile loop walk will get you acquainted with some of the current avian residents of this salt marsh, including a fair number of herons, egrets, and grebes, and even a few peregrine falcons and endangered snowy plovers. Self-tours are free, and guided tours are available on the first Saturday of the month (9–10.30am; $1; groups by reservation at ☎714/840-1575, ⊛www.amigosdebolsachica.org).

Newport Beach and Corona del Mar

Ten miles south from Huntington Beach, **NEWPORT BEACH,** with its ten yacht clubs and ten thousand yachts, is upmarket even by Orange County standards. The town is spread around a natural bay that cuts several miles inland, and although there are hardly any conventional "sights" in town, the obvious place to hang out is on the thin **Balboa Peninsula**, an artificial formation created from infill, accessed along Balboa Boulevard, which runs parallel to the three-mile-long beach. The most socially active section, with a number of bars and restaurants, is about halfway along, around **Newport Pier** at the end of 20th Street. To the north, beachfront homes restrict access; to the south, around **Balboa Pier** (the second of the city's piers), there's a marina from which you can hop on the *Catalina Flyer*, which leaves for Santa Catalina Island (1hr 15min trip, leaves daily 9am, returns 4.30pm; $61 total; ☎949/673-5245, ⊛www.catalinainfo.com).

On the peninsula itself, the highlight is the modernist **Lovell Beach House**, 1242 Ocean Ave, a private home designed by Rudolph Schindler and finished in 1926. Raised on five concrete legs, its living quarters cantilevered over the sidewalk, the house made the architect's international reputation and could easily pass for a product of the 1950s or 60s. On very rare occasions, it's even open for tours (contact ☎323/651-1510, ⊛www.makcenter.org to check).

Across the main harbor channel from the peninsula, the Newport Beach district of **CORONA DEL MAR** is mainly worth a stop for its **Sherman**

Library and Gardens, 2647 E Pacific Coast Highway (daily 10.30am–4pm; $3; ☎949/675-5458, ⊛www.slgardens.org), devoted to the horticulture of the American Southwest. Among the many vivid blooms raised in its botanical gardens are cacti, orchids, roses, and an array of different herbs. Due north from the gardens, Newport Beach is home to the **Orange County Museum of Art**, 850 San Clemente Drive (Tues–Sun 11am–5pm, Thurs closes 8pm; $10, free Tues; ☎949/759-1122, ⊛www.ocma.net), a fine institution that presents regular lectures, events, and art and architecture tours. Its collection focuses on contemporary work from LA artists like Lari Pittman, Edward Ruscha, and Ed Kienholz, and there are periodical exhibits of work by video pioneers like Nancy Thater and Bill Viola.

A short distance west, San Joaquin Hills Road leads you to Backbay Drive, which makes a marvelous trip around the edge of one of Orange County's natural wonders, the **Upper Newport Bay Ecological Reserve**, 2301 University Drive (daily 7am–dusk; $3 weekdays, $5 weekends; ☎949/923-2290, ⊛www.ocparks.com/uppernewportbay) In the idyllic thousand-acre preserve and renowned bird-watching spot, you can see a great range of birds, including falcons, pelicans, terns, and rails, some of them endangered. The preserve – and its hills, wetlands, and inlets – also presents excellent opportunities for hiking, kayaking, horseback riding, and cycling. The **interpretive center** (Tues–Sun 10am–4pm; free) gives an overview of the area's ecology and geology.

Crystal Cove State Park

Back along PCH, the area between Newport and Laguna beaches offers an inviting, unspoiled three-mile chunk of coastline, **Crystal Cove State Park** (⊛www.crystalcovestatepark.com). Its two thousand acres of rugged inland terrain around El Moro canyon are good for hiking, horseback riding, and biking, on trails that cross hilly peaks and ravines. Bluffs tower over the beach, and a fascinating twelve-acre, federally protected "Historic District" contains 46 beachside bungalows and cottages ($31–41; see "Accommodation", p.256) that provide an eerie hint of the rustic character of the shoreline when they were constructed in the 1920s and 30s. Crystal Cove also has some excellent stretches for surfing, diving, and snorkeling, exploring the aquaculture of the offshore "underwater park," or just poking around on the beach among the coves and tide pools.

Laguna Beach

Six miles south of Crystal Cove, nestled among the crags around a small sandy beach, **LAGUNA BEACH** grew up late in the nineteenth century as a community of artists drawn by the beauty of the location. You need a few million dollars to live here nowadays, but there's a relaxed and tolerant feel among the inhabitants, who range from millionaires to upper-middle-class gays and lesbians. The scenery is still the great attraction, along with a still-flourishing arts scene in the many streetside galleries.

PCH passes through the center of Laguna, a few steps from the small main **beach**. From the beach's north side, an elevated wooden walkway twists around the coastline above a protected **ecological area,** enabling you to peer down on the ocean and, when the tide's out, scamper over the rocks to observe the tide-pool activity. From the end of the walkway, make your way through the legions of posh beachside homes and head down the hill back to the center. You'll pass the **Laguna Art Museum**, 307 Cliff Drive (daily 11am–5pm; $10; ☎949/494-8971, ⊛www.lagunaartmuseum.org), which has

The festivals of Laguna Beach

Laguna Beach hosts a number of large summer **art festivals** over six weeks in July and August. The best-known – and most bizarre – is the **Pageant of the Masters**, in which the participants pose in front of a painted backdrop to portray a famous work of art. It might sound ridiculous, but it's actually quite impressive and takes a great deal of preparation – something reflected in the prices: $20–100 for shows that sell out months in advance. You may, however, be able to pick up cancellations on the night (shows begin at 8.30pm; ℡949/494-1145 or 1-800/487-3378, ⊛www.foapom .com). The idea for the pageant was hatched during the Depression as a way to raise money for local artists, and the action takes place at the Irving Bowl, close to where Broadway meets Laguna Canyon Road, a walkable distance from the bus station. The pageant is combined with the **Festival of the Arts** (daily 10am–11.30pm; $7; information as above) held at the same venue, featuring the work of 150 local artists.

The excitement of both festivals waned in the 1960s, when a group of hippies created the alternative **Sawdust Festival**, 935 Laguna Canyon Rd (July–Aug 10am–10pm; $7, season pass $13; ℡949/494-3030, ⊛www.sawdustartfestival.org), and stole some of the thunder from the other events; these days, it's just as estab- lished as the other two, but easier to get into, featuring artists setting up makeshift studios to demonstrate their skills.

changing exhibitions from its stock of Southern California art from the 1900s to the present. A few miles south is relaxed **South Laguna**, where the secluded **Victoria** and **Aliso beaches** are among several below the bluffs.

About two-and-a-half miles inland from downtown Laguna Beach is one sight not to be missed by lovers of sea life, the **Friends of the Sea Lion Marine Mammal Center**, 20612 Laguna Canyon Rd (daily 10am–4pm; free; ℡949/494-3050, ⊛www.pacificmmc.org), a rehabilitation center that lets you watch as underweight, injured, or otherwise threatened seals and sea lions are nursed back to health.

Dana Point

DANA POINT, a town and promontory jutting into the ocean, lies about four miles south of South Laguna. It was named after sailor and author Richard Henry Dana Jr, whose *Two Years Before the Mast* described how cattle hides were flung over these cliffs to trading ships waiting below, and did much to romanti- cize the California coast while still viewing it with a wary eye. He ended his voyaging career here in 1830, and there's a statue of him and a replica of his vessel, *The Pilgrim*, at the edge of the harbor on the grounds of the **Ocean Institute**, 24200 Dana Point Harbor Drive (Sat & Sun 10am–4.30pm; $6; ℡949/496-2274, ⊛www.ocean-institute.org). Marine-biology cruises are offered here as well as public visits, during which you can view oceanic wildlife, from lobsters to anemones, in glass-enclosed tanks.

San Juan Capistrano

Three miles inland from Dana Point along the I-5 freeway, most of the small suburb of **SAN JUAN CAPISTRANO** is built in a Spanish Colonial style derived from the **Mission San Juan Capistrano**, right in the center of town at Ortega Highway and Camino Capistrano (daily 8.30am–5pm; $6; ℡949/234- 1300, ⊛www.missionsjc.com), a short walk from the Amtrak stop. The seventh of California's missions, founded by Junípero Serra in 1776, the mission was so well populated within three years that it outgrew the original chapel. Soon after, the **Great Stone Church** was erected, the ruins of which are the first thing you see as you walk in. The huge structure had seven domes and a bell tower, but was destroyed by an earthquake soon after its 1812 completion. For an idea of how it might have looked, see the full-sized replica – now a church – just northwest of the mission.

The mission's main **chapel** is small and narrow, decorated with Indian drawings and Spanish artifacts from the mission's earliest days, and set off by a sixteenth-century altar from Barcelona. In a side room is the chapel of **St Pereguin**, a tiny room kept warm by the heat from the dozens of candles lit by hopeful pilgrims who arrive here from all over the US and Mexico. Other restored buildings include the kitchen, smelter, and workshops for dyeing, weaving, and candlemaking.

The complex is also noted for its **swallows**, popularly thought to return here from their winter migration every March 19. They sometimes do arrive on schedule, but the birds are more likely to show up as soon as the weather is warm enough, and when there are enough insects on the ground to provide a decent homecoming banquet.

San Clemente

Five miles south of San Juan Capistrano down I-5, the sleepy town of **SAN CLEMENTE** is a pretty little place, its streets contoured around the hills, creating an almost Mediterranean air. Because of its proximity to one of the largest military bases in the state, **Camp Pendleton**, it's a popular weekend retreat for military personnel. It's also home to some of Orange County's better surfing beaches, especially toward the south end of town, and a reasonable campground, too (see "Accommodation," p.256). Around the city's southern tip, San Clemente had a brief glimmer of fame when President Richard Nixon convened his **Western White House** here from 1969 to 1974, regularly meeting with cronies and political allies. The 25-acre estate is located off Avenida del Presidente and visible from the beach, but off-limits to interlopers.

Listings

Listings

Accommodation

F inding **accommodation** in Los Angeles is easy, and whether you seek budget motels or world-class resorts, the city has plenty of options. Finding somewhere that's good value *and* well located can be much trickier, but it's far from impossible, especially if you don't mind a short drive or light-rail trip between your hotel room and your destination. If money is *the* issue and you must stay in an ultra-budget motel farther from the action, you'll need to be choosy about the district you pick, as getting across town can be a time-consuming business. Either that or stay in a better-located hostel.

You can often find worthwhile deals by shopping around or booking online. Minimally acceptable digs in a **motel** or low-end **hotel** will start at $60 for a double, and if you're comfortable in the familiar two-story, neon-lit 1960s motel built around a shallow swimming pool, you'll find many options. For pricier accommodations, LA has a seemingly limitless collection of mid-level to high-end **hotels** and **resorts** that rival the best in the world for views, comfort, and amenities – and you can expect to pay a small fortune for some of them (from $500–1000 a night in some cases). **Bed-and-breakfasts** are slowly becoming more common in LA (typically based on a Victorian-architecture or country-cottage theme), but the few that do exist tend to be expensive.

For those on a tight budget, **hostels** are dotted all over the city, many in good locations with desirable amenities – though at some, stays are limited to a few nights, and at others, the nonstop party atmosphere can be grating. **Camping** is also an option – from the beach north of Malibu, throughout Orange County, on Santa Catalina Island, and in the San Gabriel Mountains – but you'll need a car (or a boat) to get to these campgrounds.

Since there are few booking agencies, and visitor centers don't make hotel reservations (they will offer information and advice), **book a room** through a travel agent, by phoning the hotel directly or through its online Web page – if it has one – or by using an Internet reservations site (see p.23 for a list of options).

Where to stay

LA is so big that if you want to avoid constantly having to cross huge, congested expanses, it makes sense to divide your stay between several districts. Prices and options vary by area, and except for the most desirable spots – Beverly Hills, West Hollywood, Malibu, beachside Santa Monica – you can find standard chain hotels that are reasonably affordable. **Downtown** has both swank hotels and drab, basic dives, with cheaper accommodations west of Downtown, across the 110 freeway, in much dicier neighborhoods. **Hollywood** provides a good range of choices, a few of them historic hotels and many more classic old

The **accommodation prices** quoted are for the least-expensive double room in each establishment throughout most of the year. As with most major cities, however, rates can fluctuate wildly, rising steeply during the busiest periods – holidays, summer weekends, popular conventions, etc. – or dropping similarly when chance discounts are offered. The steepest fluctuations are noted in the review. Bear in mind also that in Los Angeles all room rates are subject to a fourteen-percent **room tax** in addition to the rates listed below.

roadside motels, along Hollywood and Sunset boulevards, while **West Hollywood** has some of the most chic and trendy accommodations in town, with predictably high prices. **West LA** and **Beverly Hills** are predominantly upper-range territory, with very expensive establishments in Century City and the relatively few bargains around the Westwood campus of UCLA, and better deals in more out-of-the-way locations. Staying in **Santa Monica** can be costly near the ocean and inexpensive further inland, while just south, **Venice** offers a cheaper alternative, with quite a few decent hostels and the occasional funky hotel, higher-ticket properties are making headway in recent years. Although not a destination by itself, **Marina del Rey** to the south has a number of clean chain hotels, if all else fails.

Among options further out from central LA, the **South Bay** has a fair selection of low- to mid-range hotels strung along the Pacific Coast Highway, with higher-end hotels sitting by the bay in **Long Beach**. The upscale choices in the **San Gabriel** and **San Fernando valleys** are around Pasadena and Universal City, respectively, and basic chain alternatives can be found everywhere else, including North Hollywood, Burbank, and further out. The limited selections in **Malibu** are almost all upper-end resorts or inns (worth the trip if you have the money), except for several roadside motels along Pacific Coast Highway – located well out of town. Finally, the dreariest accommodations in **Orange County** tend to be around Disneyland, where an array of faded motels competes for tourist dollars, while the county coast has many more appealing choices, from luxury hotels to quirky motels to inexpensive youth hostels.

Note that accommodation listings appear in the relevant chapter maps throughout the guide.

Hotels and motels

Hotels and **motels** are listed by neighborhood, with specific accommodation options for gay and lesbian travelers listed in Chapter 16, "Gay and lesbian LA"– though most LA hotels are gay friendly. We've also listed a few affordable places to stay near the airport should you be arriving late or leaving early (see box, p.248).

On the whole, you can comfortably stay throughout LA by **spending** around $125 a night, but there are plenty of bare-bones spots charging far less. Paying $250 will get you an elegant, entry-level room in a swank hotel, and beyond that anything is possible, with suites often going for $350 and up. Lower on the food chain, many affordable chain hoteliers offer basic suites for around $150. Prices increase at tourist-oriented establishments during peak travel periods, typically over the summer and on weekends, especially those near major attractions like Disneyland and Universal Studios. Conversely, weekend rates at business-oriented hotels can be much cheaper than weekday prices, often to the tune of $100–120.

Listed **amenities** include features that are not always standard to hotel rooms in the area, such as hot tubs, DVD players, flatscreen TVs, fireplaces, Internet access, kitchenettes, on-site gyms, and saunas. More common in-room amenities – the likes of ironing boards, hairdryers, cable TV, free parking, free morning bagels and juice, etc. – are not listed, except in truly low-end accommodations where their presence comes as a surprise.

Downtown

Cecil 640 S Main St ☎213/624-4545. Grand old 1920's hotel that's been spruced up as a serviceable, low-budget property; rooms are basic, but there's Internet access. The place to stay if you're really short on cash; the surrounding neighborhood is on the grim side. (Name change planned in 2008.) $50

Downtown LA Standard 550 S Flower St ☎213/892-8080, ⊛www.standardhotel.com. The downtown branch of LA's self-consciously trendy chain features sleek, modern furnishings and quirky decor, but is best for its rooftop bar. Although billed as a "business hotel," the party scene is pretty much constant. Avoid the posy, depressing West Hollywood branch. $165

Hilton Checkers 535 S Grand ☎213/624-0000 or 1-800/HILTONS, ⊛www.hiltoncheckers.com. One of the great LA hotels, with sleek modern appointments in historic 1920's architecture, and a gym, rooftop deck with pool and spa, and swank Checkers restaurant. Terrific Downtown views, too. $229

Holiday Inn LA City Center 1020 S Figueroa St ☎213/748-1291, ⊛www.holiday-inn.com. Located south of Downtown near the Harbor Freeway, this blocky chain hotel is part of the Staples Center–Convention Center complex, and provides an affordable stay with pool, gym, and Internet access, as well as easy access to most Downtown sights. $169

Kawada 200 S Hill St at Second St ☎213/621-4455 or 1-800/752-9232, ⊛www.kawadahotel.com. Small but clean rooms in a bland hotel near the Civic Center; as at the Cecil, come here if you want an adequate room and don't care about the seedy digs outside. $109 for three-night minimum stay.

Los Angeles Athletic Club 431 W Seventh St ☎213/625-2211, ⊛www.laac.com. Beaux Arts brick-and-terracotta charmer that's home to an exclusive club, but the top three floors make up a hotel with 72 serviceable rooms and nine expensive suites; a real plus is free use of the club's track, pool, exercise equipment, and handball and basketball courts, plus a whirlpool and sauna. $199

Marriott Downtown 333 S Figueroa St ☎213/617-1133, ⊛www.marriott.com. Palm-tree-laden pool area, spacious rooms, and health club add some charm to this chain business hotel, centrally located near the 110 and 101 freeways, and Bunker Hill sights such as Disney Hall and MOCA. $259

🏃 **Millennium Biltmore** 506 S Grand Ave at Fifth St ☎213/624-1011 or 1-800/245-8673, ⊛www.thebiltmore.com. Renaissance Revival architecture from 1923, combined with modern luxury: a health club modeled on a Roman bathhouse, cherub and angel decor, and a view overlooking Pershing Square. The well-appointed rooms match the stateliness of the design. All things considered, Downtown LA's best deal for luxury. $189

Miyako Inn and Spa 328 E First St ☎213/617-2000, ⊛www.miyakoinn.com. Despite the grim, concrete-box exterior, this mid-priced hotel offers comfortable rooms with fridges, plus onsite gym, spa, massage room, and Internet access, and there's a karaoke bar. $149

New Otani 120 S Los Angeles St ☎213/629-1200 or 1-800/421-8795, ⊛www.newotani.com. Business hotel that's seen better days, featuring spacious suites but unexciting rooms, a good restaurant with Asian cuisine (see p.267), and, up on the roof, the small Japanese Garden in the Sky, which uses the traditional technique of "borrowed scenery" to incorporate existing views into the design. $195

Omni Los Angeles 251 S Olive St at Fourth St ☎213/617-3300 or 1-800/327-0200, ⊛www.omnilosangeles.com. Fancy Bunker Hill hotel with plush, elegant rooms, swimming pool and weight room. Adjacent to MOCA and the Music Center. A good deal for $169.

Ritz Milner 813 S Flower St ☎213/627-6981, ⓦwww.milner-hotels.com. Somewhat bare-bones rooms at this restored old building south of Bunker Hill, but still cheap and clean, with Net access and in a prime location. Larger suites also available. $79

Sheraton Downtown 711 S Hope St ☎213/488-3500, ⓦwww.sheraton.com. A block from the Metrorail line, this chain hotel offers smart but standard corporate rooms just south of Bunker Hill, with a spa and health club on site, and Internet access. Safe, predictable lodgings geared for the business traveler. $249

Westin Bonaventure 404 S Figueroa St, between Fourth and Fifth Sts ☎213/624-1000 or 1-800/228-3000, ⓦwww.westin.com. Modernist luxury hotel with five glass towers that resemble cocktail shakers, a six-story atrium with a "lake," and elegant, conic-shaped rooms. A breathtaking exterior elevator ride ascends to a rotating cocktail lounge. $159

▲ Westin Bonaventure

Wilshire Grand 930 Wilshire Blvd ☎213/688-7777 or 1-888/773-2888, ⓦwww.wilshiregrand.com. Large Bunker Hill hotel with health club and pool. Mainly geared toward business travelers heading to the nearby convention center; rack rate is overpriced for rather bland rooms, but special discounts can knock up to $60 off the price. $219

Around Downtown

Comfort Inn 2717 W Sunset Blvd ☎213/413-8222, ⓦwww.comfortinn.com. Central to Silver Lake and Echo Park, a solid chain bet for clean and modern furnishings, with gated parking and free breakfast. There's also a

nearby branch west of downtown, **1710 W 7th St** (☎213/616-3000), with similar prices and amenities, plus a pool. $95

Mayfair 1256 W Seventh St ☎213/484-9789 or 1-800/528-1234, ⓦwww.mayfairla.com. Grand 1920's building with clean but faded rooms and suites, and sundeck and exercise room, but watch the edgy neighborhood. Wide range of rates, depending on size and amenities, starting from $90.

Vagabond Inn 3101 S Figueroa St ☎213/746-1531 or 1-800/522-1555, ⓦwww.vagabondinn.com. The best place to stay near USC and the Shrine Auditorium, a few miles south of Downtown. Clean and basic chain-motel rooms, with an on-site pool. $99

Mid-Wilshire

Beverly Laurel 8018 Beverly Blvd at Laurel Ave ☎323/651-2441. While the coffee shop here, Swingers, attracts most of the attention, the motel has nice retro-1960s touches, albeit plain rooms. Good location, not far from the Fairfax District and Beverly Hills. $95

Bevonshire Lodge 7575 Beverly Blvd at Curson Ave ☎323/936-6154, ⓦwww.bevonshire.com. Ultra-basic, but well situated for West LA, across from Pan Pacific Park and the black cube of CBS Studios. All the basic rooms come with a fridge; for a few dollars more you can have a kitchenette. $65

Farmer's Daughter 115 S Fairfax Ave ☎323/937-3930 or 1-800/334-1658, ⓦwww.farmersdaughterhotel.com. Conveniently located across from (naturally) the Farmers Market and recently tarted up to boutique level, with Internet access, DVD players, and elements of the Midwestern kitsch the place was always known for. $209

Orlando 8384 W Third St ☎323/658-6600, ⓦwww.theorlando.com. Elegant, well-appointed rooms make this one of the area's better boutique hotels, with plasma TVs, DSL access, swimming pool, hot tub, and fitness center. Good location for accessing the Beverly Center mall. $229

Oxford Palace 745 S Oxford Ave ☎213/389-8000, ⓦwww.oxfordhotel.com. Solid choice for business travelers with nicely furnished lobby, good, clean rooms and a few suites. Located near the heart of Koreatown, just around the corner from the Wiltern Theater. $160

Wilshire Crest 6301 Orange St ☎323/936-5131, ⓦwww.wilshirecrestinn.com. Small, cheap hotel with drab, mildly depressing rooms, but located in a charming, period-revival residential area, conveniently sited just west of Fairfax Ave and Museum Row. $100

Hollywood

Best Western Hollywood Hills 6141 Franklin Ave between Gower and Vine ☏323/464-5181, ⓦwww.bestwesterncalifornia.com. Reliable chain hotel, with Internet access, microwaves, fridges and heated pool, at the foot of the Hollywood Hills. $119

Comfort Inn and Suites 2010 N Highland Ave ☏1-800/809-0065, ⓦwww.cisuiteshollywood.com. Good chain-motel rooms with microwaves, fridges, complimentary breakfast, and heated pool. Just three blocks north of the center of Hollywood. $149

Dunes Sunset 5625 Sunset Blvd ☏323/467-5171. On the dingy eastern side of Hollywood, but far enough away from the weirdness of Hollywood Blvd to feel safe; adequate motel rooms with high-speed Net access. Convenient to major sights. $78

Hollywood Hills Magic Hotel 7025 Franklin Ave ☏323/851-0800, ⓦwww.magiccastlehotel.com. One of the unheralded deals in these parts, a hotel with studios and suites with kitchens, CD and DVD players, high-speed Net access, plus continental breakfast. An added plus is that guests can buy tickets to the adjacent Magic Castle (see p.102) – otherwise off-limits to the general public. $165

Holiday Inn Hollywood 2005 N Highland Ave ☏323/876-8600 or 1-800/465-4329, ⓦwww.holiday-inn.com. Massive and well placed, near the heart of Hollywood Boulevard and the Chinese Theatre. Basic rooms, but amenities include pool, spa, gym, and Internet access. $145

Hollywood Celebrity 1775 Orchid Ave ☏323/850-6464 or 1-800/222-7017, ⓦwww.hotelcelebrity.com. Recent arrival on the affordable boutique scene, with a great location in central Hollywood and rooms with charming furnishings and high-speed Internet. Guests have access to the Hollywood Magic Castle (see p.102). $129

Hollywood Liberty 1770 Orchid Ave ☏323/962-1788, ⓦwww.hollywoodliberty hotel.com. Creaky but clean old spot near the center of the tourist district, featuring wireless Net access and free breakfast. Not too sexy, but good value considering the situation. $99

Hollywood Metropolitan 5825 Sunset Blvd ☏323/962-5800 or 1-800/962-5800, ⓦwww.metropolitanhotel.com. Sleek high-rise in central Hollywood. Good value for the area, with serviceable rooms with mini-fridges. $110

Hollywood Roosevelt 7000 Hollywood Blvd ☏323/466-7000, ⓦwww.hollywoodroosevelt.com. The first hotel built for the movie greats, in 1927. The place reeks of atmosphere, with recently renovated boutique rooms, cabanas, and suites, plus a Jacuzzi, fitness room, and swimming pool. $179

Orchid Suites 1753 Orchid Ave ☏323/874-9678 or 1-800/537-3052, ⓦwww.orchidsuites.com. Roomy, if spartan, suites with cable TV, kitchenettes, laundry room, and heated pool. Very close to the most popular parts of Hollywood and adjacent to the massive Hollywood & Highland mall; good value. $109

Renaissance Hollywood 1755 N Highland Blvd ☏323/856-1200, ⓦwww.renaissance hollywood.com. The centerpiece of the Hollywood & Highland mall, with arty, boutique-style rooms and suites and a prime location in the heart of Tinseltown. You're guaranteed to pay top dollar for a room. $249

Saharan 7212 Sunset Blvd at Poinsettia Place ☏323/874-6700, ⓦwww.saharanmotel.com. A classic 1950s-style motel: double-decker layout with standard rooms built around a pool, plus cheesy neon sign and brash color scheme. The cheapest decent digs you'll find in Hollywood. $69

Sunset–La Brea Travelodge 1401 N Vermont St ☏323/665-5735, ⓦwww.travelodge.com. A cheap bet east of Hollywood's major sights, with adequate rooms, sundeck, and pool. Two blocks south of Barnsdall Park and a Metrorail stop. $85

West Hollywood

Chamberlain 1000 Westmount Drive ☏310/657-7400, ⓦwww.chamberlainwesthollywood.com. Sumptuous hotel just off the Strip, within easy walking distance of major clubs and attractions, but just far enough away from the chaos and noise. The impressive suites include sunken living rooms, Internet access, DVD players, fireplaces, balconies, and refrigerators. $279, suites $379

Chateau Marmont 8221 Sunset Blvd at Crescent Heights Blvd ☎323/626-1010, ⓦwww .chateaumarmont.com. Iconic Norman Revival hotel, which resembles a dark castle or Hollywood fortress and has hosted all manner of celebrities. A bit worn these days, despite the glamour. Come for the history, but don't expect any kind of deal. $350

Elan Hotel Modern 8435 Beverly Blvd ☎323/658-6663, ⓦwww.elanhotel.com. Semi-upscale boutique hotel, located in a busy shopping zone just north of the Beverly Center mall. Rooms are appointed in smart style, and there's also an on-site fitness center and spa. $189

Grafton 8462 Sunset Blvd ☎323/654-6470, ⓦwww.graftononsunset.com. Mid-level boutique hotel with bright and trendy furnishings, CD and DVD players, plus a pool, fitness center, and complimentary shuttle to nearby malls and businesses. $219

Hyatt West Hollywood 8401 Sunset Blvd ☎323/656-1234, ⓦwesthollywood.hyatt.com. Big and boxy on the outside, but also the legendary site of outlandish rock-star antics by bands from Led Zeppelin to the Who to Guns N' Roses. Now an upscale business hotel, with nice, spacious rooms that offer balconies, but sadly (or perhaps happily) without the same hip edge as before. $240

Le Montrose 900 Hammond St ☎310/855-1115, ⓦwww.lemontrose.com. Excellent spot with Art Nouveau stylings, featuring upscale restaurant and rooftop tennis courts, pool, and hot tub. Most rooms are suites with full amenities. $290

Le Parc 733 N West Knoll Drive ☎310/855-8888 or 1-800/578-4837, ⓦwww.leparcsuites.com. Graceful apartment hotel in a residential area not far from major sights (including the Beverly Center mall), with simple studios, more spacious one- and two-bedroom suites, stereos, refrigerators, plasma TVs, and rooftop pool and hot tub with views of the hills. $299

London West Hollywood 1020 N San Vicente Blvd ☎310/854-1111, ⓦwww.thelondonla.com. Arty, Euro-flavored hotel whose lovely rooms have upscale decor, balconies, and kitchens. Public areas include an exquisite lobby, pool, Jacuzzi, and gym. Recent renovation into a suites-only site (complete in 2008) promises to drive prices into the stratosphere, probably $325 and up.

Standard West Hollywood 8300 Sunset Blvd ☎323/650-9090, ⓦwww.standardhotel.com. Lots of style, but not much substance, at this famed hipster "party hotel" offering extra-spartan rooms furnished with platform beds and beanbag chairs, plus an outdoor pool with drinks service, and two lounges. A better place to pose than stay, and thus unavoidable in some circles. $225

Sunset Marquis 1200 N Alta Loma Rd ☎310/657-1333 or 1-800/858-9758, ⓦwww .sunsetmarquishotel.com. A hangout for musicians, with private cabanas around two pools, plus a hot tub, sauna, and weight room. There are very pricey villas set in gardens; most rooms are smart suites with kitchens, balconies, and patios. Prices start at $350 and can top out over $2000.

Sunset Tower 8358 Sunset Blvd ☎323/654-7100, ⓦwww.sunsettowerhotel.com. An Art Deco landmark now converted into an upper-end luxury hotel, featuring automotive radiator-grill decor and 1930's Zigzag Moderne style, but also modern boutique amenities, 24hr gym and pool, along with marble-floored bathrooms and prime views of the Sunset Strip. $345

Beverly Hills and Century City

Avalon 9400 W Olympic Blvd ☎310/277-5221, ⓦwww.avalonbeverlyhills.com. Located in south Beverly Hills, three long blocks from the Golden Triangle, this hipster hotel boasts cozy rooms and modern furnishings, along with in-room CD players, fax machines, and fitness club. The poolside bar is where Entourage types pose in their silk shirts. $200

Beverly Hills Hotel 9641 Sunset Blvd ☎310/276-2251 or 1-800/283-8885, ⓦwww.beverlyhillshotel.com. The pinnacle of hotels in LA and the classic Hollywood resort, with a bold pink-and-green color scheme and Mission-style design, surrounded by its own exotic gardens. Rooms have marbled bathrooms, VCRs, Jacuzzis, and other such luxuries, and the famed Polo Lounge restaurant is here. $335

Beverly Hilton 9876 Wilshire Blvd ☎310/274-7777 or 1-800/922-5432, ⓦwww.hilton.com. Prominent white, geometric hotel at the corner of Wilshire and Santa Monica boulevards. In-room plasma TVs, boutique decor, and many rooms with balconies. $220

Beverly Terrace 469 N Doheny Drive ☎310/274-8141, ⓦwww.beverlyterracehotel.com. A good, clean motel with complimentary breakfast, a few boutique touches, and some balconies. Central location on the border between Beverly Hills and West Hollywood makes it one of the area's better deals. $195

Beverly Wilshire 9500 Wilshire Blvd ☎310/275-5200, ⊛www.fourseasons.com. Located near the heart of Rodeo Drive, amid countless boutiques and chic department stores, this 1928 hotel has stylish modern rooms, three restaurants, palatial architecture, and views overlooking Beverly Hills. $525 weekends, $450 weekdays

Century Plaza 2025 Avenue of the Stars ☎310/277-2000, ⊛www.centuryplaza.hyatt .com. In the middle of Century City, a huge, crescent-shaped hotel offering stylish rooms with outstanding views from Beverly Hills to the ocean. Amenities include multiple pools, health club, business center, car rental outlets, and so on. $289

Crescent 403 N Crescent Drive ☎310/247-0505 or 1-800/451-1566, ⊛www.crescentbh.com. Near Beverly Hills City Hall and Rodeo Drive, a formerly low-end property that's been smartened up a bit, though it still has its creaky side. Now offers boutique furnishings and Internet access. Considering the price, it's mainly worth it if you're after a central location over all else. $295

Four Seasons Beverly Hills 300 S Doheny Drive ☎310/273-2222 or 1-800/332-3442, ⊛www .fourseasons.com/losangeles. One of the most famous luxury hotels in town, featuring designer-furnished rooms with balconies, elegant traditional decor, and decent artworks, along with pool and health-club facilities. Ultra-high prices attract A-list celebs in droves. Weekdays $425, weekends $395

Intercontinental Century City 2151 Avenue of the Stars ☎310/284-6500 or 1-800/496-7621, ⊛www.intercontinental.com. Century City stalwart with access to sights in West LA and Beverly Hills. Business-oriented rooms with balconies and on-site pool and spa. $260

Luxe Hotel Rodeo Drive 360 N Rodeo Drive, Beverly Hills ☎310/273-0300, ⊛www .luxehotels.com. The self-appointed bastion of luxury on central Rodeo, where the rooms have all the amenities you'd expect. You might even spot a celebrity, or at least a lot of rich tourists. $289

Maison 140 140 S Lasky Drive ☎310/281-4000, ⊛www.maison140.com.

High-profile entry for swank hipsters, boasting rooms with CD and DVD players, Internet access, salon, bar, fitness room, and complimentary breakfast. $219

Mosaic 125 S Spalding Drive ☎310/278-0303, ⊛mosaichotel.com. Boutique hotel featuring rooms with CD players, plasma TVs, Internet access, fridges, and pool, sauna and fitness room. Located near the Golden Triangle shopping zone, but far enough away to sit in its own quiet, leafy setting. $350, though multi-night specials can knock $50 off.

Peninsula Beverly Hills 9882 Little Santa Monica Blvd ☎310/551-2888 or 1-800/462-7899, ⊛beverlyhills.peninsula.com. Luxury celebrity digs featuring ultra-chic rooms, suites, and villas thick with graceful furnishings and decor, along with pool, sundeck, cabanas, rooftop gardens, whirlpool, and weight room. $495; more than double for suites

Tower Beverly Hills 1224 Beverwil Drive ☎310/277-2800, ⊛thetowerbeverlyhills.com. Adequate accommodation if the bigger-name places are booked. This one has business-standard guestrooms, a health club, pool, gym, and some rooms with views and balconies, though it's lacking in luxury overall, considering the price. $219

West LA

Bel Air 701 Stone Canyon Rd ☎310/472-1211 or 1-800/648-1097, ⊛www.hotelbelair.com. Perhaps LA's poshest hotel, and the only commercial business in Bel Air, located in a thickly overgrown canyon, with lush gardens and waterfall. Go for a beautiful brunch by the Swan Pond if you can't afford the rooms, which will cost you at least $540 for their exquisite decor, spaciousness, and luxury amenities.

▲ Bel Air

Best Western Royal Palace 2528 S Sepulveda Blvd ☎310/477-9066, ⓦwww.bestwestern royalpalace.com. The name overstates it more than a little, but if you want a cheap room and don't mind staying near the junction of the 405 and 10 freeways, this is the place: with microwaves and a pool, hot tub, and fitness center. Westside Pavilion shopping mall is a mile away. $109

Brentwood Inn 12200 Sunset Blvd ☎310/476-9981, ⓦwww.thebrentwood.com. Unassuming little spot that's been around since 1947, but recently spruced up with boutique furnishings, including flatscreen TVs and high-speed Internet access. $209

Carlyle Inn 1119 S Robertson Blvd ☎310/275-4445, ⓦwww.carlyle-inn.com. Just north of Pico Boulevard, a hotel close enough to Beverly Hills to make an affordable visit worthwhile; basic rooms include fridges, and there's also high-speed Net access and a smallish gym. $169

Comfort Inn and Suites 4922 W Century Blvd ☎310/671-7213, ⓦwww.comfortinn.com. Modern facility near Inglewood with Internet access, in-room fridges, complimentary breakfast, and airport transportation. $99

🏃 **Culver Hotel** 9400 Culver Blvd ☎310/838-7963 or 1-800/888-3-CULVER, ⓦwww .culverhotel.com. A restored historic landmark, once the offices of town founder Harry Culver and lodgings of the midget cast during filming of The Wizard of Oz. Today it features red-and-black decor, checkered marble floors, and old-time iron railings in the lobby, and cozy rooms with good views of the city. $119

Airport hotels

If you're catching an early-morning flight and want to beat the traffic, or if you're just getting into town late, you may want to stay at a **hotel near LAX**. The most conspicuous choices are arrayed along and around Century Boulevard east of the airport, but there are also pockets of motels and hotels in the suburb of El Segundo to the south, and in the dodgier turf of Inglewood a mile northeast. The following represent some of the better value in the immediate airport area.

Embassy Suites LAX North 9801 Airport Blvd, just east of LAX ☎310/215-1000 or 1-800/695-8284, ⓦwww.embassysuites.com. Affordable luxury from this hotel giant, offering in-room wet bars, refrigerators, Internet access, and microwaves in spacious, two-room suites. Other features include spa, weight room, sauna, pool, and airport shuttle. $229. There's another good, cheaper branch a bit further from LAX to the south, at 1440 Imperial Ave, El Segundo (☎310/640-3600). $115

Holiday Inn Express West LA 10330 W Olympic Blvd ☎310/553-1000, ⓦwww.holiday-inn.com. Located between Century City and the Westside Pavilion mall, offering adequate rooms with VCRs and fridges, and suites with lofts and spiral stairways. $159

Hotel Angeleno 170 N Church Lane at Sunset Blvd and 405 freeway ☎310/476-6411, ⓦwww .jdvhotels.com/angeleno. Cylindrical concrete eyesore that pokes out of a hillside below the Getty Center, but recently upgraded with good comfort and boutique furnishings, plus pool, spa, weight room, and rooftop restaurant. All rooms have balconies, some with terrific views across the Westside. $179

Luxe Sunset Boulevard 11461 Sunset Blvd ☎310/476-6571 or 1-800/HOTEL-411, ⓦwww .luxehotels.com. Upper-end spot with impeccable, smartly designed rooms with marble bathtubs, Internet access, and refrigerators. There are two on-site pools, tennis courts, and a health club, plus a free shuttle to nearby Getty Center. $269

La Quinta Inn and Suites 5249 W Century Blvd, just east of LAX ☎310/645-2200, ⓦwww .lq.com. Renovated chain choice featuring ten floors of comfortable and well-equipped rooms with Net access, plus pool, gym, laundry room, two restaurants, a bar, and free 24hr LAX shuttles. $99

Renaissance 9620 Airport Blvd ☎310/337-2800 or 1-800/228-9898, ⓦwww.renaissancehotels .com. One of the best of the LAX-area hotels: swanky wood-and-marble decor, ample rooms, and pool, spa, and health club. As low as $99 weekdays, but up to three times as much on weekends. For an extra $10–30, elegant suites are available with tasteful appointments and good views.

Travelodge LAX 5547 W Century Blvd ☎310/649-4000, ⓦwww.travelodge.com. Reliable, basic chain motel with continental breakfast, gym, pool, and airport shuttle. $79

Westwood and UCLA

Hilgard House 927 Hilgard Ave ☎310/208-3945
or 1-800/826-3934, ⊛www.hilgardhouse.com.
Much more affordable than the W Hotel
across the street, a pleasant, friendly spot
with clean, tasteful rooms and excellent
location for UCLA. Some higher-end units
come with Jacuzzis and kitchens. $169

Sky Hotel 2352 Westwood Blvd ☎310/475-
4551, ⊛www.skyhotella.com. In an area thick
with cheap (but mostly fleabag) hotels, this
is one of the better ones, offering simple
boutique furnishings, rooms with high-speed
Internet and iPod stations, gym and
business center. $179

UCLA Guest House 330 Young Drive E ☎310/825-
2923, ⊛www.hotels.ucla.edu. Excellent choice
for anyone visiting the UCLA campus, with
rooms offering basic amenities (including
complimentary breakfast), use of nearby
university recreation center, and kitchenettes
available for only $5 extra. Parking nearby for
$9 per day. $113

W Los Angeles 930 Hilgard Ave ☎310/208-8765
or 1-800/421-2317, ⊛www.whotels.com.
Chain luxury in Westwood, featuring well-
decorated – though not huge – suites with
CD players and Internet access, plus on-site
pool, spa, health club, and ample parking.
Popular with parents visiting kids at adjacent
UCLA. $339

Santa Monica and Venice

🏃 **Ambrose** 1255 20th St, Santa Monica
☎310/315-1555, ⊛www.ambrosehotel
.com. Excellent recent arrival in inland
Santa Monica that beats the coastal spots
for value and luxury. Craftsman-styled
decor and boutique rooms have DSL
access and include continental breakfast.
$229

Bayside 2001 Ocean Ave at Bay St, Santa
Monica ☎310/396-6000, ⊛www.baysidehotel
.com. Just a block from Santa Monica beach
and Main Street. Bland exterior, but
generally comfortable rooms; higher-priced
units offer ocean views, fridges, Internet
access, and kitchenettes. $125

Cal Mar 220 California St, Santa Monica
☎310/395-5555, ⊛www.calmarhotel.com.
Good for its central location (two blocks
from the beach, one from the Promenade).
Garden suites have CD/DVD players and
dining rooms, kitchens, and balconies, and

there's a heated kidney-shaped pool, fitness
room, and airport shuttle. $154

Carmel 201 Broadway at Second St, Santa
Monica ☎1-800/445-8695, ⊛www.hotelcarmel
.com. Drab and only functional, but these
are the cheapest adequate rooms for the
immediate area, with the ocean two blocks
away and the Third Street Promenade a
block in the other direction. $149

Casa del Mar 1910 Ocean Way, Santa Monica
☎310/581-5503 ⊛www.hotelcasadelmar.com.
Another luxury item on a beachside strip
crowded with upscale hotels, not far from the
pier and Promenade. Tasteful rooms feature
California-modern decor and Internet access,
and there's an on-site pool, spa, and garden.
Gloriously restored from an old landmark
building. For all this, rates start at $400.

Custom Hotel 8639 Lincoln Blvd, Playa del Rey
☎310/645-0400, ⊛www.customhotel.com. A
new arrival in a dreary spot not known for its
hotels, but offering rooms with iPod,
stations, flatscreen TVs, DVD players and
free Wi-Fi access, plus pool with cabanas,
fire pit and gym. $119

🏃 **Fairmont Miramar** 101 Wilshire Blvd,
Santa Monica ☎310/576-7777, ⊛www
.fairmont.com. Swanky hotel that's a classic
fixture near the north end of the Promenade,
with designer-furnished suites and tropical-
flavored bungalows near the pool, salon,
spa, fitness center, and fine views over the
Pacific. One of the best luxury choices in
town. $349

Georgian 1415 Ocean Ave, Santa Monica
☎310/395-9945 or 1-800/538-8147, ⊛www
.georgianhotel.com. A stunning blue-and-gold
Art Deco gem, renovated with an airy
Californian interior design. Rooms are
elegant, if small, though pricier suites offer
more space and better views, from Malibu
to Palos Verdes. Take the stairs instead of
the creaky elevator. $235

Huntley Santa Monica Beach 1111 Second St,
Santa Monica ☎310/394-5454, ⊛www
.preferredhotels.com. Rooms feature Internet
access, DVD players, and superb vistas,
plus a flashy exterior elevator that brings
you up twenty stories to a lounge on top.
Inflated rates are worth it only if you really
want a room with a view. $379

Inn at Venice Beach 327 Washington Blvd,
Venice ☎310/821-2557 or 1-800/828-0688,
⊛www.innatvenicebeach.com. A good choice
for visiting the beach and the Venice canals,
with simple, tasteful rooms with balconies

and refrigerators. Other choices in the area are mostly chain-oriented. $189

Loew's Santa Monica Beach 1700 Ocean Ave at Pico Blvd, Santa Monica ☎ 310/458-6700, ⊛ www.loewshotels.com. One of Santa Monica's chicest hotels, a deluxe edifice overlooking the ocean and Santa Monica pier. The rooms can be a bit cramped and overpriced, though they come with boutique furnishings and high-speed Net access. $349

Oceana 849 Ocean Ave, Santa Monica ☎ 310/393-0486 or 1-800/777-0758, ⊛ www.hotel oceanasantamonica.com. Almost all-suite hotel with courtyard, good oceanside views, pool, spa, fitness room, in-room kitchens, and CD players. Located at the base of trendy Montana Avenue, giving some explanation for the overly steep prices. $375

Ramada Limited 3130 Washington Blvd, Venice ☎ 310/821-5086, ⊛ www.ramada.com. Located between Venice and Marina del Rey, a good budget choice with basic, clean rooms and a pool, spa, weight room, and complimentary breakfast – a much better option than the grubby, low-end motels littering nearby Lincoln Boulevard. $90, with weekend rates $20 more.

Ritz-Carlton Marina del Rey 4375 Admiralty Way ☎ 310/823-1700, ⊛ www.ritzcarlton.com. One of the few good reasons to come to this unappealing district, a beautiful luxury hotel with all the high-end accoutrements, including rooms with balconies, swimming pool, spa, weight room, and garden terrace overlooking the marina. $359

Shangri-La 1301 Ocean Ave, Santa Monica ☎ 310/394-2791, ⊛ www.shangrila-hotel.com. Formerly the Shangri-La Apartments, a terrific, 1930's Art Deco structure with wraparound Streamline Moderne windows and railings, and alluring white-and-black design, with some original fixtures. Remodeling into Art Deco chic (complete in 2008) promises to drive rates up around $300.

🏃 **Shutters on the Beach** 1 Pico Blvd at Appian Way, Santa Monica ☎ 310/458-0030 or 1-800/334-9000, ⊛ www.shuttersonthe beach.com. The seafront home to the stars, a white-shuttered luxury resort south of the pier. Amenities include hot tubs (with shuttered screens), pool, spa, sundeck, ground-floor shopping, and ocean views. $450

Su Casa Venice Beach 431 Ocean Front Walk ☎ 310/452-9700, ⊛ www.sucasavenicebeach .com. Fine, centrally located beach digs that

can be booked by the day, week or month, with a dozen studio rooms and suites, flatscreen TVs, Net access, and on-site laundry (limited maid service, though). $225

Travelodge Santa Monica – Pico Blvd 3102 Pico Blvd ☎ 310/450-5766, ⊛ www.travelodge.com. Clean and basic chain lodging on the eastern edge of town, in a grim, colorless building. Good as a fallback if you don't want to pay top dollar for a beachfront spot. $100

Venice Beach House 15 30th Ave, Venice ☎ 310/823-1966, ⊛ www.venicebeachhouse .com. A quaint bed-and-breakfast in a 1915 Craftsman house, with nine comfortable rooms and suites finished with lush period appointments and named for famous guests – Charlie Chaplin, Abbot Kinney, etc. True to the name, it's right next to the beach. $145

🏃 **Venice on the Beach** 2819 Ocean Front Walk ☎ 310/437-4103, ⊛ www .veniceonthebeachhotel.com. Groovy beachside spot whose simply furnished rooms boast microwaves, fridges, and Net access; some with patios by the sands. Excellent, hard-to-find value for the area. Daily $100, weekly $500

▲ Viceroy

Viceroy 1819 Ocean Ave, Santa Monica ☎ 310/451-8711, ⊛ www.viceroysantamonica .com. Luxury item with great bay views and rooms with CD players, on-site pool, and lounge. The high-end rooms reach $500. Otherwise $315.

The South Bay and LA Harbor

Beach House at Hermosa 1300 Strand, Hermosa Beach ☎ 310/374-3001, ⊛ www.Beach-House .com. The height of luxury in the South Bay, offering two-room suites with fireplaces, wet bars, balconies, hot tubs, stereos, and refrigerators, with many rooms overlooking the ocean. On the beachside concourse of the Strand. $289

Guesthouse International 5325 E PCH, Long Beach ☎562/597-1341, ⓦwww.guesthouse.net. Convenient to Cal State-Long Beach and a bit inland from major sights, but still a solid chain motel with clean, agreeable rooms, and a swimming pool. $119

Hilton Long Beach 710 W Ocean Blvd ☎562/983-3400, ⓦwww.hilton.com. Chic corporate property whose rooms have the usual style and amenities, though with the added plus of prime location near many Downtown sights; also with gym and business center. $289

Holiday Inn San Pedro 111 S Gaffey St, San Pedro ☎310/514-1414, ⓦwww.holidayinn.com. While not in an ideal spot – several blocks from the end of the 110 freeway – the cheap rates, creaky but quaint design, and adequate rooms and suites (all with fridges and some with kitchens) make this chain hotel worth considering. $90

Hotel Hermosa 2515 PCH, Hermosa Beach ☎310/318-6000, ⓦwww.hotelhermosa.com. In a bustling part of town, off a busy stretch of PCH between Hermosa and Manhattan beaches, one of the cheaper hotel options. Bland rooms variously have balconies, sea views, and Jacuzzis, and there are some suites with lofts. A short walk to the beach. $119–189

Manhattan Beach Marriott 1400 Parkview Ave ☎310/546-7511, ⓦwww.marriott.com. One of the biggest hotels along the coast, with some four hundred rooms and suites at a variety of price levels. Many of the units have Internet access, and there's a pool, gym, hot tub, and nine-hole golf course for visiting duffers. $149, though rates jump by $70 or so on weekdays.

Motel 6 5665 E 7th St, Long Beach ☎562/597-1311, ⓦwww.motel6.com. Solid, basic rooms at cheap prices; good mainly for travelers motoring their way south to Orange County or San Diego. Just a few blocks from Cal State Long Beach. $76

Portofino Hotel and Yacht Club 260 Portofino Way, Redondo Beach ☎310/379-8481, ⓦwww.hotelportofino.com. Elegant suite-hotel by the ocean. The best choices are the well-furnished, comfortable two-room suites with hot tubs and vistas over the elite playground of King Harbor. Rooms $239, suites $339.

Rodeway Inn 50 Atlantic Ave at Ocean Blvd, Long Beach ☎562/435-8369, ⓦwww.rodewayinn.com. Inoffensive, inexpensive chain-motel, a block from the beach and a serviceable base for exploring Long Beach and its downtown and harbor area. Also with Internet access. $109

Shade 1221 N Valley Drive, Manhattan Beach ☎310/546-4995, ⓦwww.shadehotel.com. The bleeding edge of trendiness in the South Bay, this boutique property's designer lobby and smart rooms — many with hot tubs — resemble an upscale salon. It offers a chic lounge, pool, and spa, though there are better deals around for this price. $295

Vagabond Inn 150 Alamitos Ave, Long Beach ☎562/435-7621, ⓦwww.vagabondinn.com. One of the cheapest, most reliable of the chain-lodging options in the area, with a pool, located just a few blocks west of the main downtown action. $50. Also in San Pedro at 215 Gaffey St (☎310/831-8911). Both $70.

Westin Long Beach 333 E Ocean Blvd, Long Beach ☎562/436-3000, ⓦwww.westin.com. A solid bet for bayside luxury at surprisingly affordable prices (cheaper when reserved online), right by the convention center, with spa, fitness center, pool, and business-oriented rooms. $199

The San Gabriel and San Fernando valleys

Artists Inn 1038 Magnolia St, South Pasadena ☎626/799-5668 or 1-888/799-5668, ⓦwww.artistsinns.com. Themed B&B with ten rooms and suites (some with spas) honoring famous painters and styles. Best of all is the Italian Suite, with an antique tub and sun porch. Located just two blocks from a Gold Line Metro stop. $135

Best Western Pasadena Inn 3600 E Colorado Blvd ☎626/793-0950, ⓦwww.bestwesterncalifornia.com. Comfortable chain lodging with clean rooms, jetted tub, Internet access, fridges, and pool. Much closer to Arcadia's LA County Arboretum than to Old Pasadena. $95. Also a branch very close by at 3570 E Colorado Blvd (☎626/796-9100). $85

Beverly Garland's Holiday Inn 4222 Vineland Ave, North Hollywood ☎818/980-8000 or 1-800/972-2576, ⓦwww.beverlygarland.com. Two-tower complex with standard chain-style rooms (some with balconies), but also with pool, tennis courts, gym, sauna, and screening room for guests, and close to Universal Studios CityWalk. The proprietor played maternal character roles on TV. $170

Graciela Burbank 322 N Pass Ave ☎818/842-8887, 🅦www.thegraciela.com. Ultra-modern boutique accommodations. Many rooms have fridges, DVD and CD players, and high-speed Net access. Also with onsite pool, gym, sauna, and rooftop sundeck with Jacuzzi. $199

Motel 6 12775 Encinitas Ave, Sylmar ☎818/362-9491, 🅦www.motel6.com. At the northern tip of the Valley near the 5 freeway, a budget chain motel with small, clean rooms, but best for providing good access to sights near San Fernando and, further north, to Magic Mountain. $62

🏃 **Ritz-Carlton Huntington** 1401 S Oak Knoll Ave, Pasadena ☎626/568-3900, 🅦www.ritzcarlton.com. Utterly luxurious landmark 1906 hotel, located in residential Pasadena on an imposing hilltop. Palatial grounds, ponds, and courtyards, three restaurants, expansive rear lawn, and terrific San Gabriel Valley views. The elegant rooms are a bit on the small side (though they start at $379). For even bigger bucks, inquire about the private bungalows.

Safari Inn 1911 W Olive St, Burbank ☎818/845-8586, 🅦www.safariburbank.com. A classic mid-century motel, renovated but still loaded with pop-architecture touches (Tiki and "Googie" styles). Features a pool, fitness room, Burbank airport shuttle, and in-room fridges, with some suites also available. $139

Sheraton Universal 333 Universal Terrace, Universal City ☎818/980-1212 or 1-800/325-3535, 🅦www.starwoodhotels.com/sheraton. A large and luxurious high-rise hotel on the south end of the Universal Studios lot, with health club, spa, pool, and good restaurant, and spacious rooms with superior valley views. Easily accessible off the 101 freeway. $259

Tarzana Inn 19170 Ventura Blvd, San Fernando Valley ☎818/345-9410. A half-mile south of the 101 freeway, a handy motel for exploring the Santa Monica Mountains that lie further south, with rooms featuring high-speed Net access and fridges. Pool. $99

Universal City Hilton 555 Universal Terrace, Universal City ☎818/506-2500, 🅦www.hilton.com. A sleek high-rise neighbor to the Sheraton Universal, with similar appointments and amenities – pool, spa, and health club – though a much better-looking, sparkling steel-and-glass edifice. Rooms are nicely furnished within an easy stroll of CityWalk. $239

Vagabond Inn 1203 E Colorado Blvd at Michigan Ave, Pasadena ☎626/449-3170, 🅦www.vagabondinn.com. Friendly budget chain motel, usefully placed for exploring Pasadena, with kitchenettes, pool, and continental breakfast. $88

Westin Pasadena 191 N Los Robles Ave, Pasadena ☎626/792-2727, 🅦www.westin.com. Located in the cheesy, postmodern Plaza de las Fuentes, an imposing pastel creation with Spanish Revival touches such as Mission-style arches and bright, fancy tiling. Luxury rooms have Internet access and stylish decor, but location is the best feature, near Old Pasadena and City Hall. $189

Malibu and the Santa Monica Mountains

Casa Malibu Inn 22752 PCH ☎310/456-2219. Located opposite Carbon Beach and featuring superb, well-appointed rooms – facing a courtyard garden or right on the beach – with great modern design and some in-room fireplaces, Jacuzzis, and balconies. $129

🏃 **Channel Road Inn** 219 W Channel Rd at PCH ☎310/459-1920, 🅦www.channelroadinn.com. B&B rooms in a romantic getaway nestled in lower Santa Monica Canyon (northwest of Santa Monica), with ocean views, a hot tub, and free bike rental. Enjoy complimentary grapes and champagne in the sumptuous rooms, each priced according to its view. Rooms $215, suites $325

Good Nite Inn 26557 Agoura Rd, Calabasas ☎818/880-6000, 🅦www.goodnite.com/calabasas. A good deal if you don't mind driving, this double-decker chain motel boasts a pool and spa, and offers simple rooms at affordable rates in a rustic suburb on the north side of the Santa Monica Mountains. A fifteen-minute drive to the ocean. $69

Homewood Suites 28901 Canwood St Agoura Hills ☎818/865-1000, 🅦www.hwsagourahills.com. Although the suburban location off the 101 freeway is hardly exciting, it's well placed for easy travel down Kanan Road to Point Dume, Malibu Creek State Park, and other great sights. The suites are smart and clean with kitchens, and there's a pool, gym, laundry, and putting green. $139

Malibu Beach Inn 22878 PCH ☎310/456-6445 or 1-800/4-MALIBU, ⓦwww.malibubeachinn .com. Sunny Spanish Colonial resort by the Malibu Pier on chic, celebrity-thick Carbon Beach, with in-room fireplaces, tiled bathtubs, seaward balconies, DVD players, continental breakfast, and oceanside hotel deck. Late-2007 renovation promises to add more upscale touches, and prices. $325, weekend rates leap up to $490.

Malibu Shores Motel 23033 Pacific Coast Highway ☎310/456-6559. Best for its location across from Surfrider Beach, this basic, no-frills spot is a cheap and decent place to lay your head with a minimum of hassle. $119

Anaheim around Disneyland

Comfort Inn 300 E Katella Way ☎714/772-8713, ⓦwww.comfortinn.com. Chain spot offering rooms with continental breakfast, Internet access, fridges and microwaves, on-site pool and spa, and shuttle to Disneyland, a mile away. $80

Courtyard by Marriott 7621 Beach Blvd, Buena Park ☎714/670-6600, ⓦwww.courtyard.com /snabp. The best bet for visiting Knott's Berry Farm, and a good choice for its business-oriented accommodations, with in-room fridges and Internet access, plus free parking, pool, spa, bar, and restaurant. $109

Desert Palms 631 W Katella Ave, Anaheim ☎1-888/788-0466, ⓦwww.desertpalmshotel.com. Rooms and suites with fridges, microwaves, high-speed Net access, and continental breakfast – and suites also with kitchenettes. The hotel usually offers agreeable rates, even during conventions. $165

Disneyland Hotel 1150 W Cerritos Ave at West St, Anaheim ☎714/956-6400, ⓦdisneyland .disney.go.com/disneylandresort. A thousand cookie-cutter rooms in a huge, monolithic pile – but an irresistible stop for many. Also with pools, faux beach, and interior shopping. The Disneyland monorail stops outside – though park admission is separate. The most fun of three similarly overpriced Disney hotels. Basic rooms begin at $235, one-bedroom suites at $500.

Holiday Inn Buena Park 7000 Beach Blvd ☎714/522-7000, ⓦwww.holidayinn.com. Good lodging not far from the Magic Kingdom and Knott's Berry Farm, offering standard rooms with limited amenities, plus gym, pool and spa, and much cheaper rates than the Disney equivalent. $80

Motel 6 100 W Disney Way, at Katella Ave ☎714/520-9696, ⓦwww.motel6.com. Less than a mile from the Disneyland gate, with pool, hot tub, and standard cleaning facilities. $63. **Also at 2920 W Chapman Ave** (☎714/634-2441), near Anaheim Stadium. $57

Park Place Inn 1544 S Harbor Blvd ☎714/776-4800, ⓦwww.parkplaceinnandminisuites.com. Best Western chain hotel across from Disneyland, with the customary clean rooms with fridges and microwaves, plus pool, sauna, Jacuzzi, and continental breakfast. $138

Pavilions 1176 W Katella Ave ☎714/776-0140, ⓦwww.pavilionshotel.com. Convenient chain hotel offering basic rooms with fridges and microwaves, as well as a pool, spa, sauna, and shuttle to Disneyland. $85

Stovall's Inn 1110 W Katella Ave ☎714/778-1880, ⓦwww.stovallsinn .com. Tasteful, clean chain accommodation near Disneyland, with fitness center, pools, and two spas, and in-room fridges and microwaves. $95

The Orange County coast

Best Western Huntington Beach 800 PCH ☎714/536-7500, ⓦwww.bestwesterncalifornia .com. You can almost smell the sand from this chain hotel, and it's not far from the pier, either. Rooms are unexceptional, but the property does have a rooftop hot tub and a gym. $139

Fairmont Newport Beach 4500 MacArthur Blvd ☎949/476-2001, ⓦwww.fairmont.com. Hard to top this brand of luxury on the coast — plasma TVs, CD/DVD players and marble baths are some of the chic amenities offered, with pool, gym and spa, and much cheaper rates than at the company's similarly swanky Santa Monica location. $199

Hilton Waterfront Beach Resort 21100 PCH, Huntington Beach ☎714/960-7873, ⓦwww .waterfrontbeachresort.hilton.com. A towering high-rise whose rooms have private balconies, and there's a serpentine pool, spa, and rentals of everything from surfboards to rollerblades; rooms have views of gardens or ocean. $229

ACCOMMODATION | Hotels and motels

Inn at Laguna Beach 211 N Coast Hwy ☎949/497-9722, ⊛www.innatlaguna-beach.com. Great spot right on the beach, featuring many luxury rooms with ocean views, plus CD players, boutique decor, and free continental breakfast; there's also a pool and spa and easy access to the main downtown sights. $349

Newport Coast Villas 23000 Newport Coast Drive ☎949/464-6000, ⊛www.marriott.com. Among the swankiest of Marriott's Orange County properties, boasting luxury villas and suites chock full of amenities. $429. If you want a cheaper option closer to the main city action, try the more corporate, but still nice, **Newport Beach Marriott at 900 Newport Center Drive** (☎949/640-4000). $209

Mission Inn 26891 Ortega Hwy at I-5, San Juan Capistrano ☎949/234-0249, ⊛www .missioninnsjc.com. Plush and comfortable rooms come with continental breakfast, CD players, and fridges (some units with fireplaces), Internet access, plus use of hot tub and pool. Located in a distant Orange County city, but close enough to the main draw, the old Spanish Mission. $175

Ritz-Carlton Laguna Niguel PCH at One Ritz-Carlton Drive ☎949/240-2000, ⊛www.ritzcarlton.com/resorts/laguna_niguel. Another stunning Ritz-Carlton, this one perhaps the best in Orange County for its oceanside beauty (on the cliffs overlooking the sea around Dana Point) and rooms and suites chock full of luxury. The high-end amenities – swank decor, pool, spa, racquet club, etc. – are everything you'd expect when paying $525 a night.

▲ Ritz-Carlton Laguna Niguel

Pacific Inn 600 Marina Drive, Seal Beach ☎1-866/466-0300, ⊛www.sealbeachinn.com. Sited between Long Beach and the major Orange County coastal cities, an unassuming spot with pleasant rooms and suites which have, at a minimum, high-speed Net access and complimentary breakfast. Some units with Jacuzzis, fridges, and wet bars, and there's an on-site pool and gym. $130

Sun 'n Sands Motel 1102 PCH, Huntington Beach ☎714/536-2543, ⊛www.sunnsands .com. Just a relaxed, good-time motel right across from the beach, within easy distance of the pier and other city attractions. Rooms are on the drab side, though they do have Net access. The location is what you're paying for, after all. $129

Surf and Sand Resort 1555 S Coast Hwy, Laguna Beach ☎1-888/869-7969, ⊛www .surfandsandresort.com. Among the best of the coast's hotels, with terrific oceanside views, easy beach access, and luxurious rooms and suites with many features, including balconies. Rates begin at $500.

Hostels

As you might expect, **hostels** occupy the bottom of the price scale, offering dorm rooms and beds for somewhere around $18–25, depending on whether you're a member of their organization. Many hostels also offer cut-rate single and double rooms for $45–80. You can expect little more from your stay than a clean, safe bed, somewhere to lock your valuables, and a typically colorful crowd of visitors – sometimes making for quite the party atmosphere. Some hostels also offer tours of local sights, while others organize volleyball, pizza parties, and the like. There's often a three-to-five-night maximum stay, though this is generally enforced only when demand outstrips supply.

Adventure Hostel 527 Knickerbocker Rd, Big Bear Lake ☎1-866/866-5255, ⊛www.adventurehostel .com. One of the region's best bets if you've got a car, a mountainside spot with plenty of activities, from skiing and snowboarding in winter to jet-skiing, hiking, and parasailing in summer. Two-hour drive from LA; remodeled in 2007. Call for current prices.

Banana Bungalow 2775 Cahuenga Blvd W, in the Cahuenga Pass ☎323/851-1129 or 1-800/446-7835, ⓦwww.bananabungalow.com. Popular large hostel near Universal City and US-101, with free airport shuttles, city tours to Venice Beach and theme parks, and a relaxed atmosphere. Outdoor pool, free parking, café and movie lounge. Dorms $19–20, private doubles $69–75.

HI-Anaheim/Fullerton 1700 N Harbor Blvd at Brea, Fullerton ☎714/738-3721, ⓦwww .hihostels.com. Convenient and comfortable, five miles north of Disneyland on the site of a former dairy farm. The hostel's excellent facilities include a grass volleyball court, golf driving range, and picnic area. There are only twenty dorm beds, so reservations are a must. OCTA bus #43 stops outside. $25

HI-LA/Santa Monica 1436 Second St, Santa Monica ☎310/393-9913, ⓦwww.hilosangeles .org. A few blocks from the beach and pier, the building was LA's Town Hall from 1887 to 1889, and retains its historic charm, with a pleasant inner courtyard, Internet café, movie room, and 260 beds. $32–34. Reservations essential in summer; open 24hr.

HI-LA/South Bay 3601 S Gaffey St, Bldg #613, San Pedro ☎310/831-8109, ⓦwww.hihostels .com. Sixty beds in old US Army barracks, with a panoramic view of the Pacific Ocean. Ideal for seeing San Pedro, Palos Verdes, and the Harbor Area. Dorms $26; private rooms $48. MTA bus #446 passes by, but it's a two-hour journey from Downtown. During Oct–May only open to groups of 20 or more.

Hollywood International Hostel 6820 Hollywood Blvd ☎1-800/750-6561, ⓦwww .hollywoodhostels.com. Centrally located, with game room, gymnasium, patio garden, kitchen, and laundry. Offers tours of Hollywood, theme parks, Las Vegas, and Tijuana. Dorms $17, private rooms $40.

Orange Drive Manor 1764 N Orange Drive, Hollywood ☎323/850-0350, ⓦorangedrive hostel.com. Centrally located hostel (right behind the Chinese Theatre), offering tours to film studios, theme parks, and homes of the stars. Members $25, others $29, private rooms $55–69.

🏃 Orbit Hotel and Hostel 7950 Melrose Ave ☎323/655-1510 or 1-877/ORBIT-US, ⓦwww.orbithotel.com. Retro-1960s hotel and hostel with sleek Day-Glo furnishings and ultra-hip modern decor, offering complimentary breakfast, movie screening room, patio, café, private baths in all rooms, and shuttle tours. The area, while central to the Melrose District, can get dicey at night. Dorms $22, private rooms $69–79.

Surf City Hostel 26 Pier Ave, Hermosa Beach ☎310/798-2323 or 1-800/305-2901, ⓦwww .surfcityhostel.ws. Good location near popular beachside strip, the Strand, and numerous restaurants, clubs, and bars. Also with kitchen, laundry, and shuttles to Disneyland and other major theme parks and shopping zones. Shared rooms from $23 or private doubles from $56.

USA Hostels – Hollywood 1624 Schrader Blvd ☎323/462-3777 or 1-800/LA-HOSTEL, ⓦwww .usahostels.com. A block south of the center of Hollywood Boulevard, near major attractions, and with a game room, private baths, main bar, Internet access, and garden patio, as well as airport and train shuttles. Shared rooms $23–27 and private rooms from $62–68.

Venice Beach Cotel 25 Windward Ave, Venice ☎310/399-7649, ⓦwww.venicebeachcotel .com. Located in a historic beachside building near Muscle Beach, this colonnaded hostel (or "cotel") has dorm rooms for $22–26, and private rooms for $52–70.

Campgrounds

Reserve America (☎1-800/444-7275, ⓦwww.reserveamerica.com) processes reservations at many of the **campgrounds** listed below and can help you find an alternative if your chosen site is full. It charges a $7 fee per reservation per night up to a maximum of eight people per site, including one vehicle.

Mainland

Bolsa Chica ☎714/846-3460. Facing the ocean in Huntington Beach, near a thousand-acre wildlife sanctuary and birdwatchers' paradise, with fishing opportunities as well. $34–44 for campers with a self-contained vehicle. No tent camping.

Chilao Recreation Area on Hwy-2, 26 miles north of I-10 ☎818/899-1900, ⓦwww.fs.fed.us /r5/angeles. The only campground in the San Gabriel Mountains reachable by car, though there are others accessible on foot. Bears are active in the area. For details, contact the Angeles National Forest Ranger Station at 701 N Santa Anita Ave, Arcadia (☎626/574-5200). $12, with $5 vehicle pass; open April to mid-Nov.

Crystal Cove State Park 8471 Pacific Coast Hwy, north of Laguna Beach ☎949/494-3539 or 1-800/444-7275. Two thousand acres of woods and nearly four miles of coastline (rich with tidepools) make this tent-camping park a good, and affordable, choice for all manner of hiking, horseback riding, snorkeling, scuba diving, and surfing. $11–15. Also with restored vintage beach cottages ($31–41), which are often reserved many months in advance.

Dockweiler Beach County Park 8255 Vista del Mar ☎310/322-4951 or 1-800/950-7275, ⓦbeaches.co.la.ca.us. On a noisy coastal strip, almost at the western end of the LAX runways, this site is mainly for RVs. It's on a popular urban beach that can get a little dicey on weekends. $28–32.

Doheny State Beach 25300 Dana Point Harbor Drive ☎949/496-6171 or 1-800/444-7275. Often packed with families, especially on weekends. Located at southern end of Orange County, not far from Dana Point Harbor. $25, add $10 for beachfront sites.

Leo Carrillo State Beach Park northern Malibu ☎818/706-1310 or 1-800/444-7275. Pronounced "Ca-REE-oh", it's near one of LA's best surfing beaches, with campsites in sight of the ocean. About 25 miles northwest of Santa Monica on Pacific Coast Hwy, not far from the end of Mulholland Highway. $25.

Malibu Creek State Park 1925 Las Virgenes Rd, in the Santa Monica Mountains ☎818/706-8809 or 1-800/444-7275. A rustic campground in a park that can become crowded at times. Sixty sites in the shade of huge oak trees, almost all with fire pits, solar-heated showers, and flush toilets. One-time filming location for TV show *M*A*S*H*. $25.

San Clemente State Beach 3030 Avenida del Presidente, two miles south of San Clemente ☎714/492-7146 or 1-800/444-7275. A prime spot for hiking, diving, and surfing, around an area that was once home to Richard Nixon's "Western White House." $25, add $9 for beachfront sites.

Santa Catalina Island

Campgrounds on **Santa Catalina Island** are all processed through the Catalina Island Company (☎310/510-8368, ⓦwww.scico.com/camping), which charges $12 for adult use, $6 for kids, and usually requires reservations. Island transportation by boat or bus is not included; see box on p.186 for more details on getting around the area.

Blackjack Not for the timid – an isolated site high up near the island's center, poised at 1600 feet. It's a rugged nine-mile trek from the nearest town, Avalon (which has its own, much tamer Hermit Gulch, below), with limited facilities except for barbecues, fire pits, toilets, and showers.

Boat-in Sites If you have access to water-craft, use it to reach these fine, secluded spots northeast of Avalon, where you have to bring your own cooking implements (fires not allowed) and all facilities are primitive, without running water. Nine locations with seventeen specific sites.

Hermit Gulch Only a mile and a half from the boat launch at Avalon, this campground is popular and easy to access, with barbecues, picnic tables, and a few tepees. Provides a good jumping-off point for exploring the island.

Little Harbor Sited on the island's south side, it's accessible by hiking or by bus. Fire rings are available, but the main draw is the pair of sandy beaches, good for swimming in a relaxed, isolated setting.

Parsons Landing Remote site on the island's northern tip; eight camp sites with no showers or fresh water, but offering fire rings, picnic tables, and, for a fee from a lockbox, firewood and bottled water. Boating is the obvious choice for arrival, though the site is accessible on foot. Seven miles from Two Harbors.

Two Harbors Located on a lovely isthmus near the island's center, a tourist-oriented campground offering standard tent sites, along with "Catalina Cabins" ($25 weekdays, $40 weekends), which provide amenities like fridges and heaters.

⑪

Eating

Since the arrival of California cuisine in the 1980s, LA has been one of the major nodes on the country's dining map, its **restaurants** and **cafés** attracting high-profile chefs and generating a national culinary buzz. Even 25 years later, the city's gastronomic trendsetters are still going strong, from old favorites such as *Michael's* and *Spago*, which helped get the ball rolling, to newcomers specializing in a variety of Cal-cuisine hybrids, incorporating everything from Northern Italian to pan-Asian. The range of cuisines in LA stretches far beyond the influence of California-style dishes like salmon glazed with saffron and shiitake mushrooms. Almost everyplace, from exclusive supper clubs to the dingiest burger shacks, doles out delicious meals. Beside the fast-food drive-ins that were invented here, LA is the birthplace of such enduring favorites as the cheeseburger, hot fudge sundae, French dip sandwich, and Caesar salad, and all are worth a tasty try in their hometown.

For many of the restaurants listed, you won't need to **reserve** ahead, though you should make the effort on weekends, during major holidays, and at the most expensive or trendy places, provided they allow it. For **dinner**, expect to pay $6–10 per person for simple fast food, $15–25 for most ethnic and old-fashioned, steak-and-potatoes American restaurants, and $35–70 for the latest hot spots of any sort (and this doesn't include wine or cocktails). To sample great food without paying a bundle, go for **lunch** at those upscale eateries that offer it, where you can typically eat for about half of what you might shell out at dinner and the menu is often a reduced version of that available for dinner. The price breaks do not, however, continue downward at those establishments that offer **breakfast**, and unless you're going for a rock-bottom meal at *Denny's* or at *Norm's* diners, you'll end up paying $10–15 for any sort of edible morning repast.

No matter where you choose to eat, though, don't reach for a cigarette – in 1993, health-conscious LA banned **smoking** in restaurants, and the state of California then followed with a blanket tobacco prohibition in restaurants and bars.

Cuisines

Budget food is both iconic and plentiful in LA, ranging from good sit-down meals in street-corner coffee shops to eat-with-your-hands grub at burger chains – so much so that we've included a special section that leads off the reviews. Almost as common, and just as cheap, is **Mexican food**, the closest thing you'll get to an indigenous LA cuisine. Mexican burrito stands and lunch-trucks are often the city's best deals, serving tasty and filling food for as little as $5 per person; they're at their most authentic in East LA, although there's a broad selection of more Americanized examples all over the city. The cuisines of the rest of **Latin America** have made plenty of inroads, too, from the flavors of Honduras and Nicaragua and the blending of Peruvian cuisine with local seafood (aka "Peruvian seafood"), to the hot, garlicky platters of Argentine beef available throughout the Westside.

The city lacks a wide selection of **African** restaurants, other than those based on the cuisines of North Africa. Those that do exist are mainly found in small strips around Hollywood and Mid-Wilshire. **Moroccan** food is typically flavorful, often with a little belly dancing thrown into the mix, though not concentrated in any one neighborhood. The best **Ethiopian** restaurants are in a small pocket around Olympic Boulevard in Mid-Wilshire, and are fairly inexpensive. Aside from such singular cuisines, pan-African hybrids have made some headway on the menus of adventurous restaurants, mixing the grains, spices, and vegetables of Africa with the foods of the Caribbean, Europe, and the American South.

Old-fashioned **American** cuisine, with its massive steaks, baked potatoes, and mountainous salads, doesn't ride the wave of LA food trendiness, but does attract the broadest swath of the city's chow-hounds – everyone from Armani-wearing executive to the most benighted tourist likes a good prime rib. The fare is available across LA, costing as little as $10 for a gut-busting blowout in a roadside diner, to well over $100 for a full meal with a choice porterhouse served amid chandeliers in a luxury steakhouse.

Much more conspicuous, and trendier, is the juggernaut of **California cuisine**, which not only adds bold new twists to American cooking, but often combines with other cuisines (Japanese, Indian, etc) to produce some unusual variations. In its original form, "Cal-cuisine" uses fresh, locally available ingredients, more likely grilled or poached than fried, and is stylishly presented with a nod to French *nouvelle cuisine*. In its more recent and decadent incarnation, it's an excuse to mix-and-match discordant flavors on the same plate, with varying results – there's only so much apple-cinnamon-glazed beef heart one can stand.

As a side avenue of American cuisine, spicy **Cajun** food is affordable as well as enjoyable, and there are a number of serviceable establishments sprinkled throughout the region.

Unlike many ethnic cuisines in LA, those from the **Caribbean** – namely Jamaican – are more visible in West LA and Santa Monica than in Hollywood. With few exceptions, local Caribbean restaurants leave subtlety behind in exchange for sweat-inducing flavors and spices, added to staples like plantains, yucca root, and jerked chicken; however, **Cuban** restaurants (and bakeries, where you can find them) offer more complex flavors, and number among the city's finest restaurants, sometimes in Cal-cuisine hybrids.

LA's most fashionable districts offer many delicious **Chinese** and dim sum restaurants, which can easily set you back $30. More authentic and less pricey outlets tend to be located Downtown, notably in Chinatown, where you can get a good-sized meal for around $10–20. The more jade-and-bamboo kitsch you see, the less authentic and more tourist-centric the place is; the more it looks like a cafeteria, the more authentic it may be. **Vietnamese** food is quite solid here, both in its authentic variety – namely in the Orange County suburbs of Santa Ana or Westminster – and in its Cal-cuisine incarnation, often employed as a hybrid with *nouvelle* French fare.

French restaurants proper are among LA's fanciest; look to those on the Westside for the most expensive prices, and unexpected spots in the San Gabriel Valley and Downtown for cheaper fare, usually in the bistro mold. On the other hand, LA's **Greek** restaurants provide fairly traditional dishes for inexpensive prices, but are fairly thin on the ground, sometimes better known for their frenetic nightly singing and dancing than for their menus.

Indian restaurants are growing in popularity, with restaurant menus embracing California dishes to create hybrids like curry polenta and duck tandoori, though more traditional meals are almost always offered as well. Most of the Indian restaurants in Hollywood or West LA charge $15–20 for a full meal, less for a vegetarian dish. **Pakistani** variants on Indian cuisine can be equally delicious, though of course without pork ingredients (or alcohol), and are located in roughly the same areas as Indian eateries.

After decades of settling for nothing more exotic than takeout pizza chains, LA in the 1980s became home to some of the country's best regional **Italian** restaurants, with those specializing in Northern Italian food usually being the most expensive. That said, as common as it is, Italian food can also be quite low in quality, often little more than bland, mealy piles of pasta. A more appealing phenomenon is the **designer pizza**, invented at Hollywood's (now Beverly Hills') *Spago* restaurant by celebrity chef Wolfgang Puck, and topped with duck, shiitake mushrooms, or whatever comes to mind. None of this comes cheap, however: the least elaborate designer pizza will set you back $15–20. On the other hand, LA's **traditional pizza** joints are generally tasty and affordable, with their checkered table cloths and thatch-wrapped chianti bottles.

Japanese cuisine is available throughout LA, and not surprisingly, Little Tokyo is among the top choices. *Udon* and *soba* spots are more noticeable as you head further west, and more authentic fare is concentrated in the drab immigrant center of Gardena. Along with French cooking, Japanese cuisine is one of the favorites used by Cal-cuisine chefs for their culinary experiments, making many "Japanese" restaurants more international in style, and fair representatives of the city's latest cultural trends, especially on the Westside. By contrast, outside the giant mini-malls and diners of Koreatown, **Korean** cuisine tends to be limited to isolated pockets in the Westside and the northern suburbs. Spicy barbecued ribs and *kim chee* (pickled cabbage) are among the more traditional dishes; expect to pay under $20 per person for a good-sized meal.

LA's various **Middle Eastern** restaurants can be affordably palate-pleasing. Aside from citywide falafel and pita chains, excellent examples of this cuisine are found in strip-mall eateries. In health-food or vegetarian restaurants, the old-style Levantine cooking becomes all but unrecognizable, containing ingredients such as avocado, bean sprouts, tofu, and kasha.

Russian and **Eastern European** restaurants are uncommon in LA outside of isolated ethnic enclaves – particularly present in Mid-Wilshire, the eastern side of West Hollywood, and in the San Fernando Valley around Ventura Boulevard. Although **seafood** is offered throughout LA in a variety of cuisine mixes, there are plenty of worthwhile seafood-only restaurants, predominantly along the coast, with a strong concentration near Malibu, Santa Monica, and Newport Beach. However, some oceanside restaurants are better for their views than their food, and by venturing just a mile or so inland, you can find a better meal than you might at a restaurant located within sight of whales and seagulls.

Spanish cooking, along with **tapas bars**, has made a growing dent in LA's culinary culture. While classic Spanish restaurants are choice spots for a pitcher of sangría and savory seafood and pork dishes, the latest tapas bars offer "little plates" of anything that comes to mind – meatballs, sushi, garlic fries – hardly Spanish, often quite salty, and definitely expensive, once you finish counting all the plates you need to make a meal.

Considering all of LA's options for Asian cuisines, authentic **Thai** food might be the best deal, both for its spicy flavors and reasonable prices. Thai food is at its best and least pretentious in the less trendy sections of town, such as mini-malls in Hollywood and run-down storefronts in Mid-Wilshire. If you don't mind sacrificing atmosphere for delicious food, a trip to such environs is usually well rewarded.

Mind- and body-fixated LA has a wide variety of **vegetarian** and **wholefood** restaurants, the bulk of them on the Westside and many along the coast as well. Some vegetarian places can be very good value ($5–10 or so), but watch out for those that pipe in New Age music and include a gift shop selling crystals and pyramids – these can be three times as costly. If you'd rather have a picnic than visit a restaurant, try the area's frequent **farmers' markets**, loaded with organic produce and frequently advertised in the press.

Finally, LA is littered with **celebrity-owned** outfits, but the food is usually so unremarkable and the prices so steep we haven't listed them. For chowing down, celebrity-watching, or just enjoying a nice view, you're better off practically anywhere else.

Coffee shops, delis, and diners

At its best, budget food in LA is doled out in the many small **coffee shops**, **delis**, and **diners** that offer soups, omelets, sandwiches, and a slew of comfort food. It's easy to eat this way and never have to spend much more than $10 for a full meal. There are, of course, the usual fast-food franchises on every street; better are the local chains of **hamburger stands**, most open 'til midnight or 1am. Some, such as *Fatburger* and *In-N-Out Burger*, are now extending their reach across the US; others, like the ever-popular *Tommy's*, are only-in-LA favorites and sworn by their proponents to be the greatest in the city, in the state or in the West.

Sadly, the best of the 1950s "Googie"-style **drive-ins** have either been torn down or remodelled beyond recognition, such as *The Wich Stand*, now a health-food store. However, some spots, including *Pann's* near Inglewood, continue to cater to fans of old-fashioned formica-countered diners, with their neon signs, boomerang roofs, and belly-stuffing steak-and-eggs breakfasts.

All restaurants and cafes are listed in the relevant chapter maps throughout the guide; the exceptions are restaurants in West Hollywood and Beverly Hills, which appear in this chapter on maps on p.275 and p.277.

Downtown

Clifton's Cafeteria 648 S Broadway ⓣ213/627-1673. Classic 1930's cafeteria, the last remaining in a chain of six quirky eateries, with plenty of bizarre decor: redwood trees, a waterfall, even a mini-chapel. The food is less daring – traditional meat-and-potatoes American – and cheap, too. Daily 6.30am–7.30pm.

Cole's Pacific Electric Buffet 118 E Sixth St ⓣ213/622-4090. In the same seedy spot for a hundred years, this is LA's oldest extant restaurant. The decor and food haven't changed much over the decades, and the rich, hearty French dip sandwiches – a dish invented at this very spot – are still loaded with steak, pastrami, or brisket. Daily 9am–10pm.

Emerson's 606 S Olive St ⓣ213/623-3006, 862 S Los Angeles St ⓣ213/623-8807. Solid breakfast-and-lunch spot with some of the city's best cheap sandwiches; the croque monsieur and chicken-salad baguette are among the highlights. Sip espresso and munch on a regular salad, too, or sample the clam chowder or jambalaya, for less than $10 each. Mon–Fri 7am–5pm.

Grand Central Market 317 S Broadway ⓣ213/624-9496. Selling plenty of tacos, deli sandwiches, and Chinese food, plus a few more exotic items, like pigs' ears and lamb sweetbreads. A fun, cheap place to eat. Daily 9am–6pm.

Langer's Deli 704 S Alvarado St ☎213/483-8050. "When in doubt, eat hot pastrami" says the sign. Helpful, but you still have to choose from over twenty ways of eating what is easily LA's best pastrami sandwich. Located in a dicey spot, but curbside pick-up available. Mon–Sat 8am–4pm.

Mitsuru Café 117 Japanese Village Plaza ☎213/613-1028. Features old-time favorites like squid balls, teriyaki rice, and ramen, but the highlight is the imagawayaki – red-bean paste baked in batter resembling a pancake. Mon–Sat 8am–10pm, Sun 8am–7pm.

Original Pantry 877 S Figueroa St ☎213/972-9279. There's always a queue for the hearty portions of meaty American cooking – chops and steaks, mostly – in this diner owned by former mayor Dick Riordan. Breakfast is the best option. Mon–Fri 24hr.

Original Texas Barbeque King 867 W Sunset Blvd ☎213/437-0885. Delicious and heaping platters of ribs and chicken served up Lone Star State–style, with smoked, goopy sauce and more napkins than you can shake a drumstick at. Just west of Chinatown. Sun–Mon 6am–8pm, Tues–Sat 6am–10pm.

Philippe the Original French Dip 1001 N Alameda St, Chinatown ☎213/628-3781. Renowned sawdust café/cafeteria, a block north of Union Station, where you can tuck into juicy, artery-clogging French dips – loaded with turkey, pork, beef, or lamb – at one of the long communal tables. A filling treat for less than $6. Daily 6am–10pm.

The Yorkshire Grill 610 W Sixth St ☎213/623-3362. New York–style deli and neighborhood fave since 1947, with big sandwiches, patty melts, and friendly service for under $10. Mon–Fri 6am–4pm, Sat 6am–2pm.

Mid-Wilshire

C&J's Cafe 5501 W Pico Blvd ☎323/936-3216. Completely off the tourist circuit, but has a savory selection of cheap breakfasts and lunches with burgers, chops, eggs, fried chicken, and French toast, plus lots of Mexican dishes. Mon–Sat 6am–5.30pm, Sun 7am–4pm.

Canter's Deli 419 N Fairfax Ave ☎323/651-2030. Iconic LA deli with huge sandwiches and excellent kosher soups served by famously aggressive waitresses in pink uniforms and running shoes. Live music

nightly in Canter's adjoining "Kibitz Room" 'til 1.40am. Deli open 24 hours.

Cassell's Hamburgers 3266 W Sixth St ☎213/480-8668. No-frills takeout hamburger stand that some swear by, serving up nearly two-thirds of a pound of beef per bun. Mon–Sat 11am–4pm.

Du-Par's 6333 W Third St ☎323/933-8446. A long-standing LA institution, located in the Farmers Market, which draws a whole host of old-timers for its tasty hotcakes and heavy-duty cheeseburgers. Make sure to sample a piece of pie – they come in a full range of bright colors and flavors. Daily 6am–10.30pm.

Maurice's Snack 'n Shack 5068 W Pico Blvd ☎323/931-3879. Fill up on pan-fried chicken, hush puppies, and sides like string beans, candied yams, and corn pudding, plus apple pie. Take-out only; Sun offers a $10 combination of the top choices. Mon–Thurs noon–9pm, Fri noon–10pm, Sat noon–4pm, Sun 2–8pm.

Oki Dog 5056 W Pico Blvd ☎323/938-4369. An essential LA stop for all lovers of "red hots," in this case wieners wrapped in tortillas and stuffed with all manner of gooey, super-caloric ingredients – from pastrami to cheese to chili. Daily 10am–10pm. Also a branch closer to Hollywood at 860 N Fairfax Ave (☎323/655-4166); Mon–Thurs 7.30am–2am, Fri–Sat 7.30am–3am.

Swingers in the Beverly Laurel Motor Lodge, 8018 Beverly Blvd at Laurel Ave ☎323/653-5858. Affordable American comfort food – with a few eclectic vegan and pan-Asian offerings – served in a strangely trendy motel environment, luring a large crowd of hipsters and poseurs, as well as a few movie-star wannabes. Mon–Sat 6.30am–4am, Sun 6.30am–midnight.

Hollywood

25 Degrees 7000 Hollywood Blvd, inside Hollywood Roosevelt Hotel ☎323/785-7244. Bring your creativity to this fancy spot, while you pile your own home-made burger high with onions, chili, eggs, cheese, and even sirloin steak. Worth it to when you've got a bad case of the munchies. Mon–Wed 11.30am–1am, Thurs–Sat 11.30am–3am, Sun 11.30am–10pm.

Back Door Bakery 1710 Silver Lake Blvd ☎323/662-7927. Popular for its healthful breakfasts of pancakes and French toast, this Silver Lake favorite also serves lunch fare (soups, sandwiches, quesadillas), along with nice desserts. Daily 7am–6pm.

Fred 62 **1854 N Vermont Ave, Los Feliz** ①**323/667-0062.** Designed like something out of the 1950s – with a soda fountain, streamlined booths, and 24-hr operation – this restaurant offers stylish, affordable Cal-cuisine twists on familiar staples like salads, burgers and fries, and a tempting array of pancakes and omelets, too.

▲ Fred 62

KFC **340 N Western Ave** ①**323/467-7421.** Chain-food chicken meals are generic as ever, but the postmodern architecture is striking: a giant, 40-foot-high "bucket" and a little white cube, featuring the Colonel's face, balancing precariously on top. The towering interior ceiling and spiral staircases inside reward a look. Daily 10am–11pm.

Pink's Hot Dogs **709 N La Brea Ave** ①**323/931-4223.** The quintessence of chili dogs. Depending on your taste, these monster hot dogs – topped with anything from bacon and chilli cheese to pastrami and swiss cheese – are lifesavers or gut bombs. Mon–Thurs 9.30am–2am, Fri & Sat 9.30am–3am, Sun 9.30am–midnight.

Roscoe's Chicken and Waffles **1514 N Gower St** ①**323/466-7453.** An unlikely spot for Hollywood's elite, this diner attracts all sorts for its fried chicken, greens, goopy gravy, and thick waffles. Listen to the ringing pagers and cell phones as you wait in line for breakfast with movie-industry big shots. One of five area locations. Daily 8.30am–midnight, weekends closes at 4am.

Tiny's K.O. **6377 Hollywood Blvd** ①**323/462-9777.** The latest among the slew of LA diners to get a big reputation for its hipster vibe and pseudo-dive atmosphere. Various savory and veggie burgers are on the bill, plus fries, salads and nachos. Daily 11am–2am.

Tommy's **2575 Beverly Blvd** ①**213/389-9060.** One of the prime LA spots for big, greasy, tasty burgers and scrumptious fries – and, many would say, the best. Located right off the 101 freeway in a somewhat grim section of East Hollywood. Even though there are 30 other metro locations, this is the one you should visit. 24hrs.

West Hollywood

Astro Burger **7475 Santa Monica Blvd** ①**323/874-8041.** Not just burgers, but garden burgers, as well as sandwiches and other veggie meals, are the appeal of this diner – along with the late hours: Sun–Thurs 7am–3am, Fri–Sat 7am–4am. Also in Hollywood at 5601 Melrose Ave (①323/469-1924).

Barney's Beanery **8447 Santa Monica Blvd** ①**323/654-2287.** Two hundred bottled beers, plus hot dogs, hamburgers, and bowls of chili served in a hip, grungy environment, which used to be a haunt of Jim Morrison, among others. Angelenos can be divided up by those who love or hate the place – but everybody knows it. Daily 11am–2am.

Duke's **8909 Sunset Blvd** ①**310/652-3100.** A favorite of visiting rock musicians (the Roxy and Whisky-a-Go-Go clubs are nearby), this basic coffee shop also attracts a motley crew of night owls and bleary-eyed locals who've managed to hang on 'til daybreak. Mon–Fri 7.30am–8.30pm, Sat & Sun 7.30am–3.30pm.

Griddle Café **7916 Sunset Blvd** ①**323/874-0377.** The postmodern Hollywoodized version of a diner, where the pancakes, chili, and omelets come with various outlandish toppings, the cheesecake French toast will make you cheer (while you eat it), and half the crowd is there hoping to be seen by slumming producers and casting directors. Mon–Fri 7am–4pm, Sat-Sun 8am–4pm.

Hamburger Haven **8954 Santa Monica Blvd at Robertson Blvd** ①**310/659-8796.** A funky burger shack serving up hot patties in its cramped dining room and at outdoor patio tables (with a view of traffic whipping by at full volume). Especially busy on weekend nights, when the B-listers come by to drip grease off their chins like everyone else. Sun 11am–7pm, Mon–Thurs 10.30am–9pm, Fri–Sat 10.30am–10pm.

Irv's Burgers 8289 Santa Monica Blvd ☎323/650-2456. A divey, old-time burger joint where you can sup on rib-stuffers like cheese-, bacon- and fishburgers, patty and tuna melts, and the ever-popular chorizo and egg breakfast. Mon–Fri 7.30am–8pm, Sat 8am–7pm.

Mel's Drive-In 8585 Sunset Blvd ☎310/854-7200. Calorie-packing milkshakes, fries, and, of course, burgers make this fun 24-hour diner a must if you've got the late-night munchies. Everyone from curious tourists to jaded locals makes an appearance at this iconic spot.

Topz 8593 Santa Monica Blvd ☎310/659-8843. One in a local chain of fast-food joints that focuses, somehow, on the healthier side of eating burgers, hot dogs, and french fries, with lo-cal cooking oils and lean meats on the culinary agenda. Mon–Thurs 11am–9pm, Fri–Sun 11am–10pm.

Yukon Mining Co 7328 Santa Monica Blvd ☎323/851-8833. Divey coffee shop, best known for its omelets, with a diverse clientele – don't be surprised to see a crowd of hard-bitten Russians, neighborhood old-timers, and glammed-up drag queens. Open 24hr.

Beverly Hills and West LA

The Apple Pan 10801 W Pico Blvd, West LA ☎310/475-3585. Grab a spot at the counter and enjoy freshly baked apple pie and greasy hamburgers across from the imposing Westside Pavilion mall. An old-time joint that opened just after World War II. Tues–Sun 11am–midnight, weekends closes 1am.

Benito's Taco Shop 11614 Santa Monica Blvd, West LA ☎310/442-9924. Beef, pork, or fish rolled up in a flour tortilla, for just a few bucks. Most combos are also under $5, making this a good spot to gulp and run. One of three 24hr Benitos in the area.

Brighton Coffee Shop 9600 Brighton Way, Beverly Hills ☎310/276-7732. This simple eatery provides welcome relief from the smugness of the district – it's located right in the middle of the Golden Triangle – by offering solid diner food, with especially fine omelets, quesadillas, and sandwiches. Mon–Sat 7am–5pm, Sun 9am–3pm.

In-N-Out Burger 922 Gayley Ave, Westwood ☎1-800/786-1000. The best-looking fast-food place in town, selling wonderfully greasy hamburgers in an award-winning pop art building – a red-and-white modern box with zingy yellow boomerang signs and an oversized interior logo looming behind the diners. Daily 10.30am–1am, Sun closes midnight.

Islands 10948 W Pico Blvd, West LA ☎310/474-1144. The prototypical "dude" burger joint, one in a chain of many in the region, where you can knock back brewskis, chow on decent burgers, and stuff your maw with nachos, fries, and all kinds of other appealingly greasy grub. Daily 11.30am–10pm.

Jerry's Famous Deli 8701 Beverly Blvd, Beverly Hills ☎310/289-1811. Unavoidable are the many Jerry's locations in LA, and this one like the others has a sizeable deli menu, and is open 24hr. Occasionally, celebrities stop in to nosh.

John o' Groats 10516 W Pico Blvd, West LA ☎310/204-0692. Excellent breakfasts and lunches (mostly staples like bacon and eggs, oatmeal, and waffles), but come at an off hour; the morning crowd can cause a headache. Prices aren't cheap, either. Daily 7am–3pm.

Johnnie's Pastrami 4017 S Sepulveda Blvd, Culver City ☎310/397-6654. A wonderful 1950s diner where fans line up for the massive pastrami sandwiches, which cost around $8 and are prepared before your eyes in all their dripping, steaming glory. Sun & Mon 10am–1am, Tues–Thurs 10am–2.30am, Fri & Sat 10am–3.30am.

Nate 'n' Al's 414 N Beverly Drive ☎310/274-0101. The best-known, and perhaps best, deli in Beverly Hills, popular with movie people and one of the few reasonably priced places in the vicinity. Get there early (opens daily 7am) to grab a booth. Daily 7am–9pm.

The Nosh of Beverly Hills 9689 Little Santa Monica Blvd, Beverly Hills ☎310/271-3730. Filling breakfasts and home-made bagels, pies, and deli fare are the favorites at this unassuming diner, a hangout of bigwig movie-industry lawyers and producers, none of whom you'll recognize. Mon–Fri 7am–4pm, weekends closes at 3pm.

Santa Monica, Venice, and Malibu

Bagel Nosh 1629 Wilshire Blvd, Santa Monica ☎310/451-8771. Drab ambience may be left over from the 1960s, but this neighborhood favorite appeals for its sizable breakfasts of omelets and bagel sandwiches, picked up from an old-fashioned short-order counter. Daily 6.30am–2.30pm.

Café 50's 838 Lincoln Blvd, Venice ☎310/399-1955. Grubby little diner that's nonetheless kept going for years because of its savory eats – pancakes, French toast, milkshakes – and rock 'n' roll jukebox. Mon–Thurs 7am–midnight, Fri–Sat 7am–1am, Sun 8am–midnight.

Café Montana 1534 Montana Ave, Santa Monica ☎310/829-3990. The eclectic menu is highlighted by solid breakfasts, excellent salads, and tasty grilled fish, in an upmarket section of Santa Monica. Daily 8am–10pm.

Mo's Place 203 Culver Blvd ☎310/822-6422. The kind of good-time dive where you can get slapped on the back by an old-timer while sinking your teeth into a burger, listening to the jukebox and watching sports on TV. Just about the only gig in Playa del Rey. Daily 10am–1am.

Norm's 1601 Lincoln Blvd, Santa Monica ☎310/450-0074. One of the last remaining diners with "Googie"-style architecture, this local chain has 16 other LA branches and serves breakfasts and lunches for around $7. Open 24hrs.

Rae's Diner 2901 Pico Blvd, Santa Monica ☎310/828-7937. Solid 1950s diner with heavy comfort food. Its turquoise-blue facade and interior have been seen in many films, notably True Romance. Daily 5.30am–10pm.

Reel Inn 18661 PCH, Malibu ☎310/456-8221. Seafood diner by the beach, with unsurprising food, but cheap prices and a fun atmosphere. Also at 1220 W Third St, Santa Monica ☎310/395-5538. Daily 11am–10pm.

South Central and East LA

Chips 11908 Hawthorne Blvd, south of Inglewood ☎310/679-2947. A solid array of comfort food from sandwiches to burgers, served in a classic diner with a fabulous neon sign. Daily 7am–5pm.

The Donut Hole 15300 Amar Rd, La Puente ☎626/968-2912. Pop art fans will want to make the twenty-mile drive east from Downtown LA to see this eye-popping favorite which, like Randy's Donuts (see below), is shaped like a giant donut – except this one you can actually drive through, picking up a hot sack of fried,

sugared dough from deep inside a tunnel of comfort food. 24hrs.

Pann's 6710 La Tijera Blvd, Inglewood ☎310/337-2860. One of the all-time great "Googie"-style diners, where you can't go wrong with the burgers or biscuits and gravy – and you can always jog off the calories amid the oil wells of Baldwin Hills, just to the north. Daily 7am–11pm.

Randy's Donuts 805 W Manchester Ave, Inglewood ☎310/645-4707. This folk-art fixture is hard to miss, thanks to the colossal donut sitting on the roof. Excellent for its piping-hot treats, which you can pick up at the drive-through on your way to or from LAX. One of four South Central locations, though the only one with a giant donut on top. 24hrs.

The South Bay and LA Harbor

East Coast Bagels 5753 E PCH, Long Beach ☎562/985-0933. Located in a mini-mall, but with an excellent, wide selection of bagels, ranging from New York staples to California hybrids like the jalapeno-cheddar bagel stuffed with cream cheese. Daily 7am–5.30pm.

Hof's Hut 6257 E 2nd St, Long Beach ☎562/598-4070. Part of a local chain that serves up reliable, affordable burgers, salads, sandwiches, and pies, plus steak and pork chops. Daily 6am–midnight.

Johnny Reb's 4663 N Long Beach Blvd ☎562/423-7327. The waft of BBQ ribs, catfish, and hush puppies alone may draw you to this prime Southern spot, where the portions are large and the price is cheap. Daily 7am–9pm, weekends closes at 10pm.

The Local Yolk 3414 Highland Ave, Manhattan Beach ☎310/546-4407. As the name suggests, everything here is made with eggs, and there are airy muffins and pancakes, too. Breakfast and lunch only. Daily 6.30am–2pm.

Ocean View Café 229 13th St, Manhattan Beach ☎310/545-6770. Enjoyably light breakfasts, and soup and baguettes for under $10, in a pleasant hillside setting on a quiet pedestrian path overlooking the Pacific. Mon–Thurs 10.30am–4pm, Fri & Sat 9am–5pm, Sun 10am–5pm.

Pier Bakery 100-M Fisherman's Wharf, Redondo Beach ☎310/318-5348. A small but satisfying menu, featuring the likes of jalapeno-cheese bread, churros, and cinnamon rolls. Probably the best food around in this touristy area. Daily 8am–7pm.

The San Gabriel and San Fernando valleys

Art's Deli 12224 Ventura Blvd, Studio City ☎818/762-1221. Long-time film-industry favorite (mainly for old-timers, not for the nubile), with a range of hefty, scrumptious sandwiches and soups like the traditional chicken-noodle. Daily 7am–9pm.

Bob's Big Boy 4211 W Riverside Drive, Burbank ☎818/843-9334. The inimitable chain diner, fronted by the plump burger lad, was saved from demolition through the efforts of "Googie"-style architecture preservationists. See also p.206. 24hrs.

Carney's 12601 Ventura Blvd, Studio City ☎818/761-8300. The place to come if you really want to get your fill of burgers and chili dogs in an old railway car. Sun–Thurs 11am–10pm, Fri–Sat 11am–midnight. A neighborhood institution, as is the branch on the Sunset Strip at 8351 Sunset Blvd ☎323/654-8300. Sun–Wed 11am–midnight, Thurs-Sat 11am-3am.

Conrad's 861 E Walnut St, Pasadena ☎626/577-7603. Functional diner that has barely adequate burgers and sandwiches. Most come here for the late hours (in a sleepy part of town) and convivial atmosphere. Daily 5am–1am, weekends 24hrs.

Coral Café 3321 W Burbank Blvd ☎818/566-9725. A few miles north of Burbank's studios, this 24-hr diner draws a mix of movie-crew workers and locals with its filling breakfasts, chicken tortilla soup, and lunchtime burgers and steaks.

Dr Hogly-Wogly's Tyler Texas Bar-B-Q 8136 Sepulveda Blvd, Van Nuys ☎818/780-6701. Long lines snake out the door here for some of the best chicken, sausages, ribs, and beans in LA, despite the depressing surroundings in the middle of nowhere. Daily 11.30am–10pm.

Fair Oaks Pharmacy and Soda Fountain 1526 Mission St, South Pasadena ☎626/799-1414. A fabulously restored soda fountain, with many old-fashioned drinks, from lime rickeys to egg creams – a historic 1915 highlight along the former Route 66. Daily 9am–11pm, Sun 11am–9pm.

The Hat 491 N Lake Ave, Pasadena ☎626/449-1844. Very popular spot selling agreeable burgers, "world-famous pastrami," and French dip sandwiches. Several Valley locations. Daily 8am–5.30pm.

Jim's Famous Quarterpound Burger 915 W Duarte Rd, Arcadia ☎626/447-5993. If you hang out in the San Gabriel Valley, you could do a lot worse than to stop here. They've been doling out giant burgers, fries, and ice cream for what seems like ages, to mostly locals who know where to get their fast-food fix. Daily 7am–10pm.

Lamplighter 5043 Van Nuys Blvd, San Fernando Valley ☎818/788-5110. A divey, old-style diner serving gutbuster portions of "broasted chicken" that bring in a cast of assorted, colorful characters. Daily 6am–11pm.

Pie 'n' Burger 913 E California Blvd, Pasadena ☎626/795-1123. Classic coffee shop, with primo cheeseburgers and excellent fresh fruit pies, served fresh and hot to your gullet. Mon–Sat 6am–10pm, Sun 7am–9pm.

Porto's Bakery 315 N Brand Blvd, Glendale ☎818/956-5996. Popular and cheap café serving flaky Cuban pastries, scrumptious sandwiches, cheesecakes soaked in rum, croissants, tarts and tortes, and cappuccino. Mon–Sat 7am–6pm, Sun 7am–2pm.

Rose Tree Cottage 395 E California Blvd, Pasadena ☎626/793-3337. Scones, shortbread, and high tea in a thoroughly English country-home setting. Reservations are essential. Daily 10am–6pm, afternoon tea Tues–Sun 1pm, 2.30pm & 4pm.

Wolfe Burgers 46 N Lake St, Pasadena ☎626/792-7292. Knockout gyros, chili, tamales, and burgers – a longstanding Valley favorite. Daily 7am–10pm, Sun opens at 8am.

Orange County

Angelo's 511 S State College Blvd, Anaheim ☎714/533-1401. Straight out of TV's Happy Days, a drive-in complete with roller-skating car-hops, neon signs, vintage cars, and good burgers. Daily 10am–11pm, until 1am on weekends.

Duke's 317 PCH, Huntington Beach ☎714/374-6446. Best to stick to staples like steak and salad at this frenetic beachside favorite, known more for its prime location near the pier. Mon–Sat 11.30am–2.30pm & 5–9.30pm, Sun 11.30am–2.30pm & 4.30-9pm.

Harbor House Café 34157 PCH, Dana Point ☎949/496-9270. Excellent breakfasts, particularly its overstuffed omelets – a slew of them, with a veritable laundry list of options. 24hrs.

Heroes 125 W Sante Fe Ave, Fullerton
☎714/738-4356. The place to come if you're starving after hitting the theme parks. Knock back one of the 100 beers available or chow down on items like hamburgers, chili, ribs, or meatloaf. Daily 11am–11pm, weekends closes at 1am.

Mrs Knott's Chicken Dinner Restaurant just outside Knott's Berry Farm at 8039 Beach Blvd, Buena Park ☎714/220-5080. Serving cheap and tasty meals for over 65 years. People flocked here for delicious fried-chicken dinners long before Disneyland was around, and they still do; there's also a mean boysenberry pie. Outside the theme park entrance. Daily 7am–9.30pm.

Mimi's Cafe 1400 S Harbor Blvd, Anaheim
☎714/956-2223. Huge servings, low prices,

and solid breakfasts and lunches. Part of a sizeable chain in Los Angeles and Orange counties, and popular in both. Daily 7am–11pm.

Ruby's 1 Balboa Pier, Newport Beach
☎949/675-RUBY. The first and finest of the retro-streamline 1940s diners in this chain – in a great location at the end of Newport's popular pier. Mostly offers the standard burgers, fries, and soda fare. Daily 7am–9pm, weekends open until 11pm.

Zinc Café 344 Ocean Ave, Laguna Beach
☎949/494-2791. A popular breakfast spot also offering simple soup-and-salad meals and other vegetarian fare, with some tasty desserts. Daily 7am–4.30pm.

Restaurants

The listings below generally follow the chapter divisions of our guide, grouping **restaurants** first by neighborhood, then by cuisine. A number of specialty categories (24hr celebrity watching, etc) appear in boxes.

All restaurants and cafes are listed in the relevant chapter maps throughout the guide; the exceptions are restaurants in West Hollywood and Beverly Hills, which appear in this chapter on maps on p.275 and p.277.

Downtown

American, Californian, and Cajun

Arnie Morton's of Chicago 735 S Figueroa
☎213/553-4566. The place to come for a predictably succulent steak experience, this swank chain restaurant serves sizable slabs of beef, salads, and desserts, with predictably steep prices. Daily 5.30–11pm, also Mon–Fri 11.30am–2.30pm.

Café Metropol 923 E Third St ☎213/613-1537. One of several restaurants attempting to bring eateries (and people) back to a formerly grim part of town. The area may still be industrial, but this artsy, affordable spot is worth a visit for its hearty sandwiches, salads, pizza, and pasta. Mon–Sat 8am–10pm, Sun 9am–10pm.

Checkers in the Hilton Checkers hotel, 535 S Grand Ave ☎213/624-0519. One of the most elegant Downtown restaurants, serving top-rated California cuisine, with lamb and seafood among the better offerings. If you're careful, you and a companion can escape with a bill under $100. Daily 5.30–9pm, also Mon–Fri 6.30am–2.30pm, Sat–Sun 7am–2pm.

Engine Co. No. 28 644 S Figueroa St
☎213/624-6996. Longtime favorite for all-American fare, featuring expensive grilled steaks and seafood, served with great fries in a renovated 1912 fire station. A solid wine list rounds out this excellent eatery. Mon–Fri 11.30am–9pm, Sat & Sun 5–9pm.

L.A. Prime inside the Westin Bonaventure hotel, 404 S Figueroa St ☎213/612-4743. Plump slabs of tender Midwestern beef are the draw at this pricey New York–style steak-house, while the side orders and desserts hold their own. Killer views from the hotel's 35th floor. Daily 4pm–1am, Sun closes at midnight.

New Moon 102 W Ninth St ☎213/624-0186. Worthwhile mainly for its location near the Garment District and its reasonably priced mix of American cooking – salads, soups, steaks, and the like – and serviceable Chinese dishes. Mon–Fri 11am–5pm, Sat 11am–3pm.

Pacific Dining Car 1310 W Sixth St
☎213/483-6000. Here since 1921, a would-be English supper club where the Downtown elite used to cut secret deals.

▲ Pacific Dining Car

Located inside an old railroad carriage, it's open 24hrs for very expensive and delicious steaks. Breakfast is the best value.

Patina 141 S Grand Ave ☎213/972-3331. Fancy, ultra-swank Disney Hall branch of one of LA's top eateries, where you can devour pheasant, pork loin medallions, and other rotating items on the menu, if you're prepared to drop a wad of cash. Mon–Fri 6pm–9.30pm, Sat 5.30-10.30pm.

Water Grill 544 S Grand Ave ☎213/891-0900. One of the top-priced, top-notch spots for munching on California cuisine in LA, or anywhere, with the focus on seafood prepared in all manner of colorful and ever-changing ways. Mon–Tues 11.30am–9pm, Wed–Fri 11.30am–10pm, Sat 5–9.30pm, Sun 4.30–8.30pm.

Chinese and Vietnamese

ABC Seafood 708 New High St ☎213/680-2887. Pork buns, egg tarts, and dim sum are the reasons to schlep to this Chinatown joint, which looks like it's been around for eons. Doles out decent dumplings and rolls no matter how creaky the surroundings. Daily 8am–10pm.

Grand Star 934 Sun Mun Way ☎213/626-2285. While the traditional Chinese soups and meat dishes here are flavorful and authentic, the real appeal is the lively video-karaoke scene. Also offers takeout. Daily 5pm–1.30am, Sun closes midnight.

Mandarin Deli 727 N Broadway #109 ☎213/623-6054. Delectable and cheap noodles, pork and fish dumplings, and other hearty staples in the middle of Broadway's riot of activity. Also at **356 E Second St, Little Tokyo** ☎213/617-0231. Daily 11am–7.30pm, closed Thurs.

Ocean Seafood 747 N Broadway ☎213/687-3088. Busy Cantonese restaurant serving inexpensive and excellent food – dim sum, crab, shrimp, and duck are among many standout choices. Daily 9am–10pm.

Pho 79 29 S Garfield Ave, Alhambra ☎626/289-0239. Consider venturing out to this ethnic suburb northeast of Downtown to sample some excellent Vietnamese food, including, of course, their signature pho soups. Daily 9am–9pm, weekends 'til 10pm.

Yang Chow 819 N Broadway ☎213/625-0811. Solid, affordable Chinese restaurant, where you can't go wrong with the Szechuan beef or any shrimp dish. Sun–Thurs 11.30am–9.30pm, weekends closes at 10.30pm.

French

Angelique Café 840 S Spring St ☎213/623-8698. A marvelous and affordable Continental eatery in the middle of the Garment District, where you can sit on the quaint patio and dine on well-crafted pastries for breakfast or savory sandwiches, rich casseroles, and fine salads for lunch. Mon–Fri 7am–4pm, Sat 8am–4pm.

Café Pinot 700 W Fifth St ☎213/239-6500. Located next to the LA Public Library, this elegant restaurant adds a touch of French to its nouvelle California cuisine. Mon–Fri 11.30am–9.30pm, Sat 5–10pm, Sun 4.30–9pm.

Italian and pizza

Ciao Trattoria 815 W Seventh St ☎213/624-2244. Housed in a striking Romanesque building, full of lovely historic-revival decor, a good choice for upscale, Northern Italian dining. Somewhat pricey, but not as steep as you might think. Mon–Fri 11am–9.30pm, Sat–Sun 5–9.30pm.

Cicada 617 S Olive St ☎213/488-9488. Lodged in the stunning Art Deco Oviatt Building (see p.63), this Northern Italian restaurant offers fine pasta for half the price of its fish and steak entrees – but still very expensive. Daily 5.30–9.30pm.

Tesoro Trattoria 300 S Grand Ave ☎213/680-0000. This comfortable Italian spot has adequate if bland pastas, salads, and sandwiches. Still, it's convenient for visiting MOCA. Mon–Fri 11.30am–8.30pm, Sat–Sun 5–9pm.

Zucca 801 S Figueroa St ☎213/614-7800. Italian bistro setting near the Convention Center that serves up Cal-cuisine-styled Italian fare, making pasta, salads, and desserts with real flair for hungry conventioneers. Daily 5–9pm, also Mon–Fri 11.30am–2.30pm.

Japanese

Daikokuya 327 E 1st St ☎213/626-1680. One of a number of affordable Little Tokyo restaurants congregated in the same general area (let your nose be your guide). This one's nice menu of noodle soups, rolls, gyoza, and various combos merit a taste or two. Mon–Thurs 11am–midnight, Fri–Sat 11am–1am, Sun noon–7pm.

Kagaya 418 E 2nd St ☎213/617-1016. A solid staple of the Little Tokyo area, which provides a range of choices of beef wraps, various noodles and more oddball dishes with fried eel and egg custard — almost all good, almost all expensive. Tues–Sat 6–10.30pm, Sun 6–10pm.

Shibucho 3114 Beverly Blvd ☎213/387-8498. Tasty, affordable sushi bar west of Downtown. The squid and eel are quite fine,

along with the famed toro, an expensive but delicious tuna delicacy. Mon–Sat 6pm–midnight.

A Thousand Cranes 120 S Los Angeles St, Little Tokyo ☎213/253-9255. Located beside the Japanese Garden in the Sky of the *New Otani* Hotel (see p.243), this is dining at its most refined, with pleasant views of water and greenery, and multiple courses – notably tempura – served in an elegant setting. Daily 7–10am & 11.30am–2pm & 6–9pm, Sun opens 11am.

Zip Fusion Sushi 744 E Third St ☎213/680-3770. Bringing color back to a former dead zone, this somewhat overpriced Cal-cuisine-styled sushi bar has decent takes on the usual fish staples, plus an arty vibe and occasional live music and DJs. Mon–Fri 11.30am–2.30pm & 5–10.30pm, Fri closes at 11.30pm, Sat 5–11.30pm.

Mexican and Latin American

Burrito King 2109 W Sunset Blvd at Alvarado, Echo Park ☎213/484-9859. Excellent, cheap burritos and tasty tostadas from this small stand. Also nearby at 2827 Hyperion Ave ☎323/663-9378. Daily 9am–3am, Sun closes midnight.

El Taurino 2306 W 11th St ☎213/738-0961. Tacos, burritos and especially tostadas are the draw at this popular and authentic eatery – where the green and red salsas burn all the way down. Daily 11am–11pm.

King Taco 2904 N Broadway ☎323/222-8500. The most centrally located diner in a chain of many ultra-basic shops around Downtown (this one north of Chinatown), with many varieties of inexpensive, savory tacos. Daily 8am–11pm, weekends 'til 2am.

La Luz del Día 107 Paseo de la Plaza ☎213/628-7495. Authentic Mexican eatery on Olvera Street with fiery burritos, enchiladas, and stews, served in sizeable enough portions to make you sweat with a smile. Mon–Thurs 11am–9pm, Fri–Sun 10am–10pm.

Wood Spoon 107 W 9th St ☎213/629-1765. Recent Brazilian arrival that kicks up its heels with a range of interesting items like shrimp dumplings, pork burgers, and yam fries. Mon–Fri 11am–9pm, Sat 9am–9pm.

Spanish

Ciudad 445 S Figueroa St ☎213/486-5171. Ceviche and paella are some of the

Fine dining

At the following restaurants – good for business dinners or impressing your date – you'll need to book ahead and, likely, dress up too. Meals can easily run about $100 or more per head, including drinks.

Checkers p.266
Chinois on Main p.281
Cicada p.268
Claes Seafood p.289
Cut p.278
Engine Co. No. 28 p.266
Geoffrey's p.283
Grace p.269
Hatfield's p.269
L'Orangerie p.276

LA Farm p.281
L.A. Prime p.266
Lucques p.275
Matsuhisa p.280
Mr Chow p.278
Pacific Dining Car p.266
Saddle Peak Lodge p.286
Sona p.276
Valentino p.282
Water Grill p.267

highlights at this colorful, if pricey, Mexican-influenced spot, where the live Latin music competes with the delicious food for your attention. Mon–Thurs 11.30am–9pm, Fri 11.30am–10pm, Sat 5–11pm, Sun 5–9pm.

Mid-Wilshire

African

Nyala 1076 S Fairfax Ave ☎ 323/936-5918. One of several reasonably priced Ethiopian favorites along Fairfax, serving staples like doro wat (marinated chicken) and kitfo (chopped beef with butter and cheese) with spongy injera bread. Daily 11.30am–10.30pm.

Rosalind's 1044 S Fairfax Ave ☎ 323/936-2486. Spicy goat meat, beef stew, and pepper chicken are among the highlights at this moderate Ethiopian spot, a neighborhood favorite for many years. Daily 11am–2am, Sun closes midnight.

American, California cuisine, and Cajun

Ca' Brea 346 S La Brea Ave ☎ 323/938-2863. One of LA's best-known, and best, choices for Italian cuisine, with especially solid osso buco and risotto. Getting in is difficult, so reserve ahead and expect to pay a bundle. Daily 5.30–10.30pm, also Mon–Fri 11.30–2.30pm.

Flora Kitchen 460 S La Brea Ave ☎ 323/931-9900. Connected to a flower shop, this restaurant's key attractions are the California

cuisine–style sandwiches made with a host of tasty, fresh ingredients. Mon–Sat 7am–10pm, Sun 7am–3pm.

Grace 7360 Beverly Blvd ☎ 323/934-4400. Expensive but delicious Cal-cuisine that inspires great confidence, not least for its red pork belly, wild-boar tenderloin, and very inventive range of desserts, from butterscotch donuts to passion-fruit caramel cake. Tues–Thurs 5.30–11pm, Fri–Sat 5.30–midnight, Sun 5.30–10.30pm.

Hatfield's 7458 Beverly Blvd ☎ 323/935-2977. A relatively recent arrival on the local food scene that's whipped up a big (deserved) reputation — for its rack of lamb, duck breast, smoked pork belly and outstanding desserts. Expensive, but the seven-course menu ($78) is great. Mon–Sat 6–10pm.

The Gumbo Pot 6333 W Third St, in the Farmers Market ☎ 323/933-0358. Ever-popular, delicious, and dirt-cheap Cajun cooking. Try the full-flavored gumbo yaya of chicken, shrimp, and sausage, along with the fruit-and-potato salad. Daily 9am–9pm, Sun closes at 8pm.

Luna Park 672 S La Brea Ave ☎ 323/934-2110. Reliable Cal-cuisine spot that serves up smart versions of diner items like burgers, mac 'n' cheese and grilled sandwiches for lunch, and chic seafood, steak, and pasta for dinner. Daily 11.30am–2.30pm & 5.30–10.30pm.

Taylor's 3361 W Eighth St ☎ 213/382-8449. Old-fashioned American meat in a darkly lit, old-school steakhouse ambience, priced a bit more reasonably – though still expensively – than at similar Westside spots. Mon–Fri 11.30am–9.30pm, Sat 4-10.30pm, Sun 4.30–9.30pm.

Caribbean

Prado's 244 N Larchmont Blvd ⊤ 323/467-3871. A stylish, affordable spot in the Larchmont Village shopping zone, better than the standard Caribbean offerings in LA, with a broad range of tasty items, from spicy seafood and jerk chicken to plantains and pizza. Mon–Fri 11.30am–3pm & 5.30–10pm, Sat–Sun 4.30–10.30pm.

Chinese and Vietnamese

Genghis Cohen 740 N Fairfax Ave ⊤ 323/653-0640. Familiar Chinese dishes with a Yiddish touch: the menu features fine Szechuan beef, dumplings, and kung pao chicken. Sun–Thurs noon–11pm, weekends noon–midnight.

Pho 2000 215 N Western Ave ⊤ 323/461-5845. One of four Koreatown restaurants specializing in hot, spicy bowls of the Vietnamese soup pho. Cheap and authentic, it draws a loyal crowd of regulars. Mon–Sat 11am–7.30pm.

Pho Western 425 S Western Ave ⊤ 213/387-9100. You won't have to look hard in Koreatown to find solid Vietnamese eateries, and this one's no different – offering the spicy soup pho, along with rice-noodle bowls and other authentic entrees – and cheap, too. Mon–Fri 10am–8pm.

French

Mimosa 8009 Beverly Blvd ⊤ 323/655-8895. Mid-priced bistro cooking with a strong French accent, making for savory offerings like rack of lamb, sweetbreads, and beef bourguignon. Mon–Thurs 6–10pm, Fri–Sat 6–11pm.

Ortolan 8338 W Third St ⊤ 323/653-3300. New favorite on LA's French cuisine map, mixing up the old style with inventive quirks, which may include the likes of foie gras confit, eggs and caviar (in hot ash!), scallop ceviche, and roasted sweetbreads. None of this comes cheap — either $125 fixed or plates at $20–50. Mon–Sat 6–10pm.

Greek

Le Petit Greek 127 N Larchmont Blvd ⊤ 323/464-5160. Sizable, mid-priced servings of Greek staples in a quiet Larchmont Village location. Nothing exceptional, but will do in a pinch. Daily 11.30am–10.30pm.

Papa Cristos 2771 W Pico Blvd ⊤ 323/737-2970. Consider venturing to this grim neighborhood near the 10 freeway to sample the authentic delights at this Greek joint, including delicious gyros, Greek sausage, caviar, and hefty portions of lamb chops or roast chicken for under $10. The real thing. Tues–Sat 9am–8pm, Sun 9am–4pm.

Sofi 8030 W Third St ⊤ 323/651-0346. A pleasant, comfortable place near the Farmers Market, serving well-prepared Greek items like stuffed grape leaves and moussaka to a loyal crowd — which will soon include you. Daily 11.30am–3pm & 5.30–11pm, Sun opens at 5.30pm.

Indian

India's Oven 7231 Beverly Blvd ⊤ 323/936-1000. Friendly, inexpensive Indian restaurant where you'll get large, delicious portions of old favorites like stuffed naan, veggie samosas, chicken balls, and vindaloo. Daily 10.30am–10pm.

Italian and pizza

Amalfi 143 N La Brea Ave ⊤ 323/938-2504. Sample appetizers like tuna tartare and black sausage, many fine pizzas and pastas, and pricier items like rack of lamb and roasted duck. The eclectic menu even includes risotto and a sirloin burger. Mon–Fri 11.30am–3pm & 6pm–midnight. Sat 6pm–1am.

Angelini Osteria 7313 Beverly Blvd ⊤ 323/297-0070. The kind of authentic place that knows the difference between its primi and secondi, and offers a fine selection of pasta, as well as veal and lamb chops, Dover sole, and rotating items like oxtail, veal shank, and porchetta. Not as expensive as you might think. Tues–Fri noon–2pm & 5.30–10pm, Sat 5.30–11pm, Sun 5.30–10pm.

Campanile 624 S La Brea Ave ⊤ 323/938-1447. Incredible but very expensive Northern Italian food. If you can't afford a full dinner, just try the dessert or pick up some of the city's best bread at La Brea Bakery next door (see p.355). Mon–Fri 11.30am–2.30pm & 6–10pm, Sat 9.30am–1.30pm & 5.30–11pm, Sun 9.30am–1.30pm.

Japanese

Ita-Cho 7311 Beverly Blvd ⊤ 323/938-9009. Not the most authentic fare around, but still appealing for the tasty and affordable sashimi, sushi, grilled squid, and eggplant dishes, served in a chic Westside setting. Tues–Sat 6–11pm.

Mishima 8474 W Third St ☎323/782-0181. Great miso soup, softshell crab salad, and udon and soba noodles, at very affordable prices, at this popular Westside eatery. Daily 11am–10pm.

Sushi Roku 8445 W Third St ☎323/655-6767. This upscale, slightly stuffy eatery is worth visiting for its fine lobster potstickers, octopus sashimi, and crab rolls. One of several Westside locations. Mon–Fri 11.30am–2.30pm & 5.30–11.30pm, Sat noon-11.30pm, Sun 5–10pm.

Wako Donkasu 3377 Wilshire Blvd #112 ☎213/381-9256. Somewhat hard-to-find Koreatown joint in a mini-mall. Features fine Japanese fare on the menu, highlighted by pork and fish cutlets, crispy chicken, and bowls of soba and udon noodles — all cheap and very tasty. Mon–Sat 11am–9.30pm, Sun noon–8pm

Korean

Dong Il Jang 3455 W Eighth St, Koreatown ☎213/383-5757. Cozy, affordable little restaurant where the meat is cooked at your table and the food is consistently appealing, especially the grilled chicken and BBQ beef. Tempura dishes and a sushi bar are an added draw. Daily 11am–11pm.

Kobawoo House 698 S Vermont Ave #109, Koreatown ☎213/389-7300. Korean fishhouse where the seafood comes in spicy soups or made into pancakes. There are also a good kimchee, pork belly, barbequed beef, and other authentic choices. Daily 11am-midnight.

Soot Bull Jeep 3136 W Eighth St, Koreatown ☎213/387-3865. A genuine Korean BBQ joint, where you'll appreciate just how delicious slow-cooked, heavily spiced slabs of chicken, pork, and steak really are, for moderate prices. Fans of this type of cooking will rejoice. Daily 11am–10.30pm.

Mexican and Latin American

Casa Carnitas 4067 Beverly Blvd ☎323/667-9953. Delicious and cheap Mexican food from the Yucatán, inspired by Cuban and Caribbean cooking, and including lots of seafood, too. Tues–Sun 11am–10pm.

El Cholo 1121 S Western Ave ☎323/734-2773.

One of LA's first big Mexican restaurants and still one of the best, despite the wait to get in during peak hours. Offers a solid array of staples like enchiladas and tamales, with some vegetarian options. Mon–Thurs 11am–10pm, Fri–Sat 11am–11pm, Sun 11am–9pm.

El Coyote 7312 Beverly Blvd ☎323/939-2255. Labyrinthine restaurant serving gut-busting Mexican fare, almost more than you can stand. Cheap and lethal margaritas are the primary draw to the gloomy setting. Daily 11am–10pm, weekends until 11pm.

Guelaguetza 3014 Olympic Blvd, Koreatown ☎213/427-0608. Primo eatery that appeals for its cheap, authentic Mexican fare from Oaxaca – delicious molés, savory stews, and soups, and all manner of south-of-the-border staples, from chile rellenos to horchata. Daily 9.30am–10pm, Sun closes 9.30pm.

Pampas Grill 6333 W Third St, in the Farmers Market ☎323/931-1928. Delivers on the promise of spicy, delicious Brazilian fare with its selection of hearty churrasco, including linguica, leg of lamb and various barbeque temptations. It's served in a cafeteria setting, but still quite appealing, especially for the price. Daily 10.30am–9pm.

Middle Eastern

Haifa 8717 W Pico Blvd ☎310/888-7700. Located south of Wilshire, this affordable Mediterranean spot rewards a visit if you love falafel, kabobs, and shawarma, all of it prepared kosher. Daily 11.30am–9.30pm.

Shah-Abbas 400 S San Vicente Blvd ☎310/659-3242. Solid Iranian dining south of the Beverly Center, where you can get your fill of rich and savory kabobs, chicken, and walnut stew, and other staples for reasonable prices; plus, there's belly dancing regularly. Daily 11.30am–10pm.

Spanish

Cobras and Matadors 7615 Beverly Blvd ☎323/932-6178. Expensive tapas restaurant just down the street from Pan Pacific Park. You can sample all your favorite Castilian delights in a hushed, intimate setting. Daily 6–11pm, weekends until midnight.

Tasca 8108 W Third St ☎323/951-9890. Another solid choice for tapas, with faves like risotto fritters, braised short ribs, and tuna tartare, along with a nice selection of salads and wines. Tues–Thurs 6–10pm, Fri–Sat 6–11pm, Sun 10am–3pm.

Thai and Southeast Asian

Singapore's Banana Leaf 6333 W Third St, in the Farmers Market ☎323/933-4627. A fine hole in the wall where you can sample Malaysian cuisine at its spiciest and most savory: delectable curry soups, satay, and tandoori dishes. Mon–Fri 9am–9pm, Sat 9am–8pm, Sun 10am–7pm.

Vim 831 S Vermont Ave ☎213/386-2338. Authentic Thai and Chinese food at low prices; the seafood soup and pad Thai are especially pleasing. Daily 11am–11pm, until midnight on weekends.

Vegetarian and wholefood

Erewhon 7660 Beverly Blvd ☎323/937-0777. An old-fashioned juice bar and deli, where you can gobble down as much raw food and gulp down as many wheatgrass concoctions and bee-pollen smoothies as you can stand – for high prices. Mon–Sat 8am–10pm, Sun 9am–9pm.

Inaka Natural Foods 131 S La Brea Ave ☎323/936-9353. Located in the trendy La Brea district and featuring vegetarian and macrobiotic food with a strong Japanese theme. Tues–Fri noon–2.30pm & 6–10pm, Sat 5.30–10pm, Sun 5.30–9pm.

Hollywood

African

Dar Maghreb 7651 Sunset Blvd ☎323/876-7651. Set in a faux-African palace, done up in ogee arches and antique decor, this eatery's rich, pricey Moroccan dishes, including b'stilla (a pastry stuffed with chicken, chickpeas, and spices), almost take a backseat to the belly-dancing. Mon–Sat 6–11pm, Sun 5.30–10.30pm.

Moun of Tunis 7445 Sunset Blvd ☎323/874-3333. Mouthwatering Tunisian fare presented in huge, multicourse meals, heavy on the spices and rich on the exotic flavors – plus belly-dancing regularly. Daily 5.30–11pm.

American, Californian, and Cajun

The Foundry on Melrose 7463 Melrose Ave ☎323/651-0915. Among the greatest of pricey Cal-cuisine arrivals in the neighborhood, serving such succulent and unexpected dishes as skate wing, black cod with mussels, glazed pork belly, and persimmon salad; also compelling desserts such as apple fritters and white-chocolate nougat. Tues–Sat 6–11pm.

Grub 911 Seward St ☎323/461-3663. Set in a little house south of Central Hollywood, this is a fine spot for affordable comfort food, especially for breakfast: cinnamon-vanilla French toast, chorizo burritos, and inventive omelets. Flavorful soups, chili and salads are on the lunch menu. Mon–Fri 11am–3pm, Sat–Sun 9am–2pm.

Hollywood Canteen 1006 N Seward St ☎323/465-0961. A dark club scene with fish, steak, and clam chowder – just the right ambience to make you feel like a big shot. Also with nightly dance music and on-site "trailer" to accommodate schmoozer overflow. Mon–Fri 11.30am–3pm & 7pm–2am, Sat 6pm–2am.

Musso and Frank Grill 6667 Hollywood Blvd ☎323/467-7788. A 1919 classic, loaded with authentic atmosphere and history in a dark-paneled dining room. The drinks (see p.292) are better than the costly, mostly upscale diner food. Tues–Sat 11am–11pm.

Off Vine 6263 Leland Way ☎323/962-1900. Dine on eclectic Cal cuisine – pecan chicken, duck sausage, and steak with Roquefort cabernet sauce – in a renovated but still funky Craftsman bungalow. Daily 11.30am–2.30pm & 5.30–11pm, weekends opens at 5.30pm.

Pig 'n' Whistle 6714 Hollywood Blvd ☎323/463-1473. Historic 1927 eatery refurbished as a posy Cal-cuisine restaurant, with the emphasis on all things porcine, from ribs to pork roast to bacon. Although much of the old spirit and decor are the same, the prices are not: no diner has food this pricey. Sun–Thurs 11.30am–10.30pm, weekends until 11pm.

Providence 5955 Melrose Ave ☎323/460-4170. Near the top of the LA pricey-food heap, and for good reason: the place is swarming with foodies, who come for the black sea bass, salmon risotto, lump blue crab, and plenty of other tremendous choices. In a word — go. Mon–Fri 6–10pm, also Fri noon–2.30pm, Sat 5.30–10pm, Sun 5.30–9pm.

vermont 1714 N Vermont Ave ☎323/661-6163. One of the better Cal-cuisine eateries in the area. The entrees are predictable enough – roasted chicken, crab cakes, ravioli, etc – but the culinary presentation is effective and, on occasion, inspired. Tues–Sun 5.30–10.30pm, also Tues–Fri 11.30am–3pm.

Caribbean

El Floridita 1253 N Vine St ☎323/871-8612.
Lively Cuban restaurant where the dance
floor swings on the weekends and there's
live music regularly throughout the week.
The menu features solid standards like
plantains, croquetas, and yucca, all affordably priced. Mon–Wed & Fri 11.30am–1am,
Tues & Thurs 11.30am–9pm, Sat noon–
1am, Sun 2–9pm.

Chinese and Vietnamese

Hong Kong Deli 1645 N Cahuenga Blvd
☎323/957-1998. Appealing for its cheap and
traditional Szechuan and Mandarin entrees,
but also for its serviceable sushi. Daily
11.30am–10pm.
Hunan Cafe 7986 W Sunset Blvd ☎323/822-
1208. Powerful tasty eats in Central
Hollywood. You can sup on spicy chicken
and beef and noodle dishes for not more
than a couple of bucks. Mon–Sat noon–
10pm, Sun 4–10pm.
Pho Café 2841 Sunset Blvd ☎213/413-0888.
Traditional Vietnamese restaurant transformed by Silver Lake trendiness into a
hipster hangout, with the usual pho soup
and egg rolls, plus a decent selection of rice
noodle dishes. It's cheap, but cash only.
Daily 11am–midnight.
Taipan 7075 Sunset Blvd ☎323/464-2989. An
affordable neighborhood eatery offering
appetizing shrimp and chicken entrees, plus
a few surprises like black-bean catfish. Daily
11am–10pm.

French

Café des Artistes 1534 N McCadden Place
☎323/469-7300. With a French chef at the
helm and French customers at the tables,
this cozy, pricey spot is at its best in such
treats as osso buco, braised ribs, and an
array of seafood dishes. Daily 5.30pm–
midnight, also Mon–Fri 11.30am–3pm,
closes at 2am Thurs–Sat, midnight Sun.

Indian

East India Grill 345 N La Brea Ave
☎323/936-8844. Southern Indian
cuisine given the California treatment:
impressive specialties include tomato-chili
chicken wings, lamb stir fry, mango ribs,
and parmesan naan. Daily 11am–10.30pm.
Electric Lotus 4656 Franklin Ave, Los Feliz
☎323/953-0040. While somewhat cramped

and located in a mini-mall, a fine choice for
traditional staples – pakoras, vindaloo,
curries, stuffed naan, etc. DJs and private
booths create a clubby atmosphere. Daily
11.30am–midnight, weekends until 1am.
Tantra 3705 Sunset Blvd ☎323/663-8268.
Popular and reasonably priced Silver Lake
eatery where you can dig into favorites like
lamb curry and vindaloo, chicken tikka, and
much more. There's a mild hipster vibe, so
try to grab a seat before it fills up. Tues–Sun
5-11pm, weekends 'til midnight.

Italian and pizza

Angeli 7274 Melrose Ave ☎323/936-9086.
Refreshingly basic pizza styles – baked in a
wood-burning oven – make this a worthwhile, affordable stop, as do the tasty
frittatas and croquettes. Tues–Thurs
11.30am–10pm, Fri 11.30am–11pm, Sat &
Sun 5–11pm.
Miceli's 1646 N Las Palmas St ☎323/466-3438.
Hefty, old-style pizzas that come laden with
gooey cheese and plenty of tomato sauce.
It's hardly nouvelle cuisine, but you'll be too
busy scarfing it down to notice. Mon–Thurs
11.30am–midnight, Fri 11.30am–1am, Sat
5pm–1am, Sun 5–11pm.
Palermo 1858 N Vermont Ave ☎323/663-1178.
As old as Hollywood, and with as many
devoted fans, who flock here for the rich
Southern Italian pizzas, cheesy decor, and
gallons of cheapish red wine. Wed–Mon
11am–midnight.
Tomato Pie Pizza Joint 7751 Melrose Ave
☎323/635-9993. Despite the curious name,
a really solid place to grab a slice, including
the usual staples, plus pies with pesto,
eggplant parmigiana, spicy buffalo-style
chicken, and rib-eye steak. Also serves
decent pastas, subs, and salads. Daily
11am–9pm.
Vivoli Cafe 7994 Sunset Blvd ☎323/656-5050.
A fine spot for dining on fairly authentic,
affordable Italian fare including caprese,
calamari, pastas, pizza, and palate-pleasing
chicken, beef, and veal entrees. Daily
11.30am–10pm, weekends 'til 11pm.

Japanese

Shintaro Sushi 1900 N Highland Ave ☎323/882-
6524. Just north of the center of Hollywood,
some of the town's best sushi, and not too
pricey, with a selection of rolls, sushi and
sashimi, and other favorites, including
enjoyable cooked presentations of salmon,

scallops, and albacore tuna. Mon–Sat 5.30–11pm, also Mon–Fri 11.30am–2.30pm.
Yamashiro 1999 N Sycamore Ave ☎323/466-5125. Although the food can be an overpriced letdown, this place is still a must-see for its outstanding gardens, koi ponds, palatial design, and terrific view of LA from the Hollywood Hills – making it a perfectly romantic attraction. Daily 5–10pm, weekends until 11pm.

Mexican and Latin American

Cactus Mexican 950 Vine St ☎323/464-5865. A good spot to keep the evening going while you're club-hopping in Hollywood, with rib-stuffing tacos, quesadillas, and burritos that'll make you hiccup with a smile. Daily 10.30am–3am, Sun closes midnight.
El Compadre 7408 W Sunset Blvd ☎323/874-7924. With potent margaritas, live mariachi bands, and cheap Mexican standards, this is a music-loving gourmand's delight. One of several locations, most of them in more distant parts of the metropolis. Daily 11am–2am.
Mario's Peruvian & Seafood 5786 Melrose Ave ☎323/466-4181. Delicious and authentic Peruvian fare: supremely tender squid, rich and flavorful mussels, among many other compelling choices. Inexpensive, too. Mon–Thurs 11.30am–8pm, Fri–Sat 11.30am–9.30pm, Sun 9.30am–8pm.
Mexico City 2121 N Hillhurst Ave ☎323/661-7227. Spinach enchiladas and other Califor-nian versions of Mexican standards, including a mean pollo verde chicken dish, with prices that are easy to stomach. Daily noon–midnight.
Yuca's Hut 2056 N Hillhurst Ave ☎323/662-1214. A small, hidden jewel serving consid-erable burritos, marinated pork dishes, and beef tacos al fresco, opposite the more popular Mexico City (see above). Mon–Sat 11am–6pm.

Middle Eastern

Marouch 4905 Santa Monica Blvd ☎323/662-9325. Although located in a nondescript part of town, this fine Lebanese restaurant provides rich sustenance with its flavorful kabobs, baba ganoush, stuffed grape leaves, and shawarma, at very manageable prices. Tues–Sun 11am–11pm.
Zankou Chicken 5065 Sunset Blvd ☎323/665-7845. The top Middle Eastern value in town

(and part of a citywide chain), with delicious garlicky chicken cooked on a rotisserie and made into a sandwich, plus all the traditional salads – tabouli, hummus, and the like. Daily 10am–midnight.

Russian and Eastern European

Csardas 5820 Melrose Ave ☎323/962-6434. Located a few blocks from Paramount Studios, this funky and affordable Hungarian joint serves up spicy old-world flavors in hearty stews and goulash, dumplings, stuffed cabbage rolls, and roasted chicken and pork. Daily noon–10pm.
Uzbekistan 7077 Sunset Blvd ☎323/464-3663. Savory, though very heavy, servings of mostly lamb-based Uzbekistani food, especially big on dumplings. Daily 11am–11pm.

Thai and Southeast Asian

Chan Darae 1511 N Cahuenga Blvd ☎323/464-8585. Terrific Thai food, and the locals know it, flocking here for a mid-priced range of scrumptious staples such as tom yum soup and pad Thai. Daily 11am–11pm, weekends opens at 5pm.
Jitlada 5233 Sunset Blvd ☎323/667-9809. In a dreary mini-mall, but the spicy chicken, squid, and seafood curries more than make up for the setting. Affordable prices, too. Mon–Sat 11am–10.30pm, Mon opens 5pm.
Palms Thai 5273 Hollywood Blvd ☎323/461-7053. A popular only-in-LA locale, swamped nightly not due to the dishes served – though the fairly priced Thai standards are well done – but for the kitschy entertainment, namely "Thai Elvis," a surprisingly convincing King. Daily 11am–2am.
Sanamluang Café 5176 Hollywood Blvd ☎323/660-8006. You can't beat the cheap, excellent and plentiful noodles at this nearly-all-night Thai eatery. Daily 10.30am–3.30am, Sun closes midnight.

West Hollywood

American, Californian, and Cajun

Arnie Morton's 435 N La Cienega Blvd ☎310/246-1501. A 1950s-style homage to the old days of American eats, where hefty steaks and scrumptious sides of creamed spinach and baked potatoes pull in grizzled veterans of Tinseltown. Part of the upper-end Morton's chain. Mon–Sat 5.30–11pm, Sun 5–10pm.

WEST HOLLYWOOD
EATING & DRINKING

N

EATING & DRINKING

7969	26	Fenix	4	Lola's	27	Roxy	13
Ago	45	Flowering Tree	20	Lucques	42	Snake Pit	28
Angeli	41	Frankie and Johnnie's	14	Marix Tex-Mex		Sona	54
Arnie Morton's	53	French Quarter	23	Playa	10	Spanish Kitchen	35
Astro Burger	24	Griddle Café	3	Mel's Drive-In	9	Swingers	58
Barney's Beanery	18	Hamburger Haven	46	Melrose Bar & Grill	51	Taste	43
Café La Boheme	22	House of Blues	6	Miyagi's	1	Topz	31
Carlitos Gardel	39	Irv's Burgers	19	Mother Lode	40	The Troubadour	48
Cat Club	17	Jar	57	Normandie Room	32	Ultra Suede	49
Champagne French		Jerry's Famous Deli	55	Nova Express	29	Urth Caffé	44
Bakery	38	Jones	25	Poquito Mas	7	Viper Room	21
Chin Chin	8	Katana	5	Rage	37	Vito's Pizza	34
Duke's	15	Key Club	11	Rainbow Bar and		Whisky-a-Go-Go	16
El Compadre	2	King's Road Espresso		Grill	12	Yukon Mining Co.	30
The Factory	47	House	56	Real Food Daily	52		
Fat Fish	50	L'Orangerie	33	Red Rock	36		

Café La Boheme 8400 Santa Monica Blvd
⊕323/848-2360. The dark, somewhat
spooky decor is matched by the indulgent
melange of Cal-cuisine flavors enlivening the
pasta, risotto, and steak entrees. Daily
5.30pm–11.30pm, weekends until 12.30am.
Jar 8225 Beverly Blvd ⊕323/655-6566. An
upper-end steakhouse featuring all the usual
red-meat fare – prime rib, T-bone, even a
pot roast – with an inspired Cal-cuisine flair,

throwing in different spices and exotic
flavors to create an unusual, yet traditional,
result. Mon–Sat 5.30–11pm, Sun 10am–
2pm & 5.30–9.30pm.
Lucques 8474 Melrose Ave ⊕323/655-6277.
Expensive but tasty eatery that doles out
comfort food for the culinary elite – veal
cheeks, wild mushroom lasagna, and the
"devil's chicken" are but a few of the items
that helped its lead chef win a 2006 James

Beard award. Tues–Sat noon–2.30pm & 6–11pm, weekends closes midnight, Sun 5.30–10pm.

Melrose Bar and Grill 8826 Melrose Ave ☎310/278-3684. The place to come if you want savory pizzas, pasta, seafood, or burgers, prepared in a mildly upscale environment without too much pretension. Mon–Fri 11.30am–9.30pm, Sat 6–10pm.

Taste 8454 Melrose Ave ☎323/852-6888. Fancy nouveau diner fare with plenty of panache, with the seafood, watermelon salad, pizzas, and lamb chops among the favorites. Mon–Fri 11.30am–10pm, Sat 5.30–11pm, Sun 5.30–10pm.

Chinese and Vietnamese

Chin Chin 8618 Sunset Blvd ☎310/652-1818. Flashy but affordable dim sum café, a long-standing favorite and one of several around town. Daily 11.30am–11pm.

Kung Pao China 7853 Santa Monica Blvd ☎323/848-9888. Back-to-basics spot for tasty and affordable Chinese fare. The pork ribs, wontons, and pan-fried chicken keep regulars coming back. Sun–Thurs 11am–10.30pm, Fri–Sat 11am–11.30pm.

French

L'Orangerie 903 N La Cienega Blvd ☎310/652-9770. Super-upscale nouvelle California–style French cuisine; if you can't afford around $50 per entree (or a good suit and tie), enjoy the view from the bar. Tues–Sun 6–11pm.

Sona 401 N La Cienega Blvd ☎310/659-7708. A reminder of why French food in this part of town can bankrupt the unwary: the most creative and delicious nouvelle cuisine you can imagine, with six courses for $95, nine courses for $169. Tues–Fri 6–10.30pm, Sat 5.30–11.30pm.

Italian and pizza

Ago 8478 Melrose Ave ☎323/655-6333. Though there are better fancy Italian restaurants in LA, this one has the irresist-ible combo (to some) of excellent pasta, risotto, lamb, and veal, with regular celebrity appearances thrown in for good measure. Mon–Fri noon–11.30pm, Sat 6–11.30pm, Sun 6–10.30pm.

Frankie & Johnnie's 8947 Sunset Blvd ☎310/275-7770. Amid all the big rock clubs, an old favorite for its sizable pizzas loaded with greasy and healthy ingredients alike.

Check out the ink-scrawled messages on the walls, which include praise from famous regulars, from Don Knotts to Fred Durst. Mon–Sat 11am–2am, Sun noon–midnight.

Vito's Pizza 846 N La Cienega Blvd ☎310/652-6859. A neighborhood staple that, while not large, draws the crowds for its delicious pies, which include a mean Margherita and slices that recall East Coast pizza in all its thin-crusted and succulent glory. Sun–Thurs 11am–10.30pm, Fri–Sat 11am–midnight.

Japanese

Katana 8439 Sunset Blvd ☎323/650-8585. A notable example of a prototypical Westside sushi house – stunning ambience with high production values, fine and tasty sashimi rolls, and sushi, and a killer price tag. The swank atmosphere is hard to beat. Mon–Wed 6–11pm, Thurs–Sat 6pm–12.30am, Sun 6–11pm.

Miyagi's 8225 Sunset Blvd ☎323/650-3524. A hip sushi complex with a mid-priced menu of traditional and hybrid raw-fish offerings, served on three floors to piped-in dance music. Also a major pick-up joint for the area. Restaurant daily 5.30–11.30pm, bar until 2am.

Mexican and Latin American

Carlitos Gardel 7963 Melrose Ave ☎323/655-0891. Rich, affordable, and delectable Argentine cuisine – ie, heavy on the beef and spices, with sausages and garlic adding to the potent kick. Mon–Fri 11.30am–2.30pm & 6–11pm, Sat 6–11pm, Sun 5–10pm.

Poquito Mas 8555 Sunset Blvd ☎310/652-7008. Grab a chicken enchilada or burrito, the top choices at this popular low-priced LA chain. Daily 11am–10pm.

Spanish Kitchen 826 N La Cienega Blvd ☎310/659-4794. Swank but fun Mexican eatery that doles out a heavy selection of tamales, quesadillas, tortilla soup, and other staples – sometimes authentic, sometimes not. Daily 11am–1.30am, Sun closes midnight.

Thai and Southeast Asian

Galanga Thai Fusion 7440 Santa Monica Blvd ☎323/851-4355. Very fine, affordable Thai spot that serves some seriously tasty fish and noodle dishes, green papaya salad, curries, soups, and plenty more for a mostly local crowd. Daily 11am–10pm.

Michelia 8738 Third St ☎310/276-8288.
Located between Beverly Hills and West
Hollywood, this is something of a nouveau
Southeast Asian eatery, with Cal-cuisine
versions of traditional spicy salads and fish
dishes. Mon–Fri 11.30am–3pm & 5.30–
9.30pm, Sat 5.30–10.30pm.

Vegetarian and wholefood

Flowering Tree 8253 Santa Monica Blvd
☎323/654-4332. Nothing exceptional, but
the various veggie soups, faux burgers,
sandwiches, and salads merit a try, with
healthy drinks as well. Daily 9am–10pm.
Real Food Daily 414 N La Cienega Blvd
☎310/289-9910. Tempeh burgers, hemp
bread, and various soups and salads
draw a crowd at this vegan restaurant,
which also operates a branch at **514
Santa Monica Blvd, Santa Monica** (☎310/451-
7544). Mon–Sat 11.30am–11pm, Sun
10am–3pm.

Beverly Hills and West LA

African

Koutoubia 2116 Westwood Blvd, West LA
☎310/475-0729. Authentic Moroccan lamb,

couscous, and seafood, in a comfortable
environment enlivened by belly-dancing and
a touch of North African style. Can be
expensive, though. Daily 11.30am–10pm,
weekends 'til 11pm.

American, Californian, and Cajun

Aphrodisiac 10351 Santa Monica Blvd, West LA
☎310/282-8870. An elegant choice for lobster
tail, steak, seafood, and rack of lamb, with
middle-high prices for entrees, but if you
want to splurge, the eight-course "Bedroom
Menu" is the way to go ($395 for two).
Tues–Thurs 6–10pm, Fri–Sat 5.30–11pm.
Barney Greengrass 9570 Wilshire Blvd, Beverly
Hills ☎310/777-5877. Though dining in a
department store while stargazing might not
be everyone's idea of fun, the added plus at
this Barney's eatery is its consistently
pleasing Cal-cuisine, including delicious
sandwiches, bagels, and drinks. You will,
however, pay handsomely to eat here.
Mon–Sat 8.30am–6pm, weekends 'til 7pm,
Sun 9am–6pm.
Cheesecake Factory 364 N Beverly Drive, Beverly
Hills ☎310/278-7270. The flagship branch of
what's now a national chain of eateries,
which serves up adequate all-American fare.

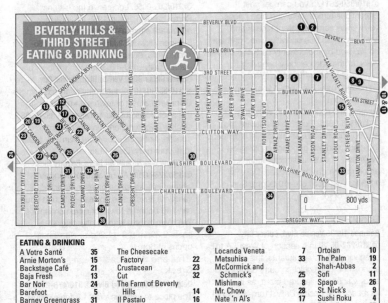

EATING & DRINKING

A Votre Santé	35	The Cheesecake		Locanda Veneta	7	Ortolan	10
Arnie Morton's	15	Factory	22	Matsuhisa	33	The Palm	19
Backstage Café	21	Crustacean	23	McCormick and		Shah-Abbas	2
Baja Fresh	13	Cut	32	Schmick's	25	Sofi	11
Bar Noir	24	The Farm of Beverly		Mishima	8	Spago	26
Barefoot	5	Hills	14	Mr. Chow	28	St. Nick's	9
Barney Greengrass	31	Il Pastaio	16	Nate 'n Al's	17	Sushi Roku	4
Brighton Coffee		Jacopo's	36	Newsroom Café	29	Talesai	37
Shop	27	Jerry's Famous Deli	1	Nic's Restaurant/		Third Stop	6
Café Flor	34	Kate Mantilini	30	Martini Lounge	12		
Chaya Brasserie	3	Le Palais des Thes	18	The Nosh of Beverly Hills	20		

277

Possibly the most popular restaurant in Beverly Hills, so come at an off-hour if you want a table. Mon–Thurs 11am–11pm, Fri & Sat 11am–midnight, Sun 10am–11pm.

Cut 9500 Wilshire Blvd, Beverly Hills ⊤310/276-8500. This Wolfgang Puck steakhouse designed by Richard Meier looks like the Getty Center cafeteria – nonetheless, if you like (and can afford) $50 steaks, Kobe short ribs and Maine lobsters, this is the place. Daily 5.30–10pm.

The Farm of Beverly Hills 439 N Beverly Drive ⊤310/273-5578. The name and decor are, of course, ironic, since this is a fundamentally urban Beverly Hills Cal-cuisine power diner, where the rotating menu may feature items such as steak, braised duck, and ham, at mid-to-high prices. Also in the Grove mall, **Third St at Fairfax Ave** (⊤323/525-1699). Daily 9am–11pm.

Kate Mantilini 9101 Wilshire Blvd, Beverly Hills ⊤310/278-3699. Tasty, upscale versions of American diner food, served up in a stylish interior designed by edgy architectural firm Morphosis. Mon–Thurs 7.30am–midnight, Fri 7.30am–2am, Sat 11am–2am, Sun 10am–midnight.

The Palm 9001 Santa Monica Blvd, Beverly Hills ⊤310/550-8811. It you can get past the pretentious atmosphere and high prices, you'll enjoy these excellent steaks and seafood at this little operation, and perhaps be amused by the celebrity cartoons on the walls, or the odd celebrity behaving cartoonishly. Mon–Thurs noon–10pm, Fri noon–11pm, Sat 5pm–11pm, Sun 5pm–9.30pm

Spago 176 N Cañon Drive, Beverly Hills ⊤310/385-0880. Flagship restaurant that helped nationalize Cal-cuisine (in a different location), and still good for supping on Wolfgang Puck's latest concoctions, among them designer pizzas. Daily 11.30am–2.30pm & 6–10.30pm, Sun opens at 6pm.

Caribbean

Bamboo 10835 Venice Blvd, Culver City ⊤310/287-0668. In a section of West LA full of enticing ethnic restaurants, this one stands out for its chicken curry dishes and spicy Caribbean-flavored pizza, as well as its reasonable prices. Daily 11am–10.30pm, weekends 'til 11pm.

Versailles 10319 Venice Blvd, Culver City ⊤310/558-3168. Bustling, authentic Cuban restaurant with hearty dishes, including excellent and affordable fried plantains, paella, and black beans and rice. Also nearby at **1415 S La Cienega Blvd** ⊤310/289-0392. Daily 11am–10pm, weekends 'til 11pm.

Zabumba 10717 Venice Blvd, Culver City ⊤310/841-6525. In a colorful building amid drab surroundings, this Brazilian is a favorite for its bossa nova music, Latin American–inflected pizzas, tasty seafood, cheap prices, and convivial atmosphere. Mon–Sat 6pm–1am, Sun 6pm–midnight.

Chinese and Vietnamese

Chung King 11538 W Pico Blvd, West LA ⊤310/477-4917. Chinese restaurant serving spicy, mid-priced Szechuan food: don't miss out on the bum-bum chicken and other house specialties. Daily 11am–10pm, weekends until 11pm.

Feast from the East 1949 Westwood Blvd ⊤310/475-0400. The pad Thai, Chinese chicken salad, spicy tofu, stir fries, and other favorites always please at this appealing neighborhood eatery, and the prices are under control, too. Mon–Sat 11am–9pm.

Eurochow 1099 Westwood Blvd, Westwood ⊤310/209-0066. Located in the historic Dome building (see p.125), this stylish restaurant offers a melange of Chinese and European flavors, with dumplings, pasta, shrimp rolls, seafood, and even designer pizzas. Daily 5.30–10.30pm.

Golden China 9000 Venice Blvd, Culver City ⊤310/559-0116. A decent place to eat Chinese in a part of town not known for it, this spot doles out old favorites like orange chicken, wontons, and various veggie options. Not great, but more than adequate to fill your belly. Daily 11am–10pm.

Mr Chow 344 N Camden Drive, Beverly Hills ⊤310/278-9911. An ultra-pricey hangout where Chinese food comes in a wide variety of flavors and spices — though you can find better in town for much cheaper. The main appeal is the stargazing. Daily noon–2.30pm & 6–11.30pm, weekends opens at 6pm.

Greek

Delphi 1383 Westwood Blvd ⊤310/478-2900. The place to come in West LA for authentic Greek cooking, from flavorful dolmas and tabouli to the hearty pitas and souvlaki – an unpretentious joint that offers plenty of food

for a reasonable price. Mon–Fri 11.30am–
2.30pm & 5–9.30pm, Sat 5–10pm.

Indian

Bombay Café 12021 Pico Blvd, West LA
⊕**310/473-3388.** One of LA's finest
Indian restaurants, with terrific traditional
and nouveau offerings and helpful, friendly
staff. Mon–Fri 11.30am–3pm & 5–10pm,
Sat 5–11pm, Sun 5–9.30pm.
Nizam 10871 W Pico Blvd, West LA ⊕**310/470-
1441.** Small Indian haunt, where hefty
portions of curried lamb and tandoori
chicken go for fairly cheap prices, with a
buffet for less than $8. Daily 11.30am–
2.30pm & 5.30–10pm, weekends 'til 11pm.

Italian and pizza

Anna's Italian 10929 W Pico Blvd ⊕**310/474-
0102.** If those nuovo italiano joints just aren't
for you, saunter into this comfy haven of
old-school cooking, where the sauces are
rich, red, and drippy (or white and gooey),
the pastas are piled on, and you might even
spot a pinkie ring or two. Mon–Fri 11.30am–
11pm, Sat 4pm–midnight, Sun 4–11pm.

Barefoot 8722 W Third St, Beverly Hills
⊕**310/276-6223.** Enjoyable pasta, pizza, and
seafood between Beverly Hills and the
Beverly Center. Affordable prices, considering the upscale location. Daily 11am–
11.30pm, weekends 'til 12.30am.

Il Pastaio 400 N Canon Drive ⊕**310/205-
5444.** Ever-popular Beverly Hills fave
serving fine, affordable food – tasty
Northern Italian offerings such as risotto
(prepared in a range of ways), many
traditional pastas, and veal, pork, and
seafood entrees. Mon–Thurs 11.30am–
11pm, Fri–Sat 11.30am–midnight, Sun
11.30am–10pm.

**Jacopo's 326 S Beverly Drive, Beverly
Hills** ⊕**310/858-6446.** Favorite local
spot that has some of LA's best pizza,
served piping hot and fairly cheap. Also in
Pacific Palisades at 15415 Sunset Blvd
(⊕310/454-8494). Daily 11.30am–11pm.

**Locanda Veneta 8638 W Third St, Beverly
Hills** ⊕**310/274-1893.** Whether it's the
scrumptious ravioli, risotto, veal or
carpaccio, you can't go wrong at one of
LA's culinary joys (near the Beverly Center).

Best restaurants for celebrity-watching

If you're less interested in eating fine cuisine than in catching a glimpse of your
favorite film and TV stars, there are a number of places where you can watch
celebrities go through their paces of alternately hiding from, and then mugging for,
the public. Practically any upper-end eatery is a likely spot to find the stars –
especially in Beverly Hills, Santa Monica, and Malibu – but some places just have
that special cachet. Note that the few restaurants listed below without page references are recommended for their star-spotting potential, not their overpriced food,
and are not reviewed in the Guide.

Ago p.276
Barney Greengrass p.277
Chinois on Main p.281
Cut p.278
Drago p.282
Eurochow p.278
The Farm of Beverly Hills p.278
Frankie & Johnnie's p.276
Geoffrey's p.283
The Ivy 113 N Robertson Blvd, Beverly
   Hills ⊕310/274-8303
Jerry's Famous Deli p.263
Koi 730 N La Cienega Blvd, West
   Hollywood ⊕310/659-9449.
LA Farm p.281
Locanda Veneta p.279
Matsuhisa p.280

Mr Chow p.278
Morton's 8764 Melrose Ave, West
   Hollywood ⊕310/276-5205
Musso and Frank Grill p.272
Nate 'n' Al's p.263
The Palm p.278
Patina p.267
Patrick's Roadhouse 106 Entrada
   Drive, Pacific Palisades
   ⊕310/459-4544
Pig 'n' Whistle p.272
Roscoe's Chicken and Waffles p.262
Spago p.278
Sunset Room 1430 N Cahuenga Blvd,
   Hollywood ⊕323/463-0004
Valentino p.282

Expensive, but not unreasonably so. Mon–Fri 11.30am–2.30pm & 5.30–10pm, Sat 5–11pm, Sun 5–10pm.

Japanese

Matsuhisa 129 N La Cienega Blvd, Beverly Hills ☎310/659-9639. The biggest name in town for sushi, charging the highest prices. Essential if you're a raw-fish aficionado with a wad of cash; otherwise, for the same price you can dine two or three times at other fine, and much cheaper, Japanese restaurants. Mon–Fri 11.30am–2pm & 5.30–10pm, Sat–Sun 5.30–10pm.

Mori Sushi 11500 W Pico Blvd, West LA ☎323/479-3939. A subtly stylish spot that resists trendiness, but still offers up some of the city's finest sushi, almost always delicious and always fresh and not farmed. Mon–Fri 11.30am–2pm & 6–10pm, Sat 6.30–10.30pm.

Mexican and Latin American

Baja Fresh 475 N Beverly Drive, Beverly Hills ☎310/858-6690. Cheap and enjoyable Mexican food served to a hungry crowd of window-shoppers and movie-industry wannabes. Many other area locations. Daily 10.30am–9pm.

Eduardo's Border Grill 1830 Westwood Blvd, Westwood ☎310/475-2410. Quietly appealing neighborhood Mexican restaurant that serves up a tasty range of meaty tacos and burritos and other staples to a following of local customers. Mon-Sat 11am-10pm, Sun 11am-9pm.

La Salsa 1154 Westwood Blvd ☎310/208-7083. The place to come for fresh, delicious soft tacos and burritos, on the lower end of the price scale. One of many Westside branches. Daily 11am–8pm.

Monte Alban 11927 Santa Monica Blvd, West LA ☎310/444-7736. Forget the tacky mini-mall setting and focus on the fine, affordable selection of mole sauces and Mexican staples that make any trip here a reward. Daily 8am–midnight.

Middle Eastern

Magic Carpet 8566 W Pico Blvd, West LA ☎310/652-8507. Unexpected treats like pan-fried dough with mushrooms and other toppings, and more traditional falafel – both in generous portions for fair prices – bring loyal customers to this excellent Yemeni

restaurant. Mon–Thurs 11am–10pm, Fri 11am–2.30pm, Sun 9am–10pm.

Shamshiri 1712 Westwood Blvd, West LA ☎310/474-1410. Top Iranian restaurant in the area, offering delicious kebabs, pilafs, and exotic sauces for moderate cost. Daily 11.30am–10.30pm, weekends 'til 11pm.

Seafood

Crustacean 9646 Little Santa Monica Blvd, Beverly Hills ☎310/205-8990. Dressy eatery that draws the swells and a few tourists for its array of savory crab, shrimp, salmon, and other seafood entrees. Jacket required. Mon-Fri 11.30am–2.30pm & 5.30–10.30pm, Sat 5.30–11.30pm.

J.R. Seafood 11901 Santa Monica Blvd ☎310/268-2468. West LA seafood with a Chinese flair; without dropping a wad, you can chow down on platefuls of spicy shrimp, lobster, mussels, and fish, with the added boost of lip-smacking soups. Mon–Fri 11am–3pm & 5–10pm, Sat 11.30am–11pm, Sun 11.30am–10pm.

McCormick and Schmick's 206 N Rodeo Drive, Beverly Hills ☎310/859-0434. Swank seafood joint for business types, known for great weekend dinner specials; part of an esteemed national chain. Daily 11am–11pm.

Thai and Southeast Asian

Chaya Brasserie 8741 Alden Drive, Beverly Hills ☎310/859-8833. Pan-Asian bistro with moderate-to-expensive prices and a chic clientele that munches on fancy noodles, curry, and fish dishes. Try a splurge if you like your Asian fare with LA trendiness. Daily

Rough Guide favorites

Round-the-clock dining
Benito's Taco Shop p.263
Bob's Big Boy p.265
Canter's Deli p.261
Coral Café p.265
The Donut Hole p.264
Fred 62 p.262
Harbor House Café p.265
Jerry's Famous Deli p.263
Norm's p.264
Original Pantry p.261
Pacific Dining Car p.266
Randy's Donuts p.264
Tommy's p.262
Yukon Mining Co p.263

11.30am–2.30pm & 6–11.30pm, weekends until midnight.

Talesai 9198 Olympic Blvd, Beverly Hills ☎310/271-9345. Excellent curried seafood, corncakes, and Cal-cuisine-leaning noodle dishes served to knowing gourmets in a drab strip mall. Daily 5.30–10pm, also Mon–Fri 11.30am–2.30pm.

Vegetarian and wholefood

À Votre Santé 13016 San Vicente Blvd, Brentwood ☎310/451-1813. Scrambled tofu and fried vegetables are on the menu – along with veggie and turkey burgers – at this mid-priced Westside chain. Mon–Fri 8am–9.30pm, Sat & Sun 9am–9pm.

Newsroom Café 120 N Robertson Blvd, Beverly Hills ☎310/652-4444. A prime spot to eat veggie burgers and drink wheatgrass "shooters." Especially popular for lunching; also offers magazine racks (thus the name) and Internet terminals. Mon–Thurs 8am–9.30pm, Fri 8am–10pm, Sat 9am–10pm, Sun 9am–9.30pm.

Santa Monica, Venice, and Malibu

American, Californian, and Cajun

17th Street Café 1610 Montana Ave, Santa Monica ☎310/453-2771. Seafood, pasta, sandwiches, eggs, and burgers at moderate prices in a casual, unpretentious atmosphere in a chic part of town. Best for breakfast or lunch. Daily 8am–10pm.

Aunt Kizzy's Back Porch 4325 Glencoe Ave, Marina del Rey ☎310/578-1005. Serving up the likes of hushpuppies, chicken, and collard greens, this is one of the few places to get decent soul food in this part of LA. Daily 11am–9pm, weekends until 11pm.

Hal's 1349 Abbot Kinney Blvd, Venice ☎310/396-3105. Popular restaurant in a hip shopping zone in Venice, with a range of well-done, somewhat expensive American standards, including marinated steaks, turkey burgers, and salmon dishes. Daily 11.30am–3pm & 5.30–10.30pm, weekends closes 11pm.

Houston's 202 Wilshire Blvd, Santa Monica ☎310/576-7558. Mid- to upper-end chain dining with savory salads, burgers, and international cuisine, but especially good for its prime location a block from the Third Street Promenade. Mon-Sat 11.30am–11pm.

Joe's 1023 Abbot Kinney Blvd, Venice ☎310/399-5811. One of the less heralded of LA's better upscale eateries, offering appealing Cal-cuisine dishes (mixed with a dash of French cookery) using staples like crispy chicken, pork, and salmon. Daily 11.30am–2.30pm & 6–10pm, weekends until 11pm.

LA Farm 3000 W Olympic Blvd, Santa Monica ☎310/453-2204. Delicious, though very expensive, California cuisine, with an accent on crab cakes and lobsters. The main draw is the celebrity-watching: here the stars dine in peace, away from the flashier precincts. Mon–Fri 11.30am–2.30pm & 5.30-9.30pm, Sat 5.30–10pm.

Michael's 1147 Third St, Santa Monica ☎310/451-0843. Long-standing favorite for California cuisine, served here amid modern art. This venerable establishment always attracts the crowds with its succulent steak, pasta, and fowl. Reservations are essential, and prices are steep. Mon–Sat 11.30am–2.30pm & 6–10.30pm.

Uncle Darrow's 2560 Lincoln Blvd, Venice ☎310/306-4862. A bit east of the main beach action, but worth a stop if you like savory and affordable catfish, gumbos, and other down-home Cajun and Creole cooking. Mon–Fri 11am–9pm, Sat 7am–10pm, Sun 7am–9pm.

Caribbean

Babalu 1002 Montana Ave, Santa Monica ☎310/395-2500. The pumpkin pancakes at this pan-ethnic, Caribbean-influenced restaurant are delightful, as are the sweet potato tamales and fried plantains. Service can be erratic, especially at peak times. Mon–Thurs 11am–9.30pm, Fri 11am–10.30pm, Sat 8am–10.30pm, Sun 8am–9.30pm.

Chinese and Vietnamese

Chinois on Main 2709 Main St, Santa Monica ☎310/392-9025. Expensive Wolfgang Puck restaurant, skilfully mixing nouvelle French and Chinese cuisine with dash for a ravenous yuppie crowd. Mon–Sat 6–10pm, also Wed–Fri 11.30am–2pm, Sun 5.30–10pm.

Indian

Nawab 1621 Wilshire Blvd, Santa Monica ☎310/829-1106. Though there are few surprises on the menu, pleasing renditions of Indian standards like chicken vindaloo and tikka masala do the trick. Mon–Fri 11.30am–2.30pm & 5.30–10pm, Sat & Sun noon–3pm & 5.30–10pm.

Pradeep's 1405 Montana Ave, Santa Monica ☎310/393-1467. Modest and reasonable spot on a swank shopping strip, which serves up vegetarian-oriented Indian cuisine (without ghee) to rail-thin diners; not exactly authentic, but tastier than you'd expect around here. Daily 11am–9.30pm.

Italian and pizza

Abbot's Pizza Company 1407 Abbot Kinney Blvd, Venice ☎310/396-7334. Named after the old-time founder of the district, this home of the bagel-crust pizza gives you your choice of seeds, tangy citrus sauce, or shiitake and wild mushroom sauce. Also at 1811 Pico Blvd, Santa Monica ☎310/314-2777. Daily 11am–11pm.

Drago 2628 Wilshire Blvd, Santa Monica ☎310/828-1585. Among LA's better superchic Italian eateries, this one serves various Cal-cuisine–oriented dishes and pastas in an appropriately stuffy setting. Daily 11.30am–3pm & 5.30–11pm, weekends opens 5.30pm.

Giorgio Baldi 114 W Channel Rd, Pacific Palisades ☎310/573-1660. Very fine Italian food just north of Santa Monica; great for its pastas and seafood entrees, with a correspondingly high price tag. Tues–Sun 6–11.30pm.

Valentino 3115 W Pico Blvd, Santa Monica ☎310/829-4313. Some call this the best Italian cuisine in the US, served up in classy surroundings with great flair. The specialties, especially veal, duck, and venison, are sure to please, though your pocketbook won't be quite so lucky. Reservations and formal wear mandatory. Mon–Thurs 5.30–10.30pm, Fri & Sat 5.30–11pm.

Wildflour Pizza 2807 Main St, Santa Monica ☎310/392-3300. Serving up a great and cheap thin-crust pizza, this cozy little spot has been drawing crowds since the early 1970s (apparently the last time the place was renovated). Sun–Thurs 11.30am–10.30pm, Fri & Sat 11am–11.30pm.

Japanese

Chaya Venice 110 Navy St, Venice ☎310/396-1179. Elegant mix of Japanese and Mediterranean foods in an arty sushi bar, with plenty of Cal-cuisine

elements and a suitably snazzy clientele. Mon–Fri 11.30am–midnight, Sat 5pm–midnight, Sun 5–10pm.

Musha 424 Wilshire Blvd, Santa Monica ☎310/576-6330. Among the top choices on the LA sushi scene, this spot prepares fish with striking invention and culinary precision; the results are almost uniformly great. Unfortunately, the word is out, so during a busy time you'll find yourself waiting up to an hour for a table. Mon–Sat 6-11.30pm.

Sushi Roku 1401 Ocean Ave, Santa Monica ☎310/458-4771. While the ambience here can be a bit on the stuffy side, this upscale eatery has fine Spanish mackerel sushi, monkfish, octopus sashimi, and crab rolls. Mon–Fri 11.30am–2.30pm & 5.30–11.30pm, Sat noon–11.30pm, Sun 5.30–10.30pm.

Korean

Monsoon Café 1212 Third St, Santa Monica ☎310/576-9996. Stylish space offering a mid-priced mix of Pacific Rim cuisines: expect anything from sushi to Szechuan to Malaysian to Korean barbecued beef. Mon–Thurs 11.30am–10.30pm, Fri & Sat 11.30am–11.30pm, Sun 3–9.30pm.

Mexican and Latin American

Border Grill 1445 Fourth St, Santa Monica ☎310/451-1655. Nice place to sup on delicious shrimp, pork, plaintains, and other

▲ Border Grill

nuevo Latin American–flavored fixings, with excellent desserts, too. Prices are on the expensive side, but the ambience is always swinging. Daily 11.30am–10pm, weekends 'til 11pm.

Gaucho Grill 1251 Third St, Santa Monica ☎310/394-4966. A link in a fine local chain of mid-level Argentine beef-houses, where the steaks come rich and garlicky. Located along the Third Street Promenade. Daily 11.30am–10pm, weekends until 11.30pm.

Mariasol 401 Santa Monica Pier, Santa Monica ☎310/917-5050. Cervezas with a view, perched at the end of the pier, with straightforward Mexican staples. The small rooftop deck affords a sweeping panorama from Malibu to Venice. Mon–Thurs 10am–10pm, Fri & Sat 10am–11pm, Sun 9am–10pm.

Marix Tex-Mex Playa 118 Entrada Drive, Pacific Palisades ☎310/459-8596. Flavorful fajitas and big margaritas are the best picks at this rowdy beachfront cantina. Also at 1108 N Flores St, West Hollywood ☎323/656-8800. Daily 11.30am–midnight, weekends until 2am.

Russian and Eastern European

Warszawa 1414 Lincoln Blvd, Santa Monica ☎310/393-8831. Pleasant, if a bit pricey, establishment with fine Polish cuisine. Don't miss the hearty potato pancakes, pierogi, and borscht. Tues–Sat 6–11pm, Sun 5–10pm.

Seafood

Geoffrey's 27400 PCH, Malibu ☎310/457-1519. One of Malibu's most upscale spots for steak, seafood, and sunset-watching. The Cal-cuisine–inspired menu is almost secondary to the fun of watching the Tinseltown luminaries drop in. Mon–Fri 11.30am–9.30pm, Sat 11am–10.30pm, Sun 10am–9pm.

I Cugini 1501 Ocean Ave, Santa Monica ☎310/451-4595. One of the city's more prominent seafood restaurants is also, luckily, one of its best, offering delectable Italian-influenced dishes such as seafood risotto, seared salmon, and the usual complement of pastas. Not quite as pricey as some of its counterparts in Malibu. Daily 11.30am–3pm & 4–10pm.

Killer Shrimp 523 Washington St, Marina del Rey ☎310/578-2293. When all you want is shrimp, and lots of it, this popular, somewhat dreary-looking spot is the place

to come. For a pretty cheap price, you can happily stuff your maw with fistfuls of crustaceans. Daily 11.30am–10pm, weekends 'til 11pm.

The Lobster 1602 Ocean Ave, Santa Monica ☎310/458-9294. Other than the sub-mediocre Gladstone's (not listed), there are few seafood eateries in town with a fine view — but this one has it, along with excellent upscale cuisine: the crab cakes, sea bass, and titular crustacean are among the top choices. Mon–Sat 11.30am–3pm & 5–10pm, weekends 'til 11pm.

Ocean Avenue Seafood 1401 Ocean Ave, Santa Monica ☎310/394-5669. One of the more reliable of the upscale fishhouse choices in town, with a nice selection of fresh, raw oysters, lobster, steak, and crab cakes, among other delights. Sun–Thurs 11.30am–10pm, Fri–Sat 11.30am–11pm.

Thai and Southeast Asian

Thai Dishes 1910 Wilshire Blvd, Santa Monica ☎310/828-5634. Very basic Thai meals geared toward diners unfamiliar with the spicier, more extreme versions of the cuisine. Part of a citywide chain. Daily 11am–10.30pm, weekends opens at noon.

Vegetarian and wholefood

Figtree's Café 429 Ocean Front Walk, Venice ☎310/392-4937. Tasty veggie food and grilled fresh fish on a sunny patio just off the Boardwalk. Health-conscious yuppies come in droves for inexpensive breakfasts. Daily 9am–9pm.

Good Karma 1809 Ocean Front Walk ☎310/827-2955. Little hole in the wall along the Venice Boardwalk where you can pick up a flavorful veggie burger, faux hot dogs, or sweet-potato fries, all of it simple and affordable. Daily 11am–8pm.

Inn of the Seventh Ray 128 Old Topanga Rd, Topanga Canyon ☎310/455-1311. The ultimate New Age restaurant in a supremely New Age area, serving vegetarian and other wholefood meals in a relatively secluded setting. Excellent desserts, too. Daily 11.30am–3pm & 5.30–10pm, Sun opens at 9.30am.

South Central and East LA

American, Californian, and Cajun

Harold and Belle's 2920 Jefferson Blvd, South Central ☎323/735-9023. One of the most authentic and affordable of the Cajun-cuisine restaurants in town, offering a rich gumbo, excellent po' boy sandwiches, and heaping portions of crayfish, catfish, and shrimp, along with sides like corn on the cob. Daily 11.30am–10pm, weekends until 11pm.

Phillips 4307 Leimert Blvd ☎323/292-7613. An excellent, and cheap, Southern barbeque joint that appeals for its authentic smoky sauces and spicy marinades, full set of sides like potato salads, and fine desserts. Visit Leimert Park for a taste. Mon–Thurs 11am–10pm, Fri & Sat 11am–midnight. Also at 2619 Crenshaw Blvd (☎323/731-4772; same hours except closed Sun, open Mon 11am-6pm).

Woody's 3446 W Slauson Ave ☎323/294-9443. What some claim as LA's best barbeque is, unfortunately, located in one of its grimmer corners – but still, if you come during the day, you can get your fill of some rich beef ribs and gut-stuffing pork sausages. Pretty inexpensive, too. Also at 475 S Market St in Inglewood (☎310/672-4200). Daily 11am–11pm.

Mexican and Latin American

Ciro's 705 N Evergreen Ave, East LA ☎323/267-8637. A split-level cave of a dining room, serving enormous platters of shrimp and mole specials. The garlic shrimp and flautas are the main draw, and they also offer takeout. Tues–Sun 7am–9pm.

El Tepayac 800 S Palm Ave, Alhambra ☎626/281-3366. Huge, luscious burritos and hot salsa bring true lovers of Mexican food out to this rather removed section of the San Gabriel Valley. Also at 812 N Evergreen Ave, East LA (☎323/267-8668). Mon & Wed–Thurs 6am–9.30pm, Fri & Sat 6am–11pm, Sun 6am–10pm.

Luminarias 3500 Ramona Blvd, Monterey Park ☎323/268-4177. Dance to salsa and merengue between bites of seafood-heavy, mid-priced Mexican food, surprising for an area best known for its Chinese cuisine. Mon–Thurs 11am–3pm & 4–10pm, Fri & Sat 11am–3pm & 4–11pm, Sun 9.30am–3pm & 4–10pm.

Paco's Tacos 6212 W Manchester Ave, Westchester ☎310/645-8692. Potent margaritas and filling burritos are the highlights at this affordable local chain. Also at 4141 S Centinela Ave (☎310/391-1616). Daily 11am–10pm, weekends until 11pm.

The South Bay and LA Harbor

American, Californian, and Cajun

Lasher's 3441 E Broadway, Long Beach ☎562/433-0153. Set in a little house east of Downtown, a New American choice for steak, rack of lamb, seafood, and pasta, at the upper end of what you'll pay in this town. Sun 10am–3pm & 5–9pm, Mon–Thurs 5–9pm, Fri 5–10pm.

New Orleans 140 Pier Ave, Hermosa Beach ☎310/372-8970. From the looks of this authentic diner, you wouldn't expect to find Deep-South Cajun cuisine here, but it's a welcome respite anyway, serving up lip-smacking jambalaya, gumbo, po' boy sandwiches, and fried oysters, all of them plenty tasty and cheap. Mon, Thurs & Fri 11.30am–2pm & 5–9pm, Sat–Sun noon–10pm.

Rock 'n' Fish 120 Manhattan Beach Blvd, Manhattan Beach ☎310/379-9900. Whether you're in the mood for halibut, sea bass, shrimp, or just a good old prime rib, this cozy surf 'n turf eatery is a decent, affordable spot to indulge. Just make sure to reserve ahead. Daily 11.30am–10pm, weekends until 11pm.

Caribbean

Cha Cha's 762 Pacific Ave, Long Beach ☎562/495-4242. Paella, black-pepper shrimp, plantains, and jerk chicken are all recommended here, in one of Long Beach's better and more colorful mid-priced restaurants. Daily 11.30am–10pm, weekends 'til 11pm.

Greek

George's Greek Cafe 318 Pine Ave, Long Beach ☎562/437-1184. Centrally located and affordable eatery where you can indulge in some tasty gyros, dolmas and souvlaki, as well as several fine combo plates. Mon–Thurs 8am–10pm, Fri–Sat 9am–11pm, Sun 9am–10pm.

Papadakis Taverna 301 W Sixth St, Long Beach ☎310/548-1186. A rich and hearty reminder of the good old days, when this part of town was thick with Mediterranean immigrants; eating fine lamb loin, grape leaves, veal fillets, and other Old World favorites here, it's like nothing has changed. Daily 5–10pm.

Italian and pizza

L'Opera 101 Pine Ave, Long Beach ☎562/491-0066. Very swank Italian dining – mixed with a fair bit of Cal-cuisine style – in a historic old building near the center of Long Beach's downtown activity. Mon–Thurs 11.30am–10.30pm, Fri & Sat 5pm–midnight, Sun 5–11pm.

La Sosta Enoteca 2700 Manhattan Ave, Hermosa Beach ☎310/318-1556. Among the best options for Italian fare in the South Bay, with a broad swath of excellent pasta and seafood choices, as well as supreme wine and desserts. Tues–Thurs 6–11.30pm, Fri–Sun 6pm–midnight.

Mangiamo 128 Manhattan Beach Blvd, Manhattan Beach ☎310/318-3434. Like the name says, "Let's eat!" Fairly pricey but interesting for the specialty Northern Italian seafood – and near the beach, too. Mon–Thurs 11.30am–9.30pm, Fri & Sat 11.30am–10.30pm, Sun 11am–8pm.

Mexican and Latin American

By Brazil 1615 Cabrillo Ave, Torrance ☎310/787-7520. Hearty and affordable Brazilian fare, mostly grilled chicken and beef dishes; go to inland Torrance for a taste. Tues–Sun 11.30am–9.30pm, weekends until 10pm.

El Pollo Inka 1100 PCH, Hermosa Beach ☎310/372-1433. Cheap Peruvian-style chicken, catfish, and hot and spicy soups to make your mouth water. Closer to central LA, try the one at 11701 Wilshire Blvd, Westwood ☎310/571-3334. Daily 11am–11pm.

Pancho's 3615 Highland Ave, Manhattan Beach ☎310/545-6670. Big portions of old favorites like tacos and burritos, and fairly cheap for the area. Adequate and convenient, if far from great. Daily 11am–10pm, weekends until 11pm.

Taco Beach 211 Pine Ave, Long Beach ☎562/983-1337. As you might guess, fish tacos are the main draw here, though the rest of the eatery's low-priced south-of-the-border fare is also quite palatable. Sun–Thurs 11am–10pm, Fri & Sat 11am–midnight.

Seafood

Bluewater Grill The South Bay outpost of an Orange County favorite (see p.289), featuring a slew of mid-priced fresh fish – salmon and catfish to crabs and oysters – though it brings in a few more tourists than the other branch. Daily 11.30am–10pm, weekends 'til 11pm.

Kincaid's Bay House 500 Fishermans Wharf, Redondo Beach ☎310/318-6080. A dramatically placed fishhouse serving old-fashioned meals of crab, lobster, and prawns, and drawing equal numbers of locals and tourists. Mon–Thurs 11.30am–10pm, Fri-Sat 11.30am–11pm, Sun 11am–9pm.

King's Fish House 100 W Broadway #500, Long Beach ☎562/432-7463. Esteemed seafood restaurant with a full selection of salmon, tuna, oysters, and sea bass. One in a local chain of upmarket eateries. Sun & Mon 11.30am–9pm, Tues–Thurs 11.30am–10pm, Fri & Sat 11.30am–11pm.

Quality Seafood 130 Intl Boardwalk, Redondo Beach ☎310/372-6408. Seafood eateries are just about the only reason to hang out in this seaside town, and here you can indulge in a fine oyster bar and pick from a great selection of crabs, clams, shrimp and other shellfish, prepared while you watch. Daily 10am-8pm, weekends 'til 9pm.

Spanish

Alegria Cocina Latina 115 Pine Ave, Long Beach ☎562/436-3388. Tapas, gazpacho, and a variety of platos principales served with sangría on the patio, to the beat of live flamenco on weekends. Central location near the harbor in Downtown Long Beach. Mon–Thurs 11.30am–11pm, Fri 11.30am–2am, Sat noon–2am, Sun noon–11pm.

Thai and Southeast Asian

Thai Dishes 1015 N Sepulveda Blvd, Manhattan Beach ☎310/546-4147. Basic but decent Thai fare, with the usual noodle dishes and soups presented in a no-frills manner. Local chain that makes an excellent stop if you're in the area. Daily 11am–10pm, weekends 'til 10.30pm.

Vegetarian and wholefood

Good Stuff 1286 The Strand, Hermosa Beach ☎310/374-2334. Many veggie choices, as well as healthy seafood, wraps, and sandwiches, at this link in a chain of reliable South Bay restaurants. Daily 7am–4pm.

The Spot 110 Second St, Hermosa Beach ☎310/376-2355. A staggering selection of inexpensive vegetarian dishes, based on Mexican and other international cuisines and free of refined sugar and any animal products. Daily 11am–10pm.

The San Gabriel and San Fernando valleys

African

Marrakesh 13003 Ventura Blvd, Studio City
℡818/788-6354. Moroccan restaurant in the Valley, where filling couscous and lamb dishes are served amid lush furnishings and belly dancing, for moderate to high prices. Daily 5–9.30pm, weekends until 10pm.

American, Californian, and Cajun

Arroyo Chophouse 536 S Arroyo Pkwy, Pasadena
℡626/577-7463. A refreshing break from LA's chain steakhouses, this one offers an elegant atmosphere and a mouth-watering selection of filet mignon, prime rib, savory soups, and desserts. Bring several credit cards, though. Sun–Thurs 5pm–9.30pm Fri–Sat 5pm–10pm

Granville Cafe 121 San Fernando Blvd, Burbank
℡818/848-4726. Tasteful atmosphere provides a pleasant setting for eating straightforward pizza, pasta, burgers, sandwiches, and soups. One of a dozen in a Valley chain. Mon–Thurs 11am–10pm, Fri 11am–11pm, Sat 8am–11pm, Sun 8am–10pm.

Marston's 151 E Walnut St, Pasadena
℡626/796-2459. A little house makes fine digs for breakfast and lunch, with the omelets, French toast, pancakes, and other scumptious comfort food among the highlights. Tues–Fri 7am–2.30pm & 5.30–9.30pm, Sat–Sun 8am–2.30pm, also Sat 5.30–9.30pm.

Saddle Peak Lodge 419 Cold Canyon Rd, Calabasas ℡818/222-3888. On the San Fernando Valley side of the Santa Monica Mountains, this is elite LA's nod to rustic hunting lodges, where you can elegantly, and expensively, devour anything from venison to boar to antelope. Wed–Sun 5–10pm, also Fri–Sat 11am–3pm.

Caribbean

Xiomara 69 N Raymond Ave, Pasadena
℡626/796-2520. An upscale Old Pasadena restaurant serving delicious Cuban and Latin American meals, mainly beef, pork, and fish entrees with colorful sauces, plus a solid range of stews. Daily 11.30am–11pm, Sat & Sun opens at 5pm.

Chinese and Vietnamese

City Wok 10949 Ventura Blvd, Studio City
℡818/506-4050. A little establishment selling Chinese food without frills or attitude. From the tasty wonton soup to the garlic chicken to the potstickers, most of the dishes are flavorful and the prices cheap. Mon–Sat 11am–10pm, Sun 4–9.30pm.

Lee's Garden 1428 S Atlantic Blvd, Alhambra
℡626/284-0320. As with many of the Chinese restaurants in the vicinity, a fine neighborhood eatery that has a range of staples – pork dumplings, kung pao dishes, etc – at affordable prices. Daily 11.30am–10pm.

🏃 **Ocean Star 145 N Atlantic Blvd, Monterey Park** ℡626/308-2128.
One of the prime names in a city bursting with excellent Chinese restaurants, this rather huge venue specializes in dim sum, with the fried shrimp, dumplings, and salty chicken among the highlights. Very popular and affordable, too. Mon–Fri 10am–10pm.

French

Café Bizou 14016 Ventura Blvd, San Fernando Valley ℡818/788-3536. Bringing affordable French cuisine to the northern valleys, this delightful, busy restaurant serves succulent pork tenderloin, risotto, seafood, and salads. Also at 91 N Raymond Ave, Pasadena ℡626/792-9923. Daily 5.30–10pm, weekends until 11pm, also Mon–Fri 11.30am–2.30pm.

Julienne 2649 Mission St, San Marino
℡626/441-2299. While the pâté and apricot chicken are decent, the chicken salad, sirloin burger, and rich desserts like crème brulee French toast are even better at this excellent, mid-to-high-priced French restaurant. Mon–Sat 7am–3.30pm.

Greek

Café Santorini 70 W Union St, Pasadena
℡626/564-4200. A fine mix of mid-range Greek and Italian food – capellini, souvlaki, risotto, baba ganoush, hummus, and the like. Located in a relaxed plaza and offering some patio dining. Daily 11.30am–10pm, weekends until midnight.

Great Greek 13362 Ventura Blvd, Sherman Oaks ℡818/905-5250. A busy, mid-range old-world enterprise serving delicious dolmas, kebabs, meatballs and moussaka to ethnic music beats and fervent dancing. Daily 11.30am–11pm, weekends until midnight.

Indian

Passage to India 14062 Burbank Blvd, Van Nuys ☎818/787-8488. Savory and affordable Indian cooking with a British flair, covering South Asian staples such as spicy vindaloos, tandoori chicken, tikka masala, stuffed naan, and beef and lamb kebabs. Daily 11.30am–2.30pm & 5–10pm.

Italian and pizza

Avanti Cafe 111 N Lake Ave, Pasadena ☎626/577-4688. A lip-smacking place to get your (affordable) gourmet pizza fix, in styles ranging from glazed apple, prosciutto, or shiitake mushroom to good old pepperoni, sausage, and anchovies. Mon–Thurs 11am–10pm, Fri–Sat 11am–11pm, Sun 11am–10pm.

Market City Caffè 36 W Colorado Blvd #300, Pasadena ☎626/568-2303. Southern Italian cuisine featuring a range of Mediterranean delights, along with a supreme antipasto bar. Also at **164 E Palm Ave, Burbank** ☎818/840-7036. Daily 11.30am–10pm, weekends until midnight.

Panzanella 14928 Ventura Blvd, Sherman Oaks ☎818/784-4400. Some of the best Italian cuisine in LA adds a dash of California creativity, but stays true to the simple, delicious character of traditional pasta, rice, and beef dishes. Mon–Sat 5.30–11.30pm, Sun 5.30–10.30pm.

Japanese

Kyoto Sushi 4454 Van Nuys Blvd, Sherman Oaks ☎818/986-7060. Has several types of sushi, sashimi, and seasonal macrobiotic dishes. Decent food for moderate cost, especially the all-you-can-eat platters. Mon–Sat noon–2.30pm & 5.30–10.30pm, Sun 5–10pm.

Shiro 1505 Mission St, South Pasadena ☎626/799-4774. One of the few top-notch restaurants in South Pasadena, perhaps the only one. The seafood – particularly the grilled catfish and smoked salmon – is best here, prepared in rich, tangy flavors. Tues–Sun 6–9pm, weekends until 9.30pm.

Sushi Nozawa 11288 Ventura Blvd, Studio City ☎818/508-7017. Excellent, if expensive, sushi dishes served to trendy regulars who don't mind being berated by the imperious chef: if you sit at the bar, he will decide what

▲ Sushi Nozawa

you'll eat. Period. Mon–Fri noon–2pm & 5.30–10pm.

Tama Sushi 11920 Ventura Blvd, Studio City ☎818/760-4585. Presents a formidable array of sushi, sashimi, rolls, and soups at a price that won't leave you gasping. Daily 11.30am–2.30pm & 5–9.30pm, Sun opens 5pm.

Mexican and Latin American

Don Cuco 3911 W Riverside Drive, Burbank ☎818/842-1123. Mainly familiar Mexican staples, as well as reliable fish, seafood, and margaritas. One of several in a Valley chain, the other closest at 214 N Brand Blvd, Glendale (☎818/553-1123). Daily 11am–10pm, weekends 'til 11pm.

Izalco 10729 Burbank Blvd, North Hollywood ☎818/760-0396. Salvadoran cuisine presented with style, from plantains and pork ribs to corn cakes and pupusas. Daily 10am–10pm.

La Estrella 502 N Fair Oaks Ave, Pasadena ☎626/792-8559. Ultra-cheap and delicious favorite for Mexican cuisine, where you can get great tacos, burritos, ceviche, and tostadas for not more than a few bucks. Daily 10am–midnight.

Señor Fish 618 Mission St, South Pasadena ☎626/403-0145. Somewhat drab-looking joint with great fish tacos, seafood burritos, and charbroiled halibut for inexpensive prices. Daily 11.30am–9pm.

Middle Eastern

Azeen's 110 E Union St, Pasadena ☎626/683-3310. Esteemed, stylish haunt for rich and flavorful Afghani cuisine such as kebabs, meat pastries, and dumplings, representing an appealing mix of Persian and Indian foodways. Daily 5.30-9.30pm, also Mon–Fri 11.30am–2pm.

Burger Continental 535 S Lake Ave, Pasadena
☎626/792-6634. Although it sounds like a
fast-food joint, this is actually one of LA's
better Middle Eastern restaurants, where
you can get mounds of chicken and lamb
kebabs for affordable prices. Daily
7am–10.30pm.
Carousel 304 N Brand Ave, Glendale ☎818/246-
7775. A Lebanese charmer in downtown
Glendale, chock full of Levantine cultural
artifacts and deliciously authentic food, from
roasted chicken and quail to several
different kinds of kebab. Daily 11.30am–
10pm, weekends 'til 1am, Sun 'til 9pm.

Spanish

La Luna Negra 44 W Green St, Pasadena
☎626/844-4331. An affordable spot for
tapas, including fine croquetas, paellas,
and spicy seafood dishes, regularly
accompanied by Latin music and dancing.
Daily 11am–10pm, weekends until
midnight.

Thai and Southeast Asian

Kuala Lumpur 69 W Green St, Pasadena
☎626/577-5175. Curried soups and tangy
salads are a few of the highlights at this
Malaysian eatery, along with coconut rice
and spicy chicken, plus other inexpensive
Southeast Asian dishes. Daily 11.30am–
2.30pm & 5.30–9.30pm.
Saladang 363 S Fair Oaks Ave, Pasadena
☎626/793-8123. Don't miss out on
the pad Thai, curry, and salmon at this chic
and delicious spot, or the spicy noodles
that would pass muster anywhere. The
restaurant's annex, Saladang Song, offers
even spicier Thai concoctions. Daily
7am–10pm.
**Sanamluang Café 12980 Sherman Way, North
Hollywood** ☎818/764-1180. The cheap, plentiful
noodles at this nearly all-night Thai eatery are
unbeatable. Daily 10.30am–3.30am.

Orange County

American, Californian, and Cajun

The Cottage 308 N Coast Hwy, Laguna Beach
☎949/494-3023. Hungry beachgoers can
choose from filling American breakfasts In
the morning, and affordable seafood, pasta,
and chicken dishes at lunch and dinner.
Daily 7am–3pm & 5–8.30pm.
Five Crowns 3801 E Coast Hwy, Corona del Mar
☎949/760-0331. A steak and rib joint that

doles out ample meaty fare amid mildly
kitschy Olde English decor. Mon–Thurs
5–10pm, Fri & Sat 5–11pm, Sun 10am–
2.30pm & 4–9pm.
Jack Shrimp 2400 W Coast Hwy, Newport Beach
☎949/650-5577. One in a chain of Cajun
dinner establishments along the Orange
County coast, offering an appealing assortment of spicy seafood and Louisiana
staples. Mon–Sat 5.30–9.30pm, weekends
'til 10.30pm, Sun 3.30–9.30pm.
Memphis Cafe 2920 Bristol St, Costa Mesa
☎714/432-7685. A fine spot for Southern
dining, with a range of shrimp, fried chicken,
cornbread and more; set in a trendy club
environment with higher prices than you
might expect. Mon–Sat 11am–3pm &
5–10.30pm, weekends 'til 11pm, Sun
5–9.30pm.
Sage 2531 Eastbluff Drive, Newport Beach
☎949/718-9650. Fancy eatery catering to
Cal-cuisine lovers, featuring savory delights
like blue crab cakes, steelhead trout, flatiron
steak, and roasted duck breast. Mon–Sat
11.30am–9.30pm, weekends 'til 10pm, Sun
11am–9.30pm.

Chinese and Vietnamese

**Anh Hong 10195 Westminster Ave, Garden
Grove** ☎714/537-5230. Terrific Vietnamese
restaurant known for its slew of traditional,
affordable favorites (including broiled pork
with vermicelli noodles) and "seven
courses of beef," a panoply of red meat
in all its glory. Mon–Thurs 4.30–9.30pm,
Fri & Sat 11am–10pm, Sun 11am–
9.30pm.
Favori 3502 W First St, Santa Ana ☎714/531-
6838. What may be LA's best Vietnamese
food: delicious garlic shrimp, barbequed
pork, salty squid, and baked catfish, all for
decent prices. Sun–Thurs 11.30am–
9.30pm, Fri & Sat 11.30am–10pm.

Italian

Antonello 3800 Plaza Drive, Costa Mesa
☎714/751-7153. Although Orange County is
hardly prime turf for quality Italian fare, this is
one of the exceptions – a fine, upper-crust
eatery where the ravioli and fettuccini
(among other pastas) are always well-
prepared, and the beef and salmon entrees
rarely disappoint. Mon–Fri 11.30am–2pm &
5–9.30pm, Sat 5–10pm.
Villa Nova 3131 W Coast Hwy, Newport Beach
☎949/642-7880. Old-time Italian seafood

presented in a classy setting for locals and out-of-towners alike; the pastas (including a fine gnocchi) and seafood risotto draw crowds, so reserve ahead. Daily 5pm–midnight, weekends 'til 1am, Sun opens at 4pm.

Korean

In Chon Won 13321 Brookhurst St, Garden Grove ☎714/539-8989. One of the best spots outside of LA's Koreatown for rich, tasty barbecue – from pork and chicken to wild boar – prepared before your very eyes, for reasonable cost. Sun–Thurs 11am–9.30pm, Fri & Sat 11am–10pm.

Mexican and Latin American

Don Jose's 15101 Goldenwest St, Huntington Beach ☎714/894-5519. A Mexican eatery doling out the usual staples – rellenos, burritos, and the like – for cheap prices, this is a valuable spot for a gut-stuffer after a day on the sands. One of several in an Orange County chain. Daily 11am–10pm.

Los Primos Cantina 488 E 17th St, Costa Mesa ☎949/650-1486. If you find yourself roving around the county looking for cheap, authentic Mexican fare, stop at this joint for very filling burritos, tostadas, and other reasonable choices. Daily 11am–10pm.

Taco Mesa 647 W 19th St, Costa Mesa ☎949/642-0629. Cheap, tasty burritos, quesadillas, chilaquiles, and tacos, as well as more unexpected choices like lobster bisque and calamari, at this reliable Orange County chain. Daily 7am–11pm.

Middle Eastern

Zena's 2094 N Tustin St, city of Orange ☎714/279-9511. A friendly Lebanese spot offering a selection of gyros, kebabs, baba ganoush, stuffed grape leaves, shawarma, and other traditional, inexpensive favorites. Daily 11am–10pm, Sun closes at 8pm.

Seafood

Bluewater Grill 630 Lido Park Drive, Newport Beach ☎949/675-3474. Delectable, relatively affordable seafood standards – ahi tuna, salmon, oysters, lobster, and the like – accompanied by appealing ocean views from the patio. Daily 11am–10pm, weekends 'til 11pm.

Claes Seafood in the Hotel Laguna, 425 S Coast Hwy, Laguna Beach ☎949/376-9283. One of the county's best seafood eateries, where you can sample pricey and delicious ahi tuna and halibut with a Cal-cuisine spin, indoors with a fine view of the Pacific. Tues–Sat 7am–2pm & 5.30–9.30pm, Sun 9am–2pm & 5.30–9.30pm.

Crab Cooker 2200 Newport Blvd, Newport Beach ☎949/673-0100. The hefty plates of crab legs and shrimp and steaming bowls of chowder at this small diner make the long lines a bit more bearable. Daily 11am–10pm.

Oysters 2515 E Coast Hwy, Corona del Mar ☎949/675-7411. Another Orange County stab at California cuisine–style seafood; not quite as expensive as Claes Seafood, but the food here looks and tastes almost as good, especially the titular bivalve. Mon–Thurs 5–10pm, Fri & Sat 5–11pm, Sun 4–9pm.

Bars and clubs

N**ightlife** here counts as some of the best and most frenetic in the country, and the image of swingin' singles or bleary-eyed drunks ensconced in their favorite LA watering holes is just as iconic to the city as anything produced by Hollywood. Weekend nights are the busiest at the various bars and clubs, but during the week things are cheaper and often just as enjoyable. For uninterrupted drinking, there are **bars** and lounges on seemingly every other corner, especially in Hollywood, where lower-end dives welcome a mixed crowd of grizzled old-timers and slumming hipsters, and shameless velvet-rope scenes cater to wannabe celebrities who feel the need to pay $200 for a bottle of fancy vodka. **Smoking is banned** under California law.

Bar styles tend to go in and out of fashion quickly, changing from month to month, often according to music and showbiz trends. What follows are descriptions of some of the more established bars in LA, generally those that have been around for at least a year or two; the trendiest joints sometimes only last a few months, disappearing once they lose their buzz and their exorbitant overhead finally catches up with them.

If you want something of the bar atmosphere without the alcohol, visit one of LA's many **coffeehouses**, which can be relaxed and fun, but sometimes carry a bit of the attitude, whether self-consciously hip, studious, or pretentious. Given the West Coast's taste for expensive coffee concoctions, coffeehouses can offer a refreshing break from the bar scene, especially if you want some culture– in the form of alternative music and performing arts.

LA's many **clubs** often double as live music venues (for which, see Chapter 14), but in this section we've tried to focus on entertainment that's readily available from night to night, and especially on weekends. When big-name touring DJs pull up, door charges can be as much as going to a live rock concert; more often, however, such big names are the exception and the usual scene will be based around local DJs — who in LA may even be national caliber. There will often be a bar attached to the club (allowing for overlap with that category), but unless the lounge itself is the reason people come, we've tried to focus on the beats.

Bars

As you'd expect, LA's **bars** reflect their locality: a clash of artists, musicians, and yuppies Downtown; serious hedonists and leather-clad rockers in Hollywood; actual or (more often) pretend movie stars and self-styled producers in West Hollywood and West LA; a mix of tourists and locals in Santa Monica; a more oddball selection in Venice; and the random assortment of interesting characters in the valleys. A few hard–bitten bars are open the legal maximum hours (from 6am until 2am daily), though the busiest hours are between 9pm and midnight. During **happy hour**, usually from 5–7pm, drinks are cheap and there'll often be a selection of snacks like taco dips, chips, buffalo wings, and sometimes more substantial appetizers.

Downtown

Barragan's 1538 W Sunset Blvd, Echo Park ☎213/250-4256. Actually a Mexican restaurant with serviceable food, but producing one of the stronger margaritas in LA. Be alert to the dicey neighborhood.

Bona Vista at the Westin Bonaventure hotel, 404 S Figueroa St ☎213/624-1000. Thirty-five floors up, this constantly rotating cocktail lounge spins faster after a few of the expensive drinks, and offers an unparalleled view of the sun setting over the city.

Casey's Bar 613 S Grand Ave ☎213/629-2353. Old-time Irish pub with white floors and dark wood-paneled walls, and a friendly, rousing ambience that has made it something of a local institution.

Little Cave 5922 N Figueroa St ☎323/255-6871. One of the few solid places to booze in dodgy Highland Park, but worth a visit for its killer drinks, much cheaper than in swankier parts of town, and self-consciously divey atmosphere.

🏃 **Mountain Bar 475 Gin Ling Way** ☎213/625-7500. Hidden in a nook in Chinatown, this bar is hard to find off Bamboo Lane, but if you want to knock back your well drinks and cocktails in a colorful environment loaded with Asian decor, this is the spot.

Mr T's Bowl 5621 N Figueroa Ave, Highland Park ☎323/960-5693. Former bowling alley whose inspired dumpiness draws a regular crowd of hipsters, and local characters. Cheap prices, karaoke, and rockin' live shows add to the allure.

Pete's Café and Bar 400 S Main St ☎213/617-1000. A retro-flavored Deco bar (with upscale diner food) located in an old bank building, which despite the dicey environs draws a nightly crowd of business types and a few artsy loft-occupiers.

Redwood 316 W Second St ☎213/617-2867. Not overly flashy or lively, but a solid Downtown choice for serious drinking and cheap all-American grub since 1943. Attracts a mix of imbibers for its dark and cozy setting and affordable drinks.

Standard Hotel Bar 550 S Flower St ☎213/892-8080. LA's poseur pinnacle: a rooftop, alcohol-fueled playpen where the silk-shirted-black-leather-pants crowd goes to hang out in red metallic "pods" with waterbeds and sprawl out on an Astroturf lawn, against a backdrop of corporate towers. You'll have to navigate the velvet-rope scene and $20 cover charge.

Mid-Wilshire

🏃 **El Carmen 8138 W Third St** ☎323/852-1552. Groovy faux dive-bar with a south-of-the-border theme pushed to the extreme, with black-velvet pictures of Mexican wrestlers, steer horns, stuffed snakes, and much tongue-in-cheek grunge, as well as signature margaritas.

H.M.S. Bounty 3357 Wilshire Blvd ☎213/385-7275. An authentic dive experience. Advertising "Food and Grog," the scruffy bar is a hot spot for hipsters and grizzled old-timers who come for the dark ambience, cheap and potent drinks, and kitschy nautical motifs dating from 1937.

Molly Malone's Irish Pub 575 S Fairfax Ave ☎323/935-1577. Self-consciously authentic Irish bar, from the food (corned-beef sandwiches, burgers, and other belly-fillers) to the music (mostly grinding rock and Celtic folk) to the shamrocks swirled into the creamy head of your Guinness.

St. Nick's 8450 W Third St ☎323/655-6917. A few blocks from the colossal Beverly Center mall sits this oddly popular dive bar, good for getting sloshed for cheap, if little else.

The Third Stop 8636 W Third St ☎310/273-3605. One of the best places in LA to find a broad selection of national and international beers, with the emphasis on microbrewing. Also offers decent pizzas and a relaxed atmosphere.

🏃 **Tom Bergin's 840 S Fairfax Ave** ☎323/936-7151. Old-time drinking joint from 1936, a great place for Irish coffee (supposedly invented here), and less rough-and-ready than Molly Malone's down the road. You can spot the regulars in the pictures on the walls.

Hollywood

4100 **4100 Sunset Blvd, Silver Lake** ☎323/666-4460. Although it continues the annoying LA trend of naming itself after its street address, this darkly colorful bar does boast inventive pan-Asian decor, moody lighting, and a mix of gays, straights, and imbibing tourists.

Akbar **4356 Sunset Blvd** ☎323/665-6810. A diverse crowd – workers and bohemians, gays and straights, old-timers and newbies – frequents this cozy, unpretentious Silver Lake watering hole. Also presents occasional dance events.

Beauty Bar **1638 N Cahuenga Blvd** ☎323/464-7676. A drinking spot devoted to hair, nails, and cosmetics, featuring 1950s-style retro-decor and a cocktail list to match; there's also dancing. One of three in a national mini-chain.

Blue Goose **5201 Sunset Blvd** ☎323/667-1400. Comfortable lounge where you can plunge into a soft couch (or a potent cocktail) or try your luck at karaoke or a video game. A good, functional drinker's hangout with minimal pretension.

Boardner's **1652 N Cherokee Ave** ☎323/462-9621. Formerly one of Hollywood's premier dive bars, now remade into more yuppie-friendly digs that reflect the sanitization and gentrification of this stretch of Tinseltown. Have a cosmo if you're exhausted from mall-hopping.

Burgundy Room **1621 Cahuenga Blvd** ☎323/465-7530. A classic place to get down and dirty with the old Hollywood dive-bar vibe, with minimal decor, stiff drinks, a growling crowd of regulars, decent DJs, and a rocking jukebox.

Cat n' Fiddle Pub **6530 Sunset Blvd** ☎323/468-3800. Boisterous but comfortable and convivial pub with darts, British food, English beers on tap, and live jazz on Sun nights. See also "Live music," p.305.

Cheetah's **4600 Hollywood Blvd** ☎323/660-6733. One of LA's biggest lurid attractions, with strong drinks, (almost) topless enter-tainment, and a crowd of both men and women. Hooting and hollering are encouraged.

The Dresden Room **1760 N Vermont Ave** ☎323/665-4298. One of the neighbor-hood's classic bars, best known perhaps for its nightly show (except Sun), in which the husband-and-wife lounge act of Marty and Elayne takes requests from the crowd of old-timers and goateed hipsters.

Formosa Café **7156 Santa Monica Blvd** ☎323/850-9050. Started in 1925 as a watering hole for Charlie Chaplin's adjacent United Artists studios, this creaky old spot is still alive with the ghosts of Bogie and Marilyn. Imbibe the potent spirits, but stay away from the insipid food.

Frolic Room **6245 Hollywood Blvd** ☎323/462-5890. Classic LA bar decorated with Hirschfeld celebrity cartoons and steeped in a dark, old-time ambience. Right by the Pantages Theater.

Good Luck Bar **1514 Hillhurst Ave** ☎323/666-3524. A hip Los Feliz retro-dive, this hangout is popular for its cheesy Chinese decor and tropical drinks straight from the heyday of *Trader Vic's*. Located near the intersection of Sunset and Hollywood blvds.

Highlands **6801 Hollywood Blvd** ☎323/461-9800. If you're a tourist who likes to drink and dance (and doesn't mind paying $20 to get in), this two-story spot on the fourth floor of the Hollywood & Highland mall is the place for you. Pose and preen as if your life depends on it.

Lucy's El Adobe Café **5536 Melrose Ave** ☎323/462-9421. Something of a celebrity hotspot in the 1970s for figures such as (then-Governor, now-Attorney General) Jerry Brown, this Mexican restaurant serves only adequate food, but the house specialty is worth a try: lethal green margaritas.

Musso and Frank Grill **6667 Hollywood Blvd** ☎323/467-7788. Simply put, if you haven't had a drink in this landmark 1919 bar, you haven't been to Hollywood. It also serves pricey diner food. For more details, see p.272.

The Powerhouse **1714 N Highland Ave** ☎323/463-9438. Enjoyable, long-standing hard-rockers' watering hole just off Hollywood Blvd. Few people get here much before midnight.

The Room **1626 N Cahuenga Blvd** ☎323/462-7196. Small, dark bar with acceptably stiff drinks and decent music. Recently renovated, and excellent if you like to imbibe to the sound of reggae and dub.

Smog Cutter **864 N Virgil Ave** ☎323/667-9832. Dive bar that attracts a mix of boozers and hipsters. Don't miss the karaoke scene, which, like the liquor, can be pleasantly mind-numbing.

Tiki Ti 4427 W Sunset Blvd ☎323/669-9381. Tiny grass-skirted cocktail bar straight out of *Hawaii-Five-O*, packed with kitschy pseudo-Polynesian decor and no more than a handful of patrons – it's pretty cozy inside.

The Well 6255 W Sunset Blvd ☎323/467-9355. Good-time lounge with a fine central bar, murky mood lighting, and not too much pretension. Come during the cheap Happy Hour and start slurring your words with the best of 'em.

The Woods 1533 N La Brea Ave ☎323/876-6612. Formerly the iconic Lava Lounge, this well-placed bar keeps to its eponymous bucolic theme with a dash of kitsch. A decent jukebox and strong drinks keep its faithful fans satisfied.

West Hollywood

Bar Lubitsch 7702 Santa Monica Blvd ☎323/654-1234. Despite the German-film-director name, this fun, moody lounge has a Russian theme and the drinks lean heavily on all things vodka, either served in cocktails or straight-up as cold as Moscow.

Barney's Beanery 8447 Santa Monica Blvd ☎310/654-2287. Well-worn pool room/bar, stocking over 100 beers, with a solid, rock'n'roll-hedonist history. It also serves all-American, rib-stuffing food; see p.262.

Jones 7205 Santa Monica Blvd ☎323/850-1726. Groovy, youthful scene with a colorful atmosphere and decent American cuisine, though the main draw is the head-spinning drinks named after rock stars.

Lola's 945 N Fairfax Ave ☎213/736-5652. It has beer and wine, but martinis are the theme at this swanky joint, with more than 50 interesting, inventive choices on offer, from the Big Banana to the Caramel Apple to the Garlic Mashed Potato.

The Palms 8572 Santa Monica Blvd ☎310/652-6188. Comfortable mixed, leaning toward lesbian-oriented, scene (see p.321), with pool tables and a patio making for a relaxed vibe; also has dance music most nights of the week.

Rainbow Bar & Grill 9015 Sunset Blvd ☎310/278-4232. A down-and-dirty lounge that for decades has been catering to the metal-and-thrash set on the Sunset Strip – it's a lot more authentic (and generous with its pours) than the posier lounges to the east.

Red Rock 8782 Sunset Blvd ☎310/854-0710. Energetic watering hole with a wide array of drafts on tap and a similarly broad assortment of customers – everyone from bleary-eyed club kids to slumming preppies.

Snake Pit 7529 Melrose Ave ☎323/653-2011. One of the better bars along the Melrose shopping strip, small and not too showy, with a mix of jaded locals and inquisitive tourists who come to slurp down tropical concoctions and other drinks.

Beverly Hills and West LA

Bar Noir in the Maison 140 hotel, 140 S Lasky Drive, Beverly Hills ☎310/271-2145. A swank lounge with much effort spent on the quasi-Asian decor and dark and atmospheric "set design." Worth a look to see how the beautiful people imbibe.

The Joint 8771 Pico Blvd, West LA ☎310/275-2619. Something of an antidote to the stuffier attitudes often found in more northerly Beverly Hills, this joint is good for both its affordable, old-school cocktails and regular indie bands, who perform in a cramped but relaxed setting.

Liquid Kitty 11780 Pico Blvd, West LA ☎310/473-3707. As its quirky name might suggest, this bar is aimed solidly at the hipster contingent, with a fine selection of cocktails and nightly lounge and dance music to set the mood.

Nic's Restaurant and Martini Lounge 453 N Canon Dr ☎310/550-5707. Although it has the pricey drinks, rubberneckers eager to spot celebs, and self-consciously hip decor common to most Beverly Hills bars, this one appeals for its ice-cold vodka tastings (in a separate room) and primo Cal-cuisine, much better than your average bar fare. By default the best bar in this town.

Q's Billiards 11835 Wilshire Blvd, Brentwood ☎310/477-7550. Not exactly free of the pretension or meatmarket vibe that plagues West LA bars, but close enough – a good spot to knock back a brew in a packed college atmosphere, play a game of pool, and listen to DJs mix.

Santa Monica and Venice

The Brig 1515 Abbot Kinney Blvd, Venice ☎310/399-7537. One of the more conspicuous lounges along this stretch of interior Venice, and not a bad place to stop in to soak up the stylish decor and decent cocktails, though other bars around town have a more authentic vibe.

Encounter 209 World Way, at LAX ☎310/215-5151. A Space Age–themed bar inside architect Eero Saarinen's futuristic Theme Building, overlooking the LAX parking lot. Well worth a visit to sample the potent Day-Glo drinks while watching the jets land. Recently under renovation; due to reopen by the end of 2008.

Finn McCool's 2700 Main St, Santa Monica ☎310/452-1734. Despite the dubious name, a worthwhile Irish pub with neo-Celtic artwork, a tasty selection of Emerald Isle brews, and hefty platters of traditional fare that calls for a pint of Guinness.

Hinano Café 15 Washington Blvd, Venice ☎310/822-3902. Low-attitude chill bar by the beach, with pool tables and shambling decor. A good place to drink without too many tourists breathing down your neck.

Library Alehouse 2911 Main St, Santa Monica ☎310/314-4855. Presenting the choicest brews from West Coast microbreweries and beyond, this is spot offers a nice range of well-known and obscure labels and a decent selection of food.

Makai 101 Broadway, Santa Monica ☎310/434-1511. A magnet for the trendy, located by the Pier and Promenade, where the prices are predictably high. The cocktails and Asian food almost merit the cost.

O'Brien's 2226 Wilshire Blvd, Santa Monica ☎310/829-5303. A fun, tub-thumping scene serving Irish food and brews to an animated crowd of locals and Irish expats.

The Otheroom 1201 Abbot Kinney Blvd, Venice ☎310/396-6230. Bring your dog (allowed inside) and a taste for good beer, and you'll enjoy this relaxed hipster scene, with murky lighting, comfy sofas, and low-energy buzz that are well suited for making friends (or more) with the locals.

Rick's Tavern 2907 Main St, Santa Monica ☎310/392-2772. Dark and humming neighborhood joint off the Main Street shopping strip, with sports on TV and boisterous regulars on the bar stools.

Ye Olde King's Head 116 Santa Monica Blvd, Santa Monica ☎310/451-1402. Very British joint with jukebox, dartboards, and signed photos of all your favorite rock dinosaurs; don't miss the steak-and-kidney pie, afternoon tea, or the fish and chips.

The San Gabriel and San Fernando valleys

Amazon 14649 Ventura Blvd, San Fernando Valley ☎818/986-7502. A small wonderland of kitsch, in which you can knock back *Trader Vic's*–type tropical concoctions amid pseudo South American and Polynesian decor: waterfalls, ferns, and so on.

Aura 12215 Ventura Blvd, Studio City ☎818/487-1488. What passes for hip in the San Fernando Valley: a trendy lounge/nightclub atop a strip mall, with plush decor, DJs and live music, and serviceable cocktails.

Clear 11916 Ventura Blvd, Studio City ☎818/980-4811. An attempt to draw Westsiders up to the Valley, this chic lounge has the requisite minimal-but-swanky decor, overpriced cocktails, and preening crowd of beautiful types. Worth a visit to see the Valley at its maximum pose.

Clearman's North Woods 7247 N Rosemead Blvd, San Gabriel ☎626/286-3579. A kitsch-lover's delight with fake snow on the outside and moose heads on the walls inside; a great place for devouring steaks while throwing peanut shells on the floor.

The Colorado 2640 E Colorado Blvd, Pasadena ☎626/449-3485. A bright spot along a bleak Pasadena stretch, offering salty bartenders, cheap drinks, and a couple of pool tables amid hunting-based decor.

Cozy's Bar & Grill 14048 Ventura Blvd, Sherman Oaks ☎818/986-6000. Listen to an excellent range of blues musicians (see p.306), or come by any time to throw darts, shoot pool, or knock back a few. A friendly, laid-back San Fernando Valley spot with a devoted clientele.

Ireland's 32 13721 Burbank Blvd, Van Nuys ☎818/785-5200. One of the San Fernando Valley's better spots for quaffing Irish drafts, powering down traditional stews and chops, and soaking up a fair amount of traditional atmosphere, shamrocks, and all.

Old Towne Pub 66 N Fair Oaks Ave, Pasadena ☎626/577-6583. Somewhat hard-to-find location that, for its cheap drinks, lack of pretension, and easygoing vibe, ranks first among the dive bars in town, much better than the posier lounges littering Old Pasadena.

The Sapphire 11938 Ventura Blvd, Studio City ☎818/506-0777. About as enticing as Valley watering holes get if you don't like your bars divey – in this case the mod furnishings, comfortable couches, inventive drinks, and

(reasonably) laid-back clientele make for an appealing, toasty vibe.

Coffeehouses

You can find **coffeehouses** throughout LA, from bitter hole-in-the-wall dives to sanitized yuppie magnets. Although straightforward java joints are alive and well throughout the metropolis, well-trafficked tourist routes such as Melrose Avenue and Santa Monica's Main Street boast more inventive spots to grab a jolt. The listings below go beyond java, focusing on unique establishments that, while serving coffee (and perhaps tea, food, and alcohol), also offer diversions like art, music, poetry, or eye-popping decor. You can find the best of these coffee joints in Hollywood, West LA, Santa Monica, and the valleys – which have more appealing coffeehouses than you might expect. If you feel safer in a chain coffee-house, try LA's own *Coffee Bean & Tea Leaf*, which has outlets everywhere (see Ⓦ coffeebean.com), before resorting to the ubiquitous java mermaid.

Hollywood and West Hollywood

Bourgeois Pig 5931 Franklin Ave, Los Feliz ☎ 323/962-6366. Self-consciously hip environment and overpriced cappuccinos – you really pay for the artsy atmosphere, but the agreeable java and colorful people-watching might make it worthwhile.

Coffee Table 2930 Rowena Ave, Los Feliz ☎ 323/644-8111. Casual, unpretentious space with affordable coffees and relaxed surroundings; good for its breakfasts, too.

CyberJava 7080 Hollywood Blvd ☎ 323/466-5600. Located near the corner of La Brea Avenue, this spot offers DSL Internet access and the usual range of smoothies, java drinks, and assorted sweets.

Downbeat Cafe 1202 N Alvarado St, Echo Park ☎ 213/483-3955. East of Silver Lake, this local favorite appeals for its flavorful sandwiches, bagels, and desserts, and serves a fine batch of java to a crowd of mostly local hipsters.

Intelligentsia 3902 W Sunset Blvd, Silver Lake ☎ 323/663-6173. A new arrival that's more stylish than your average coffeehouse, and linked to a fine seller of beans, which come in many varieties and from many places. The scene is more yuppie than bohemian — a surprise given the surrounding area.

King's Road Espresso House 8361 Beverly Blvd, West Hollywood ☎ 323/655-9044. Sidewalk café in the center of a busy shopping strip, with good breakfasts and lunches. Popular

with the hipster crowd as well as a few interloping tourists.

Stir Crazy 6917 Melrose Ave ☎ 323/934-4656. Cozy haunt that provides a glimpse of what this stretch of Melrose used to be like before the chain retailers moved in. Mellow attitudes, decent java, and Western-themed decor.

Yonni's 1714 Wilcox Ave ☎ 323/962-1020. Organic is the theme at this friendly spot, whether in coffee beans or tea leaves, with the added plus of organic sandwiches, salads, pizza, and other light meals; there are also smoothies for those averse to caffeine.

Beverly Hills and West LA

Cacao Coffee 11609 Santa Monica Blvd, West LA ☎ 310/473-7283. Fun and friendly joint with all kinds of kitsch and retro-Tiki bric-a-brac for decor, and good snacks and coffee served to an amenable crowd of regulars.

Café Flore 214 S Robertson Blvd, Beverly Hills ☎ 310/659-6877. "Vive la France!" you'll cheer (maybe) after devouring the scrumptious French bistro fare — sandwiches, crepes, tartines, and the like — and sampling the espresso and cappuccino at this Gallic-themed cafe.

Café Zinio 1731 Westwood Blvd, West LA ☎ 310/575-9999. Potent espresso is the main draw at this Westwood-area joint, which also features a good array of pastries and panini and the opportunity to puff on a hookah.

Insomnia 7286 Beverly Blvd, north of Mid-Wilshire ☎323/931-4943. A chic spot for chugging cappuccinos while sitting on comfy sofas and admiring the vivid art on the walls — or tapping out a screenplay on a laptop like the other regulars. Cash only.

Le Palais des Thes 401 N Canon Dr, Beverly Hills ☎310/271-7922. If you don't mind dropping a wad for some of the city's best tea — in countless varieties and flavors — come to this upscale vendor of the leaf, where you can also drink its many fine offerings.

Nova Express 426 N Fairfax Ave, south of West Hollywood ☎323/658-7533. Designed in a retro-futuristic sci-fi style, with weird colors and lighting, and additional curiosities like lava lamps and angular lounge and dance music most nights. Other than the look, coffee and pizza are the main draws. Open weekdays till 2am, weekends till 4am.

Urth Caffè 8565 Melrose Ave ☎310/659-0628. Customers at this high-priced tea-and-java vendor tend toward navel-gazing and celebrity-watching, but the coffees are certainly tasty enough, and the atmosphere is pleasant and fairly well-scrubbed. Also at 267 S Beverly Drive, Beverly Hills (☎310/205-9311), and 2327 Main St, Santa Monica (☎310/314-7040).

Santa Monica and Venice

Abbot's Habit 1401 Abbot Kinney Blvd, Venice ☎310/399-1171. Prototypical coffee house for this part of Venice – rich, tasty coffee and homemade snacks and desserts, assorted artwork on the walls, occasional music and spoken-word events, and a friendly neighborhood vibe.

Café Bolivar 1741 Ocean Park Blvd, Santa Monica ☎310/581-2344. Just as much as the coffee, the small and delightful sandwiches and salads, thoughtful artworks, and welcoming air are the draw at this South American-themed cafe.

Caffe Luxxe 925 Montana Ave, Santa Monica ☎310/394-2222. Carefully prepared espressos, macchiatos, and the like draw loyal locals to this fine, homespun place, which stands out on a busy strip thick with chain coffee-grinders.

Funnel Mill 930 Broadway, Santa Monica ☎310/597-4395. Somewhat spare digs create the right atmosphere for the purity of the drink — coffee or tea — at this smart cafe where the technique of the barista is refined to an art.

▲ Novel Café

Novel Café 212 Pier Ave, Santa Monica ☎310/396-8566. Used books and high-backed wooden chairs set the tone; good coffees, teas, and pastries hit the spot, even though many of the patrons are self-consciously studious. Located near the Venice border. Also at 1101 Gayley Ave, Westwood ☎310/208-6410.

Rose Café 220 Rose Ave, Venice ☎310/392-4191. A somewhat pricey, though not pretentious, place for coffee, meals, pastries, and occasional music. A neighborhood favorite, located near the Santa Monica border.

Tanner's Coffee 200 Culver Blvd, Playa del Rey ☎310/574-2739. Free Wi-Fi and good coffee and desserts make this cafe quite appealing to locals — that and the fact it's just about the only place to get a decent cup o' joe in the neighborhood.

UnUrban Coffee House 3301 Pico Blvd, Santa Monica ☎310/315-0056. A combination alternative coffeehouse and performance space, worth a look for its open-mike, music and comedy nights.

World Cafe 2820 Main St, Santa Monica ☎310/392-1661. More of a tourist scene than other spots in town, but has adequate Cal-cuisine and drinks, and a very central location — around which there are better lounges altogether.

The South Bay and LA Harbor

Coffee Cartel 1820 S Catalina Ave, Redondo Beach ☏ 310/316-6554. Somewhat unremarkable coffeehouse that nonetheless presents some interesting acoustic music and poetry readings.

Java Man 157 Pier Ave, Hermosa Beach ☏ 310/379-7209. Tables lit by halogen lamps, plus rotating displays of work by local artists, are the visuals at this coffeehouse not far from the beach. Also serves sandwiches and decent desserts.

North End Café 3421 Highland Ave ☏ 310/546-4782. A fancy spot for swillin' mud in Manhattan Beach, with the added allure of hearty sandwiches and a solid breakfast menu for those headed to the beach, which happens to be only a few blocks away.

Portfolio 2400 E Fourth St, Long Beach ☏ 562/434-2486. The kind of place where you're encouraged to browse the artworks for sale as you sip your demi-tasse. Occasional open-mike nights, plus poetry readings.

Sacred Grounds 468 W Sixth St, San Pedro ☏ 310/514-0800. Although located far from central LA, this combo coffeehouse and club offers periodic open-mike nights, music jams, and even some marginally funny comedy acts.

San Gabriel and San Fernando valleys

Aroma Coffee and Tea 4360 Tujunga Ave, Studio City ☏ 818/508-6505. In a remodeled house, this is an unfussy, mellow spot where you can enjoy beverages with cakes and scones, either on the patio near the gardens or in a living room with an old-fashioned fireplace.

Cobalt Café 22047 Sherman Way, Canoga Park ☏ 818/348-3789. Grungy but hip coffeehouse in the San Fernando Valley, with food and live music, and poetry readings, too.

Coffee Connection 4397 Tujunga Ave #B, Studio City ☏ 818/769-3622. Enjoyable joint in a strip mall, regularly presenting open-mike sessions and weekend acoustic music.

Coffee Gallery 2029 N Lake Ave, Altadena ☏ 626/398-7917. An appealing spot to lounge on sofas, munch on pastries, and browse artworks and various art and culture books while you sip your espresso.

Coffee Junction 19221 Ventura Blvd, Tarzana ☏ 818/342-3405. If you end up trapped in this remote corner of the Valley, the tasty coffee and music here are worth a stop. Located in a minimall.

iBrowse Coffee and Internet 11 W Main St, Alhambra ☏ 626/588-2233. Browse the Web to the sounds of eclectic music while downing supercharged coffee, at this spot off the main tourist path. Open 'til 2am.

Lulu's Beehive 13203 Ventura Blvd, Studio City ☏ 818/986-2233. Good not only for a jolt of java, but also for a dose of artwork, along with regular musical performances – not to mention comedy and poetry.

Zephyr 2419 E Colorado Blvd, Pasadena ☏ 626/793-7330. Charming old Craftsman house converted into coffee central, where you can lounge on sofas, view art on the walls, and guzzle java in a buzzy, convivial environment.

Zona Rosa 15 El Molino Ave, Pasadena ☏ 626/793-2334. One of the city's high points for excellent, inventive coffee drinks (often brewed from South American beans), an arty atmosphere, and periodic live music of the jazz and salsa variety.

Clubs

The **club** scene in LA is one of the finest in the country, ranging from posey yuppie hangouts to industrial noise cellars, with everybody claiming to be a rock musician or movie industry insider. Some of the hottest clubs – especially those catering to the house, ambient, techno or hip-hop scenes – are the most transient, disappearing within a few months of emerging as an "essential stop" for club-hoppers. As a result, you should always check the *LA Weekly* before setting out.

Weekend nights are the busiest, but during the week things are often cheaper and just as fun. Always, the best time to turn up is between 11pm and midnight. **Cover charges** range widely (anywhere from $5 to $20; call ahead), depending on the venue and night. The **minimum age** is 21, and it's normal for ID to be checked, so bring your passport or other photo ID. (Some establishments that don't serve alcohol or that separate the bar from the rest of the club admit patrons ages 18–21.) Prohibitive dress codes are common only at the "velvet rope" clubs that supposedly cater to movie brats and starlets, but more often to drunken suburban kids playing dress-up (and paying $12 for watered-down drinks).

Most of the top clubs are either in Hollywood or along a ten-block stretch of the Sunset Strip in West Hollywood. Beverly Hills and West LA are a lifeless desert, Downtown is home to a handful of itinerant clubs operating above and below board, Santa Monica has a smattering of compelling spots, and the San Fernando Valley's more rough-and-ready scene is usually confined to the weekends. (For gay and lesbian clubs and discos, see p.320.)

Downtown and Mid-Wilshire

Bordello 901 E First St ☎213/687-3766. True to its name, this is an extravagantly decorated, plush set for serious drinking and partying, where the nightly entertainment may be anything from an up-and-coming indie band to a jazz or blues concert to a cabaret freakshow.

Club 740 760 S Broadway ☎213/627-6277. Based out of the striking *Globe Theater*, a 1913 Beaux Arts movie palace, this frenetic multistory nightclub is worth a visit both for its Latin electronica and its historic architecture.

El Rey Theater 5515 Wilshire Blvd ☎323/936-4790. Favorite old neighborhood movie palace turned into a club and performing-arts space; check listings for periodic dance-club nights and special events.

🕺 **Jewel's Catch One 4067 W Pico Blvd** ☎323/734-8849. Sweaty barn catering to a mixed crowd of gays and straights on two wild dance floors. A longtime favorite for club-hoppers of all sorts. Especially busy Fri–Mon, though located in the middle of nowhere.

▲ Jewel's Catch One

La Cita 336 S Hill St ☎213/687-7111. A sweaty, hip-shaking scene in the heart of Downtown, this dance club draws a crowd with its great bar, thumping electronica — both Euro and

Latin — and the opportunity to dance your drunk off.

🕺 **Mayan 1038 S Hill St** ☎213/746-4287. Formerly a pre-Columbian–styled movie palace, now hosting Latin rhythms and nonstop disco and house tunes on three dance floors.

Velvet Room 3470 Wilshire Blvd ☎213/381-6006. A curious Koreatown experience, where the DJs spin like mad, the atmosphere is intense, the crowd young and buzzing, and it costs several hundreds dollars to "rent" a table to sit down. Bring your best credit card.

Hollywood

Arena 6655 Santa Monica Blvd ☎323/462-0714. Work up a sweat to funk, hip-hop, Latin, and house sounds on a massive dancefloor inside a former ice factory. Gay-friendly scene, playing host to different, ever-changing club nights.

Avalon 1735 N Vine St ☎323/462-3000. Major dance club spinning old-school faves along with the usual techno and house, with the occasional big-name DJ dropping in. Prices are among the most expensive in town.

Bar Sinister 1652 N Cherokee ☎323/769-7070. A collection of sprightly dance beats most nights of the week, then memorably spooky goth music and anemic-looking vampire types on Sat ($10 if in costume). Connected to *Boardner's* bar (see p.292).

The Derby 4500 Los Feliz Blvd ☎323/663-8979. Supper club with gorgeous high wooden ceilings and a round bar. One of the originators of the retro-swing craze, it now plays all sorts of indie tunes, mostly Wed & Fri.

Dragonfly 6510 Santa Monica Blvd ☎323/466-6111. Murky decor, two large dance rooms, and a mix of house and disco club nights and live music; also presents oddball cabaret shows and various retro-themed evenings.

King King 6555 Hollywood Blvd ☎323/960-5765. A solid Hollywood bet for live dance music, with house, funk, rap, and retro-pop all on the DJ docket.

🏃 **Little Temple** 4519 Santa Monica Blvd ☎323/660-4540. A Silver Lake scene with moody Asian decor, atmospheric lighting, tasty beverages (like the coconut martini), and an expressive, shmoozy clientele, this place draws the smarter club-hoppers around town.

The Ruby 7070 Hollywood Blvd ☎323/467-7070. Wide-ranging, feverish dance nights take turns Thurs–Sun, covering everything from goth and grinding industrial to perky house and garage.

Three Clubs 1123 N Vine St ☎323/462-6441. Dark, perennially trendy bar and club where the usual crowd of hipsters drops in for retro, rock, and funk music — and gets pleasingly plastered. Colorless exterior and lack of good signage makes the joint even hipper.

Vanguard 6021 Hollywood Blvd ☎323/463-3331. Fans of house music may revere this signature house club — especially at Deep, on Sundays — though others may find the meatmarket scene, $12 drinks, and steep cover charge less than appealing.

West Hollywood

7969 7969 Santa Monica Blvd ☎323/654-0280. Classic WeHo dance club – a landmark for its frenetic assortment of gay-themed (but straight-friendly) shows, from go-go girls to male strippers to drag queens. Always one of LA's most colorful spots for dancing and grinding.

The Factory 652 N La Peer Drive ☎310/659-4551. Mixed straight and gay crowd grooving to DJs spinning house and retro most nights of the week. One of West Holly-wood's more popular clubs.

🏃 **Key Club** 9039 Sunset Blvd ☎310/274-5800. A hot spot on the liveliest stretch of the Strip's west side, attracting a young, happening group for hip-hop and electronica. Music scene is quite varied, often including live-music acts (see p.303) and special events.

Hyde Lounge 8029 W Sunset Blvd ☎323/655-8000. Completely overpriced poser scene

where people nonetheless beg to get past the velvet rope — mainly to get a glimpse of celebrities boozing, dancing, or otherwise embarrassing themselves.

Tempest 7323 Santa Monica Blvd ☎323/850-5115. After 10pm on weekends, the eclectic grooves start to spin here, from retro-funk and disco to Britpop, drawing a mixed, energetic gay and straight crowd.

Ultra Suede 661 N Robertson Blvd ☎310/659-4551. The spot for superior retro-dancing, heavy on 1970s disco and 80s technopop, with a mixed gay and straight crowd. Neighbor to *The Factory*, and draws much of the same mixed crowd.

The Viper Room 8852 Sunset Blvd ☎310/358-1880. Excellent live acts, with occasional DJs spinning a mix of dance and other styles. See also "Live music," p.304.

West LA

Backstage Café 9433 Brighton Way ☎310/777-0252. Epitomizing nightlife on the Westside, a Cal-cuisine bar and restaurant where the nice decor and well-made cocktails are offset by pretension, high prices, and a corporate feel.

Carbon 9300 Venice Blvd ☎310/558-9302. Though hardly central, a good spot for eclectic nightly DJs, whose turntables glow with Latin, retro, jungle, drum & bass, hip-hop, soul, and rock beats, depending on the night.

Santa Monica and Venice

217 Lounge 217 Broadway, Santa Monica ☎310/394-6336. A little slice of West LA by the bay, complete with snotty attitudes, smart decor, decent cocktails, and, of course, posy regulars.

Circle Bar 2926 Main St, Santa Monica ☎310/392-4898. Old-fashioned dive that mainly draws a crowd of high-fiving party dudes who get plastered on the pricey but potent drinks and struggle to keep the beat on the dance floor. Venice is well within staggering distance.

Mor 2941 Main St, Santa Monica ☎310/396-6678. Nightly selections of techno, trance, house, and soul, mixing it up for groovy club nights most evenings in a hip lounge setting.

🏃 **Temple Bar** 1026 Wilshire Blvd, Santa Monica ☎310/392-1077. Popular dance club, with doses of world beat thrown in as well, and all manner of electronica. A fun, engaging scene.

Zanzibar 1301 Fifth St, Santa Monica ☎310/451-2221. DJs spinning sounds with a house, hip-hop, and soul bent, but also with a bit of funk and bossa nova thrown in on selected nights.

San Gabriel and San Fernando valleys

Bigfoot Lodge 3172 Los Feliz Blvd, Atwater Village ☎323/662-9227. On the far side of East Hollywood in dreary Atwater, this is nevertheless a prime draw for its nightly DJs, who set feet to stomping with retro-rock and punk tunes, with glam, goth, thrash, and rockabilly sounds thrown in as well.

CIA 11334 Burbank Blvd, North Hollywood ☎818/506-6353. A truly odd venue where art and music collide, with curious visual installations (often with circus clown and freak show themes) and sounds from punk to avant-garde.

Coda 5248 Van Nuys Blvd, Sherman Oaks ☎818/783-7518. Its brushed-steel, vaguely industrial decor is fairly hip for the Valley, but not as pose as you might think, drawing locals for its bouncy blend of rap, pop, and electronica.

Menage 54 Colorado Blvd ☎626/793-0608. Pasadena is hardly prime turf for dance clubs, but this will do in a pinch — a two-story pop/electronica club where the price and pretension can occasionally get out of hand, although it's mostly a scene for locals and interloping tourists.

The Mix 2612 Honolulu Ave, Glendale ☎818/248-3040. Fairly safe sounds at this dance club and restaurant (located on the northern edge of Glendale), mainly country and middle-of-the-road tunes with plenty of retro-pop thrown in.

Live music

os Angeles has an overwhelming choice of **live music** venues. Besides local acts, there are always plenty of big stateside and European names on tour, from major artists to independents. Most venues open at 8pm or 9pm; headline bands are usually onstage between 11pm and 1am. Cover charges range widely from $3 to $75, and you should phone ahead to check set times and whether the gig is sold out. For admission, you will often need to be 21 and will likely be asked for ID. As ever, *LA Weekly* and the "Calendar" section of the *Los Angeles Times* are the best sources of **listings**. Seats for concerts are often purchased from Ticketmaster (℗213/480-3232 or 714/740-2000).

The music scene

Just about any musical form can be heard in LA, whether on the biggest concert stages or in the dingiest bars. Ever since the nihilistic punk bands of thirty years ago drew the city away from its spaced-out slacker image, LA's **rock** scene has been second to none, peaking in popularity in the 1980s with the Sunset Strip's own brand of "hair metal" and more recently having an alternative or indie tinge. The old **punk** scene has been revitalized with up-and-coming bands, and heavy metal can still be found here and there. The influence and popularity of **hip-hop** is also considerable, whether mixed in dance music by Westside DJs or in its more authentic form in inner city clubs (best avoided by out-of-towners).

Surprisingly, **country music** is fairly common, at least away from trendy Hollywood, and the valleys are hotbeds of **bluegrass** and **swing**. There's also **jazz**, played in a few genuinely authentic downbeat clubs, though more commonly found in diluted form in upscale restaurants. Latin **salsa** music is immensely popular in some circles, and can be found in a few Westside clubs; and there's a small live **reggae** scene, occasionally featuring big names but more often sticking to local bands.

Concert halls and performance spaces

LA's **concert halls** and **performance spaces** are scattered throughout the region.

Major concert venues

Carpenter Performing Arts Center 6200 Atherton St, on the campus of Cal State Long Beach ℗562/985-7000, ⓦwww.carpenterarts .org. A major arts space in the South Bay, attracting mostly mid-level entertainers in pop, traditional rock, folk, jazz, and country, it puts on toe-tapping musicals as well.

Cerritos Center for the Performing Arts 12700 Center Court Drive ☎1-800/300-4345, ⓦwww .cerritoscenter.com. North of downtown Long Beach, a top draw for mainstream country, gospel, classical, pop, and jazz acts – usually nothing too quirky or adventurous.

Ford Amphitheatre 2850 Cahuenga Blvd, Hollywood ☎323/461-3673, ⓦwww .fordamphitheater.org. An open-air venue presenting eclectic productions that include a range of pop and rock concerts.

The Forum 3900 W Manchester Blvd, Inglewood ☎310/330-7300, ⓦwww.thelaforum.com. Despite being converted into a mega-church for Sunday services, this huge venue with giant columns still hosts the occasional sinful rock and pop bands.

Gibson Amphitheatre 100 Universal City Plaza ☎818/622-4440, ⓦwww.hob.com/venues /concerts/universal. A huge but acoustically excellent auditorium putting on regular rock shows by headline groups. Located on the Universal Studios lot.

Greek Theatre 2700 N Vermont Ave, Griffith Park ☎323/665-1927 ⓦwww.greektheatrela.com. Outdoor, summer-only venue (May–Oct) hosting mainstream rock and pop acts, with seating for five thousand. Parking can be a mess, so come early.

Grove of Anaheim 2200 E Katella Ave ☎714/712-2700, ⓦwww.thegroveofanaheim .com. Orange County concert space showcasing old-time performers and mid-level entertainers in soul, country, pop, rock, and jazz.

Hollywood Palladium 6215 Sunset Blvd, Hollywood ☎323/962-7600, ⓦwww .hollywoodpalladium.com. Once a big-band dance hall, with an authentic 1940s interior, now a venue for all manner of hard rock, punk, and rap outfits.

Honda Center 2695 E Katella Blvd, Anaheim ☎714/704-2400, ⓦwww.hondacenter.com. A 19,000-seat sports arena that draws the usual big-ticket events in music and entertainment, and also features a separate

"Theatre" – about a third the size – for smaller-scaled rock groups.

Kodak Theatre 6801 Hollywood Blvd, Hollywood ☎323/308-6300, ⓦwww.kodaktheatre.com. Part of the colossal Hollywood & Highland mall, a media-ready theater partly designed to host the Oscars, as well as major and minor pop and rock acts.

Nokia Theatre 777 Chick Hearn Court ☎714/740-2000, ⓦwww.nokiatheatrelalive .com. Grand new auditorium that's part of the colossal LA Live complex (see p.67). To pay off the overhead, it's doubtful the theater will be booking anything but the safest pop, country, and rock acts.

Orpheum Theatre 842 S Broadway, Downtown ☎1-877/677-4386, ⓦwww.laorpheum.com. Terrific old movie palace (see p.62) that's now been spruced up as a major-league concert venue, hosting a broad range of acts including the latest big- and mid-name alternative bands.

Staples Center 865 S Figueroa St, Downtown ☎213/742-7340, ⓦwww.staplescenter.com. Big, glassy sports arena (home to the LA Lakers) with millions of municipal and corporate dollars behind it. A good showcase for Top 40 rock and pop acts.

Wiltern Theater 3790 Wilshire Blvd, Mid-Wilshire ☎323/388-1400, ⓦwww.wiltern.com. A striking blue Zigzag Art Deco movie palace, converted into a top performing space for standard pop acts as well as edgy alternative groups.

▲ Wiltern Theater

Small venues

You can hear live music in small venues, such as bars and clubs, all over LA, though most major rock and alternative spots are in Hollywood or West Hollywood, with many right on the Sunset Strip.

Rock and pop

Downtown and Mid-Wilshire

The Echo 1822 Sunset Blvd ☎213/413-8200.
Like the name says, an Echo Park club with
scrappy indie-rock bands playing in a dark,
intense little hole for a crowd of serious
rockers. A good place to catch what's
bubbling up in the underground music
scene.

El Rey Theater 5515 Wilshire Blvd, Mid-Wilshire
☎323/936-4790. Although not as famous as
its Sunset Strip counterparts, this rock and
alternative venue is possibly the best spot to
see explosive new bands and enduring
oldsters.

Largo 432 N Fairfax Ave, north of Mid-Wilshire
☎323/852-1073. Cozy cabaret with some
unusual live acts, though mostly jazz, rock,
and pop, often of the acoustic variety; some
comedy as well.

Mr T's Bowl 5621 N Figueroa Ave,
Highland Park ☎323/960-5693. Former
bowling alley remodelled into a quirky bar
with a regular crowd of hipsters and local
characters. On weekends, there's live
music, with a strong punk-rock-surfer bent.

The Smell 247 S Main St, Downtown ☎213/625-
4325. A funky space with cool art grunge,
including frenetic rock and punk music, and
a notoriously grim location.

Hollywood

Gabah 4658 Melrose Ave ☎323/664-8913.
Eclectic spot serving up a mix of reggae,
funk, dub, and rock, with a mix of club and
live-music nights. Don't walk through the
dicey neighborhood unless you like a good
clonk to the head; always let the valet take
charge of your car.

The Gig 7302 Melrose Ave ☎323/936-4440.
Central Melrose hot spot for hard-rocking,
venom-spitting, and fist-shaking, with a
regular line-up of spirited groups and a
good group of spirits, too.

Music Box @ Fonda 6126 Hollywood Blvd
☎323/464-0808, ⓦwww.henryfondatheater
.com. A charming, renovated old theater that
began life in 1926 and still hosts theatrical
productions, but more typically alternative
rock and dance musicians.

Silver Lake Lounge 2906 Sunset Blvd
☎323/666-2407. A hole in the wall popular
for its energetic punk and alternative shows,
plus some weekends featuring drag and
dance music.

Spaceland 1717 Silver Lake Blvd
☎213/661-4380. Doesn't have the
national rep of places like the Roxy and
Whisky, but you're unlikely to find a better
spot in LA to catch up-and-coming rockers
and other acts, including punk and alternative musicians. Cover often less than $10.

▲ Spaceland: performance by The Gift

West Hollywood

Cat Club 8911 Sunset Blvd ☎310/657-0888.
Hard, meaty jams can be heard here every
night of the week, mainly rock, punk, and
rockabilly – which should come as no
surprise, since the owner's a former
Stray Cat.

Key Club 9039 Sunset Blvd ☎310/274-5800. A
hot spot in the liveliest section of the strip,
attracting young hipsters for its regular
concerts in the rock, punk, and metal vein,
with occasional lighter fare as well.

The Roxy 9009 Sunset Blvd ☎310/276-2222.
An intimate club showcasing the music
industry's new signings and boasting a great
sound system, too. On the western – but
still hectic – end of the strip.

The Troubadour 9081 Santa Monica
Blvd ☎310/276-6168. Fabled 1960s
mainstay that's been through a lot of
incarnations in its forty-plus years. Used
to be known for folk and country rock,
then metal, now for various flavors of
indie rock.

The Viper Room 8852 Sunset Blvd ☎310/358-1880. Great live acts, plus a famous owner (Johnny Depp) and a headline-grabbing past have helped boost this club's hipness quotient. Expect almost any musician to show up onstage.

Whisky-a-Go-Go 8901 Sunset Blvd ☎310/652-4202. Legendary spot in the 1960s, and still important for LA's rising music stars. Mainly hard rock, though you might catch an alternative act now and then.

West LA

Cinema Bar 3967 Sepulveda Blvd, Culver City ☎310/390-1328. If you want a break from the Hollywood posers, but want to get down 'n' dirty with an underground band (of any stripe), this small, out-of-the-way spot is a great bet — pretty much the only thing going on in this part of town.

The Joint 8771 Pico Blvd, West LA ☎310/275-2619. A dark, small neighborhood venue with assorted punk screamers and occasionally decent rock and alternative groups. Posers need not apply.

Santa Monica

14 Below 1348 14th St ☎310/451-5040. At this tiny bar, pool tables and a fireplace compete for your attention with rangy rock, folk, and blues acts that perform nightly.

Temple Bar 1026 Wilshire Blvd ☎310/392-1077. Along with its dance club scene (see p.299), you can catch a chaotic mix of popular styles here, from funk and soul to rap and R&B, as well as forays into rock, pop, and world beat.

South Bay and Long Beach

The Lighthouse 30 Pier Ave, Hermosa Beach ☎310/376-9833. Near the beach, this old favorite has a broad booking policy that spans rock, jazz, and reggae as well as karaoke and occasional comedy.

San Gabriel and San Fernando Valleys

Cobalt Café 22047 Sherman Way, Canoga Park ☎818/348-3789. Valley outpost for all kinds of kid musicians thrashing, head-banging, and behaving badly, with nightly bands and decent coffee drinks, too (see p.297).

Sagebrush Cantina 23527 Calabasas Rd, Calabasas ☎818/222-6062. About as close as the western San Fernando Valley gets to having a live-music scene, this Mexican restaurant offers 1970s-leaning rock cover bands several nights of the week to an appreciative crowd.

The Scene 806 E Colorado St, Glendale ☎818/241-7029. Head-scratching booking policy features punks on some nights, experimental noise or country crooners on others, and rockabilly swingers on the next. Call ahead to find out what you're in for.

Country and folk

Hollywood and West LA

Boulevard Music 4136 Sepulveda Blvd, Culver City ☎310/398-2583. This unglamorous music store manages to host some fairly interesting folk acts on weekends, from roots country to delta blues, with international groups adding even more to the mix.

Hotel Café 1623 N Cahuenga Blvd, Hollywood ☎323/461-2040. Comfortable spot for acoustic acts and earnest singer-songsmiths, as well as the occasional indie band. Tunes nightly.

Molly Malone's Irish Pub 575 S Fairfax Ave, west of Mid-Wilshire ☎323/935-1577. Local favorite for its colorful clientele and mix of traditional Irish music, American folk, indie rock, bluegrass, country, and reggae. See also p.291.

Santa Monica

Finn McCool's 2702 Main St ☎310/452-1734. A serviceable spot for quaffing draughts, this Irish bar also offers twice-weekly performances of folk tunes from the Emerald Isle; see "Bars," p.294.

McCabe's 3103 W Pico Blvd ☎310/828-4497. LA's premier acoustic guitar shop; long the scene of some excellent and unusual folk and country shows, with the occasional alternative act thrown in as well.

Rusty's Surf Ranch 256 Santa Monica Pier ☎310/393-7437. Offers not only surf music – and displays of old-time longboards – but also rock, pop, folk, and even karaoke. Always a popular spot for tourists, near the end of the pier.

South Bay and Long Beach

Cowboy Country 3321 E South St, Long Beach ☎562/630-3007. Pull out your best line-dancing moves and your fanciest boots for this two-story country scene with three dance floors. Very popular with self-styled cowpokes for its country DJ sets and live performances.

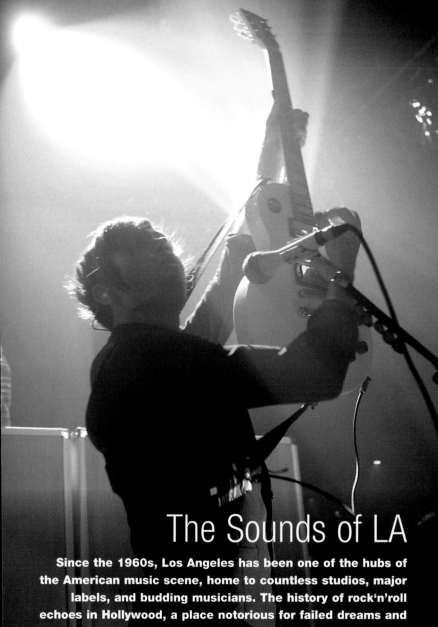

The Sounds of LA

Since the 1960s, Los Angeles has been one of the hubs of the American music scene, home to countless studios, major labels, and budding musicians. The history of rock'n'roll echoes in Hollywood, a place notorious for failed dreams and hollow myths, but it's always been easier for an up-and-comer to grab a guitar and start a band than to land a movie role or direct a film. In Los Angeles, music has long been an essential part of the cultural landscape, especially among the young.

Ritchie Valens ▲

The Beach Boys ▼

Linda Ronstadt ▼

Early years

In the 1950s, LA witnessed the **birth of rock'n'roll**, with the emergence of such homegrown talent as Ritchie Valens and The Platters, and the efforts of local producers such as Phil Spector and Jack Nitzsche. At the time, the major New York labels, backed by Wall Street financial resources, dominated the industry and propped up graying big-band crooners and insipid teen idols.

Stylistically, the LA sound was defined in the early 1960s by **surf rock**, exemplified by the pleasant harmonies of the **Beach Boys** and Jan and Dean, and by pop vocalists like Frankie Avalon, who sang anodyne tales of apple-cheeked youth and puppy love.

The gold rush, and after

It wasn't until the mid-1960s that the major-label recording industry really took root in town, as The Doors, Buffalo Springfield, Frank Zappa, and Love rose to the top of the club scene. The 1967 **Monterey Pop Festival** brought LA and San Francisco bands to prominence, and a flood of record deals went to once-obscure acid-rockers. "After the Gold Rush" (as Neil Young would put it), the Sunset Strip was awash in drugs and criminals, of which Charles Manson was the most infamous. At the same time, super-agents like David Geffen and Elliot Roberts began building their empires, taking the music-money muscle away from New York.

By the early 1970s, stupefied by a blizzard of cocaine, LA's musicians spawned the **country-rock** sound, defined by the Eagles, Jackson Browne, Gram Parsons, and Linda Ronstadt, who sang about the city as a spaced-out pleasure zone, to great commercial success.

Famous LA music sites

Barney's Beanery (see p.262) – An LA staple since 1920, this bar really became (in)famous for the drunken antics of Jim Morrison and Janis Joplin in the 1960s, and the Olympian drinking of Charles Bukowski.

"Beatle Manor," 356 St Pierre Rd, Bel Air – One of three hideouts where the Fab Four decamped during their mid-60s tours, when playing at the Hollywood Bowl.

Chateau Marmont (see p.246) – A grand Norman castle that hosted a slew of spectacles, among them Jim Morrison's painful attempt to play Tarzan on a drain pipe and John Belushi's overdose on a coke-and-heroin speedball.

Dead Man's Curve, Sunset Blvd west of Groverton Pl, near UCLA – The pop world's most notable road bend, which Jan and Dean sang about in their eponymous 1964 hit, and where a number of drivers died before the city regraded it.

Hyatt West Hollywood (see p.246) – The "Riot House": a Sunset Strip hotel frequented by Led Zeppelin, The Who, Jim Morrison, and the Rolling Stones, who variously dropped TVs out of windows, raced motorcycles down hallways, and did unspeakable things to groupies.

Landmark Hotel, 7047 Franklin Ave, Hollywood – Now the Highland Gardens, a dreary spot where Janis Joplin overdosed on heroin, three years after her astonishing debut at the Monterey Pop Festival.

Laurel Canyon Country Store, 2108 Laurel Canyon Blvd, Hollywood – The grocery-store epicenter of the late-1960s singer-songwriter movement, frequented by Joni Mitchell, Frank Zappa, Crosby, Stills and Nash, and many others.

Viper Room (see p.304) – Opened by Johnny Depp in 1993, a great showcase for indie music. Actor River Phoenix met his end on the sidewalk outside, a drug casualty on a Halloween morning.

▲ Indie group performs at Viper Room

▼ Joni Mitchell in Laurel Canyon

Rock reactions

The music haze cleared around 1978, with the emergence of an energetic **punk** scene first headed by groups such as the Germs and X, later dominated by Orange County hardcore bands like Black Flag, Circle Jerks, Fear, and The Adolescents. Huntington Beach was a notable birthplace of violent trends like **slam dancing**.

The major labels reacted to the threat of punk with **heavy metal**, which had been around since Led Zeppelin's first American tour at the dawn of the 1970s. At the end of the decade, LA's own Van Halen rose to the top of the charts. The style really hit its commercial stride in the 1980s, with Mötley Crüe and Guns N' Roses; many lesser imitators like Ratt and Poison found chart success as well.

A rocker on Sunset Strip ▲

Rap group NWA ▼

Rap and beyond

Near the end of the "hair metal" era, by the late 1980s, the city's **hip-hop** artists created their own unique sound. Leading the way were rappers such as NWA, Snoop Dogg, Ice Cube, Ice T, and especially Dr Dre, who almost single-handedly elevated the **West Coast sound** to prominence: Laid-back beats, an undertone of funk and soul, and a lyrical emphasis on violence and hedonism.

Since then, alternative or **indie rock** has claimed the creative mantle, its roots extending back to bands like Jane's Addiction, Hole, and Red Hot Chili Peppers. These days, with the exception of major-name artists like Beck, many LA bands are content with more limited success in exchange for creative freedom via self-distribution, online promotions, and Web-based fan clubs.

San Gabriel and San Fernando Valleys

Celtic Arts Center 4843 Laurel Canyon Blvd, Studio City ☎818/760-8322. A celebration of all things Celtic and Gaelic (and not just Irish, either), offering monthly concerts, dance lessons and, best of all, free Sunday night Céili dances followed by traditional-music jam sessions.

Cowboy Palace Saloon 21635 Devonshire St, Chatsworth ☎818/341-0166. Worth a trip to this distant corner of the San Fernando Valley for plenty of tub-thumping country-and-western concerts and down-home helpings of Sunday BBQ.

CTMS Center 16953 Ventura Blvd, Encino ☎818/817-7756, ⓦwww.ctmsfolkmusic.org. The home base for the California Traditional Music Society, which throughout the year puts on periodic performances of ancient and modern folk music. The center also offers education and training and monthly jam sessions (open to the public).

Kulak's Woodshed 5230 Laurel Canyon Blvd, North Hollywood ☎818/766-9913, ⓦwww .kulakswoodshed.com. Puts on nightly shows in a cramped but colorful space, ranging from acoustic and spoken-word to performance art and poetry. Must be a member to enter ($5 fee); join via the website.

Oil Can Harry's 11502 Ventura Blvd, Studio City ☎818/760-9749. Gay cowboy bar strongly oriented to country music, with occasional down-home performances, line-dancing, and a mildly cornpone atmosphere.

Viva Fresh Cantina 900 Riverside Drive, Burbank ☎818/845-2425. A Mexican restaurant on the far side of Griffith Park, where you can hear some of LA's most engaging country, bluegrass, and honky-tonk artists performing nightly.

Jazz, blues, and reggae

Hollywood and West Hollywood

Cat 'n' Fiddle Pub 6530 Sunset Blvd, Hollywood ☎323/468-3800. An English-style pub with worthwhile jazz performers on Sun from 7pm until 11pm; no cover. See also "Drinking," p.292.

Catalina Bar and Grill 6725 W Sunset Blvd ☎323/466-2210. This central Hollywood jazz institution offers a wide range of sounds from many big-name performers, as well as good acoustics, filling meals,

and potent drinks. It can get pricey, though.

House of Blues 8430 Sunset Blvd, West Hollywood ☎323/848-5100. Over-commercialized mock sugar shack, with good but pricey live acts. Very popular with tourists, as it's the flagship of a national chain. Cover can reach $40 or more.

🎷 **Knitting Factory** 7021 Hollywood Blvd, Hollywood ☎323/463-0204. West Coast branch of the landmark New York City club, housed in a minimall and featuring a wide range of eclectic music, much of it experimental or avant-garde.

West LA

🎷 **Jazz Bakery** 3233 Helms Ave, Culver City ☎310/271-9039. More performance space than club, and the brainchild of singer Ruth Price, here the best local musicians play alongside big-name visitors in a former bakery building.

The Mint 6010 W Pico Blvd, south of Mid-Wilshire ☎323/954-9400. What places like the Echo are to rock, this place is to jazz — a small, intense spot that's off the beaten path but worth the ramble to hear the latest in the city's brass/keys/bass/drums sound, with decent food and drink, too.

Vibrato Grill and Jazz 2930 Beverly Glen Circle, West LA ☎310/474-9400. You're not going to find anything too challenging at this Bel Air club, but for traditional and smooth jazz sounds, it may fit the bill.

Santa Monica

Harvelle's 1432 Fourth St ☎310/395-1676. Near the Third Street Promenade, a stellar blues joint that for more than seven decades has offered different performers nightly, with a little funk, R&B, and burlesque thrown in as well.

South Central LA

🎷 **Babe and Ricky's Inn** 4339 Leimert Blvd ☎323/295-9112. Long a top spot for blues on Central Avenue, this premier music hall continues to attract quality, nationally known acts at its more recent Leimert Park location.

Fais Do-Do 5247 W Adams Blvd ☎323/954-8080. Though it often hosts DJ nights of the dance, funk, and rap variety, this spot, between Downtown and Culver City, also presents concerts from regional reggae, jazz, and R&B acts.

World Stage 4344 Degnan Blvd, South Central LA ☎323/293-2451. Informal, bare-bones rehearsal space that attracts top-name players like drummers Billy Higgins and Max Roach. Thursday jams, Friday, and Saturday gigs.

South Bay and Long Beach

Blue Café 210 Promenade, Long Beach ☎562/983-7111. A range of nightly blues near the harbor, plus a slew of pool tables and an upstairs dance floor. No cover.
Café Boogaloo 1238 Hermosa Ave, Hermosa Beach ☎310/318-2324. One of the better spots in the South Bay for nightly blues, with occasional New Orleans jazz and swing.

San Gabriel and San Fernando Valleys

The Baked Potato 3787 Cahuenga Blvd W, North Hollywood ☎818/980-1615. A small but near-legendary contemporary jazz spot, where many reputations have been forged. Don't come looking for bland lounge jazz/muzak – expect to be surprised.

▲ Jazz musicians at The Baked Potato

BB King's Blues Club 1000 Universal Center Drive, Universal City ☎818/6-BBKING. Set up in the mallified precinct of CityWalk, this two-story club offers the blues you'd expect many nights, mixed in with the odd R&B, indie, or soul performer.
Cozy's Bar and Grill 14048 Ventura Blvd, Sherman Oaks ☎818/986-6000. Listen to very good blues on the weekend, or periodically during the week, at this restaurant and lounge that also features karaoke, funk, and soul performances.

Jax 339 N Brand Blvd, Glendale ☎818/500-1604. A combination restaurant and performing stage where you can take in a good assortment of jazz, from traditional to contemporary. No cover.
Spazio 14755 Ventura Blvd, 2nd Floor, Sherman Oaks ☎818/728-8400. Swank Italian eatery that's one of the bigger-name spots for mainstream jazz, hosting nightly performances.

Latin and salsa

Conga Room at LA Live complex, Downtown ☎323/938-1696. Former Mid-Wilshire favorite for live Cuban, salsa, and South American music that closed its doors in 2006 and is set to reopen at the colossal LA Live (see p.67) in 2008.
El Floridita 1253 N Vine St, Hollywood ☎323/871-8612. Decent Mexican and Cuban food complements a fine line-up of Cuban and salsa artists, who play on weekends and jam on other nights.
King King 6555 Hollywood Blvd ☎323/960-5765. Though better known as a dance club (see p.299), this Hollywood staple has Tuesday-night salsa lessons, which precede a long night of dancing where you can show off your newly acquired skills.
Luminarias 3500 Ramona Blvd, Monterey Park ☎323/268-4177. Hilltop restaurant with live salsa reckoned to be as good as its Mexican food. No cover.
Mama Juana's 3707 Cahuenga Blvd W, Studio City ☎818/505-8636. Spanish/Mexican restaurant that also serves up nightly helpings of live salsa, merengue, and other Latin-flavored tunes. Also has salsa lessons on weekends before the shows begin.
Rio Lounge and Grill 15910 Ventura Blvd, Encino ☎818/205-9799. Weekend salsa, samba, and bossa nova set the scene for a fun atmosphere in the San Fernando Valley, with salsa lessons offered on Sun before the music.
Zabumba 10717 Venice Blvd, West LA ☎310/841-6525. In a colorful building amid drab surroundings, this venue is more bossa nova Brazilian than straight salsa, but it's still great, and very lively.

Performing arts and film

L os Angeles offers a wealth of **performing arts** options all over the basin. While it's true that the city's range of highbrow cultural offerings was at one time quite limited, confined to art-house cinemas and a handful of mainstream playhouses, LA has now firmly established itself in the performing-arts field thanks to a solid push from old-money and corporate interests. The city boasts a world-class classical-music **orchestra** with a renowned conductor, along with several less-familiar entities like a cappella and chamber-music groups. The fields of **opera** and **dance** are represented by several noteworthy companies, with the chief alternative entity (Long Beach Opera) consistently surpassing the mainstream one (LA Opera). **Theater** is always a growth industry here, with more than a thousand shows produced annually (and more than one hundred running at any one time), plenty of actors to draw from, and a burgeoning audience for both mainstream and fringe productions. **Cabaret** caters to a smaller crowd of lounge-act, torch-song and kitsch fans, but **comedy** is a much bigger draw – especially for first-time visitors to the metropolis. Not surprisingly, though, it's **film** that is still the chief cultural staple of the region, and there is no shortage of excellent theaters in which to catch a flick.

Classical music

Believe it or not, LA's **classical-music** scene is second to none in the US. Under the guidance of conductor Esa-Pekka Salonen, and housed in the stunning Disney Hall, the **LA Philharmonic** should be one of the first tickets you buy if you're interested in the performing arts. Less well known, though still intriguing, are the city's smaller performing groups, which tend to float from art centers to universities to church venues, drawing a loyal, though limited, audience. Your best bet for following the cultural trends is to watch the press, especially the *LA Times*, for details. In any case, you can expect to pay from $10 to $120 for most concerts, and more for really big names.

Classical-music companies

Da Camera Society rotating venues ☎213/477-2929, ⊛ www.dacamera.org. This organization's

"Chamber Music in Historic Sites" series provides a great opportunity to hear classical, Romantic, and modern chamber works in stunning settings, from grand churches to private homes, including such inspired sites as Doheny Mansion near USC. Ticket prices vary widely, depending on the venue, and can run anywhere from $35 to $95.

Long Beach Symphony office at 110 W Ocean Blvd, Suite 22, Long Beach ☎562/436-3203, ⓦwww.lbso.org. Not quite up to the level of Long Beach Opera, but a light alternative to LA's heavier repertoire, playing mainstream favorites like Tchaikovsky and Beethoven, interspersed with crowd-pleasing pops selections. Venues rotate between the **Terrace Theater, Long Beach Arena, and Long Beach Performing Arts Center.** $15–107.

Los Angeles Chamber Orchestra rotating local venues ☎213/622-7001 ext 215, ⓦwww .laco.org. Appearing at venues such as UCLA's Royce Hall, Glendale's Alex Theatre, and Culver City's Jazz Bakery, the orchestra presents a range of chamber works, not all canonical, from different eras. Concerts vary widely by price and seating choices. $17–69. (For a monumental interpretation of the orchestra's musicians, check out Kent Twitchell's colossal *Harbor Freeway Overture* mural in Downtown LA; see p.66.)

Los Angeles Master Chorale Disney Hall, 1st St at Grand Ave, Downtown; also at rotating venues ☎213/972-2782, ⓦwww.lamc.org. Classic works, along with lighter madrigals and pops favorites, are showcased by this choral institution, now performing in Disney Hall. $19–114.

Los Angeles Philharmonic Disney Hall, Downtown, and Hollywood Bowl ☎323/850-2000, ⓦwww.laphil.org. The one big name in the city performs regularly during the year, and conductor Esa-Pekka Salonen always provides a diverse, challenging program, from powerful Romantic works to craggy modern pieces, with regular appearances by celebrity conductors and musicians. Not to be missed if you have even the slightest interest in "longhair" music. $18–142.

Pacific Serenades office at 1201 W 5th St, Downtown ☎213/534-3434, ⓦpacser.org. Chamber-music concerts taking place Jan–June in the LA area, usually highlighting new composers and taking place at historic sites like Pasadena's Neighborhood Church and the UCLA Faculty Center (both $32) and various private homes ($50).

Pacific Symphony Orchestra Orange County Performing Arts Center, 615 Town Center Drive, Costa Mesa ☎714/755-5788 ⓦwww .pacificsymphony.org. Although not as groundbreaking as the LA Philharmonic, this suburban orchestra nonetheless draws big crowds for its excellent, stylish performances of mostly canonical works, performed in the sparkling Segerstrom Concert Hall or,

▲ Disney Hall

in summer, at the outdoor Verizon Wireless Amphitheater. $25–95.

Pasadena Symphony at Pasadena Civic Auditorium, 300 E Green St ☏ 626/793-7172, ⓦ www.pasadenasymphony.org. Veering between the standard repertoire and more contemporary pieces, this esteemed symphony plays at the stately Pasadena Civic Auditorium, a 1932 Renaissance Revival gem, once a month from October to April. $15–75, $10 for students.

Southwest Chamber Music ☏ 1-800/726-7147, ⓦ www.swmusic.org. A nationally recognized performing and recording troupe that offers a wide range of music, from medieval to modern. Venues include the wintertime (Oct–April) series at the Norton Simon Museum and Downtown's Colburn School of Performing Arts, summer concerts at the Huntington Library, and regular open rehearsals at Pasadena's Armory Center. $38; students $10.

Classical-music venues

Bing Theater 5905 Wilshire Blvd, Mid-Wilshire ☏ 213/473-8493 or 213/473-0625, ⓦ www.lacma.org. When it isn't hosting movie revivals, this auditorium at the LA County Museum of Art provides a fine space for classical concerts, which occur periodically during the year ($25). Plus, free Friday-night jazz in the courtyard April–Nov.

Disney Hall First St at Grand Ave, Downtown ☏ 323/850-2000, ⓦ wdch.laphil.org. LA's most renowned cultural attraction (along with the Getty Center) and home of the LA Philharmonic. A striking Frank Gehry design that hosts a range of music and arts groups.

Dorothy Chandler Pavilion at the Music Center, 135 N Grand Ave, Downtown ☏ 213/972-7211 or 972-7460, ⓦ www.musiccenter.org. Long-standing warhorse of the arts community, used by LA Opera and other top names, though no longer by the LA Philharmonic.

The Hollywood Bowl 2301 N Highland Ave, Hollywood ☏ 323/850-2000, ⓦ www.hollywoodbowl.org. Hosts LA Philharmonic concerts, usually of the pops variety, and various jazz and world-beat groups, for open-air concerts during the summer.

John Anson Ford Theater 2850 Cahuenga Blvd, Hollywood ☏ 323/461-3673, ⓦ www.fordamphitheater.org. An open-air venue that has eclectic productions by local classical and operatic groups as well as sporadic pop and rock concerts.

Orange County Performing Arts Center 600 Town Center Drive, Costa Mesa ☏ 714/556-ARTS, ⓦ www.ocpac.org. Home of the Pacific Symphony Orchestra and Opera Pacific, and also showcasing traveling pop and jazz acts.

Pasadena Civic Auditorium 300 E Green St, Pasadena ☏ 626/449-7360, ⓦ www.pasadenacal.com/civic.htm. A bit more appealing than it sounds, this 3000-seat municipal hall hosts award shows and the esteemed Pasadena Symphony.

Royce Hall on the UCLA campus in Westwood ☏ 310/825-2101, ⓦ www.uclalive.org. Classical concerts, often involving big names, occur at this splendid historic-revival structure throughout the college year (Sept–June). Call or go online to find out about other on-campus productions arranged by the UCLA Center for the Performing Arts.

Shrine Auditorium 665 W Jefferson Blvd, South Central ☏ 213/749-5123; box office at 655 S Hill St; ⓦ www.shrinela.com. Huge 1926 Moorish-domed curiosity that hosts touring pop acts, choral gospel groups, and countless award shows – though not the Oscars any more.

▲ Shrine Auditorium

Thornton School of Music **On the USC campus, South Central** ☎213/740-6935, ⊛www.usc .edu/music. A fine array of venues, from 90–1200 seats, for sonatas, concertos, and other works (usually Sept–May), with most tickets less than $20. During the season (Sept–May), weekly concerts are broadcast on KUSC 91.5 FM and sometimes feature name guest conductors.

Opera and dance

The few major **opera** companies in LA and Orange counties are either old-line institutions that focus on the warhorses of the repertoire, or newcomers that make more of an effort to cross artistic boundaries and program contemporary works. **Dance** performances tend to be grouped around major events, so check cultural listings or call the venues listed below for seasonal information. Otherwise, check for performances at universities like UCLA (☎310/825-4401, ⊛www.uclalive .org), where some of the most exciting names in dance have residencies.

Opera companies and venues

Casa Italiana Opera Company **at St Peter's parish church, 1051 N Broadway, Downtown** ☎310/451-6012, ⊛www.casaitaliana.org. About four times during the year, this alternative company stages workshops in which singers in training perform popular Romantic Italian operas, from Puccini to Verdi and Mascagni, for an affordable price. $48.

LA Opera **at the Music Center, 135 N Grand Ave, Downtown** ☎213/972-8001, ⊛www.laopera .com. With Plácido Domingo at the helm, this institution stages mainstream productions between Sept and June, from heavy *opera seria* to lighter operettas. For better or worse, the undisputed opera heavyweight in town. $20–238.

Long Beach Opera **at the Carpenter Center, 6200 Atherton St** ☎562/439-2580, ⊛www.lbopera .com. Although eight years older than LA Opera, this company presents the freshest and edgiest work in town, from lesser-known pieces by Monteverdi to craggy new works by local composers to bizarre hybrids of hitherto unrelated pieces (e.g., Strauss Meets Frankenstein!). One of the most groundbreaking companies in the nation — and cheap, too. $45–95.

Opera Pacific **Orange County Performing Arts Center, 600 Town Center Drive, Costa Mesa** ☎714/546-6000 or 1-800/34-OPERA, ⊛www .operapacific.org. Performs mostly mainstream grand opera and tub-thumping operettas. $27–200.

Dance companies and venues

Carpenter Center **6200 Atherton St, on the campus of Cal State Long Beach** ☎562/985-7000, ⊛www.carpenterarts.org. The South Bay's major arts space, hosting the Long Beach Opera and mainstream pop concerts, as well as periodic dance performances and touring arts groups.

Cerritos Center for the Performing Arts **12700 Center Court Drive, Southeast LA** ☎1-800/300-4345, ⊛www.cerritoscenter.com. Located in distant Cerritos on the Orange County border, this is one of LA's better-known and funded venues, home to mainstream classical, opera, and dance performances, as well as big-name pop and jazz performers.

Japan America Theater **244 S San Pedro St, Little Tokyo** ☎213/680-3700, ⊛www.jaccc .org. Intriguing theatrical, dance, and performance works drawn from Japan and the Far East, mixing traditional and contemporary styles.

Los Angeles Ballet **office at 2525 Michigan Ave, Suite T4B, Santa Monica** ☎310/998-7782, ⊛www.losangelesballet.org. In 2006, this company arrived to fill a serious hole in the LA cultural scene, with a Nov–May program featuring standards like the Nutcracker and a surprising number of new and modern works. Shows at Glendale's Alex Theatre, UCLA sites, and a few other venues.

Pasadena Dance Theater **1985 Locust Ave, Pasadena** ☎626/683-3459, ⊛www .pasadenadance.org. One of the San Gabriel Valley's more prominent dance venues, hosting diverse groups throughout the year.

UCLA Center for the Performing Arts **on UCLA campus** ☎310/825-4401, ⊛www.uclalive.org. Hosts a wide range of touring companies in music, theater, and dance (Sept–June), and runs a fine dance series between Sept and June, often with an experimental bent.

Theater

LA has an active and energetic **theater** scene. You can expect to find most any kind of stage production on any given night in one of the city's venues, including huge, Broadway juggernauts, obscure hole-in-the-wall events, avant-garde carnivals, edgy political melodramas, and even revivals of classic works by the likes of Shaw and Ibsen. Aside from the nationally touring mega-hits, some of the productions to attract the most attention are multicharacter one-person shows and irreverent stagings of canonical works, with Shakespeare often in the crosshairs.

Since the region is home to a wealth of **film actors**, most of them unemployed in the movie biz, there is always a good pool of thespians for local productions. Depending on the play, you may even find semi-popular TV actors or big celebrity names on stage, their presence occasionally impromptu and unannounced. While the bigger venues host a predictable array of shopworn musicals and hidebound classics, there are over a hundred "Equity waiver" theaters with fewer than a hundred seats – typically 99 – enabling non-Equity cardholders (who don't belong to Actors' Equity, the theatrical labor union) to perform. This means a lot of fringe performances take place, for which prices can be very low, and the quality can vary greatly. But you may catch an electrifying surprise now and again — check the *LA Weekly* for a sense of what's out there.

Tickets are less expensive than you might expect: a big show will set you back at least $40–50, or up to $100 for some blockbusters (matinees are cheaper), with smaller shows around $10 to $25. A quick way through the maze of LA's **theaters** is to phone the **LA Stage Alliance** (☏213/614-0556, ⓦ www.lastagealliance.com) and ask for the availability of discount tickets for a given show, under its LA Stage Tix program.

Major theaters

Actors' Gang Theater 9070 Venice Blvd, Culver City ☏310/838-GANG, ⓦ www.theactorsgang .com. A cross between a major and an alternative theater; having fewer than a hundred seats keeps it cozy, though it does host the odd spectacular production that features semi-famous names from film or TV.

Ahmanson Theatre at the Music Center, 135 N Grand Ave, Downtown ☏213/628-2772, ⓦ www.taperahmanson.com. A two-thousand-seat theater hosting colossal traveling shows from Broadway. If you've seen a major production advertised on TV and on the sides of buses, it's probably playing here.

Alex Theatre 216 N Brand Blvd, Glendale ☏818/243-7700, ⓦ www.alextheatre.org. A gloriously restored movie palace – with a great neon spike and quasi-Egyptian forecourt – hosting a fine range of musical theater, dance, comedy, and film.

Coronet Theatre 366 N La Cienega Blvd, West Hollywood ☏310/657-7377, ⓦ www .coronet-theatre.com. A spot where mid-level Hollywood actors come to test new material before crowds of supportive fans; you can occasionally see big names in the theater's Writer's Lab workshop.

Freud Playhouse in MacGowan Hall on the UCLA campus, Westwood ☏310/825-2101, ⓦ www .uclalive.org. A nearly 600-seat venue that features a mix of mainstream and contemporary pieces – plus risk-taking experimental works. Along with Royce Hall (see p.309), occasionally hosts performances by visiting major troupes, such as the Royal Shakespeare Company.

Geffen Playhouse 10886 Le Conte Ave, Westwood ☏310/208-5454, ⓦ www .geffenplayhouse.com. A 500-seat, Spanish Revival building that often hosts one-person shows. There's a decided Hollywood connection, evident in the crowd-pleasing nature of many of the productions and the frequent presence of semi-familiar names from television and the movies.

International City Theatre 300 E Ocean Ave, Long Beach ☏562/436-4610, ⓦ www .ictlongbeach.org. Part of the Long Beach Performing Arts Center, this is an enjoyable, affordable spot for mainstream comedy and drama. Nothing too challenging, but makes for a reasonably fun night in the South Bay.

Mark Taper Forum at the Music Center, 135 N Grand Ave, Downtown ☎213/628-2772, ⊛www .taperahmanson.com. Theater in the three-quarter round, with familiar classics and, less frequently, assorted new plays. Don't expect fringe-theater radicalism; this high-culture spot is mostly known for its conservatism and adherence to the mainstream repertoire.

Pantages Theater 6233 Hollywood Blvd, Hollywood ☎323/468-1770, ⊛www .nederlander.com/wc. Quite the stunner: an exquisite, atmospheric Art Deco theater, in the heart of historic Hollywood, hosting major touring Broadway productions.

Pasadena Playhouse 39 S El Molino Ave, Pasadena ☎626/792-8672 or 356-PLAY, ⊛www.pasadenaplayhouse.org. A grand old space that has been refurbished to provide enjoyable mainstream entertainment. Actors are often a mix of youthful professionals and aging TV and movie stars.

Ricardo Montalbán Theatre 1615 N Vine St, Hollywood ☎323/462-6666, ⊛www .ricardomontalbantheatre.org. The former James Doolittle Theatre, now restored and renamed for the actor best known as Mr Roarke from *Fantasy Island*. Presents a range of productions dealing with social politics and Latino ethnic identity, in a classic building in the heart of Hollywood.

South Coast Repertory 655 Town Center Drive, Costa Mesa ☎714/708-5555, ⊛www.scr.org. Orange County's major theater entry, where you can watch well-executed performances of the classics on the main stage, and edgier works by new writers on the smaller, 150-seat second stage. Adjacent to the Orange County Performing Arts Center (see p.309).

Small and alternative theaters

A Noise Within 234 S Brand Blvd, Glendale ☎818/240-0910, ⊛www.anoisewithin.org. A very mainstream performance space in downtown Glendale, focusing heavily on the classics, with a strong emphasis on Shakespeare, Molière, and the like.

Actors Forum Theatre 10655 Magnolia Blvd, North Hollywood ☎818/506-0600, ⊛www .actorsforumtheatre.org. Unpredictable venue that hosts a range of topical dramas, one-person shows, and the odd production from nontraditional actors and playwrights. Dramatic workshops are also offered.

The Complex 6476 Santa Monica Blvd, Hollywood ☎323/465-0383, ⊛www .complexhollywood.com. A group of alternative companies west of Cahuenga Blvd, centered on a group of five small theaters, where you're likely to see any number of dynamic productions.

Highways 1651 18th St, Santa Monica ☎310/315-1459, ⊛www.highwaysperformance .org. Located in the 18th Street Arts Complex, an adventurous performance space that offers a range of topical drama and politically charged productions, with a strong bent toward the angry, polemical, and subversive.

Hudson Theaters 6539 Santa Monica Blvd, Hollywood ☎323/856-4252, ⊛www .hudsontheatre.com. Socially conscious "message" plays alternate with more satiric, comedic works at this venue for upcoming actors. The complex consists of four stages, each with less than a hundred seats, plus a coffeehouse.

Kirk Douglas Theatre 9820 Washington Blvd ☎213/628-2772, ⊛www.centertheatregroup .org. Exhibit A in the renovation of downtown Culver City, a nice sprucing up of the long-closed Culver Theatre into a 300-seater that hosts modern, irreverent, and offbeat productions. Part of the Center Theatre Group, which also runs the stodgier Ahmanson Theatre and Mark Taper Forum.

Knightsbridge Theatre 1944 Riverside Drive, Glendale ☎323/667-0955, ⊛www .knightsbridgetheatre.com. On the edge of Griffith Park, Knightsbridge is a prime spot for classical theater, from Shakespeare to Molière. While you won't recognize most of the names in the cast, you'll likely enjoy the fresh spins on familiar standards.

Latino Theater Company 514 S Spring St, Downtown ☎213/489-0994, ⊛www .latinotheater.com. A new bid to bring modern theater en Espanol into the heart of a gentrifying part of town, in the classic 1907 Security Trust and Savings Bank building. Productions are infrequent, but sometimes interesting.

Lee Strasberg Creative Center 7936 Santa Monica Blvd, West Hollywood ☎323/650-7777, ⊛www.strasberg.com. Although Method acting as once taught by the master Strasberg is plentiful here, all types of plays are performed, with a strong bent toward character-driven pieces. You can sometimes spot stars in the crowd.

Lonnie Chapman Group Repertory 10900 Burbank Blvd, North Hollywood ☏818/700-4878. A troupe that tends toward plays involving serious social themes – though some musicals and comedies are staged, too.

Matrix Theater 7657 Melrose Ave ☏323/852-1445, ⓦwww.matrixtheatre.com. Melrose theater offering good, uncompromising productions that often feature some of LA's better young actors and playwrights, with the occasional Broadway or Hollywood director dropping in to supervise.

Odyssey Theater Ensemble 2055 S Sepulveda Blvd, West LA ☏310/477-2055, ⓦwww.odysseytheatre.com. Well-respected Westside theater company with a modernist bent, offering a range of quality productions on three stages for decent prices.

Open Fist Theatre 1625 N La Brea Ave, Hollywood ☏323/882-6912, ⓦwww.openfist.org. As you might expect from the name, biting and edgy works are often the focus at this small theater company, employing a limited cast of spirited unknowns.

Pacific Resident Theatre 703 Venice Blvd, Venice ☏310/822-8392, ⓦwww.pacificresidenttheatre.com. Solid mix of productions, leaning toward the classics, at this compelling small venue. A ways from the center of the theater action, but worth a visit if you like good, old-fashioned drama.

Powerhouse Theatre 3116 Second St, Santa Monica ☏310/396-3680, ⓦwww.powerhousetheatre.com. On the border of Venice, this alternative theater presents risk-taking experimental shows; perhaps the best of its kind in town. Located in a former electrical station for the old Red Car transit line.

Redcat 631 W 2nd St, Downtown ☏213/237-2800. ⓦwww.redcat.org. Multidisciplinary arts space in Disney Hall and overseen by the estimable California Institute of the Arts (CalArts). A terrific venue for seeing a range of visual art, hearing risk-taking and experimental music, and enjoying multimedia productions that may incorporate dance, theater, poetry, cinema and other forms.

Stages Theatre Center 1540 N McCadden Place, Hollywood ☏323/465-1010, ⓦwww.stagestheatrecenter.com. With three stages offering twenty to one hundred seats, this is an excellent place to catch a wide range of comedies and dramas, including restagings of canonical works and contemporary productions.

Theatre West 3333 Cahuenga Blvd W, Hollywood ☏323/851-7977, ⓦwww.theatrewest.org. A classic venue that's always a good spot to see inventive, sometimes odd, productions by a troupe of excellent young up-and-comers.

Theatricum Botanicum 1419 N Topanga Canyon Blvd, Topanga Canyon ☏310/455-3723, ⓦwww.theatricum.com. Terrific spot showing a range of classic (often Shakespeare) and modern plays amid an idyllic outdoor setting. Founded by Will Geer – TV's Grandpa Walton.

Zephyr Theatre 7456 Melrose Ave ☏323/653-4667. Although featuring a range of acting troupes and plays, the playbill here leans toward socially relevant, issue-related content, occasionally with a bit of irreverence.

Comedy

LA has a broad range of **comedy** clubs. While rising stars and beginners can be spotted on the "underground" open-mike scene, most of the famous comics, both stand-up and improv, appear at the more established clubs in Hollywood, West LA, or the valleys. These venues usually have a bar, charge a $5–20 cover, and put on two shows per evening, generally starting at 8pm and 10.30pm – the later one being more popular. The better-known places are open nightly, but are often solidly booked on weekends.

Acme Comedy Theater 135 N La Brea Ave, Mid-Wilshire ☏323/525-0202, ⓦwww.acmecomedy.com. A fancy venue with mostly sketch and improv comedy, as well as variety and theme-comedy shows. $10–16.

Bang Improv Theater 457 N Fairfax Ave, Mid-Wilshire ☏323/653-6886, ⓦwww.bangstudio.com. One-person shows and long-form improvisation are the specialties at this small theater/comedy club, with the more popular shows running on weekends. $10.

Comedy & Magic Club 1018 Hermosa Ave, Hermosa Beach ⊤310/372-1193, ⊛www .comedyandmagicclub.info. Notable South Bay comedy space where Jay Leno sometimes tests material. Tickets can run up to $30, depending on the performer.

Comedy Store 8433 W Sunset Blvd, West Hollywood ⊤323/656-6225, ⊛www .thecomedystore.com. LA's premier comedy showcase, and popular enough to comprise three rooms – which means there's usually space, even at weekends. Run by Pauly Shore's mom. $15–20.

Empty Stage 2372 Veteran Ave, West LA ⊤310/470-3560, ⊛www.emptystage.com. Sometimes funny, sometimes irritating sketch comedy that draws upon long improv routines, with the odd short comic play as well. Cast mainly with up-and-comers of varying hilarity. $10–15.

Groundlings Theater 7307 Melrose Ave ⊤323/934-4747, ⊛www.groundlings.com. Pioneering venue where only the gifted survive, with furious improv events and high-wire comedy acts that can inspire greatness or groans. Most notable as a training ground for future Saturday Night Live regulars. $12–20.

Ha Ha Café 5010 Lankershim Blvd, North Hollywood ⊤818/508-4995, ⊛www.hahacafe .com. Amateur and a few professional comedians face off for your amusement nightly, at this combination comedy club and café space around the NoHo Arts District. $15.

The Ice House 24 N Mentor Ave, Pasadena ⊤626/577-1894, ⊛www.icehousecomedy .com. The comedy mainstay of the Valley, very established and fairly safe; often amusing, with plenty of old names and the occasional big name. $15–20.

The Improv 8162 Melrose Ave, Mid-Wilshire ⊤323/651-2583, ⊛www.improv.com. Long-standing brick-walled joint known for hosting some of the best acts working in the area, in both stand-up and improv. One of LA's top comedy spots, and the forerunner of a national chain of such clubs – so book ahead. $10–20.

Improv Olympic West 6366 Santa Monica Blvd, Hollywood ⊤323/962-7560, ⊛www.iowest .com. In the heart of old Hollywood, a spot for those who like their improv drawn out and elaborate, with comedy routines more like short theater pieces than a set of wacky one-liners. $5-10.

LA Connection 13442 Ventura Blvd, Sherman Oaks ⊤818/710-1320, ⊛www.laconnection comedy.com. Cozy space for sketch comedy, group antics, and individual jokesters. Often memorable. $7–12.

LA Theatresports 1727 N Vermont Ave #211, Hollywood ⊤323/401-6162, ⊛www.theatre sports.com. As you might guess, comedy competitions here are arranged like sports contests, with plenty of feedback from the audience and all kinds of high-spirited theatrics. Operates a school of comedy and offers lessons in being funny. $5–15.

The Laugh Factory 8001 Sunset Blvd, West Hollywood ⊤323/656-1336, ⊛www .laughfactory.com. Nightly stand-ups of varying standards and reputation, with the odd big name. $18–30.

Second City Studio Theatre 6560 Hollywood Blvd, Hollywood ⊤323/464-8542, ⊛www .secondcity.com. Groundbreaking comedy troupe with numerous branches, this one hosting nightly improv and sketch comedy sometimes built around lengthy routines and theme performances. Mostly up-and-comers. $5–15.

Cabaret

The rediscovery of retro lounge music has transformed LA's **cabaret** scene into a favorite hangout for young, trendy SoCal hipsters (as well as the requisite grizzled old-timers and lounge lizards). The food at most of the venues leaves much to be desired, but it hardly matters to those who attend. Most of the best and biggest cabarets are in Hollywood.

Canter's Kibitz Room 419 N Fairfax Ave, Mid-Wilshire ⊤323/651-2030, ⊛www.cantersdeli .com/kibitzroom. Located next to *Canter's Deli*, one of the more bizarre versions of cabaret in

LA, featuring an assortment of pop, rock, and jazz artists – as well as audience members on open-mike nights – performing in a retro-1950s lounge space. Free.

The Dresden Room 1760 N Vermont Ave, Hollywood ☎323/665-4294, ⊛www.thedresden. com. Iconic local singers doing your favorite easy-listening hits from Wayne Newton to Tom Jones on Tues nights (see "Bars," p.292), as well as a regular husband-and-wife lounge act the rest of the time. No cover, but two-drink minimum.

Gardenia Room 7066 Santa Monica Blvd, Hollywood ☎323/467-7444. Straight-up jazz and adult contemporary tunes presented to a gracious crowd nightly. The odd comedian provides some variation, but music is the real attraction. $10–20, plus two-drink minimum.

Largo 432 N Fairfax Ave, Mid-Wilshire ☎323/852-1073, ⊛www.largo-la.com. Intimate cabaret venue that features a colorful range of singers and acts, along with some of LA's more unusual live bands (though mostly jazz, rock, and pop). Cover varies.

Masquers Cabaret 8334 W Third St, Mid-Wilshire ☎323/653-4848, ⊛www .masquerscabaret.com. Zany comedies, slap-dash variety acts, and energetic drag queens at this spirited nightly dinner theater near the Beverly Center mall. Although not

always successful, the performers here rarely quit trying to amuse the crowd. $8–15.

Ms. Kitty's 6510 Santa Monica Blvd, Hollywood ☎323/466-6111. Strange combination dance club-freakshow where the theme nights may involve club-goers in anything from cartoon character dress-ups to sexual fetish escapades. The entertainment matches the atmosphere, with burlesque, gender-bending cabaret, postmodern erotica, and other things you'll never see on TV back home.

vermont 1714 N Vermont Ave ☎323/661-6163. Chic Cal-cuisine restaurant plays host to Monday-night open-mike cabaret, with a mix of slumming pros and (more commonly) ear-jangling, would-be Streisands screeching to hit the high notes. $5, one-drink minimum.

Vitello's 4349 Tujunga Ave, Studio City ☎818/769-0905. Broadway toe-tappers, old-time jazz, and operatic showstoppers are the norm in this cozy lounge with decent singers, passable Italian food, and just the right sort of funky, downmarket atmosphere. Nightly performances; $10 minimum food and drink purchase.

Film

Some feature **films** are released in LA months (or years) before they play anywhere else in the world, sometimes only showing here and nowhere else. A huge number of cinemas focus on new releases, though there are also plenty of venues for silver-screen classics, independent or art-house films, and foreign movies. Tickets tend to be around $8–11, with cheaper prices for matinees and screenings of films that aren't current releases (around $5–7). **Drive-ins** are rare these days, with a few still left in distant burgs miles from anywhere you might want to find yourself. For **cheap** or **free films**, the USC campus often has interesting free screenings aimed at film students (announced on campus notice-boards), and UCLA's James Bridges Theater shows films drawn from the school's extensive archive (☎310/206-FILM or ⊛www.cinema.ucla.edu).

Of the countless venues for **mainstream cinema**, the most notable are in Westwood and Hollywood. For **art houses** and **revival theaters**, there are a few worthwhile choices, mostly scattered across the Westside. Finally, the grand **movie palaces**, described in greater depth elsewhere in this guide, are here listed only as actual movie theaters; many others have been converted into performing-arts venues, music halls, churches or, depressingly, swap meets and flea markets. The still-functional movie palaces Downtown are still open, once a year in June, for the "Last Remaining Seats" festival (see p.335), run by the LA Conservancy, which you should catch if you have the chance.

Mainstream cinema

AMC Century 15 in the Century City mall, 10250 Santa Monica Blvd, Century City ☎310/289-4AMC. Never mind that it's in a mall – this is one of the best places to see new films in LA. The theaters are somewhat boxy, but if you're after crisp projection, booming sound, comfy seating, and a rapt crowd, there are few better choices.

AMC Loews CityWalk 19 end of Universal City Drive, Burbank ☎818/508-0588. At Universal CityWalk, one of LA's better multiplexes, including a pair of pseudo-Parisian cafés. Despite all the screens, though, only five or six films are typically shown, with multiple theaters reserved for each.

ArcLight 6360 Sunset Blvd, Hollywood ☎323/464-1478. ⓦwww.arclightcinemas.com. Probably the most carefully shown films in LA (for a commercial venue), with all-reserved seats in 14 theaters, top-of-the-line projection, good sightlines, wide seats, and — best of all — the iconic Cinerama Dome, a white hemisphere that has the biggest screen in California.

Beverly Cinemas 13 in the Beverly Center mall, Beverly and La Cienega blvds, Mid-Wilshire ☎310/652-7767. A big mall-house of mostly small screens that show first-run blockbusters and the usual Hollywood product.

Bruin 948 Broxton Ave, Westwood ☎310/208-8998. Aggressive remodelling has made it smaller than it used to be, but this 1930s moviehouse remains a city landmark for its wraparound marquee and sleek Moderne styling.

Fine Arts 8556 Wilshire Blvd, Beverly Hills ☎310/360-0455. Proof that moviehouses that show current releases don't have to be ugly concrete boxes. The simple exterior and lobby give way to a grandly opulent 1936 theater showing a mix of mainstream and art-house films.

IMAX Theater 600 State Drive, at the California Science Center in Exposition Park ☎213/744-7400. Six-story, hemispheric screen showing short, eye-popping documentaries, including the occasional 3D presentation. Mostly science and nature films for kids.

Majestic Crest 1262 Westwood Blvd, Westwood ☎310/474-7866. A riot of neon and flashing lights outside, with glowing murals of Old Hollywood inside. Typically shows Disney flicks.

National 10925 Lindbrook Drive, Westwood ☎310/208-4366. In every way a period piece from the 1960s, a giant, curvaceous 70mm theater that may be on its last legs.

One Colorado 8 42 Miller Alley, Pasadena ☎626/744-1224. Comfortable Old Pasadena venue showing a mix of mainstream and independent productions; convenient for shopping and dining, too.

Regency Fairfax 7907 Beverly Blvd, Mid-Wilshire ☎323/655-4010. Three screens and great old decor, refurbished for independent and art films; located in the middle of the Fairfax District.

Regent 1045 Broxton Ave, Westwood ☎310/208-3259. Restored by the Landmark chain, a fine old favorite for a mainstream flick, in the heart of a neighborhood teeming with great movie theaters.

Village 961 Broxton Ave, Westwood ☎310/248-6266. One of the most enjoyable places to watch a movie in LA, with a giant screen, fine seats, good balcony views, and a modern sound system; it's a frequent spot for Hollywood premieres. Come early and take a look at the marvelous 1931 exterior, particularly the white spire on top.

Arthouses and revival theaters

Aero 1328 Montana Ave, Santa Monica ☎310/466-FILM, ⓦwww.aerotheatre.com. The American Cinematheque film organization, presents classic and art-house movies in this fine old venue from 1940 (often the same fare playing at the organization's Egyptian; see below). The fare is eclectic and intelligently programmed.

Bing at the LA County Art Museum, 5905 Wilshire Blvd, Mid-Wilshire ☎323/857-6010. Offers engaging retrospectives highlighting famed actors and directors, as well as full-priced evening programs of classic, independent, foreign, art-house, and revival cinema.

Los Feliz 1822 N Vermont Ave, Hollywood ☎323/664-2169. Having successfully avoided a descent into the porn-movie market in the 1960s, this theater now shows international and low-budget American independent fare on its three small screens.

Monica 4-Plex 1332 Second St, Santa Monica ☎310/394-9741. An antidote to the big houses showing mainstream schlock on the Third Street Promenade, this is the closest nearby theater (a block away) where you can see a mix of indie and art-house fare.

New Beverly Cinema 7165 Beverly Blvd, Mid-Wilshire ☎323/938-4038. Worthwhile for its excellent art films and revival screenings, with some imaginative double bills.

Nuart 11272 Santa Monica Blvd, West LA ☎310/281-8223. Showing rarely seen classics, documentaries, and edgy foreign-language films, this is the place to catch independent filmmakers testing their work. Sometimes offers brief December previews of Oscar contenders weeks or months before they're released nationwide.

NuWilshire 1314 Wilshire Blvd, Santa Monica ☎310/394-8099. With a solid booking policy, this is one of LA's better venues for indie and foreign films, located a mile east of Palisades Park.

Old Town Music Hall 140 Richmond St, El Segundo ☎310/322-2592, ⓦwww.otmh.org. An old-fashioned spot to see historic movies, with accompanying organ or piano music on some nights; unfortunately sited in a grim industrial location south of LAX. Tickets $20.

Royal 11523 Santa Monica Blvd, West LA ☎310/477-5581. Though it doesn't quite live up to its regal name, this is still a prime spot for independent fare in a spacious, classically ornamented theater.

Silent Movie 611 N Fairfax Ave, Mid-Wilshire ☎323/655-2520, ⓦwww.silentmovietheatre.com. Offers an enjoyable mix of silent comedies and adventure flicks – Douglas Fairbanks swashbucklers and the like – along with darker fare like Fritz Lang's Metropolis and even the occasional talkie.

Sunset 5 8000 Sunset Blvd, West Hollywood ☎323/848-3500. This arthouse complex sits on the second floor of the Sunset Plaza shopping center – former site of the legendary Schwab's drugstore – and shows a good assortment of edgy, independent flicks.

Vista 4473 Sunset Drive, Hollywood ☎323/660-6639. A nicely renovated moviehouse with very eclectic offerings – from mindless action flicks to micro-budgeted indie productions – located near the intersection of Sunset and Hollywood boulevards.

Movie palaces

Listed here are historic theaters where you can see regularly scheduled films amid the splendor of the golden age of theatrical architecture. For information on movie palaces that are generally closed, such as the Los Angeles (see p.62), Orpheum (see p.62), Palace (see p.62), Rialto (see p.198), and refer to individual descriptions in the guide.

Avalon 1 Casino Way, Santa Catalina Island ☎310/510-0179. Located in the stunning Casino building, this great old moviehouse is a riot of mermaid murals, gold-leaf motifs, and an overall design sometimes called "Aquarium Deco." Also presents regular mainstream movies and a yearly silent-film fest.

Chinese 6925 Hollywood Blvd, Hollywood ☎323/464-8111. Its forecourt thick with tourists and wild chinoiserie design, this Hollywood icon shows relentlessly mainstream films, but is still worthy of all the postcard images (see p.101). Part of the Hollywood & Highland complex.

Egyptian 6712 Hollywood Blvd, Hollywood ☎323/466-FILM, ⓦwww.americancinematheque.com. Thanks to the American Cinematheque film group, this historic 1922 moviehouse has nightly showings of revival, experimental, and art films, and has been lovingly restored as a kitschy masterpiece of Egyptian Revival – all grand columns, winged scarabs, and mythological gods (see p.100).

El Capitan 6834 Hollywood Blvd, Hollywood ☎323/467-7674. Whether or not you enjoy the typically kiddie-oriented fare offered in this Disney-owned venue, the twice-restored splendor of this classic Hollywood movie palace is bound to impress.

Warner Grand 478 W Sixth St, San Pedro ☎310/548-7672, ⓦwww.warnergrand.org. Definitely worth a trip down to LA Harbor to see the glory of this restored 1931 Zigzag Moderne masterpiece, with its dark geometric details, majestic columns, and sunburst motifs – a style that almost looks pre-Columbian. Having fallen into disuse for many years, the theater is now a repertory cinema and performing-arts hall.

Gay and lesbian LA

lthough nowhere near as nationally prominent as San Francisco's, LA's **gay and lesbian scene** is similarly well-established, and the city as a whole is generally quite welcoming in its urban core and inner suburbs (though the further into the exurbs you go, the less tolerance you'll find). The best known gay-friendly area is the city of **West Hollywood**, which has become synonymous with the (affluent, white) gay lifestyle, not just in LA but all over California. Santa Monica Boulevard, east of Doheny Drive and west of Fairfax Avenue, in particular has a wide range of restaurants, shops, and bars aimed at gay men, though less flashy lesbian-oriented businesses can also be found here and there. West Hollywood is also the site of LA's exuberant **Gay Pride Parade**, held annually in June. Another well-established community with a strong gay and lesbian presence is **Silver Lake**, especially along Hyperion Boulevard and part of Sunset Boulevard. Even Orange County has its pockets of gay and lesbian culture, mainly on the coast, and especially in the upscale confines of **Laguna Beach's** trendy restaurants and bars.

Gay couples will find themselves readily accepted at most LA **hotels**, but there are a few that focus on gay travelers, and they can also be useful sources of information on the scene in general. Listed below, too, are **restaurants**, **bars**, and **clubs** that cater mainly to gay men and lesbians.

▲ Gay Pride Parade participants

The most-read local gay publication, though it's also distributed nationally, is *The Advocate* (® www.advocate.com); other gay-oriented publications feature weekly club and event listings, community information and topical articles, and can be found at eateries and retailers around LA – often for free.

Accommodation

See the box on p.242 for information on accommodation pricing.

Coral Sands 1730 N Western Ave, Hollywood ® 1-800/467-5141, ® www.coralsands-la.com. Cruisy spot exclusively geared towards gay men. All rooms face the inner courtyard pool. Also with on-site sauna, Jacuzzi, and gym. $79.

Holloway Motel 8465 Santa Monica Blvd, West Hollywood ® 323/654-2454, ® www .hollowaymotel.com. Typical clean roadside motel, if rather dreary looking. Rates include complimentary breakfast. Add $50 during key holidays like Halloween and Gay Pride. $95.

Hollywood Metropolitan 5825 Sunset Blvd ® 323/962-5800, ® www.metropolitanhotel .com. Spanish-style hotel hotel with a mix

of small, comfortable rooms with mini-fridges, and larger suites. Just off the 101 freeway. $95.

Ramada Plaza Suites 8585 Santa Monica Blvd, West Hollywood ® 310/652-6400 or 1-800/845-8585, ® www.ramadaweho.com. A modern place that has clean and comfortable rooms with high-speed Net access, a pool and a gym; located in the center of the community. $149.

San Vicente Inn 854 N San Vicente Blvd, West Hollywood ® 310/854-6915, ® www.gayresort .com. Small and comfortable bed-and-breakfast located just north of Santa Monica Boulevard, with pool, spa, and sauna. $119 per night, $149 with private bath.

Restaurants and cafés

The Abbey 692 N Robertson Blvd ® 310/289-8410. A popular spot for excellent, all-American food and drink that increasingly caters to a mixed crowd, with a positive,

upbeat vibe and sizable lounge with convivial atmosphere. Often packed, though.

Champagne French Bakery 8917 Santa Monica Blvd, West Hollywood ® 310/657-4051.

Convenient bakery and coffee shop with serviceable pastries and baked treats in a central location – good for an inexpensive breakfast or lunch on the main drag. One of several LA locations.

Coffee Table **2930 Rowena Ave, Los Feliz** ☎323/644-8111. A neighborhood coffeehouse with low-fat sandwiches and health food, along with a smattering of tasty desserts.

Fat Fish **616 N Robertson Blvd, West Hollywood** ☎310/659-3882. Enjoyable and upscale pan-Asian and Cal-cuisine restaurant with inventive cocktails and good sushi.

French Quarter **7985 Santa Monica Blvd, West Hollywood** ☎310/654-0898. Inside the French Market Place, a New Orleans–themed restaurant that's more of a draw for its convivial atmosphere than its inauthentic cuisine.

Golden Bull **170 W Channel Rd, Pacific Palisades** ☎310/230-0402. Old-style steak-and-seafood restaurant and bar with a relaxed atmosphere near the ocean, not far from Santa Monica.

Marix Tex-Mex Playa **118 Entrada Drive, Pacific Palisades** ☎310/459-8596. Flavorful fajitas and big margaritas in this rowdy beachfront cantina, which attracts mixed gay and straight crowds. An even livelier branch at 1108 N Flores St, West Hollywood ☎323/656-8800.

Mark's **861 N La Cienega Blvd, West Hollywood** ☎310/652-5252. Familiar stand-by for Cal-cuisine, dishing up the likes of crab cakes, osso bucco, and lamb chops.

Woody's at the Beach **1305 S Coast Hwy, Laguna Beach** ☎949/376-8809. Upscale bar and restaurant in Orange County, serving quality California cuisine to a fairly well-heeled clientele.

Yukon Mining Co **7328 Santa Monica Blvd, West Hollywood** ☎323/851-8833. Colorful 24-hr coffee shop doling out basic diner food, where you're likely to see an odd mix of drag queens, Russian immigrants, and old-timers.

Bars and clubs

Mid-Wilshire

Faultline **4216 Melrose Ave** ☎323/660-0889. Denim-and-leather bear scene with plenty of frenetic action inside – driving house beats and testosterone-fueled mayhem. Near Koreatown.

Jewel's Catch One **4067 W Pico Blvd** ☎323/734-8849. Longtime favorite on the local club scene, a sweaty barn catering to a mixed crowd and covering two wild dance floors.

The Plaza **739 N La Brea Ave** ☎323/939-0703. Nondescript joint hosts wild, mind-blowing drag shows before a Latino, mostly gay crowd. Power up for the night by munching on monster hot dogs from neighboring *Pink's* (see p.262).

Silver Lake

Akbar **4356 Sunset Blvd** ☎323/665-6810. A mellow and unpretentious Silver Lake watering hole that draws a diverse, bohemian crowd, including a loyal coterie of gay visitors. No cover.

Cobalt Cantina **4326 Sunset Blvd** ☎323/953-9991. A low-key, elegant bar and restaurant where the stylish interior and well-scrubbed yuppie patrons contrast dramatically with the scruffy neighborhood outside.

Eagle LA **4219 Santa Monica Blvd** ☎323/669-9472. Very popular hairy/daddy scene with grungy but friendly vibe and various fetish nights. Male-dominated, but open to women, too.

Le Bar **2375 Glendale Blvd** ☎323/660-7595. Quiet and welcoming bar in a bland section of Silver Lake. Not as much attitude as in some West Hollywood spots. No cover.

MJ's **2810 Hyperion Ave** ☎323/660-1503. Thumping neighborhood hangout with diverse gay-male customers, along with a few bohemian straights. Theme nights include jaw-dropping dance scenes like Tuesday night's "Rim Job" and Thursday's "Porn Palace."

Hollywood

Arena **6655 Santa Monica Blvd** ☎323/462-0714. Many clubs under one roof, large dance-floors throbbing to funk, house, and hi-NRG grooves, and sometimes live bands and outrageous drag shows (also see p.298). Cover can reach $20 or more.

Dragstrip 66 at Safari Sam's, 5214 Sunset Blvd ☎ 323/969-2596. Although it's moved around in recent years, this upbeat drag party is worth following (second Sat of the month) for all the pouting and preening you'd expect, to a soundtrack of punchy electronica and rock 'n roll sleaze. $15.

Spotlight 1601 N Cahuenga Blvd ☎ 323/467-2425. The place to be if you want the feel of an old-time 1970s gay bar, with a mildly raunchy dive atmosphere, affordable drinks, and a gently buzzing scene. The place has somehow endured since the 1960s.

West Hollywood

7969 7969 Santa Monica Blvd ☎ 323/654-0280. Legendary club offering high-energy dance tunes, frenetic DJs, and colorful theme-party nights.

The Factory 652 N La Peer Drive ☎ 310/659-4551. DJs spin house music most nights of the week at what is one of West Hollywood's more popular clubs. Friday-night Girl Bar is a long-established lesbian party scene.

FUBAR 7994 Santa Monica Blvd ☎ 323/654-0396. If you recognize the acronym, you'll know what you're in for at this high-energy club, a popular scene that offers regular karaoke and dance events, plus "Locker Room Saturdays" that are better seen than described.

Micky's 8857 Santa Monica Blvd ☎ 310/657-1176. Lively, pulsating scene with a full range of club nights, including the usual retro-70s and -80s dance-pop, thundering house, and hip-hop beats, and twice-weekly drag shows. A draw for straights as well.

Miyagi's 8225 Sunset Blvd ☎ 323/650-3524. Three-story dance club with house and

electronica sounds, free-spirited crowd, five liquor bars, and assorted sushi bars.

Mother Lode 8944 Santa Monica Blvd ☎ 310/659-9700. Strong drinks, wild dancing to house and hi-NRG music, karaoke, and periodic drag antics make this one of the more colorful area clubs.

Normandie Room 8737 Santa Monica Blvd ☎ 310/659-6204. Long-standing, if smallish, lesbian hangout that draws a big weekend crowd for its stiff drinks, pool table, comfortable atmosphere, and relaxed neighborhood vibe.

The Palms 8572 Santa Monica Blvd ☎ 310/652-6188. Usually house and pop-music dance nights at West Hollywood's most established lesbian bar, which increasingly caters to a mixed crowd.

Rage 8911 Santa Monica Blvd ☎ 310/652-7055. Very flashy gay men's club and neighborhood favorite, playing the latest house to a long-established crowd.

Ultra Suede 661 N Robertson Blvd ☎ 310/659-4551. Featuring various club nights where a mixed gay and straight crowd gyrates to new wave, rock, house, and retro-pop music.

San Fernando Valley

Club Fuel 11608 Ventura Blvd, Studio City ☎ 818/506-0404. San Fernando Valley club that regularly hosts theme dance parties, with electronica, retro-disco, and garage among the musical offerings.

Oil Can Harry's 11502 Ventura Blvd, Studio City ☎ 818/760-9749. Engaging San Fernando Valley club with a mix of theme nights, including country-and-western line dancing, 1970s disco, a leather scene, and more.

16

GAY AND LESBIAN LA | Bars and clubs

Sports and outdoor activities

os Angeles has plenty of **sports** and **outdoor activities** to keep you occupied, wherever your interests may lie. Angelenos don't have the same feverish, die-hard enthusiasm for spectator sports as do, say, New Yorkers or Chicagoans, they still often make a good showing at basketball, baseball, and hockey games, as well as college football contests; the hometown USC Trojans are consistent national performers. If you can't make it to a sporting event, there are always **sports bars** where you can catch local teams on television and knock back a few brews as well.

However, when most people think about LA sports, it's not team sports but participatory sports like **surfing**, along with more self-conscious pursuits like bodybuilding, that comes to mind. Much of the stereotype of Southern California as a body-fixated culture can be depressingly accurate at times, but you can usually enjoy yourself without worrying about clothes, attitude, or abs.

Water and **beach sports** are still the city's main claims to fame, be they swimming or surfing along the coast, snorkeling or scuba diving around Santa Catalina Island, or even kayaking and jet-skiing. If you'd rather not get wet, you can always try a bit of in-line skating, skateboarding, or bicycling along strips like the Venice Boardwalk, or simply suntanning at the beach. **Airborne activities** include ballooning above the LA basin, hang gliding off precarious seaside cliffs, or just taking a safe helicopter tour. If you want to sweat, you can choose from **fitness sports** such as jogging, rock climbing, and hiking – not to mention working out in a fitness club. Just as strenuous, **skiing** and **snowboarding** are both possible in the mountains east of LA, especially around the Big Bear region, a favorite weekend getaway for many locals. If all this sounds like too much work, there are plenty of other **leisure activities**, like horseback riding, fishing, and bowling, to keep you occupied.

Spectator sports

LA's **spectator sports** are just as exciting to watch as any in the country – though you can expect less enthusiasm here for the home squad than you'd find on the East Coast. For most LA locals, team sports are a diversion, not a way of life.

Baseball

LA has two area major-league **baseball teams**, playing from mid-April to early October: the **Dodgers** (☎323/224-1-HIT, ⓦwww.dodgers.com), who play at the top-notch Dodger Stadium in Chavez Ravine, northwest of Downtown, and the **Angels** (☎714/663-9000 or 1-888/796-4256, ⓦwww.angelsbaseball.com), who play at drab, ugly Anaheim Stadium out in Orange County; the Angels' owner renamed them for Los Angeles instead of Anaheim in the 2005 season.

The Dodgers are historically the more triumphant and beloved franchise, having relocated from Brooklyn in the late 1950s and pulled off a number of glory years in the 1970s and 80s – though they've taken some hits in recent years for being consistently overpaid and underachieving. Whereas the Dodgers last won a world championship back in 1988, the Angels had their best season in 2002, getting to and winning the World Series for the first time. Unlike the Dodgers, the Angels have made the playoffs regularly in recent years – most recently in 2007. Tickets for both teams are easy to get, with games generally running $8–45 for most seats.

Basketball

Basketball's flashy **LA Lakers** (☎213/480-3232 or 310/426-6000, ⓦwww.lakers.com) have boasted such luminaries through the years as Kareem Abdul-Jabbar, Magic Johnson, and Shaquille O'Neal, and have won a total of thirteen championships, including three in a row through 2002. Led by Kobe Bryant after the departure of O'Neal, the current version of the team is not that great, but games are still a hot ticket. They play at the Staples Center in Downtown LA; tickets run from $13 to more than $275, but can be hard to come by.

The lesser light in LA's basketball galaxy, the **LA Clippers** (☎213/742-7430, ⓦwww.clippers.com), have a

▲ LA Lakers vs New Orleans Hornets at the Staples Center

history of shocking ineptitude, and rarely make the playoffs; games are also held at the Staples Center, with seats running $12–250, and you should have no problem getting a ticket – unless the Lakers are the opponent. The NBA **season** runs from November through late April, not including the playoffs.

The **Los Angeles Sparks** (☎1-877/44-SPARKS, ⓦwww.wnba.com/sparks) is one of fourteen teams playing nationally in the WNBA women's basketball league. As with the other local basketball squads, the Sparks play their home games at the Staples Center, though on a summertime schedule (May–Aug).

Football

Los Angeles has had no professional **football** teams since 1995, and few locals seem to care. However, college ball is another story: Pasadena's 102,000-seat **Rose Bowl** (☎626/577-3101, ⓦwww.rosebowlstadium.com) hosts one of the four Bowl Championship Series games to decide the championship, and is also the home field for UCLA's respectable football team (tickets $17–47; ☎310/825-2101, Ⓦuclabruins.cstv.com), who play there a half-dozen times during the autumn. The top-notch USC squad also plays in historic digs, at the LA Coliseum in South Central (tickets $35–60; ☎213/740-GOSC, Ⓦusctrojans.ocsn .com), site of the 1932 and 1984 Olympics. Ticket prices can vary widely depending on the opponent (usually $50 and up) and whether the school has recently won a championship. All games are played on Saturdays throughout fall.

Hockey

Hockey in LA didn't mean much until the late 1980s, when the **LA Kings** (☎1-888/KINGS-LA, Ⓦwww .lakings.com) traded for superstar Wayne Gretzky from the champion Edmonton Oilers. Gretzky's long gone from these parts, and the Kings have since moved from the Forum to the Staples Center; seats are $29–126. The **Anaheim Ducks**, in Orange County, play at Honda Center in Anaheim (☎714/704-2500, Ⓦducks.nhl.com)

and won the Stanley Cup in 2006; tickets $17–175. The NHL season lasts throughout the winter and into early spring, when the playoffs take place.

Soccer

One of the newer teams in town, the **LA Galaxy** (☎1-877/3-GALAXY, Ⓦwww.lagalaxy.com) plays **soccer** in the MLS (Major League Soccer), and games take place at the Home Depot Center, in the city of Carson in the South Bay. The season runs much of the year, save winter; tickets $20–75.

Horse racing

Horse racing is a fairly popular spectator sport in the LA area, which has two main tracks. **Santa Anita**, in the San Gabriel Valley town of Arcadia at 285 W Huntington Drive, has an autumn and winter season (☎626/574-7223, Ⓦwww.santaanita.com); while **Hollywood Park**, 1050 S Prairie Ave in Inglewood, has a spring-to-autumn season (☎310/419-1500, Ⓦwww .hollywoodpark.com).

Water and beach sports

Many visitors to LA head straight for the ocean. Along the sands from Malibu to Orange County, you can find any number of options for **water** and **beach sports** to keep you busy. Among more passive pleasures at the seaside, **suntanning** with the crowds is always a popular option.

Swimming, snorkeling, and scuba diving

Although you'd never believe it from watching TV, **swimming** in many LA coastal areas is definitely not recommended. As a rule, the further you go from most city piers, the better off you are. Piers, along with run-off pipes and channels, are sources of water-borne contamination, particular after heavy rains. (For more info, see Ⓦwww.healthebay.org, or the box on p.138.)

The beaches closer to Malibu, Palos Verdes, and Orange County are usually less crowded and safer than those around Santa Monica and Venice, though any spots near LA Harbor are to be avoided. **Parking** at major strips of sand will cost you upwards of $6-8, even for a short time, but you can usually find roadside spots where you can park if you want to take a dip along the rockier coves and crags. Similarly, **snorkeling** and **scuba diving** are better experienced well away from LA in places like Santa Catalina Island.

Prices for excursions to see Catalina's astounding undersea life, kelp forest, and shipwrecks can vary widely, but expect to pay at least $90–120 for any trip. Lover's Cove, a marine preserve just east of Avalon, is the best spot to view the local sea life close-up, though only snorkeling is allowed.

Catalina Dive Shop at Lover's Cove, Santa Catalina Island ☎1-877/SNORKEL, ⊛www .catalinadiveshop.com. Provides ecological tours, snorkeling equipment for rent (generally $35 per day for a decent package), and underwater cameras for sale.

Catalina Divers Supply Avalon Casino and pier, Avalon ☎310/510-0330 or 1-800/353-0330, ⊛www.catalinadiverssupply.com. Leads undersea tours ($50–110) around Santa Catalina and rents scuba and snorkeling equipment; $27 per day for a complete snorkel set, and $55 for the full scuba package.

Descanso Beach Ocean Sports PO Box 386, Avalon 90704 ☎310/510-1558, ⊛www .kayakcatalinaisland.com. Offering kayaking and snorkeling trips and hourly, half-day, or two-day rental packages, running anywhere from $16 to $64.

Scuba Luv 126 Catalina Ave, Avalon ☎310/510-2350, ⊛www.scubaluv.com. Good introductory dives for beginners, daily snorkel tours for $50–60, and basic, overnight trips to the island, running $238–377 per person – though more elaborate versions are available, too.

Sundiver 5901 Warner Ave #410, Huntington Beach ☎562/594-6968 or 1-800/955-9446, ⊛www.sundiver.net. Popular package deals include boating trips to area islands for one or two days of scuba diving; prices vary widely.

Surfing, windsurfing, kayaking, and jet-skiing

Since railroad magnate Henry Huntington first began importing Hawaiian talent in 1907 to publicize his Red Car route in the South Bay, **surfing** has been big business in LA and has made a major impact on the city's culture and image. If you want to give the sport a try, head to where the surfers are: along the Malibu section of the Pacific Coast Highway from Surfrider to Leo Carrillo beaches and around Point Dume; along the South Bay in towns like Manhattan Beach and Hermosa Beach; and at Orange County beaches from Huntington to San Clemente. Don't worry about buying equipment, though: **surfboards** are available for rent by the hour from rental shacks up and down the coast.

If you've never been **windsurfing**, a trip to LA might not be the ideal time to start, given the often challenging conditions. But for the confident, several coastal outlets rent windsurfers by the hour or day. The newer sport of **kiteboarding** may be even more challenging: you hold onto a large kite while standing on a board, and let the wind pull you along the waves. Lessons can be very expensive. Somewhat easier is **kayaking**, and the ocean-going kayaks that you can rent are more basic and manageable than river kayaks; many are two-seaters. Finally, there's **jet-skiing**, a popular choice. It will cost you around $100 to rent a machine for a half-day of splashing around Santa Monica Bay or elsewhere.

Alfredo's Beach Rentals ten locations citywide, info at ☎562/434-6121, ⊛www.alfredosbeach club.com. Rents kayaks for around $10–20 per hour, bikes and inline skates for $10 and hour, and pedal boats for $15 an hour.

Catalina Ocean Rafting 103 Pebbly Beach Rd, Avalon ☎1-800/990-RAFT or 310/510-0211, ⊛www.catalinaoceanrafting.com. Takes groups out in small, flat "ocean rafts" to tour the seaside world. Half-day trips for $99 per person, or $189 for a full day.

Kayaks on the Water 5411 E Ocean Blvd, Long Beach ☎562/434-0999, ⊛www.kayakrentals .net. Good location for affordable kayak rentals, with singles at $8 per hour and doubles for $12–15. April–Sept only.

Long Beach Windsurf Center 3850 E Ocean Blvd, Long Beach ☎562/433-1014, ⊛www .windsurfcenter.com. Located near the Belmont Pier, this operator rents in-line skates and kayaks for $10–20 per hour; windsurfers run upwards of $25–30 per hour.

Offshore Watersports 128 E Shoreline Drive, Long Beach ☎562/436-1996, ⊛www .owsrentals.com. Has new jet skis, or wave runners, for $125 per hour, or fishing boat rental for $85 per half-day.

Southwind Kayak Center 17855 Sky Park Circle, Irvine ☎1-800/SOUTHWIND, ⊛www.south windkayaks.com. Orange County operator with rental spots in Newport Beach (call for location). Kayak rentals from $14–20 per hour for singles and doubles, or $50–65 per day. Excellent for beaches further south.

West End Dive Center Santa Catalina Island, at Two Harbors ☎310/510-0303 ext 272 or 1-800/785-8425, ⊛www.visitcatalinaisland.com /twoharbors. Specializes in kayak and scuba trips, with an array of package deals starting at $49 for a basic guided dive. Kayaks and bikes rent for $15–20 per hour, or $48–68 for a full day.

Zuma Jay Surfboards 22775 Pacific Coast Hwy, Malibu ☎310/456-8044, ⊛www.zumajays.com. Solid choice for boards near some major waves. Expect to pay $20–25 per day, plus $10 for a wetsuit in winter months.

Rollerblading and bicycling

Inline skating, or **rollerblading**, is enormously popular along the Venice Boardwalk and other beachside paths, and in certain parks and recreation zones. The famed **cycling path** from Santa Monica to Palos Verdes is a terrific route for exploring the seacoast of the metropolis. This oceanside path is also the main choice for **bicycling** in LA, even though there are myriad bike paths throughout the region, from the peaceful, leafy setting of the Arroyo Seco to the post-apocalyptic landscape of the LA River. You can rent a bike for as little as $6–8 per hour off the beaten trail, but the beachfront is the only place with a good selection of dealers, who may charge $10–15 an hour for skates or bikes, depending on the equipment. (Note also the kayak, rafting and diving operators listed above, many of

which also rent bikes and skates.)

Bikestation 221 E First St, Long Beach ☎562/436-BIKE, ⊛www.bikestation.org. Offers bicycle rental, repair, and storage, and even valet bike-parking.

California Association of Bicycling Organizations ☎310/639-9348, ⊛www.cabobike.org. Good online source of maps and information, plus regular updates of California laws and municipal strategies affecting cyclists.

California Department of Transportation (CalTrans) LA office at 100 S Main St, Downtown ☎213/897-3656, ⊛www.dot.ca.gov. Perhaps the most comprehensive source of guides and maps for the LA urban area and region, showing which commuter arterials are best for cycling, and which should be avoided.

Perry's Café and Rentals 100, 2500 & 3100 Ocean Front Walk, Venice ☎310/904-4849, ⊛www .perryscafe.com; 930 Pacific Coast Hwy, Santa Monica ☎310/260-1114; 1200 PCH, Santa Monica ☎310/458-3975; and on the Santa Monica Pier ☎310/393-9778. A mini-chain of oceanside rental spots where the bikes and skates go for $20–25 per day or $7–10 per hour.

Sea Mist 1619 Ocean Front Walk, Venice ☎310/395-7076. Located opposite the Venice Pier, with affordable bike and skate rentals for $5–7 per hour, or around $15 per day.

Segway LA 1660 Ocean Ave, Santa Monica ☎310/395-1395 ⊛www.segway.la. If you don't mind looking a bit goofy, you can rent one of these peculiar upright cycles ($75 per two hours) for tooling around the city or oceanfront. Your standup travel is sure to attract plenty of attention.

Spokes 'n' Stuff 1715 Ocean Front Walk, Santa Monica ☎310/395-4748. Among the better choices among many similar bike-rental agents along the sands; $8–10 per hour minimum. In Griffith Park, the outfit has a branch near the LA Zoo, at 4400 Crystal Springs Drive (☎323/662-6573).

Airborne activities

If you want to rise above the smog, LA has several worthwhile **airborne activities** of interest. The most affordable is **hang gliding**, in which you hang from a flexible or rigid-wing glider to drift down from a hill, mountain, or cliff on air currents, and slowly come to a safe landing. experienced hang gliders bring their gliders to the bluffs overlooking the Pacific near Point Fermin for a strikingly picturesque trip over the sea cliffs and toward the beach.

An appealing alternative is **soaring** in enclosed gliders, again using air currents to rise and fall. A ride in one of these simple craft can be memorable, if not quite as awe-inspiring as that of hang gliding. You'll doubtless spend most of your time watching from the back seat of the glider, while the pilot controls the flight, but it's bound to be a vivid experience.

A **helicopter ride** may provide all the airborne excitement you need, allowing you to view some of LA's premier sights, like the Hollywood sign, from thousands of feet above the ground. There are a number of different packages and tours available, all at fairly steep prices. The most expensive, and most conventional, mode of flying is also available – an **airplane trip** in a single- or twin-engine craft flying from private or commercial airports.

Blue Skies Aviation 7535 Valjean Ave #4, Van Nuys, San Fernando Valley ☏818/901-1489, ⓦwww.blueskiesaviation.com. For those who have at least a student pilot's license, a wide range of prop-plane rentals, including aerobatic models, for $84–210 per hour.

Bravo Aviation Berth 75, Ports 'o Call Village, San Pedro ☏310/263-7669, ⓦwww.bravoair .com. Short, 20min helicopter excursions in the South Bay for $109, and half-hour-long overhead tours of Long Beach's and San Pedro's top sights for $159.

Great Western Soaring 32810 165th St E, Llano, north of LA in the Antelope Valley ☏661/944-9449, ⓦwww.greatwesternsoaring.com. Provides gliders and lessons, at a cost of

$96 for a basic lesson, up to $176 for a more involved ride.

Group 3 Aviation 16425 Hart St, Van Nuys Airport, San Fernando Valley ☏818/994-9376, ⓦwww.group3aviation.com. Takes movie-oriented helicopter trips from central LA to various points along the coast (from $160–275).

Windsports Soaring Center 12623 Gridley St, Sylmar ☏818/367-2430, ⓦwww.windsports .com. A well-known hang-gliding tour and rental outlet. For around $120, they will give you the basic experience, but if you want a greater challenge, more expensive package deals are available for $200.

Fitness activities and extreme sports

LA's preoccupation with tanned, muscular, and silicone-boosted physiques is most evident in the city's vigorous pursuit of **fitness activities**. For some, the goal is simply to keep their body in shape, while others zealously worship it or test its physical limits with **extreme sports**.

Fitness activities

For a dose of LA's health mania, try **working out** at a fitness club or along the beach. Whether you've come to pump iron yourself or to watch the weightlifters go through their paces, there are few better spots than **Muscle Beach** near the Venice Boardwalk – although having well-developed abs and biceps is essential if you're planning to participate. Contact the Venice Beach Recreation Center, 1800 Ocean Front Walk (☏310/399-2775), for more information on bench-pressing with the local iron-pumpers. If you're not quite there yet,

the exercise and training equipment just south of the **Santa Monica Pier** should start you on your way, but for less conspicuous bodybuilding and training, LA's numerous **health clubs** are everywhere, with Gold's Gym among the most prominent.

If you want to go **jogging**, stick to the safer Westside. Although Hollywood would at first seem like a dubious choice for exercising, the steeply inclined paths and fine views of Runyon Canyon Park make for an excellent workout (enter off Mulholland Drive or Fuller Avenue), as does the circuit around Lake Hollywood. Elsewhere, the best paths for joggers include the green median strip of San Vicente Boulevard from Brentwood to Santa Monica; Sunset Boulevard through Beverly Hills and Westwood (not Hollywood); the Arroyo Seco in Pasadena; and most stretches along the beach – except near the LA Harbor.

Also along the beach, you may be able to join a **volleyball** game at any of the sandy courts from Santa Monica to Marina del Rey. Hermosa Beach is another good choice for volleyball (the city famously hosts competitions throughout the year), as are Orange County's Huntington and Laguna beaches. There are **tennis** courts all over LA, with space available for visitors at city parks (notably Griffith Park) and universities. Call the city's Department of Recreation and Parks for more information on reserving a court (℡213/485-5555).

The best workout in town is also one of the cheapest. **Hiking** in LA doesn't have the same reputation as it does in other parts of California, but you can do some serious hiking here. The Santa Monica Mountains – a huge natural preserve west of LA and north of Malibu – have many different trails and routes for exploration, most of which feature jaw-dropping scenery, copious wildlife, and interesting rustic sights. In the mountains, the section of Mulholland Highway west of the 405 freeway is known as "Dirt Mulholland," and is closed to auto traffic for seven rutted, uneven miles that are popular with hikers and bikers.

Audubon Society **at Plummer Park, 7377 Santa Monica Blvd, West Hollywood** ℡323/876-0202, Ⓦwww.laaudubon.org. Provides periodic guided hikes (event line ℡323/874-1318) through the Santa Monica Mountains and other LA-area nature zones, as well as information on their various chirping and warbling denizens. Operates a bookstore and library at its headquarters; Mon–Thurs 9.30am–4pm.

California Department of Parks ℡818/880-0350, Ⓦwww.parks.ca.gov. Good source of information and maps, especially online, where you can get an overview of each state park and its resources.

Hiking in LA **15230 Ventura Blvd, Sherman Oaks, San Fernando Valley 91403** ℡818/501-1005. A private group that offers treks through the Santa Monica Mountains in several foreign languages, as well as English. Part of JRT International.

LA Trails Ⓦwww.latrail.com. Good, all-around website for exploring the paths and trails of the region, from simple paved concourses to steep mountain scrambles.

Santa Monica Mountains Conservancy ℡310/589-3200, Ⓦlamountains.com. The leader in efforts to preserve land in the mountains and ensure public access. Also a good source of information about the region at visitor centers in Franklin Canyon, Downtown, Pacific Palisades, and Ramirez Canyon.

Santa Monica Mountains Visitor Center **401 W Hillcrest Drive, Thousand Oaks** ℡805/370-2301, Ⓦwww.nps.gov/samo. Offers maps and information on hiking trails and parks in the area. Located in a neighboring city just north of LA. Daily 9am–5pm.

Sierra Club **3435 Wilshire Blvd #320, Mid-Wilshire** ℡213/387-4287, Ⓦangeles.sierraclub .org. Major political and environmental advocacy group that offers information on local natural areas, and conducts hikes and tours of key ecological zones.

Extreme sports

Sports such as hang gliding or kayaking can be taken to death-defying limits, but LA also has a taste for some other daring **extreme sports**.

The original "extreme sport" was arguably **skateboarding**, and in the 1970s LA quickly became a trailblazer and dominant force in the high-flying version of this sport. Slightly more sedate, though potentially just as thrilling, **rock climbing** is offered in private rock "clubs" or "gyms" where you can scale vertical surfaces to your heart's content (rental equipment is available for an additional fee). For a closeup look at the sport without paying a dime, turn up at Stony Point near Chatsworth, in the San Fernando Valley, to watch crowds of hardcore rock enthusiasts dangling by their fingertips.

For sheer terror, **bungee jumping** is hard to beat, though it's lost a little

SPORTS AND OUTDOOR ACTIVITIES | Fitness activities and extreme sports

328

luster since its 1990s heyday, and there are far fewer operators in the business nowadays. Powering a **motocross** dirtbike around desert washes and boulder-strewn valleys can be a thrill if you've got excellent balance and aren't scared of taking a nasty spill. If that isn't extreme enough for you, though, there's always **skydiving**, over the desert north of Los Angeles.

Bungee America ℡310/322-8892, Ⓦwww .bungeeamerica.com. Long-standing bungee operator that offers thrilling weekend jumps from the so-called "Bridge to Nowhere" in the Angeles National Forest, an abandoned span only accessible by a two-hour walk; package deals start from $69 for one leap to $165 for five.

California City Skydive 22521 Airport Way, in California City in the Mojave Desert ℡1-800/2-JUMPHI, Ⓦwww.calcityskydive.com. A good introduction to the sport, at a cost of $199 if you jump yourself (with 4–5hr training), and $140 more for two assistants to help you on the way down. If you fall with one instructor ($239), only a half-hour introductory session is required before you make your ten-thousand-foot airborne journey to the desert floor.

MotoVentures Glen Helen Raceway Park (check for directions), Temecula ℡951/767-0991, Ⓦwww.motoventures.com. Motorcycle ranch two hours east of LA that offers instruction in motocross for novices and exhilarating two-wheel tours of the surrounding mountains and desert. If you have your own dirtbike, day-long tours are $195; it's $100 more if you need a rental.

The Rock Gym 2599 E Willow St, near Long Beach ℡562/981-3200, Ⓦwww.therockgym .com. One of LA's top climbing venues, with a 12,000-square-foot space for scaling. One climb is $15 ($12 for kids) and rental of a full climbing gear package is $6. Find other, similar operators around town by looking under "Rock Gyms" or "Rock and Mountain Climbing Instruction" in the *Yellow Pages*.

RockReation 11866 La Grange Ave, West LA ℡310/207-7199, Ⓦwww.rockreation.com. Not the most thrilling spot, but good for its "bouldering cave" and 9000 square feet of rock-climbing surfaces.

Skateboard Parks Ⓦskateboardparks.com. Although you can certainly earn a daring reputation skateboarding illegally in city plazas and the like, to find a list of above-board skateboard parks in LA, visit this national website, which puts special emphasis on LA and Southern California.

Skiing and snowboarding

On the fringe of the LA region, the mountainside lake and hamlet of **Big Bear** is prime territory for **skiing** and **snowboarding** about two hours east of Downtown LA, north of San Bernardino near state highways 18 and 38. Along with Mount Baldy and other locations in or near the San Bernardino Mountains, Big Bear and its several appealing resorts is deservedly a top winter draw. Thousands of Angelenos drive out here (there are hardly any public transit options, except from San Bernardino itself) to experience the excellent ski and snowboard conditions from November through April. In summer, there is excellent hiking, boating, fishing, and jet-skiing. Hotels and motels are plentiful, and the fine *Adventure Hostel* (see p.254) provides cheap accommodation. Expect to pay around $30–35 for a full ski or snowboard package rental.

Bear Mountain 43101 Goldmine Drive, Big Bear Lake ℡909/585-2519, Ⓦwww.bearmountain .com. Major ski area with twelve chairlifts, plus the added attraction of some of the country's top terrains parks, as well as all the summer activities. Lift tickets $52, kids $21; also good for use at Snow Summit.

Mount Baldy off Mountain Avenue in the Angeles National Forest ℡909/981-3344, Ⓦwww.mtbaldy.com. Located on the edge

of LA County, with a nice assortment of straightforward skiing trails and routes, along with decent snowboarding. Lift tickets $49, kids $19; half-day tickets for $39 and $14.

Mountain High near Wrightwood at 24512 Hwy-2 ℡760/249-5803, Ⓦwww.mthigh.com. Caters to dedicated winter athletes with two high-speed chairlifts (out of 12), plus night skiing every day of the week until 10pm. Also has terrain parks for snowboarders. Lift tickets $51, kids $21.

Snow Summit 880 Summit Blvd, Big Bear Lake ☎909/866-5766, Ⓦwww.snowsummit.com. One of the best ski areas, with twelve chair-lifts, one of which operates in summer for hikers and mountain bikers ($10 round trip rides). Thrilling terrain park for snowboarders, with a halfpipe and

Superpipe. Winter lift tickets $49, kids $19; also good for use at Bear Mountain.

Snow Valley 35100 Hwy-18 near Running Springs ☎909/867-2751, Ⓦwww.snow-valley .com. Located further from Big Bear Lake, a spot for the usual snow sports, with a terrain park and twelve chairlifts. Lift tickets $52, kids $21.

Leisure activities

You can enjoy LA's great outdoors without a lot of grunting and sweating, thanks to the city's diversity of **leisure activities**.

Fishing

Fishing is encouraged at a few locations, like the northern beaches around Malibu. Elsewhere, however – especially near the Santa Monica and Venice piers – any fish you catch is likely to contain a lifetime's worth of nasty chemicals. A better, though more costly, alternative is to charter a **sport-fishing cruise** out to sea and cast your line there. Prices run from one to two thousand dollars for a six-hour trip on a winter weekday, to three thousand or more for an eight-hour cruise during a summer weekend.

A California state **fishing license** is required for pier casting, ocean fishing, and any other type of angling. It costs nonresidents $12, $19, or $37, for one, two, or ten days of fishing, with annual licenses running $100 ($37 for residents). **Special permits** are required for salmon ($1.60 extra), steelhead ($6), and abalone ($18) fishing. Many cruise operators and fishing-supply dealers provide short-term fishing licenses. For more information, check Ⓦwww.dfg .ca.gov/licensing.

Joe's Rent-a-Boat on Green Pleasure Pier, Avalon ☎310/510-0455, Ⓦwww.catalina.com /rent-a-boat.html. Operator that has basic runabouts starting at $45/hour or $225/day, as well as kayaks ($15/hr) and pedal boats ($15/hr) for pleasure cruising.

LA Harbor Sportfishing 1150 Nagoya Way, Berth 79, San Pedro ☎310/547-9916, Ⓦwww .laharborsportfishing.com. Partial ($33 per

person) or full-day ($50) trips to offshore waters, along with overnight trips ($115), and seasonal whale-watching cruises (2hr 30min; $20).

Long Beach Sportfishing 555 Pico Ave, Berth 55, Long Beach ☎562/432-8993, Ⓦwww.longbeach sportfishing.com. Organizing full-day ($50) and half-day ($36) fishing expeditions to deep-sea waters, as well as whale-watching trips ($12).

Marina del Rey Sportfishing 13759 Fiji Way, Marina del Rey ☎310/822-3625, Ⓦmarinadelreysportfishing.com. Somewhat more touristy than the other operators, though the tour prices and packages are much the same (rental equipment, licenses, day or half-day trips for $50 and $35, whale watching for $20, etc).

Redondo Sportfishing 233 N Harbor Drive, Redondo Beach ☎310/372-2111, Ⓦwww .redondosportfishing.com. Half- and full-day trips are offered ($35–55), sailing to waters near Palos Verdes all the way out to more distant islands off the California coast. Also offers whale-watching cruises ($17).

Golf

Southern California is a prime spot for **golfing**, with links throughout the region. Unfortunately, the most notable and upscale of the courses in LA tend to be off-limits unless you're chummy with a member. The courses listed below are all open to the public, and are much more affordable than the big names but no less centrally located (with the exception, on both counts, of the course in Malibu). A full list of LA-area courses, public and private, can be found at ⓦthegolf courses.net. The thirteen operated by the City of Los Angeles, which supposedly runs more links than any other US city, require an annual Los Angeles City Card ($40 for nonresidents; call for information) if you want to reserve ahead. For information call ☎818/246-1135 or visit ⓦwww.ci.la.ca.us/RAP.

Griffith Park 4730 Crystal Springs Drive, north of Hollywood ☎323/664-2255, ⓦwww .griffithparkgolfshop.com. Set over four thousand acres in one of LA's best outdoor settings, the four courses of Griffith Park – Wilson, Harding, Roosevelt, and Los Feliz – mostly date from the eras of their respective presidents (with the latter from 1952), though all are kept in good shape and quite busy throughout the week. Regular fees are $24–31 per eighteen holes.

Malibu Country Club 901 Encinal Canyon Rd, Malibu t818/889-6680, ⓦwww.malibucountry club.net. If you have the money to spend on an upper-crust public course, this is the place to spend it: in the Santa Monica Mountains amid some of LA's most beautiful rustic scenery. Keep in mind that you must check in twenty minutes before your tee time and wear appropriate golf attire. Eighteen holes $70–95, nine for $40–55.

Penmar 1233 Rose Ave ☎310/396-6288. On the border of Santa Monica and Venice, this pocket-sized course only has nine holes, but it's the most central to the Westside beach of any municipal course — and has cheap rates, too ($13–17).

Rancho Park 10460 W Pico Blvd, West LA ☎310/839-4374. Set in one of the most convenient areas for visitors on the Westside, this inexpensive course offers undulating terrain. The greens are packed at peak hours on weekends, but it's still a local favorite after almost sixty years. $24–31 for eighteen holes, $13–17 for nine holes.

Bowling

Best exemplified by the crazy characters in the film *The Big Lebowski*, **bowling** in LA attracts a diehard crowd of local enthusiasts, and all around town you can find bowling alleys, from grungy old linoleum-and-formica lanes to newer bowl-o-ramas where flashy bowling nights feature glow-in-the-dark lanes and sparkly bowling balls. Costs start around $4–7 per game, with shoe rental a few bucks extra.

All Star Lanes 4459 Eagle Rock Blvd ☎323/254-2579. Located between Glendale and Pasadena in the little burg of Eagle Rock, this retro-styled alley features a bar, dance floor, video games, and pool tables to keep you busy when you're not prowling the lanes. Rockabilly bands and karaoke warblers provide the live soundtrack.

Brunswick West Covina 675 S Glendora Ave, West Covina, San Gabriel Valley ☎626/960-3636. Lovers of "Googie"-style pop architecture will not want to miss this colorful, faux-Polynesian alley – with its own coffee shop and cocktail lounge – though it's located out in the middle of nowhere.

Corbin Bowl 19616 Ventura Blvd, Tarzana ☎818/996-BOWL. Solid site in the San Fernando Valley for inspired rolling, with 26 lanes, video arcade, café, and weekend music, lights, and fog.

Jewel City Bowl 135 S Glendale Ave, Glendale ☎818/243-1188. Bowling purists may hate it, but casual fans will enjoy this popular Valley spot, where glowing balls, heavy metal music, artificial fog, and pulsing lights all serve to distract you from hitting strikes.

Lucky Strike 6801 Hollywood Blvd ☎323/467-7776. Bowling Hollywood-style, with a smirky hipster atmosphere, higher prices than elsewhere, drunken karaoke, loud music, and the usual rash of celebrity spottings.

Pickwick Bowling 921 W Riverside Drive, Burbank ☎818/842-7188, ⓦwww.pickwick gardens.com. With twenty-four lanes and a mixed crowd of young and old, this colorful Valley spot has gimmicks like Friday dance-music nights and Saturday's "Electric Fog" bowling, featuring copious amounts of dry ice and wild lighting.

Pinz Bowling Center 12655 Ventura Blvd, Studio City ☎818/769-7600, ⓦwww.pinzbowling center.com. The place to be seen on the Valley bowling scene, with 32 lanes, plenty of arcade games, and a rock'n'roll atmosphere. Don't be surprised to see a B-list TV actor or recent Hollywood has-been in the lane next to you.

Horseback riding

You can go **horseback riding** at several ranches and stables throughout the greater LA region, principally around the Santa Monica Mountains and the hills of Griffith Park. Most businesses give you a choice of packages that may include evening outings, individual or group rides, easy or difficult routes, and various added amenities like dinners or barbecues. Costs can be anywhere from $15 to $50 per hour, depending on the location and package.

Bar S Stables 1850 Riverside Drive, Glendale ☎818/242-8443. A Griffith Park–area operator that provides guided equine tours during the daylight or evening hours, and occasionally under moonlight, starting at $20 per hour.

Catalina Stables 600 Avalon Canyon Rd, Avalon ☎310/510-0478. Offers guided tours of gorgeous Santa Catalina Island, with simple half-hour tours starting around $42, hour-long treks for $65, and two-hour journeys costing $82.

Circle K Stables 910 Mariposa St, Burbank ☎818/843-9890. Located near the LA Equestrian Center, these stables provide affordable rides for $25 per person for the first hour, $15 for each subsequent hour.

Dude's Ranch Tarzana, San Fernando Valley ☎818/497-7468, ⓦwww.dudesranch.com. Many tours through varying terrain around the Santa Monica Mountains – from hills and canyons to waterfalls and beaches – with most rides one to five hours long, at $50–65 per hour, per person. Rides at sunset and under moonlight are the same cost. Lessons $55 per hour.

LA Equestrian Center 480 Riverside Drive, Burbank ☎818/840-8401, ⓦwww.la-equestriancenter.com. Across the LA River from Griffith Park, this outfit offers horse rentals for $20 an hour or evening rides for $40.

Sunset Ranch 3400 N Beachwood Drive, Hollywood ☎323/469-5450, ⓦwww.sunsetranchhollywood.com. A Griffith Park operator providing evening horse rides through the surrounding area on a first-come first-served basis, sometimes with dinner; regular one- or two-hour rides $25 and $40.

Will Rogers State Historic Park 1501 Will Rogers State Park Rd, Pacific Palisades ☎310/455-2900. Watch a polo match on the park's front lawn (April–Oct Sat 2–5pm, Sun 10am–1pm; free) before enjoying a guided horseback ride in the vicinity for $50.

▲ LA Equestrian Center

Festivals and events

L os Angeles throws a lot of **parades** and **festivals**, from proud displays of ethnic culture to internationally famous spectacles to oddball street fairs and quirky bohemian gatherings. No matter when you come, you'll likely find some sort of event or celebration, especially in summer, when beach culture is in full bloom. This selective list concentrates on some of the more notable observances, along with smaller, local events that provide unusual or nontraditional festivities. For a list of national **public holidays**, see Basics, p.43.

January

Japanese New Year (1st) Art displays, ethnic cuisine, cultural exhibits, and more at this annual Little Tokyo festival, centered around the Japanese American Community and Cultural Center. ☎213/628-2725, ⓦwww.jaccc.org.

Tournament of Roses Parade (1st) Pasadena's famous procession of floral floats and marching bands along a five-mile stretch of Colorado Blvd, coinciding with the annual Rose Bowl game. ☎626/795-9311 or 449-ROSE, ⓦwww.tournamentofroses.com.

Martin Luther King Parade and Celebration (mid) The civil-rights hero is honored with activities at King Park, Baldwin Hills, Crenshaw, and many other city locations. ☎323/290-4100, ⓦwww.sclclosangeles.org.

Golden Globe Awards (mid to late) As the annual run-up to the Oscars, this awards show is held by the Hollywood Foreign Press Association, and attracts ever-increasing (some say undeserved) attention. Tourists are encouraged to watch the stars arrive, and gape accordingly. ☎310/657-1731, ⓦwww.hfpa.org.

February

Chinese New Year (early to mid) Three days of dragon-float street parades, tasty food, and various cultural programs, based in Chinatown, Alhambra, and Monterey Park. ☎213/617-0396, ⓦwww.lachinesechamber.org.

Bob Marley Reggae Festival (mid) A two-day event that exalts the reggae legend with food, music, and plenty of spirit. At the Long Beach Convention and Entertainment Center. ☎310/515-3322, ⓦwww.bobmarleydayfestival.com.

Mardi Gras (mid) Floats, parades, costumes, and lots of singing and dancing at this Latin fun fest, with traditional ceremonies on Olvera Street downtown (☎213/625-7074) and colorful antics in West Hollywood (☎310/289-2525).

Queen Mary Scottish Festival (mid) All the haggis you can stand at this two-day Long Beach celebration, along with peppy Highland dancing and bagpipes. ☎562/499-1650, ⓦwww.queenmary.com.

The Academy Awards **(end)** The top movie awards, presented at the Kodak Theater at the Hollywood & Highland mall. Bleacher seats are available to watch the limousines draw up and the stars emerge for the ceremony. ☎310/247-3000, ⓦwww.oscars.org.

March

LA City Marathon **(early)** Cheer on the runners all around town, or sign up to participate in this 26-mile run, which covers a course from Downtown to the Westside and South Central LA. ☎310/444-5544, ⓦwww.lamarathon.com.

Route 66 Art Auction **(early)** A good opportunity to get a look at the latest and most engaging artworks to come out of the vibrant gallery scene northeast of Downtown; held at the Center for the Arts in Eagle Rock. $20. ☎323/226-1617, ⓦwww.centerartseaglerock.org.

Television Festival **(early to mid)** Few things could be more appropriate to LA than this two-week celebration at the Directors' Guild honoring the idiot box. If you love TV, it's one event you shouldn't miss, honoring shows from the past and present with clips, cast reunions, lectures, and more. Each night's program focuses on a different TV show, but can be pricey at $30 each. ☎1-888/464-2468, ⓦwww.mtr.org/festivals/paleyfest2008.

St Patrick's Day **(mid)** No parade in LA, but freely flowing green beer in the "Irish" bars along Fairfax Ave in Mid-Wilshire. Parade along Colorado Boulevard in Old Town Pasadena, and another in Hermosa Beach. ☎310/376-0951, ⓦwww.stpatricksday.org.

Spring Festival of Flowers **(mid)** A floral explosion of color at Descanso Gardens, including different types of tulips, lilies and daffodils, among many others. ☎818/949-4200, ⓦwww.descansogardens.org.

April

Blessing of the Animals **(early)** A long-established ceremony, Mexican in origin, in which

▲ Attendee at the California Poppy Festival

locals come to Olvera Street to have their pets blessed, then watch a parade. ☎213/625-5045, ⓦolvera-street.com/html/fiestas.html.

California Poppy Festival **(mid to late)** Although it's in a bleak northern valley, Lancaster's 1800-acre poppy reserve draws big crowds with its blinding orange colors each spring. To go with the blooms, the town throws a festival featuring local foodstuffs, folk art, and crafts. ☎661/723-6075, ⓦwww.poppyfestival.com.

Jimmy Stewart Relay **(mid)** The late great actor – and star of such classics as *Vertigo* and *Mr. Smith Goes to Washington* – is honored with a 26.2-mile marathon run by five-person relay teams. It's fun to watch the runners charge through the hills and valleys of Griffith Park, but if you want to participate, it'll cost your team $200. ☎310/829-8968.

Long Beach Grand Prix **(mid)** Some of autoracing's best drivers and souped-up vehicles zoom around Shoreline Drive south of Downtown in the city's biggest annual event, which takes place over three days. ☏562/981-2600, ⓦwww.longbeachgp.com.

Songkran Festival (Thai New Year) (weekend nearest 13th) The Wat Thai Temple in North Hollywood is the focus for this cultural event, with spicy food, authentic music, and plenty of monks. ☏818/997-9657, ⓦwww.watthaiusa.org.

Cowboy Poetry and Music Festival (late) Folk music from the Old West and accompanying cowboy poems – some excellent, some cornpone – are the highlights of this three-day Santa Clarita celebration, just north of LA. ☏661/286-4021, ⓦwww.cowboyfestival.org.

Fiesta Broadway (late) Along Broadway in Downtown, this street fair presents lively Latino pop singers and delicious Mexican food. ☏310/914-0015, ⓦwww.fiestabroadway.la.

May

Cinco de Mayo (5th) A day-long party to commemorate the 1862 Mexican victory at the Battle of Puebla. Besides a spirited parade along Olvera Street, several blocks of Downtown are blocked off for Latino music performances. There are also celebrations in most LA parks. ☏213/628-1274, ⓦolvera-street.com/html/fiestas.html.

LA Modernism (early) This annual show, at Santa Monica Civic Auditorium, is a fine opportunity to see a wealth of modernist art and design from the twentieth century. ☏818/244-1126, ⓦwww.lamodernism.com.

Renaissance Pleasure Faire (weekends, plus Memorial Day) Dress up in your Tudor best for this celebration of olden times, which includes dancing, theater, food, and the inevitable jousting. Held in distant Irwindale near the Sante Fe Dam. $25. ☏626/969-4750, ⓦrenfair.com/socal.

NoHo Theater and Arts Festival (mid) Music, food, poetry, theater, and dance fill the streets of this artsy district in North Hollywood in the San Fernando Valley. ☏310/537-4240, ⓦwww.nohoartsdistrict.com/festival.

Venice Art Walk (mid) A great chance to peer into the private art studios in town, where you can see the work of both big-name local artists and lesser-known up-and-comers – though it will cost you $50. ☏310/392-9255.

Strawberry Festival (late) Garden Grove in Orange County is the setting for this huge, old-fashioned shindig of carnival rides, games, parades, and other festivities – all in celebration of the humble strawberry. ☏714/638-0981, ⓦwww.strawberryfestival.org.

UCLA Jazz and Reggae Festival (late) Two days of jazz and reggae concerts, plus heaps of food, on the UCLA campus. ☏310/825-9912, ⓦwww.jazzreggaefest.com.

June

Last Remaining Seats (throughout) An excellent film festival that draws huge crowds to the grand Los Angeles, Orpheum, and other movie palaces to watch revivals of classic Hollywood films. Also offers films at Glendale's eye-opening Alex Theatre. Tickets to each screening $20, often with live entertainment. ☏213/623-CITY, ⓦlaconservancy.org.

Irish Fair and Music Festival (mid to late) Sizable Irish music, food, and culture celebration held in the Orange County town of Irvine ☏949/489-1172, ⓦwww.irishfair.org.

Los Angeles Film Festival (mid) Although Hollywood is better at making generic films than honoring good ones, this ten-day festival is an exception, screening notable independent and art-house films across West LA at a variety of venues. ☏1-866/FILMFEST, ⓦwww.lafilmfest.com.

Playboy Jazz Festival (mid) Renowned event held at the Hollywood Bowl, with a lineup of traditional and not-so-traditional musicians. ☏213/480-3232, ⓦwww.playboy.com/arts-entertainment/features/jazzfest2008.

Bayou Festival (late) Heaps of Creole food, wild parades, and plenty of high-spirited Cajun and Zydeco music at this colorful Long Beach event. ☏562/427-3713, ⓦwww.longbeachfestival.com.

Gay Pride Celebration (late) Raucous parade along Santa Monica Blvd in West Hollywood, with hundreds of vendors, an all-male drag football-cheerleading team and a heady, carnival atmosphere. ☏323/969-8302, ⊛www.lapride.org.

July

Festival of the Arts/Pageant of the Masters (early July to late Aug) Laguna Beach's signature street festival, featuring food, arts, and dancing, but most memorable for its living tableaux, which re-create classic paintings – a true Southern California spectacle (see box, p.236). ☏949/494-1145, ⊛www.foapom.com.

Independence Day (4th) The *Queen Mary* in Long Beach hosts a particularly large fireworks display, as well as colorful entertainment (☏562/435-3511). Other fireworks displays throughout LA, including West Hollywood's Plummer Park (☏323/848-6530).

Lotus Festival (first weekend after 4th) An Echo Park celebration featuring dragon boats, ethnic food, pan-Pacific music and, of course, the resplendent lotus blooms around the lake. ☏213/485-1310, ⊛www.laparks.org/grifmet/lotus.htm.

South Bay Greek Festival (mid) Three days of food and music at St Katherine Greek Orthodox Church in Redondo Beach, with arts and crafts displays and energetic dancing adding to the festivities. ☏310/540-2434, ⊛www.sbgreekfestival.com.

Central Avenue Jazz Festival (late) Jazz and blues concerts by big names and lesser-known performers, held in front of the historic *Dunbar Hotel* in South Central. ☏323/234-7882, ⊛www.centralavenuejazzfestival.com.

Festival of the Chariots (late) A strange and unique LA phenomenon: giant decorated floats parade down Venice Boardwalk to the sound of lively music and the smell of vegetarian Indian food. Sponsored by the International Society for Krishna Consciousness. ☏310/836-2676, ⊛www.festivalofchariots.com.

Jazzfest West (late) West of Pasadena in the town of San Dimas' Bonelli Park, an event mixing mid- to big-name acts in mainstream jazz with appetizing foodstuffs and arts and crafts displays. $45. ☏949/360-7800, ⊛www.omegaevents.com.

August

International Surf Festival (early) Newcomers and old-time fans party at this surfing tournament and festival in the South Bay. The exciting three-day spectacle also includes volleyball, fishing, and sandcastle design. ☏310/305-9546, ⊛www.surffestival.org.

Long Beach Jazz Festival (mid) Relax and enjoy famous and local performers at the Rainbow Lagoon park in downtown Long Beach. ☏562/424-0013, ⊛www.longbeachjazzfestival.com.

Nisei Week (mid to late) A celebration of Japanese America, with martial arts demonstrations, karaoke, Japanese brush painting, baby shows, and performances. ☏213/687-7193, ⊛www.niseiweek.org.

Sunset Junction Street Fair (mid) A spirited neighborhood party, and one of LA's most enjoyable fêtes, along Sunset Boulevard in Silver Lake. The live music, ethnic food, and carnivalesque atmosphere draws a big crowd of locals in the know. ☏323/661-7771, ⊛www.sunsetjunction.org.

African Marketplace and Cultural Faire (late Aug to early Sept) Hundreds of arts and crafts booths and many different entertainers at this annual celebration at Rancho Cienega Park in South Central LA. ☏323/293-1612, ⊛www.africanmarketplace.org.

September

Fiesta Hermosa (early) Labor Day weekend is a great time to visit this fun-loving beach town, which puts on a bash with food vendors, music, oceanside sports, and other activities. ☏310/376-0951, ⊛www.fiestahermosa.com.

Long Beach Blues Festival (early) Hear some of the country's top blues performers at this annual event at Cal State University at Long Beach. ☎562/985-5566, ⓦwww.kkjz .org/events.

Los Angeles County Fair (early to late) In the San Gabriel Valley, Pomona hosts the biggest county fair in the US, with livestock shows, pie-eating contests, rodeos, and fairground rides. ☎909/623-3111, ⓦwww .fairplex.com.

LA's birthday (early) A civic ceremony and assorted street entertainment around El Pueblo de Los Angeles, to mark the founding of the original pueblo in 1781. ☎213/625-5045, ⓦolvera-street.com/html/ fiestas.html.

Festival of Philippine Arts and Culture (second Sun) Good food, music, dancing, theater, and film at this annual Point Fermin event in San Pedro. ☎323/913-4663, ⓦfilamarts.org.

Manhattan Beach Arts Festival (second Sun) Colorful arts and crafts are on display at this South Bay event, accompanied by food and music. ☎310/545-5621 or 802-5440.

LA Korean Festival (mid) Dancing, parading, and tae kwon do exhibitions are the main events at this Mid-Wilshire event held in Seoul International Park (☎213/487-9696). A similar event takes place in Pasadena around the same time (☎626/449-2742).

Oktoberfest (late Sept through Oct) Venture into Alpine Village, in the South Bay suburb of Torrance, to revel in Teutonic culture, from hearty German food to music and dancing. ☎310/327-4384, ⓦwww.alpinevillage.net. Also a spirited event in Huntington Beach, Orange County. ☎714/895-8020, ⓦwww .oldworld.ws.

Watts Towers Day of the Drum/Jazz Festival (late) Two days of community spirit and free music – African, Asian, Cuban, and Brazilian – with the towers as the striking backdrop. Taking place at the same time, and in the same location, the Jazz Festival is the oldest such event in LA. ☎213/485-1795, ⓦwww .wattstowers.org.

October

Catalina Island Jazz Trax (first three weekends) A huge line-up of major and rising jazz stars performs in the beautiful Art Deco ballroom of the historic Avalon Casino. ☎1-866/872-9849, ⓦwww.jazztrax.com.

Detour (early) Symbolizing the revitalizing of Downtown LA, this recently inaugurated music fest features some of the top names in indie rock — thirty bands spread over four stages — a great deal at $36. ☎818/380-0400 #248, ⓦwww.laweekly .com/detour.

Eagle Rock Music Festival (early) This funky district, due north of Downtown LA near Glendale, hosts a freewheeling festival of food, crafts, and a widely eclectic assortment of music. ☎323/226-1617, ⓦwww .myspace.com/eaglerockmusicfestival.

Lithuanian Fair (early) Traditional music and food, and Easter egg painting, are some of the highlights of this Los Feliz fair, held at St Casimir's Church. ☎323/664-4660.

Los Angeles Bach Festival (mid) Revel in the Baroque master's music at the First Congregational Church, just north of Lafayette Park in Westlake. ☎213/385-1345, ⓦwww .fccla.org.

Antique Street Fair (late) One of the bigger antiques shows around, giving you a chance to hunt for bargains in the distant town of Whittier. ☎562/696-2662, ⓦwww .whittieruptown.com.

Halloween (31st) A wild procession in West Hollywood, featuring all manner of bizarre and splashy costumes and characters (☎310/289-2525). Or you can opt for the Halloween-themed events on the *Queen Mary*. ☎562/435-3511.

November

Dia de Los Muertos (2nd) The "Day of the Dead," celebrated authentically throughout East LA and more blandly for tourists on Olvera Street and elsewhere. Mexican traditions, such as picnicking on the family burial spot and making skeleton puppets, are faithfully upheld. ☎213/625-5045, ⓦolvera-street.com/html/fiestas.html.

AFI Film Festival (early) Arguably LA's most influential film festival, with a mix of engaging up-and-comers and Hollywood veterans testing the indie-film waters; showings can be popular and venues sell out early, so plan ahead. ☎323/856-7600, ⓦwww.afi.com/onscreen/afifest/2007.

LA Mariachi Festival (mid) Munch on Mexican food or take a music workshop, all to the sounds of nonstop mariachi bands; appropriately enough, held in Mariachi Plaza in Boyle Heights. ☎323/466-1156.

Doo-dah Parade (Sun before Thanksgiving) Absurdly costumed characters marching through Pasadena are the main attraction at this immensely popular event, which began as a spoof of the Tournament of Roses parade. ☎626/205-4029, ⓦwww.pasadenadoodahparade.info.

Griffith Park Light Festival (late) A huge favorite, this spectacle stretches a mile along Crystal Springs Road, complete with drive-through tunnels of light, thematic displays, and representations of familiar LA sights like the Hollywood sign. ☎323/913-4688 ext. 9.

December

Hollywood Christmas Parade (1st) The biggest of LA's many Yuletide events, with a procession of mind-bogglingly elaborate floats, marching bands, and famous and semi-famous names from film and TV. ☎323/469-2337.

Belmont Shore Christmas Parade (early) Homemade floats and marching bands kick off the holiday season at this East Long Beach event. ☎562/434-3066.

Holiday Boat Parade (early) Marina del Rey is the site for this annual, ocean-going procession of brightly lit watercraft, supposedly the largest of its kind on the West Coast (☎310/670-7130, ⓦwww.mdrboatparade.org). A similar event takes place along

Shoreline Village in Long Beach. ☎562/435-4093.

Las Posadas (late) An Olvera Street re-enactment of the biblical tale of Mary and Joseph seeking a place to rest on Christmas Eve, culminating with a piñata-breaking. ☎213/625-5045, ⓦolvera-street.com/html/fiestas.html.

LA County Holiday Celebration (Christmas Eve) Thousands of people pack the Dorothy Chandler Pavilion in Downtown LA to catch this juggernaut of multicultural entertainment, including everything from Japanese dance to Jamaican reggae. ☎213/974-1396, ⓦwww.lacountyarts.org/holiday.html.

19

Kids' LA

A lthough most of LA's attractions are geared for adults, the city does
hold some appeal for **kids**, from popular **museums** and **aquariums**
to the outdoor fun of the region's excellent **parks and beaches**. If
these don't hold the kids' interest, treat them to a stop at one of the
many worthwhile **toy shops** in town (not just in the huge, numbing malls),
where they can pick out something bright and shiny. Most, if not all, kids will
doubtless want to go to major theme parks like **Disneyland**, **Knott's
Berry Farm**, and **Magic Mountain**, but the thrill fades after only a
couple of days – or even hours – of being jostled by massive crowds, waiting
in interminable lines, and eating crummy theme-park food. Some of the
selections below are good alternatives.

Museums

Some LA **museums** feature kid-friendly exhibits and hands-on, interactive
displays with lots of flashing lights and bright colors. Although the
Children's Museum of Los Angeles, located in the San Fernando Valley,
has yet to be built (no set date for opening; see Ⓦ www.childrensmuseumla
.org for the latest), youngsters can have fun at several existing museums.
Exposition Park (see p.160), south of Downtown, has the **California
Science Center**, with lots of flashy displays and pressable buttons; the
associated **Air and Space Gallery**, where aircraft hang from the ceiling; and
the huge, all-encompassing nature films of the **IMAX Theater**. Meanwhile,
visitors of all ages enjoy the neighboring **Natural History Museum of Los
Angeles County**; like the **George C. Page Discovery Center** in Mid-
Wilshire (p.80), it's a fine place to view the colossal bones of extinct creatures,
featuring mammoths, sloths, wolves, and saber-toothed cats dredged up from
the adjacent **La Brea Tar Pits**.

For Western-tinged fun, **Will Rogers State Historic Park** (p.215) has a
great ranch house loaded with lariats, cowboy gear, and even the mounted
head of a Texas Longhorn. Kids with a taste for roping and riding may also
warm to the **William S. Hart Ranch and Museum** (p.212), for its wide
range of Western duds, cowboy equipment, and Tinseltown memorabilia, as
well as the meatier exhibits at the **Museum of the American West** (p.95) in
Griffith Park.

If all else fails, you can take older kids with a taste for the surreal to the
Museum of Jurassic Technology (p.135), an institutional haunted house of
sorts filled with all manner of bizarre displays, including creepy bugs.

▲ Denizen of the Aquarium of the Pacific

Aquatic attractions

The region's biggest and most comprehensive collection of marine life is kept at the **Aquarium of the Pacific** (p.181) in Long Beach, where there are plenty of sharks, tide-pool creatures, jellyfish, and other creatures to tantalize kids. Less crowded is the smaller **Cabrillo Marine Aquarium** (p.179) in San Pedro, while the Orange County coast is the home of the **Friends of the Sea Lion** (p.236) – where kids can watch injured animals being nursed back to health.

Further north, along the rugged coastline of Palos Verdes, the **Point Vicente Interpretive Center** has simple exhibits on local marine life (p.175), but is best for its **whale watching** during the winter months. These massive creatures can also be spotted from other promontories along the Santa Monica Bay, and **whale-watching cruises** operate from Santa Catalina Island and Long Beach (see p.186 and p.181).

North of Point Vicente, Manhattan Beach's **Roundhouse and Aquarium** (p.172) offers an inexpensive look at the region's ocean flora and fauna, but for a much more in-depth view, the **Santa Monica Pier Aquarium** (p.140) is a good choice, where kids can eyeball sea creatures and learn about marine biology and ecology.

Finally, if you're on your way south toward San Diego, bring the kids to the **Ocean Institute** (p.236) in Dana Point, where the highlight isn't any sea creature, but a full-sized replica of a tall ship anchored just offshore.

Parks

The most prominent of LA's outdoor recreation areas is **Griffith Park** (p.92), where you can find an excellent network of hiking, biking, and horse-riding trails in the large, mountainous green space. The park has numerous attractions to pique children's interest, including a pleasant **Fern Dell**, as well as the imposing

Griffith Observatory, chock full of astronomical and scientific exhibits that will entrance young and old alike. The observatory will probably appeal to older children more than the **LA Zoo** on the other side of the park, where a standard array of animals is shown before the public in mostly outdated displays and cramped environments. Near the zoo, **Travel Town** is geared to smaller tots, who like to walk around the disused old trains sitting near the LA River.

The **Santa Monica Mountains** are a good place to visit for the many hiking trails and buzzing wildlife. One sight in the mountains, **San Vicente Mountain Park** (p.222), a decommissioned missile base, is a fascinating excursion for older kids, who can get great views of LA by clambering atop a tower that used to cover a launch center.

Paramount Ranch (p.223) is equally interesting for kids and adults as the filming site of numerous Hollywood Westerns. Nearby, the **Peter Strauss Ranch** is an idyllic natural landscape that was once the site of a colorful resort. Not far away, **Malibu Creek State Park** (p.222) is a good choice for a half-day family outing into some of LA's more rugged, unspoiled terrain, while closer to the Westside, above Beverly Hills, **Franklin Canyon** (p.121) has pleasant nature walks and a nature center.

Both parents and kids may enjoy spending time in the city's **ecological reserves**, which offer fine opportunities for hiking, birdwatching, and sometimes horseback riding and bicycling. The action on **Santa Catalina Island** (p.185) includes hiking, camping, and bus tours around the island's unspoiled interior. Orange County, too, has several worthwhile options, including the striking **Crystal Cove State Park** (p.235) along the coast, and the **Bolsa Chica** (p.234) and **Upper Newport Bay** (p.235) ecological reserves, where kids can see nature in its sublime, undeveloped state.

Beaches and water parks

Of course, LA has a number of popular **beaches**. The best, and least polluted, are around **Malibu** and along the **Orange County coast,** while Santa Catalina Island is great for its many snorkelling sites. One beach is no good for swimming, but nevertheless caters to kids (at least during the daytime): the **Santa Monica Pier** is chock-full of cotton candy, video games, and carnival rides (other city piers are mainly useful for fishing).

For freshwater amusement, the region's quartet of **water parks** are sure to delight kids with a yen for hydrotubes and splash pools. These include the excellent, often expensive, rides at Magic Mountain's **Hurricane Harbor** (p.212), Knott's Berry Farm's **Soak City U.S.A.** (p.230), **Raging Waters** in the eastern San Gabriel Valley (p.202), and **Wild Rivers** in the Orange County city of Irvine, at 8770 Irvine Center Drive (June–Aug hours vary, generally daily 10am–8pm; May & Sept Sat & Sun 10am–5pm; $30, kids $19; ☎949/788-0808, ⓦwww.wildrivers.com), loaded with water tubes, pools, and flumes, and a short distance from the 405 freeway.

Toy and game shops

Dinosaur Farm 1510 Mission St, South Pasadena ☎1-888/658-2388, ⓦwww.dinosaurfarm.com. A paradise for little dino-lovers, bursting with games, puzzles, lunchboxes, and models relating to the giant reptiles – not to mention clothing, masks, and outfits for dressing like a Tyrannosaurs rex.

Brainy or creative children will not be disappointed by LA. Though the **Getty Center, Getty Villa**, and **Los Angeles County Museum of Art** are not specifically geared toward children, they both offer headphones and "listening tours" for kids on occasion, and also sell children's guides to art in their bookstores. The Getty Center's **Central Garden** has attractive foliage and short paths for kids to walk off some of their excess energy.

One museum in the region, the **Bowers Museum of Cultural Art** (p.230), features a separate institution – the **Kidseum** – designed for the little ones, with simplified displays on native and world cultures. Better, perhaps, is the **Muckenthaler Cultural Center** (p.231) in nearby Fullerton, a whole mansion loaded with cultural treasures.

Children may be interested in the **decorative art and commercial design** displayed in several of the city's galleries. Bizarre clocks, chairs, and televisions are but a few of the novelties to look at, and perhaps even touch and tinker with, at places like the **Gallery of Functional Art** (p.145) in Santa Monica's Bergamot Station.

For art out in the open, away from confining museums and galleries, the **Franklin Murphy Sculpture Garden** on the UCLA campus is without peer, a treasure-trove of twentieth-century abstract sculpture, all set amid bright sunshine and grassy lawns. For a strange twist on "living art," reserve tickets for Laguna Beach's **Pageant of the Masters** (see p.236), in which people dress up and pose as characters from famous paintings and sculptures.

Budding musicians may want to attend the **LA Philharmonic**'s (p.308) seasonal "youth symphonies," either at Disney Hall or the Hollywood Bowl. The concerts feature child-oriented staples like Prokofiev's *Peter and the Wolf*, Saint-Saëns' *Carnival of the Animals*, and accessible works from Bach, Mozart, and Vivaldi.

A trip Downtown to Disney Hall can be combined with a visit to the **Bob Baker Marionette Theater**, 1345 W First St (shows Tues–Fri 10.30am, Sat & Sun 2.30pm; $15, toddlers free; by reservation only at ☏213/250-9995, ⊛www.bobbakermarionettes .com), one of LA's best puppet shows for 47 years running, performed by a classic puppeteer. The only downside is the theater's dicey location on the west side of the 110 freeway – don't linger after dark — though the marionettes make regular appearances around town, too (details at ☏213/250-4093). An alternative puppet experience in a more hospitable location is the tiny **Santa Monica Puppet and Magic Center**, 1014 Broadway, which has displays of historic puppets and a performance space for the long-running spectacle of *Puppetolio!* (shows Tues & Thurs 10.30am, Wed 1pm, Sat & Sun 2pm; $7.50; ☏310/656-0483, ⊛www.puppetmagic.com), a one-man production featuring whimsical characters.

Giant Robot 2015 Sawtelle Blvd, West LA ☏310/478-1819, ⊛www.giantrobot.com. If your kids have a flair for the surreal, this is the place to come, loaded with Asian-themed wind-up dolls, comic books, freakish dolls, miniatures, and curiosities beyond description.

Gregory's Toys and Adventures in the Encino Place mall, 16101 Ventura Blvd #135, Encino ☏818/906-2212. This San Fernando Valley retailer stocks a fine selection of action figures, puzzles, electric trains, old-fashioned blocks, and more – all at prices lower than the big names.

Hollywood Toys and Costumes 6600 Hollywood Blvd, Hollywood ☏323/464-4444, ⊛www.hollywoodtoys.com. A classic, one-of-a-kind LA business, with not only an array of dolls and action figurines, but also dress-up treats – wigs, masks, Halloween outfits, costume jewelry, and all kinds of colorful trinkets and eye-catching junk.

Kip's Toyland in the Farmers Market, 6333 W Third St, Mid-Wilshire ☏323/939-8334. Venerable dealer in assorted toys, dolls, stuffed animals, puzzles, and games – not always the flashiest items around, but the store maintains a loyal following in a central location.

Monkeyhouse Toys 1618 Silver Lake Blvd, Silver Lake ☏323/662-3437 ⊛www.monkeyhouse toys.com. Great stop for designer toys and oddities like MC Escher puzzles, Keith Haring pull toys, and plush monkey puppets — all of it fascinating, and expensive.

Robotoys in the Sherman Oaks Galleria, 15301 Ventura Blvd, Studio City ☏ 818/788-3344, ⓦ www.robotoys.com. Nothing but robots to suit every taste, ranging from cheesy tin toys to slick Transformers-types, and even kit-sets that allow you to build your own mechanical man.

San Marino Toy and Book Shoppe 2424 Huntington Drive, San Marino ☏ 626/309-0222, ⓦ www.toysandbooks.com. Excellent, pricey selection of puppets, dollhouses, and building blocks, along with odd items like woolly-mammoth skeleton puzzles and kids' "mood lamps."

Would You Believe? 1118 Fair Oaks Ave, South Pasadena ☏ 626/799-3828, ⓦ www.wyb.com. Magic supplies, novelties, balloons, and juggling equipment, as well as toys. Kids and adults can also rent costumes and go around town dressed as a moose, monk, or mummy.

Wound & Wound Toy Company Universal CityWalk, Universal City ☏ 818/509-8129, ⓦ www.thewoundandwound.com. Packed with all kinds of wind-up toys, from goofy aliens and tin trucks to burgers with feet. The display cases full of rare collectibles – *Star Wars* dolls prominent among them – are worth a look.

20

Shopping

S hopping in LA is serious business. The level of disposable income in the wealthy parts of the city is astronomical, and an expedition to some of the ritzy **shopping districts** and outrageous stores can offer some insight into LA life – revealing who's the money and what they're capable of blowing it on. Besides the run-of-the-mill chain retailers you'll find anywhere, there are big, only-in-LA **department stores** and mega-**malls** where most of the hard-core shopping goes on.

If you have bags of money to spend, you should feel right at home in LA's fashionable **art galleries**, where you can spot the latest works from the city's hottest artists offered at jaw-dropping prices.

Shopping districts

While you can find souvenirs and touristy merchandise in most retail zones, there are a few notable **shopping districts** worth mentioning. In Downtown, the main shopping area is the **Fashion District**, where you can pick up a variety of fabrics and clothes, including designer knockoffs and markdowns – at some of the lowest prices on the West Coast.

Although its signature Miracle Mile has seen better days, Mid-Wilshire has no less than three major shopping areas: **La Brea Avenue**, just north of Wilshire, a stretch of clothing, furniture, and antiques stores; **Third Street**, a strip of boutiques and restaurants east of the Beverly Center mall and west of the Grove mall; and **Larchmont Village**, a pocket of small retailers and chain stores on the edge of Hancock Park.

Just north in Hollywood, the irrepressible **Melrose Avenue** is LA's most conspicuously hip area, where the quirky shops are increasingly being displaced by high-end boutiques. Further north, **Hollywood Boulevard** is one big cut-rate shopping zone, especially for movie memorabilia and discount T-shirts, with merchants thickest between La Brea Avenue and Gower Street, and the giant Hollywood & Highland mall anchoring the whole scene. To the east is the short **North Vermont Avenue** strip in Los Feliz, with its idiosyncratic boutiques and good restaurants. By contrast, West Hollywood is more self-consciously chic, and you can expect to find small boutiques along the western end of **Santa Monica Boulevard**, and numerous music and bookstores (and more than a few sex shops) along the **Sunset Strip**.

Beverly Hills is, of course, the pinnacle of high-end shopping, with strat-ospheric retailers concentrated in the downtown core known as the **Golden Triangle**, which includes **Rodeo Drive**. West LA retail is anchored by the colossal *Westside Pavilion* and *Century City* malls; Brentwood's **San Vicente**

Boulevard, another ritzy zone; and **Westwood Village**, a student haven full of inexpensive bookstores, clothing outlets, and used-record stores.

Out in Santa Monica, the **Third Street Promenade** is one of LA's busiest shopping strips, with a mix of small retailers and, increasingly, mega-chain stores; linked from the Promenade by a free bus (in summer), Santa Monica's **Main Street** is popular for its book dealers, clothing stores, and gift shops. The same types of retailers, though of a funkier and more downmarket character, cluster further south, around Venice's **Windward Arcade**.

In the outlying areas, there are countless malls, minimalls, and chain-store outlets, but only a few truly interesting places to shop or browse. **Downtown Long Beach**, especially around Pine Avenue, is appealing for its used-book stores and scattered clothing shops; **Old Pasadena** – notably Colorado Boulevard – offers music stores, clothing boutiques, and used-book sellers; **Ventura Boulevard**, running through Studio City in the San Fernando Valley, is a good place to buy new and used music, assorted souvenirs, colorful trinkets, and cheap clothing; the so-called **NoHo Arts District** in North Hollywood in the Valley has a clutch of boutiques and souvenir stores; and along Newport Beach's **Balboa Peninsula**, on the Orange County coast, you can pick up expensive designer duds and similarly pricey outfits at numerous boutiques. The South Bay, San Fernando Valley, and Orange County are also littered with overgrown malls. Oddly enough, the high-profile city of Malibu has relatively few unique shopping attractions that are open to the general public.

Department stores and shopping malls

You won't have to travel far to find LA's flagship **department stores**. Bloomingdale's, Macy's, Nordstrom, and Saks Fifth Avenue are located in malls throughout the region. For addresses, refer to "Shopping malls", p.346.

Department stores

Barneys 9570 Wilshire Blvd, Beverly Hills ☎310/276-4400, ⌨www.barneys.com. At the base of the Golden Triangle, this high-end retailer offers five levels of dapper shoes and clothing – and an exclusive restaurant, Barney Greengrass (see p.277) on the fifth floor; if you don't look like you belong there, expect the sales clerks to ignore you.

Bloomingdale's 10250 Santa Monica Blvd, in the Century City Marketplace, Century City ☎310/772-2100, ⌨www.bloomingdales.com.

This major chain features all the standard men's and women's apparel, kitchen items, and assorted jewelry and kidswear. Also in the Beverly Center, Sherman Oaks Fashion Square, and Newport Beach Fashion Island.

Macy's 8500 Beverly Blvd, in the Beverly Center mall ☎310/854-6655, ⊛www.macys .com. One of the big boys on the US department store scene, at Century City Marketplace; 920 W Seventh St, Downtown; the Santa Monica Place mall; Westside Pavilion; Paseo Colorado mall; 401 S Lake Ave, Pasadena; 3400 Sepulveda Blvd, Manhattan Beach; Del Amo Fashion Center, South Bay; Glendale Galleria; Newport Beach Fashion Island; South Coast Plaza, Costa Mesa; and other Orange County locations.

Neiman-Marcus 9700 Wilshire Blvd, Beverly Hills ☎310/550-5900, ⊛www.neimanmarcus .com. Loaded with attitude and (overly) high prices, with three fancy restaurants, opulent displays of jewelry, and a plethora of fur coats, this store is quintessential Beverly Hills, located at the base of the Golden Triangle. Also in Orange County at Newport Beach Fashion Island ☎949/759-1900.

Nordstrom 10830 Pico Blvd, in the Westside Pavilion mall, West LA ☎310/470-6155, ⊛www.nordstrom.com. Mostly clothing and accessories at this Westside department store. If you can't decide on the right party dress or power tie, a "personal shopper" can help you – for a steep price. Also at the Grove mall, Mid-Wilshire; Glendale Galleria; South Coast Plaza; and many other branches in the valleys and Orange County.

Saks Fifth Avenue 9600 Wilshire Blvd, Beverly Hills ☎310/275-4211, ⊛www.saksfifthavenue. com. An upmarket chain with expensive perfume, eye-popping jewelry, and high fashion. Also at South Coast Plaza ☎714/540-3233.

Shopping malls

Beverly Center 8500 Beverly Blvd, between Mid-Wilshire and West Hollywood ☎310/854-0070. Seven acres of boutiques, Macy's and Bloomingdale's, and a multiplex cinema, all in one complex that resembles a giant brown concrete bunker – built over a parking garage.

Burbank Town Center 201 E Magnolia Blvd at N San Fernando Rd, Burbank ☎818/566-8617.

Branches of Sears, Mervyn's and Macy's occupy this complex of buildings just outside the heart of old Burbank, right beside the I-5 freeway.

Century City Marketplace 10250 Santa Monica Blvd, Century City ☎310/553-5300. An outdoor mall with one hundred upscale shops and one of the better food courts around. The place to come to see stars do their shopping, and a spot to catch a first-run movie in excellent surroundings at the AMC Century 15 Theaters (see p.316).

Del Amo Fashion Center Hawthorne Blvd at Carson St, Torrance ☎310/542-8525. The South Bay's own super-mall, one of the country's largest, with five major anchor stores and a wealth of mid-level retailers and shoppers.

Glendale Galleria Central Ave at Colorado St, Glendale ☎818/240-9481. A sprawling downtown complex with Nordstrom and Macy's, and a broad selection of clothiers.

The Grove 6301 W Third St, Mid-Wilshire ☎323/571-8830. A giant, open-air mega-structure by the Farmers Market; has all the usual chain retailers and restaurants, movie theaters, and a more stylish design than the typical "dumb-box" construction found elsewhere.

▲ The Grove

Hollywood & Highland **at the same intersection in Hollywood** ⊕323/960-2311. A mega-mall modeled after an elaborate silent-film set, but offering the usual corporate boutiques and trendy shops, and a multiplex connected to the Chinese Theatre.

Newport Beach Fashion Island **401 Newport Center Drive** ⊕949/721-2000. A reasonable alternative to Orange County's South Coast Plaza, though not as large, with an appealing outdoor setting. Anchored by Bloomingdale's, Macy's, and Neiman-Marcus.

Paseo Colorado **E Colorado Blvd at S Los Robles Ave, Pasadena** ⊕626/795-8891. Two levels of (mostly chain) stores, including Macy's, beneath several levels of housing, with street-front entrances and an open-air design that invites strolling.

Santa Monica Place **Broadway at Second St, Santa Monica** ⊕310/394-5451. Sunny, skylit mall with three tiers of shops and an outdated postmodern-pastel decor. The chain-link-walled parking garage is of minor note as an early Frank Gehry design experiment.

Sherman Oaks Galleria **15301 Ventura Blvd, Sherman Oaks** ⊕818/382-4100. Sleek mall – and nothing like the original Galleria – with a handful of restaurants and shops, plus a multiplex; only worthwhile if you're in the neighborhood.

South Coast Plaza **3333 Bristol St, north of 405 freeway, Costa Mesa** ⊕714/435-2000. Orange County's main super-mall, where you'll get a good workout navigating the nearly three hundred shops and huge crowds of locals and tourists. Includes seven anchor stores – among them Macy's, Saks Fifth Avenue, and Nordstrom — and many top-name designer boutiques.

Third Street Promenade **Third St between Broadway and Wilshire Blvd, Santa Monica.** Major outdoor mall, packed on weekend evenings with mobs scurrying about the fashion retailers, restaurants, and cinemas. Throngs of itinerant musicians, homeless people, and gaping tourists round out the picture. In recent years, though, chain retailers have replaced independent businesses.

Westfield Fashion Square **14006 Riverside Drive, San Fernando Valley** ⊕818/783-0550. The famed Galleria – the original Sherman Oaks home to the notorious "Valley girls" – no longer exists, so this nearby mall now suffices for Valley denizens. Macy's and Bloomingdale's are the anchors, with around 120 other chain stores vying for your attention.

Westside Pavilion **Pico and Westwood blvds, West LA** ⊕310/474-6255. The obligatory chain stores at this postmodern shopping complex centered around Nordstrom and Macy's; the outdoor, western side of the mall is more engaging to stroll through, but has the same familiar retailers.

Clothes and fashion

In LA's iconic **clothing** stores, you can reinvent yourself with a freshly bought Hermès bag, velvet cape, or gold lamé dog collar. Apart from the usual chain-clothing stores, you'll find hordes of slick designer boutiques along Rodeo Drive, on the western side of West Hollywood, and increasingly along Melrose Avenue. Much more relaxed are the funky clothing stores for which LA is famous, many of them located along La Brea and north Vermont avenues and Santa Monica and Sunset boulevards. If you're just looking for cheap duds, however, LA has a good selection of secondhand and vintage clothiers to choose from.

Upscale chain stores

Bernini **8500 Beverly Blvd, in the Beverly Center mall** ⊕310/659-0228. Any money you haven't spent elsewhere in the mall will quickly evaporate at this pricey shop, which offers chic men's and women's clothing, notably fancy suits and tuxedos, plus colognes and perfumes. Also at 346 N Rodeo Drive, Beverly Hills ⊕310/273-8786.

Chanel **400 N Rodeo Drive, Beverly Hills** ⊕310/278-5500. As you'd expect, a pricey selection of swanky clothes and perfumes from Paris. You'll get a healthy dose of attitude, too, if you've only come to browse.

Christian Dior 309 N Rodeo Drive, Beverly Hills ☏ **310/859-4700.** Top-flight high fashion for predictably high prices – but you knew that already. Show up wearing jeans and sneakers and expect to be shown the door. Also at Beverly Center ☏310/659-5875, and South Coast Plaza ☏714/549-4700.

Façonnable 9680 Wilshire Blvd, Beverly Hills ☏ **310/247-8277.** An upper-bracket clothing merchant at the base of the Golden Triangle, selling sleek casual and dress wear, and an assortment of colognes and fragrances; a shade less pretentious than some of its bigger-name neighbors. Also at South Coast Plaza ☏714/966-1140.

Fendi 355 N Rodeo Drive, Beverly Hills ☏ **310/276-8888.** Ultra-chic designer shirts, sportswear, and watches for Americans who want to look vaguely European, but not be too showy about it. Also at South Coast Plaza ☏714/751-1111.

Giorgio Armani 436 N Rodeo Drive, Beverly Hills ☏310/271-5555 **or Beverly Center** ☏310/289-3610. One of LA's most elite fashion houses, featuring sleek, well-cut suits that are standard issue to movie agents, lawyers, and other self-anointed big shots. For slightly cheaper clothing, try Emporio Armani at 9533 Brighton Way ☏310/271-7790, or Armani Exchange, at 8700 Sunset Blvd, West Hollywood ☏310/659-0171.

Gucci 347 N Rodeo Drive, Beverly Hills ☏310/278-3451. Aside from the outlandishly priced shoes, wallets, and accessories that you can find here, there's also a fair assortment of upscale men's and women's clothing. Also at Beverly Center ☏310/652-0375, and South Coast Plaza ☏714/557-9600.

Hugo Boss 414 N Rodeo Drive, Beverly Hills ☏310/859-2888. The place to go if you're looking for a thousand-dollar suit. Also at the Beverly Center mall ☏310/657-0011; Century City Marketplace ☏310/553-7171; Newport Beach Fashion Island ☏949/759-1622; and South Coast Plaza ☏714/641-8661.

Kenneth Cole Broadway at Second Street, in the Santa Monica Place mall ☏310/458-6633. Leather jackets, tapered boots, sleek earrings, and hip-hugging pants – all in black – to help you get into the chic nightclubs in town. Also a branch at Beverly

Center ☏310/659-2396; Century City Marketplace ☏310/282-8535; and Newport Beach Fashion Island ☏949/219-0671.

Louis Vuitton 295 N Rodeo Drive, Beverly Hills ☏310/859-0457. Designer wallets and luggage in plenty of expensive styles. Also at the Beverly Center mall ☏310/360-1506; Century City Mall ☏310/551-0090; Hollywood & Highland mall ☏323/962-6216; Newport Beach Fashion Island ☏949/759-1900; and South Coast Plaza ☏714/662-6907.

Prada 469 N Rodeo Drive, Beverly Hills ☏310/385-5959. Ultra-chic couturier in an unmarked modern building, attracting clients who don't bat an eyelash at paying thousands for a shirt.

Ralph Lauren 444 N Rodeo Drive, Beverly Hills ☏310/281-7200. The top place to get yourself outfitted to resemble a member of the English gentry. Pick up a gilded walking cane, finely tailored suit, and a smart tweed cap, all for a small fortune. Also at South Coast Plaza ☏714/556-7656 and in Malibu at 3835 Cross Creek Rd ☏310/317-9592.

St. John 9536 Wilshire Blvd, Beverly Hills ☏310/858-1116. Chock full of elite women's power outfits for crushing the competition at a corporate meeting, or for dining in smart luxury at an exclusive restaurant. A dozen other area locations.

Zegna 301 N Rodeo Drive, Beverly Hills ☏310/247-8827. Exclusive lines of menswear and the high-end men's ZegnaSport collection make this a popular spot for young celebrities and even old-money types. Also at South Coast Plaza ☏714/444-1534.

Designer boutiques

Betsey Johnson 8050 Melrose Ave, West Hollywood ☏323/852-1534. An upscale boutique where micro-miniskirts, flirty tops, and girly handbags are all part of a funky look, for which you'll pay plenty. Other branches in the Sherman Oaks Fashion Square ☏818/986-9810 and Newport Beach Fashion Island ☏949/720-0186.

Diavolina 334 S La Brea Ave, Mid-Wilshire ☏323/936-3000. Shoes in which you can really strike a "little devil" pose: killer stilettos, modest mules, and funky boots, priced anywhere from around $100 to well over $500. Also a chic location for apparel at 156 S Robertson Blvd ☏310/550-1341.

Fred Segal 8118 Melrose Ave, West Hollywood ℡323/651-1935. For those poseurs and party-hoppers who wouldn't be spotted dead in Beverly Hills, this Melrose complex – selling everything from stylish shoes and duds to cosmetics – provides just the right mix of designer gloss and funky edge. Also with several other citywide branches.

Giselle 1306 Montana Ave, Santa Monica ℡310/451-2140. Well-established designer women's clothing in a variety of styles, but with a strong emphasis on wispy, pre-Raphaelite designs for size-2 waifs.

Jimmy Choo 469 N Canon Drive, Beverly Hills ℡310/860-9045. Even if you're just looking, and can't afford the exorbitant prices, there are enough strappy sandals and slender boots to give you warm memories on your trip home. Also at South Coast Plaza ℡714/327-0644.

Kendo 7218 Melrose Ave ℡323/934-9450. The self-proclaimed women's "sneaker boutique" that really is the height of conspicuous, almost absurd consumption – selling high-priced vintage running shoes from the 1970s and 80s, along with limited-edition designer footwear of the stylish and sporty varieties.

Lisa Kline 136 S Robertson Blvd ℡310/246-0907. If you want to dress on the leading edge of trendiness (in clothes that may be out of date by the time you fly home), this is the place to come, with an array of high-end denim jeans, among other women's garments. Also a branch at 315 S Beverly Drive ℡310/691-1070 and a men's store at 143 S Robertson Blvd ℡310/385-7113.

Maxfield 8825 Melrose Ave, West Hollywood ℡310/274-8800. One of LA's most exclusive boutiques, selling big-name and lesser-known labels, and displaying pricey classic and modern antiques, expensive dresses and baubles, irreverent books, and an eye-popping array of jewelry.

Paper Bag Princess 8818 Olympic Blvd, West LA ℡310/385-9036. A cross between an elite boutique and a secondhand store: an upscale dealer in gently worn vintage designer fashions. Some items on the racks are on consignment from celebrities (who allegedly frequent the place).

Veronica M 7122 Beverly Blvd, north of Mid-Wilshire ℡323/936-3802. Tasteful boutique with a smart selection of women's attire and jewelry, a bit more affordable than at comparable designer stores around town.

Funky clothing

Agent Provocateur 7961 Melrose Ave, West Hollywood ℡323/653-0229. If Victorian-style knickers and tasteful, yet racy, boudoir skimpies are what you're seeking, this is the spot – LA's own, quirkier spin on Victoria's Secret, with a lot more spark and imagination.

Frederick's of Hollywood 6751 Hollywood Blvd, Hollywood ℡323/957-5953. Offers a panoply of frilly, lacy and leathery lingerie (prices vary). Many other branches in and around LA; this one moved from its original, legendary location a block away.

Ipso Facto 517 N Harbor Blvd, Fullerton ℡714/525-7865. Piercing supplies for serious punks, ultra-black goth clothing, and a full range of skull-emblazoned belts, rings, and boots at this retailer in, of all places, Orange County.

Necromance 7208 and 7220 Melrose Ave, north of Mid-Wilshire ℡323/934-8684. Try on the latest ghoulish clothing at this morbidly themed shop, which sells coffin ornaments, tarot cards, and goth fashions that can make you look like a spooky specter in no time.

Panty Raid 2378 Glendale Blvd, Silver Lake ℡323/668-1888. One of LA's best spots for affordable and inventive styles of lingerie and, of course, underwear, with provocative g-strings, push-up bras, and the like.

Retail Slut 7308 Melrose Ave, north of Mid-Wilshire ℡323/934-1339. An essential Melrose stop for decades, where you can pick up all the vinyl dresses, skull necklaces, leather dog collars, bondage gear, and spiked wristbands you'll ever need.

Trashy Lingerie 402 N La Cienega Blvd, West Hollywood ℡310/652-4543. Not only can you find the sort of undergarments you'd expect, you can also browse through a wide selection of more traditional satin and silk bras, teddies, and bustiers. All of the revealing items are handmade, and you'll have to pay a $5 annual "membership fee" to get in.

Uncle Jer's 4459 Sunset Blvd, Silver Lake ℡323/662-6710. Quirky shop crammed with colorful and inexpensive garments, much of it handmade, along with soaps and fragrances, incense and "magic potions," and assorted trinkets.

Secondhand and vintage clothing

Aardvark's Odd Ark 7579 Melrose Ave ☎323/655-6769. One of LA's best for used garments, whether wild psychedelic shirts, old leisure suits, goofy ball caps, and frumpy pants, or more recent – and more fashionable – shirts, skirts, dresses, and suits. Also at 1253 E Colorado Blvd, Pasadena ☎626/583-9109.

American Rag Cie 150 S La Brea Ave, Mid-Wilshire ☎323/935-3154. Not your typical secondhand clothing store; the beat-up denim jackets, floral-print dresses, and retro shoes here are often high-end designer material, sometimes restyled into new forms. This is among the most prominent of LA's vintage dealers, so be prepared to shell out.

Decades 8214 Melrose Ave, West Hollywood ☎323/655-0223. Sells elegant designer wear, but also offers expensive retro-clothes from the 1960s, with occasional detours into stylish 1950s apparel and ungainly 1970s jumpsuits.

Golyester 136 S La Brea Ave, Mid-Wilshire ☎323/931-1339. Very vintage materials, with clothes dating as far back as the nineteenth century, in every sort of fabric imaginable. Also sells antiques.

It's a Wrap 1164 S Robertson Blvd, Mid-Wilshire ☎310/246-WRAP. Fascinating place to buy garments and wardrobes from recent movies and TV shows. The prices aren't too cheap, but if you can't go another minute without owning a jacket worn by one of the Desperate Housewives, this store is for you. Also at 3315 W Magnolia Blvd, Burbank ☎818/567-7366.

Jet Rag 825 N La Brea Ave, Hollywood ☎323/939-0528. Vintage dealer selling stylish club jackets from the old Hollywood days, as well as all kinds of bargains on dresses, hats, accessories and plenty more — sometimes for as little as $1 per item.

Junk for Joy 3314 W Magnolia Blvd, Burbank ☎818/569-4903. A vintage dealer whom old-time clothing from the 1950s to the 1970s not only looks great, it's never been worn. On display are ancient, discontinued

items that have been overlooked by various fashion trends – but not by Hollywood, whose wardrobe designers sometimes use them for shoots.

Ozzie Dots 4637 Hollywood Blvd, Los Feliz ☎323/663-2867. A vintage store that's best known for its costumes, but that also has colorful and eye-catching 1930s-through-1970s attire – plus props and accessories like feather boas, Tiki cuff links, and soda-jerk hats.

Polkadots and Moonbeams 8367 Third St, Mid-Wilshire ☎323/651-1746. Dresses, swimsuits and sweaters from the pre-1970s era, most in fine condition and some quite affordable. If it's more modern clothing you crave, drift down to the pricier contemporary outlet at 8379 Third St ☎323/655-3880.

Re-Mix 7605 1/2 Beverly Blvd, Mid-Wilshire ☎323/936-6210. Stylish men's and women's shoes, from the dainty 1920s to the supper-club 1940s to the disco 1970s, many of them authentic (some reproduction) and none of them ever worn before.

Rodeo Drive Resale 11306 Ventura Blvd, Studio City, San Fernando Valley ☎818/980-9990. Purveyor of chic designer brands that you'd find on the titular Beverly Hills shopping strip, but at more affordable prices.

Squaresville 1800 N Vermont Ave, Los Feliz ☎323/669-8464. A bit off the beaten vintage path, but worth a trip for its cheap prices for mainly 1950s-through-80s wear and colorful jewelry and accessories – plus a good selection of holiday (ie, Halloween) wear during the season.

Wasteland 7428 Melrose Ave, north of Mid-Wilshire ☎323/653-3028. Solid vintage and used designer wear for a variety of prices; not the flashiest store on the block, but one of the more reliable vendors on this busy strip.

The Way We Wore 334 S La Brea Ave, Mid-Wilshire ☎323/937-0878. One of the best of the vintage clothiers in LA, stocking expensive dresses and shoes and other garments from the 1920s to the 80s, with classic shifts from Valentino and other name designers.

Spas and beauty services

As the capital of self-worship and personal transformation, LA has a large array of **hair** and **make-up salons** where you can be teased, sprayed, plucked, and painted. Cheap clip joints are everywhere, but if you're really looking to get a fancy makeover, or a massage, manicure, or pedicure, head for one of the top-notch **spas** and salons around town, or to a more affordable but smart spot.

Ball Beauty Supply 416 N Fairfax Ave, north of Mid-Wilshire ⓣ323/655-2330. A great store-house for inexpensive make-up, wigs, and other adornments, where the clientele is a mix of youthful male and female club-hoppers and old-timers who've been coming here for ages.

Beauty Bar 1638 N Cahuenga Blvd, Hollywood ⓣ323/464-7676. A fun watering-hole where you can pick from an array of beauty services, including henna tattoos, at afford-able prices – plus chill out with a neon-colored concoction. See also p.292.

Goodform 727 N Fairfax Ave, West Hollywood ⓣ323/658-8585. Whether you're primping for a night of clubbing or a power lunch, this colorful parlor will do the trick, using a variety of hair-styling and makeover techniques, along with more straightforward skin care and manicures.

Jessica's Nail Clinic 8627 Sunset Blvd, West Hollywood ⓣ310/659-9292. The place where the stars get their pedicures and manicures, and you can too. The occasional celebrity-peeping provides a small distraction.

Larchmont Beauty Center 208 N Larchmont Blvd, Mid-Wilshire ⓣ323/461-0162. Features a comprehensive, and pricey, assortment of bath products and beauty-care treatments, from hair styling, manicures and pedicures, makeovers, and skin care to massage and aromatherapy.

Le Pink & Co. 3820 Sunset Blvd, Silver Lake ⓣ323/661-7465. Cosmetics and skin-care products as well as various lotions, creams and bath items are the draw at this East Hollywood vendor of fine beauty supplies.

Ona Spa 7373 Beverly Blvd, north of mid-Wilshire ⓣ323/931-4442. Chic spa with a trendy atmosphere and a vaguely Asian-inspired design, and such options as vitality

and detox treatments for those in need of soul- as well as body-cleansing.

Robinson's Beautilities 12320 Venice Blvd, West LA ⓣ310/398-5757. Along with a good selection of hair-care products and cosmetics, this supply house stocks a fascinating assortment of designer and fright wigs, facial glitter, and special-effects make-up for the movie biz.

Rudy's Barber Shop 4451 W Sunset Blvd, Los Feliz ⓣ323/661-6535. Idiosyncratic LA salon, a super-hip joint in a converted East Hollywood garage that draws the local rocker and actor crowd. Good for an affordable trendy look. One of several locations around town.

Taka 2010 Sawtelle Blvd, West LA ⓣ310/575-6819. Hair styling with an Asian flair and a sharp modern edge that won't cost you a fortune (if it isn't entirely cheap, either), offering a full range of perms, cuts, weaves, straightenings, kinks, and anything else you can dream up.

Umberto 452 N Camden Drive, Beverly Hills ⓣ310/274-0393. Another celebrity-friendly locale, with steep prices, but not quite as much pretension as some of its neighbors. While you wait, eat a sandwich, or sip a cappuccino from the in-house food service. Also at 416 N Canon Drive, Beverly Hills ⓣ310/274-6395 and 1772 S Robertson Blvd, Mid-Wilshire ⓣ310/204-4995.

Vidal Sassoon 9403 Little Santa Monica Blvd, Beverly Hills ⓣ310/274-8791. While the full-price haircuts may seem out of reach, assistants in training charge roughly half – a very good deal considering the area. Cosmetology students can also tinker with your looks for much less at Vidal Sassoon's own "hair academy," located at 321 Santa Monica Blvd, Santa Monica ⓣ310/255-0011.

Drugstores and pharmacies

Horton & Converse 11600 Wilshire Blvd, West LA ⓣ310/478-0801. Open until midnight. Other locations open regular business hours: 2001 Santa Monica Blvd, Santa Monica ⓣ310/829-3401; 11600 Wilshire Blvd, West LA ⓣ310/478-0801; 8361 W Third St, West LA ⓣ310/659-6111; 9201 Sunset Blvd, West Hollywood ⓣ323/272-0488; 201 S Alvarado, Downtown ⓣ213/413-2424; 1127 Wilshire Blvd, Downtown ⓣ213/481-7030; 325 N Larchmont Blvd, Mid-Wilshire ⓣ323/466-7607; and 10250 Santa Monica Blvd, Century City Mall, West LA ⓣ310/557-2332.

Longs Drugs 8490 Beverly Blvd, Mid-Wilshire ☎323/653-0880. Also at 3202 Wilshire Blvd, Mid-Wilshire ☎310/829-5513; 9618 Pico Blvd, West LA ☎310/858-1070; 11941 San Vicente Blvd, West LA ☎310/440-4160; 7021 Hollywood Blvd, Hollywood ☎323/836-0304; and 255 Main St, Venice ☎310/399-2436.

Mickey Fine 433 N Roxbury St, Beverly Hills ☎310/271-6123. An only-in-LA pharmacy where the elite meet to pick up fancy European hair- and facial-care products, along with all the latest creams, ointments, gels, and any concoction promising to make the body more radiant.

Rite-Aid 463 N Bedford Dr, Beverly Hills ☎310/247-0843. Also at 5575 Wilshire Blvd, Mid-Wilshire ☎323/954-7193; 300 N Canon Drive, Beverly Hills ☎310/273-3561; 11321 National Blvd, West LA ☎310/479-5729; 7900 Sunset Blvd, Hollywood ☎323/876-4466; 1130 N La Brea Ave, Hollywood ☎323/463-8539; 1101 Westwood Blvd, West LA ☎310/209-0708; 6130 Sunset Blvd, Hollywood ☎323/467-4201. See ⓦwww.riteaid.com for more area branches.

Sav-On/Osco 201 N Los Angeles St, Downtown ☎213/620-1491. Also at 201 S Western Ave, Mid-Wilshire ☎323/386-1771; 861 N Vine St, Hollywood ☎323/466-7300; 5570 Wilshire Blvd, Mid-Wilshire ☎323/936-6121; 5510 Sunset Blvd, Hollywood ☎323/464-2169; 1747 N Cahuenga Blvd, Hollywood ☎323/463-7900; 8491 Santa Monica Blvd, West Hollywood ☎310/360-7326; 12315 Venice Blvd, West LA ☎310/390-6296; 12015 Wilshire Blvd, West LA ☎310/479-6500. See ⓦwww.savon.com for more area branches.

Food and drink

Since it's a matter of course to eat out in LA, you may never have to shop for **food** and **drink** at all. But if you're preparing a picnic, or want to indulge in a bit of home cooking, there are plenty of places to stock up. **Delis** and **groceries** can be found on many street corners. There are also a number of good **ethnic groceries** and **health-food stores**, as well as various fine **bakeries**, mainly clustered in West LA.

Delis and groceries

Art's Deli 12224 Ventura Blvd, Studio City ☎818/762-1221. Long-standing film-industry favorite, and the one deli that rarely provokes complaints among aficionados, providing a good range of sandwiches, soups, and breads.

Brent's Deli 19565 Parthenia Ave, Northridge ☎818/886-5679. This New York–style deli, in a minimall in a remote corner of the San Fernando Valley, features a huge takeout selection of meat, fish, desserts, salads, and sandwiches. Easily the best of its kind in the Valley, some would even say in LA itself.

Bristol Farms 7880 W Sunset Blvd, Hollywood ☎323/874-6301. One of the region's best grocers, with delicious meats, cheeses, wine, and caviar, but prices can be rather high. Still, a cut way above the standard gourmet supermarkets. Also at 9039 Beverly Blvd, West Hollywood ☎310/248-2804, and a half-dozen other locations. See ⓦwww.bristolfarms.com for details.

Canter's Deli 419 N Fairfax Ave, north of Mid-Wilshire ☎323/651-2030. An LA institution, next to its own unusual cabaret (see p.314), with tasty sandwiches, kosher soups, a good selection of meat and fish, and assorted sweets. Open 24-hrs.

Grand Central Market 317 S Broadway, Downtown ☎213/624-2378. One of the city's prime culinary destinations, with primo Mexican food, a warren of food stalls, and vendors of all sorts of produce, meat, cheese, snacks, and pastries from the region.

Izzy's Deli 1433 Wilshire Blvd, Santa Monica ☎310/394-1131. Long-standing favorite for straightforward deli fare, and one of the few good bets for authentic deli sandwiches along the coast. Open 24-hrs.

Jerry's Famous Deli 8701 Beverly Blvd, West Hollywood ☎310/289-1811. Not quite as good as other delis around town, but this local does sport a solid array of takeout soups, sandwiches, and meats, as well as cakes and pies. This particular branch is open 24-hrs, as is the one in Studio City at 12711

Ventura Blvd ☎818/980-4245. Also at 10925 Weyburn Ave, Westwood ☎310/208-3354. See ⓦwww.jerrysfamous deli.com for more branches.
Junior's 2379 Westwood Blvd, West LA ☎310/475-5771. This fine Westside deli and restaurant features a good bakery and deli counter that stocks all of the usual favorites – including lox, whitefish, matzo ball soup, and various egg dishes.
Langer's 704 S Alvarado St, Mid-Wilshire ☎213/483-8050. In the middle of the high-crime Westlake district, this is nevertheless one of LA's finest delis, with an excellent selection of takeout meats and baked goods, and twenty variations on LA's best (and most tender) pastrami sandwich. Closes at 4pm; curbside pickup available.
Nate 'n' Al's 414 N Beverly Drive, Beverly Hills ☎310/274-0101. This superior deli, in the middle of Beverly Hills' Golden Triangle, offers stargazing and a good array of meat and bread food stuffs – not to mention terrific blintzes, lox, and matzo-ball soup. See also p.263.
Stan's Produce 9307 W Pico Blvd, West LA ☎310/274-1865. A popular neighborhood grocer with a fine selection of fruits, vegetables, and exotic produce. Just south of Beverly Hills.
Vicente Foods 12027 San Vicente Blvd, Brentwood ☎310/472-4613. If you're in this upscale neighborhood, this is a good place to stop for a terrific selection of breads,

cheeses and meats to suit your fancy; worth the high prices.

Ethnic groceries

Alpine Village 833 W Torrance Blvd, Torrance ☎310/327-4384. Though quite a hike from LA, and in a rather drab South Bay area, this place has all the bratwurst and schnitzel you'll ever need, and plays host to one of LA's more spirited Oktoberfest celebrations.
American Armenian Grocery 1442 E Washington Blvd, Pasadena ☎626/794-9220. The place to come if you want to sample authentic food from the Caucasus region of Asia: scrumptious baked goods, pastries, nuts, spices, produce, and chocolates.
Bang Luck Market 5170 Hollywood Blvd, Hollywood ☎323/660-8000. Located in "Thai Town," a Thai grocer in Los Feliz with super-cheap prices on meat, fish, sauces, and noodles to help you make a Southeast Asian feast, or a simple snack.
Bay Cities Italian Deli 1517 Lincoln Blvd, Santa Monica ☎310/395-8279. An excellent, centrally located deli and retailer with an Italian focus. Offers piles of fresh pasta, meat, spices, and sauces, along with many French and Middle Eastern imports and terrific lunchtime sandwiches.
Bharat Bazaar 11510 Washington Blvd, Culver City ☎310/398-6766. One of several excellent

▲ Nate 'n' Al's

Indian grocers around this stretch of Culver City, providing some savory samosas and all the goods for making your own curries and vindaloo.

Claro's Italian Market 1003 E Valley Blvd, San Gabriel ☏626/288-2026. This compact but well-stocked spot has everything from Italian wines, chocolate, and crackers to frozen meals, plus a deli and a bakery offering some forty varieties of cookies. Worth the drive out to this section of the San Gabriel Valley.

Domingo's Italian Grocery 17548 Ventura Blvd, Encino ☏818/981-4466. A good reason to travel to the San Fernando Valley: a neighborhood staple for 50 years that continues to provide good and authentic Italian meats, pasta, and cheeses.

Elat Meat Market 8730 Pico Blvd, West LA ☏310/659-7070. Mainly Middle Eastern staples at cheap prices at this colorful kosher market, located near other ethnic grocers on Pico Blvd, just southeast of Beverly Hills.

Jeff's Gourmet Kosher Sausage Factory 8930 W Pico Blvd, West LA ☏310/858-8590. Despite the unassuming name, a top-notch vendor of well-crafted sausages, from mergez to jalapeno to Polish to veal bratwurst — delicious if you're in the mood for it.

Mandarin Deli 727 N Broadway, Downtown ☏213/623-6054. Very tasty and cheap noodles, pork and fish dumplings, and other hearty staples in the middle of Chinatown.

Marconda's in the Farmers Market, 6333 W Third St, Mid-Wilshire ☏323/938-5131. Longstanding favorite for its variety of excellent fresh-cut meats at affordable prices, including ribs, chops, steaks, lamb shanks, and more daring items like oxtail and tripe.

Market World 3030 W Sepulveda Blvd, Torrance ☏310/539-8899. A good selection of prepared Korean and pan-Asian meats, vegetables, and noodles at this South Bay grocery. Located off Crenshaw Blvd.

Nijiya Market 2130 Sawtelle Blvd, West LA ☏310/575-3300. Bentos – rice-and-meat combos served in a bowl – are among the succulent takeout items available at this wide-ranging Japanese grocer. Also a branch in Little Tokyo at 124 Japanese Village Plaza mall ☏213/680-3280 and three locations in the suburbs.

Olson's Deli 5560 Pico Blvd, Mid-Wilshire ☏323/938-0742. Herring, meatballs, and assorted sausages at this solid Swedish grocer, one of the few Scandinavian food stores in LA and definitely worth a try.

Thailand Plaza 5321 Hollywood Blvd, Hollywood ☏323/993-9000. This Thai supermarket and eatery has an impressive selection of Southeast Asian noodles, spices, and other delicacies for very cheap prices.

Vallarta Supermarket 10950 Sherman Way, Burbank ☏818/846-1717. San Fernando Valley chain – whose Burbank store is the closest to central LA – focusing on foodstuffs from Latin America, including special chilis and spices, with an onsite taqueria that doles out some delicious and inexpensive food. Find more stores at Ⓦ www.vallartasupermarket.com.

Health-food stores

Beverly Hills Juice Club 8382 Beverly Blvd, north of Mid-Wilshire ☏323/655-8300. Raw foods are the focus of this vegan-oriented takeout vendor and grocery, which supplies fruit, veggies, meatless sushi, sprout rolls, and, of course, ultra-healthy juices.

Co-Opportunity 1525 Broadway, Santa Monica ☏310/451-8902. A popular neighborhood store selling bulk organic and vegetarian foods, with a coffee & juice bar, plenty of macrobiotic and other specialty foodstuffs, and herbs, vitamins, and oils meant to soothe the body and soul.

Erewhon 7660 Beverly Blvd, north of Mid-Wilshire ☏323/937-0777. The epitome of health-obsessed LA, selling pricey health food, lots of vegetarian offerings, and all the wheat grass you can stand. Close to CBS Television City, so you're apt to spot a few B-actors in the aisles.

Full o' Life 2515 W Magnolia Blvd, Burbank ☏818/845-8343. This mother of all health-food stores dates back to 1959 and offers an organic market, deli, dairy, restaurant, and book department, and there are nutritionists and a naturopath on the premises daily.

Mother's Market 225 E 17th St, Costa Mesa ☏949/631-4741. A large health-food retailer in Orange County, the perfect place to stock up on bulk juice, vitamins, veggie cuisine, and even animal-friendly beauty supplies, with a nice deli and cafe on premises, too. Also at 19770 Beach Blvd, Huntington Beach ☏714/963-6667, and 2963 Michelson Drive, Irvine ☏949/752-6667.

Nature Mart 2080 Hillhurst Ave, Hollywood ☏323/660-0052. A Los Feliz storehouse for organic produce, non-sugary sweets, veggie options, hair and skin-care items, and a wealth of vitamins and herbs. Somewhat cheaper than comparable Westside retailers.

One Life 3001 Main St, Santa Monica ☎310/392-4501. Healthy eating near the bay, courtesy of this trusty old neighborhood grocer that sells organic produce, bulk foods, herbs, brown rice, unprocessed bread, and all the rest.

Simply Wholesome 4508 W Slauson Ave, South Central ☎323/294-2144. An icon of pop-modern design, the building that once housed the Wich Stand is now converted into an agreeable health-food shop. Juices, smoothies, and nutritious products, with an on-site cafe for dining on veggie food with a Caribbean flair.

VP Discount Health Food Mart 8001 Beverly Blvd, north of Mid-Wilshire ☎323/658-6506. A chain retailer that has a following of hard-core vegans willing to pay a bit more for clean, sanctified food. Also several other locations around town.

Whole Foods Market 239 N Crescent Drive, Beverly Hills ☎310/274-3360. One in a nationwide chain of high-quality megastores, this small but central branch is located in the exclusive Golden Triangle shopping zone. For other LA branches see Ⓦwww .wholefoods.com.

Baked and dairy goods

Al Gelato 806 S Robertson Blvd, West LA ☎310/659-8069. That delectable Italian version of ice cream – *gelato* – is served here with American panache: delicious flavors doled out in sizable helpings. The espresso *gelato* is particularly mouthwatering. Also offering Italian-styled soups and sandwiches.

Beverlywood Bakery 9128 Pico Blvd, West LA ☎310/278-0122. Longstanding vendor of Old World desserts and baked goods, from dense strudels to chewy, thick-crusted breads, with premium prices that reflect the store's proximity to Beverly Hills, a block north.

The Cheese Store 419 N Beverly Drive, Beverly Hills ☎1-800/547-1515 or 310/278-2855. More than four hundred types of cheese from the US and all over the world – some suspended invitingly overhead; prices can be equally out of reach.

Diamond Bakery 335 N Fairfax Ave, north of Mid-Wilshire ☎323/655-0534. In the heart of the Fairfax District, this great old Jewish bakery makes traditional favorites, including babka, challah, mandelbrot, and rugelach, and a legendary pumpernickel bread.

Doughboys Café and Bakery 1156 Highland Ave, Hollywood ☎323/467-9117. Tasty and filling pizzas, scones, and sandwiches are available for midday meals, but the real highlight of this Westside bakery is the bread: rich, hearty loaves with interesting ingredients like walnuts, olives, and various cheeses.

Fair Oaks Pharmacy and Soda Fountain 1526 Mission St, South Pasadena ☎626/799-1414. A fabulously restored soda fountain along the former Route 66, with many classic soda drinks, such as egg creams, and old-fashioned ice-cream treats like sundaes and banana splits.

Fosselman's 1824 W Main St, Alhambra ☎626/282-6533. Reason alone to visit this San Gabriel Valley town: what many, many Angelenos regard as the region's best ice cream. The very long-standing (85 years) shop churns out rich, creamy concoctions, highlighted by a delicious macadamia crunch and burgundy cherry.

Gill's Old Fashioned 6333 W Third St, north of Mid-Wilshire ☎213/936-6786. The name says it – a longtime neighborhood fave with a convenient location in the Farmers Market and a nice selection of rich ice creams, yogurts, ices, and frozen bananas.

Gourmet Cobbler Factory 33 N Catalina Ave, Pasadena ☎626/795-1005. Bakery selling a range of yummy, fruity cobblers, from blackberry and other berry flavors, to apple and peach, to pecan and sweet potato. Occupies a prime spot near Old Pasadena.

LA Desserts 113 N Robertson Blvd, Beverly Hills ☎310/273-5537. If you don't mind a few snide looks from the Hollywood swells, step into this terrific bakery inside the swank *Ivy* restaurant and try the delicious cakes, cookies, and tarts, among the best on the Westside.

La Brea Bakery 624 S La Brea Ave, Mid-Wilshire ☎323/939-6813. This bakery (adjacent to the upscale *Campanile* restaurant; see p.270) is a serious treat for anyone with an interest in fine breads, from sourdough rolls to fancier olive- and cherry-laden loaves, as well as scrumptious cookies, tarts, and cheeses.

Mäni's Bakery 519 S Fairfax Ave, Mid-Wilshire ☎323/938-8800. This vegetarian- and vegan-oriented bakery provides sugarless brownies and meatless sandwiches to local bohemians and wholefood-oriented yuppies.

Mousse Fantasy/Beard Papa's 2130 Sawtelle Blvd #110, West LA ☎310/479-6665. Pair of combined patisseries featuring a range of tasty tarts and pastries, highlighted by the eclairs, cream puffs, and various mousses and cakes.

Portos Bakery 315 N Brand Blvd, Glendale ☎818/956-5996. In a town that used to be filled with Cuban immigrants, this great throwback to the old days offers tasty baked goods and desserts, along with flaky Cuban pastries, cheesecakes soaked in rum, muffins, Danishes, croissants, and tortes.

Röckenwagner 12835 W Washington Blvd, Culver City ☎310/578-8171. A Westside culinary delight that offers chocolate desserts, rich pastries and scones, donuts, rolls, and hearty breads like the signature pretzel bread. No credit cards.

Say Cheese 2800 Hyperion Ave, Silver Lake ☎323/665-0545. A distinctive array of French and other international cheeses, priced from moderate to expensive. The delicious sandwiches may be your best bet.

Scoops 712 N Heliotrope, north of Mid-Wilshire ☎323/906-2649. Located right off the freeway in a drab location, a terrific place to sample inventive, unexpected ice cream flavors for cheap prices. Everything from pumpkin brandy to lychee to maple oreo to brown bread (!) may tempt your tongue if you let it.

Viktor Benes Continental Pastries 8330 Santa Monica Blvd, West Hollywood ☎310/654-5543. The place to go for freshly baked bread, coffee cakes, Danish pastries, and chocolaty treats, and appreciative local fans know it. Fifteen other area locations as well.

Beer, wine, and spirits

Cañon Liquor and Deli 1586 E Chevy Chase Drive, Glendale ☎818/547-1764. Pick up a bottle of wine or a pound of Italian meat at this excellent local grocer.

Greenblatt's Deli & Fine Wine 8017 Sunset Blvd, West Hollywood ☎323/656-0606. A Sunset Strip kosher deli and liquor mart that's a neighborhood favorite, best known for its excellent sandwiches and wide assortment of wine, brandy, Champagne, and Scotch. Open 'til 2am.

Hi-Time Wine Cellars 250 Ogle St, Costa Mesa ☎949/650-8463 or 1-800/331-3005, ⊛www .hitimewine.com. Despite the unimpressive name, this has been one of Southern California's finest purveyors of wine and spirits for 50 years, and perhaps its best overall choice for buying microbrewed and European beers.

Red Carpet Wine 400 E Glenoaks Blvd, Glendale ☎818/247-5544 or 1-800/339-0609. Besides having a comfortable wine bar and a sizable stock of vino and beer, this store is also a fine spot to purchase spirits, cigars, Champagne, and chocolates.

Silver Lake Wine 2395 Glendale Blvd ☎323/662-9024. Favorite Hollywood vino vendor that has a wealth of regional brands, including some obscure ones, which you can sample during regular Sunday wine tastings at 3pm, with other primo tastings on Mondays and Thursdays at 5pm.

Valley Beverage Company 14901 Ventura Blvd, Sherman Oaks ☎818/981-1566. Offering an excellent selection of California and international wines, many at discounted prices, with a special emphasis on kosher wines, Scotch, tequila, and brandy.

Wally's 2107 Westwood Blvd, West LA ☎310/475-0606. A gourmet grocery that has a good assortment of international wines and beers, plus caviar, cheeses, and other fancy treats; sells hard liquor and cigars, too.

Wine and Liquor Depot 16938 Saticoy St, Van Nuys ☎818/996-1414. Promising the lowest area prices on blended and single malt Scotch, this Valley dealer is also worth a look for its international wines, port, sherry, bourbon, and beer.

Bookstores

It can seem like LA has almost as many **bookstores** as people, with enough variety to suit every taste, whether you want chain **superstores**, cozy local bookstores, or **specialist** and **secondhand** places that may reward several hours' browsing along miles of dusty shelves. Megastores like Barnes and Noble (Ⓦwww .bn.com) have branches all over the place, but locally operated stores often have a more well-chosen selection and intelligent advice on your purchases.

General interest and new books

Book Soup 8818 W Sunset Blvd, West Hollywood ☎310/659-3110. Great selection, right on Sunset Strip. Narrow, winding aisles stuffed with books, strong in art, entertainment, travel, politics, and photography. Celebs are sometimes known to come in, attempting to look studious.

▲ Book Soup

Dutton's 11975 San Vicente Blvd, Brentwood ☎310/476-6263. One of the better general-interest stores in town, an ungainly complex built around a central courtyard. Its aisles tend to be cluttered, but it's a fine store; try to visit during the less-crowded weekdays. **Equator Books** 1103 Abbot Kinney Blvd, Venice ☎310/399-5544. Former garage-turned-hipster-bookseller that has a chic and inviting atmosphere, art on the walls, and a broad but well-selected range of titles; the art, alternative, fiction, and magazine sections are the strongest. **Illiterature** 452 S La Brea Ave, Mid-Wilshire ☎323/937-3505. This smallish bookstore has a limited, but well-chosen, selection of general-interest titles; it also appeals for its quality soaps, candles, toys, and other gifts near the back of the store.

Skylight Books 1818 N Vermont Ave, Hollywood ☎323/660-1175. Just north of Barnsdall Park in a trendy shopping zone, this Los Feliz bookseller has a broad range of mainstream and alternative literature, plus a fine selection of film books and regularly scheduled author readings. **Small World Books** 1407 Ocean Front Walk, Venice ☎310/399-2360. A modest neighborhood dealer by the beach that's strong on mystery novels and literature from local and national authors, including publications from small presses. **Vroman's** 695 E Colorado Blvd, Pasadena ☎1-800/769-2665 or 626/449-5320. One of the San Gabriel Valley's major retailers, offering a good selection and a café. Although there are no real bargains here, smaller bookstores (below) selling used and specialist books can be found within a few blocks.

Secondhand books

Acres of Books 240 Long Beach Blvd, Long Beach ☎526/437-6980. Worth a trip down the Blue Line Metrorail just to wallow in LA's largest, and most disorganized, secondhand collection. You may not be able to find the exact title you're looking for, but chances are you'll stumble across something good. **Alias Books** 1650 Sawtelle Blvd, West LA ☎310/473-4442. Not the hugest or cheapest selection of used titles in town, but among the most carefully chosen, with strengths in scholarly titles, art, architecture, textbooks, comics, and rare items. **Atlantis Book Shop** 144 S San Fernando Rd, Burbank ☎818/845-6467. Specializes in history, fiction, politics, and – as the name might suggest – the paranormal, extrater-restrial, and mythological. **Berkelouw Books** 830 N Highland Ave, Hollywood ☎323/466-3321. An easy-to-miss dealer with voluminous stacks of titles in fiction, biography, entertainment, and history – plus a knowledgable owner who'll be glad to help you sift through his well-chosen collection. **Book Alley** 611 E Colorado Blvd, Pasadena ☎626/683-8083. A handsomely designed bookstore with a large stock of affordable used books on a wide variety of subjects.

You'll find a similar selection at the store's annex, Book Alley Too!, nearby at 696 E Colorado Blvd ☏626/795-0818.

Brand Book Shop 231 N Brand Blvd, Glendale ☏818/507-5943. Excellent Valley used-book seller with a huge range of liberal-arts titles and particular strengths in entertainment, history, and politics. Located in the pulsing heart of downtown Glendale.

Cliff's Books 630 E Colorado Blvd, Pasadena ☏626/449-9541. This long-standing used-bookseller, with narrow aisles stacked with titles on a wide assortment of subjects, has a bigger selection than some other bookstores in the vicinity, with slightly higher prices as well.

Cosmopolitan Book Shop 7017 Melrose Ave, north of Mid-Wilshire ☏323/938-7119. The cozier Westside equivalent to Acres of Books, a dealer loaded with thousands of titles stacked high in oversized bookcases, on a variety of subjects but especially strong on film and media.

Iliad Bookshop 5400 Cahuenga Blvd, San Fernando Valley ☏818/509-2665. Easily one of LA's best used booksellers, and meriting a trip out to North Hollywood. Features a broad selection of titles, including rare, out-of-print, and bizarre titles you probably won't find anywhere else.

Kulturas 1700 Ocean Park Blvd, Santa Monica ☏310/450-8707. The personification of the small-time independent bookseller, with interesting, sometimes oddball, titles, and a focus on paperback fiction and the liberal arts. Not as selective as other stores' inventory, though.

Wilshire Books 3018 Wilshire Blvd, Santa Monica ☏310/828-3115. An excellent used-bookstore for its size, which is quite small and cramped. Features an intelligent collection of tomes on art, politics, religion, and music – all of them coherently organized and accessible.

Specialist bookstores

Arcana 1229 Third Street Promenade, Santa Monica ☏310/458-1499. Among the very last independent holdouts in the face of corporate chain store takeover of this strip, this is a fine place to choose from a nicely curated array of art books, with a particular strength in photography.

Bodhi Tree 8585 Melrose Ave, West Hollywood ☏310/659-1733. Ultra-trendy Westside book retailer in an ultra-chic part of Melrose, with a range of New Age, occult, and self-improvement titles, including plenty of information on the healing power of crystals, pyramids, and the like.

Circus of Books 4001 Sunset Blvd, Silver Lake ☏323/666-1304. Take a trip through LA's seamier side at this well-known (mainly magazine) dealer in weird murder tales, serial-killer exposés, S/M diaries, and assorted pornography. Also a more gay-oriented branch at 8230 Santa Monica Blvd, West Hollywood ☏323/656-6533.

Cook's Library 8373 W Third St, north of Mid-Wilshire ☏323/655-3141. It's all about eats at this top-notch dealer in culinary content. Whether you want to whip up a mean steak tartare or are trying to hunting down that 1950s recipe for apple brown betty, the info you need is probably on one of the eight thousand titles.

Dawson's 535 N Larchmont Blvd, north of Mid-Wilshire ☏323/469-2186. Dating back a hundred years, supposedly the longest-operating bookstore in LA (though at different sites), and known for its excellent stock of vintage books on California and Western US history. Holds regular salons on social and city politics, and runs an attached photography gallery of some note.

A Different Light 8853 Santa Monica Blvd, West Hollywood ☏310/854-6601. The city's best-known gay and lesbian bookstore, in the heart of the city's main gay district, with monthly art shows, readings, and women's music events. See also "Gay and lesbian LA," p.319.

Distant Lands 56 S Raymond Ave, Pasadena ☏626/449-3220. Well-stocked travel bookstore in Old Pasadena, with some fairly hard-to-find titles, as well as maps and travel gear. Also hosts the occasional public speaker and globe-trotting slide show.

Geographia 4000 Riverside Drive, Burbank ☏818/848-1414. Solid San Fernando Valley choice for an array of travel titles, from the basic guides to detailed maps and other publications.

Hennessey and Ingalls 214 Wilshire Blvd, Santa Monica ☏310/458-9074. An impressive range of coffee-table art and architecture books makes this bookstore among the best of its kind in LA. Rare posters, catalogs, and hard-to-find books are also in stock. While there are many cut-rate remainders, the books you'll likely want will be priced at a premium.

Hollywood Book and Poster Co. 6562 Hollywood Blvd, Hollywood ☎323/465-8764. A great place to stop if you're hunting for any kind of media memorabilia, including film stills of famous and obscure actors, books on "psychotronic" cinema and TV history, various screenplays, and, of course, splashy old movie posters.

Larry Edmunds Book Shop 6644 Hollywood Blvd, Hollywood ☎323/463-3273. Many stacks of books, a large number of them out of print, are offered on every aspect of film and theater, with movie stills and posters. Located at the center of touristy Hollywood.

Mitchell Books 1395 E Washington Blvd, Pasadena ☎626/798-4438. A favorite San Gabriel Valley dealer in detective and mystery novels, where you can grab a copy of Raymond Chandler, Walter Moseley, or James Ellroy to use as a fictional travel-guide to LA's dark side.

Norton Simon Museum Bookstore 411 W Colorado Blvd, Pasadena ☎626/449-6840. One of LA's better museum bookstores, with a superb stock of material – often with sizeable volumes on artists in the museum's collection.

Psychic Eye 1011 W Olive Ave, Burbank ☎818/845-8831. Small chain of book shops focusing on New Age and occult topics, including astrology and Wicca, plus various candles, tools, and oils for sale. Psychics give personal on-site readings ($20+).

Samuel French Theatre & Film Bookshop 7623 Sunset Blvd, Hollywood ☎323/876-0570. LA's broadest selection of theater books is found in this local institution, along with a good collection of movie and media-related titles.

Taschen 354 N Beverly Drive, Beverly Hills ☎310/274-4300. Fun, edifying, and weird titles that focus on everything from Renaissance art to kitsch Americana to fetish photography. Cheap volumes on both familiar and obscure subjects, and even the coffee-table books are occasionally afford-able. Also right outside the Farmers Market, 6333 W Third St, Mid-Wilshire ☎323/931-1168.

Traveler's Bookcase 8375 W Third St, Mid-Wilshire ☎323/655-0575. A bookseller with a limited but well-chosen selection of travel guides, maps, and publications, along with a fine array of literary travel stories, novels, trip diaries, and personal memoirs and essays.

Wacko 4633 Hollywood Blvd, Hollywood ☎323/663-0122. Although also great for its eclectic gift selection, this East Hollywood favorite stocks an excellent array of titles leaning toward the alternative: art and archi-tecture, bizarre fetishes, alternative history, music guides, and conspiracy rants.

Music stores

As elsewhere, many **record stores** have closed in LA in recent years due to competition from the Internet. While CDs are the dominant format, vinyl fans will be happy to find LPs here and there, thanks in equal parts to diehard collectors and club DJs. The selection below leans toward LA's more unusual record stores.

Amoeba Music 6400 W Sunset Blvd, Hollywood ☎323/245-6400. Arguably the greatest record store in Southern California, featuring a vast selection of titles – supposedly numbering around half a million – on CD, tape, and vinyl, which you can freely hear at listening carrels throughout the store. Also presents occasional in-store live music.

Backside Records 139 N San Fernando Rd, Burbank ☎818/559-7573. Though very much oriented toward DJs and the vinyl-minded, this two-level store stocks both LPs and CDs with a broad range of electronica, plus some jazz, rap, and soul.

Counterpoint 5911 Franklin Ave, Hollywood ☎323/957-7965. Although not the highest-profile dealer in town, it has a terrific smorgasbord of used vinyl, CDs, movies on cassette and DVD, books, and even antique 78 records. Also connected to its own underground art gallery.

DMC Records 7619 Melrose Ave, Hollywood ☎323/651-3520. A prime spot to buy used CDs and, especially, vinyl. Local club-hoppers and DJs come here to stock up on the latest dance records and find more obscure tracks by little-known artists.

Fingerprints 4612 E Second St, Long Beach ☎562/433-4996. A formidable indie outfit in the South Bay, offering alternative-leaning CDs and vinyl, plus in-store performances from local rockers, and a mellow, soft-sell attitude. Located in the Belmont Shore district.

Headline Records 7706 Melrose Ave, Hollywood ⊤323/655-2125. The last gasp of grungy old Melrose, this book, T-shirt, and record joint is oriented toward all things punk, from proto-punk 60s garage kings to latter-day thrashers and pogoers, with current CDs and hard-to-find vinyl rarities both making appearances.

Orphaned CDs 7401 Sunset Blvd, Hollywood ⊤323/874-0198. Broad selection of all kinds of used CDs, good and bad, for some of the city's cheapest prices.

Penny Lane 1661 E Colorado Blvd, Pasadena ⊤626/535-0949. New and used records at reasonable prices. Often crowded, this local chain features listening stations and has a good number of LPs as well. Also at 569 S Lake Ave, Pasadena (⊤626/568-9999).

Poo-Bah Records 2636 E Colorado Blvd, Pasadena ⊤626/449-3359. Plenty of American and imported New Wave sounds, along with 1980s technopop and various other genres.

Record Surplus 11609 W Pico Blvd, West LA ⊤310/478-4217. A massive LP collection of surf music, early rock'n'roll, 1960s soundtracks, and unintentionally hilarious spoken-word recordings. Prices are excellent, with many CDs and cassettes offered at ridiculously low prices. Anyone with an interest in classic, alternative, or offbeat music knows this place.

Rockaway Records 2395 Glendale Blvd, Silver Lake ⊤323/664-3232. Great place to come for both used CDs and LPs, as well as DVDs. Also offers old magazines, posters, and memorabilia. Located just east of the Silver Lake reservoir.

Vinyl Fetish 1614 N Cahuenga Blvd, Hollywood ⊤323/957-2290. Loaded with punk, alternative, and indie sounds – plus plenty of vinyl for budding DJs – this is also a good place to discover what's new on the ever-changing LA music scene.

Virgin Megastore 8000 Sunset Blvd, West Hollywood ⊤323/650-8666. A Sunset Strip corporate-music giant with steep retail prices, but well worth a look for the extensive selection spread over two levels, including CDs, DVDs, books, and video games. On the former site of legendary Schwab's drugstore.

Specialty stores

The **specialty stores** below are some of the more colorful you'll find in LA.

Cinema Secrets Beauty Supply 4400 W Riverside Drive, Burbank ⊤818/846-0579. If you're disappointed that Halloween only comes one day of the year, come to this emporium crammed with over-the-top glam and glitz —stage make-up, fake eyelashes, wigs, masks, and other accessories, including effects make-up such as fake blood and scars.

Family 436 N Fairfax Ave, north of Mid-Wilshire ⊤323/782-9221. Offbeat name is appropriate to the many bizarre items here: limited-edition surrealist art books and artworks, weird and little-known CDs and movies, various comics and zines, and many alternative-press publications.

G.A.L.A.X.Y. Gallery 7224 Melrose Ave ⊤323/938-6500. An LA original: an upscale head-shop with arty pipes and elaborate bongs, and tasteful paraphernalia aimed at the discriminating toker. The "wacky tabacky" is, of course, not available, but

you're encouraged to smoke an alternative, legal drug (say, tobacco) at the store's *Chronic Café* espresso bar.

Le Sex Shoppe 12323 Ventura Blvd, Studio City ⊤818/760-9352. LA's prime sex-paraphernalia dealer, with everything from magazines and videos to handcuffs and lingerie, catering to a mix of curious Westsiders and seedy regulars. One of several branches citywide.

Noisy Toys 8728 S Sepulveda Blvd, Westchester, just north of LAX ⊤310/670-9957. A cacophonous shrine to percussion, loaded with drums and other instruments from around the world, including zithers, rain sticks, bongos, maracas, castanets, wooden whistles, tambourines, and didgeridoos. You can play around with the instruments before you buy.

Off the Wall 7325 Melrose Ave, north of Mid-Wilshire ⊤323/930-1185. Appealing mid-twentieth-century antiques cleaned up and sold as high-priced goods, from Bakelite jewelry to Fiestaware dishes, as well as faded consumer items like outdated board games and old telephones.

Plastica 8405 W Third St, Mid-Wilshire T 323/655-1051. A one-of-a-kind shrine to all things plastic: shoes, boots, shirts, tanktops, spectacles, and accessories, along with jewelry, furniture, handbags, pillows, and countless other cheap knick-knacks.

Show 1722 N Vermont Ave, Los Feliz T 323/644-1960. Loaded with all kinds of clever, if pricey, home furnishings, lights, and oddments. Stop by for a look at antler sconces, quirky jewelry, and salt shakers shaped like bones, as well as a few more conventional items.

Skeletons in the Closet 1104 N Mission Rd, Downtown T 323/343-0760. Believe it or not, this is the LA County Coroner Gift Shop, selling everything from skeleton-adorned beach towels and T-shirts to toe-tag key chains – a great place to buy unique LA merchandise.

Vidiots 302 Pico Blvd, Santa Monica T 310/392-8508. Easily one of LA's best video stores, providing an excellent selection of classics and current flicks, but also a good range of cult and bizarre films, strange government propaganda, and experimental art movies.

Wacko 4633 Hollywood Blvd, Hollywood T 323/663-0122. The name says it all – freakish alternative comic books, odd-smelling candles, funky posters and toys, and various underground magazines. Part of a complex that includes the Soap Plant, where, along with soap, you can find body creams, fragrant oils, and bubble baths.

Y-Que Trading Post 1770 N Vermont Ave, Los Feliz T 323/664-0021. All kinds of cheap but essential junk at this clearinghouse for oddities, including toy action figures, weird stickers and books, furry handcuffs, and T-shirts with the latest and strangest messages to capture the LA zeitgeist.

Zipper 8316 W Third St, north of Mid-Wilshire T 323/951-9190. The height of chic and trendy gifts for Angelenos, and a good spot to pick up a gift from La-La Land for the folks back home: lacquered stone candles, stylish cocktail shakers, glazed terracotta bowls, quirky trinkets, sleek lamps, glasses, and teacups.

Galleries

The Westside is the province of LA's top art **galleries** for painting, mixed-media, sculpture and, especially, photography. Indeed, snapping pictures is what a city based on the movie industry does best, and you're likely to find terrific retrospectives of photographers like Weston and Stieglitz among the breakout shows of up-and-coming local shutterbugs. Keep in mind that the galleries listed below are among LA's established art-houses, and that by wandering through the right parts of Venice, Silver Lake, and Downtown's northeast fringe, you can often find art that's just as interesting and much cheaper – long before it reaches the walls of the big-name galleries.

Armory Center for the Arts 145 N Raymond Ave, Pasadena T 626/792-5101. Shows by young artists and retrospectives of local painters and photographers at this enjoyable, fairly unpretentious spot. Located just north of Old Pasadena.

Ben Maltz Gallery 9045 Lincoln Blvd, Westchester T 310/665-6905. Perhaps the most renowned of LA's university galleries, overseen by the Otis College of Art and Design. Presents broad-ranging shows by established names and rising locals, incorporating media from traditional to multimedia and video.

Beyond Baroque 681 Venice Blvd, Venice T 310/822-3006. A gallery and art center that's as interesting and unpredictable as any place in town, with a wide spectrum of performance art, fiction and poetry readings, assemblage and mixed-media, painting, drawing, photography and more. Also offers classes and expensive tours of LA murals.

Center for Land Use Interpretation 9331 Venice Blvd, Culver City T 310/839-5722, W www.clui.org. Narrowly focused but fascinating museum/gallery that looks at land use from various angles, notably time-lapse photography, satellite images, and evocative exhibits on mudslide catch basins, aviation graveyards, and windswept eastern deserts.

DiRT Gallery 7906 Santa Monica Blvd #218, West Hollywood ☎323/822-9359. One of the better places on the Westside to discover the edgiest and most cutting-edge artworks in a variety of media. Some works are compelling, some aren't for the faint of heart.

Fahey-Klein 148 N La Brea Ave, Mid-Wilshire ☎323/934-2250. One of LA's heavyweight institutions, featuring much contemporary work, especially black-and-white photography. Don't be deterred by the forbidding, windowless exterior – the gallery is open and accessible most days of the week.

Gagosian Gallery 456 N Camden Drive, Beverly Hills ☎310/271-9400. A major name in LA art that occasionally shows big names, and is housed in a memorable modern shed designed by Richard Meier. Prices in the stratosphere.

Gallery 825 825 N La Cienega Blvd, West Hollywood ☎310/652-8272. Affiliated with the Los Angeles Art Association, this long-standing space is devoted to ground-breaking exhibits by emerging artists and thoughtful career retrospectives, in a variety of media, including photography, installation, and multimedia.

Gallery of Functional Art 2525 Michigan Ave, Santa Monica ☎310/829-6990. Noise-emitting clocks, ornamental wooden furniture, and funky, Space Age wall sconces are for sale at this Bergamot Station gallery, where form and function mix with intriguing results. One of the few galleries good for (well-behaved) kids to browse in.

Iturralde Gallery 116 S La Brea Ave, Mid-Wilshire ☎323/937-4267. Established and emerging Latino artists are usually on display here, with shows alternating between the work of talented locals and international figures.

Jan Kesner Gallery 164 N La Brea Ave, north of Mid-Wilshire ☎323/938-6834. This excellent and well-respected gallery features retrospectives of noted artists – most of them photographers – as well as openings by up-and-comers. By appointment only.

Judson Gallery 200 S Ave 66, Highland Park ☎1-800/445-8376, ⓦ www.judsonstudios.com. A good place for checking out what's going on in Downtown's artsy northeastern fringe, heavy on contemporary stained glass as well as periodic exhibitions in a variety of media. Located in USC's former art and architecture school.

Koplin Del Rio 6031 Washington Blvd, Culver City ☎310/836-9055. Elite art dealer specializing in etchings, sculptures, paintings, and drawings, with an eye toward contemporary art from LA and focusing strongly on representational pieces.

La Luz de Jesus 4633 Hollywood Blvd, Hollywood ☎323/666-7667. Connected to the Wacko strange-gift emporium (see above), and sharing its taste for the bizarre, perverse, experimental, and quirky in a variety of media, with many affordable prints and posters.

Los Angeles Contemporary Exhibitions 6522 Hollywood Blvd, Hollywood ☎323/957-1777. Also known as LACE, this esteemed institution hosts a wide-ranging selection of mixed-media, painting, drawing, installation, and video work, while its community-outreach events and programs bring art to the masses.

Margo Leavin Gallery 812 N Robertson Blvd, West Hollywood ☎310/273-0603. This eclectic gallery is worth a look for its exhibitions of modern and postmodern stalwarts, from David Smith to John Baldessari and Donald Judd, and features a Claes Oldenburg facade, *Knife Slicing Through Water* – ie, the stucco.

Robert Berman Gallery 2525 Michigan Ave, Santa Monica ☎310/315-1937. A solid Bergamot Station dealer of artworks in a variety of media, focusing on multimedia, photo retrospectives, group shows, and conceptual pieces.

Rosamund Felsen Gallery 2525 Michigan Ave, Santa Monica ☎310/828-8488. One of the bigger names in Bergamot Station, featuring established Southern California artists and more recent arrivals. The eclectic selection is often striking, but you can forget about buying anything: the prices here are always sky-high.

Susanne Vielmetter/Los Angeles Projects 5795 W. Washington Blvd, Culver City ☎323/933-2117. Compelling gallery showing contemporary artists, particularly those working in nontraditional media, installations, and conceptualism, with a strong Southern California bent.

Track 16 2525 Michigan Ave, Bergamot Station, Santa Monica ☎310/264-4678. Politically oriented and subversive artworks tending toward mixed-media and assemblage, though you can also find traditional painted and sculpted works.

Southern California

Southern California

San Diego

et around a gracefully curving bay, **SAN DIEGO** is relatively free from the smog and byzantine freeways famously found in Los Angeles, and while its residents are for the most part affluent and libertarian, they're also easygoing and far from smug. Despite being the site of the first Spanish mission in the state, the city – the second most populous in California – only really took off with the arrival of the Santa Fe Railroad in the 1880s, and in many aspects it has long been in the shadow of Los Angeles. During World War II, however, the US Navy made San Diego its Pacific Command Center, and the military (along with tourism) continues to dominate the local economy. Ultimately, with its long white beaches, sunny weather, and bronzed bodies – which have given rise to the city's nickname, "Sandy Ego" – San Diego is like LA in miniature, though with a more manageable size and transportation system, and a tamer and more family-oriented vibe. If these things are important to you, definitely consider adding the place to your itinerary. (Note that the mountains and canyons north and east of the city suffered a series of calamitous fires in autumn 2007, but this has affected few of the sights listed below.)

Arrival, information, and transportation

Amtrak **trains** on the Pacific Surfliner route from LA use the Santa Fe Railroad Depot, close to the western end of Broadway at 1050 Kettner Boulevard (℡1-800/872-7245), while the Greyhound **bus** terminal is six blocks east at Broadway and First Avenue (℡619/239-6737). Lindbergh Field **airport** (aka San Diego International; ℡19/400-2400, ⓦwww.san.org) is only two miles from Downtown, and is connected to it by buses #923 ($1.75) and #992 ($2.25). By car, San Diego is easily accessible via the I-5 freeway; the drive south from central Los Angeles takes about two hours.

Once you arrive, **getting around** without a car is comparatively easy. The overarching **bus** system within San Diego County is called the Metropolitan Transit System (MTS), the most convenient and accessible means of public transport in the region. By far the most prominent entity of the system is San Diego Transit Corporation, or SDTC (℡1-800/266-6883, ⓦwww.sdcommute .com), which offers typical one-way fares of $1.75 and $2.25, $2.50–4.00 for more distant routes, and $5–10 for the most lengthy journeys into rural terrain; the exact fare is required when boarding (dollar bills are accepted). The **Transit Store**, at First and Broadway (Mon–Sat 9am–5pm; ℡19/234-1060), has

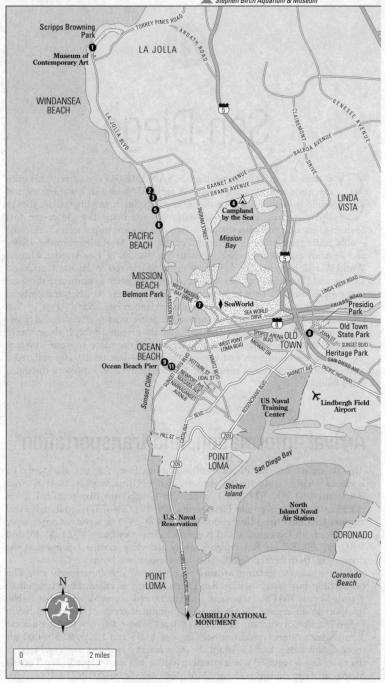

Scripps Browning
Park

TORREY PINES ROAD

ARDATH ROAD

LA JOLLA

❶
Museum of
Contemporary Art

WINDANSEA
BEACH

LA JOLLA BLVD

5

CLAIREMONT DRIVE

GENESEE AVENUE

BALBOA AVENUE

LINDA
VISTA

GARNET AVENUE

GRAND AVENUE

INGRAHAM STREET

❷
❸
❺
❻

❹
Campland
by the Sea

Mission
Bay

5

PACIFIC
BEACH

MISSION
BEACH
Belmont Park

WEST MISSION BAY DRIVE

MISSION BLVD

❼ ♦ SeaWorld

SEA WORLD
DRIVE

SPORTS ARENA BLVD

8

LINDA VISTA ROAD

FRIARS ROAD

Presidio
Park

Old Town
State Park

❽

JUAN ST

SUNSET BLVD

Heritage Park

SAN DIEGO AVE

OCEAN
BEACH
Ocean Beach Pier

❾
⓫

SUNSET CLIFFS BLVD
VOLTAIRE ST
NEWPORT AVE
UDAL ST
NIAGARA AVE

NARRAGANSETT
AVENUE

WEST POINT
LOMA BLVD

MIDWAY DR

NIMITZ BLVD

CATALINA BLVD

BARNETT AVE

PACIFIC HIGHWAY

ROSECRANS BLVD

US Naval
Training
Center

Lindbergh Field
Airport ✈

Sunset Cliffs

HILL ST

209

POINT
LOMA

209

CABRILLO MEMORIAL DRIVE

U.S. Naval
Reservation

Shelter
Island

San Diego Bay

North
Island Naval
Air Station

CORONADO

Coronado
Beach

POINT
LOMA

▼ CABRILLO NATIONAL
MONUMENT

N

0   2 miles

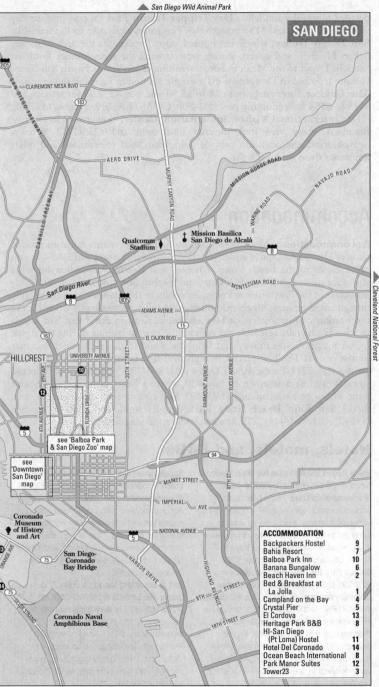

▲ San Diego Wild Animal Park

CLAIREMONT MESA BLVD

SAN DIEGO FREEWAY

805

AERO DRIVE

MURPHY CANYON ROAD

163

MISSION GORGE ROAD

NAVAJO ROAD

WARING ROAD

8

Qualcomm
Stadium ◆

Mission Basilica
San Diego de Alcalá

MONTEZUMA ROAD

San Diego River

8

805

15

ADAMS AVENUE

EL CAJON BLVD

163

HILLCREST

UNIVERSITY AVENUE

30TH STREET

FAIRMOUNT AVENUE

EUCLID AVENUE

6TH AVE

4TH AVENUE

FLORIDA DRIVE

⑩

⑫

see 'Balboa Park
& San Diego Zoo' map

see
'Downtown
San Diego'
map

94

MARKET STREET

47TH ST

IMPERIAL   AVE

HIGHLAND   AVENUE

Coronado
Museum
of History
and Art

5

NATIONAL AVENUE

HARBOR DRIVE

8TH AVENUE

⑬

ORANGE AVE

75

San Diego-
Coronado
Bay Bridge

18TH STREET

⑭

75

SILVER STRAND

Coronado Naval
Amphibious Base

ACCOMMODATION	
Backpackers Hostel	9
Bahia Resort	7
Balboa Park Inn	10
Banana Bungalow	6
Beach Haven Inn	2
Bed & Breakfast at La Jolla	1
Campland on the Bay	4
Crystal Pier	5
El Cordova	13
Heritage Park B&B	8
HI-San Diego (Pt Loma) Hostel	11
Hotel Del Coronado	14
Ocean Beach International	8
Park Manor Suites	12
Tower23	3

▼ Imperial Beach

detailed timetables and sells a **Day Tripper Transit Pass** for one- to four-day visits ($5, $9, $12, and $15, respectively). The passes apply also to the tram-like **San Diego Trolley**, which has limited stops throughout the area (one-way tickets $1.25–3) and covers, among other routes, the sixteen miles from the Santa Fe Depot to the Mexican border-crossing at San Ysidro. North San Diego County is linked to Downtown via a simple commuter light-rail system called **The Coaster**. Fares range from $4 to $5.50 one way, $2–2.75 for seniors, and $115 to $154 for a monthly pass (T1-800/COASTER, Wwww.gonctd.com).

The **International Visitor Information Center,** downtown at 1040 W Broadway (daily 9am–4pm, summer until 5pm; T19/236-1212, Wwww .seeyouinsandiego.com), can provide help with hotel reservations and offers numerous flyers on local sights.

Accommodation

Accommodation is plentiful throughout San Diego, with a range of upscale choices Downtown and a wider selection of motels, resorts and B&Bs as you move closer to the beach towns. Choose your location depending on what you want to see – historic sites, ships, and baseball downtown, or the surf-and-sun scene of the beach towns. Prices, especially in the summer, tend to be high, though some business hotels may offer good value on weekends when they're not hosting conventioneers or businesspeople. Keep in mind that San Diego weather is generally agreeable throughout the year, so coming during the down season may save you money and help you avoid some of the thick summer tourist crowds. The best-placed, though mall-like, **campground** is Campland on the Bay, 2211 Pacific Beach Drive (T1-800/422-9386, Wwww.campland .com), linked to downtown by bus #30, where a basic site starts at $39, with more elaborate sites running $150–250. For a more serene camping option, there's **San Elijo Beach State Park**, Rte-21 south of Cardiff-by-the-Sea ($11–25; T1-800/444-7275, Wwww.reserveamerica.com).

Hotels, motels, and B&Bs

Bahia Resort 998 W Mission Bay Drive, Mission Beach T858/488-0551 or 1-800/576-4229, Wwww.bahiahotel.com. Prime beachside accommodation with expansive ocean views, watersport rentals, a pool, and a Jacuzzi. Units range from cozy but pleasant rooms in a palm-garden setting to pricier bayside suites. Off-season $169, summer $229.

Balboa Park Inn 3402 Park Blvd, Hillcrest T19/298-0823, or 1-800/938-8181, Wwww .balboaparkinn.com. Spanish Colonial, gay-oriented B&B within walking distance of Balboa Park and the museums. The 26 themed suites (with oceanside, Impressionist, and jungle motifs, to name a few) have microwaves and mini-fridges. Prices vary, depending on size and level of kitsch. Rooms $99, add $40 for a suite.

Beach Haven Inn 4740 Mission Blvd, Pacific Beach T858/272-3812 or 1-800/831-6323, Wwww.beachhaveninn.com. Clean motel accommodation with comfortable, tasteful rooms around a heated pool; continental breakfast included. One of the nicest places to unwind at the beach, and plenty cheap to boot. Off-season $70, but can double in summer.

Bed & Breakfast Inn at La Jolla 7753 Draper Ave, La Jolla T858/456-2066 or 1-800/582-2466, Wwww.innlajolla.com. A collection of fifteen themed rooms – topped by the $459-a-night Irving Gill Penthouse, inexplicably decorated in Victoriana – with tranquil gardens, great service, and nice proximity to the beach and art museum. $199

Bristol 1055 First Ave, Downtown ℡ 19/232-6141, ⓦ www.thebristolsandiego.com. Centrally located boutique hotel with stylish modern decor and boutique amenities such as in-room CD players and high-speed Internet access. A good deal, especially considering the area. $179

Crystal Pier 4500 Ocean Blvd, Pacific Beach ℡ 858/483-6983 or 1-800/748-5894, ⓦ www.crystalpier.com. Quaint, deluxe cottages built in the 1920s and situated right on the pier. All units are suites with private decks and most have kitchenettes. Can get pricey, but the location makes it worth it. $229

El Cordova 1351 Orange Ave, Coronado ℡ 19/435-4131 or 1-800/229-2032, ⓦ www.elcordovahotel.com. The best deal in Coronado (see p.372), comprising Spanish Colonial buildings from 1902 arranged around lovely gardens. There's a pool, and many rooms have kitchenettes. Huge price spread, from cheap and basic units without a/c to grandly elegant suites for $839. Save $40 on basic rooms in winter, otherwise $149.

Heritage Park B&B 2470 Heritage Park Row, Old Town ℡ 19/299-6832 or 1-800/995-2470, ⓦ www.heritageparkinn.com. A restored Queen Anne mansion in Heritage Park, chock-full of Victorian trappings. The twelve rooms and suites are in the usual lace-and-chintz style, and breakfast and afternoon tea are included in the price. One small unit goes for $140 per night; otherwise most units are $170–180.

🏃 **Horton Grand** 311 Island Ave at Third Ave, Downtown ℡ 19/544-1886 or 1-800/542-1886, ⓦ www.hortongrand.com. Classy amalgam of two century-old hotels, with fireplaces in most of the 132 antique-flavored rooms (some with balconies), an on-site restaurant, a piano bar, and Saturday-afternoon high tea from 2.30 to 5pm. $155

Hotel del Coronado 1500 Orange Ave, Coronado ℡ 19/522-8000 or 1-800/468-3533, ⓦ www.hoteldel.com. This luxurious spot put

Coronado on the map and is still the area's major tourist sight (see p.372), thanks to its striking rooms and suites, expansive bay views, and old-fashioned Victorian charm. $280

Manchester Grand Hyatt One Market Place, at Harbor Drive, Downtown ℡ 19/232-1234, ⓦ www.manchestergrand.hyatt.com. The most prominent hotel along the waterfront (and among the biggest in the state). Its two gleaming white towers offer all the top-notch amenities: pool, spas, a health club, several restaurants and lounges, and rooms with expansive views of the bay. Also ground zero for conventioneers. $289

Park Manor Suites 525 Spruce St, near Balboa Park ℡ 19/291-0999 or 1-800/874-2649, ⓦ www.parkmanorsuites.com. Tasteful hotel suites – housed in a renovated apartment complex that's around eighty years old – feature kitchens and nice, large sitting areas. Continental breakfast is included. $169

Tower23 723 Felspar St, Pacific Beach ℡ 1-866/TOWER23, ⓦ www.tower23hotel.com. Despite being named for a lifeguard tower, this is among the most chic of the local boutique hotels, offering stylish rooms with flatscreen TVs, Internet access, and designer furnishings. The even more stylish suites variously come with balconies, cabanas, and whirlpool tubs. Off-season $229, summer $389

🏃 **US Grant Hotel** 326 Broadway between Third and Fourth aves, Downtown ℡ 19/232-3121 or 1-800/237-5029, ⓦ www.usgrant.net. Across from Horton Plaza, it's been Downtown's poshest address since 1910, with a grand Neoclassical design, chandeliers, marble floors, and cozy but comfortable guestrooms (with Internet access) and more capacious suites. The elegant ballrooms and swank conference rooms are worth a peek. $300

Hostels

Banana Bungalow 707 Reed Ave, Pacific Beach ℡ 858/273-3060 or 1-800/5-HOSTEL, ⓦ www.bananabungalow.com. Although the rooms are small and drab, the beachside location, beach volleyball, BBQ cookouts, and lively atmosphere make this place worthwhile. There's also Internet access for a small fee. Breakfast, and a communal kitchen are

included. Six-person dorms $20–25 by season; private rooms $65–105. Take bus #30, then it's a five-minute walk.

HI-Pt Loma 3790 Udall St, Ocean Beach ℡ 19/223-4778, ⓦ sandiegohostels.org. Well-run and friendly, though without the party atmosphere prevailing in other hostels. Located a few miles from the beach and six miles from Downtown (via bus #923). Has a large kitchen, a patio, and weekly bonfires; breakfast is included in the price. Eight-bed (or smaller) dorms $17–22, private rooms for three or more $42–48.

HI-San Diego Downtown 521 Market St at Fifth, Downtown ☎19/525-1531, ⓦsandiegohostels.org. Centrally located spot, especially convenient to the Gaslamp District and Horton Plaza. Free wireless Internet access and breakfast, plus a library and regular trips to Tijuana. No curfew. $19–24 for HI members, $22–27 for non-members; private doubles $50–57.

Ocean Beach International Backpackers Hostel 4961 Newport Ave, Ocean Beach ☎19/223-7873 or 1-800/339-7263, ⓦmembers.aol.com/OBIhostel/hostel. Lively spot a block from the beach, offering barbecues, bike and surfboard rentals, airport transport, and nightly movies. Space in a four-bed dorm $17–24, with sheets, showers, and continental breakfast. Tax included; must reserve online.

USA Hostels – San Diego 726 Fifth Ave between F and G sts, Downtown ☎19/232-3100 or 1-800/438-8622, ⓦwww.usahostels.com /sandiego/s-index.html. Well-placed hostel on the edge of the Gaslamp District. Six to eight beds (with sheets) per room for $20–25 by season; private rooms $42–57. Free breakfast, cheap Internet access, and organized tours to Tijuana make this one of the best city hostels.

㉑ The City

Loosely bordered by the curve of San Diego Bay and the I-5 freeway, **Downtown** is, for those not headed straight to the beach, the inevitable nexus of San Diego and the best place to start a tour of the city. Various preservation and restoration projects, kick-started in the late 1970s, have improved many of the area's older buildings, producing several pockets of stylishly renovated turn-of-the-century architecture. Corporate towers left over from the boomtown 1980s and 90s showcase the city's bustling trade with the Pacific Rim, as well as its inflated real-estate market. Beyond Downtown, San Diego's lovely **Balboa Park** and compelling **Old Town** make for interesting cultural diversions. The sun-and-surf crowd will no doubt gravitate to the fun, hedonistic **beach cities**, where you can have a tropical drink while lounging by the sands, or perhaps play a game of volleyball or take a ride on a surfboard.

Downtown

At the western end of Broadway, the tall Moorish archways of the **Santa Fe Railroad Depot**, built in 1915 for the Panama-California Exposition, still evoke a sense of grandeur. The depot is contiguous with the Downtown branch of the **Museum of Contemporary Art**, or MCA San Diego, 1001 Kettner Blvd (Sat–Tues 11am–6pm, Thurs & Fri 11am–9pm; $10; ☎858/454-3541, ⓦwww .mcasd.org), a fine first-stop for anyone interested in contemporary art with a California twist. Although its permanent collection focuses on American minimalism, pop art, and the indigenous art of Mexico, the museum's temporary shows are the real appeal here, often involving irreverent imagery drawn from the intersection of pop-culture surrealism and socioeconomic concerns, among many other topics. Further west, **Broadway** slices through the middle of Downtown, becoming its most hectic between Fourth and Fifth avenues. Many visitors linger around the fountains on the square outside **Horton Plaza**, between First and Fourth avenues south of Broadway (hours vary; often Mon–Fri 10am–9pm, Sat 10am–8pm, Sun 11am–7pm; ☎19/239-8180, ⓦwww .westfield.com/hortonplaza), a giant open-air mall of some 140 stores and

① & Little Italy (1 block) ▲   ▲ **Hillcrest (20 blocks)**

CEDAR STREET

BEECH STREET

ACCOMMODATION
Bristol	A
HI-San Diego Downtown	D
Horton Grand	E
Manchester Grand Hyatt	F
The U.S. Grant	B
USA Hostel – San Diego	C

Maritime Museum

ASH STREET   ASH STREET

A STREET

N

Balboa Park

San Diego Bay Ferry Docking Stage

Santa Fe Railroad Depot & American Plaza

B STREET

Copley Symphony Hall

Coronado

USS Midway

NORTH HARBOR DRIVE

PACIFIC HIGHWAY

KETTNER BOULEVARD

INDIA STREET

COLUMBIA STREET

STATE STREET

UNION STREET

FRONT STREET

FIRST AVENUE

THIRD AVENUE

FOURTH AVENUE

FIFTH AVENUE

SEVENTH AVENUE

Civic Theatre/ San Diego Opera

Greyhound Station

C STREET

Transit Store

Trolley Line

Museum of Contemporary Art

BROADWAY

Newtown Park

E STREET

Library

Balboa Theatre

Horton Plaza

F STREET   F STREET

0   200 yds

G STREET

GASLAMP DISTRICT

EATING & DRINKING
4th and B	3
Anthony's Fish Grotto	2
Café 222	8
Candelas	9
de' Medici	6
Dobson's	4
Dublin Square	7
Filippi's Pizza Grotto	1
Onyx Room	5

MARKET STREET

FIRST AVENUE

THIRD AVE

FIFTH AVENUE

EIGHTH AVENUE

William Heath Davis House

ISLAND AVENUE

Trolley Line

EMBARCADERO

HARBOR DRIVE

J STREET

San Diego Convention Center

DOWNTOWN SAN DIEGO

Embarcadero Marina Park

▼ **Coronado & Petco Park**

San Diego's de facto city center. The complex's broad array of shops and eateries makes it a colossal tourist draw, but its whimsical postmodern style, loaded with quasi-Art Deco and southwestern motifs, also makes it worth a look.

The Gaslamp District

South of Broadway, a few blocks from Horton Plaza, lies the sixteen-block **Gaslamp District**, once the seedy heart of frontier San Diego but now filled with smart streets lined with cafés, antique stores, art galleries, and, of course, "gas lamps" – powered by electricity. The area's history is best gleaned during the two-hour **walking tour** (Sat 11am; $10, includes admission to the William Heath Davis House; ☎19/233-4692, ⊛www.gaslampquarter.org/tours). Beginning at the small cobbled square at Fourth and Island avenues, the walk takes you through San Diego's original city center, which in the 1880s became a notorious red-light district called the Stingaree. You'll hear about the exploits of the gunslinger Wyatt Earp, the more colorful of the town's Victorian-era whores, and other assorted miscreants who made the Stingaree the dynamic town it once was. The square where the walking tour starts is within the grounds of the **William Heath Davis House**, 410 Island Ave (Tues–Sat 9am–6pm, Sun 9am–3pm; $5; ☎19/233-4692), whose owner founded modern San Diego and built his saltbox-styled home here in 1850.

The energy of San Diego **nightlife**, especially on the weekend, has been ensured by the construction of **Petco Park**, Seventh Ave at Harbor Drive (☎19/795-5000, ⊛www.sandiego.padres.mlb.com), which draws plenty of Padres baseball fans

SAN DIEGO | The City

㉑

despite its limited options for parking. If you've come to play spectator, make an early trip on the Blue Line trolley (which passes alongside) – mass transit around game time resembles a rail-bound journey into deepest tourist hell.

The bayfront

Along San Diego's curving, enjoyable **bayfront**, the pathway of the **Embarcadero** runs a mile or so along the bay, curling around to the western end of Downtown; along this stretch, the expansive green lawn of **Embarcadero Marina Park South** provides some summertime amusement for its mainstream concerts. For those with an interest in the US military, clamber aboard for a tour of the **USS Midway**, 910 N Harbor Drive (daily 10am–5pm, last admission 4pm; $15, kids $8; ☎19/544-9600, ⓦwww.midway.org), which shows off its formidable collection of naval hardware and weapons to the public. To see some vintage ships, go further north to the **Maritime Museum**, 1492 Harbor Drive (daily 9am–9pm, winter closes 8pm; $12; ☎19/234-9153, ⓦwww.sdmaritime .com). Among the seven ships there, the highlights are the 1863 **Star of India**, the world's oldest iron sailing ship still afloat; the **Californian,** a modern replica of an 1847 cutter, which served as a federal lawboat patrolling the Pacific during the Gold Rush; the **HMS Surprise**, a replica of an eighteenth-century, 24-gun frigate, built for the film *Master and Commander*; and a creaky Soviet diesel submarine, the **B-39**, which was only decommissioned in the 1990s, well into the nuclear-sub era.

Coronado

Across San Diego Bay from downtown, the isthmus of **Coronado** is a well-scrubbed resort community with a major naval station occupying its western end. It's reached by the majestically modern **Coronado Bay Bridge**, a curving 11,000-foot span that's one of the area's signature images, or on the **San Diego Bay ferry** (daily 9am–9pm; $3 each way, $3.50 with bikes; ☎19/234-1111, ⓦwww.sdhe.com), which leaves Broadway Pier on the hour, returning on the half-hour. The town of Coronado grew up around the **Hotel del Coronado** (see "Accommodation," p.369), a Victorian whirl of turrets and towers erected as a health resort in 1888. The "Del" is where Edward VIII (then Prince of Wales) first met Coronado housewife Wallis Warfield Simpson in 1920, and where *Some Like It Hot* was filmed in 1958, posing as a Miami Beach hotel. A less grandiose place to explore Coronado's past is the **Coronado Museum of History and Art**, 1100 Orange Ave (Mon–Fri 9am–5pm, Sat & Sun 10am–5pm; $5; ☎19/435-7242, ⓦwww.coronadohistory.org), which chronicles the town's early pioneers and first naval aviators, as well as its history of yachting and architecture.

Balboa Park and the San Diego Zoo

Northeast of Downtown, sumptuous **Balboa Park** contains one of the largest groups of **museums** in the US, as well as charming landscaping, traffic-free promenades, and stately Spanish Colonial-style buildings. The **Balboa Park Passport**, a week-long pass that allows one-time admission to all thirteen of the park's museums and its Japanese garden (plus the San Diego Zoo, for an extra $25), is available for $35 from the **visitor information center** (daily 9.30am–4.30pm; ☎619/239-0512, ⓦwww.balboapark.org), inside the on-site House of Hospitality. Near the center, the **Spreckels Organ Pavilion**

▲ San Diego's Embarcadero

(concerts June–Aug Sun 2pm; free; Ⓦ www.serve.com/sosorgan) is worth a look as the home of one of the world's largest organs, with no less than 4500 pipes.

Most of the major museums flank **El Prado**, the pedestrian-oriented road that bisects the park. Minor works by Rembrandt and El Greco and a stirring collection of Russian icons make the stifling formality of the **Timkin Museum of Art** (Tues–Sat 10am–4.30pm, Sun 1.30–4.30pm; closed Sept; free; Ⓣ 19/531-9640, Ⓦ www.timkenmuseum.org) worth enduring. The **San Diego Museum of Art** (Tues–Sun 10am–6pm, Thurs closes at 9pm; $10, kids $4; Ⓣ 19/232-7931, Ⓦ www.sdmart.org) is the main venue for any big traveling shows – collections from Egypt, China, and the Vatican (to name a few) that usually charge a $5–10 premium beyond museum admission. In the permanent collection, there's a solid stock of European paintings from the Renaissance to the nineteenth century, highlighted by Hals and Rembrandt, matched by curious modern works by California artists. Straddling El Prado, the **Museum of Man** (daily 10am–4.30pm; $8; Ⓣ 19/239-2001, Ⓦ www.museumofman.org) offers demonstrations of Mexican loom-weaving, replicas of huge Maya stones, interesting Native American artifacts, and various Egyptian relics.

Close to the Park Boulevard end of El Prado, the **Reuben H. Fleet Science Center** (Mon–Thurs 9.30am–5pm, Fri 9.30am–9pm, Sat 9.30am–8pm, Sun 9.30am–6pm; Science Center $7, Science Center and theater or simulator $11.75, all three $15.75; Ⓣ 19/238-1233, Ⓦ www.rhfleet.org) presents an assortment of child-oriented exhibits of varying interest, focusing on the glitzier aspects of contemporary science, as well as the expected IMAX theater and virtual-reality simulator. Across Plaza de Balboa, the **Natural History Museum** (daily 10am–5pm; $9; Ⓣ 19/232-3821, Ⓦ www.sdnhm.org) features a great collection of fossils, a curious array of stuffed creatures, hands-on displays of minerals, and entertaining exhibits on dinosaurs and crocodiles. South of El Prado, the **Casa de Balboa** houses three museums that are worth a look. The **Museum of Photographic Arts** (Tues–Sun 10am–5pm, Thurs closes 9pm; $6; Ⓣ 19/238-7559, Ⓦ www.mopa.org) offers a fine permanent collection that includes the work of Matthew Brady, Alfred Stieglitz, Paul Strand, and other big names. In the **San Diego Historical Society Museum** (daily 10am–5pm; $5; ℡19/232-6203, ⓦwww.sandiegohistory.org), the main exhibit charts the booms that have elevated San Diego from scrubland into the seventh-largest city in the US within 150 years. Covered in other exhibits are topics such as the city's use as a Hollywood backlot and the architectural and historical background of Balboa Park. Also in Casa de Balboa is the **Model Railroad Museum** (Tues–Fri 11am–4pm, Sat & Sun 11am–5pm; $6; ℡19/696-0199, ⓦwww.sdmodelrailroadm.com), that displays tiny, elaborate replicas of cityscapes, deserts, and mountains, as well as the little trains that chug through them.

At the southern end of Pan American Plaza, the **Aerospace Museum** (daily 10am–4.30pm; $12; ℡19/234-8291, ⓦwww.aerospacemuseum.org) recounts the history of aviation with its nearly seventy planes, including the *Spitfire*, the *Hellcat*, and the mysterious spy plane *Blackbird*. Next door at the **Automotive Museum** (daily 10am–5pm; $8, kids $4; ℡19/231-2886, ⓦwww.sdautomuseum.org) car enthusiasts will enjoy lingering over a host of classic cars and motorcycles, from old-time Model Ts and fancy Rolls

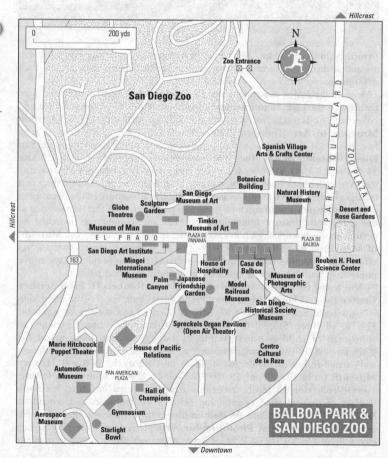

Royces to more obscure models like the 1912 Flying Merkle cycle and the 1948 Tucker Torpedo – one of only fifty left.

Immediately north of the main museums is the enormous **San Diego Zoo** (daily: mid-June to early Sept 9am–8pm; early Sept to mid-June 9am–4pm; one-day ticket $23, kids $15.50; two-day ticket $39, kids $27; ⊤19/231-1515, Ⓦwww.sandiegozoo.org), one of the world's most renowned. You can easily spend a full day here, taking in the major sections devoted to the likes of chimps and gorillas, sun and polar bears, lizards and lions, flamingos and pelicans, and habitats such as the rainforest and savanna. Take a bus tour early on to get a general idea of the layout, or survey the scene on the vertiginous **Skyfari**, an overhead tramway. Bear in mind, though, that many of the creatures get sleepy in the midday heat and retire behind bushes to take a nap. Moreover, the giant **pandas** Bai Yun and Shi Shi and four others spend a lot of time sleeping or being prodded by biologists in the park's Giant Panda Research Station. In addition to the main zoo facility, there's also a **children's zoo** in the park, with walk-through birdcages and an animal nursery. Regular **admission** only covers entry to the main zoo and the children's zoo; to add a 35-minute bus tour and a round-trip ticket on Skyfari, you'll need the $33 Deluxe Ticket Package. A $59 ticket (kids $39) also admits you to the San Diego Wild Animal Park near Escondido (daily 9am–4pm, summer closes 8pm; $28.50 adults, $17.50 kids), a two-thousand-acre preserve for big cats, rhinos, giraffes, and the like, which roam about outside your car's windows.

On the northern border of Balboa Park, **Hillcrest** is a lively and artsy area at the center of the city's **gay community**; the neighborhood is about as close as San Diego gets to having a bohemian air. Visit either for something to eat – there's a selection of interesting cafés and restaurants around University and Fifth streets – or simply to stroll past the fine collection of Victorian homes.

Presidio Hill and Old Town San Diego

In 1769, Spanish settlers chose **Presidio Hill** as the site of the first of California's missions. They soon began to build homes at the foot of the hill, which was dominated in turn by Mexican officials and then by early arrivals from the eastern US. **Old Town San Diego**, reachable from Downtown via the Trolley, is now a state historical park and the site of several original adobe dwellings – as well as the inevitable souvenir shops. The old buildings themselves are generally open 10am to 5pm and have free admission, but most things in the park that aren't historical – the shops and restaurants – open around 10am and close at 9 or 10pm. Highlights include the **Casa de Estudillo** on Mason Street, one of the poshest of the original adobes; it was built by the commander of the **presidio**, José Mariá de Estudillo, in 1827. Next door, the **Casa de Bandini** was the home of the politician and writer Juan Bandini and acted as the social center of San Diego during the mid-nineteenth century. Details on the many structures here are available from the **visitor center**, inside the Robinson-Rose House, near Taylor and Congress streets (daily 10am–5pm; ⊤19/220-5422, Ⓦwww.sandiegohistory.org or Ⓦwww.oldtownsandiego.org).

The Spanish-style building now atop Presidio Hill is only a rough approximation of the original mission – moved in 1774 – but its **Junipero Serra Museum**, 10818 San Diego Mission Rd (Mon–Fri 11am–3pm, Sat & Sun 10am–4.30pm; $5; ⊤19/297-3258), offers an intriguing examination of Junípero Serra, the padre who led the Spanish colonization and Catholic conversion of California. The **Mission San Diego de Alcalá** itself was relocated six miles north to 10818 San Diego Mission Rd (daily 9am–4.45pm;

donation; ℡19/283-7319, Ⓦwww.missionsandiego.com), to be near a water source and fertile soils, and to be safer from attack. The present building is still a working parish church, with a small **museum**; among the objects and artifacts from the mission is the crucifix held by Serra at his death in 1834.

Ocean Beach and Point Loma

Ruled by the Hell's Angels in the 1960s, **OCEAN BEACH**, six miles northwest of Downtown via bus #35 or #923, or via the I-5 and I-8 freeways, is a fun and relaxed beach town whose quaint, old-time streets and shops have preserved some of their ramshackle appeal and funky character. The two big hangouts include **Newport Street**, where backpackers haunt snack bars, surf and skate rental shops, and some of the best secondhand music stores around, and **Voltaire Street**, which, in line with its name, has a good range of independent-minded local businesses. There is often good surf, and the beach itself can be quite fun – especially on weekends, when the local party scene gets cranking. South from the pier rise the dramatic **Sunset Cliffs**, a prime spot for twilight vistas.

South of Ocean Beach, at the southern end of the hilly green peninsula of **Point Loma**, the **Cabrillo National Monument** (daily 9am–5pm; seven-day pass $5 per vehicle, $3 per pedestrian or cyclist; ℡19/557-5450, Ⓦwww.nps .gov/cabr) marks the spot where Juan Cabrillo and crew became the first Europeans to land in California, albeit briefly, in 1542. The startling views from this high spot easily repay a trip here. A platform atop the western cliffs of the park makes it easy to view the November-to-March **whale migration**, when scores of gray whales pass by en route to their breeding grounds off Baja California, Mexico. The nearby visitor center (same hours as the park) contains information on the history and wildlife of the point, and lies near the **Old Point Loma Lighthouse**, which offers tours that lead past replica Victorian furnishings and equipment from the 1880s.

Sea World, Mission Beach, and Pacific Beach

North of Ocean Beach, **Mission Bay** is the site of San Diego's most popular tourist attraction: **SeaWorld** (hours vary, often mid-June to Labor Day 9am–dusk; rest of year 10am–dusk; $57, children $47, parking $10; ℡1-800/25-SHAMU, Ⓦwww.seaworld.com), the local branch of an entertainment colossus that stretches from Texas to Florida; it's reachable by bus #9 from Downtown, or via the I-5 and I-8 freeways. SeaWorld has numerous exhibits and events, including the Shamu Show and Shamu Rocks!, an unfortunate pairing of orcas with flashing lights and rock music; Forbidden Reef, stocked with moray eels and stingrays; the Wild Arctic, populated by walruses, beluga whales, and polar bears; and the Shark Encounter, where sharks circle menacingly around visitors walking through a viewing tunnel.

The biggest-name public beaches in San Diego are **Mission Beach**, the peninsula that separates Mission Bay from the ocean, and its northern extension, **Pacific Beach**. If you aren't up for bronzing on the sands, you can always nurse a beer at one of the many beachfront bars, or you can rollerblade or bike down **Ocean Front Walk**, the concrete boardwalk running the length of both beaches, and observe the toasty sands overrun with scantily clad babes and surfboard-clutching dudes. A mile north of Pacific Beach's Crystal Pier, **Tourmaline Surfing Park**, or "Turmo," La Jolla Blvd at Tourmaline St, is reserved exclusively for surfing and windsurfing – no swimmers are allowed. If you don't have a board, **Windansea Beach**, a few miles north, is a good alternative. This favorite surfing hot spot is also fine for swimming as well as hiking alongside the oceanside rocks and reefs.

Near the southern end of Ocean Front Walk at 3146 Mission Blvd (hours vary, often Mon–Thurs 11am–8pm, Fri–Sun 11am–10pm; rides $2–6; ℡858/228-WAVE, ⊛www.belmontpark.com), once-derelict **Belmont Park** has been renovated with eleven official rides, though the two main attractions are both from 1925: the **Giant Dipper** roller coaster, one of the few of its era still around, and the **Plunge**, once the largest saltwater plunge in the world, and a regular film set for famous Hollywood swimmers Johnny Weismuller and Esther Williams.

La Jolla

A more pretentious air prevails in **La Jolla** (pronounced "La Hoya"), an elegant beach community just to the north. Stroll its immaculate, gallery-filled streets, fuel up on some California cuisine at one of the many sidewalk cafés, or visit the local outpost of the **Museum of Contemporary Art**, 700 Prospect St (daily 11am–5pm, Thurs closes 7pm; $10, free third Tues of month; ⊛www .mcasandiego.org), which has a huge, regularly changing stock of paintings and sculptures from 1955 onwards, highlighted by California pop and minimalism. On the seaward side of the museum lies the small and tasteful **Ellen Scripps Browning Park**, named for the philanthropist whose Irving Gill–designed home now houses the museum. Where the park meets the coast is the popular **La Jolla Cove**, much of it an ecological reserve whose clear waters make it perfect for snorkeling.

Further north, the **Stephen Birch Aquarium and Museum**, part of the Scripps Institute of Oceanography, 2300 Expedition Way (daily 9am–5pm; $11, kids $7.50; ℡858/534-FISH, waquarium.ucsd.edu), provides up-close views of captive marine life. Highlights include the Hall of Fishes, a huge kelp forest home to countless sea creatures, and the Shark Reef, displaying a nice range of the fearsome creatures, including a few pint-sized versions. Altogether, the museum is a much more edifying experience than anything at SeaWorld, and a lot cheaper, too.

Eating

Wherever you are in San Diego, you'll have few problems finding some place good to **eat** at reasonable prices. Everything, from crusty coffee shops to stylish ethnic restaurants, is in copious supply here, with seafood at its best around Mission Beach and the Gaslamp District, and the latter also home to the greatest concentration of restaurants.

Anthony's Fish Grotto 1360 Harbor Drive, Downtown ℡19/232-5103. Fish-and-chips and other fish-related favorites from oysters to lobster tail are the draw at this longstanding bayside haunt with a good range of prices. Lunch or dinner; one of several area locations.
Bella Luna 748 5th Ave, Downtown ℡19/239-3222. A romantic, moon-themed bistro with

an artsy feel, serving up mid-priced dishes from different regions of Italy, with hefty servings of pasta and calamari.
Berta's 3928 Twiggs St, Old Town ℡19/295-2343. A far cry from a conventional south-of-the-border restaurant, offering well-priced, authentic cooking from all over Latin America. The affordable and savory dishes include chimichurri steak, and paella, and

there's a range of hot and spicy concoctions to help you knock it all back.

Café 222 222 Island Ave, Downtown ☎19/236-9902. Hip café serving great breakfasts and lunches, with excellent pancakes, French toast, and pumpkin waffles. Also has inventive twists on traditional sandwiches and burgers (including vegetarian), all at reasonable prices.

Candelas 416 3rd Ave, Downtown ☎19/702-4455. A Gaslamp District restaurant offering swank, pricey Mexican fare with creative seafood and meat dishes demonstrating a California-cuisine influence. Try the halibut, Serrano ham, or any dessert.

Chez Loma 1132 Loma Ave, Coronado ☎19/435-0661. Romantic, upscale, and delicious French cuisine; especially strong on old-line favorites, though with nouvelle influences too. Good for its rack of lamb, sea scallops, black mussels, onion soup, and, of course, filet mignon.

Cody's La Jolla 8030 Girard Ave, La Jolla ☎858/459-0040. Innovative California cuisine; especially notable are the bouillabaise, ling cod, duck breast, and scrumptious burgers. Dinner entrees are about twice as expensive as the affordable lunch dishes.

de' Medici 815 5th Ave, Downtown ☎19/702-7228. Upscale Italian fare that draws plenty of suits for the Old World style. The food is scrumptious, with the oysters rockefeller, *langostino* lobster, crab legs, and saltimbocca rounding out a fine menu.

Dobson's 956 Broadway Circle, Downtown ☎19/231-6771. A chic restaurant in an old building, loaded with business types in power-ties, and the cuisine leans toward Continental, and ranges from crab hash and oyster salad to flat-iron steak and rack of lamb.

Filippi's Pizza Grotto 1747 India St at Date St, Downtown ☎19/232-5094. A good spot for devouring affordable, no-nonsense favorites like thick, chewy pizzas and various pasta dishes, including a tasty lasagna. Meals are served in a small room at the back of an Italian grocery.

Ichiban 1449 University Ave, Hillcrest ☎19/299-7203. Scrumptious Japanese cuisine for a reasonable charge, featuring a range of good rolls, bentos, soups, and sushi. An unpretentious and popular spot.

Old Town Mexican Café 2489 San Diego Ave, Old Town ☎19/297-4330. Lively, inexpensive, and informal Mexican diner where the crowds line up to dine on Mexican ribs, chile Colorado, and steak Azteca; only at breakfast are you unlikely to have to wait for a table.

Point Loma Seafoods 2805 Emerson St, Ocean Beach ☎19/223-1109. Fast, cheap counter serving up San Diego's freshest fish in a basket, along with mean crab cake and scallop sandwiches that make the locals cheer.

Primavera 932 Orange Ave, Coronado ☎19/435-0454. Swank and scrumptious Italian cuisine that's among the best in town. There's carpaccio, pasta, and risotto for those a little lighter in the wallet and steak and lamb chops for the big spenders

Sportsmen's Seafood 1617 Quivira Rd, Mission Beach ☎19/224-3551. A combo diner/market for the serious fish-lover, where the catch of the day is laid out before your eyes. The environment is no-frills and the food is affordable and delicious – the shrimp cocktail, squid steak, tuna burger, fish'n'chips, crab or lobster platters, and fish tacos are all worth a try.

Nightlife

Although San Diego's municipal money is lavished on **classical music**, **opera**, and **theater** (half-priced tickets and information at the **Arts Tix** booth, Broadway at Third Avenue, at Broadway Circle; Tues–Thurs 11am–6pm, Fri & Sat 10am–6pm, Sun 10am–5pm; ☎19/497-5000, ⓦwww.sandiegoperforms .com), the crowds flock instead to beachside **discos** and boozy Gaslamp District **music venues**. For full listings, pick up the free *San Diego Reader* (ⓦwww.sdreader.com), the Thursday edition of the *San Diego Union-Tribune* (ⓦwww.signonsandiego.com), or the youth-oriented *Slamm/San Diego CityBeat* (ⓦwww.sdcitybeat.com).

Bars, coffeeshops, and clubs

The Alibi **1403 University Ave, Hillcrest** ⊤ **19/295-0881.** The place to hit when you just want to get ripped – a classic dive bar with potent drinks, pool tables, occasional live acts, and a grungy but cozy decor.

Claire de Lune **2906 University Ave, Hillcrest** ⊤ **19/688-9845.** The prototypical coffeehouse, with steaming java, teas, sandwiches, comfy seating, and entertainment that runs from smooth jazz to spoken-word to avant-garde.

Dublin Square **554 4th Ave, Gaslamp District** ⊤ **19/239-5818.** Get your fill of leek soup, shepherd's pie, and lamb-shank stew as you quaff Irish beer and spirits at this Emerald Isle-styled pub. Even the breakfast steak is marinated in Guinness, and the chocolate cake is given a whiskey boost.

Kensington Club **4079 Adams Ave, Kensington District, north of Hillcrest** ⊤ **19/284-2848.** This divey joint (aka "The Ken") is great for beer, wine, and cocktails,

but also for wide-ranging music selections from thumping-dance DJs to head-banging rockers.

Live Wire **2103 El Cajon Blvd, just east of Hillcrest** ⊤ **19/291-7450.** An interesting, mixed crowd is drawn here for the pinball, pool, great jukebox, funky, sub-bohemian atmosphere, and impressive selection of imported beers.

Onyx Room **852 5th Ave, Gaslamp District** ⊤ **19/235-6699.** Groovy scene with lush decor and comfortable seating, where you can listen to torch songs, knock back a few cocktails, and hit the back room for live jazz and dance tunes. The swanky lounge upstairs, *Thin*, has pricier drinks and bigger attitudes. $10–15 cover on weekends (for both).

Thrusters Lounge **4633 Mission Blvd, Pacific Beach** ⊤ **858/483-6334.** Cozy bar and club where the hip-hop and dance beats come hard and heavy, and jazz and rock make occasional appearances as well.

Live-music venues

4th and B **345 B St, Downtown** ⊤ **619/231-4343,** ⊛ **www.4thandb.com.** One of the city's premier venues for live pop, rock, Latin, and other types of music, with pretty good sight lines and atmosphere, and a mix of up-and-comers with frenetic energy and old-timers playing out the string.

Belly Up Tavern **143 S Cedros Ave, Solana Beach** ⊤ **858/481-9022,** ⊛ **www .bellyup.com.** Mid-sized hall that plays host nightly to an eclectic range of live music – anything from Fergie and Les Nubians to Leon Russell and They Might Be Giants.

Brick by Brick **1130 Buenos Ave, Mission Bay** ⊤ **19/675-5483,** ⊛ **www.brickbybrick.com.** Aggressively hip lounge that's one of the better known indie spots around town, attracting nationally known alternative, blues, and hard rock acts.

Casbah **2501 Kettner Blvd, Downtown** ⊤ **19/232-4355,** ⊛ **www.casbahmusic.com.** If you're up for a night of hipstering, this is a good spot

to begin – a grungy joint that nevertheless hosts a solid, varying roster of blues, funk, reggae, rock, and indie bands.

Humphrey's Concerts by the Bay **2421 Shelter Island Drive, Point Loma** ⊤ **19/523-1010,** ⊛ **www.humphreysconcerts.com.** Mainstream concert venue that draws a range of mellow, agreeable pop, blues, jazz, country, folk, and lite-rock acts, often of national caliber.

SOMA **3350 Sports Arena Blvd, west of Old Town** ⊤ **19/226-7662,** ⊛ **www.somasandiego.com.** Favorite all-ages spot for thrashing to punk acts or head-banging to rockers, set in a former moviehouse complex with two stages. A good spot to seek out what's bubbling up in the music scene.

Winston's **1921 Bacon St, Ocean Beach** ⊤ **19/222-6822.** This local club (in a former bowling alley) has rock bands most nights, with occasional reggae and 1960s-style acts as well.

Palm Springs

Amid lush farmland replete with golf courses, condos, and millionaires, **PALM SPRINGS** embodies a strange mix of Spanish Colonial and mid-twentieth-century modernism. Massive Mount San Jacinto looms over its low-slung buildings, casting a welcome shadow over the town in the boiling summer heat. Ever since Hollywood stars first came here in the 1930s, laying claim to ranch estates and holing up in elite hotels, the clean, dry air and sunshine, just 120 miles east of LA, have made Palm Springs irresistible to the masses. In recent years, the city has also become a major **gay and lesbian** resort. The town is more widely known for its **golf**, so if you're handicap's well under 20, this should be one of your prime Southern California destinations.

Arrival, information, and getting around

Arriving by car, you drive into town on N Palm Canyon Drive, passing the **visitor center** at no. 2901 (daily 9am–5pm, Sun closes 4pm; ☎1-800/347-7746, ⓦwww.palm-springs.org), a classic piece of pop architecture with an upswept roof and boomerang design. Greyhound **buses** (4 daily from LA; 2–4hr) pull in downtown at 311 N Indian Canyon Drive, while Amtrak **trains** from LA (2 daily; 2hr 30min) stop just south of I-10 at N Indian Avenue, about ten minutes from downtown. The local operator SunBus (6am–8pm; tickets $1, day passes $3; ☎1-800/347-8628, ⓦwww.sunline.org) circulates in all the local resort towns.

Companies such as Celebrity Tours, 4751 E Palm Canyon Drive (☎760/770-2700, ⓦwww.celebrity-tours.com), offer one-hour **tours** of celebrity homes and enclaves for $30, and two-and-a half hour treks out to the region's star-studded highlights for $35. (You can also do it yourself, with a map of the stars' homes ($7) from the visitor center.) Guided tours of Palm Springs' stash of notable **modernist architecture**, among them designs by R.M. Schindler, Albert Frye, and Richard Neutra, are organized by PS Modern Tours (2hr 30min; $65; ☎760/318-6118, ⓔpsmoderntours@aol.com).

Accommodation

Luxury **hotels** outnumber the cheaper variety in Palm Springs, but prices drop by as much as seventy percent as temperatures soar in the summer. The north end of town, along Hwy-111, holds many of the lower-priced places, including countless motels, virtually all of which have pools and air-conditioning. The prices below are **spring** and **autumn rates**; expect to pay about $20–50 more or less for winter and summer, respectively.

Ballantines 1420 N Indian Canyon Drive ℡1-800/485-2808, ⌨ballantineshotels.com. Remodeled motel with modern luxuries and sporting vintage 1950s kitsch in its themed rooms (bachelor pad, Hollywood glamour, etc). $139

Casa Cody 175 S Cahuilla Rd ℡760/320-9346, ⌨www.casacody.com. Built in the 1920s, this historic, but updated, Southwestern-style B&B offers attractive rooms and a shady garden. A bit more comfortable than higher-priced retro-motels. $109

Ingleside Inn 200 W Ramon Rd ℡760/325-0046 or 1-800/772-6655, ⌨www.inglesideinn.com. Historic downtown option, where the guest list has included Dalí, Garbo, and Brando. Many rooms have antiques, and some include fireplaces, whirlpool tubs, and patios, for double the price of a standard unit. $130

Orbit Inn 562 W Arenas Rd ℡1-877/996-7248, ⌨www.orbitin.com. About the best that can be expected when remaking a 1957 motel into a suave, yuppie-friendly hotel. You can drink cutely named cocktails by the pool and lounge in stylish rooms filled with arch-modern decor. $229

Palm Court Inn 1983 N Palm Canyon Drive ℡760/416-2333, ⌨www.palmcourt-inn.com. Nice motel with two pools, a Jacuzzi and gym, plus free continental breakfast and comfortable rooms. $95

Villa Royale Inn 1620 S Indian Trail ℡760/327-2314, ⌨www.villaroyale.com. Elegant inn with nice rooms and suites, as well as in-room Jacuzzis and a good restaurant (see p.384). $199

The Willows 412 W Tahquitz Canyon Way ℡760/320-0771, ⌨www.thewillowspalmsprings.com. The very reason celebrities were first attracted to Palm Springs in the 1930s: a stunning hangout for the Hollywood elite that provides great views and opulent rooms. $295

Downtown Palm Springs

For such a notable location, Palm Springs doesn't offer a great deal in the way of conventional attractions. You may begin at **Downtown Palm Springs**, which stretches for a mile along **Palm Canyon Drive** from Tamarisk to Ramon roads, much of it a wide, bright, and modern strip of chain stores that has overrun the town's quaint Spanish Colonial–style buildings. Shops run the gamut from upscale boutiques and art galleries to tacky T-shirt emporia and bookstores devoted to dead celebrities. In the vicinity you'll find the **Agua Caliente Cultural Museum**, 219 S Palm Canyon Dr (Wed–Sat 10am–5pm, Sun noon–5pm; summer Fri–Sat only; free; ℡760/778-1079, ⌨www.accmuseum.org), with a fine selection of native baskets and pottery craftwork, as well as household objects from the local Cahuilla tribe, such as tools and utensils made from bone, reeds, and stone.

The luxuriously housed **Palm Springs Desert Museum**, 101 Museum Drive (Tues, Wed, & Fri–Sun 10am–5pm, Thurs noon–8pm; $12.50, children $5; ℡760/325-7186, ⌨www.psmuseum.org), is strong on Native American and Southwestern art, as well as grand American landscape painting from the nineteenth century. There is a modern art gallery and some lovely sculpture courts on the grounds, and the museum hosts performances of music, theater, comedy, and dance in the 450-seat **Annenberg Theater** (tickets ℡760/325-4490).

There's an anarchic piece of landscape gardening at **Moorten Botanical Gardens**, 1701 S Palm Canyon Drive (Mon–Sat 9am–4.30pm, Sun 10am–4pm;

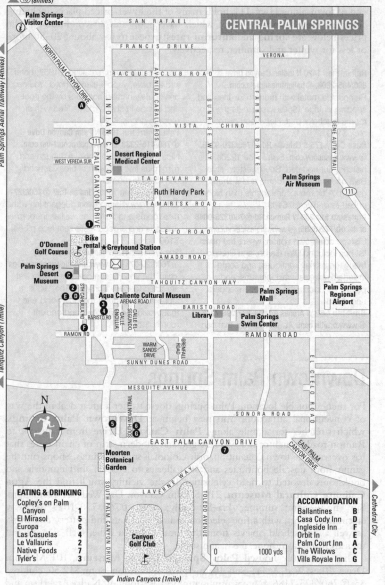

Palm Springs
Visitor Center

CENTRAL PALM SPRINGS

SAN RAFAEL

FRANCIS DRIVE

VERONA

RACQUET CLUB ROAD

AVENIDA CABALLEROS

SUNRISE WAY

FARRELL DRIVE

GENE AUTRY TRAIL

VISTA CHINO

A

B

Desert Regional
Medical Center

WEST VEREDA SUR

Palm Springs
Air Museum

TACHEVAH ROAD

Ruth Hardy Park

TAMARISK ROAD

ALEJO ROAD

O'Donnell
Golf Course

Bike
rental

★ Greyhound Station

AMADO ROAD

Palm Springs
Desert Museum

TAHQUITZ CANYON WAY

Palm Springs
Mall

Palm Springs
Regional
Airport

Aqua Caliente Cultural Museum

ARENAS ROAD

BARISTO ROAD

Library

Palm Springs
Swim Center

BARISTO RD

RAMON RD

RAMON ROAD

WARM
SANDS
DRIVE

SUNNY DUNES ROAD

MESQUITE AVENUE

N

SONORA ROAD

EAST PALM CANYON DRIVE

Moorten
Botanical
Garden

LAVERNE WAY

TOLEDO AVENUE

Canyon
Golf Club

0   1000 yds

EATING & DRINKING

Copley's on Palm Canyon	1
El Mirasol	5
Europa	6
Las Casuelas	4
Le Vallauris	2
Native Foods	7
Tyler's	3

ACCOMMODATION

Ballantines	B
Casa Cody Inn	D
Ingleside Inn	F
Orbit In	E
Palm Court Inn	A
The Willows	C
Villa Royale Inn	G

▼ Indian Canyons (1mile)

$3; ☎760/327-6555, ⓦwww.palmsprings.com/moorten), an odd cornucopia of desert plants in settings designed to simulate their natural environments. Collections of flora include native agaves, barrel cacti, and other succulents, as well as regional plants from as far away as South Africa and South America. Finally, near the airport, the **Palm Springs Air Museum**, 745 N Gene Autry Trail (daily 10am–5pm; $10; ☎760/778-6262, ⓦwww.palmspringsairmuseum.org), has an impressive collection of World War II fighters and bombers, including Spitfires, Tomcats, and a B-17 Flying Fortress.

Around Palm Springs

Most visitors to Palm Springs never leave the poolside, but desert enthusiasts still visit to hike and ride in the **Indian Canyons** (daily 8am–5pm, summer Fri–Sun only; $8; Ⓦwww.indian-canyons.com), three miles southeast of downtown along S Palm Canyon Drive, where centuries ago, ancestors of the indigenous Cahuilla people developed extensive agricultural communities. The **Palm Canyon Trading Post**, 380 N Palm Canyon Drive (same hours as canyons; ℡760/323-6018), is a gift shop that serves as the de facto visitor center, from which mile-long guided hikes (90min; $3) leave during regular canyon hours. The canyons are about fifteen miles long, and can be toured by car, although it's worth walking at least a few miles; the easiest trails lead past the waterfalls, rocky gorges, and copious palm trees of **Palm Canyon** (3 miles) and **Andreas Canyon** (1 mile). Some areas are set aside for **trail-blazing** in jeeps and four-wheel-drive vehicles: you can rent one from Off-Road Rentals, four miles north of town at 59511 Hwy-111 (Sept–June only; $40 per hour; ℡760/325-0376, Ⓦwww.offroadrentals.com), or take a guided jeep adventure around the Santa Rosa Mountains with Desert Adventures, 67555 E Palm Canyon Drive, Cathedral City (3–4hr; $129–169; ℡760/340-2345, Ⓦwww.red-jeep.com).

If the desert heat becomes too much to bear, board one of the large cable cars that grind and sway over eight thousand feet up the **Palm Springs Aerial Tramway**, Tramway Road, just off Hwy-111 north of Palm Springs (daily 10am–9pm; $22, children $15; ℡760/325-1391, Ⓦwww.pstramway.com), heading to the striking 10,815ft summit of Mount San Jacinto. In the opposite direction from Palm Springs, a few miles east of town, **PALM DESERT** is, like the sun-baked towns further east, riddled with golf courses and elite resorts. Its other claim to fame is the mile-long **El Paseo**, a boutique-rich strip that some claim as the "Rodeo Drive of the Desert," though it's doubtful that fabled Beverly Hills route ever hosted anything quite so kitschy as an annual golf-cart parade (Ⓦwww.golfcartparade.com). Beyond retirees on the green, Palm Desert is also home to the **Living Desert**, a combination garden and zoo at 47900 Portola Ave, Palm Desert (daily: summer 8.30am–1pm; rest of year 9am–5pm; $12, summer $8.75; ℡760/346-5694, Ⓦwww.livingdesert.org), which is rich with cactus and palm gardens, and throws in an incongruous section devoted to African desert animals, such as giraffes, zebras, cheetahs, and warthogs.

Finally, where the low Colorado Desert meets the high Mojave northeast of Palm Springs, **Joshua Tree National Park** ($15 per vehicle for 7 days, $5 per cyclist or hiker; www.nps.gov/jotr) protects 1250 square miles of the grotesquely gnarled plants, which aren't trees at all, but a type of **yucca**, an agave. Named by Mormons in the 1850s, who saw in their craggy branches the arms of Joshua pointing to the promised land, Joshua trees can rise up to forty feet tall, but have to contend with extreme aridity and rocky soil. From Palm Springs, the park is best approached along Hwy-62, which branches off I-10 and continues northeast for forty miles to the park. You can enter the park via the **west entrance**, on Park Blvd in the town of Joshua Tree (daily 8am–5pm;

▲ Palm Springs Aerial Tramway ascending Mount San Jacinto

☎760/366-1855), or the **north entrance** at Twentynine Palms, where you'll also find the **Oasis Visitor Center**, 74485 National Park Drive (daily 8am–5pm; ☎760/367-5500). Alternatively, if you're coming from the south, there's another entry at the **Cottonwood Visitor Center** (daily 9am–3pm; ☎760/367-5500), seven miles north of I-10.

Eating and drinking

Although most of the better **restaurants** in Palm Springs are ultra-expensive, more reasonable options can be found with a little effort; the spots preferred by locals are, as ever, to be favored over the slick, often banal cuisine served up by places catering to the tourist trade. Some of the better ones are listed below.

Copley's on Palm Canyon 621 N Palm Canyon Drive ☎760/327-9555. Hang out in Cary Grant's old digs while you sup on upscale, smartly prepared California cuisine, which may include the likes of lobster pot pie, rack of lamb, tandoori chicken, and ahi tacos.

El Mirasol 140 E Palm Canyon Drive ☎760/323-0721. Reasonable, affordable Mexican dining that offers a mix of familiar staples and more

authentic fare from Zacatecas and other regions.

Europa 1620 S Indian Trail ☎1-800/245-2314. Located in the Villa Royale Inn (see p.381), a solid bet for romantic appeal, and known for its delicious, upscale French and Italian offerings, with the added charm of intimate seating and a cozy fireplace.

Las Casuelas 368 N Palm Canyon Drive ☎760/325-3213. Local, affordable Mexican favorite that's been around since 1958, and remains popular for its hefty portions and laid-back atmosphere. The best bet in a local chain.

Le Vallauris 385 W Tahquitz Canyon Way, next to the Art Museum ☎760/325-5059. Decent contemporary California-Mediterranean cuisine in a gorgeous setting, with sky-high prices and the occasional b-list celebrity dropping in. Reservations only.

Native Foods 1775 E Palm Canyon Drive ☎760/416-0070. One of the town's better choices for cheap vegetarian cuisine, with veggie pizzas, burgers, and tacos, plus bean soups, rice bowls, and tempeh burgers for true initiates.

Shame on the Moon 69950 Frank Sinatra Drive, Rancho Mirage ☎760/324-5515. Upscale California cuisine and excellent service are the draw here, attracting a loyal gay clientele. Located eight miles east of downtown Palm Springs.

Tyler's 149 S Indian Canyon Drive ☎760/325-2990. The tasty burgers are what send residents tramping out here, but the potato salad, fries, and sandwiches aren't bad, either.

Santa Barbara

US-101 travels along the coast a hundred miles north of Los Angeles to **SANTA BARBARA**, a seaside resort beautifully situated on gently sloping hills above a curving bay. The town's low-rise Spanish Colonial Revival buildings feature red-tiled roofs and white stucco walls, a lovely background to the crescent of golden, palm-lined **beaches** below.

Once home to Ronald Reagan, and a weekend escape for much of the old money of Los Angeles and assorted celebrities, Santa Barbara has both a traditional conservative side, as well as a more relaxed libertarian character among the younger set. Still, it's a small city; local culture runs to playing volleyball, surfing, cycling, sipping coffee, or cruising in expensive convertibles along the shore.

Arrival, information, and transportation

From Los Angeles on the 101, Santa Barbara is less than an hour-and-a half drive if you're lucky. Greyhound **buses** arrive from LA and San Francisco every few hours, stopping downtown at 34 W Carrillo Street, while Amtrak **trains** stop at 209 State Street, a block west of US-101. Santa Barbara Municipal **Airport** (℡805/683-4011, ⓦwww.flysba.com), eight miles north of the town center at 500 Fowler Road (near UC Santa Barbara), has regular but often expensive scheduled service to other cities in the Western US.

For more information on Santa Barbara, or for help with finding a place to stay, contact the **visitor center**, 1 Garden Street (Mon–Sat 9am–5pm, Sun 10am–5pm; ℡805/965-3021, ⓦwww.santabarbara.com). **Getting around** central Santa Barbara mainly involves walking, though there's a 25¢ **shuttle** that loops between downtown and the beach on the "Downtown" route, and from the harbor to the zoo on the "Waterfront" line. Other areas are covered by Santa Barbara Metropolitan Transit District (SBMTD) **buses** (fares $1.25; ℡805/683-3702, ⓦwww.sbmtd.gov).

Accommodation

Home to some of the West Coast's most deluxe resorts, Santa Barbara is among California's most expensive places to **stay**, with many rooms averaging over

$250 a night. However, with a bit of advance planning, you can find that somewhere reasonable that shouldn't take too big a bite out of your wallet. The less expensive places are usually booked throughout the summer, but if you get stuck, enlist the assistance of *Hot Spots*, a hotel-reservation center that offers specials on lodging (Mon–Fri 9am–5pm, Sat 9am–4pm, summer closes Mon–Fri at 7pm; ☎1-800/793-7666, ⓦwww.hotspotsusa.com).

There is a **hostel** in Santa Barbara, and, while there are no **campgrounds** within the town limits, you'll find several sites along the coast to the north, including El Capitan and Refugio state beaches (both at ☎1-800/444-7275; $20–25), and Carpinteria State Beach to the south (☎1-800/444-7275; $25); all are accessible through ⓦwww.reserveamerica.com.

Blue Sands Motel 421 S Milpas St ☎805/965-1624. Looks like your average roadside motel at first, but this spot is actually the city's best deal for accommodation: clean rooms with gas fireplaces, free wireless Internet access, kitchenettes, and flat-screen TVs – along with the standard heated pool. $115

Cheshire Cat 36 W Valerio St ☎805/569-1610, ⓦwww.cheshirecat.com. Loaded with precious Victorian decor, this B&B has twelve rooms, two cottages, and a coach house, and features a hot tub, bikes for guests' use, and an Alice in Wonderland theme. Complimentary wine on arrival and breakfast under a palm tree. $189

Four Seasons 1260 Channel Drive ☎805/969-2261, ⓦwww.fourseasons.com/santabarbara. The apex of swanky resort style in the area, where the opulent rooms (from $550) boast such amenities as fireplaces and wrought-iron balconies, the suites have two to four bedrooms, and the complex has a spa, pool, and fitness center. $550

Inn at East Beach 1029 Orilla del Mar ☎805/965-0546, ⓦwww.innateastbeach.com. Another unexpectedly appealing find, offering a motel-like appearance but clean, good-value rooms with free wireless Internet, microwaves and fridges, and some suites with kitchens, built around a kidney-shaped pool. $160, but summer weekend rates tack on another $125.

Inn of the Spanish Garden 915 Garden St ☎805/564-4700, ⓦwww.spanishgardeninn.com. About the finest boutique lodgings the city offers, whose elegant rooms come with designer furnishings, fireplaces, high-speed Internet connections, and French presses for morning coffee. $289

Marina Beach Motel 21 Bath St ☎1-877/627-4621, ⓦwww.marinabeachmotel.com. Clean and modern motel rooms in a recently remodeled facility, with continental breakfast and options for bike rentals, kitchenettes, and Jacuzzis. A bit cheaper than comparable spots in the area. $115, but add $100 for weekend rates during the high season.

Montecito Inn 1295 Coast Village Rd ☎1-800/843-2017, ⓦwww.montecitoinn.com. Charming Spanish Revival inn with a wide range of rooms and rates, from quaint, basic units to elaborate suites, plus pool, sauna, and Jacuzzi. Sometimes has summer discounts of $50 or so. $245

Santa Barbara Tourist Hostel 134 Chapala St ☎805/963-0154, ⓦwww.sbhostel.com. Centrally located hostel near the beach and State Street, with bicycle and surfboard rentals, complimentary breakfast, and Internet access. Dorm rooms go for $20–29, with private rooms also available ($55–89), some with private bath (extra $10).

The Town

Somewhat ironically, Santa Barbara owes its current Mission-era atmosphere, with its attendant quaintness and historical "authenticity," to a devastating **earthquake** in 1925, after which the city authorities decided to rebuild virtually the entire town as an apocryphal Mission-era village – even the massive "historic" El Paseo shopping mall has a whitewashed adobe facade.

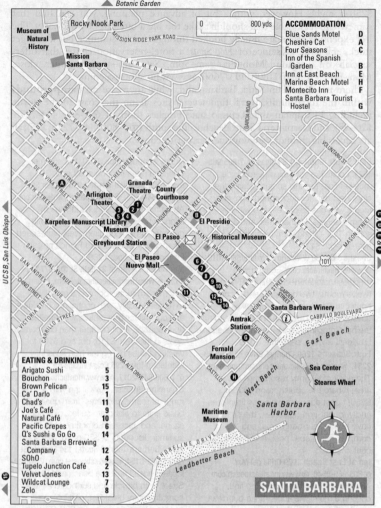

Rocky Nook Park

0   800 yds

Museum of Natural History

Blue Sands Motel   **D**
Cheshire Cat   **A**
Four Seasons   **C**
Inn of the Spanish
  Garden   **B**
Inn at East Beach   **E**
Marina Beach Motel   **H**
Montecito Inn   **F**
Santa Barbara Tourist
  Hostel   **G**

Mission Santa Barbara

Granada Theatre
County Courthouse
Arlington Theater
Karpeles Manuscript Library
El Presidio
Museum of Art
El Paseo
Greyhound Station
Historical Museum
El Paseo Nuevo Mall
Santa Barbara Winery
Amtrak Station
Fernald Mansion
Sea Center
Stearns Wharf
Santa Barbara Harbor
Maritime Museum
West Beach
East Beach
Leadbetter Beach

N

SANTA BARBARA

EATING & DRINKING

Arigato Sushi	5
Bouchon	3
Brown Pelican	15
Ca' Darlo	1
Chad's	11
Joe's Café	9
Natural Café	10
Pacific Crepes	6
Q's Sushi a Go Go	14
Santa Barbara Brrewing
Company	12
SOhO	4
Tupelo Junction Café	2
Velvet Jones	13
Wildcat Lounge	7
Zelo	8

The square-mile **historic center**, squeezed between the south-facing **beaches** and the foothills of the Santa Ynez Mountains, has one of the region's liveliest street scenes. The main drag, **State Street**, is home to an assortment of restaurants, bookstores, coffee bars, and nightclubs catering as much to the needs of locals – among them twenty thousand UC Santa Barbara students – as to visitors.

The historic center

The **historic center** of Santa Barbara lies mostly along State Street a few blocks inland from the beach and the 101 freeway. The town's few genuine Mission-era structures are preserved as **El Presidio de Santa Barbara**, two blocks east of State Street at 123 E Canon Perdido St (daily 10.30am–4.30pm;

$3; ⓦ www.sbthp.org/presidio.htm), built around the fourth and last of the Spanish military garrisons in the region, though only the living quarters of the soldiers who once guarded the site remain. One of these structures, the modest **El Cuartel**, two blocks east of State Street at 123 Canon Perdido Street, is the second oldest building in California, dating from 1782, and now houses historical exhibits and a scale model of the small Spanish colony. A block away, at 136 E De la Guerra Street, the **Santa Barbara Historical Museum** (Tues–Sat 10am–5pm, Sun noon–5pm; donation; ⓣ 805/966-1601, ⓦ www.santabarbaramuseum.com), built around an 1817 adobe, contains displays on Spanish- and Mexican-era life and presents other aspects of the city's past, from Ice Age geology to artifacts from native settlements to modern photographs. Near the museum, where De la Guerra Street meets State Street, the **Casa de la Guerra** (Thurs–Sun noon–4pm; $3; ⓣ 805/966-6961, ⓦ www.sbthp.org/casa.htm) preserves what was, in the 1820s, one of the more upscale residences in town (though still built in the spartan Spanish Colonial style), home to one of the Presidio's commanders. These days, it holds spurs, saddles, toys, and weapons, plus exhibits of antique tools, furniture, and religious icons. After it survived the 1925 earthquake that otherwise obliterated much of downtown, the Casa became a template for the type of Spanish Colonial style that continues to dominate the town's design.

On the corner of State and Anapamu, at 1130 State Street, the fine **Santa Barbara Museum of Art** (Tues–Sun 11am–5pm; $9; ⓣ 805/963-4364, ⓦ www.sbmuseart.org) features some classical Greek and Egyptian statuary, a smattering of French Impressionists, an Asian collection of some note, and interesting modern photography. There's an appealing if scattershot selection of European greats, from minor works of Picasso and Matisse to more engaging pieces from Chagall, Kandinsky, and Miró. Its main features, though, come from its **American collection**, which is particularly strong in nineteenth-century landscape painters such as Albert Bierstadt and postwar California modernists like Richard Diebenkorn. Just east, the still-functioning **County Courthouse**, at 1100 Anacapa Street (Mon–Fri 8.30am–4.30pm, Sat & Sun 10am–4.30pm; free tours Mon–Sat 2pm, also Mon, Tues & Fri 10.30am; ⓣ 805/962-6464), is a Spanish Revival gem, an idiosyncratic 1929 variation on the Mission theme that's widely known as one of the finest public buildings in the US, with striking murals, tilework, and a fountain. Take a break in the sunken gardens, explore the quirky staircases, or climb the seventy-foot "**El Mirador**" clocktower for a nice view out over the town.

Two blocks up State Street, at no. 1317, the landmark 1930s **Arlington Theater** (ⓣ 805/963-4408) is an intact and functional movie palace and performance venue, with a trompe l'oeil interior modeled after an atmospheric Spanish village plaza. It is also home to the modest but respected Santa Barbara Symphony (tickets $28–60; ⓣ 805/898-9526, ⓦ www.thesymphony .org). Keep in mind that in 2008 the symphony is making its long-awaited move a block away to the 1924 Moorish-flavored **Granada Theatre**, 1216 State Street, gloriously renovated to serve as the town's main performing arts center (information at ⓣ 805/899-3000, ⓦ www.granadasb.org). Nearby, at 21 W Anapamu Street, the beautifully decorated **Karpeles Manuscript Library** (daily 10am–4pm; free; ⓣ 805/962-5322, ⓦ www.rain.org/~karpeles) is home to a diverse array of original documents, such as the Constitution of the Confederate States of America, Napoleon's battle plans for his Russian invasion, and manuscripts by famous figures such as Mark Twain, Thomas Edison, John Locke, and Jorge Luis Borges.

The beaches and around

Half a mile down State Street from the town center, Cabrillo Boulevard runs along the south-facing shore, a long, clean strip stretching from the yacht and fishing harbor beyond palm-lined **West Beach** to the volleyball courts and golden sands of **East Beach**. At the foot of State Street, an outdoor **arts-and-crafts market** (Sun 10am–dusk; free) presents the work of some 250 local artisans every week. Also here is the touristy 1872 **Stearns Wharf** (Ⓦwww.stearnswharf.org), the oldest wooden pier in the state. The victim of several earthquakes and fires, it was nearly destroyed most recently in November 1998 when a third of it was engulfed by flames, but it has since been restored to its former glory. The wharf is lined with knick-knack shops, seafood restaurants, ice cream stands, and the **Ty Warner Sea Center** (daily 10am–5pm; $7; Ⓣ805/962-2526), an annex of the Museum of Natural History (see below), offering a tot-friendly selection of touch tanks, interactive exhibits, whale bones, and tide pools.

Just west, overlooking the marina, the **Santa Barbara Maritime Museum**, 113 Harbor Way, Suite 190 (daily except Wed 10am–5pm, summer closes 6pm; $7; Ⓣ805/962-8404, Ⓦwww.sbmm.org) occupies the site of the old Naval Reserve Center and showcases old-fashioned ship models and exhibits on the whaling and tallow trade, seal hunting, native Chumash canoes, and the current nautical practices of recovering shipwrecks and communicating with shore. A few vessels are outside, including a bathyscaphe submersible for plumbing the deep.

Mission Santa Barbara and beyond

The mission from which the city takes its name, **Mission Santa Barbara** (daily 9am–5pm; donation; Ⓣ805/682-4713 ext 121, Ⓦwww.sbmission.org), is located in the hills above town at 2201 Laguna Street. Known as the "Queen of the Missions," its imposing 1820 twin-towered facade – facing out over a perfectly manicured garden towards the sea – combines Romanesque and Mission styles, giving it a formidable character lacking in some of the prettier outposts. A small **museum** displays artifacts from the mission archives, and the cemetery contains the remains of some four thousand Native Americans. Many of them helped build the original complex, which includes aqueducts, waterworks, a grist mill, and two reservoirs, with the old pottery kiln and tanning vats now in ruin. To get to the mission, take SBMTD bus #22 from the Courthouse along Anapamu Street downtown, or walk or drive the half-mile from State Street up Mission Street and Mission Canyon.

Just beyond the mission at 2559 Puerta del Sol Road, the **Museum of Natural History** (daily 10am–5pm; $8; Ⓣ805/682-4711, Ⓦwww.sbnature.org) showcases intriguing artifacts from Chumash culture, various dioramas of mammals, birds, reptiles, and insects, a planetarium, and actual skeletons of such extinct creatures as the pygmy mammoth, taken in 1994 from Santa Rosa Island, off the Santa Barbara coast in Channel Islands National Park. For a closer glimpse of nature, continue on into the hills from the mission until you come to the splendid **Botanic Garden**, 1212 Mission Canyon Road (Mar–Oct daily 9am–6pm, rest of year closes 5pm; $8; Ⓣ805/682-4726, Ⓦwww.sbbg.org), whose 65 acres feature pleasant hiking trails amid indigenous cacti, manzanita, trees, and wildflowers – a relaxing respite among hillside meadows and glades.

▲ Stearns Wharf

Eating

Santa Barbara has a number of very good and very expensive **restaurants**, but it also has many more affordable options offering a range of cuisines. Since it's right on the Pacific, you'll find a lot of seafood and sushi; Mexican places are numerous, and smoothies – blended fruit shakes – are everywhere, a welcome snack on a hot summer day. Throughout, you'll also see local wine that comes from the vineyard-blanketed countryside northwest of the city.

Arigato Sushi 1225 State St ☎ 805/965-6074.
The main draw for sushi in town, this boutique Japanese spot is a bit on the pricey side – with the requisite modernist chic and

hipster diners – but the fresh, delicious raw fish tends to justify the expense.
Bouchon 9 W Victoria St ☎ 805/730-1160.
Among the town's top choices for elite

dining is this California cuisine favorite, which presents a rotating menu of dishes such as citrus-marinated quail, rack of lamb or venison, maple-glazed duck breast, and a full selection of fresh seafood.

Brown Pelican 2981 Cliff Drive ☎805/687-4550. One of the more affordable of the better Santa Barbara eateries, offering a good array of seafood and wine from the local region, plus enjoyable breakfasts and lunches. It has an unbeatable location smack on a secluded beach a bit north of downtown.

Ca' Dario 37 E Victoria St ☎805/884-9419. Although there are a number of upscale Italian haunts in town, this is one of the few that lives up to its prices, with fine cheeses like bocconcini and pasta like ziti, and main dishes that include roasted quail, veal chops, and fresh fish.

Chad's 625 Chapala St ☎805/568-1876. A local favorite serving modern American cuisine – with seafood and steak among the highlights – in the intimate atmosphere of a historic Victorian home.

Joe's Café 536 State St ☎805/966-4638. Long-established bar and grill, still a great place to stop off for a burger, chowder, and a strong drink. More or less midway between the beach and the downtown museums.

Natural Café 508 State St ☎805/962-9494. Scrumptious, cheap veggie meals – with pasta, sandwiches, salads, falafel, and desserts – in a prime spot for people watching. Also at 361 Hitchcock Way, ☎805/563-1163.

Pacific Crêpes 705 Anacapa St ☎805/882-1123. About as close to a decent crêpe as you're going to get here, prepared by real French cooks, who do an especially good job on the dessert crêpes. Expect to wait for service.

Tupelo Junction Cafe 1218 State St ☎805/899-3100. One of the town's best spots for breakfast, focusing on such stick-to-your-ribs items as bacon-spinach-onion scrambles, crab cake and potato hash, vanilla French toast, and pumpkin waffles. Also serves lunch and dinner.

Bars and clubs

There are quite a few **bars** and **clubs** along State Street, especially downtown; for the most up-to-date **nightlife** listings, check out a copy of the free weekly *Santa Barbara Independent* (ⓦwww.independent.com), available at area bookstores, record stores, and convenience marts.

Q's Sushi a Go Go 409 State St ☎805/966-9177. Four bars – including one for sushi – plus a dance floor in a three-story location make this lounge and restaurant a big draw if you're ready to drink and boogie; the sushi, though, is just average.

Santa Barbara Brewing Company 501 State St ☎805/730-1040. Serviceable American fare – burgers, seafood, and sandwiches – with solid microbrewed beers and live music on weekends. The Rincon Red and State Street Stout are both worth a swig.

Soho 1221 State St ☎805/962-7776, ⓦwww.sohosb.com. Favorite local place to catch a jazz show, with nightly performances and the occasional big name. Mixes the vibe with frequent rock, acoustic, and world-beat artists and bands.

Velvet Jones 423 State St ☎805/965-8676, ⓦwww.velvet-jones.com. Among the few good places in town to catch a show, typically of the indie variety, on the weekends and perhaps comedy and reggae at other times, drawing the usual crowd of students and would-be hellraisers.

Wildcat Lounge 15 W Ortega St ☎805/962-7970, ⓦwww.wildcatlounge.com. A good spot for seeing electronica DJs and various bands, in a chic atmosphere with a mix of locals, students, and out-of-towners.

Zelo 630 State St ☎805/966-5792, ⓦwww.zelo.net. One of Santa Barbara's more fashionable bars and restaurants, the Zelo evolves into a dance club as the night wears on, offering alternative, Latin, retro, and other eclectic rhythms throughout the week.

Contexts

Contexts

History

To casual observers, Los Angeles is a place with no sense of **history**, an ultramodern urban sprawl that lives up to its vapid stereotypes, nothing but sunny skies, surfer dudes, and movie stars. However, a potent countermyth has also emerged of dystopic LA, in which violent outbreaks and scandals are commonplace, and lying beneath the city's sunny surface is a dark and dangerous underbelly. Although both of these myths have some validity, what they most reveal is the sense of drama (and not just the Hollywood variety) in LA's self-image. Whether they see their city as a sunshine paradise or a necropolis, Angelenos tend to agree that their chosen city is a harbinger of things to come for the rest of America.

Prehistoric LA

Like other parts of the West Coast, the underlying **geology** that makes up the LA basin began as an **oceanic terrane**, basically a mobile chunk of land that pushed toward the North American landmass along the Pacific Plate. For 120 to 160 million years, the terrane came closer, drifting northward, and repeatedly rose above and sank below sea level, until it reached its current, above-ground position around five million years ago. By the time of the **Ice Age**, around 25,000 years ago, the LA region was literally an arcadia – a sylvan land of fertile, tree-covered plains, crystalline brooks and lakes, untamed rivers, and a temperate climate. Despite the idyllic conditions, a natural peril awaited the region's creatures in the form of the **La Brea Tar Pits**: dark, boggy pools that were visible evidence of the copious petroleum deposits in the region and which spelled doom for any animals that wandered into them. Sinking into the murky ooze, they remained preserved in the tar until they were unearthed in the modern era by **William Orcutt**, giving a vivid picture of the rich ecology of the time, when prehistoric LA was populated with the likes of saber-toothed tigers, giant ground sloths, mammoths, and even camels. The wide array of fauna and pristine environment would not last long, for as soon as humans began crossing into North America via the temporary land-bridge at the Bering Strait (about 18–25,000 years ago), such creatures were doomed to be prey for hunters or driven out of the area entirely, to become extinct.

Native peoples

For thousands of years prior to the arrival of Europeans, **native peoples** subsisted in different parts of the Los Angeles basin without too much difficulty. The dominant groups in the area were **Tataviam**, **Chumash**, and **Tongva** (whom the Spanish called Gabrieleño) peoples. Of these, the dominant tribes were the Chumash, who lived along the coast around modern-day Malibu and Ventura, and the Tongva, who occupied much of the central LA basin. Both tribes fished and traded by sea in pitch-blackened canoes, and were skilled enough navigators to meet explorer Juan Cabrillo before his 1542 landfall off San Pedro. Otherwise, these tribes had little in common, and were an easy target for later **Spanish** conquerors and missionaries – although it's also true that they were wiped out by European-borne epidemics as much as by outright Spanish aggression.

Today, LA County is home to the greatest number of native peoples of any county in the US – up to two hundred thousand by some estimates, many migrating from other parts of the US. Indeed, most Native Americans in these parts are now Navajo, and little remains to mark the existence of the early tribes, aside from the faded remnants found at scattered archeological digs and the cultural treasures locked up behind glass in folk-art museums.

European discovery and colonization

After sighting San Diego harbor, Cabrillo continued north along the coast to Santa Catalina Island and the Channel Islands off Santa Barbara. He bestowed a number of other place names that survive, including, in the LA area, Santa Monica, and San Pedro Bay, named for the first Bishop of Rome. Other European explorers followed, charting the California coast and naming more of the islands, bays, and coastal towns, but it was the **Spanish**, moving up from their base in Mexico, who were to colonize Southern California and map out the future city of Los Angeles.

The Spanish occupation of California began in earnest in 1769 as a combination of military expediency (to prevent other powers from gaining a foothold) and missionary zeal (to convert Native Americans to Roman Catholicism). **Padre Junípero Serra** began the missions, setting off from Mexico and going all the way up to Monterey; assisting him was **Gaspar de Portola**, a soldier who led the expedition into LA.

The first mission sited in Los Angeles was **Mission San Gabriel**, in 1771; from that beginning, Spanish military garrisons served to hold the natives subject to the demands of Franciscan friars who ordered them to abandon their religious beliefs, cultural rituals, and languages. The penalties for disobedience were stiff: flogging with twenty to forty lashes was standard practice. While the Spanish were trying to "convert the savages," they were also eradicating the native population, reducing their ranks by 95 percent over the course of 150 years. By World War I, fewer than 17,000 of them remained.

The Spanish era

Aside from abusing the natives, the Spanish who colonized Southern California effected the first crude designs for LA, which they established in 1781 at a site northwest of the current Plaza in Downtown. The city's original **pobladores**, or settlers, of which there were less than fifty, set a multicultural precedent for the region, as they were made up of a majority of black, mestizo, mixed-race, and native peoples, with the white Spanish being a distinct, though powerful, minority. The early **pueblo** (town), designed by California's governor **Felipe de Neve**, grew in short spurts, aided by the creation of the *zanja madre*, or "mother ditch," that brought water into town. Despite half-hearted efforts by

▲ Statue of Padre Junípero Serra at Mission San Gabriel

the Spanish to make the settlement grow, it took a devastating 1815 flood for large-scale development to begin, starting with the construction of the current Plaza and its Plaza Church – La Placita – and the Avila Adobe.

As the town grew from remote outpost to regional centerpiece, the power of the Spanish Crown began to fade. While the military and missions exercised official power, the functional operation of the little burg was increasingly the province of a small group of mestizo families whose names are still reflected in LA's street names – Sepulveda, Pico, and so on – along with a few white American expatriates who for various reasons found the region to their liking. By the early 1800s, the Spanish were playing only a *de jure* role in city administration; soon after, they would be forcibly removed from power.

Mexican rule

Mexico gained independence in 1821, calling itself the United States of Mexico, and over the next four years, the Mexican residents of Southern California evicted the Spanish and made the region into a territory of Mexico itself – Alta California.

The 24 subsequent years of Mexican rule upended the political and social order – causing the destruction and looting of many missions – but provided no end to the oppression of native peoples. The Tongva and others now found themselves at the bottom level of an oppressive new hierarchy, where rich land barons controlled huge parcels of land known as **ranchos** and reduced the natives to a state of near-serfdom. (Despite the ugliness that took place there, many of these ranchos survive in a reasonably preserved state, with copious gardens and elegant adobe architecture, making for an excellent starting point on any trip into LA history.)

Due to widespread social oppression and frequent clashes between the wealthy land bosses (often linked to internal politics in southern Mexico), the period was largely a chaotic one, well described by Richard Henry Dana, Jr in his book *Two Years before the Mast*. By the time Governor **Pio Pico** successfully established his Alta California capital in Los Angeles (long his preferred spot for governance), the period of Mexican rule was almost at an end, its demise assured by the factional struggles and undisciplined ways of the rancho owners.

The Mexican–American War

From the 1830s onward, driven by the concept of **Manifest Destiny**, the popular, often religious, belief that Americans had a divine or moral charge to occupy the country from coast to coast, the US government's stated policy regarding California was to buy all of Mexico's land north of the Rio Grande, the river that now divides the US and Mexico. When President James K. Polk went ahead and annexed Texas – still claimed by Mexico – war broke out. Most of the fighting in the **Mexican–American War** took place in Texas, though a few skirmishes occurred in Southern California.

By the summer of 1846, after the American capture of Monterey and San Diego, Pico and his colleagues had difficulty even finding significant numbers of loyal Mexicans to defend LA against the US. A truce was signed to avoid bloodshed and American troops walked into the city virtually unopposed. However, despite this relatively pacific start, the military chieftains left local government in the hands of the incompetent **Archibald Gillespie**, who promptly instituted martial law and just as quickly turned the populace against the American presence. The situation further degenerated, with outbreaks of local hostilities, and by the time Mexican general Andreas Pico and American "pathfinder" John C. Fremont signed the final **peace treaty** in January 1847 at Campo de Cahuenga, after several battles and much bloodshed, the chasm between the Mexican residents and their new American conquerors had grown considerably.

Early American rule

California was admitted to the US as the 31st state in 1850, a move quickly followed by the **1851 Land Act**, through which the new white settlers targeted the rancho owners, forcing them to legally prove their right to the land they had been granted. The ensuing legal battles left many of the owners destitute, and while the rancho boundaries and some of their elemental chunks continued to linger for up to a century or more, the central goal of the new settlers had been accomplished: the old-line Mexicans were driven out and replaced by a gringo elite. However, even as this process was taking place, and the latest real-estate magnates were consolidating their power, the city's social structure continued its slide into chaos.

For many good reasons, LA was called "**Hell Town**" in the middle of the nineteenth century. The lives of the native peoples got even worse, as they were subject to all manner of mob aggression and legal disenfranchisement. Because the city had no effective municipal authority, and because it was crowded with hordes of aggressive fortune-hunters who had failed in the northern gold rush, it became a magnet for violent criminals and other ne'er-do-wells, and was peppered with gambling halls, saloons, and brothels – a Wild West town decades before such a thing existed. The bellicose citizenry usually focused their rage against the groups at the bottom of the social hierarchy, tactics that eventually backfired when roving groups of Mexican bandidos, such as Tiburcio Vasquez, emerged to counter the threats.

The local situation got so bloody that "**vigilance committees**" were created to deal with the crime, which had reached the same levels as San Francisco even though LA only had a tenth as many people. The vigilantes summarily executed 32 people, and gave rise to even more extreme groups who would hunt down lawbreakers, real or imagined, and severely maim or kill them. The El Monte Rangers, an imported gang of Texas thugs, was perhaps the most notorious, though there were many others, and LA remained a city solidly under the thumb of mob rule until after the Civil War.

During the height of its social strife, the region managed to sketch the outlines of what would later become the metropolitan area. Post offices, banks, newspapers, and churches were a few of the emblems of encroaching civilization, and the activity of such pioneering entrepreneurs as **Phineas Banning** – the developer of the Wilmington harbor plan, whose elegant estate is still worth a look – also brought early growth to the city.

In 1860, LA's citizens chose the wrong side in the **Civil War**, casting a meager 18 percent of their ballots for Abraham Lincoln, and soon became possessed by secessionist rage and racial hatred. Adding to the rancor, many in the city and region were clamoring to split from northern California and create an autonomous enclave where they wouldn't be subject to state or federal power. Thirteen thousand soldiers were stationed in Wilmington's Drum Barracks to ensure domestic order, act against Southwest rebel activity, and, later, quash native uprisings. Just as tellingly, a crowd of revelers gathered in LA after hearing news of Lincoln's assassination. Their celebration was broken up – but only with the aid of the federal soldiers.

Late-nineteenth-century growth

The last three decades of the nineteenth century were an era of **rapid growth** and **technological change** in LA, principally because of three key factors: periodic real-estate booms that led to the subdivision of the old ranchos into smaller, more profitable chunks; the building of railroad lines externally, to places like San Francisco, and internally, from Downtown to the port at San Pedro; and most importantly, the mass arrival of Midwesterners.

From the 1870s, LA gained a reputation as a bastion of healthy living. While eastern American cities were notorious for sooty air and water pollution, LA was touted as a sunny, clean-air paradise where the infirm could recover from their illnesses and everyone could enjoy the fruits of the invigorating desert lifestyle. The **orange** was the perfect symbol of this new arcadia, and trees and citrus groves were planted by the thousands, ultimately leading to towns being named for oranges and walnuts, and streets for magnolias and white oaks. Huge numbers of Iowans and Kansans moved to the city in the Victorian era, spurred on as well by cheap one-way railroad tickets: thanks to a price war between the Santa Fe and Southern Pacific railroads, fares from Kansas City to LA briefly dropped to a mere dollar; before long, the passenger cars were full of church-going Protestants seeking desert salvation.

The Midwesterners of the 1880s did much to displace lingering Hispanic influences, meanwhile exacerbating racial tensions, which flared up in such instances as the **anti-Chinese riot of 1871**. After a disagreement left a white man dead at the hands of a Chinese shopkeeper, a mob assembled and quickly set about attacking and murdering what Chinese residents it could get its hands on. While there were only about two hundred Chinese in LA at the time, the mob managed to strangle, shoot, stab, and hang 22 of them. In an ominous portent of LA-style justice to come, few of the perpetrators faced jail time, and those that did only served a year or so.

Beyond its racial animus and Midwestern migrations, LA was becoming an attraction of sorts for a few of the nation's more colorful characters. **Charles Fletcher Lummis** was the first of these, a fervent supporter of the rights of native peoples, yet also an isolationist who saw a looming threat from foreign immigration. Aside from that, Lummis was a bit of a crank who was so committed to his own notion of healthy living that he created a boulder house, "El Alisal," which still stands in Highland Park, and he took the unusual step of coming to LA from Cincinnati **on foot** – a distance of nearly three thousand miles. Lummis would be just one of many individualists to inhabit the LA region, including others like the Pasadena artisans who created "**Arroyo culture**" just after the turn of the century (an Arts-and-Crafts philosophy that owed much to Lummis; see box, p.197), and left-wing political activists like **Job Harriman**, whose commune in the northern desert town of Llano del Rio was intended to be the blueprint for a socialist utopia.

While the dreamers and artists experimented with alternative living, the politicians and businessmen were busy expanding the city by every means possible: the **harbor** was developed at San Pedro; **railway lines** were added throughout the region by Henry Huntington, through his electric Red Car transit system; and other entrepreneurs like Edward Doheny grew rich drilling for **oil** practically everywhere.

The early twentieth century: water and power

Around the turn of the century, LA's population reached 100,000; perhaps more important to the city's development, however, **William Mulholland** was put in charge of the city's water department. Mulholland was the catalyst for a water-stealing scheme that even now remains legendary: various bankers, publishing magnates, and railway bosses purchased large land holdings in the San Fernando Valley, and shortly thereafter, a small cadre of city bankers secretly began buying up land in California's distant Owens Valley, 250 miles away. By the time the northern farmers realized what had happened, the bankers had consolidated control over the valley watershed and were making plans to bring the bulk of the region's water to the drought-stricken citizens of LA — or so it seemed. Modern evidence suggests that massive amounts of water were being deposited into the city sewers so area dams and reservoirs could drop precipitously, thus making it look like the region was on the verge of a severe drought.

Following the land grab, Mulholland built a **giant canal system** – one of the country's biggest public-works projects (see box, p.203) – that carried the stolen water to Southern California, but not LA proper. Instead, the aqueduct mysteriously ended in the San Fernando Valley and city politicians **annexed** the valley for housing, thus wiping out thousands of acres of fertile agricultural land and making the real-estate interests there – actually Downtown bankers and political powerbrokers who secretly bought up the land – wealthy beyond imagination. The entire enterprise surely ranks as one of the country's biggest municipal swindles, and one that the Owens Valley farmers did not soon forget. In the 1920s, when Mulholland and company set about acquiring more property for the canal system, the farmers responded by destroying sections of the system with carefully placed dynamite charges. This violence, coupled with the unrelated bursting of the St Francis dam north of LA – a catastrophe that killed more than four hundred people – destroyed Mulholland's reputation. However, by that time, his main work had already been accomplished: the aqueduct helped turn LA into a metropolis.

Accompanying the development of the modernizing city was the growth of **organized labor**. In 1910, a series of strikes at breweries and foundries crippled the city, and local labor was also responsible for nearly bringing socialist Job Harriman to power. However, when the main building of the *Los Angeles Times* – the right-wing organ of labor's archenemy **Harrison Gray Otis** – was bombed, a slow erosion of leftist support took place and ultimately led to defeat for Harriman, who then retreated to his northern desert commune.

World War I to the Great Depression

Metropolis or not, LA continued to display its regressive, provincial character in many ways, especially in its treatment of **minorities**. Chinese residents were still subject to all manner of exclusionary laws, as were the Japanese, and both were among the Asian immigrants targeted by the **1913 Alien Land Bill**, which kept them from purchasing further land tracts and limited their lease tenures. Finally, even though industrial production during World War I doubled the black population of the city, the total number of **African–Americans** was still fairly small (less than three percent of the population).

Despite its lack of progressive ideas, rapid growth continued, and after World War I, LA became quite a **tourist magnet** – long before the arrival of Disneyland. Sights like Abbot Kinney's pseudo-European Venice and the carnival midways in Santa Monica and Long Beach all drew good numbers of seasonal visitors, as did Santa Catalina Island and the Mount Lowe Railroad in the San Gabriel Mountains.

Soon, another great **wave of newcomers** began arriving, from all across America. By the 1920s, LA was gaining residents by one hundred thousand per year, most coming by car and flocking to **suburbs** such as Glendale, Long Beach, and Pasadena. **Petroleum** was adding to the boom, from places like Signal Hill to Venice, with oil wells popping up all over the region, usually without regard to aesthetics or pollution. Naturally, the wells helped fuel the explosive growth of the local **car culture**, which even in the 1920s had become a potent force. The quintessential symbol of the dynamic, forward-looking atmosphere of the time was **City Hall**, built in 1928 as a mix of classical and contemporary elements, and topped by none other than a small replica of one of the long-lost ancient wonders of the world – the Mausoleum at Halicarnassus. This was civic ego on a grand scale, a fitting reflection of the attitudes of the time, but also a symbolic portent of the 1930s.

Into this highly charged environment also came the first **movie pioneers**, whose typically Jewish backgrounds, and origins in the Eastern garment industry, were looked down on by the Downtown elite. Because of exclusionary housing laws, film titans like Adolph Zukor and Samuel Goldwyn developed the Westside as their base of operations, an action that had long-lasting effects. Even today, West Hollywood, Beverly Hills, and West LA remain the cultural focus of the city, with Downtown still well behind, despite the constant financial efforts of the remaining Downtown elite to remedy the situation.

The boom years ended with the onset of the **Great Depression**. Banks collapsed, businesses went bankrupt, and Midwestern drought brought a new round of immigrants to Southern California, much poorer and significantly more desperate than their forebears. By 1936 the LAPD — in its seemingly infinite powers — imposed a typically draconian solution: posting officers at the California state border to deter any more "damn Okies" from coming. Those that weren't sufficiently persuaded by the police department's strong-arm tactics faced six months in jail.

These hard times spawned a number of movements. Led by fiery evangelists like **Aimee Semple McPherson**, religious **cults** gained adherents by the thousands, Communist and Fascist organizations trawled for members among the city's more frustrated or simple-minded ranks, and the muckraker **Upton Sinclair** emerged as the greatest threat to LA's ruling hierarchy since Job Harriman. With his **End Poverty in California (EPIC)** campaign, Sinclair frightened the upper crust across the region, and was countered not only by the usual Downtown stalwarts, but also by their Westside adversaries, the Hollywood movie bosses, who rightly perceived a danger in Sinclair's message to their control over the film industry and film-crew labor. Fraudulent newsreel propaganda (showing hordes of homeless men and various halfwits testifying their allegiance to Sinclair) helped speed Sinclair's demise in the gubernatorial contest, but no one could stop the tide of reform, which brought down LA's corrupt mayor **Frank Shaw** and his attendant cronies. The entire political and social mess was reflected in the most famous literary works of the time: Nathanael West's *Day of the Locust* and Raymond Chandler's detective fiction, all of which portrayed a morally decayed society on the verge of collapse.

World War II and after

By the time of **World War II**, LA was emerging as one of the top US sites for military hardware production and coastal defense. In San Pedro, Fort MacArthur, named after the father of one of the war's most famous generals, was the site of Battery Osgood, home to anti-aircraft guns on the watch for Japanese fighter planes. Similarly, at the man-made Terminal Island, the harbor area itself was a shipbuilding center, still embodied by the presence of the hulking SS *Lane Victory*, one of the huge cargo ships that carried supplies for the Navy during the war.

The misery of the continuing Depression and the dark, paranoid atmosphere in the early part of the war exacerbated the underlying social tensions and unleashed yet more rounds of violence and oppression against the perceived enemies of white Protestants. Although Chinese citizens had suffered after Union Station was plunked on top of the destroyed, former site of Chinatown, it was the city's Japanese population who now received the full brunt of the region's, as well as the nation's, racial animus. One of Franklin Roosevelt's executive orders gave the green light to mass deportations of Japanese-American citizens, who were forcibly relocated to bleak desert **internment camps** for the duration of the war. Minorities who hadn't been shipped away made for fat targets as well, especially Mexican-Americans.

The **Sleepy Lagoon Murder case** – in which seventeen Hispanics were rounded up and sent to jail for a single murder, only to be later released by a disgusted appellate court – was but a prelude to the turmoil that would come to be known as the **Zoot Suit Riots**, named for the popular apparel Hispanic youth wore at the time, with wide stripes, broad, shoulders, and accessories like dangling watch-chains and low-slung hats. Over the course of several days in early June 1943, two hundred sailors on leave attacked and beat up a large number of Mexican-Americans – with the handy assistance of local police, who made sure that the black-and-blue victims were promptly arrested on trumped-up charges. The violence continued until it became a federal issue, causing a rift in international relations between the US and Mexico. After the chaos ended, the LA City Council responded aggressively to the ugly events – by banning the wearing of zoot suits.

Although anti-Asian and -Hispanic feelings still remained, the end of the war brought a shift in hostilities. A growing contingent of **black migrants**, drawn by the climate and defense-related jobs, became the focus of white wrath, and the reason was clear: from 1940 to 1965, the number of blacks in LA increased from 75,000 to 600,000. The white elite did what it could to marginalize the new residents – keeping blacks confined to eastern sections of town around Central Avenue and "redlining" them out of personal loans and business financing – but these tactics only served to heighten the hostility that would later erupt in mass violence.

In the meantime, LA was becoming one of the USA's largest cities, with the nonstop arrival of newcomers from across the country, the rebirth of the local economy, and the construction of a **vast freeway network** to replace the old Red Cars – due principally to a decline in public-transit users and active subversion by oil, gas, and automotive interests. Defense industries, notably in aerospace, began a decades-long dominion over the local economy, superseding, most notably, the movie industry, which experienced a sharp decline in the 1950s because of television's impact and governmental antitrust actions (see "The rise of Hollywood," p.407). Not surprisingly, with the rise of the military-industrial complex, the LA region became a focus of Cold War defense as many hilltop sites, from San Pedro to the Santa Monica Mountains, were converted into command centers for launching missiles against nuclear bombers, and installations like the Jet Propulsion Laboratory and Edwards Air Force Base became the focus of a local economy still on a war footing. At the top of the military-industrial heap was the shadowy figure of **Howard Hughes**, who became well-known for his dabbling in Hollywood B-flicks and flying the oversized "Spruce Goose," but whose real contribution to the economic growth of LA was as the head of Hughes Aircraft and Hughes Aerospace, which led the way in the development of air-to-air missiles to fight the next war against the Soviet foe.

Concurrently, suburbs like **Orange County** drew old-time residents from the heart of the city into expanding towns like Garden Grove, Huntington Beach, and Anaheim – where **Disneyland** also acted as a pop-culture beacon. The northern valleys traded orange groves for subdivisions and asphalt, and before long, the entire LA basin was swelling with people in every conceivable direction. In contrast, much of the wealth in the Hollywood and Mid-Wilshire sections of town, areas that had first been developed by middle-class automotive travel in the 1920s and 1930s, left with the "white flight" of bourgeois residents to the outlying suburbs, and the old commuter suburbs west of Downtown increasingly became part of the inner city and the new home of working-poor minorities.

The 1960s to the 1980s

As elsewhere in the country, the face of Los Angeles began changing dramatically in the 1960s. Not only was the freeway system stitching the entire basin into an interconnected network of automobile suburbs, but LA's own classic Art Deco and Historic Revival buildings were quickly disappearing to make way for the promise of shiny new superstructures. Places like **Bunker Hill** changed from shambling Victorian neighborhoods into auto-oriented corporate enclaves, poor Hispanic families were cleared out of Elysian Park to make way for Dodger Stadium, the old 20th-Century Fox movie lot was sold off to make way for the colorless highrise towers of Century City, and the quaint homes of Playa del Rey were demolished to make way for expansion of LAX. However unpopular they were, many of these deals were, predictably, sealed behind closed doors, in the continuing atmosphere of secrecy and intrigue that pervaded city politics.

However, the type of right-wing leadership evident in LA's postwar politicians, such as the race-baiting mayor Sam Yorty, and the city's so-called **Committee of 25**, a business cabal that acted as a sort of shadow government from its California Club headquarters, got its comeuppance with 1965's **Watts Riots**. The riots – which started with the arrest of one Marquette Frye for speeding, lasted a week and ended with the arrival of 36,000 police and National Guard troops – caused $40 million worth of property damage and permanently dismantled white LA's beliefs about the perceived laziness of minorities and willingness to accept overt subjugation. While many blacks did not see, and still have not seen, a diminution in poverty levels, the old municipal overlords couldn't help but take notice at the potent brew of anger and frustration they had helped create.

Along with this, the late 1960s **protests** by student radicals, mostly against the involvement in Vietnam, and the emergence of flower power and hippie counterculture caused a dramatic break between generations – the staid Orange County parents versus their rebellious, pot-smoking kids. The colorful result led to an explosion of psychedelic music, left-wing political diatribe, untamed sexuality, and, occasionally, bursts of violence – evident with the Manson Family killings of 1969. These freewheeling attitudes were most evident in places like the Sunset Strip, then as now famed for its rock-music scene, and Topanga Canyon, which became a rich musicians' hippie commune in places.

After much effort, the progressive forces in LA politics finally began to undermine the corrupt power structure that had ruled LA for nearly a century. Eight years after the riots, LA's first black mayor, **Tom Bradley**, was elected by a coalition of black, Hispanic, and Westside Jewish voters. The political success of these groups galvanized others into action on the LA political scene, notably women and gays. Accordingly, the *LA Times*, long a paragon of reactionary yellow journalism, underwent a historic change through the efforts of **Otis Chandler**, son of archconservative former publisher Harry Chandler, who turned the paper into a liberal icon with a range of world-class writers and critics.

Bradley's twenty-year tenure was also marked, less fortuitously, by the disappearance of LA's manufacturing base. South Central and Southeast LA ceased to be centers for oil, rubber, and automotive production, San Fernando Valley car plants closed, and heavy industries like Kaiser's mammoth steel-making operation in Fontana shut down. Though this was somewhat tempered in the 1980s by the heavy investment of Japanese and Canadian money into Downtown real estate, the decade ended hard with the **demise of aerospace jobs**, which had been the region's military-industrial meal ticket since the early Cold War era. As one telling symbol of the change, the old Westside site of Hughes Aircraft is now occupied by a massive condominium development.

Modern LA: the 1990s to the present

The early Nineties continued the hard times, which only got bleaker when black motorist **Rodney King** was videotaped being beaten by uniformed officers of the LA Police Department. The officers' subsequent acquittal by jurors in conservative Simi Valley sparked the April 1992 **riots**, which highlighted the economic disparities between rich and poor, along with the more obvious abuses of police power and privilege. Sixteen years on, the aftermath of the riots (which involved all races in mass chaos from South Central to Koreatown and were not simply black versus white) has not yet been fully realized or understood, and new initiatives promised by local and federal authorities to combat LA's endemic violence and poverty have not materialized. Meanwhile, episodes like the **O.J. Simpson trial** have only served to further confuse matters. In 1995, Simpson, a black former football star, was acquitted of killing his wife and her friend, in what was termed the "Trial of the Century," an ugly and protracted affair in which public opinion was split along racial lines.

All these factors combined to make the first five years of the 1990s perhaps the bleakest since the Great Depression, and **natural calamities** – regional flooding, Malibu fires and mudslides, and two dramatic earthquakes – only added to the general malaise.

The rest of the decade was not nearly as dramatic. **Richard Riordan**, a multimillionaire technocrat, was mayor for eight years in the mid- to late-1990s and presided over a major **revival** in the city's economic fortunes and a **restructuring** of its economic base – aerospace and automotive industries giving way to tourism, real estate, and, as always, Hollywood. New property developments attempted to revitalize blighted sections of town, and even crime and violence tailed off marginally. However, the city's old demons continued to stir. More than anything else, the allegations behind the **Rampart police scandal** – where a group of corrupt police officers acted worse than the gangs they were trying to shut down – made people realize what truly awful elements still lurked under LA's glossy surfaces.

The 2001 mayoral election of bland, uninspiring bureaucrat James Hahn didn't help matters, but his appointment of former New York police reformer **William Bratton** to head the LAPD surprised many, giving hope that an outsider with no connection to the department's entrenched ways might be just the person to reform it, though this still remains more hope than reality. Four years later, Hahn was defeated in his re-election bid by **Antorio Villaraigosa** – amazingly, LA's first Latino mayor since 1872 – but the city's core problems remain the same as they ever have: a huge gap between the richest and poorest Angelenos (even more extreme than the national rate); much lingering hostility between the races; and the difficulty of expunging gang violence, drive-by shootings, and all those other nasty elements of urban life that have been more effectively dealt with in cities such as, New York. To add to all this, the **fires of 2007** – burning acreage from Griffith Park to Santa Catalina Island – gave everyone a swift reminder that natural disasters weren't just limited to the 1990s.

Nonetheless, the metropolis is back on a much firmer economic footing, and the ugly character of much LA design from the 1960s into the 1990s – a mix of concrete Brutalism and corporate glass towers – is slowly changing with the arrival of a slew of high-profile **signature buildings**, including the Getty Center, Disney Hall and the CalTrans building. At the same time, the preservation of classic sections of town like Old Pasadena and Downtown's Spring Street and Broadway offer a little hope that the city may have finally learned from its mistakes in trying to demolish its past, even while demolitions like that of the Ambassador Hotel (death site of RFK) suggest otherwise.

Considering all these factors, and with the movies again showcasing LA as a stereotypical land of ultra-brite smiles and perfect bodies, it may only be a matter of time before the migrants – white, black, and Hispanic – start arriving in droves once more. Despite the occasional rain and gloom, the Southern California dream is too vivid and blinding ever to be fully obscured.

The rise of Hollywood

To this day, the word **Hollywood** remains synonymous with the motion picture industry, even if the reality of that association has not always held true. What follows is a brief history of the movie business in Los Angeles and how the studio system took root, from its genesis to the beginning of its decline.

Westward migration

While we now think of Hollywood's emergence as a simple matter of abundant sun, low taxes, and cheap labor – all important factors, to be sure – the original reason the first filmmakers established themselves here was due to something much simpler: **fear**. But for the strong-arm tactics of Thomas Edison and company, the movie business might never have come to Southern California.

Edison and his competitors (companies like Biograph, Vitagraph, and Pathé, among many others) had by 1909 consolidated their various patents on film technology and processing to form what was known as "**the Trust**": the Motion Picture Patents Company (the MPPC). Although it didn't even last a decade (thanks to bad business practices and a federal antitrust suit), the MPPC did manage to scare off many directors and producers in the first years of its existence, including producer William Selig and director Francis Boggs, both of whom wanted to get as far away from the MPPC's seat of power, New York City, as they possibly could. Southern California was their choice, and more prominent film-industry figures soon followed, finding the taxes, labor costs, and abundant shooting locations much to their liking.

Early Hollywood

Thomas Ince, **Mack Sennett**, and **D.W. Griffith** were the early film legends who helped to establish Hollywood as the focus of the American movie business. Ince, with his studios in Culver City and Edendale, and his coastal "Inceville" north of Santa Monica, founded the elemental model of the studio system that was to hold sway for many decades: writers would prepare scripts in collaboration with directors and Ince himself, after which a tightly budgeted production would be filmed at prearranged locations, and a final cut of the movie would be edited. This sort of precise planning minimized the possibility of surprises during shooting, as well as ground-breaking or idiosyncratic storytelling, and contributed to the factory-like character of Ince's operation.

By comparison, Sennett's **Keystone Film Company** in Edendale, in East Hollywood, produced Keystone Kops comedies in less rigorous fashion. However, with production needs mounting, Sennett adopted his former colleague's model (both had worked for Culver City's Triangle Films, on the lot that now houses Sony Studios) and went on to a two-decades-long career making his signature brand of wacky entertainment.

The largest creative presence in early Hollywood was, however, D.W. Griffith, who began as a theatrical actor and director of one-reel shorts and reached the peak of his fame with *Birth of a Nation*, a runaway hit in 1914 – despite its glamorization of the Ku Klux Klan, its epic length (2hr 40min), and its unprecedented $2 admission fee. Woodrow Wilson praised the film for "writing history with lightning," overlooking that its source was not actual history, but the bigoted ramblings of Southern preacher Thomas Dixon, on whose book, *The Clansman*, the movie had been based.

Generating a firestorm of controversy with the film, Griffith fired back at his critics with his next film, *Intolerance* – a bloated historical epic – but only succeeded at permanently damaging his career. With its preachy moralizing and colossal sets loaded with Babylonian columns and squatting elephants, *Intolerance* became a buzzword for box-office failure and directorial narcissism. Griffith would make a slow slide into obscurity in the 1920s, but not before he perfected the essential aesthetic components he developed with *Birth of a Nation*: close-ups, flashbacks, cross-cutting, and the like – essential elements of modern cinema storytelling to this day.

The birth of the big studios

In 1913, **Cecil B. DeMille**, an itinerant theatrical actor and director, came west to rent a horse barn for a movie. From this simple act, DeMille and his partners, glove-maker Sam Goldfish (soon to be renamed Goldwyn) and vaudeville producer Jesse Lasky, established the basis for the big studios that would follow. The film made in the barn (even as there were horses still in it) was *The Squaw Man*, which became a huge commercial triumph; DeMille became one of the early industry's most bankable directors of historical and biblical epics, and Lasky and Goldwyn later teamed with Adolph Zukor to create the colossus known as **Paramount Studios**.

Like other studios in the coming decades, Paramount used a number of tactics to push its product, including "block booking" (in which film packages, rather than individual films, were sold to exhibitors, thus maximizing studio revenue) and buying up theater chains across the country (to ensure exhibition spaces for its films). These influential practices served to consolidate the industry. By the end of World War I, three major studios had risen to dominance: Paramount, **Loew's**, and **First National** – though only Paramount would survive in name during the height of the studio system.

The 1919 creation of **United Artists (UA)** looked promising for actors and directors. This studio, formed by Douglas Fairbanks Sr, Mary Pickford, D.W. Griffith, and Charlie Chaplin, seemed to suggest a greater role might be in store for the creative individuals who actually made the films, instead of just the studio bosses and executive producers. Things didn't quite work out that way: the next decade saw UA in the role of bit player, along with Columbia and Universal, principally because it didn't own its own theaters and had to rely on one of the major studios for booking its films. The one major development UA prefigured was the dominance of the **star system**, by which big-name actors (such as Fairbanks and Pickford), rather than writers, directors, or the story itself, would drive the production and marketing of studio product – a scheme that has barely changed in 90 years.

The golden age

The five largest studios from the 1920s to the 1940s were **Paramount**, the **Fox Film Corporation** (later 20th-Century Fox), **Warner Bros**, **Radio–Keith–Orpheum** (later RKO), and the biggest of them all, **Metro–Goldwyn–Mayer**, or MGM, which was controlled by the still-powerful Loew's corporation in New York. The majors used every method they could to rigidly control their operations, and they did much to industrialize the business, breaking down the stages of production and using specialists (editors, cinematographers, and so on) to create the product, which was often exhibited in lavish, company-owned "**movie palaces**" that even today are regarded as the greatest spaces ever built for movie-watching. The arrival of **sound** in the late 1920s further specialized the industry, and the possibility of a lone professional with a camera shooting a nationally released film vanished.

Ince's original system had been perfected into rigorous, clinical efficiency. Even the content of the movies was controlled, in this case because of **Will Hays**, formerly postmaster general in the corrupt Harding administration, when a series of 1920s scandals (not least, Fatty Arbuckle's three trials for the murder-rape of actress Virginia Rappe) tarnished the industry and raised the specter of government censorship. Hays' major claim to fame was as the developer of the 1930 "**Hays Code**," a series of official proscriptions and taboos that the studios were supposed to follow, involving intimations of sex, miscegenation, blasphemy, and so on. Although Hays is often credited with enforcing movie-industry censorship, it was actually **Joseph Breen** who wielded the real censorial power starting in the mid-1930s, when the Code first began to be rigidly enforced. With Breen and the Catholic organization the **Legion of Decency** looking over its shoulder, Hollywood produced a brand of entertainment that was safe, fun, and mostly noncontroversial. That filmmakers like John Ford, Orson Welles, Howard Hawks, and Preston Sturges were able to make classic films in such a stifling environment says much about the degree of talent the studios were employing during this time – although the industry also produced many tepid, cloying melodramas and tiresome serials that followed the Code precisely and remain almost unwatchable.

Although Hollywood was, as an industrial system, unmatched by any other production complex in the world, it was, even at its height, something of an illusory power. For while the most visible and glamorous of the movie industry's stars and bosses smiled for the paparazzi in Hollywood, the real **financial muscle** continued to come from New York City. Companies like Loew's, which were based there, had the power – infrequently used until the 1950s – to command studios like MGM to change their policies and even films, simply by applying pressure in the corporate boardroom. It was only the financial discipline of the Southern California tycoons, their ability to turn a handsome profit and their fear of the Wall Street honchos that kept Hollywood with a reasonable degree of autonomy. And when times turned bad, New York took over – firing even the all-powerful Louis B. Mayer in 1951.

The demise of the studios

The emergence of the **film noir** style at the end of World War II should have sounded a warning to the old studio system. With bleak storylines, chiaroscuro

A case study: Hollywood's first and last major studio

Riding high on the heels of the success of their 1913 film, *The Squaw Man*, Cecil B. DeMille, Sam Goldwyn, and Jesse Lasky created **Paramount Studios** by merging their operation with **Adolph Zukor's Famous Players**, which owned property across Melrose Avenue at 650 N Bronson. By adopting the Paramount name and merging with twelve other movie companies three years later, the young company quickly became second in stature only to Culver City's MGM. It subsumed the facilities of **RKO Studios** when that company went under, and in its heyday, Paramount churned out more than a hundred films a year, and had biggies like the Marx Brothers, Cary Grant, D.W. Griffith, Marlon Brando, and countless others under contract. Moreover, it even possessed a "**house style**" of glossy cinematography, sleek sets, and smart dialogue, with impeccable directors like Ernst Lubitsch and Josef von Sternberg helping to define the very notion of the sophisticated, intelligent Paramount film.

Eventually, as with the other majors, Paramount's unique style would fade by the 1950s and the company found itself foundering. By 1967, the conglomerate **Gulf + Western** devoured the studio but later adopted its name to fully cash in on its snow-capped image and reputation. A surprising rebound was soon led by studio executive, and later independent producer, **Robert Evans**, who with his freewheeling style and mountainous ego would do much to recall the glory days of the company's golden age, this time in the late 1960s and early 70s. With Evans bringing the studio back to prominence with a slew of commercially and/or critically successful films like *Rosemary's Baby, Love Story, The Godfather,* and *Chinatown*, Paramount regained its stature as a major force in Hollywood. Today, as with its house style of old, Paramount's critical and commercial luster has dimmed considerably, until its movies now resemble those of any other studio owned by a media conglomerate – faceless, sterile diversions. However, even though it's now owned by another giant corporation, Viacom, Paramount continues to maintain one unique aspect that other studios have long since forsaken: its original Hollywood location.

photography, morally questionable antiheroes and dark endings, *film noir* was an abrupt departure from many of Hollywood's previous aesthetic conventions. This stylistic change, and the postwar disillusion it reflected, preceded several major transformations that permanently altered the way the studios did business.

The greatest threat to the system, the **federal government**, in its antitrust prosecution of Paramount, was beginning to dismantle the practices of block booking and theatrical ownership that had kept the majors in firm control over the exhibition of their films. The increasing power of independent producers, helped by this and other structural changes, also removed some of the majors' control over the industry, as did the increasing ability of actors to finally use the star system to their advantage by not allowing the studios to lock up their careers for interminable lengths of time (starting with Olivia de Havilland, who sued Warner Bros to get out of her contract and won in California's supreme court after a three-year legal battle). Along with these changes, **television** reduced film viewership by great numbers and the studio bosses had to resort to desperate devices like 3D, widescreen, and Cinerama to try to lure back their audiences.

Furthermore, the institution that the Hays Code had censored, with the blessing of Congress, began to come under direct attack from McCarthyite politicians. The House Un-American Activities Committee (HUAC) dredged up information on the alleged presence of Communist and left-leaning groups in Hollywood, as well as supposed "hidden pro-Communist" messages in certain films, and many screenwriters, actors, and directors were either humiliated into testifying or found themselves on an internal **blacklist** that kept them from working.

After the HUAC proceedings, Hollywood was creatively damaged, but the government's activities didn't keep directors like Otto Preminger from challenging the Hays Code. Through a series of legendary battles, on films like *The Moon is Blue* and others, Preminger and other filmmakers succeeded in throwing off the yoke of the Code, which had been in place for more than thirty years. This change, combined with the diminishment of pressure groups like the Legion of Decency, further loosened the control of the studio bosses over movie content and later led to the late-1960s establishment of the **ratings system** in place today.

The aftermath

By the end of the 1950s, the studio system, at least as it had been known, was finished, and it took many years for the majors to regain much of the ground they had lost. However, while the industry eventually **rebounded** – through greater international sales and the development of ancillary markets like cable TV and home video – and moviemaking has become profitable once more to the studios (if not necessarily for their investors), it's unlikely that the industry will see a return to Depression-era days, when each studio churned out hundreds of films per year and could afford to experiment occasionally with quirky low-budget projects or off-kilter genre pictures.

Currently, Hollywood only manages to pump out a few big-budget spectacles and a declining number of medium-budget flicks – often cumulatively less than twenty annual films per studio. Modern American filmmaking, driven by exorbitant **talent costs**, is quite different from the old mechanized industry between the wars. With much of today's production budgets going into the

▲ The gates of Paramount Studios

wallets of the top actors, many of the formerly essential costs – elaborate sets, casts of thousands, and so on – have been scaled back as expensive luxuries, especially on fantasy, sci-fi and historic pics that rely on expensive computer-enhanced **CGI** technology. Moreover, television–film studio mergers, videotape sales, and multimedia production have only served to highlight the differences from the old way of doing business. In one way, though, the studios have reasserted their dominance: by buying innovative independent companies like Miramax, or establishing their own "art-house" divisions such as Fox Search-light, they have ensured that risky, lower-budget productions come under their direct control, to their direct benefit – just like the old days.

LA on film

Since its birth in the 1910s, Hollywood has often searched its own back-yard for compelling scenes and interesting stories. While not always successful in conveying the truth of LA to a film audience, Hollywood **films** have nevertheless helped define the city for domestic and foreign audiences alike. The list below focuses on films that best use their LA backdrop as well as key works in Hollywood film history, and films tagged with a 🏃 are particularly recommended.

Hollywood does Hollywood

Autofocus (Paul Schrader 2003). Memorably creepy portrait of mid-level actor Bob Crane, who played the sunny title character on TV's *Hogan's Heroes*, but was in reality a sex addict who ended up being murdered in a Scottsdale motel, in one of Tinsel-town's still-unsolved mysteries.

The Bad and the Beautiful (Vincente Minnelli 1952). Kirk Douglas shines in one of his best roles, a megalomaniacal Hollywood producer whose machinations are described in retrospect by his associates and victims.

Barton Fink (Joel Coen 1991). Tinseltown in the 1940s is depicted by the Coen brothers as a dark world of greedy movie bosses, belligerent screenwriters, and murderers disguised as traveling salesmen. Allegedly based on the experience of playwright Clifford Odets.

The Big Knife (Robert Aldrich 1955). An incisive portrayal of Holly-wood politics, in which a weak-willed actor can't get free from the tentacles of a hack director, despite the pleas of his wife. Based on a play by Clifford Odets and filmed like one as well.

Day of the Locust (John Schles-inger 1975). Somewhat awkward realization of the classic satire by Nathanael West. The author's vivid colors are rendered here as bland

pastels. See "Books," p.431, for a review of the source.

Ed Wood (Tim Burton 1994). The low-budget fringes of Fifties Holly-wood are beautifully re-created in this loving tribute to the much-derided auteur of *Plan 9 from Outer Space* and *Glen or Glenda*. Gorgeously shot in black and white, with a magnificent performance by Martin Landau as an ailing but vulgar Bela Lugosi.

Gods and Monsters (Bill Condon 1998). An interesting, fact-based tale of the final days of 1930s horror-film director James Whale, ignored by the moviemaking elite and slowly dying of malaise by his poolside in Hollywood. The title refers to a memorable Ernest Thesiger line from Whale's classic *Bride of Frankenstein*.

Good Morning, Babylon (Paolo and Vittorio Taviani 1987). Two restorers of European cathedrals find themselves in 1910s Hollywood, working to build the monstrous Babylonian set for D.W. Griffith's *Intolerance*, in this Italian story of the contribution of immigrants in early Tinseltown. Oddly enough, that same set has now been rebuilt in Holly-wood – as part of a mall (see p.101).

Hollywood Canteen (Delmer Daves 1944). Based on an actual, eponymous Hollywood establishment where popular movie stars from the World War II era sang and danced to a bevy of toe-tapping tunes. Most of Warner Bros' stars were featured in the picture – those that wouldn't appear were labeled "unpatriotic."

Hollywood on Trial (David Helpern Jr 1976). This interesting documentary examines the early 1950s witch-hunts in Hollywood and the blacklisted screenwriters, actors, and directors.

The Last Tycoon (Elia Kazan 1976). F. Scott Fitzgerald's unfinished, would-be masterpiece is here rendered as an interesting failure: a rich, opulent world of Hollywood gloss that translates into slow, clumsy storytelling.

The Player (Robert Altman 1992). Tim Robbins is a studio shark who thinks a disgruntled screenwriter is out to get him; he kills the writer (at South Pasadena's Rialto theater), steals his girlfriend and waits for the cops to unravel it. A wickedly sharp satire about contemporary Hollywood, with some great celebrity cameos.

Postcards from the Edge (Mike Nichols 1990). Written by Carrie Fisher, an insider's look at behind-the-scenes Hollywood, with Meryl Streep as the drug-addicted daughter of pushy glamour-queen Shirley MacLaine – thinly veiled versions of Fisher and her mother, Debbie Reynolds.

Singin' in the Rain (Stanley Donen/Gene Kelly 1952). A merry trip through Hollywood set during the birth of the sound era. Gene Kelly, Donald O'Connor, and Debbie Reynolds sing and dance to many classic tunes, including *Good Morning*, *Moses*, and *Broadway Melody*.

A Star Is Born (William Wellman 1937; George Cukor 1954). Based on the film *What Price Hollywood?*, these adaptations tell the story of the rise of a starlet mirroring the demise of her Svengali. Janet Gaynor and Fredric March star in the 1930s

version, Judy Garland and James Mason in the later. Both are worthwhile, while a 1977 remake with Barbra Streisand and Kris Kristofferson runs a very distant third.

The State of Things (Wim Wenders 1982). A European filmmaker sees his financing disappear while stranded in LA and is beset by boredom in his mobile home. Essential if you're a fan of Wenders or of music by the punk band X – then near their peak.

Sullivan's Travels (Preston Sturges 1941). A high-spirited comedy about a director who wants to stop making schlock pictures and instead create gritty portrayals of what he thinks real life to be. The first two-thirds are great, though the film ends in mawkish fashion.

Sunset Boulevard (Billy Wilder 1950). Award-winning film about a screenwriter falling into the clutches of a long-faded silent-movie star. William Holden was near the beginning of his career, Gloria Swanson well past the end of hers. Erich von Stroheim fills in nicely as Swanson's butler, and even Cecil B. DeMille makes a cameo appearance.

The Way We Were (Sydney Pollack 1973). Aside from the Barbra Streisand–Robert Redford pairing and cloyingly memorable songs, a worthwhile portrait of the dark days of the Red Scare and Hollywood blacklist of the 1950s.

What Price Hollywood? (George Cukor 1932). The template for the *A Star Is Born* movies that followed: Constance Bennett is the starlet, an ambitious waitress, and Lowell Sherman is the drunken director.

Whatever Happened to Baby Jane? (Robert Aldrich 1962). Bette Davis and Joan Crawford are former child stars who plot against one another in a rotting Malibu house. A fine slice of horror.

LA crime stories

Beverly Hills Cop (Martin Brest 1984). Still-amusing Eddie Murphy flick, in which the actor plays an unorthodox, fast-talking Detroit detective who takes LA by storm while trying to solve a murder case.

The Big Sleep (Howard Hawks 1946). One of the key *film noirs* of the 1940s, with Humphrey Bogart playing Philip Marlowe, and featuring a wildly confused plot – even screenwriter Raymond Chandler admitted he didn't know who killed a particular character. Still, there's crackling chemistry between Bogie and Lauren Bacall.

Chinatown (Roman Polanski 1974). One of the essential films about the city. Jack Nicholson hunts down corruption in this dark criticism of the forces that animate the town: venal politicians, black-hearted land barons, crooked cops, and a morally bankrupt populace. Great use of locations, from Echo Park to the San Fernando Valley.

Devil in a Blue Dress (Carl Franklin 1995). Terrific modern *noir*, in which South Central detective Easy Rawlins (Denzel Washington) navigates the ethical squalor of elite 1940s white LA and uncovers a few ugly truths about the city's leaders.

Double Indemnity (Billy Wilder 1944). The prototypical *noir*. Greedy insurance salesman Fred MacMurray collaborates with harpy wife Barbara Stanwyck to murder her husband and cash in on the settlement. Edward G. Robinson observes on the sidelines as MacMurray's boss.

The Glass Shield (Charles Burnett 1995). Institutionalized racism in the LAPD is brought under the harsh glare of director Burnett, one of the great chroniclers of LA's black urban underclass.

The Grifters (Stephen Frears 1990). A memorable film with Annette Bening, John Cusack, and Anjelica Huston playing the title characters – con artists hunting through the LA underworld for their next victims.

He Walked by Night (Alfred Werker 1948). This vérité-style crime story set in "the fastest growing city in the nation" starts with a random cop-killing in Santa Monica and ends with a manhunt through the 700-mile subterranean city storm-drain system, stunningly shot by torch-light by peerless *noir* cinematographer John Alton.

Heat (Michael Mann 1995). Stars big names like De Niro and Pacino, but this crime drama, which does include some stunning set-pieces (eg a Downtown LA shootout), is ultimately less than the sum of its parts, with a predictable ending.

In a Lonely Place (Nicholas Ray 1950). One of the all-time great *noirs*, and an unconventional one at that. Humphrey Bogart is a disturbed, violent screenwriter who causes trouble for those around him, particularly girlfriend Gloria Grahame – at the time, the director's real-life ex-wife.

Jackie Brown (Quentin Tarantino 1997). A glorious return to form for Pam Grier, who, as a tough airline stewardess, plays the perfect foil for Samuel L. Jackson's smooth gangster.

LA Confidential (Curtis Hanson 1997). Easily the best of the contemporary *noir* films, a perfectly realized adaptation of James Ellroy's novel about brutal cops, victimized prostitutes, and scheming politicians in 1950s LA. Even the good guys, Russell Crowe and Guy Pearce, are morally questionable.

The Long Goodbye (Robert Altman 1973). Altman intentionally mangles *noir* conventions in this Chandler adaptation. Elliott Gould plays Marlowe as a droning schlep who wanders across a sun-drenched landscape of casual corruption, encountering bizarre characters like nerdy mobster Marty Augustine, played with relish by movie director Mark Rydell, and Sterling Hayden as a hulking alcoholic writer. Cameo by future governor Arnold Schwarzenegger – in his underwear.

Murder My Sweet (Edward Dmytryk 1944). One-time Busby Berkeley crooner Dick Powell changed his tune and became a grim tough-guy detective in the best work from this director, who was briefly blacklisted for his former communist ties, then ratted on his colleagues once he was released.

One False Move (Carl Franklin 1991). A disturbing early role for Billy Bob Thornton, as a murderous hick who kills some people in an LA bungalow with his girlfriend and a psychotic, nerdy colleague, then gets pursued by the LAPD and a small-town Arkansas sheriff.

Point Blank (John Boorman 1967). Engaging, somewhat pretentious art-house flick with Lee Marvin as a hit man out for revenge. Begins and ends in Alcatraz, but in between

successfully imagines LA as an impenetrable fortress of concrete and glass.

The Postman Always Rings Twice (Tay Garnett 1946). Lana Turner and John Garfield star in this seamy – and excellent – adaptation of the James M. Cain novel, first brought to the screen as *Ossessione*, an Italian adaptation by Luchino Visconti. Awkwardly remade by Bob Rafelson in 1981 with Jessica Lange and Jack Nicholson.

To Live & Die in LA (William Friedkin 1985). A violent cult film with a plot involving morally dubious characters and counterfeiting, but most remembered for its kinetic car chases and dark portrait of the sleek, cold LA of the 1980s.

Touch of Evil (Orson Welles 1958). Supposedly set at a Mexican border town, this *noir* classic was actually shot in a seedy, decrepit Venice. A bizarre, Baroque masterpiece with Charlton Heston playing a Mexican official, Janet Leigh as his beleaguered wife, and Welles himself as a bloated, corrupt cop addicted to candy bars.

True Romance (Tony Scott 1993). With a Quentin Tarantino plot to guide them, Patricia Arquette and Christian Slater battle creeps and gangsters amid wonderful LA locations, from seedy motels to the classic *Rae's Diner* in Santa Monica.

Apocalyptic LA

Blade Runner (Ridley Scott 1982). The first theatrical version may have flopped, but the fully re-cut director's version (released in December 2007) confirms the film's stature as a sci-fi classic, in which dangerous "replicants" roam the streets of a dystopic future LA and soulless corporations rule from pyramidal towers.

Earthquake (Mark Robson 1974). Watch the Lake Hollywood dam collapse, people run for their lives, and chaos hold sway in the City of Angels. Originally presented in "Sensurround!"

Falling Down (Joel Schumacher 1993). Fired defense-worker Michael Douglas tires of the traffic jams on the freeways and goes on a rampage through some of the city's less picturesque neighborhoods, railing at petty injustices, and wreaking havoc at every turn.

Kiss Me Deadly (Robert Aldrich 1955). Perhaps the bleakest of all *noirs*, starring Ralph Meeker as brutal detective Mike Hammer, who tramples on friends and enemies alike in his search for the great "whatsit" – a mysterious and deadly suitcase.

Lost Highway (David Lynch 1997). A lurid, frightening take on the city by director Lynch, using nonlinear storytelling and actors playing dual roles, and which had critics screaming for the exits – but if you like Lynch, this is essential viewing.

LA lifestyles

Bob & Carol & Ted & Alice (Paul Mazursky 1969). Once-daring, but still funny zeitgeist satire about wife-swapping and bed-hopping in hedonistic Southern California, starring Natalie Wood, Robert Culp, Elliott Gould, and Dyan Cannon as the titular foursome.

Boyz N the Hood (John Singleton 1991). An excellent period piece that cemented the LA stereotype as a land of gangs and guns, starring Cuba Gooding Jr in his first big role, and Laurence Fishburne as his dad.

Clueless (Amy Heckerling 1995). Jane Austen's *Emma* transplanted to a rich Southern California high school, with a fine performance by Alicia Silverstone as a frustrated matchmaker.

Crash (Paul Haggis 2005). An overly sentimental flick that somehow won a Best Picture Oscar, involving characters of various races and classes trying to get chummy and rediscover their humanity.

Dogtown & Z-Boys (Stacy Peralta 2002). Even if you have no interest

Strange Days (Kathryn Bigelow 1995). In a chaotic, nightmarish vision of LA, Ralph Fiennes, Angela Bassett, and Juliette Lewis run around the city screaming-in the new millennium. More interesting as a reflection of mid-1990s LA angst than as compelling cinema.

The Terminator (James Cameron 1984). Modern sci-fi classic, with Arnold Schwarzenegger as a robot from the future sent to kill the mother of an unborn rebel leader. Bravura special effects and amazing set-pieces here were followed up with the director's 1989 sequel, *T2: Judgment Day*, in which Arnold becomes a good robot, and the less-inspired *T3*.

in skateboarding, this is a fun, high-spirited look at the glory days of the sport, when a daring group of LA kids took to using the empty swimming pools of the elite as their own private skate-parks.

Endless Summer (Bruce Brown 1966). Still the template for all surf films, a riveting portrait of the sport at its 1960s zenith, when catching a killer break could mean the world, and the waves teemed with legends. Good photography and portrait of the surfing world from one of its movie pioneers.

Faces (John Cassavetes 1968). A vivid, unforgettable portrait of middle-aged angst in upper-middle-class LA, in which a married couple breaks apart amid a nocturnal landscape of dive bars, dance clubs (the early *Whisky-a-Go-Go*), and handsome estates – one of them the director's own home.

Ghost World (Terry Zwigoff 2001). Sardonic portrait of alienated high-schooler Thora Birch trying to find her place in a grim LA world of strip malls, pointless jobs, and adult lies. Based on an equally effective and groundbreaking comic strip.

Go (Doug Liman 1999). A kinetic joyride through LA's rave subculture told from three perspectives, including Sarah Polley's botching of an aspirin-for-Ecstasy drug sale, and Jay Mohr and Scott Wolf – as two secretly gay TV soap stars – stuck in a police sting operation.

The Limey (Steven Soderbergh 1999). Gangster Terence Stamp wanders into a morally adrift LA looking for his daughter's killer, and finds the burned-out husk of former hippie Peter Fonda. Arguably this director's best work.

The Loved One (Tony Richardson 1965). An effective adaptation of Evelyn Waugh's pointed satire about the dubious practices of the funeral industry, inspired by a trip to Forest Lawn.

Magnolia (Paul Thomas Anderson 1999). A dark travelogue of human misery starring Jason Robards and Tom Cruise, among many others. The San Fernando Valley serves as an emotional inferno of abusive parents, victimized children, haunted memories, and a mysterious plague of frogs.

Mi Familia (Gregory Nava 1994). The saga of the Sanchez family, featuring fine performances by a range of Hollywood's best Hispanic actors, including Jimmy Smits, Edward James Olmos, and Esai Morales. Overly earnest and sentimental in places, though.

Mi Vida Loca (Alison Anders 1993). Depressing ensemble piece about the hard lives of Latinas in Echo Park girl-gangs and the central reason the director won a prestigious MacArthur Fellowship.

Pulp Fiction (Quentin Tarantino 1994). A successful collection of underworld stories by cult director Tarantino. Set against a backdrop of downtrodden LA streets, bars, diners, and makeshift torture chambers. Arguably the best American movie of the 1990s.

The Rapture (Michael Tolkin 1991). Mimi Rogers plays an LA telephone operator who abandons her hedonistic lifestyle after hearing a fundamentalist group talking about the impending "Rapture," and becomes born again, ultimately heading into the desert to await Armageddon. Michael Tolkin's wonderfully literal film takes his premise just as far as it can go, and then some.

Riding Giants (Stacy Peralta 2004). One of the best of the current batch of surfing documentaries, showing the glories of the sport (with modern, high-tech equipment), the life stories of some of its bigger names, and that perennial California backdrop of sun and waves.

Safe (Todd Haynes 1995). In Haynes' brilliant tale of millennial unease and corporeal paranoia, Julianne Moore plays a San Fernando Valley homemaker with seemingly little inner-life and an opulent outer one, who is diagnosed with environmental sickness and finds refuge at a New Age desert retreat.

Short Cuts (Robert Altman 1993). Vaguely linked vignettes tracing the lives of LA suburbanites, from a trailer-park couple in Downey to an elite doctor in the Santa Monica Mountains. Strong ensemble cast bolsters the intentionally fractured narrative.

Slums of Beverly Hills (Tamara Jenkins 1998). Troubled teen Natasha Lyonne deals with growing pains in a less-than-glamorous section of town, where a pill-popping cousin, manic uncle, weird neighbors, and her own expanding bustline are but a few of her worries.

Speed (Jan de Bont 1994). Ultimate LA action flick, in which a bus careens through the freeways and boulevards of the city – and will blow up if it slows below 50mph. Much better than its sequels.

Star Maps (Miguel Arteta 1997). Melodrama of immigrant life on the fringes of Hollywood. Carlos, who has grandiose dreams of movie stardom, is doing time in his father's prostitution ring, standing on street corners ostensibly selling maps to stars' homes – in reality selling his body for cash.

Swingers (Doug Liman 1996). Cocktail culture gets skewered in this flick about a couple of dudes who flit from club to club to eye "beautiful babies" and shoot the breeze like Rat Pack–era Sinatras. Many LA locales shown, including the *Dresden Room* and *The Derby*.

"Way-out" West

Barfly (Barbet Schroeder 1987). Mickey Rourke channeling writer Charles Bukowski in this liqor-soaked romp through LA's seedy world of low-lifes, fistfights, and general depravity.

Beach Blanket Bingo (William Asher 1965). A cult favorite – the epitome of sun-and-surf movies, with Frankie Avalon and Annette Funicello singing and cavorting amid hordes of wild-eyed teenagers.

The Big Lebowski (Joel Coen 1998). A bizarre Coen foray into LA, exploring the lower-class under-belly of the city – Jeff Bridges' "The Dude" and his pal John Goodman uncover mysteries, meet peculiar characters, and do lots and lots of bowling.

Boogie Nights (Paul Thomas Anderson 1997). A suburban kid from Torrance hits the big time in LA – as a porn star. Mark Wahlberg, Julianne Moore, and Burt Reynolds tread through a sex-drenched San Fernando Valley landscape of the disco years.

Down and Out in Beverly Hills (Paul Mazursky 1986). A West Coast adaptation of Jean Renoir's classic *Boudu Saved from Drowning*, with homeless Nick Nolte salving the nerves of *nouveau riche* neurotics.

Escape from LA (John Carpenter 1996). In John Carpenter's alterna-tive vision of the future, LA is cut off from the mainland by an earthquake and has been turned into a deport-ation zone for undesirables. Sent in to uproot insurrection, Kurt Russell battles psychotic plastic surgeons and surfs a *tsunami* to a showdown in a netherworld Disneyland.

Gidget (Paul Wendkos 1959). One of the most influential films about life in Southern California, for better or worse, establishing the emblematic LA images of teenagers playing in the sun, carefree romance, and easy-as-pie surfing. The first of several in a series.

House on Haunted Hill (William Castle 1958). Not the clumsy remake, but the glorious Vincent Price original, with the King of Horror as master of ceremonies for a ghoulish party thrown at his Hollywood Hills estate – actually, Frank Lloyd Wright's Ennis House (see p.92).

Mayor of the Sunset Strip (George Hickenlooper 2003). Great, disturbing documentary about the title character, a former stand-in for one of the Monkees, legendary DJ, lounge denizen, and apparent man-child who can't seem to get his life together, despite being pals with people like David Bowie.

Minnie and Moskowitz (John Cassavetes 1971). Strange and amusing tale of two loners who find a very strained romance amid the city's hot-dog stands, low-rent theaters, and LA County Museum of Art. The director himself pops up in a dark cameo as a snide, cheating husband.

Mulholland Drive (David Lynch 2001). Told in the director's inimitable style, a nightmarish tale of love, death, glamour, and doom in LA – in which elfin cowboys mutter cryptic threats, elegant chanteuses lip-sync to phantom melodies, and a blue key can unlock a shocking double identity.

Permanent Midnight (David Veloz 1998). A grim tour through the city's drug subculture, with Ben Stiller as your heroin-addicted guide. Based on the autobiographical novel by former sitcom-writer Jerry Stahl, who was responsible for *Alf*.

Point Break (Kathryn Bigelow 1991). Cult pop favorite set in the surfer-dude world, with Keanu Reeves as a robbery-investigating FBI agent and Patrick Swayze as his rebel-surfer quarry

Repo Man (Alex Cox 1984). Emilio Estevez is a surly young punk who repossesses cars for Harry Dean Stanton. Very imaginative and fun, and darkly comic.

Seconds (John Frankenheimer 1966). One of Rock Hudson's better performances, as a bored suburbanite who gets a second chance at life transplanted into the body of a younger man. Bleak in its treatment of Southern California's swinging Sixties.

Shampoo (Hal Ashby 1975). Using LA as his private playground, priapic hairdresser Warren Beatty freely acts on his formidable, though nonchalant, libido. A period piece memorable for its 1970s look.

They Live (John Carpenter 1988). Ludicrous but entertaining horror flick, in which a drifter living on the outskirts of LA discovers that aliens are subliminally encouraging the city's rampant consumerism.

Three Women (Robert Altman 1977). A fascinating, hypnotic, film in which Sissy Spacek and Shelley Duvall, co-workers at a geriatric center in Desert Springs, mysteriously absorb each other's identity.

Valley Girl (Martha Coolidge 1983). Early Nicolas Cage flick, in which the actor winningly plays a new-wave freak trying to woo the title character (Debra Foreman) in a clash of LA cultures. Good soundtrack, too.

Who Framed Roger Rabbit? (Robert Zemeckis 1988). On the surface a lightweight live-action/cartoon hybrid, it's actually a revealing film about 1940s LA, where cartoon characters suffer abuse like everyone else and the big corporations seek to destroy the Red Car transit system.

Drama and history

The Aviator (Martin Scorsese 2004). In mid-century LA, aircraft pioneer Howard Hughes builds some of the world's fastest and biggest planes, dates Hollywood starlets, and battles rival executives and politicians, all while obsessively washing his hands and collecting jars of his own urine.

The Doors (Oliver Stone 1991). Val Kilmer plays the great Jim Morrison at the height of his 1960s debauchery, under the frenetic direction of Oliver Stone.

Fat City (John Huston 1972). Great, late-Huston film starring Stacy Keach as a washed-up boxer and Jeff Bridges as his young, incompetent charge. Quietly and effectively depressing.

The Killing of a Chinese Bookie (John Cassavetes 1976). Perfectly evoking the sleazy charms of the Sunset Strip, Cassavetes' behavioral crime story is about a club-owner (Ben Gazzara) in hock to the mob – just one of his many great LA character studies.

La Bamba (Luis Valdez 1987). The fictionalized story of Ritchie Valens, the LA rocker who died in an untimely plane crash with Buddy Holly. Lou Diamond Phillips gives a compelling performance, despite looking nothing like Valens.

Nixon (Oliver Stone 1996). A long, dark look at the first president from Southern California (played by Anthony Hopkins), and the old-time LA suburbs where he grew up.

🏃 **Rebel Without a Cause** (Nicholas Ray 1955). Troubled-youth film, starring, of course, James Dean. A Hollywood classic with many memorable images, notably the use of the Griffith Park Observatory as a shooting location.

Stand and Deliver (Ramon Menendez 1988). Inspired by the story of East LA's miracle-working teacher Jaime Escalante, played effectively by Edward James Olmos. A somewhat moving film better suited for TV than the big screen.

They Shoot Horses, Don't They? (Sydney Pollack 1969). Gloomy story set during the Depression, in which contestants desperately try to win money in an exhausting dance marathon. Aptly reflects the fatalistic attitudes of the late 1960s.

To Sleep with Anger (Charles Burnett 1990). An interesting view of LA's overlooked black middle-class, directed with polish by a very under-rated African-American filmmaker.

Tupac and Biggie (Nick Broomfield 2002). In-your-face documentary about the murders of rappers Tupac Shakur and Notorious B.I.G., implicating hip-hop producer Suge Knight and rogue elements of the LAPD.

Zabriskie Point (Michelangelo Antonioni 1970). Muddled, pretentious misfire that nonetheless features some promising early work by Jack Nicholson and visually interesting shots of the LA basin.

Zoot Suit (Luis Valdez 1981). A simplified overview of the Sleepy Lagoon Murder case and resultant anti-Hispanic violence, told as a musical.

Books

I n the **book** reviews below, publishers are listed in the format UK/US, unless the title is available only in one country, in which case the country has been specified. Single listings mean the book is printed in both countries by the same publisher. Highly recommended titles are signified by ⚐. Out-of-print titles are indicated by o/p.

Travel and general

Mike Davis *Ecology of Fear* (Vintage US). Despite containing certain factual errors, a compelling read about LA's apocalyptic style, focusing on gloom and doom in movies and literary fiction, the danger of earthquakes and fires, mountain-lion attacks, and even tornadoes.

Steve Grody *Graffiti LA* (Abrams). If you're inclined to probe LA's poorer neighborhoods, you might discover many of the colorful pieces of home-grown art depicted here, which the author dissects according to their ethnic, cultural, and (in places) gang affiliation. Includes CD-ROM.

Robert Koenig *Mouse Tales* (Bonaventure Press). All the Disneyland dirt that's fit to print: a behind-the-scenes look at the ugly little secrets – from disenchanted workers to vermin infestations – that lurk behind the happy walls of the Magic Kingdom.

Anthony Lovett and Matt Maranian *LA Bizarro* (St Martin's Press o/p). Without a doubt the best alternative, off-kilter guide to the city: indispensable reading if you're touring LA's dingiest motels, grungiest bars, goofiest architecture, and most infamous death sites.

Erin Mahoney *Walking L.A.: 36 Walking Tours…* (Wilderness Press US). Three dozen fascinating treks through the city, from the well-trod districts to obscure places off the radar of most locals and all tourists; well worth the journey.

⚐ **Leonard Pitt and Dale Pitt** *Los Angeles A to Z* (University of California Press US). If you're truly enthralled by the city, this is the tome for you: six hundred pages of encyclopedic references covering everything from conquistadors to movie stars.

Jerry Schad *Afoot and Afield in Los Angeles* (Wilderness Press US). Some two hundred excellent hikes are presented in this compendium of the long and short, steep and easy, gut-wrenching and easy-going trails that are laced around the metropolis and on its wild fringes.

Surfer Magazine Guide to Southern California Surf Spots (Chronicle US). A handy, comprehensive reference to the best places in the state to ride the pipeline and find a killer break — even better, the pages are waterproof

Alexander Vertikoff and Robert Winter *Hidden LA* (Gibbs-Smith o/p). An architecture photographer and writer present their favorite unheralded sights in the metropolis, using glossy photos to highlight such spots as Monrovia's *Aztec Hotel* and the tomb of Henry Huntington.

John Waters *Crackpot* (Simon & Schuster; Scribner). The irreverent director of cult classics like *Pink Flamingos* and *Hairspray* takes you on a personalized tour of the city's seamy underside.

left margin:

C

CONTEXTS | Books

bottom left:

422

History and politics

Oscar Zeta Acosta *Revolt of the Cockroach People* (Vintage). The legendary model for Hunter S. Thompson's bloated "Dr. Gonzo," the author was in reality a trailblazing Hispanic lawyer who used colorful tactics to defend oppressed and indigent defendants. A striking, semi-autobiographical portrait of 1970s East LA, written just before the author's mysterious disappearance.

Erik Davis *Visionary State: A Journey Through California's Spiritual Landscape* (Chronicle Books US). A look at the various cults, New Agers, and Zen philosophers that have illuminated LA and the state in recent decades, along with older shamans and showmen, all highlighted by evocative, tantalizing photographs.

Margaret Leslie Davis *Dark Side of Fortune: Triumph and Scandal in the Life of Oil Tycoon Edward L. Doheny* (University of California Press US). The best and most comprehensive volume available about a business giant of early twentieth-century LA, covering his rise to power via local petroleum fields, to his downfall in the Teapot Dome scandal.

Gordon DeMarco *A Short History of Los Angeles* (Lexicos o/p). A 180-page summary of the major events and phenomena that have shaped the city, with particular regard to class and racial struggles. Excellent reading.

Joan Didion *Slouching Towards Bethlehem* (Farrar Straus & Giroux US). One of California's most polar-izing writers takes a critical look at 1960s California, from the acid culture of San Francisco to American tough guy John Wayne. In a similar style, *The White Album* (Flamingo US) traces the West Coast characters and events that shaped the 1960s and 70s.

The current, lesser memoir, *Where I Was From* (Harper Perennial; Vintage), may be too sour for many.

Robert Fogelson *The Fragmented Metropolis: Los Angeles 1850–1930* (University of California Press US). Deftly covers a hefty chunk of local history, with significant insight. A sweeping story from the early "Hell Town" to the go-go days of the 1920s.

Paul Greenstein et al *Bread and Hyacinths: The Rise and Fall of Utopian Los Angeles* (California Classics o/p). A chronicle of efforts to create communal living by some city activists, particularly the socialist and near-mayor Job Harriman.

Abraham Hoffman *Vision or Villainy: Origins of the Owens Valley–Los Angeles Water Controversy* (Texas A&M University Press US). An introduction to the messy business of water politics *c.*1900, a topic that still engenders debate and anger more than a century later.

Lisa McGirr *Suburban Warriors: The Origins of the New American Right* (Princeton University Press US). The tale of how once-fringe right-wing activists in Southern California rose from the ashes of the 1960s to dominate state and, later, national politics, culminating with the presidency of Ronald Reagan and his various minions.

Carey McWilliams *Southern California: An Island on the Land* (Gibbs Smith). One of the most important books about the city ever written, detailing the social clashes and intrigues that rocked LA in the first half of the twentieth century. The author brings special insight as the lead defense attorney in LA's shameful prosecution of the Sleepy Lagoon Murder case.

Don Normark *Chavez Ravine, 1949* (Chronicle). Black-and-white photographs and a compelling narrative provide a vivid look at life in a rural Hispanic community on the fringes of Downtown LA, just before the area was paved over to make way for Dodger Stadium.

Mark Reisner *Cadillac Desert* (Penguin US). An essential guide to water problems in the American West, with special emphasis on LA's schemes to bring upstate California water to the metropolis. One of the best renderings of this sordid tale.

Kevin Roderick *The San Fernando Valley: America's Suburb* (Los Angeles Times Publishing US). A surprising and occasionally intriguing view of the history, geography, and culture of "The Valley," provided by one of its former denizens. Also good is the author's *Wilshire Boulevard: Grand Concourse of Los Angeles* (Angel City Press), analyzing and saluting the development of the nation's first "linear city."

Kevin Starr *California: A History* (Modern Library). The latest round of Golden State history from the state's pre-eminent chronicler, this one more bite-sized and overarching than the other seven in the series, which focus on decades and details. Of those, the best overall is *Material Dreams: Southern California through the 1920s* (Oxford University Press), on the city's boom interwar years of celebrities and scandals.

Urban theory

Mike Davis *City of Quartz: Excavating the Future in Los Angeles* (Verso). A leftist counterpoint to Kevin Starr's mainstream history (see above). Written in the early 1990s, Davis's descriptions of racial hatred, security-system architecture, shifty politicians, and industrial decay have dated somewhat, and his fact-finding methods have been questioned, but there's still plenty here worth reading.

Umberto Eco *Travels in Hyperreality* (Vintage; Harvest). A pointed examination of "simulacra," and a nice literary time-capsule of Southern California life several decades ago, discussing such things as a now-closed museum in Orange County that re-created the great works of art as wax figurines.

William Fulton *The Reluctant Metropolis: The Politics of Urban Growth in Los Angeles* (Johns Hopkins University Press US). A highly readable account of political and economic conflicts in contemporary LA, with notable sections on modern Chinatown and the aftermath of the 1992 riots.

Blake Gumprecht *The Los Angeles River: Its Life, Death and Possible Rebirth* (Johns Hopkins University Press US). The downhill history of the LA River, from its early days as a meandering stream to its final transformation into a bleak, lifeless flood-channel.

Norman Klein *A History of Forgetting* (Verso). A good companion to Mike Davis's *City of Quartz*, uncovering some of the political ugliness and minority oppression that have characterized LA's past.

Merry Ovnick *Los Angeles: The End of the Rainbow* (Princeton Architectural Press US). A riveting account of the city's political and social struggles, as seen through its institutions and architecture.

Architecture

🏃 **Reyner Banham** *Los Angeles: The Architecture of Four Ecologies* (University of California Press US). The book that made architectural historians take LA seriously, and still an enjoyable read. Valuable insights on the city's freeways, vernacular buildings, and cultural attitudes.

Margaret Leslie Davis *Bullocks Wilshire* (Princeton Architectural Press US). A long-overdue tribute to the hallmark example of LA's stunning Zigzag Moderne architecture, a Mid-Wilshire department store that's now been reincarnated as a law-school library.

David Gebhard and Harriette Von Breton *Los Angeles in the Thirties: 1931–1941* (Hennessey & Ingalls US). Great old black-and-white photos documenting LA's Streamline Moderne architecture.

🏃 **David Gebhard and Robert Winter** *Los Angeles: An Architectural Guide* (Gibbs Smith US). For many years the essential guide to LA architecture, from historical treasures to contemporary quirks. Some of the quality has been lost with Gebhard's death, so try the 1994 edition (his last) for the best writing on modernist structures.

Jim Heimann *California Crazy and Beyond: Roadside Vernacular Architecture* (Chronicle Books US). This fun volume is still a favorite after twenty years, and has now been updated to include the latest of the state's bizarre-chitecture, from diners shaped liked hot dogs to wigwam motels, and the influence it has had nationally.

Sam Hall Kaplan *LA Lost and Found* (Hennessey & Ingalls US). Of interest for the excellent pictures that accompany this former newspaper critic's lament for the good old days of local architecture.

Esther McCoy *Five California Architects* (Hennessey & Ingalls US). This still-relevant 1960s book was the first to draw attention to LA's Irving Gill, an early twentieth-century forerunner of the modern style, as well as Bernard Maybeck, R.M. Schindler, and the Greene brothers.

Richard Meier *Building the Getty* (University of California Press US). Highly readable account of the conception and creation of the Getty Center, as told by its architect, the prince of modernism.

Charles Moore *The City Observed: Los Angeles* (Hennessey & Ingalls US). Classic volume that's still worth a look for its maps, pictures, and anecdotes, plus recommendations to set you on your way to exploring the old-time nooks and crannies of LA.

Elizabeth A.T. Smith *Blueprints for Modern Living: History and Legacy of the Case Study Houses* (MIT Press o/p). An excellent compendium of essays and articles about the built and unbuilt homes of the Case Study Program (see box, p.110), with descriptions, diagrams, and photographs of each.

Music

Clora Bryant et al *Central Avenue Sounds: Jazz in Los Angeles* (University of California Press US). Vividly re-creating the bouncy, kinetic scene on Central Avenue in the mid-twentieth century, and telling a long-overdue story in LA's, and the nation's, musical history.

Vincent Bugliosi *Helter Skelter: The True Story of the Manson Murders* (WW Norton). The late 1960s wouldn't have been complete without the Manson Family, and here the prosecutor-author lays out the full story of the horrifying crimes carried out by the gang, inspired by their cult leader, formerly a Sunset Strip hippy and would-be pop songwriter.

Barney Hoskyns *Waiting for the Sun: Strange Days, Weird Scenes and the Sound of Los Angeles* (Bloomsbury o/p). Ironic, detached overview of pop and rock music history in LA, with well-written perspectives on such seminal figures as Brian Wilson and Arthur Lee, and a vivid account of how it all went wrong – thanks to drugs and violence – in the late 1960s and 70s. Also good is the author's *Hotel California* (Harper Perennial; Wiley), covering the rise of LA-style country rock pioneered by the Eagles, Linda Ronstadt, Gram Parsons, et al.

Don Snowden *Make the Music Go Bang: The Early LA Punk Scene* (St Martin's Press). One of the few volumes on a critical stage in local music history, this book is most valuable for its striking pictures from the 1970s, highlighting such bands as Black Flag, the Germs, and X.

Mark Spitz and Brendan Mullen *We Got the Neutron Bomb: The Untold Story of LA Punk* (Three Rivers Press). Long-overdue recollection of the frenzied glory days of the local punk and thrash scene in the 1970s.

Danny Sugarman *Wonderland Avenue* (Abacus; Little Brown). The former Doors' publicist gives a mind-bending tour of the local rock scene from the late 1960s on, providing lurid accounts of famous and infamous figures.

Hollywood and the movies

Kenneth Anger *Hollywood Babylon* (Dell US). Deliciously dark and lurid stories of sex scandals, bad behavior, and murder in Tinseltown, written by the *enfant terrible* of 1960s experimental films. Not especially well written, but it holds your attention throughout.

Jeanine Basinger *Silent Stars* (Wesleyan University Press). Great ode to the still-famous and long-forgotten Hollywood figures of the silent era, with brief biographies that outline the careers of movie cowboys, vamps, and sheiks.

Robert Berger *The Last Remaining Seats* (Hennessey & Ingalls US). An excellent photo guide to the extant movie palaces of Los Angeles, including many shots of theaters that are now closed to the public.

Peter Biskind *Easy Riders, Raging Bulls* (Bloomsbury; Simon & Schuster). Fascinating, gossipy

account of the great wave of American filmmakers in the 1970s, among them Spielberg, Scorsese, and Coppola, who redefined Hollywood cinema as a potential art form at the same time they were indulging in lots of bad behavior. The author's later *Down and Dirty Pictures* (Simon & Schuster US) artfully picks apart the indie film and festival scene.

Peter Bogdanovich *Who the Devil Made It* (Ballantine o/p). Acclaimed book of conversations with great old Hollywood filmmakers, including Alfred Hitchcock, Fritz Lang, and Howard Hawks. A newer volume, *Who the Hell's in It* (Ballantine US), covers major actors of the Golden Age.

Kevin Brownlow and John Kobal *Hollywood: The Pioneers* (Knopf o/p). An intriguing look at the founders of American cinema in the silent era, told from the points of view of an esteemed film historian and preservationist, and a prolific writer on movie topics.

Robert Evans *The Kid Stays in the Picture* (Faber & Faber; Hyperion). Spellbinding insider's view of the machinations of Hollywood after the demise of the studio system, written with verve by one of LA's biggest egos and, it turns out, most compelling writers – the head of Paramount when that company was at its modern peak.

Carrie Fisher *Postcards from the Edge* (Pocket US). The real-life Princess Leia had serious problems: a mother from hell, the pressures of teenage stardom, and the unstoppable Hollywood Movie Machine. After caving in to chemical comfort, she cleaned up her act, rebuilt her relationship with Mom, and wrote this memorable book – a *Heart of Darkness* for 1980s Hollywood.

Otto Friedrich *City of Nets: A Portrait of Hollywood in the 1940s* (University of California Press US). Descriptions of the major actors, directors, and studio bosses of the last good years of the studio system, before TV, antitrust actions, and Joe McCarthy ruined it all.

Ian Hamilton *Writers in Hollywood: 1915–1951* (HarperCollins o/p). A revealing look at screenwriters from the early days of the studio system up to its decline, with special focus on literary heavyweights like F. Scott Fitzgerald and William Faulkner.

Gerald Horne *Class Struggle in Hollywood: 1930–1950* (University of Texas Press US). Excellent exploration of a commonly overlooked aspect of Tinseltown – the ongoing strife between labor unions and the studios, which culminates here with strike and subsequent violence.

Ephraim Katz *The Film Encyclopedia* (Harper US/UK). The essential reference guide for anyone interested in the movies, providing valuable information on the old movie companies and countless studio-system bit players, along with more contemporary figures. The first, 1980, edition is the best — the original author died soon after.

Colin McArthur *Underworld USA* (Viking/Secker & Warburg both o/p). One of the best analyses of the Hollywood gangster film, as realized by directors from Fritz Lang to Don Siegel.

Thomas Schatz *The Genius of the System* (Owl Books/Faber & Faber). A laudatory account of the big studios and bosses of the golden age of movies, covering the structure of the industry and detailing the major and minor players. A bit overboard in its praise, but still a very worthwhile read.

Alain Silver and Julia Ward *Film Noir: An Encyclopedic Reference to the American Style* (Overlook). A large-format guide to the bleak films of the 1940s to the present, and an essential title that has gone through many editions. The best of author Silver's many excellent *noir*-related volumes.

Jerry Stahl *Permanent Midnight* (Process, UK). When his employers on TV's *Alf* heard that star writer Stahl was spending more than his already-huge paycheck to support his heroin and other habits, they gave him a raise to cover the difference and keep him on the job. The result is another gritty descent into (and recovery from) Tinseltown drug hell.

Gregory Paul Williams *The Story of Hollywood* (BL Press US). Perhaps the best modern take on the rise and international conquest of America's movie capital — well-detailed but also very readable.

Fiction

Eve Babitz *Eve's Hollywood*; *Slow Days, Fast Company*; *LA Woman* (all o/p). Eye-opening, thinly veiled autobiographical portraits of Southern California in the 1960s and 70s, with all the drugs, sex, and rock 'n' roll you can imagine, but described in a relaxed, sometimes wistful, manner. Only the first is difficult to find online.

T.C. Boyle *Tortilla Curtain* (Bloomsbury; Penguin). Set in LA, this book boldly borrows its premise – a privileged white man running down a member of the city's ethnic underclass – from Tom Wolfe's *Bonfire of the Vanities*, but carries it off to great satiric effect.

James Brown *The Los Angeles Diaries* (Bloomsbury; Harper Perennial). Difficult-to-stomach but strangely compelling memoir about life in the dark underbelly of drug abuse, child molestation, arson, suicide and Hollywood striving. A memorable self-view from a talented author and screenwriter.

Charles Bukowski *Post Office* (Virgin; Ecco). An alcohol- and sex-soaked romp through some of LA's festering back alleys, with a mailman surrogate for Bukowski as your guide. One of several books by the author exploring his encounters with the city's dark side.

James M. Cain *Double Indemnity*, *The Postman Always Rings Twice*, *Mildred Pierce* (Orion; Everyman's Library). With Raymond Chandler, the ultimate writer of dark, tough-guy novels. His entire oeuvre is excellent reading, but these three are the best explorations of LA.

Raymond Chandler *Farewell, My Lovely*; *The Long Goodbye*; *The Lady in the Lake* (Penguin; Library of America). All of these books, and several more, have been adapted into movies, but Chandler's prose is inimitable: terse, pointed, and vivid. More than just detective stories (centered on gumshoe detective Philip Marlowe), these are master-pieces of fiction.

Susan Compo *Life After Death and Other Stories* (Faber & Faber o/p). The club life of the black-clad members of the local goth-rock scene is the subject here, and the author's prose brings it to life in sordid detail.

Michael Connelly *Angels Flight* (Orion; Grand Central). A sixth volume of contemporary detective fiction featuring the LAPD investigator Harry Bosch, a keen observer of LA's blood-curdling mix of corruption, public scandals, and violence.

Philip K. Dick *A Scanner Darkly* (Gollancz; Vintage). Erratic but brilliant author evokes the mid-1990s split between the Straights, the Dopers, and the Narks – a dizzying study of identity, authority, and drugs. Among the pick of the rest of Dick's vast legacy is *Do Androids Dream of Electric Sheep?* (Gollancz; Library of America), set in San Francisco, which gave rise to the film *Blade Runner*, set in LA.

Joan Didion *Play It as It Lays* (Farrar, Straus & Giroux US). Holly-wood rendered in booze-guzzling, pill-popping, sex-craving detail. Oddly, the author went on to write the uninspired script for a third adaptation of *A Star is Born*.

James Ellroy *The Black Dahlia*, *The Big Nowhere*, *LA Confidential*, *White Jazz* (Arrow; Vintage). The LA Quartet: an excellent saga of city cops from the postwar era to the 1960s, with each novel becoming progressively more complex and elliptical in style. The author's other

LA-based works are also excellent — but start here.

Steve Erickson *Amnesiascope* and *Arc d'X* (Quartet Books UK). The two best of the author's wildly florid, postmodern novels about the city, featuring bizarre characters in surreal settings.

John Fante *Ask the Dust* (Canongate; Harper Perennial). The first and still the best of the author's stories of itinerant poet Arturo Bandini, whose wanderings during the Depression highlight the city's faded glory and struggling residents. Made into a subpar recent film.

Robert Ferrigno *The Horse Latitudes* (Arrow Books UK). A drug-dealer-turned-academic begins a descent into a bizarre LA world when he encounters a corpse at his home, possibly left by his missing ex-wife.

F. Scott Fitzgerald *The Last Tycoon* (Penguin). The legendary author's unfinished final work, a major novel on the power and glory of Hollywood. Intriguing reading that gives a view of the studio system at its height. US edition features a reconstruction of what the finished version may have looked like.

Chester Himes *If He Hollers Let Him Go* (Serpent's Tail; Thunder's Mouth Press). A fine literary introduction to mid-twentieth-century race relations in LA, narrated by one Bob Jones, whose struggles mirror those of author Himes, who eventually ended up living in Spain.

Aldous Huxley *Ape and Essence* (Ivan R. Dee US). Imaginative depiction of post-nuclear LA, in which books are burned in Pershing Square for warmth and the *Biltmore* hotel is the site of an annual orgy.

Helen Hunt Jackson *Ramona* (Signet Classics US). Romanticized depiction of mission life that rightfully criticizes the American government's treatment of Indians while showing the natives to be noble savages and glorifying the Spanish exploiters. Not particularly good reading, but a valuable period piece – and perhaps the most influential piece of fiction ever written about LA.

Gavin Lambert *The Slide Area* (Serpents Tail UK). Seven short tales focusing on the dark side of Hollywood and LA's beachside towns, first published over forty years ago but still absorbing for its urban insights and lurid details.

Elmore Leonard *Get Shorty* (Penguin). Ice-cool mobster Chili Palmer is a Miami debt collector who follows a client to Hollywood, and finds that the increasing intricacies of his own situation are translating themselves into a movie script.

David Levien *Wormwood* (Allison & Busby UK). Get a glimpse of the seamier side of the contemporary movie biz, following an up-and-coming story editor through the corporate ranks until he achieves utter exhaustion and, curiously, an addiction to absinthe.

Ross MacDonald *Black Money* (Orion; Vintage); *The Blue Hammer* (o/p); *The Zebra-Striped Hearse* (Vintage, US); *The Doomsters* (o/p); *The Instant Enemy* (o/p). Following in the footsteps of Spade and Marlowe, private detective Lew Archer looks behind the glitzy masks of Southern California life to reveal the underlying nastiness of creepy sexuality and manipulation.

Walter Mosley *Devil in a Blue Dress*, *A Red Death*, *White Butterfly*, *Black Betty*, *A Little Yellow Dog*, *Bad Boy Brawly Brown* (Mask Noir; Washington Square). Excellent modern *noir* novels featuring black private detective Easy Rawlins, who "does favors" from his South Central base. Mosley compellingly brings to life Watts and, later, Compton.

Kem Nunn *Tapping the Source* (No Exit Press; Thunder's Mouth). One of the most unexpected novels to emerge from California beach culture, this eerie murder-mystery is set amid the surfing scene of Orange County's Huntington Beach.

Thomas Pynchon *The Crying of Lot 49* (Vintage; Harper Perennial). The hilarious adventures of techno-freaks and potheads in Sixties California, revealing among other things the sexy side of stamp collecting.

John Ridley *Love is a Racket* (o/p). A delightful slice of Hollywood hell, in which protagonist Jeffty Kittridge, slumming through the dregs of local society and being abused by count-less predators, leads us on a darkly comic journey through LA's many bleak corners.

Luis J Rodriguez *Republic of East LA* (Harper Perennial). Stark, memorable tales of life in the barrio, where struggling romantics and working-class strivers face the inequities of class and race, and gang crime looms ever-present.

Theodore Roszak *Flicker* (No Exit Press; Chicago Review Press). In an old LA movie house, Jonathan Gates discovers cinema and becomes obsessed by the director Max Castle – a genius of the silent era who disappeared under mysterious circumstances in the Forties – leading Gates into a labyrinthine conspiracy rooted in medieval heresy.

Geoff Ryman *Was* (Gollancz UK). A pop-lit masterpiece that bizarrely updates and twists the *Wizard of Oz* for more contemporary times, creating a fascinating work of Southern Californian magical realism.

Danny Santiago *Famous All Over Town* (Plume US). A compelling portrayal of life in a struggling Hispanic community, set in the barrio of East LA, and featuring a cast of street gangs.

Budd Schulberg *What Makes Sammy Run?* (Vintage US). Classic anti-Hollywood vitriol by one of its insiders, a novelist and screenwriter whose acidic portrait of the movie business is unmatched.

Mona Simpson *Anywhere but Here* (Atlantic Books, UK). Engaging story of a mother's desire to put her daughter on the fast track to Hollywood stardom. Made into a less-inspired movie.

Upton Sinclair *The Brass Check* (University of Illinois Press US). The failed California gubernato-rial candidate and activist author's vigorous critique of LA's yellow journalism and the underhanded practices of its main figures. Sinclair also wrote *Oil!* (o/p), about the city's 1920s oil rush.

Terry Southern *Blue Movie* (Grove Press US). Sordid, frequently hilar-ious take on the overlap between high-budget moviemaking and pornography, with the author's vulgar themes and characters cheerfully slashing through politically correct literary conventions.

Michael Tolkin *The Player* (Grove). A convincing portrayal of the depravity and cutthroat dealings of the filmmaking community, with special scorn reserved for venal movie execs. Made into a classic flick by Robert Altman.

Gore Vidal *Hollywood* (Abacus; Vintage). The fifth volume in the author's "Empire" series about emerging US power on the world stage, this one focusing on the movie industry, its interaction with Washington bigwigs, and boundless capacity for propaganda.

Evelyn Waugh *The Loved One* (Penguin). The essential literary companion to take with you on a trip to Forest Lawn – here rendered as Whispering Glades, the pinnacle of funerary pretension and a telling symbol of LA's status-obsessed ways.

Nathanael West *The Day of the Locust* (Penguin; Signet). The best novel about LA not involving detectives; an apocalyptic story of the characters on the fringes of the film industry, culminating in a glorious riot and utter chaos.

Karen Tei Yamashita *Tropic of Orange* (Coffee House Press US). Successful melding of the apocalyptic, noir, and surreal styles that characterize LA, in the form of a vitriolic satire about the media, cultural dissonance, and social disintegration.

Glossaries

Architectural terms

Art Deco Catch-all term for Zigzag Moderne, Streamline Moderne, governmental WPA, and other styles, often identified by geometric motifs, sharp lines, and sleek ornamentation. See the Miracle Mile, pp.78-79.

Beaux Arts Turn-of-the-century movement imported from New York and Europe emphasizing Neoclassical symmetry, imposing dimensions, grand columns, and stairways, and other features now associated with old-time banks. See the monumental Hall of Justice, p.56.

Brutalist Late-modern extreme architectural style first popularized in Britain and poorly executed in LA, emphasizing concrete, box-like construction, and utter lack of ornament and aesthetic interest. See any parking garage or 1960s government building.

Bungalow Prototypical style of home design in the early twentieth century, originating in the Far East but finding popularity in LA for its use of shingles, porches, and sloped roofs, and compact design. Although it was most often linked to the Arts-and-Crafts movement, many varieties can be spotted with Spanish Colonial, Mission, Continental, and even Moderne influences. See Bungalow Heaven in Pasadena, p.195.

Case Study Program Postwar design project initiated by *Arts and Architecture* magazine, which planned and sometimes constructed modern, affordable homes made principally of steel and glass. See box on p.110 for more details, or the Eames House in Pacific Palisades, p.214.

Corporate Modern Bland reduction of the original modern aesthetic,

with glass curtain walls, boxy geometry, and an inhuman scale. Usually found with towering office blocks Downtown or in Century City, though sometimes inventive, as with the Library Tower, p.66.

Craftsman Early twentieth-century style, using exposed wood beams, overhanging rooflines, large shingles, cobblestones, and prominent fireplaces to create a rough-hewn look. See the Gamble House, p.196.

Deconstructivist Architecture that looks like it's falling apart or incomplete, characterized by irregular shapes, aggressive asymmetry, and lack of obvious coherence. See box on the work of Eric Owen Moss, p.136.

Folk Architecture Home-made structures created by untrained, self-taught builders, the Watts Towers being a glorious example, p.165.

Googie Free-spirited coffee-shop architecture, with bright colors, sharp curves and boomerang shapes, pitched roofs and neon trim. See *Pann's* in South Central, p.155, or *Bob's Big Boy* in Burbank, p.206.

High-Tech 1970s and 1980s variant on the machine aesthetic, characterized by exposed pipes and ducts and industrial decor. Few good examples survive locally, although the post-industrial Carlson-Reges Residence, p.70, comes close.

Historic-Revival The early twentieth-century use of various older architectural styles – notably Spanish Colonial in the 1920s. See box on the architectural firm of Morgan, Walls and Clements, p.78.

Mission Originally the unimposing, ranch-style buildings put up by the Spanish in the eighteenth and early nineteenth centuries, such as Mission San Fernando, p.211. Later a period-revival style that reached its height with 1920s housing; see Union Station, p.53, for its most monumental form.

Modern Clean, geometric design aesthetic, beginning in the 1920s and 1930s with houses built by R.M. Schindler, such as the architect's own home, p.114, and Richard Neutra, the Lovell House, p.92, and continuing on to today's Getty Center, p.129, and Caltrans building, p.55.

Moderne A popular architectural style that used Art Deco ornamentation and sleek lines to convey quiet elegance. See any glossy movie set from the 1930s, or Crossroads of the World, p.104.

Period-Revival See "Historic-Revival."

Postmodern Contemporary rehash/mishmash of Neoclassicism, often in pastel colors. See Charles Moore's Civic Center in Beverly Hills, p.119.

Pre-Columbian Quirky 1920s architecture, employing blocky sunbursts, abstract floral motifs and stylized faces to create an ancient look for the modern city. See the *Aztec Hotel*, p.202, or almost any LA work by Frank Lloyd Wright.

Programmatic Buildings taking a particular, nonarchitectural shape, such as dogs, boots, rockets, and hats. See *The Donut Hole*, p.264.

Ranch Quintessential style of Southern California design, typically found in suburban homes with low-slung, single-story plans, open layouts with few interior walls, and abundant windows. Best seen in its grandest form at the ranch at Will Rogers State Historic Park, p.215.

Sculptural Architecture as art, often "molded" by the architect using computer-assisted design to create structures that would not be possible at a drafting table. Quite striking when successful, as in much of the work of Frank Gehry, especially Disney Hall, p.64.

Spanish Colonial Perhaps the quintessential style for housing architecture in LA, especially in the period-revival 1920s, emphasizing tiled roofs, wrought-ironwork, whitewashed walls, and romantic landscaping. See Villa Aurora, p.215.

Streamline Moderne Buildings resembling ocean liners and sometimes airplanes, borne of a 1930s worship of all things mechanical. See the Coca-Cola Bottling Plant, p.163.

Victorian General term for late-1800s housing styles – Eastlake, Queen Anne, Stick – few of which remain in the city. See Angelino Heights, p.169, or Heritage Square, p.71.

Zigzag Moderne A late-1920s version of Art Deco that had particular popularity in LA, with strong verticality, narrow windows, geometric ornamentation, and occasional use of pre-Columbian or Egyptian motifs. See Bullocks Wilshire, p.74.

Movie-industry terms

Above the line Budgeted costs for actors, writers, directors, and producers.

Above the title Adjective or adverb referring to the placement of a major actor's film credit in studio advertising, often a contractual requirement.

Below the line Budgeted costs for camera, lighting, and all other technical and behind-the-scenes costs.

Below the title Except for major actors, where everyone else – supporting players, writer, director, and so on – gets named in studio advertising for a film, typically near the bottom in fine print.

Block booking Old studio-system practice of forcing exhibitors to carry whole "blocks" of studio films, including many awful titles they would otherwise reject. Since declared an illegal monopoly practice by the US Supreme Court.

Blockbuster Now the term for a big hit, its original meaning meant a film that appealed to all audiences and thus "busted" the "blocks" of disparate segments of viewers.

Box office The weekly money generated by a particular film. Also called the "take."

Completion bond Finishing funds for a film project, given by a financial entity who in return gets some degree of control over the film.

Development The branch of a film company responsible for bringing projects into existence in pre-production, often through working with writers to re-craft their scripts for the big screen and getting notable actors and directors, and sometimes producers, on board.

Development hell The much-feared limbo during a film's pre-production, when the script suddenly requires multiple, contradictory revisions, prospective actors quit, or the studio loses interest. Every screenwriter's nightmare.

Green light A verb meaning to approve the actual production of a given film.

Gross profit The raw financial returns of a film before costs are subtracted, published on Mondays in the trade press and watched eagerly by Hollywood players.

High concept A movie plot that can be summarized on a cocktail napkin, or more specifically, by a single, basic sentence, eg "A chimpanzee detective solves crimes in Hollywood."

In the can A finished film project, symbolically sitting in its reel or canister. However, term does not mean the film is about to be released – projects can sit "in the can" for years, or never be released at all.

Independent Once applied to small companies operating outside the studio mainstream. Since such companies are now mostly controlled by the majors, the term currently refers to ultra-low-budget films and filmmakers. Also called "indie."

Lens Verb, mostly employed by the trade-industry press, meaning "to film." Possibly used this way only in Hollywood.

Lunch Verb meaning "to conduct business," and the place where business is conducted.

MPAA Acronym for the Motion Picture Association of America, the body that oversees the film-rating and classification board.

Oater Pejorative slang for Westerns – a nearly defunct genre.

Open Verb meaning "to begin playing" and, more importantly, "to draw an audience."

Player 1980s term for an important studio executive, film producer, or top director able to command financial respect throughout town and get a movie project "green lighted."

Points A percentage of profits taken from the gross earnings of a film, often as payment by actors and directors in lieu of salary.

Post Short for post-production: editing, adding sound effects, redubbing dialogue, and the like.

Preview Outside of LA, a short advertising clip, also known as a "trailer," preceding a film viewing. Within LA, an advance screening of a movie used to gauge an audience's response – positive or negative.

Scale Union-minimum wages that supporting players must accept to be involved with many productions, and that big-name actors will sometimes accept to be associated with a prestigious low-budget work or acclaimed director.

Sleeper A familiar term for an unheralded flick that manages to be a surprise hit.

Turnaround Occurs when a production company loses interest in a film project and either pawns it off on another company or shelves it for an indefinite period.

Vehicle Not an automobile, but a motion picture – often of limited creative value – that is used to forward the career of a major celebrity or rising actor. In the extreme, is known as a "vanity project."

Vertical integration The practice in the film world of owning the production, distribution, and exhibition parts of the industry – studios controlling every step of the process. Declared an illegal practice by the US Supreme Court in the 1950s but since loosened by Congress with the rise of cable TV, videotape, and digital filmmaking, and their financial overlap.

Travel
store

D: Rough Guide
DIRECTIONS for
short breaks

Kenya
Marrakesh **D**
Morocco
South Africa, Lesotho
  & Swaziland
Syria
Tanzania
Tunisia
West Africa
Zanzibar

Travel Specials
First-Time Africa
First-Time Around
  the World
First-Time Asia
First-Time Europe
First-Time Latin
  America
Travel Health
Travel Online
Travel Survival
Walks in London
  & SE England
Women Travel
World Party

Maps
Algarve
Amsterdam
Andalucia
  & Costa del Sol
Argentina
Athens
Australia
Barcelona
Berlin
Boston & Cambridge
Brittany
Brussels
California
Chicago
Chile
Corsica
Costa Rica
  & Panama
Crete
Croatia
Cuba
Cyprus
Czech Republic
Dominican Republic
Dubai & UAE
Dublin
Egypt

Florence & Siena
Florida
France
Frankfurt
Germany
Greece
Guatemala & Belize
Iceland
India
Ireland
Italy
Kenya & Northern
  Tanzania
Lisbon
London
Los Angeles
Madrid
Malaysia
Mallorca
Marrakesh
Mexico
Miami & Key West
Morocco
New England
New York City
New Zealand
Northern Spain
Paris
Peru
Portugal
Prague
Pyrenees & Andorra
Rome
San Francisco
Sicily
South Africa
South India
Spain & Portugal
Sri Lanka
Tenerife
Thailand
Toronto
Trinidad & Tobago
Tunisia
Turkey
Tuscany
Venice
Vietnam, Laos
  & Cambodia
Washington DC
Yucatán Peninsula

Dictionary
Phrasebooks
Croatian
Czech
Dutch
Egyptian Arabic
French
German
Greek
Hindi & Urdu
Italian
Japanese
Latin American
  Spanish
Mandarin Chinese
Mexican Spanish
Polish
Portuguese
Russian
Spanish
Swahili
Thai
Turkish
Vietnamese

Computers
Blogging
eBay
iPhone
iPods, iTunes
  & music online
The Internet
Macs & OS X
MySpace
PCs and Windows
PlayStation Portable
Website Directory

Film & TV
American
  Independent Film
British Cult Comedy
Chick Flicks
Comedy Movies
Cult Movies
Film
Film Musicals
Film Noir
Gangster Movies
Horror Movies
Kids' Movies
Sci-Fi Movies
Westerns

Lifestyle
Babies
Ethical Living
Pregnancy & Birth
Running

Music Guides
The Beatles
Blues
Bob Dylan
Book of Playlists
Classical Music
Elvis
Frank Sinatra
Heavy Metal
Hip-Hop
Jazz
Led Zeppelin
Opera
Pink Floyd
Punk
Reggae
Rock
The Rolling Stones
Soul and R&B
Velvet Underground
World Music
  (2 vols)

Popular Culture
Books for Teenagers
Children's Books,
  5-11
Conspiracy Theories
Crime Fiction
Cult Fiction
The Da Vinci Code
His Dark Materials
Lord of the Rings
Shakespeare
Superheroes
The Templars
Unexplained
  Phenomena

Science
The Brain
Climate Change
The Earth
Genes & Cloning
The Universe
Weather

Visit us online
www.roughguides.com
Information on over 25,000 destinations around the world

BROADEN YOUR HORIZONS

Avoid Guilt Trips

Buy fair trade coffee + bananas ✓

Save energy - use low energy bulbs ✓

- don't leave tv on standby ✓

Offset carbon emissions from flight to Madrid ✓

Send goat to Africa ✓

Join Tourism Concern today ✓

Slowly, the world is changing.
Together we can, and will, make a difference.

Tourism Concern is the only UK registered charity fighting exploitation in one of the largest industries on earth: people forced from their homes in order that holiday resorts can be built, sweatshop labour conditions in hotels and destruction of the environment are just some of the issues that we tackle.

Sending people on a guilt trip is not something we do. We know as well as anyone that holidays are precious. But you can help us to ensure that tourism always benefits the local communities involved.

Call 020 7133 3330
or visit **tourismconcern.org.uk** to find out how.

A year's membership of Tourism Concern costs just £20 (£12 unwaged) - that's 38 pence a week, less than the cost of a pint of milk, organic of course.

Fighting Exploitation in Tourism

TourismConcern

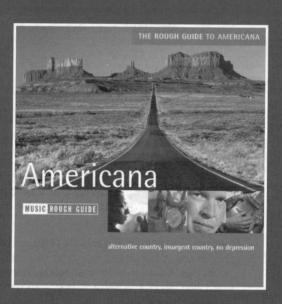

Small print and
Index

A Rough Guide to Rough Guides

Published in 1982, the first Rough Guide – to Greece – was a student scheme that became a publishing phenomenon. Mark Ellingham, a recent graduate in English from Bristol University, had been traveling in Greece the previous summer and couldn't find the right guidebook. With a small group of friends he wrote his own guide, combining a highly contemporary, journalistic style with a thoroughly practical approach to travelers' needs.

The immediate success of the book spawned a series that rapidly covered dozens of destinations. And, in addition to impecunious backpackers, Rough Guides soon acquired a much broader and older readership that relished the guides' wit and inquisitiveness as much as their enthusiastic, critical approach and value-for-money ethos.

These days, Rough Guides include recommendations from shoestring to luxury and cover more than 200 destinations around the globe, including almost every country in the Americas and Europe, more than half of Africa, and most of Asia and Australasia. Our ever-growing team of authors and photographers is spread all over the world, particularly in Europe, the USA, and Australia.

In the early 1990s, Rough Guides branched out of travel, with the publication of Rough Guides to World Music, Classical Music, and the Internet. All three have become benchmark titles in their fields, spearheading the publication of a wide range of books under the Rough Guide name.

ROUGH
GUIDES

SMALL PRINT

Including the travel series, Rough Guides now number more than 350 titles, covering: phrasebooks, waterproof maps, music guides from Opera to Heavy Metal, reference works as diverse as Conspiracy Theories and Shakespeare, and popular culture books from iPods to Poker. Rough Guides also produce a series of more than 120 World Music CDs in partnership with World Music Network.

Visit www.roughguides.com to see our latest publications.

Rough Guide travel images are available for commercial licensing at www.roughguidespictures.com

Rough Guide credits

Text editor: Constance Jones
Layout: Umesh Aggarwal
Cartography: Swati Handoo
Picture editor: Harriet Mills
Production: Rebecca Short
Proofreader: Andy McCullough
Cover design: Chloë Roberts
Photographer: Dan Bannister, Demetrio Carrasco
Editorial: London Ruth Blackmore, Alison
Murchie, Karoline Thomas, Andy Turner, Keith
Drew, Edward Aves, Alice Park, Lucy White,
Jo Kirby, James Smart, Natasha Foges, Róisín
Cameron, Emma Traynor, Emma Gibbs, James
Rice, Kathryn Lane, Christina Valhouli, Monica
Woods, Mani Ramaswamy, Joe Staines, Peter
Buckley, Matthew Milton, Tracy Hopkins, Ruth
Tidball; **New York** Andrew Rosenberg, AnneLise
Sorensen, Steven Horak, April Isaacs, Ella Steim,
Anna Owens, Sean Mahoney, Paula Neudorf,
Courtney Miller; **Delhi** Madhavi Singh, Karen
D'Souza
Design & Pictures: London Scott Stickland,
Dan May, Diana Jarvis, Nicole Newman, Mark
Thomas, Sarah Cummins, Emily Taylor; **Delhi**
Ajay Verma, Jessica Subramanian, Ankur Guha,

Pradeep Thapliyal, Sachin Tanwar, Anita Singh,
Nikhil Agarwal
Production: Vicky Baldwin
Cartography: London Maxine Repath, Ed
Wright, Katie Lloyd-Jones; **Delhi** Jai Prakash
Mishra, Rajesh Chhibber, Ashutosh Bharti, Rajesh
Mishra, Animesh Pathak, Jasbir Sandhu, Karobi
Gogoi, Amod Singh, Alakananda Bhattacharya,
Online: Narender Kumar, Rakesh Kumar,
Amit Verma, Rahul Kumar, Ganesh Sharma,
Debojit Borah, Saurabh Sati, Ravi Yadav
Marketing & Publicity: London Liz Statham,
Niki Hanmer, Louise Maher, Jess Carter, Vanessa
Godden, Vivienne Watton, Anna Paynton, Rachel
Sprackett, Libby Jellie, Jayne McPherson, Holly
Dudley; **New York** Geoff Colquitt, Katy Ball; **Delhi**
Ragini Govind
Manager India: Punita Singh
Reference Director: Andrew Lockett
Operations Manager: Helen Phillips
PA to Publishing Director: Nicola Henderson
Publishing Director: Martin Dunford
Commercial Manager: Gino Magnotta
Managing Director: John Duhigg

Publishing information

This first edition published July 2008 by
Rough Guides Ltd,
80 Strand, London WC2R 0RL
345 Hudson St, 4th Floor,
New York, NY 10014, USA
14 Local Shopping Centre, Panchsheel Park,
New Delhi 110017, India
Distributed by the Penguin Group
Penguin Books Ltd,
80 Strand, London WC2R 0RL
Penguin Group (USA)
375 Hudson Street, NY 10014, USA
Penguin Group (Australia)
250 Camberwell Road, Camberwell,
Victoria 3124, Australia
Penguin Books Canada Ltd,
10 Alcorn Avenue, Toronto, Ontario,
Canada M4V 1E4
Penguin Group (NZ)
67 Apollo Drive, Mairangi Bay, Auckland 1310,
New Zealand

Cover concept by Peter Dyer.
Typeset in Bembo and Helvetica to an original
design by Henry Iles.
Printed and bound in China
© JD Dickey 2008
No part of this book may be reproduced in any
form without permission from the publisher except
for the quotation of brief passages in reviews.
464pp includes index
A catalogue record for this book is available from
the British Library
ISBN: 978-1-85828-378-4

1   3   5   7   9   8   6   4   2

SMALL PRINT

Help us update

We've gone to a lot of effort to ensure that
the first edition of **The Rough Guide to Los
Angeles & Southern California** is accurate and
up to date. However, things change – places
get "discovered", opening hours are notoriously
fickle, restaurants and rooms raise prices or lower
standards. If you feel we've got it wrong or left
something out, we'd like to know, and if you can
remember the address, the price, the hours, the
phone number, so much the better.

Please send your comments with the
subject line "**Rough Guide Los Angeles &
Southern California Update**" to ©mail
@roughguides.com. We'll credit all contributions
and send a copy of the next edition (or any
other Rough Guide if you prefer) for the very
best emails.
    Have your questions answered and tell others
about your trip at ®community.roughguides.com

Acknowledgments

JD would like to thank his friends and family, as well as his contacts and facilitators in Southern California including those at LACVB and local accommodation offices. JD would also like to offer a cheerful endorsement of the yeoman work of Andrew Rosenberg and AnneLise Sorensen in the Rough Guides office, and great thanks to his editor Constance Jones, who contributed much energy, dedication, and skill to the project. Finally, others at RG who have worked so assiduously include Umesh Aggarwal, Swati Handoo, Katie Lloyd-Jones, Harriet Mills, and Ella Steim.

Photo credits

INDEX

Map entries are in color.

I

INDEX

449

M

W

Y

Z

Map symbols

maps are listed in the full index using colored text

-------	International border		☀	Marshland
-- -- --	State border		🕯	Lighthouse
--- ---	Chapter boundary		✈	Airport
80	Interstate		★	Bus stop
30	US Highway		◆	Point of interest
1	Highway		ⓘ	Information center
= = =	Road under construction		⊠	Post office
:::::	Pedestrianized road		◉	Accommodation
⊞⊞⊞	Steps		▣	Restaurant
....	Tunnel		⚠	Campsite
―――	Railway		♟	Museum
—M—	Metrorail station		⚑	Golf course
-----	Footpath		✝	Church (regional)
— —	Ferry route		▬	Building
⟋	River & dam		⊞	Church
⊠—⊠	Gate		⬭	Stadium
⊔	Bridge		⊞	Cemetery
⋀⋀	Mountain range		▦	Park
▲	Peak		▦	Beach
⅍	Rocks		▦	Forest

I

MAP SYMBOLS

SYLMAR

GOLDEN STATE FREEWAY

118 SAN FERNANDO

210

5

SIMI VALLEY - SAN FERNANDO VALLEY FREEWAY

118

23

MOORPARK FREEWAY

Santa Barbara

SIMI VALLEY

NORTHRIDGE

TOPANGA CANYON BLVD

SEPULVEDA BLVD

405

170

HOLLYWOOD FREEWAY

CANOGA PARK

San Fernando Valley

VAN NUYS
NORTH
HOLLYWOOD

Van Nuys Airport ✈

WOODLAND
HILLS

VENTURA FREEWAY

NORTH HOLLYWOOD

101

ENCINO

SHERMAN
OAKS

HOLLYWOOD
HILLS

Calabasas ●

MALIBU CREEK
STATE PARK

KANAN DUME RD

LAS VIRGENES RD

MULHOLLAND DRIVE

SAN DIEGO FREEWAY

TOPANGA CANYON BLVD

TOPANGA
STATE PARK

BEL AIR

WESTWOOD

HOLLYWOOD
W. HOLLYWOOD

SANTA   MONICA   MOUNTAINS

Getty Center

SANTA MONICA
NATIONAL
RECREATION AREA

BRENTWOOD

BEVERLY HILLS

UCLA

LACMA

MALIBU

PACIFIC
PALISADES

SANTA
MONICA

SANTA MONICA FREEWAY

1

PACIFIC COAST HIGHWAY

Getty
Villa

CRENSHAW

405

CULVER
CITY

Point Dume

1

VENICE

INGLEWOOD

LINCOLN BLVD

Marina del
Rey

Santa Monica
Bay

✈
LAX

405

EL
SEGUNDO

SEPULVEDA BLVD

BOULEVARD

MARINE
AVENUE

MANHATTAN BEACH

HERMOSA BEACH

REDONDO BEACH

HAWTHORNE

—— Red Line Subway
—— Blue Line Light Rail
···· Gold Line Light Rail
—— Green Line Light Rail
—— Orange Line Busway
○   Station

1

PALOS
VERDES
PENINSULA

PALOS VERDES DRIVE

Point
Vicente

0   100 miles

OREGON   IDAHO

5

80

NEVADA

N

UTAH

101

1

Sacramento

San
Francisco

Santa
Cruz

Sierra Nevada

Coastal Range

Las Vegas

15

PACIFIC

5

101

Los
Angeles

Santa
Barbara

Palm
Springs

40

10

ARIZONA

PACIFIC
OCEAN

CALIFORNIA

San
Diego

8

MEXICO

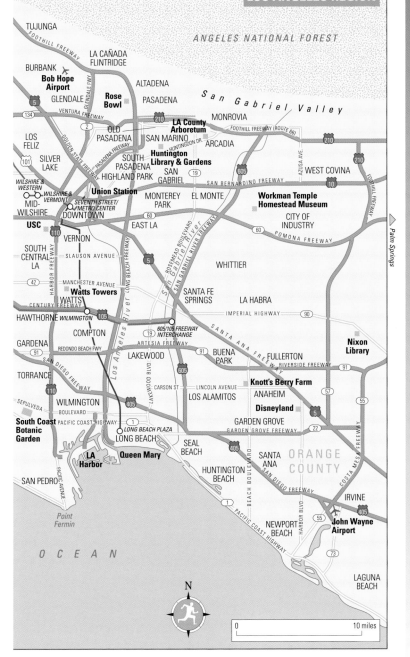

LOS ANGELES REGION

TUJUNGA

FOOTHILL FREEWAY

LA CAÑADA FLINTRIDGE

BURBANK

Bob Hope Airport ✈

GLENDALE

GLENDALE FWY

VENTURA FREEWAY

134

2

ALTADENA

Rose Bowl

PASADENA

ANGELES NATIONAL FOREST

San Gabriel Valley

210

LA County Arboretum

MONROVIA

FOOTHILL FREEWAY (ROUTE 66)

210

OLD PASADENA

SAN MARINO

ARCADIA

HUNTINGDON DR.

605

AZUSA AVE.

WEST COVINA

210

LOS FELIZ

101

SILVER LAKE

GOLDEN STATE FREEWAY

PASADENA FREEWAY

SOUTH PASADENA

Huntington Library & Gardens

HIGHLAND PARK

SAN GABRIEL

19

SAN BERNARDINO FREEWAY

10

FOOTHILL FREEWAY

WILSHIRE & WESTERN

WILSHIRE & VERMONT

MID-WILSHIRE

Union Station

MONTEREY PARK

EL MONTE

Workman Temple Homestead Museum

SEVENTH STREET/ METRO CENTER

DOWNTOWN

EAST LA

CITY OF INDUSTRY

USC

110

VERNON

SOUTH CENTRAL LA

SLAUSON AVENUE

42

HARBOR FREEWAY

LONG BEACH FREEWAY

ROSEMEAD BOULEVARD

SAN GABRIEL RIVER FREEWAY

60

POMONA FREEWAY

WHITTIER

SANTA FE SPRINGS

LA HABRA

MANCHESTER AVENUE

Watts Towers

WATTS

CENTURY FREEWAY

HAWTHORNE *WILMINGTON*

105

COMPTON

San Gabriel River

Los Angeles River

605/105 FREEWAY INTERCHANGE

19

IMPERIAL HIGHWAY

90

SANTA ANA FREEWAY

Nixon Library

GARDENA

91

REDONDO BEACH FWY

ARTESIA FREEWAY

91

BUENA PARK

FULLERTON

RIVERSIDE FREEWAY

91

TORRANCE

110

SAN DIEGO FREEWAY

LAKEWOOD

LAKEWOOD BLVD.

605

CARSON ST

LINCOLN AVENUE

LOS ALAMITOS

Knott's Berry Farm

ANAHEIM

57

55

SEPULVEDA

405

WILMINGTON

BOULEVARD

PACIFIC COAST HIGHWAY

1

Disneyland

5

GARDEN GROVE

GARDEN GROVE FREEWAY

22

South Coast Botanic Garden

LA Harbor

Queen Mary

LONG BEACH PLAZA

LONG BEACH

SEAL BEACH

405

SANTA ANA

ORANGE COUNTY

COSTA MESA FREEWAY

SAN PEDRO

PACIFIC AVENUE

HUNTINGTON BEACH

BEACH BOULEVARD

SAN DIEGO FREEWAY

HARBOR BLVD.

IRVINE

405

Point Fermin

1

PACIFIC COAST HIGHWAY

NEWPORT BEACH

55

John Wayne Airport

73

O C E A N

LAGUNA BEACH

△ *Palm Springs*

N

0   10 miles

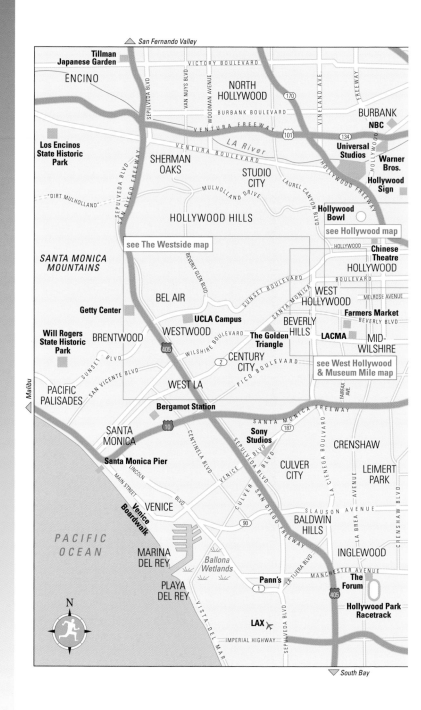

San Fernando Valley

Tillman
Japanese Garden

VICTORY BOULEVARD

ENCINO

VAN NUYS BLVD

WOODMAN AVENUE

NORTH
HOLLYWOOD

170

VINELAND AVE

FREEWAY

BURBANK BOULEVARD

BURBANK

NBC

SEPULVEDA BLVD

VENTURA FREEWAY

101

134

Los Encinos
State Historic
Park

VENTURA BOULEVARD

LA River

Universal
Studios

Warner
Bros.

SHERMAN
OAKS

VENTURA BOULEVARD

STUDIO
CITY

HOLLYWOOD FREEWAY

Hollywood
Sign

SEPULVEDA BLVD

SAN DIEGO FREEWAY

MULHOLLAND DRIVE

LAUREL CANYON BLVD

"DIRT MULHOLLAND"

HOLLYWOOD HILLS

Hollywood
Bowl

SANTA MONICA
MOUNTAINS

see The Westside map

BEVERLY GLEN BLVD

see Hollywood map

HOLLYWOOD

Chinese
Theatre

HOLLYWOOD

BOULEVARD

MELROSE AVENUE

BEL AIR

SUNSET BOULEVARD

SANTA MONICA

WEST
HOLLYWOOD

Getty Center

UCLA Campus

BEVERLY
HILLS

Farmers Market

BEVERLY BLVD

Will Rogers
State Historic
Park

BRENTWOOD

WESTWOOD

BOULEVARD

The Golden
Triangle

LACMA

MID-
WILSHIRE

405

WILSHIRE BOULEVARD

2

CENTURY
CITY

see West Hollywood
& Museum Mile map

SUNSET BLVD

PICO BOULEVARD

FAIRFAX AVE

Malibu

PACIFIC
PALISADES

SAN VICENTE BLVD

WEST LA

Bergamot Station

SANTA MONICA FREEWAY

10

187

SANTA
MONICA

CENTINELA BLVD

SEPULVEDA BLVD

Sony
Studios

CRENSHAW

Santa Monica Pier

LINCOLN

VENICE

CULVER
CITY

LA CIENEGA BOULEVARD

LEIMERT
PARK

MAIN STREET

BLVD

CULVER BLVD

SAN DIEGO FREEWAY

SLAUSON AVENUE

LA BREA AVENUE

CRENSHAW BLVD

Venice
Boardwalk

VENICE

PACIFIC
OCEAN

MARINA
DEL REY

90

BALDWIN
HILLS

Ballona
Wetlands

INGLEWOOD

PLAYA
DEL REY

Pann's

1

LA TIJERA BLVD

MANCHESTER AVENUE

The
Forum

405

N

VISTA DEL MAR

LAX

SEPULVEDA BLVD

Hollywood Park
Racetrack

IMPERIAL HIGHWAY

South Bay

△ Angeles National Forest

0   5 miles

LA CAÑADA-FLINTRIDGE

GLENOAKS BLVD

OLIVE AVENUE

ALTADENA

Rose Bowl

Gamble House

210 PASADENA

Museum of the
American West

Griffith
Park

GLENDALE 134

COLORADO ST

VENTURA FREEWAY

COLORADO BLVD

BRAND BLVD

SAN FERNANDO ROAD

GOLDEN STATE FREEWAY

FREEWAY

Eagle
Rock
●

GLENDALE

OLD
PASADENA

Griffith
Observatory

2

HIGHLAND PARK

LOS FELIZ BLVD

LOS FELIZ

BLVD

SILVER
LAKE

SUNSET BLVD

HYPERION AVE

GLENDALE FREEWAY

Southwest
Museum

5

PASADENA FREEWAY

SOUTH
PASADENA

Heritage
Square

110

HUNTINGTON DRIVE

Huntington
Library and
Gardens
SAN
MARINO

ALHAMBRA

BOULEVARD

VALLEY

GARFIELD AVENUE

San Gabriel Valley ▷

ECHO
PARK

101

see Downtown
LA map

Dodger
Stadium

CHINATOWN

WESTLAKE

WILSHIRE BOULEVARD

KOREA
TOWN

Bullocks
Wilshire
Building

PICO BLVD

Union Station

LA City Hall
DOWNTOWN

10

EAST LA
710

SAN BERNARDINO FREEWAY

ATLANTIC BOULEVARD

BOYLE
HEIGHTS

POMONA FREEWAY

60

GARFIELD AVENUE

Convention
Center

WEST ADAMS

10

Exposition Park

M.L. KING JR. BLVD

USC Campus

WHITTIER BOULEVARD

SANTA ANA FREEWAY

The Citadel

Whittier ▷

VERNON

LA River

5

WESTERN AVENUE

HARBOR FREEWAY

VERNON

AVENUE

CENTRAL AVENUE

WILMINGTON BLVD

ALAMEDA STREET

PACIFIC BLVD

SLAUSON AVENUE

SOUTHEAST LA

GARFIELD AVENUE

Orange County ▷

FLORENCE AVENUE

SOUTH
CENTRAL LA

42

FLORENCE AVENUE

FIRESTONE BOULEVARD

LONG BEACH ROAD

ATLANTIC AVENUE

710

DOWNEY

CENTURY BOULEVARD

WATTS

Watts Towers

IMPERIAL HIGHWAY

105

CENTRAL LA

Highland Park △△ Pasadena

DOWNTOWN LA

Red Line Subway
Blue Line Light Rail
Gold Line Light Rail
(M) Station

Elysian Park

AVENUE 19
AVENUE 20
AVENUE 18

ALBION ST
MOZART ST

The Brewery Complex

ACADEMY RD
SOLANO AVE
AMADOR ST
PHOENIX
SPRUCE

SOLANO

PARK DRIVE
PARK ROW DRIVE
CASENOVA ST
SOLANO AVE

MOULTON AVE
GIBBONS ST
LAMAR ST
ALHAMBRA AVE

STADIUM WAY

ACADEMY ROAD
ACADEMY RD

Silver Lake ◁

Dodger Stadium

NORTH MAIN STREET

WILHARDT ST
MESNAGER ST
SOTELLO ST

SCOTT AVENUE

BROADWAY

LA River

LILAC TERRACE
ELYSIAN PARK AVENUE
INNES AVE
STADIUM WAY
LILAC TERRACE

ELMYRA
MAGDALENA
LEROY
ALPINE STREET

Echo Park ◁

E. KENSINGTON ROAD
MARVIEW AVE
SUNSET BOULEVARD
FIGUEROA TERR.
BEAUDRY AVE
CENTENNIAL AVE

HILL STREET

RONDOUT

N

ANGELINO HEIGHTS

COLLEGE
NEW DEPT
BUNKER HILL
GRAND AVE
HILL PLACE
YALE ST
ORD ST
NEW HIGH ST
SPRING ST

CHINATOWN

VIGNES ST
AUGUSTA ST
BAUCHET ST

MISSION ROAD

DOUGLAS ST

(110)

CESAR CHAVEZ AVENUE

Union Station

RAMIREZ ST
KELLER ST

TEMPLE STREET
DOUGLAS ST
EDGEWARE ST
BOYLSTON ST
COURT STREET
COLTON STREET

(101)

The Plaza

COMMERCIAL STREET
VIGNES ST
DUCOMMUN

ANDERSON ST
MISSION JUNCTION
MYERS STREET
CENTER STREET

TEMPLE-BEAUDRY

Our Lady of the Angels Church

TEMPLE STREET

GLENDALE BLVD

Music Center

TEMPLE STREET
City Hall

TEMPLE STREET
BANNING STREET

Freight Depot (Sci Arc)

1ST STREET
WITMER AVE

Civic Center
Civic Center/Tom Bradley

Geffen Contemporary

1ST STREET

2ND STREET
EMERALD ST

Disney Hall

LOS ANGELES STREET

GAREY ST
WITT ST
SANTA FE AVENUE

MIRAMAR ST
MIRAMAR ST
3RD STREET

LA Times Building

1ST STREET

2ND STREET
ROSS ST
TRACTION AVENUE

Museum of Contemporary Art

BROADWAY
SPRING ST
MAIN STREET

2ND STREET

LITTLE TOKYO

3RD STREET AVENUE

4TH STREET
MARYLAND ST
LUCAS AVE
HARTFORD
5TH STREET
BOYLSTON ST
BEAUDRY AVENUE

BUNKER HILL

OLIVE STREET
HILL STREET

Grand Central Market
OLD DOWNTOWN

3RD STREET

4TH PLACE
HEWITT ST
MOLINO ST
MATEO ST
4TH STREET
COLYTON ST
SEATON ST
PALMETTO PLACE

6TH STREET

The Biltmore

Central Library

Pershing Square
Pershing Square

THEATER DISTRICT

WINSTON
4TH STREET
SKID ROW
5TH STREET

CENTRAL AVENUE

6TH STREET

WILSHIRE BOULEVARD
INGRAHAM STREET

Oviatt Building

Los Angeles Theatre

MAPLE AVENUE
WALL STREET
SAN JULIAN STREET

FACTORY PLACE
6TH STREET

HARTFORD
AVE
GARLAND AVE
7TH STREET
7th St/Metro Center

7TH STREET
FRANCISCO ST

7TH STREET
SPRING ST
BROADWAY
HILL STREET

6TH STREET

PRODUCE ST
WHOLESALE ST

8TH ST STREET
GARLAND AVE

8TH STREET

8TH STREET

SAN PEDRO STREET
CROCKER STREET

7TH STREET
TOWNE AVE
STANFORD AVE
GLADYS AVE
CERES AVE
KOHLER ST
MERCHANT ST

INDUSTRIAL ST
STREET
MARKET ST

ALBANY STREET
BLAINE STREET

FIGUEROA STREET
FLOWER STREET

9TH STREET

Flower Market

FASHION DISTRICT

OLYMPIC BOULEVARD

LA Live

OLYMPIC BOULEVARD

Orpheum Theatre

GEORGIA STREET

SOUTH PARK

11TH STREET

Staples Center
Convention Center

(M) Pico
PICO BOULEVARD

HOPE STREET
GRAND AVENUE
OLIVE STREET
12TH ST

MAIN STREET
SANTEE ST

11TH STREET

10TH STREET

BIRCH AVE
NAOMI AVE
HOOPER
BEACH ST

Herald Examiner Building

12TH STREET

11TH STREET

Coca-Cola Bottling Plant

PICO BOULEVARD

African-American Firefighters Museum

NEWTON STREET

14TH PL
14TH STREET
15TH STREET
16TH STREET

14TH STREET

14TH STREET

15TH STREET

18TH STREET
(10)

16TH STREET

18TH STREET

0   800 yds

WASHINGTON BOULEVARD

▽ USC   ▽ Long Beach   ▽ South Central LA

Mid-Wilshire ◁   Macarthur Park ◁   East LA ▷

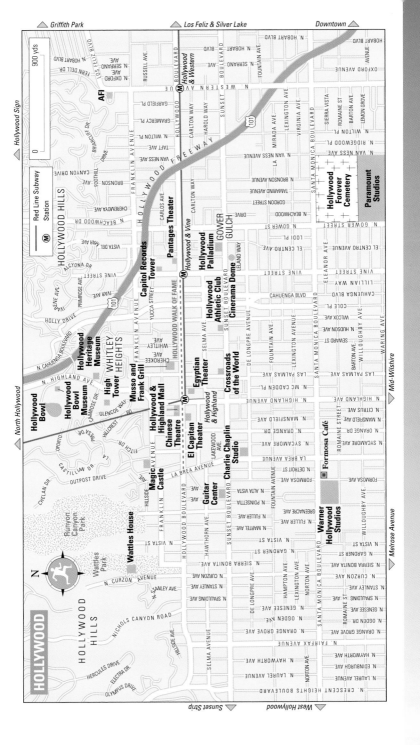

WEST HOLLYWOOD & MUSEUM MILE

0   500 yds

N

FULLER AVENUE
MARTEL AVENUE
VISTA STREET
GARDNER STREET
N. CURZON AVENUE
HAMPTON AVENUE
LEXINGTON AVENUE
NORTON AVENUE
DE LONGPRE AVENUE
OGDEN DRIVE

SANTA MONICA BOULEVARD
SUNSET BOULEVARD

N. MARTEL AVENUE
N. VISTA STREET
N. GARDNER STREET
N. SIERRA BONITA AVENUE
WILLOUGHBY AVENUE
N. STANLEY AVENUE
N. SPAULDING AVENUE
N. GENESEE AVENUE
N. OGDEN AVENUE
N. ORANGE GROVE AVENUE

N. FULLER AVENUE
CLINTON STREET
MARTEL AVENUE
N. CURZON
W. ROSEWOOD AVENUE
MELROSE AVENUE
AVENUE

N. FAIRFAX AVENUE
N. FAIRFAX AVENUE

N. HAYWORTH AVENUE
N. EDINBURGH AVENUE
N. LAUREL AVENUE

N. CRESCENT HEIGHTS BLVD
N. CRESCENT HEIGHTS BOULEVARD

WOODSHILL TRL
MONTER RD
HOLLY DR
MONTER RD

N. HAVENHURST DRIVE
ROMAINE STREET
N. LA JOLLA AVE.
N. HARPER AVE.
N. SWEETZER AVENUE
N. SWEETZER AVENUE
N. FLORES AVENUE
N. FLORES STREET
WILLOUGHBY AVENUE
N. KINGS ROAD
KINGS ROAD
N. ORLANDO AVENUE
OLIVE DR.
N. CROFT AVENUE
HACIENDA PL.
N. ALFRED STREET
WARING AVENUE
MELROSE AVENUE
CLINTON STREET
W. ROSEWOOD AVENUE
N. CROFT AVENUE
MELROSE PL.
N. ALFRED STREET
AVE.
LA CIENEGA BOULEVARD
N. MELROSE

House of Blues

Schindler House/ MAK Center

KINGS ROAD
CARLTON WAY
HARRATT WAY
QUEENS ROAD
SUNSET PLAZA DR.
LONDONDERRY PL.
ALTA LOMA RD.
SUNSET STRIP
WEST KNOLL DRIVE
HOLLOWAY DRIVE
N. WEST KNOLL ROAD
WESTMONT DRIVE
WESTBOURNE DRIVE
HANCOCK AVENUE
HUNTLEY DR.
SHERWOOD DRIVE
PALM AVENUE
HORN AVE.
LARRABEE STREET
SAN VICENTE BLVD

Whisky-a-Go-Go

Pacific Design Center

MOCA at PDC

SAN VICENTE BOULEVARD
EL TOVAR PL.
MELROSE AVE.
ROSEWOOD AVE.

The Roxy

Viper Room

ST IVES DR.
OZETA TERR.
N. WETHERLY DR.
CORDELL DR.
CAROL DR.
N. DOHENY DRIVE
CYNTHIA ST.
HAMMOND ST.
HARRATT ST.
PHYLLIS AVE.
CINTHIA ST.
VISTA GRAND ST
DICKS STREET
NORMA PLACE
ELEVADO AVE.
LLOYD PLACE
KEITH AVE.
HILLDALE AVE.
CLARK ST.

N. OAKHURST DRIVE
LA PEER DR.
MELROSE AVENUE
RANGLEY STREET
DORRINGTON AVENUE

S. FULLER AVENUE
S. MARTEL AVENUE
S. VISTA STREET
S. GARDNER STREET
COLGATE AVE.
HAUSER BLVD

OAKWOOD AVENUE
1ST STREET

BEVERLY BOULEVARD

CBS Television City

Pan Pacific Park

The Grove Mall

Farmers Market

N. STANLEY AVE.
N. SPAULDING AVE.
N. GENESEE AVE.
N. OGDEN AVE.
N. ORANGE GROVE AVE.

S. BURNSIDE AVE.
BLACKBURN AVENUE
CURZON AVE. E.
CURZON AVE. W.
S. ORANGE GROVE AVE.
CURZON AVE.
S. FULLER AVE.
S. ALANDELE AVE.

3RD STREET
COLGATE AVENUE
S. OGDEN DR.
N. OGDEN DR.

W 6TH STREET

BURNSIDE AVENUE
RIDGELEY DRIVE
HAUSER BLVD
MASSELIN AVENUE
SIERRA BONITA AVENUE
CURZON AVENUE
STANLEY AVENUE
ALANDELE AVE.
SPAULDING AVE.

WILSHIRE BOULEVARD

La Brea Tar Pits/ Page Museum
Craft and Folk Art Museum
Los Angeles County Museum of Art
Art + Design Museum
LACMA West
Museum of the Holocaust
Peterson Automotive Museum

S. FAIRFAX AVENUE

N. HAYWORTH AVENUE
S. HAYWORTH AVENUE
N. LAUREL AVENUE
S. LAUREL AVENUE

CAPISTRANO WAY

BLACKBURN AVENUE
4TH STREET
COLGATE AVENUE
DREXEL AVENUE
5TH STREET
LA JOLLA AVENUE
MARYLAND DRIVE
LINDENHURST DRIVE
6TH STREET
ORANGE STREET

MCCARTHY VISTA
DEL VALLE DR.
WARNER DR.

SLOAT DR.
CABRILLO DR.
FOSTER DR.
COMMODORE

AVENUE
1ST STREET
3RD STREET
N. SWEETZER AVENUE
S. SWEETZER AVENUE
SWEETZER AVENUE

KINGS ROAD
BEVERLY BOULEVARD
OAKWOOD

S. ORLANDO AVENUE

S. VICENTE BOULEVARD

TOWER DRIVE
GALE DRIVE
HAMILTON DRIVE
SANTA YNEZ WAY
SCHUMACHER DRIVE
GREGORY WAY

OLYMPIC BOULEVARD

WESTBOURNE DR.
HUNTLEY DRIVE
SAN VICENTE

Beverly Center

N LA CIENEGA BOULEVARD

LE DOUX ROAD
STANLEY DRIVE
CARSON ROAD
WILLAMAN DRIVE
HAMEL DRIVE
ARNAZ DRIVE
BOULEVARD

Wilshire Theater
Fine Arts Theater
Herrick Library

GREGORY WAY
CHALMERS DRIVE
S. ROBERTSON

N. ROBERTSON BLVD.
BONNER DR.

Cedars-Sinai Hospital

ASHCROFT AVENUE
ROSEWOOD AVENUE
BEVERLY BOULEVARD
ALDEN DRIVE
3RD STREET

CLARK DRIVE
SWALL DRIVE
LA PEER DRIVE
ALMONT DRIVE
WETHERLY DRIVE

Academy of Motion Picture Arts & Sciences
Music Hall Theater

WILSHIRE BOULEVARD
CHARLEVILLE BOULEVARD

CLARK DRIVE
SWALL DRIVE
LA PEER DRIVE
ALMONT DRIVE
WETHERLY DRIVE
GREGORY WAY

S. ROBERTSON
OLYMPIC BOULEVARD

DRIVE
DOHENY
OAKHURST DRIVE
OAKHURST DRIVE

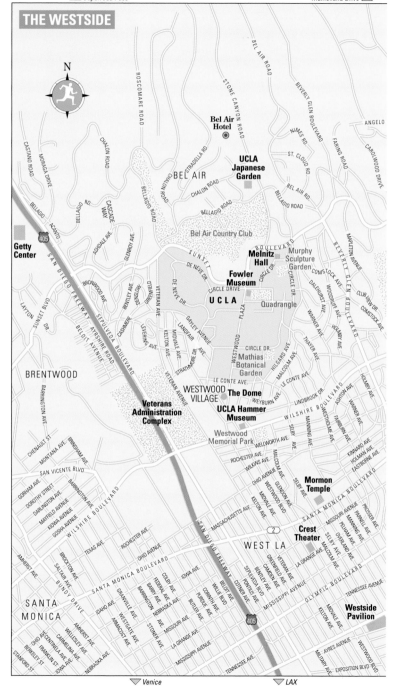

THE WESTSIDE

N

Sepulveda Pass

Mulholland Drive

ROSCOMARE ROAD

STONE CANYON ROAD

BEL AIR ROAD

BEVERLY GLEN BOULEVARD

ANGELO

CAROLWOOD DRIVE

FARING ROAD

CASTANO ROAD

MORAGA DRIVE

CHALON ROAD

Bel Air Hotel

NIMES ROAD

ST. CLOUD RD.

UCLA Japanese Garden

BEL AIR

STRADELLA RD.

CHALON ROAD

CHALON ROAD

BELLAGIO ROAD

BEL AIR RD.

BELLAGIO ROAD

BELLAGIO RD.

CASCADE WAY

ASHDALE AVE.

GLENROY AVE.

BELLAGIO ROAD

Bel Air Country Club

BELLAGIO

ACANTO

Getty Center

405

SAN DIEGO FREEWAY

BRONWOOD AVE.

BENTLEY AVE.

BENSLOW

O'BRIEN O'BRIEN AVE.

SUNSET

DE NEVE DR.

BOULEVARD

Melnitz Hall

Murphy Sculpture Garden

CIRCLE DR.

CIRCLE DR.

COMSTOCK AVE.

DALEHURST AVE.

MAPLETON AVENUE

BEVERLY GLEN BOULEVARD

WOODRUFF AVE.

CLUB VIEW DR.

COMSTOCK AVE.

Fowler Museum

U C L A

CIRCLE DRIVE

PLAZA

Quadrangle

WESTWOOD

WARNER AVE.

THAYER AVE.

LAYTON AVE.

SUNSET BLVD.

CASHMERE ST.

SEPULVEDA BOULEVARD

BELOIT AVENUE

LEVERING AVE.

GAYLEY AVENUE

LANDFAIR

MIDVALE AVE.

KELTON AVE.

STRATHMORE DR.

CIRCLE DR.

Mathias Botanical Garden

HILGARD AVE.

MALCOLM AVE.

LE CONTE AVE.

HOLMBY AVE.

BRENTWOOD

BARRINGTON AVE.

BRINGHAM AVE.

VETERAN AVENUE

LE CONTE AVE.

WESTWOOD VILLAGE

The Dome

WEYBURN AVE.

LINDBROOK DR.

WILSHIRE BOULEVARD

WESTHOLME AVE.

MANNING AVE.

SELBY AVE.

ASHTON AVE.

WARNER AVE.

FAIRBURN AVE.

HOLMBY AVE.

Veterans Administration Complex

UCLA Hammer Museum

Westwood Memorial Park

WELLWORTH AVE.

KINNARD AVE.

HOLMAN AVE.

EASTBORNE AVE.

CHENAULT ST.

MONTANA AVE.

ROCHESTER AVE.

WILKINS AVE.

MALCOLM AVE.

Mormon Temple

SAN VICENTE BLVD.

GORHAM AVE.

DOROTHY STREET

DARLINGTON AVENUE

MAYFIELD AVENUE

KIOWA AVENUE

GOSHA AVENUE

BARRINGTON AVENUE

OHIO AVENUE

WESTWOOD BLVD.

GLENDON AVE.

MIDVALE AVE.

SELBY AVE.

SANTA MONICA BOULEVARD

MISSOURI AVENUE

PRANELL AVE.

MANNING AVE.

OVERLAND AVE.

PELHAM AVE.

WILSHIRE BOULEVARD

MASSACHUSETTS AVE.

SAN DIEGO FREEWAY

2

Crest Theater

WEST LA

VETERAN AVE.

CAMDEN AVE.

GREENFIELD AVE.

BENTLEY AVE.

PONTIUS AVE.

SEPULVEDA BLVD.

SELBY AVE.

MALCOLM AVE.

OLYMPIC BOULEVARD

TENNESSEE AVENUE

ROCHESTER AVE.

OHIO AVENUE

TEXAS AVE.

AMHERST AVE.

BROCKTON AVE.

SALTAIR AVE.

BUNDY DRIVE

SANTA MONICA BOULEVARD

COLBY AVE.

BARRY AVE.

FEDERAL AVE.

BARRINGTON AVE.

NEBRASKA AVE.

CORINTH AVE.

PURDUE AVE.

BUTLER AVE.

BILOXI BLVD.

WILLIE BLVD.

LA GRANGE AVENUE

MISSISSIPPI AVENUE

WESTWOOD BLVD

MIDVALE AVE

KELTON AVE

Westside Pavilion

SANTA MONICA

OHIO AVE.

CENTINELA AVE.

CARMELINA AVE.

FRANKLIN ST.

BERKELEY ST.

STANFORD ST.

IOWA AVE.

WELLESLEY AVE.

AMHERST AVE.

GRANVILLE AVE.

IDAHO AVE.

BARRINGTON AVE.

WESTGATE AVE.

STONER AVE.

ARMACOST AVE.

MISSOURI AVE.

LA GRANGE AVE.

IOWA AVE.

MISSISSIPPI AVENUE

TENNESSEE AVE.

AYRES AVENUE

MILITARY AVE.

EXPOSITION BLVD.

405

Franklin
Canyon
Park &
Ranch

0   1 mile

TOWER RD.
SAN YSIDRO DR.

CALLE VISTA DR.
SCHUYLER RD.
LOMA VISTA DRIVE
HILLCREST ROAD
LA COLINA DR.
SIERRA ALTA WAY
DOHENY DRIVE
WETHERLY DRIVE
SUNSET PLAZA DRIVE

LAUREL WAY
BEVERLY DRIVE
WOODLAND DR.
ALPINE DRIVE

Greystone
Park

**Greystone
Mansion**

DOHENY ROAD

SUNSET STRIP
SUNSET BOULEVARD
HAMMOND
HILLDALE
LARRABEE
PALM AVE.

CYNTHIA AVE.

BENEDICT CANYON DRIVE
DRIVE
COVE WAY

MOUNTAIN DR.

SUNSET   BOULEVARD

Virginia
Robinson
Gardens

DICKS ST.
NORMA ST.
OAKHURST DRIVE
LLOYD
KEITH AVE.

**Pacific
Design
Center**

**MOCA at
PDC**

LADERA DRIVE
HARTFORD WAY

**Beverly Hills
Hotel** ◉

**Anthony
House**

CRESCENT DRIVE

LOMITAS AVENUE
PALM DRIVE
MAPLE DRIVE
ELM DRIVE
ELEVADO AVENUE
FOOTHILL DRIVE
ALPINE DRIVE
REXFORD DRIVE
HILLCREST BLVD.
ARDEN DRIVE
ALTA DRIVE
SIERRA DRIVE
CARMELITA   AVENUE
SANTA MONICA BLVD.

MELROSE   AVENUE
RANGELY AVE.
DORRINGTON AVE.
ASHCROFT AVE.
ROSEWOOD AVE.
BEVERLY BLVD.

SAN VICENTE BOULEVARD

WHITTIER DR.

CANON DRIVE
BEVERLY DRIVE

B E V E R L Y
H I L L S

②

ALDEN DRIVE

**Los Angeles
Country Club**

LOMITAS AVENUE
ELEVADO AVENUE
ROXBURY DRIVE
CAMDEN DRIVE
RODEO DRIVE
BEDFORD DRIVE
LINDEN DRIVE
WALDEN DRIVE

**Paley Center
for Media**

**City
Hall**

**GOLDEN
TRIANGLE**

**Spadena
House**

**O'Neill
House**

SANTA MONICA BLVD.
RODEO DRIVE
FOOTHILL RD.

REXFORD ROAD
ELM DR.
MAPLE DRIVE
PALM DRIVE
OAKHURST DRIVE
DOHENY DRIVE

3RD STREET

BURTON WAY

DAYTON WAY

CLIFTON WAY

ROBERTSON BLVD
ARNAZ DRIVE
HAMEL DRIVE

**Academy of
Motion Picture
Arts & Sciences**

WILSHIRE   BOULEVARD

CHARLEVILLE BOULEVARD

**Music Hall
Theater**

WETHERLY DRIVE
ALMONT DRIVE
LAPEER DRIVE
SWALL DRIVE
CLARK DRIVE

COMSTOCK AVE.
CLUB VIEW DRIVE

LASKY DRIVE
SPALDING DR.
LINDEN DR.
McCARTHY DR.
ROXBURY DRIVE
BEDFORD DRIVE
PECK DRIVE
CAMDEN DRIVE
RODEO DRIVE
EL CAMINO DRIVE
REEVES DR.
CANON DR.
CRESCENT DR.

GREGORY WAY

MORENO DRIVE

**Century City
Shopping Center**

C E N T U R Y
C I T Y ◉

OLYMPIC   BOULEVARD

BEVERLY DR.

WHITWORTH DRIVE

CENTURY PARK W.
FOX HILLS DR.
BEVERLY
PANDORA AVE.
ELLEN

**Century
Plaza
Hotel**

Fox Plaza

CENTURY PARK EAST
HEATH AVE.
SHIRLEY PL.
AVE. OF THE STARS

DANIELS
CASTELLO

PICO   BOULEVARD
ALCOTT ST.

EDRIS ST.
REEVES ST.
BEVERLY DRIVE
REXFORD DRIVE
GLENVILLE DR.
CASHIO ST.
CARDIFF AVE.
OAKHURST
CANFIELD DR.
DURANGO
CREST DRIVE
LIVONIA DRIVE

WOOSTER ST.
SHENANDOAH ST.
PICKFORD ST.

BENECIA AVE.
BEVERLY
BOULEVARD
PATRICIA AVE.

**Museum of
Tolerance**

MONTE MAR DRIVE
KIRKSIDE ROAD
OAKMORE ROAD
CRESTA DRIVE

AIRDROME STREET

ROBERTSON BLVD
PRIESS ROAD
18TH STREET
SAWYER STREET

ELONA AVE.
ALMAYA AVE.

FOX HILLS DR.

**20th Century
Fox Studios**

Hillcrest
Country Club

ROXBURY
BEVERLY DRIVE

HILLSBORO AVENUE

PICO BLVD.
AYRES AVE.
BLYTHE AVE.
CUSHDON AVE.

MOTOR AVENUE

**Rancho Park
Golf Course**

DRIVE

MONTE MAR
CRESTA DRIVE
FORRESTER DRIVE
McDONNELL DR.

CASTLE HEIGHTS AVE.
ANDASOL AVENUE

DUXBURY ROAD

BAGLEY AVENUE

CANFIELD AVENUE

GUTHRIE AVENUE

ESTHER AVENUE
ASHBY AVE.
PUTNEY RD.
ROUNTREE RD.
RADBURY RD.
NORTHVALE RD.
BUTTERFIELD RD.
CHEVIOT DR.

DRAPER
TABON DR.
DUNLEER DR.

MOTOR AVENUE

LORENZO PL.
LORENZO DR.
GLENBARR AVE.
GOSSENBERRY PL.
CAVENDISH DR.
EARLMAR DR.
CLUB DRIVE

DAVID AVENUE
24TH STREET
25TH STREET
BEVERLYWOOD ST.

SHENANDOAH ST.
HALM AVE.
HOLT AVE.

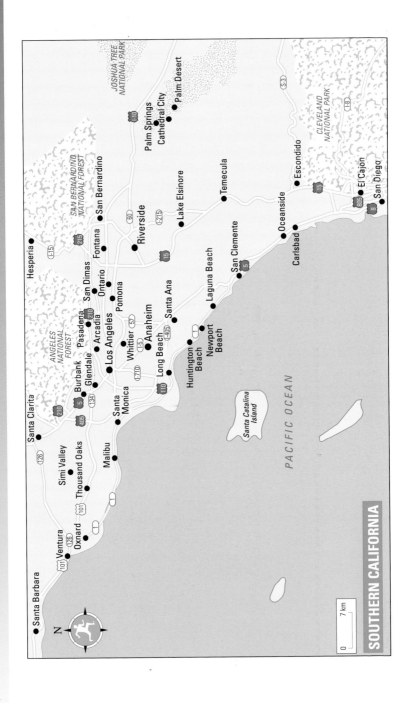

SOUTHERN CALIFORNIA

0 ___ 7 km